The Unsteady March

The Unsteady March

The Rise and Decline of
Racial Equality
in America

Philip A. Klinkner
with
Rogers M. Smith

The University of Chicago Press
Chicago and London

The University of Chicago Press, Chicago 60637
The University of Chicago Press, Ltd., London
© 1999 by The University of Chicago
All rights reserved. Published 1999
Paperback edition 2002
Printed in the United States of America
08 07 06 05 04 03 02   2 3 4 5

ISBN: 0-226-44339-6 (cloth)
ISBN: 0-226-44341-8 (paperback)

Library of Congress Cataloging-in-Publication Data

Klinkner, Philip A.
    The unsteady march : the rise and decline of racial equality in
America / Philip A. Klinkner with Rogers M. Smith.
        p.   cm.
    Includes bibliographical references and index.
    ISBN 0-226-44339-6 (cloth : alk. paper)
    1. Afro-Americans—Civil rights—History.   2. United States—Race
relations.   3. Afro-Americans—Government policy—History.
I. Smith, Rogers M., 1953– .   II. Title.
E185.K55   1999
305.896′073—dc21   99-23195
                                                                         CIP

Contents

Acknowledgments

Like its subject matter, this book has also been an unsteady march and its completion relied on the help from many quarters. The project was aided by support from Loyola Marymount University, Hamilton College, Yale University's Institute for Social Policy Studies, and the Brookings Institution. Deborah Duyan, Jon Altschul, Amy Chiou, and Elizabeth Cohen served as exemplary research assistants. We would also like to thank Cathy Cohen, Allison Dorsey-Ward, Chris Foreman, Richard Fry, Paul Frymer, Martin Gilens, Dennis Gilbert, Maurice Isserman, Glenn Loury, David Mayhew, Adolph Reed Jr., John Skrentny, Kathleen Smith, Mitchell Stevens, Thomas Sugrue, Seth Thompson, Richard Valelly, Bradford Westerfield, and Julian Zelizer for providing helpful comments and advice. In particular, we are indebted to Mary Dudziak. Not only has her pathbreaking work on the Cold War and U.S. civil rights proven crucial to the formulation of our thesis, but she has generously shared her research and insights with us. John Tryneski at the University of Chicago Press has served ably as editor and friend, and we are thankful for his support and encouragement at a critical stage. David Bemelmans did outstanding work as our copyeditor. This book, of course, would never have been possible without the love, inspiration, and indulgence of our spouses, Honorine Wallack and Mary Summers. Although each of us contributed to every chapter, the original formulation of the book's central argument and the bulk of its research and writing was by the principal author, Philip Klinkner. Consequently, the bulk of the responsibility for any errors falls to Rogers Smith.

Finally, Philip Klinkner dedicates this book to his daughter Honorine. May she continue the march and help see it through to its ultimate destination. Rogers Smith shares that hope for his children, Virginia, Caroline, and Reed; but he dedicates this book to Mary Summers, who embodies the spirit, insight, and passion needed if America's long march is ever to reach a just and peaceful journey's end.

INTRODUCTION

The Unsteady March

There is something too mean in looking upon the Negro, when you are in trouble as a citizen, and when you are free from trouble, as an alien. . . . He has been a citizen just three times in the history of this government, and it has always been in times of trouble. In time of trouble we are citizens. Shall we be citizens in war, and aliens in peace? Would that be just?

—*Frederick Douglass*, "What the Black Man Wants" (1865)

There came a time when justice seemed at hand at last. In 1965, the first president elected from a southern state since the Civil War—a proud son of that great pillar of the Confederacy, the State of Texas—responded to searing controversies over civil rights by proposing the Voting Rights Act. It aimed to make African Americans full and equal citizens of the United States in every respect. It was time, Lyndon Johnson solemnly told the nation, for America finally to "make good the promise of democracy." He insisted to his fellow white citizens that "it is not just Negroes, but really it is all of us, who must overcome the crippling legacy of bigotry and injustice." "And," he said, borrowing from the spiritual that had so greatly inspired civil rights activists, "we shall overcome."[1]

It is hard for many Americans today to understand just how astonishing and compelling it was to hear that president say those words in his unreconstructed Texas drawl. It is hard now because for more than thirty years we Americans have told ourselves that what many were then saying, with more hope than confidence, was in fact simply true. We reassure ourselves that sooner or later the United States had to have passed the Voting Rights Act and other measures overthrowing older laws that had discriminated against

1

blacks in politics and in virtually every other sphere of life. Racial discrimination, we now often believe, violates and had always violated Americans' deepest values. Many of us believe that as a result of these core values, our history has been a slow, difficult, but steady march toward laying to rest the unfortunate prejudices we inherited from our distant past. It could not, we like to think, really have been otherwise.

It is important to remember that in 1965, as for all of our nation's previous history, the statement "We shall overcome" was far more an expression of faith, hope, and prayer than a confident prediction. Many white Americans regarded any political invocation of those three words as a dangerously radical threat, usually advanced by disreputable, trouble-making blacks and their wild-eyed white agitator allies. In 1965, progress toward racial justice was still so recent and so bitterly contested that it was hard not to harbor doubts about whether the forces of white supremacy would ever truly yield. After all, Alabama, the scene of the most violent civil rights protests in 1965, was governed by another southern white man, George Corley Wallace, who had proclaimed only two years before that the policy of the "Great Anglo-Saxon Southland" was "Segregation now . . . segregation tomorrow . . . segregation forever!"[2] And in 1965, many more Americans knew that until World War II, most American leaders, north and south, had matter-of-factly defended white supremacy, segregation, and racial hierarchy in rhetoric far more similar to George Wallace's than to Lyndon Johnson's. To many reform-minded citizens, black and white, Johnson's speech seemed to be not so much a routinely predictable culmination of its egalitarian history as a breath-taking miracle.

It is not our thesis in this book that Johnson's speech or the subsequent passage of the muscular and extraordinarily effective Voting Rights Act of 1965 were miracles. Neither, however, do we share the complacent conventional wisdom that has come to prevail in its wake—that the nation's movement toward greater racial equality was somehow preordained by the characteristics and the principles of the American founding, the American national soul, or the broader tides of modern world history. That wisdom looks increasingly dubious today, a generation after enactment of the Voting Rights Act, as explosive racial divisions continue to plague American life, having only grown more complex and perplexing as the nation's racial and ethnic diversity has increased. We have been driven to write this book by concerns about current events, but it responds to a more general and enduring question: Under what circumstances has the United States made significant progress toward greater racial justice, toward more equal and meaningful opportunities for all its inhabitants, no matter how society classifies them in racial or ethnic terms?

We do not try here to explore this question in its full complexity, involving many racial and ethnic groups. We focus on the relationships between whites and blacks that have provided, we argue, the basic template for American racial hierarchies, one that has shaped the statuses of all other American groups. Nor do we attempt here an elaborate empirical causal analysis of our central question. It will take many studies to do such work persuasively. Instead, we have combed through American history and arrived inductively at what seems to us the most likely answer, for reasons we hope to make clear. It is an answer that ought to be subjected to more rigorous testing by appropriate specialists. But we also think that our answer is so significant to contemporary American race relations that we feel compelled to lay out our claims, and to do so in as emphatic and accessible a manner as possible, prior to such lengthy investigations. Although our answer is only suggestive, it is, we believe, disturbingly plausible. It is plausible because vast stretches of our national history cry out in support of our argument. It is disturbing because, if our answer is correct, we Americans must not only abandon our belief that there was anything inevitable about the overcoming of Jim Crow laws in the 1960s. We must also recognize soberly that further progress toward a just and harmonious overcoming of racial divisions and inequalities might not occur in our time unless we as a people make extraordinary efforts of a sort we have never undertaken before except under the most extreme duress.

In brief, our answer is that at least so far in American history, substantial progress toward greater (never yet full) racial equality has come only when three factors have concurred. Progress has come only

1. in the wake of a large-scale war requiring extensive economic and military mobilization of African Americans for success;
2. when the nature of America's enemies has prompted American leaders to justify such wars and their attendant sacrifices by emphasizing the nation's inclusive, egalitarian, and democratic traditions; and

3. when the nation has possessed domestic political protest movements willing and able to bring pressure upon national leaders to live up to that justificatory rhetoric by instituting domestic reforms.

We do not say that these three conditions must always be present for progress to occur. We do say that, thus far, substantial progress has never occurred without these three factors present and working together.

The essential evidence for our argument is that there have been only three eras of significant progress toward greater racial equality in U.S. history, in each of which these factors have been at work. The initial reform era was the First Emancipation following the Revolutionary War, when slavery was put on the path of extinction in the North and restrictions on free blacks and on manumissions lessened even in much of the South. The Revolution had been fought in the name of republicanism and inalienable human rights against a monarchical foe. It was won with key contributions from American blacks. And it was accompanied by white and black religious movements, especially, that highlighted the contradictions between the Declaration of Independence and the continuation of black slavery. The second significant reform era was the Reconstruction period after the Civil War. That massive struggle probably could not have been won without black soldiers. It led to the postwar constitutional amendments that ended slavery and established formally equal black citizenship, in accordance with the insistent demands of black and white abolitionists. The third reform period is the modern civil rights era, occurring in the wake of World War II and during the Cold War, including its "hot" Korean and Vietnamese phases. The years from 1941 to 1968 framed an extraordinarily prolonged period in which all three of the factors we stress remained present. Throughout these decades, the United States continuously mobilized huge numbers of black soldiers for actual or possible combat against Nazi and Communist foes, against which American leaders stressed the nation's democratic ideals. Meanwhile a broad array of civil rights protesters pushed to make those ideals realities for all Americans.

In between the first two reform eras, as we shall see, progress toward racial equality ceased in most arenas of American life. In many areas whites constructed new systems of racial hierarchy that significantly eroded previous advances. Today, after the fall of the

Soviet Union and the end of the Cold War, the forces that pressed for racial equality so powerfully for so long in modern American have again receded (though not vanished). Whether the nation will nonetheless continue to progress in a racially egalitarian direction is, we think, the most important political question facing the United States as we enter the twenty-first century. From our reading of the headlines of the present in light of the lessons of the past, we regretfully see all too abundant cause for concern.

Our story is thus consistent with the old adage of civil rights workers, "Two steps forward, one step back." We stress, however, that thus far the two steps forward have come in concentrated bursts of ten to fifteen years. The one step back, in contrast, has repeatedly been a lengthy stride covering a period of sixty to seventy-five years. Hence the normal experience of the typical black person in U.S. history has been to live in a time of stagnation and decline in progress toward racial equality. That reality helps explain the deep pessimism about race visible in the outlook even of more affluent blacks today and in much of America's past.[3]

Such pessimism is one reason why no part of our argument is wholly new with us, even though it will be uncongenial to many. Broadly speaking, specialists in international affairs have noted the relationship between international influences and domestic politics, and the ways in which wartime exigencies can lead to the expansion of citizenship rights.[4] In the case of civil rights for black Americans, many black scholars in particular have stressed the importance of war in motivating previous racial reforms. As the excerpt quoted at the beginning of this Introduction suggests, perhaps the first formulation of this thesis was offered by the great antislavery leader Frederick Douglass. He suggested blacks had been treated as citizens of the United States only in military ranks during the Revolutionary War, the War of 1812, and the Civil War (and, we would add, only the two large-scale struggles had any enduring impact on peacetime racial statuses). More recent observers, such as Mary Frances Berry and the late Benjamin Quarles, have also made the connection between blacks' military service and their citizen rights.[5] In particular, scholars such as Derrick Bell, Mary Dudziak, and John Skrentny have shown how the imperatives of the Cold War were crucial to the civil rights advances of the 1950s and 1960s.[6] The distinguished historian of American nativism, John Higham, has recently contended in a kindred vein that America has had "three Reconstructions." He sees the Revolution, the Civil War, and World War II, and the Cold War, and their accompanying defenses cast in democratic, inclusive ideological terms, as vital catalysts to periods of racial progress, decisively reinforcing the efforts of civil rights activists.[7]

But though many perceptive analysts have recognized the impact of wars on racial equality, it remains an insight many American scholars and citizens resist. Its acceptance is blocked by widespread embrace of a different view of American racial progress. That view was well summarized in a passage by historian Philip Gleason, first published in the 1980 Harvard Encyclopedia of American Ethnic Groups and subsequently both republished and widely cited by many leading scholars. Gleason argued that historically, to be an American, "a person did not have to be of any particular national, linguistic, religious, or ethnic background. All he had to do was to commit himself to the political ideology centered on the abstract ideals of liberty, equality, and republicanism. Thus the universalist ideological character of American nationality meant that it was open to anyone who willed to become an American." Gleason quickly added that, to be sure, "universalism had its limits from the beginning, because it did not include either blacks or Indians, and in time other racial and cultural groups were regarded as falling outside the range of American nationality." Thus there was "a latent predisposition toward an ethnically defined concept of nationality." But this "exclusiveness ran contrary to the logic of the defining principles, and the official commitment to those principles has worked historically to overcome exclusions and to make the practical boundaries of American identity more congruent with its theoretical universalism."[8]

We challenge this claim about the character and power of America's original "official . . . principles" and the optimistic story of steady, almost natural progress toward racial equality that scholars have built upon it. As Rogers Smith has detailed, American political thought has always contained "multiple traditions," including civic ideals presenting white Americans as in many respects God's chosen people, specially equipped by nature and providence for individual liberty and political self-governance in ways that blacks, Native Americans, and other races were not. Hence the nation's massive violations of racially egalitarian ideals and its recurring erosion of egalitarian reforms have not always been viewed by Americans as a turning away from national idealism and the common good toward a rather jaded pursuit of individual self-interest. Instead, many Americans have always been able to tell themselves that they were remaining true to their best ideals, the advancement of white Protestant civilization, a noble common cause endangered by what they genuinely believed to be misguided and destructive radical egalitarianism. If we are right that Americans have long had ample ideological resources for not only justifying but glorifying racial inequalities, then it is difficult to have so much confidence that the "national ideology" will predictably work toward the expansion of civil rights if Americans only recall it rightly.[9]

To be sure, the racialist strains in American ideology probably gained their power originally from desires to justify the institution of chattel slavery as well as the seizure of land from the native tribes, and those economic roots of racism are now part of the nation's past. But racial hierarchies were then embodied in virtually every institution of American life—political, economic, educational, religious, cultural and social—by the time of the Revolutionary War. They were supported by most American governments throughout most of our history and still persist on a de facto basis today. With the great sociologist W. E. B. Du Bois, we believe that the attachment of American whites to our country's longstanding racial ordering soon became not only and perhaps even not chiefly a matter of economic interests, although those interests are a major part of the story. Throughout most of our history, white Americans have also received a "psychological wage," to use Du Bois's term, from living in a society in which members of their racial group occupy the leading positions in most institutions.[10]

This favored status has meant that whites are commonly accepted as the "normal" and norm-setting, and hence really the most prestigious, members of American society. People who have grown up within arrangements in which their group regularly receives special social esteem as well as more material benefits, arrangements that seem so familiar as to be virtually natural, are always likely to find changes in those arrangements disquieting. Predictably, they will look for reasons to confine and condemn them. Our fellow white Americans, we firmly believe, are not people any more inherently prone to racism, selfishness, or evil than any other group in this or any other society. Their attachments to familiar ways are perfectly normal and human, and in many regards such attachments can rightly be cherished. But in American society, whites happen to be the group who have historically had the upper hand; and so many of their understandable attachments to the status quo, often accompanied by genuine good will toward others, nonetheless have always worked against overcoming real and severe injustices. We confront here almost the political equivalent of a Newtonian law: bodies in power tend to stay in power unless acted upon by outside forces.

Even if there are economic benefits to egalitarian reforms, many whites consciously or unconsciously experience the loss of the specially privileged status they have long enjoyed as a cost too high to pay. If there are not unusually strong imperatives to do so, most simply cannot be expected to pay that price.[11]

Finally, as political scientists we must insist that any analysis of the prospects for reform in America ultimately must come to grips with the incentives that shape the behavior of political parties, for little change can come without strong support from at least one major party. Even if there are powerful elements in American national ideology supporting equal rights for all, no party is likely to push with equal power for the full realization of those ideals unless it can hope to garner support in the form of votes and dollars by doing so. And in a country in which votes and dollars have always been predominantly in white hands, parties will usually have strong incentives to support equal rights symbolically, perhaps, but to back off any strong push to make substantive changes. At least, that will be the case if whites have any normal propensity to resist change in arrangements that benefit them. Again, barring exceptional circumstances, we doubt that leaders of major political parties are likely today, any more than in the past, to champion policies that erode rather than reinforce the advantages of those groups who are most numerous, most affluent, and most politically powerful. The United States is a complex and diverse society, but it is still one in which in most regards middle-class and upper-class whites are best positioned. Indeed, the political advantages of whites have in the past and the present led political leaders most often to uphold rather than condemn America's racial hierarchy.[12]

Hence we feel compelled in this book to sound a note of alarm. There is still much to overcome if we are to achieve a racially equal, free, and harmonious society. Given what it has taken to bring about meaningful and enduring change in the past, it is hard to believe that Americans will confront and master the difficult challenges we face in race relations simply as a matter of course.

There is, fortunately, reason to believe that egalitarian changes can be catalyzed today without our having to suffer anything akin to the major wars that have triggered transformations in the past. We shall see that, although racial progress has not been either inevitable or irreversible in America, it has been in significant ways cumulative. The moral and material victories of the modern civil rights movement in particular mean that it is now much harder to defend invidious racial discrimination than in the past. Demographically, economically, and intellectually, proponents of racial equality now have many more resources they can employ to push for change, even in peacetime.

Yet extensive and unjust racial inequalities persist. Precisely because so much in our circumstances makes complacency about these inequalities comfortable, there is, we think, little genuine reason for complacency about the prospects for racial progress today. Still, politics is a realm in which analysts can only discern tendencies, probabilities, obstacles, and opportunities, never certainties. It is not easy but always possible to swim against the tide, taking advantage of all available countercurrents. In the end, our political fate is something that we have significant powers to choose and determine. It is because we think Americans can and should choose to commit themselves anew to overcoming our deepest and most enduring national divisions, not because we believe they cannot or will not do so, that we have written this book.

ONE

"Bolted with the Lock
of a Hundred Keys"

The Era of Slavery, 1619–1860

In 1676, exactly one hundred years before the British American colonists would declare their independence, blacks bound to servitude for life joined landless whites in an effort to overthrow what they felt to be a repressive colonial regime in Jamestown, Virginia. They were led by a rebellious and bold gentry leader, Nathaniel Bacon, whose death from the "bloody flux" (probably dysentery) soon brought the insurgency to an ignominious close. Still, for a time colonial blacks and whites stood shoulder to shoulder in a struggle for greater opportunities. But Americans today do not celebrate Bacon's Rebellion as a milestone of interracial cooperation. Perhaps that is because its story is all too revealing of the sources, consequences, and limits of racial unity in our nation.

Nathaniel Bacon did not welcome blacks to his cause out of any commitment to racial equality. He originally formed his force to conquer the surrounding native tribes, even friendly ones, and take their lands for former indentured servants who had served their time and wanted farms. Bacon added black servants to his corps of poor whites only when he found he also had to fight William Berkeley, the colonial governor. Berkeley thought arming the Jamestown "rabble" too dangerous to be allowed. After Bacon's death, the Virginia government reacted to this spectacle of interracial servant solidarity by slowly eliminating white indentured servitude and expanding the then-new institution of black chattel slavery.[1]

The pattern thus etched—increased white acceptance of blacks as fellow contributors to a common cause during a military struggle, followed by a long period during which whites instead consolidated racial advantages at the expense of blacks—is, quite simply, the pattern of American life through most of U.S. history. This chapter shows the politics responsible for this pattern at work not only in Bacon's Rebellion but in the entire American antebellum period, from 1619 to 1860. From 1619 to 1775, white Americans developed a racial hierarchy based upon black slavery. The ideology and the crisis of the Revolutionary War undermined this hierarchy and led to the abolition of slavery in the North, its weakening in the South, and the extension of at least some of the basic rights of citizenship to free blacks in many parts of the country. Yet after the military crisis and ideological fervor of the Revolution passed, white Americans soon began to build their new nation by reinforcing their racial hierarchies, as slavery was strengthened in the South, native tribes were displaced or destroyed, and the rights of free blacks restricted throughout the land.

Slavery did not spring fully grown onto American soil when the first Africans were brought to the Jamestown colony in 1619. It appears that these Africans came not as slaves but as indentured servants who were held to labor for only a finite period of time. Moreover, black and white indentured servants were treated relatively equally at first. As late as 1651, black indentured servants who had completed their term of service were given land on an equal basis with whites of the same status. Blacks also seem to have possessed some political rights, which in a few areas included the right to vote in local elections and the right to testify in court against whites.[2]

By 1640, however, at least some blacks were being held as slaves in Virginia, and throughout the colonies the status of white and black indentured servants increasingly diverged. More and more, blacks were forced into a lifetime of labor, which was passed on to their children. Once established, the institution of slavery spread rapidly throughout the colonies in the ensuing decades, spurred on by the increasing demand for labor, the declining number of white indentured servants, and the growth of racist beliefs that Africans were uniquely qualified to serve as chattel slaves for white colonists.[3]

As slavery grew, so did its repressiveness. Blacks lost most of the rights they had possessed as indentured servants. The fear of slave revolts and of racial mixing led whites to enact harsh and punitive slave codes to ensure the stability of the slave system and to maintain the supremacy of whites over blacks. The slave codes varied from colony to colony. In the South, where slaves were most numerous and white fears of revolt most acute, the codes were elaborate and brutal. In the North, where slaves were fewer and less important to the economy, they were somewhat more lenient. In general, the codes denied slaves the right to marry, to own property, to own weapons, and to defend themselves against whites. They forbade slaves from meeting and traveling outside of the supervision of their masters. The codes also established especially harsh penalties for slaves who committed crimes, particularly those attempting escape or rebellion. African American slaves, in short, did not possess basic rights of life, liberty, or property to any meaningful extent.[4]

The small number of colonial free blacks also saw their status increasingly degraded by new laws. They had to go through burdensome procedures to prove their free status and they, too, could not own many types of property. Free blacks also had to endure higher taxes and more severe criminal punishments than whites. In 1715, North Carolina began what would become nearly three hundred years of fluctuation in black voting rights by moving to disfranchise free blacks. It would restore free black voting, subject to property qualifications, in 1734. But South Carolina also disfranchised blacks in 1716, Virginia did so in 1723, and they did not waver.[5]

By the middle of the 1700s, slavery was widespread, prominent, and widely accepted in the American colonies. There was no hiding from it: between 1680 and 1750, blacks, the overwhelming proportion of whom were slaves, grew from 4.6 percent of the population to over 20 percent. In the southern colonies, they went from 5.7 percent to nearly 40 percent of the population.[6]

And few whites sought to hide from it. To the extent that they thought twice about the institution, most white colonists saw nothing wrong with slavery, be it on humanitarian, religious, or ideological grounds. This was true in the North as well as the South. According to John Jay, the "great majority" of Northerners accepted slavery and "very few among them even doubted the propriety and rectitude of it."[7]

Yet doubts were far from unthinkable. Some did criticize slavery vigorously. Led by the Quakers, these early opponents of slavery acted most often out of religious concerns. Others, however, criticized slavery for less noble purposes, such as a fear of slave revolts or worries that slaves would undercut economic opportunities for white workers.[8] Whatever their motivations, those who condemned slavery in this era were, in the words of one historian, "like fireflies in the night," able only to highlight briefly, but not to dispel, the surrounding gloom.[9]

The coming of the American Revolution changed all this. "Almost overnight, it seemed," states historian Peter Kolchin, "an institution that had long been taken for granted came under intense scrutiny and debate."[10] In response to their perceived abuse by the English government, the colonists increasingly articulated a philosophy of natural rights positing that all humans are born free and equal, and that they possess inalienable rights to life, liberty, and property. To be sure, the revolutionaries also portrayed Americans as a special "chosen people" with a providential mission to advance the cause of liberty; but they still described that cause as not only America's but also the "cause of all mankind." The colonists saw British taxes and regulations as denying them basic liberties and, therefore, they believed that they had a right and a duty to rebel against such tyranny.[11]

In addition to putting the colonists on a collision course with the English government, the idea of natural rights had profound implications for slavery. Taken at its word, the philosophy of natural rights fundamentally contradicted the "peculiar institution." Antislavery advocates, who had previously relied mostly upon religious arguments, now began to stress slavery's violation of natural rights. In 1764, James Otis offered one of the first explicit criticisms of slavery on these grounds, stating, "The colonists are by the law of nature freeborn, as indeed all men are, white or black. . . . It is a clear truth that those who everyday barter away other men's liberty, will soon care little for their own."[12]

The example of Crispus Attucks starkly juxtaposed the colonists' fight for liberty and their treatment of blacks. On March 5, 1770, a scuffle broke out between several colonists and the British troops who were stationed in Boston to enforce the hated British taxes. A mob led by Attucks, a former slave, soon gathered and forced the soldiers back to their barracks. Attucks and the mob then marched on the Custom House and confronted a lone British sentry, accusing him of attacking a civilian and pelting him with snowballs and pieces of ice. Captain Thomas Preston and a squad of seven additional soldiers soon joined the sentry, loaded their weapons, and took aim at the crowd. As many began to back away, Attucks helped to steady them. According to one account, " 'Don't be afraid,' Attucks cried. 'They dare not fire.' "[13] In the words of an eyewitness, Attucks, who was wielding a club, "threw himself in, and made a blow at the officer; I saw the officer try to ward off the stroke; whether he struck him or not I do not know; [Attucks] then turned around, and struck the grenadier's gun at the captain's right hand, and immediately fell in with his club, and knocked his gun away and struck him over the head; the blow came either on the soldier's cheek or hat. [Attucks] held the bayonet with his left hand and twitched it and cried, kill the dogs, knock them over. This was the general cry; the people then crowded in." As the mob moved forward, the redcoats opened fire, killing Attucks first and then three others.[14]

Many white colonists acknowledged the irony of the fact that a black man was thus the first martyr of the American Revolution. In the words of historian John Hope Franklin, "It was a remarkable thing, the colonists reasoned, to have their fight for freedom waged by one who was not as free as they."[15]

Spurred, in part, by Attucks's death, antislavery advocates increasingly hammered at the contradiction between the colonists' criticism of English tyranny and their own toleration of slavery. In 1774, the Reverend Nathaniel Niles of Newbury, Massachusetts preached to his congregation, "Would we enjoy liberty? Then we must grant it to others. For shame, let us either cease to enslave our fellow men, or else, let us cease to complain of those that would enslave us."[16] The English were also quick to point out the hypocrisy of the colonists. In the words of Samuel Johnson, "How is it that we hear the loudest yelps for liberty among the drivers of negroes?"[17]

Blacks themselves, both slave and free, vocally condemned the gap between the white colonists' natural rights rhetoric and the reality of slavery. As early as 1766, blacks paraded through the streets of Charleston, South Carolina, shouting, "Liberty!"[18] In 1773, four Massachusetts slaves circulated a petition asking to be returned to Africa, stating, "We expect great things from men who have made such a noble stand against the designs of their fellow-men to enslave them."[19] The following year, "A Son of Africa" published a petition arguing, "Are not your hearts also hard, when you hold men in slavery who are entitled to liberty by law of nature, equal as yourselves? If it be so, pray, sir, pull the beam out of thine own eyes, that you may see clearly to pull the mote out of thy brother's eye; and when the eyes of your understanding are opened, then will you see clearly between your case and Great Britain, and that of the Africans. We all came from one Father, and He, by the law of nature, gave every thing that was made, equally alike to every man richly to enjoy."[20]

Prodded by such appeals, Massachusetts courts began to strike blows against slavery. They allowed slaves and their advocates to bring a growing number of successful freedom suits in the decade before the Revolution. But these cases were decided on very narrow grounds, and they failed to undermine the legal basis of slavery. Other states placed limits on the slave trade, including Rhode Island, which declared that "those who are desirous of enjoying all the advantages of liberty themselves, should be willing to extend personal liberty to others."[21] In 1774, the First Continental Congress voted to end the importation of slaves, though this step resulted as much from the general call for nonimportation of all goods as a means to retaliate against the British as from humanitarian motives.[22]

The first shots of the American Revolution at Lexington and Concord in April of 1775 heightened the ideological intensity of the colonists. As the war unfolded, it became increasingly hard to justify the mounting sacrifices entailed when the purpose was merely the reduction of taxes on imported goods. In turn, more and more colonists came to understand the Revolution as an all-encompassing struggle for freedom and liberty against tyranny. When Thomas Jefferson wrote in the Declaration of Independence, "We hold these truths to be self-evident, that all men are create equal, that they are endowed by their Creator with certain unalienable Rights, that among these are Life, Liberty, and the pursuit of Happiness," he eloquently summarized what had come to be the purpose of the Revolution.

As the colonists increasingly portrayed the Revolution in such strongly ideological terms, their contradictory treatment of blacks became more pressing and the pace of antislavery sentiment quickened.[23] Blacks remained often in the forefront in making this connection. In 1777, in a petition to the Massachusetts Assembly, "A Great Number of Blackes detained in a State of slavery" expressed

their Astonishment that It have Never Bin Considered that Every Principle from which Amarica has Acted in the Cours of their unhappy Dificultes with Great Briton Pleads Stronger than A thousand arguments in favours of your patinas they therfor humble Beseech your honours to give this petion its due weight & consideration & cause an act of the Legislatur to be past Wherby they may be Restored to the Enjoyments of that which is the Naturel Right of all men—and their Children who wher Born in this Land of Liberty may not be heald as Slaves after they arive at the age of twenty one years so may the Inhabitance of this Stats No longer chargeable with the inconsistancy of acting themselves the part which they condem and oppose in others Be prospered in their present Glorious struggle for Liberty and have those Blessing to them, &c.[24]

White colonists made similar arguments. In 1775, Thomas Paine argued, "How just, how suitable to our crime is the punishment

with which providence threatens us? We have enslaved multitudes
. . . and now are threatened with the same. And while other evils
are confessed, and bewailed, why not this especially, and publicly;
than which no other vice . . . has brought so much guilt on the
land?"[25]

Thomas Jefferson made one of the most important attempts to
link the Revolutionary cause with antislavery. In his original draft
of the Declaration of Independence, he lodged the following indictment against King George III:

> He has waged cruel war against human nature itself, violating its
> most sacred rights of life and liberty in the persons of a distant
> people who never offended him, captivating and carrying them
> into slavery in another hemisphere, or to incur miserable death
> in their transportation thither. . . . Determined to keep open a
> market where MEN should be bought and sold, he has prostituted
> his negative [veto] for supressing every legislative attempt to pro-
> hibit or restrain this execrable commerce.[26]

These words, however, failed to move Jefferson's colleagues in the
Continental Congress. Fearful of offending the sensibilities of both
northern and southern slave advocates, they deleted this clause from
the document's final version.

Jefferson himself failed to honor his own words. He continued to
own a large number of slaves throughout his life, some of them his
illegitimate children. He appeared to find the economic costs of freeing most of his slaves far too daunting for him to consider seriously.
Similarly, when Paine brilliantly rallied the colonists to support the
Revolution in his 1776 pamphlet "Common Sense," he did not risk
adding a divisive assault on slavery. Instead, he condemned Britain's
use of its "hellish power" to stir "the Indians and the Negroes to
destroy us." That passage made it clear that he was not seeking to
include "Indians and Negroes" among the new American "chosen
people," a message he doubtless saw as necessary to secure the support of the many colonists who owned slaves or who coveted tribal
lands.[27]

Beyond serving as a political springboard for much libertarian rhetoric, the Revolutionary War was also an intense military crisis. The
tasks of overcoming it, along with the revolutionary ideological fer-
ment, prompted policies of greater inclusion and equality that constituted the first significant breaches in American racial hierarchies.

The first of these upheavals began on November 14, 1775, when Lord Dunmore, the royal governor of Virginia, issued a proclamation stating, "I do hereby further declare all indented servants, Negroes, or others (apertaining to Rebels) free, that are able and willing to bear arms, they joining His Majesty's Troops, as soon as may be, for speedily reducing the Colony to a proper sense of their duty, to His Majesty's crown and dignity."[28]

Dunmore's promise of freedom in exchange for service in the British army found an enthusiastic audience among southern slaves. Within a week, over five hundred had fled to Dunmore's forces. "By the first of December nearly three hundred blacks in uniform, with the words 'Liberty to Slaves' inscribed across their breasts, were members of 'Lord Dunmore's Ethiopian Regiment.'" By the time Dunmore had to flee the following summer, eight hundred to one thousand blacks had joined him. Nonetheless, Dunmore's efforts failed. Local leaders increased slave patrols and meted out harsh punishments to slaves who were caught fleeing. Masters tried to convince their slaves that the British would later sell them in the West Indies, where they would face even harsher conditions. Furthermore, after December 1775, Dunmore's forces had to operate from ships off the Virginia coast, making it even more difficult for slaves to reach him. Most importantly, a deadly smallpox epidemic in Dunmore's camp deterred many slaves from joining him, thereby dooming his campaign.[29]

Despite its failure, Dunmore's gambit sent the colonists into a panic. They knew that if the British could enlist enough slaves into the loyalist forces, the Revolution would collapse and their property and lives would be endangered. These pragmatic fears, mixed with the egalitarian ideals of the Revolution, compelled the white colonists to begin making their first halting efforts at ensuring equality for black Americans.

Prior to December 1775, and despite the bravery of blacks in the battles of Lexington and Concord and Bunker Hill, the colonists sought to create an all-white army. Shortly after he took command of the Continental forces in July 1775, George Washington ordered recruiting officers not to enlist "any deserter from the Ministerial army, nor any stroller, negro, or vagabond." With the consent of the Continental Congress, Washington reiterated the order on November 12, declaring, "Neither Negroes, Boys unable to bare Arms, nor old men unfit to endure the fatigues of the campaign are to be inlisted." Those blacks already serving in the army would not be allowed to reenlist.[30]

When word of Dunmore's appeal reached him, however, Washington sensed the danger. On December 26, 1775, he wrote, "If that man, Dunmore, is not crushed before Spring, he will become the most dangerous man in America. His strength will increase like a snowball rolling down hill. Success will depend on which side can arm the Negroes the faster."[31] In response, on December 30, Washington rescinded his previous order and declared that blacks already serving in the army could reenlist. He reasoned that these black soldiers "are very much dissatisfied at being discarded" and that if forced out of the American forces, they "may seek employ in the Ministerial Army." Congress quickly ratified Washington's order, declaring on January 16, 1776, "That the free negroes who have served faithfully in the army at Cambridge, may be re-enlisted, but no others."[32]

Further military crises soon forced the colonists to drop this last qualification. By the end of 1776, following an unsuccessful campaign, bouts of smallpox, and widespread desertions, Washington's army numbered only a few thousand men and risked disintegrating. Congress attempted to reinforce the army by ordering the states to draft enough men for eighty-eight battalions, but this proved difficult since few wanted to serve. In order to fill their quotas, the states ignored their own requirements and began recruiting free blacks. Desperate for men, Washington also gave way on his ban against further black enlistments.[33]

Shortages of fighting men soon forced the states to go beyond this recruitment of free blacks and start enlisting slaves as well. After the disastrous winter at Valley Forge in 1777–1778, the states and the Congress began to look with increasing favor on the idea of enrolling slaves in the militia in return for their freedom. Many slaves had already filtered into the army, usually as substitutes for their masters, but their recruitment had not yet been officially sanctioned. Rhode Island took the first step. In January 1778, a group of Rhode Island officers proposed to General Washington that they be sent back to their state to find new recruits, including "a battalion of negroes." Washington agreed and sent a letter to Rhode Island's governor asking him to "give the officers employed in this business all the assistance in your power." The need for slave enlistments in Rhode Island had become even more crucial because, in addition to fulfilling its quota for the Continental army, the state also needed to raise soldiers for its own defense against a British invasion. Consequently, the state assembly voted to recruit two battalions of slaves who would be given their freedom after their term of service ended. The state would compensate their owners up to £120. But this enlistment was highly controversial; six months later the assembly reversed itself. By then, however, one battalion of slaves had already been formed and sent into battle.[34]

Despite Rhode Island's second thoughts, military necessity compelled the use of slaves and "before the end of the war most states, as well as the Continental Congress, were enlisting slaves with the understanding that they were to receive their freedom at the end of their service."[35] By 1779, the Continental Congress explicitly recommended the enlistment of slaves. Most black soldiers came from the North. Maryland, however, also authorized the recruitment of blacks, both slave and free, and Virginia allowed free blacks to serve in its forces. Virginia, along with North Carolina, also allowed slaves to serve as substitutes for their masters. Only South Carolina and Georgia refused officially to employ blacks in their forces at all. Overall, between five thousand and eight thousand black soldiers, out of a total force of three hundred thousand, served in American revolutionary armies. Thousands more worked as civilian laborers for the military, many of whom also gained freedom after the war.[36]

The military service of these blacks disrupted the racial status quo in two ways. First, it provided freedom to thousands of slaves, particularly in the North, thereby undermining slavery in those states. Second, through their service, these blacks gave lie to notions of their racial inferiority, providing evidence against the leading rationalizations of the nation's racial hierarchies.

The Revolutionary War also damaged the institution of slavery in other ways. Thousands of blacks took advantage of wartime disruptions to flee from their masters. By one estimate, nearly twenty thousand southern slaves, or roughly 5 percent of the total number of southern blacks, fled to the British.[37] Another four thousand blacks were evacuated by the British from New York in 1783.[38] Thousands of others fled to Spanish-controlled Florida or to the unsettled areas to the west. Many others who escaped remained in the states and managed to pass themselves off as free blacks. By one estimate, 30 percent of South Carolina's slaves and 75 percent of Georgia's fled, migrated, or died as a result of the war. Thomas Jefferson claimed that thirty thousand Virginia slaves ran away in 1778 alone.[39] Another estimate suggests that throughout the colonies, one hundred thousand slaves, approximately 20 percent of the total slave population, took advantage of the war to gain their freedom.[40]

The combined impact of the Revolution's ideological fervor, the service of black soldiers in the American armies, and the erosion of the slave system caused by the mass flight of blacks led white Americans to take the first steps to erode the racial hierarchies they had constructed over the previous 150 years. Most significant was the dismantling of slavery in the North during and immediately after the war. In 1777, Vermont became the first state to ban slavery, declaring in its constitution, "All men are born equally free and independent." In 1780, Massachusetts' new constitution declared, "All men are born free and equal, and have certain, essential, and unalienable rights." Three years later, the Massachusetts courts interpreted this clause to mean the abolition of slavery in the state. Many in New Hampshire read that state's constitution of 1783 as also ending slavery there, though it did not do so explicitly, and the institution dragged on until sometime after the turn of the century. In addition to these states that banned slavery outright, several others passed acts of gradual abolition. In 1780, Pennsylvania declared that all children born to slaves would be set free once they reached the age of twenty-eight. Four years later, both Rhode Island and Connecticut passed similar measures.[41]

Efforts to ban slavery in New York and New Jersey were more difficult and lengthy. In both states, wartime disruptions, an increasing number of private manumissions, and the freeing of slaves confiscated from loyalists gravely weakened the institution. Still, a gradual abolition bill narrowly failed in New York in 1785. It was not until 1799 that the state finally enacted a law freeing the children of slaves once they reached their twenty-eighth birthday. In 1804, New Jersey adopted a gradual abolition bill, becoming the last of the northern states to act against slavery. Despite the lag between the end of the war and passage of these acts, the relationship between the ideals of the Revolution and the actions of New York and New Jersey is clear. Both states chose July 4 as the day when their acts would go into effect.[42]

Northern blacks made other advances. Several northern states revised their laws to afford blacks a greater measure of legal and political rights, including, most importantly, the right to vote. The New Jersey constitution of 1776 gave the right to vote to all inhabitants who met the property qualification, without regard to race or sex. The Vermont constitution of 1777 extended the franchise to all free men without regard to race. The New York constitution of the same year allowed free black males to vote so long as they met the same property qualification set for white male voters. In 1783, Massachusetts's courts similarly declared that free black males subject to taxation had the right to vote. The Pennsylvania constitution of 1790 extended the right of suffrage to all freemen, without reference to race or property. Although some districts did not accept that blacks could truly be "freemen," most recognized blacks' right to vote.[43]

This wave of abolitionist sentiment, however, failed to sweep the South. In 1785 and 1786, the state legislatures of Maryland, Delaware, and Virginia debated but ultimately defeated plans for gradual abolition. In the rest of the South, abolition was never considered seriously. Although abolitionism may have failed in the region, the Revolution greatly altered southern race relations. The most significant change wrought in this period was the rise of the southern free black population. Prior to 1760, the words *black* and *slave* were nearly synonymous throughout the South, but by the early 1800s a sizable population of free blacks had emerged. By 1810, free blacks made up 10.4 percent of the black population in the upper South and 3.9 percent in the deep South.[44]

One factor contributing to this increase was the number of slaves in the South who had been freed in exchange for military service during the Revolution. When several masters attempted to renege on their promise of freedom to slaves who had served in their place, Virginia governor Benjamin Harrison reacted angrily. He denounced such efforts as a violation of "common principles of justice and humanity," and asked the state assembly to pass legislation "giving to those unhappy creatures that liberty which they have been in some measure instrumental in securing to us." The assembly quickly passed a bill guaranteeing the freedom of those blacks who had served in the war and ordering the state's attorney general to represent any who were still held as slaves.[45]

The egalitarian spirit of the Revolution also led many Southerners to free their own slaves. George Washington is a case in point. Prior to the war, Washington appears to have been a typical southern slave owner. While not an unusually cruel master, he did believe in the innate inferiority of blacks, and he was not above dealing with a troublesome slave by selling him off in the West Indies. But Washington changed his views as the war persisted. Not only did he reverse himself on allowing blacks to serve in the military; he also became a strong advocate of enlisting slaves into the American ranks in exchange for their freedom. Evidence that these changes reflected more than wartime exigencies came soon after the war. Washington then stated that it was "among my first wishes to see some plan adopted by which slavery may be abolished by law." Finally, Washington wrote into his will that his slaves should be set free upon the death of his wife.[46]

The rapid spread of evangelical Christianity in the South in the 1770s and 1780s combined with the Revolutionary egalitarianism of the age to further advance the antislavery cause. In a theological version of natural rights philosophy, evangelical Christians emphasized the equality of all humans in the eyes of God. Consequently, slavery was a sin that required extirpation before one could acquire salvation. The mixing of evangelical theology and the secular spirit of the American Revolution is evident in the Methodists' attack on slavery. In 1784, Methodist leaders denounced slavery as "contrary to the Golden law of God on which hang all the Law and the Prophets, and the unalienable Rights of Mankind, as well as every Principle of the Revolution," and agreed to expel members who continued to hold slaves.[47]

The rise of these antislavery sentiments led most southern states to liberalize their manumission laws. Prior to the war, legal restrictions made private manumission difficult, if not impossible. But the war brought changes, and according to historian Ira Berlin, "[b]y 1790, manumission was a slaveholder's prerogative throughout the South, except in North Carolina." Accordingly, a wave of manumissions swept the region, particularly the upper South, in the years after the war.[48]

Southern states also made it easier for blacks to attain their freedom through legal suits and by self-purchase in the immediate postwar years. Southern free blacks also saw a lessening of some of the legal and social barriers they faced. Some could even attend integrated churches and schools. A few states allowed free blacks to participate in local militias and exercise various rights in the legal system, including the right to jury trials, to bring witnesses, and to hire legal counsel. In principle, free blacks in Delaware, Kentucky, Maryland, North Carolina, and Tennessee had the vote. Although property qualifications and local prejudices served to limit actual voting by free blacks, there is evidence that it did occur in each of these states and that white politicians even campaigned for the votes of blacks.[49]

The antislavery sentiments of the 1780s also registered at the level of national government. In 1787, the Continental Congress voted to bar slavery from the Northwest Territories. Although not without its flaws (the act did not free slaves already in the territory but merely prohibited the further spread of the institution), the Northwest Ordinance was an important blow against slavery since the Northwest Territories (the current states of Ohio, Indiana, Illinois, Michigan, and Wisconsin) were the principal avenue for the nation's expansion.

Moreover, it passed the Congress with the unanimous support of the eight states present (four from the South). Only one individual member of Congress, a Northerner no less, voted against it. These facts suggest the strength of antislavery sentiment throughout the nation.[50]

By the end of the 1780s, the nation had undergone a profound transformation in its beliefs and institutions regarding slavery and race. In 1760, slavery was deeply woven into the social and economic fabric, particularly in the South, but in many areas of the North as well. Furthermore, few Americans questioned this fact, seeing slavery as a practical necessity if not a positive good. By the end of the 1780s, however, numerous critics of slavery loudly voiced their objections in every region of the country. Furthermore, the nation had, in the Declaration of Independence, established a political creed of human equality that sharply contradicted the institution of human bondage and seemed to put slavery at odds with the nation's fundamental beliefs. Versions of those beliefs that defended the institution could certainly be found, but few championed them militantly. Nor were these changes merely at the level of rhetoric. Northern laws and the Northwest Ordinance had put slavery on the path to extinction in those regions, southern laws had permitted the growth of manumissions, and many free blacks enjoyed significantly greater rights than in the late colonial era.

As significant as the changes of the Revolutionary era were, they were also incomplete. Although the politics of waging revolutionary war could drive white Americans to trumpet egalitarian principles of human liberty, the enduring economic and political interests forged by their longtime enslavement of blacks also created pressures to find ways not to carry those principles too far. As the ideological fervor of the war passed, these racially conservative forces exerted themselves with rising intensity in an effort to recraft the racial hierarchies that the war had undermined. They increasingly looked to the strands in American political ideology that defended racial exclusions and subordinations, countering unqualified adherence to principles of human rights.

Ironically, one of the most important attempts to limit the application of the principles of the Declaration of Independence came from that document's author, Thomas Jefferson. In 1787, Jefferson published one of his less acknowledged but most enduring achievements: the leading early exposition of American scientific racism. In his *Notes on the State of Virginia,* probably the most influential American book of the 1780s, Jefferson condemned slavery but insisted that legal discriminations against blacks reflected "real distinctions" in the races that were "fixed in nature." Blacks were, he suggested, "inferior" in "reason" and "imagination" to whites. Physically, they were well equipped for manual labor, "more tolerant of heat, and less so of cold," and needing less sleep. They also emitted a "very strong and disagreeable odour." And they were ruled by intense but fleeting passions: they longed for sex, especially with the more beautiful whites, just as black women were sought after by the "Oran-ootan." After rehearsing all these now-familiar racist stereotypes, Jefferson admitted that the evidence for them was questionable, especially in light of the severe conditions under which American blacks lived. Even so, he thought it most likely that black "inferiority is not the effect merely of their condition of life." It was natural. Hence it was wise for the law to "keep those in the department of man as distinct as nature has formed them." Although that admonition stopped short of endorsing slavery (or of deterring its author from interracial relations), and though as a young man Jefferson proposed a bill to ban slavery in Virginia, thereafter he never worked actively against the institution, or against any other form of black oppression, during his many years in high state and national offices.[51]

Jefferson was not the only one expressing doubts about the nation's revolutionary ideals. The war had unleashed a wave of radical sentiments generally that had profoundly shaken nearly every aspect of American society. By the middle of the 1780s, an increasing number of political and economic elites worried that, if allowed to continue, these radical sentiments would sabotage the nation's economic development and leave it vulnerable to foreign aggression or domestic uprisings such as Shay's Rebellion. Thus, whether motivated by personal financial gain or by more public-spirited reasons, the primary concern of those behind the drafting of the Constitution was not to realize further the egalitarian promise of the Declaration of Independence. It was to foster commercial development, the explicit aim of the call for the Philadelphia convention, by creating a government that could establish and maintain social order and protect the rights of property owners. Moreover, these concerns were so paramount that, almost to a man, the delegates from the ostensibly antislavery North would make common cause with those Southerners who sought to stop or roll back the racial progress of the previous decade. In doing so, the framers of the Constitution compromised the rights and liberties of those Americans held as slaves and undercut the antislavery impulse of the age in order to achieve their goals.[52]

The three-fifths clause was the most important of these compromises. Many Northerners opposed the counting of slaves at all when apportioning Representatives, since doing so would inflate the southern presence in the new House to the North's disadvantage. Southerners were strongly in favor of counting slaves on an equal basis with the whites who would control the extra Representatives these numbers would provide. On June 11, James Wilson of Pennsylvania and Charles Pinckney of South Carolina offered a compromise, by which slaves would count as three-fifths of a person for purposes of congressional representation, as a means of settling the issue. Although he opposed slavery, wrote historian Paul Finkelman, "harmony at the convention was more important to Wilson than the place of slavery in the new nation."[53]

This compromise, by which Northerners would not only recognize slavery but which would also allow the South to profit from it politically in exchange for southern support for the Union and for national commercial regulation, enjoyed widespread support among the delegates. Only Gouverneur Morris of Pennsylvania was willing to speak out against it, declaring that if the choice was between "doing injustice to the Southern States or to human nature," he "could never agree to give such encouragement to the slave trade . . . by allowing them a representation for their negroes." The three-fifths compromise, he added, "when fairly explained comes to this: that the inhabitant of Georgia and S.C. who goes to the Coast of Africa, and in defiance of the most sacred laws of humanity tears away his fellow creatures from their dearest connections and damns them to the most cruel bondages, shall have more votes in a Govt. instituted for protection of the rights of mankind, than the Citizens of Pa or N. Jersey who views with a laudable horror, so nefarious a practice." The delegates, however, were unmoved, and they voted overwhelmingly for the compromise.[54]

The willingness of the North to compromise with the slave states did not end with the three-fifths clause. The convention later voted to include provisions that barred congressional interference with the slave trade until 1808, promised federal help against any slave insurrections, and banned taxation of exports or imported slaves. The delegates also added a fugitive slave clause, requiring that slaves who escaped into free states be returned to their masters.[55] In exchange for these protections for slavery in the Constitution, the southern delegates voted for a provision to allow Congress to pass commercial regulations with the vote of a simple majority. Charles Cotesworth Pinckney noted that such regulations ran contrary to the "true interest" of the southern states; but in light of the Northerners' "liberal conduct" toward the South on slavery issues, he was prepared to go along with the commerce power.[56] According to Paul Finkelman, "On every issue at the convention, slaveowners had won major concessions from the rest of the nation, and with the exception of the commerce clause they had given up very little to win these concessions. The northern delegates had been eager for a stronger Union with a national court system and a unified commercial system. Although some had expressed concern over the justice or safety of slavery, in the end they were able to justify their compromises and ignore their qualms."[57]

By so doing, the delegates dealt a strong blow to the racial egalitarianism of the age. By leaving slavery intact, they signaled that the desire to end slavery was, at best, secondary to the desires for union, commerce, and order. Furthermore, they created a Constitution that gave slaveholders additional power in the new national legislative chambers simply because they held slaves. That system of representation provided crucial protection for their peculiar institution against further attack.

The first Congress organized under the new Constitution met in New York in February 1790. It soon confronted a petition submitted by Benjamin Franklin and other Pennsylvania abolitionists asking it to "devise means for removing this inconsistency from the character of the American people; that you will promote mercy and justice toward this distressed race; and that you will step to the very verge of the power vested in you for discouraging every species of traffic in the person of our fellow men." The petition set off a storm in the House of Representatives, as southern members denounced the abolitionists and demanded that the body ignore the petition. William Smith of South Carolina cited Jefferson's *Notes* as proof that "negroes were by nature an inferior race of beings," so that their servitude should not be questioned. He added that Pennsylvanian Quakers might favor emancipation for blacks, but none of them ever married one. In the face of this opposition and fearful that the slave states might yet reject the new union, Congress dismissed Franklin's petition, claiming it lacked the authority to interfere with slavery.[58]

Congress's refusal to consider Franklin's petition was emblematic of the nation's reluctance to carry forward the abolitionist impulse that had grown out of the Revolutionary era. Over the next two decades, abolitionism would die out as an effective force in American society. Its demise came most quickly and clearly in the South, where abolitionism was weakest and slavery, especially after the invention of the cotton gin, was crucial to the economy. Added to this was the reaction of white Southerners to the slave revolts in the West Indies during the early 1790s. Horror stories of violence against whites on the island of Saint Dominque abounded in the region, filling southern whites with dread that the same fate might await them. Rumors of slave rebellions swept through the South. These rumors had some basis in reality; between 1790 and 1800, the number of slave revolts increased 150 percent over the previous decade.[59] In 1800, Gabriel Prosser's unsuccessful rebellion in Virginia raised white anxieties to new levels.

These slave revolts, both real and imagined, eliminated abolitionism as an effective force in southern society and politics. According to historian Winthrop Jordan, "Virginia's black conspirators did not kill any whites, but they did a remarkably effective job on Virginia antislavery."[60] Between 1803 and 1825, no southern delegates attended the American Convention of Abolitionist Societies.[61] By 1805, one southern abolitionist declared, "We are in fact dead; and I may say, I have no hope of reanimation."[62]

Religious opponents of slavery also fell on hard times. In response to a Methodist antislavery petition in 1800, a mob of proslavery whites in Charleston, South Carolina accosted the town's Methodist leaders, burned their petitions, and held the head of one preacher under a pump until he nearly drowned.[63] In the face of such opposition, the Methodists, along with the Baptists and Presbyterians, reversed their previous antislavery tenets. By 1804, the Methodist General Conference was telling its preachers to "admonish and exhort all slaves to render due respect and obedience to the commands and interests of their respective masters."[64]

White Southerners also acted to tighten many of the laws regarding slaves and free blacks that had been loosened in the Revolutionary era. After 1800, most southern states placed new restrictions on private manumissions, either banning them outright or making former owners liable for the support and good behavior of their freed slaves.[65] Fearful of rebellion, especially in the aftermath of the slave revolts led by Denmark Vesey and Nat Turner, the southern states enacted even harsher slave codes. The codes varied from state to state, but, according to historians John Hope Franklin and Alfred Moss Jr., "the general point of view expressed in [the slave codes] was the same: slaves are not people but property. Laws should protect the ownership of such property and should also protect whites against any dangers that might arise from the presence of large numbers of slaves. It was also felt that slaves should be maintained in the position of due subordination in order that the optimum of discipline and work could be achieved."[66] As a result, by the 1830s, the institution of southern black slavery had evolved into its most repressive form, with few limits on the power of whites over blacks and few exceptions to the institution's rigid racial hierarchy.[67]

Fear of slave revolts also led to restrictions on southern free blacks since many white Southerners saw them as the most likely catalyst for slave unrest. According to one, "If the blacks see all their color slaves, it will seem to them a disposition of Providence, and they will be content. But if they see others like themselves free, and enjoying rights they are deprived of, they will repine."[68] By 1800, Delaware, Maryland, and Kentucky had disfranchised their free blacks. Free blacks also faced an increasing number of repressive laws that limited their economic and social autonomy. Maryland even went so far as to limit free blacks from owning more than one dog, and then only with a yearly license. Free blacks were also made to follow rigid requirements to prove their free status, with the failure to do so punishable by a return to slavery. North Carolina required its free blacks to wear a patch with the word FREE on their shoulder. Ultimately, the line between slaves and free blacks became so thin that the latter were, in the description of one historian, "slaves without masters."[69]

Not content merely to control or degrade free blacks, most southern states sought to remove them entirely. In 1806, the Virginia legislature enacted a law ordering newly freed blacks to leave the state. Fearing that they would become the dumping ground for Virginia's manumitted slaves, Kentucky, Maryland, and Delaware voted to bar the entry of free blacks in 1807, 1808, and 1811, respectively. By 1832, every southern state had enacted laws barring free blacks from entering their borders.[70]

While the reaction against racial egalitarianism came most strongly in the South, it was not confined to that region. Fears of slave revolts spreading from the Caribbean and bringing violence and disorder to the United States proved "fatal to antislavery throughout the nation."[71] Citing the horrors of the Caribbean slave revolts, one member of Congress questioned the wisdom of abolitionist petitions to Congress: "When thousands of people have been massacred, and thousands have fled for refuge in this country, when the proprietors of slaves . . . could only keep them in peace with the utmost of difficulty, was this a time for such inflammatory motions?"[72] Congress as a whole continued to turn a blind eye toward abolitionist petitions and began passing a series of laws that called into question the nation's egalitarian commitments.

In 1790, the same Congress that heard William Smith's tirade against blacks and then refused Franklin's antislavery petition went on to restrict the naturalization of immigrants to whites. Since that Congress contained many of the men who had written the Constitution, this law would long serve as a central piece of evidence for those who claimed the United States was intended to be an essentially white nation. Two years later, Congress prohibited African Americans from serving in the militia, despite the gallant service of blacks in the Revolutionary War.[73] In 1793, Congress passed the Fugitive Slave Law, which gave the aid of the federal courts to slaveowners seeking to retrieve runaways from free states. It also restricted the due process protections available to free blacks, making them even more vulnerable to being kidnapped back into slavery. In 1803, Congress voted down a gradual emancipation plan for the District of Columbia by a better than two-to-one margin.[74] In 1810, the federal government barred blacks from carrying the mail, since many whites feared that this would give free blacks greater opportunity to circulate among slaves, spreading radical ideas and organizing revolts.[75]

The retreat from racial equality was also evident at the state level in the North. Throughout the early decades of the 1800s, many northern states moved to roll back the political rights that had been granted to African Americans, particularly the right to vote. Ohio, which had a color-blind suffrage provision in its territorial constitution of 1787, restricted the vote to whites when it drew up its state constitution in 1802. In 1807, New Jersey, which until then had allowed both free blacks and women to vote, passed a law limiting the suffrage to white males. Seven years later, Connecticut, which had given blacks the right to vote in 1802, reversed itself and barred blacks from voting. In 1814, New York passed a series of voting restrictions that, while retaining the right of suffrage for blacks, placed a number of special burdens upon its exercise.[76]

Restrictions upon black voting rights were also evident in the territories. Prior to 1808, Congress provided for suffrage in the territories without regard to race. Between that year and 1860, however, Congress adopted whites-only suffrage provisions for every territory, except for Illinois in 1809.[77]

Some abolitionist sentiment lingered on through the first decade of the 1800s. Although strong enough to help push Congress to ban the slave trade in 1808 (an effort greatly aided by the proponents of the domestic slave trade), northern abolitionist sentiment had all but vanished by 1810.[78] Only in New York did abolitionists retain an active presence, and even there the principal focus was on educating and uplifting free blacks rather than on ending slavery or furthering blacks' political or legal rights.[79] Even the slave trade prohibition meant little, because for years the United States refused to sign a multination treaty of "reciprocal search and seizure" that would have rendered the ban effective. When the United States finally did so in 1842 and created an African Squadron to suppress the trade, the navy coldly instructed its sailors that the United States did "not regard the success of their efforts" as the country's "paramount interest, nor . . . paramount duty."[80]

The War of 1812, unlike the Revolution, did little to reanimate abolitionism or racial egalitarianism, despite the brave service of black soldiers and sailors in such important engagements as the Battle of Lake Erie and the Battle of New Orleans.[81] The reasons for this are two-fold. First, the War of 1812 lacked the ideological purpose and commitment of the previous war. Described as a war for "Free Trade and Sailors' Rights," it centered around American commercial interests and national pride.[82] According to Andrew Jackson:

> We are going to fight for the reestablishment of our national character, misunderstood and vilified at home and abroad; for the protection of our maritime citizens, impressed on board British ships of war and compelled to fight the battles of our enemies against ourselves; to vindicate our right to free trade, and open a market for the productions of our soil, now perishing on our hands because the *mistress of the ocean* has forbid us to carry them to any foreign nation; in fine, to seek some indemnity for past injuries, some security against future aggressions, by the conquest of all British dominions upon the continent of north america.[83]

Conspicuously lacking from Jackson's *raison d'guerre,* and from those offered by other Americans, was the passionate rhetoric of natural rights that motivated the American Revolution. Furthermore, many Americans were deeply opposed to the war. This was especially so in New England, the likely location of any serious effort to enlist African Americans into the military and to link the purposes of the war to the antislavery cause.[84]

The two wars also differed in scope and intensity. In the Revolution, the nation's very existence stood in the balance. In 1812, the stakes were much smaller. Although the British burned Washington,

D.C. to force the Americans to trade on their terms, they never seriously sought to end the United States' national existence or independence. The more limited nature of the war is seen in the fact that in it only 1,877 Americans were killed, as against at least 25,000 killed in the Revolution.[85] And for the most part, the war was fought outside the main slaveholding regions, where both the British and Americans would have been tempted to bring blacks into their forces. Consequently, America in 1812 largely avoided the military threats and pressing need for manpower that had been instrumental to the greater inclusion of blacks during the Revolution.

Still, when the military situation did seem desperate enough, the nation once again discarded its prejudices against black military service in order to meet the crisis at hand. In 1814 it seemed that the British, after capturing and burning the nation's capital, were about to move north against Philadelphia and New York City. Although the British threat never materialized, both Pennsylvania and New York quickly moved to recruit blacks to help defend against the anticipated attack, with New York promising freedom to slaves in return for their service. That same year Andrew Jackson accepted the service of the Louisiana militia's Free Black Battalion. He did this not only to augment his strength against the British but also to prevent Louisiana's blacks from giving their support to the enemy. Jackson's move was a wise one, since the Free Black Battalion played an important role in the American victory in the Battle of New Orleans in January 1815. Service such as this was lauded by many white Americans. Even Jackson, hardly a racial liberal, praised the valor of his black troops.

The military role of blacks in the War of 1812 was still too limited, however, to stem the racial revanchism that was sweeping the nation, as white Americans increasingly rejected revolutionary beliefs in human moral equality and the possibility that blacks and whites might both be equal members of the same nation. Confronted by a still-rising free black population and deepening southern dependency on slavery, many whites began elaborating the traditional anti-black themes in American political thought. One product of these changing attitudes was the rise of the colonization movement. Some whites supported colonization because they believed that free blacks constituted a perpetually inferior class of paupers, drunkards, and criminals. Eliphalet Nott, the procolonization president of Union College, pointed to the dismal condition of most northern free blacks. He claimed that they "have remained already to the third and fourth, as they will to the thousandth generation—a distinct, a degraded, a wretched race."[86] Other colonizationists rejected notions of innate black inferiority, arguing that any inferiority resulted from living in an environment of white prejudice. Even so, they believed that this prejudice was so deep-rooted that blacks could never become full and equal members of American society. Whatever the motivation, the rise of support for colonization among northern white reformers constituted a rejection of the inclusive, egalitarian spirit of the Revolutionary era.[87]

The rise of scientific racism in America reflected and reinforced these attitudes. During the eighteenth century and the early decades of the nineteenth, most American scientists endorsed "monogenesis," the belief that all races were part of the human species and that any differences among them resulted purely from environmental effects. But in 1811, Dr. Charles Caldwell attacked monogenesis, arguing that biblical chronology indicated that blacks had not been present on earth long enough to have evolved into a separate race. Rather, he claimed, the different races had resulted from "polygenesis," or the creation of the different races as distinct species. Moreover, Caldwell argued that whites' cultural and intellectual superiority was so profound that it could only have resulted from a "gift of nature" rather than the environment.[88]

The scientific racism of Caldwell, Dr. Samuel George Morton of Philadelphia, Dr. John Van Evrie of New York, and others spread throughout the American scientific community in the first half of the nineteenth century. The best known advocate of such arguments was Josiah Nott, a Pennsylvania-trained Alabama physician and self-described expert in the field of "niggerology." According to Nott, blacks and whites constituted separate and unequal species, with blacks "intended by nature for a similar dependence on the Caucasian man, in which only the ox, the ass, and the horse fulfill the intent of their creation."[89] Nott added, "No philanthropy, no legislation, no missionary labors can change this law. It is written in man's nature by the hand of his creator."[90] In 1854, Nott persuaded the nation's leading naturalist, Louis Aggasiz of Harvard, to join him and others in a magnum opus of the new scientific racism, *Types of Mankind,* the *Bell Curve* of the antebellum era. It was dedicated to proving that the "Caucasian races" had "in all ages, the largest brains and the most powerful intellect," and so were "destined eventually to conquer" and "rule" virtually "every foot of the globe." Although bulky and ponderous, the book went through seven editions in the next year.[91]

Like William Smith quoting Jefferson in 1790, many antebellum defenders of slavery readily invoked such science to support their cause. They contended that slavery did not violate the nation's creed of human equality, since blacks either weren't really human, after all, or they were so degraded a rank of humanity that they had no claim to the rights of white men. Slavery was instead the natural and mutually beneficial outgrowth of the unequal status of blacks and whites.[92]

But though the polygenesis theories of Nott and others gained a wide following among many Americans, such scientific explanations troubled the more religious among slavery's defenders, because they appeared to contradict scripture on the origins of the human race. Fortunately for these faithful whites, the Bible offered them an alternative explanation for black inferiority. Relying on the Bible's description of the curse of Ham, religious whites could argue that slavery was divinely ordained, since God had condemned blacks to be "servants unto servants."[93]

The mocking depictions of blacks long prevalent in American popular culture gained fresh credibility from these learned doctrines of black inferiority. In the early 1830s, T. D. Rice, a white performer, developed the comic, black-faced, minstrel character named "Jim Crow." Rice's Jim Crow character proved immensely popular with white audiences throughout the nation. Soon, "many plays, even some tragedies, included a Negro song act."[94]

These developments in American science, religion, and popular entertainment combined to permit most white Americans to reject the egalitarian moral premise of the Declaration of Independence, that all men were equal in basic rights, and instead to subscribe to the propriety of racial hierarchy. The first open and highly publicized congressional proclamations of this shift came during the Missouri controversy of 1819–1821. The dispute began over the issue of whether Missouri would enter into the union as a slave or free state. It quickly turned into a broader discussion of the institution of slavery and its relationship to American democracy. Antislavery advocates cited the Declaration of Independence as evidence that the nation's political creed fundamentally opposed slavery. New York Representative James Tallmadge told his colleagues, "You boast of the freedom of your Constitution and your laws; you have proclaimed, in the Declaration of Independence, 'That all men are created equal; that they are endowed by their Creator with certain inalienable rights; that amongst these are life liberty, and the pursuit of happiness;' and yet you have slaves in your country."[95]

In the past, proslavery advocates had usually allowed that slavery was incompatible with the principles of the Declaration but that practical necessity prevented emancipation, at least in the near term. During the Missouri controversy, however, defenders of slavery began to develop arguments that rejected the validity of the Declaration's egalitarian principles and made a positive defense of slavery. In 1820, Senator William Pinkney of Maryland stated, "The self-evident truths announced in the Declaration of Independence are not truths at all, if taken literally."[96] Another Southerner called the Declaration "a fanfaronade of metaphysical abstractions." Virginia congressman and later president, John Tyler, subsequently asserted, "The principle [of human equality in the Declaration], although lovely and beautiful, cannot obliterate those distinctions in society which society itself engenders and gives birth to. Liberty and equality are captivating sounds; but they often captivate to destroy."[97]

Other defenders of slavery claimed that the institution was essential to the nation's well-being. Senator Charles Pinckney declared that America's prosperity and global position derived in large part from the benefits of slavery. Destroy slavery, argued Pinckney, and you would gravely damage America's economy and national strength.[98] In contrast, Representative Louis McLane of Delaware professed to abhor slavery; but he still defended Missouri's right to maintain the institution and ban entry of free blacks. He insisted that everyone knew there was not "any possibility" that the "weaker caste" of blacks could "assimilate" with whites, any more than "oil with water." Law, "reason," and "nature" had all "drawn a line of discrimination which can never be effaced." America was at core and would always be a "white community," in which even free blacks must belong to an "inferior order." All suggestions that blacks might ever gain equal citizenship had to be firmly rejected.[99]

Slave state representatives were not the only ones expressing such views during the Missouri debates. In response to the question of whether the framers intended full political equality for blacks, including the right to vote, Senator John Holmes of Maine declared, "Gentlemen, with all their humanity, to be obliged to sit in this Senate by a black man, would consider their rights invaded." Perhaps unwittingly, Holmes's remark called into question his own status as a gentleman, since Maine was one of the few states that allowed blacks to vote and hold office.[100]

Although several Northerners argued forcefully against slavery, in the end, Congress allowed Missouri into the union as a slave state. Moreover, it accepted a new constitution that permitted the Missouri legislature to bar the immigration of free blacks and mulattos while forbidding it from emancipating slaves without the consent of their owners.[101] At the end of the Missouri controversy, according to historian Larry Tise, many Americans had developed a new and very different interpretation of their Revolutionary legacy: "Not only did the Revolution no longer require them to foster equalitarianism, emancipate slaves in the South, or incorporate the Negro in American society, their new reading of the intentions of the founders allowed them to bar both free and enslaved Negroes from certain sections of the nation wholly reserved for whites."[102]

Following the Missouri controversy, white Americans sought to ensure that their legal and political systems reflected their mounting denigration of blacks. One central target was black suffrage. New York led the way in the 1820s. Previously, all free adult male citizens of the Empire State, black or white, were allowed to vote so long as they met certain property qualifications. Then in 1821, the state's constitutional convention moved to disfranchise blacks. A committee recommended that the word *white* be inserted into the state constitution's provision on the franchise. One delegate argued that such a clause was necessary since "[t]hey [blacks] are a peculiar people, incapable, in my judgment, of exercising that privilege [voting] with any sort of discretion, prudence, or independence. They have no just conceptions of civil liberty."[103] A Colonel Young asserted that such a provision was necessary to accommodate the racist sentiments of whites: "This distinction of color is well understood. It is unnecessary to disguise it, and we ought to shape our constitution so as to meet the public sentiment."[104] Another delegate was more blunt: "But it was said that the right of suffrage would elevate them [blacks]. [I] would ask whether it would elevate a monkey, or a baboon, to allow them to vote!!"[105] While the full convention voted down complete disfranchisement by a vote of only 63 to 59, it then decided by a vote of 72 to 30 to keep the property qualification for blacks while eliminating it for whites. This move amounted to the enduring disfranchisement of most of New York's blacks, since in 1825 only 298 of a total black population of 29,701 met the property qualifications.[106]

Other states soon followed New York's example. Between 1834 and 1838, Tennessee, North Carolina, Rhode Island, and Pennsylvania eliminated free black suffrage.[107] The arguments used to support disfranchisement in these states indicates how deeply held racist ideas had become. In North Carolina, one member of the legislature contended, "This is nation of white people—its offices, dignities and privileges, are alone open to, and to be enjoyed by, white people."[108] Another raised the fearful specter of miscegenation, arguing that if given the right to vote, a black man "will not be satisfied with a black wife. He will soon connect himself with a white woman."[109] Even in Pennsylvania, the home of the Declaration of Independence and much of the abolitionist fervor of the Revolutionary age, similar sentiments abounded. In 1837, Judge John Fox of Bucks County pronounced that those who framed the state constitution "were a political community of white men exclusively."[110] A Pennsylvania legislator declared, "The elevation of the black man is the degradation of the white man."[111] Others worried that giving blacks the right to vote would only serve to attract free blacks from neighboring states, who were "more dissipated than those of any other portion of our citizens. . . . Tens of thousands of this base and degraded caste [would be] vomited upon us."[112]

As these states took the franchise away from blacks, no state made the effort to extend it. In fact, the results of several state referenda show that extending the right of suffrage to blacks was overwhelmingly unpopular (see table 1).

The loss of the franchise was but one aspect of the deteriorating condition of free blacks in the North. States and localities throughout the North passed a variety of burdens upon free blacks, including curfews, requirements for the posting of bonds to guarantee their good behavior, and restrictions on their rights to assemble. In 1828, Congress instructed the corporation it had empowered to govern Washington, D.C. to forbid blacks from entering the U.S. Capitol grounds except on "business," such as making deliveries.[113] With increasing frequency after 1820, most northern states and localities forced black children into separate and inferior schools or denied them public education altogether. The South evaded the issue by rejecting public schools for either race.[114] Popular prejudice and legal

Table 1. Result of Referenda on Black Suffrage, 1846–1860

State	Year	Vote against Black Suffrage	%	Vote for Black Suffrage	%
New York	1846	224,336	72	85,406	28
Wisconsin	1847	14,615	66	7,564	34
Michigan	1850	32,026	71	12,840	29
Wisconsin	1857	40,106	59	27,550	41
Iowa	1857	49,511	85	8,489	15
New York	1860	345,791	64	197,889	36
Total		706,385	68	339,738	32

Sources: Data compiled by the authors from Eugene H. Berwanger, *The Frontier against Slavery: Western Anti-Negro Prejudice and the Slavery Extension Controversy* (Urbana: University of Illinois Press, 1967), pp. 41–2; Emil Olbrich, *The Development of Sentiment on Negro Suffrage to 1860* (Madison: University of Wisconsin, 1912), pp. 86, 98; and Phyllis F. Field, *The Politics of Race in New York: The Struggle for Black Suffrage in the Civil War Era* (Ithaca, N.Y.: Cornell University Press, 1982), pp. 61, 127.

restrictions also limited the economic opportunities of northern free blacks. In most northern cities, blacks were isolated into impoverished ghettoes, often with names like "Nigger Hill," "Little Africa," or "Hayti."[115] Blacks were also segregated in public transportation.[116] As a consequence of these and other burdens, most northern free blacks were economically deprived, socially and geographically segregated, and politically impotent.

The most serious restrictions on free blacks were found in the frontier areas of the midwestern and western regions: Ohio, Michigan, Indiana, Illinois, Wisconsin, Iowa, Minnesota, Oregon, and California, specifically. They were free of slavery and often the most vocal in opposing its spread; but not because of white racial egalitarianism. On the contrary, these areas were the most racist in the nation outside of the South. Speaking of his fellow Hoosiers, Indiana editor and future Radical Republican Congressman George W. Julian wrote, "Our people hate the Negro with a perfect if not supreme hatred."[117]

This hatred of blacks drove numerous restrictions on free blacks, including segregated schools and public facilities, antimiscegenation laws, and denials of suffrage rights. Few of these restrictions existed prior to 1802, since the white inhabitants of these areas either felt little threat from the small number of free blacks living among them then or feared that Congress would not grant them statehood if they enacted too many racial discriminations. As the number of blacks immigrating into these areas increased and as Congress spoke volumes through its own discriminatory laws and its silence on the issues of slavery and equal rights, whites on the frontier acted against blacks with mounting severity.[118]

Ohio enacted the first restriction on black immigration in 1807 when it required free blacks to post a $500 bond before being allowed to enter. Illinois followed in 1813 by directing justices of the peace to order immigrant blacks to leave the state. Blacks who failed to comply were given thirty-nine lashes of the whip every fifteen days until they left. Those blacks already residing in the state could stay, but only if they were properly registered and had paid a fifty-cent fee to obtain their free papers. By 1840, every state of the Old Northwest had passed laws restricting the immigration of blacks, usually forcing them to post a bond of between $500 and $1,000 to ensure their good behavior.[119]

As bad as they already were, the racist attitudes of frontier whites deepened after 1840. In 1850, an Ohio legislator commented that "prejudice against the negro [was] worse than it ever [had] been, and it [was] idle to suppose that this sentiment [would] ever decrease as long as the two races remain[ed] together."[120] This worsening of white attitudes came about as increased black immigration heightened economic competition and fears of miscegenation. Such worries led many whites to believe that previous black exclusion measures were insufficient—an invitation to black men "to make proposals to marry our daughters."[121] Hoping to prevent such a calamity, in 1851 the Iowa legislature enacted a law excluding the immigration of free blacks outright. The law, first proposed by a saloonkeeper Democrat from Clinton County, Billy G. Haun, made Iowa the first northern state to bar the immigration of free blacks.[122]

Opponents of the Iowa measure pointed out that it ran counter to the nation's supposed beliefs in human equality. During the legislature's debate over the measure, one opponent attempted to change its title to "An act . . . inoperative in certain cases, so much of the constitution of this state as reads 'all men are by nature free and independent and have certain inalienable rights, among which are those of enjoying and defending life and liberty, acquiring, possessing and protecting property and pursuing and obtaining safety and happiness.' " After the measure passed, one Iowa newspaper commented, "We have always been taught to believe, and it is hard for us to forget it, 'that all men are created equal.' But according to modern ethics the quotation should read 'that all men (*except niggers*) are created equal.' "[123]

The egalitarian ideals of the Declaration of Independence proved easy to forget in Iowa and throughout the frontier. Fearful that they would become a dumping ground for free blacks unless they adopted equally severe restrictions, Illinois and Indiana quickly enacted similar exclusion laws. The popularity of such measure among whites is evident from election returns. In an 1848 referendum, Illinois voters approved by a vote of 60,585 to 15,903 (79 to 21 percent) a constitutional amendment barring the immigration of blacks, but the Illinois legislation did not pass the necessary enforcement statutes until 1853. In Indiana, a popular referendum on the state's exclusion law carried by a margin of 113,628 to 21,873 (84 to 16 percent). Overall, during the 1840s and 1850s, nearly 80 percent of the whites in Illinois, Indiana, Oregon, and Kansas voted for black exclusion laws. Except for Wisconsin, every midwestern and western state passed some form of restriction on the entry of free blacks.[124]

Ironically, this rollback in black rights coincided with a resurgence in northern abolitionism in the 1830s. But, by itself, the new abolitionism did little to change white racial attitudes. On the contrary, the nation's initial reaction was to lash out furiously against the abolitionists and to become even more adamant in its defense of slavery and racial hierarchy. The popular New York writer and pro-slavery advocate James Kirke Paulding claimed that abolition "disturbed the peace of communities and states. It menaces the disruption of our social system, and tends directly to a separation of the Union."[125] To James T. Austin, the Attorney General of the state of Massachusetts, abolition meant amalgamation:

> Is it supposed they [blacks] could amalgamate? God forbid. . . . But I fearlessly aver that if this be the tendency and the result of our moral reformation, rather than our white race should degenerate into a tribe of tawny-colored quadroons, rather than our fair and beauteous females should give birth to the thick-lipped, woolly-headed children of African fathers, rather than the Negro should be seated in the Halls of Congress and his sooty complexion glare upon us from the bench of justice, rather than he should mingle with us in the familiar intercourse of domestic life and taint the atmosphere of our homes and firesides—I WILL BRAVE MY SHARE OF ALL RESPONSIBILITY OF KEEPING HIM IN SLAVERY.[126]

To other Americans who shared Austin's sentiments, actions spoke louder than words. Widespread violence against abolitionists and free blacks marred the 1830s and 1840s. In one typical instance in St. Louis in 1836, a white mob dragged a black prisoner from a local jail and burned him alive. The aptly named Judge Lawless then freed the mob's leaders, claiming that their actions resulted from an "electric frenzy" as a result of abolitionist agitation.[127] Similar scenes were played out in cities and town throughout the nation. *Niles' Register,* the most prominent national newspaper of the time, reported 48 instances of antiabolitionist and racial violence between 1830 and 1840. Antislavery newspapers reported 209 northern antiabolitionist mobs during this same period.[128] Such violence led Abraham Lincoln, then a rising figure in Illinois politics, to warn that "whenever the vicious portion of population shall be permitted to gather in bands of hundreds and thousands, and burn churches, ravage and rob provision stores, throw printing presses into rivers, shoot editors, and hang and burn obnoxious persons at pleasure, and with impunity; depend on it, this Government cannot last."[129]

Rather than respond to the pleas of Lincoln and others, the federal government acted to limit the influence of the abolitionists. The House of Representatives in 1835 passed the infamous "gag rule," banning official discussion of antislavery petitions in the chamber. That same year, the Postal Service allowed local postmasters to confiscate abolitionist literature that local authorities deemed subversive.[130]

Even without the violence and governmental suppression that the abolitionists suffered, it seems unlikely that their efforts would have gained much ground. Notions of racial superiority were firmly entrenched in the minds of most white Americans, many of whom had come to see themselves as a chosen people with special capacities for liberty. In the words of one orator, "Out of all the inhabitants of the world, . . . a select stock, the Saxon, and out of this the British family, the noblest of the stock, was chosen to people our country."[131] Such sentiments were not at all unusual. According to historian Reginald Horsman:

> By the 1830s the Americans were eagerly grasping at reasons for their own success and for the failure of others. Although the white Americans of Jacksonian America wanted personal success and wealth, they wanted a clear conscience. If the United States was to remain in the minds of its people a nation divinely ordained for great deeds, then the fault for the suffering inflicted in the rise to power and prosperity had to lie elsewhere. White Americans could rest easier if the sufferings of other races could be blamed on racial weaknesses rather than on the white's relentless search for wealth and power.[132]

The dynamics Horsman describes became abundantly clear in the mid-1840s, as the land-hungry nation's relentless westward expansion drove it toward a conflict that emphatically did not generate support for racial equality. Instead, U.S. leaders justified the Mexican-American War of 1848 by propagating anti-Hispanic smears that have forever since been triggers of ethnic antagonisms. Because Mexico steadfastly refused to provide the United States with a substantial reason for launching hostilities, politicians and newspapers supporting James K. Polk's administration contended that the superior American Anglo-Saxon race had an inescapable "manifest destiny" to spread out "like a mighty flood" over "all Mexico" and, indeed, all the Americas. The Spanish, after all, had always been a despicable, despotic, Jesuitical people. Scientific racists attested that the degenerate Spanish habit of intermarrying with the still-lower races they conquered had, moreover, produced in Mexico "wretched hybrids and mongrels" that were "actually inferior to the inferior race itself."

For Southerners like Polk's Secretary of the Treasury, Robert Walker, the surest proof of the Mexicans' "semi-barbarous" character was that they had ended slavery and were "openly engaged in the crusade of abolition" generally. Their pernicious influence had to be stilled so that it would not "stimulate the servile population" of the United States into "revolt and massacre." Clearly, a war fought in the name of Anglo-Saxon racial destiny and the need to protect and extend slavery worked to suppress, not strengthen, the racially egalitarian elements in U.S. ideological traditions.[133]

The Mexican-American War also resulted in a tremendous shift of land, resources, and people between the two nations, as the United States ultimately acquired California, Texas, New Mexico, Arizona, Utah, Nevada, and Colorado. Basking in the glow of the greatly augmented wealth and power these shifts produced, U.S. citizens could afterwards assure themselves that their negative stereotypes of Latinos were correct. But more conscientious Americans knew even then that this war of aggression, waged partly to extend slavery, was unjust. At the time, an ambitious first-term congressman cost himself reelection by repeatedly challenging the president to show cause for the war. Years later, an old soldier who had fought in it said that there had never been a more "wicked war" than the Mexican-American War of 1848 and regretted that he had not had "courage enough to resign." By then the soldier, Ulysses S. Grant, and the former congressmen, Abraham Lincoln, had shown they were more than willing to undertake war under very different circumstances— to prevent slavery from being extended. And sadly, they had to do so, because throughout the antebellum era other white Americans, north and south, built doctrines of racial inequality ever more extensively into their political ideologies and their state and national laws.[134]

The territorial expansion of the Mexican-American War exacerbated the nation's debate over the spread of slavery, but hardly in ways that condemned slavery or supported racial equality. In fact, the strongest opposition to slavery's spread came from the frontier areas that had placed numerous restrictions on the rights of free blacks. Although this may seem contradictory, it is quite understandable if both inclinations are understood to reflect the racist desire of whites in these areas to be free of all blacks, both free and slave. David Wilmot, the Free Soil Democrat, whose Wilmot Proviso sought to keep slavery from extending into the territories acquired as a result of the Mexican-American War, embodied this attitude. He declared, "I plead the cause and rights of white freemen [and] I would preserve to free white labor a fair country, a rich inheritance, where the sons of toil, of my own race and own color, can live without the disgrace which association with negro slavery brings upon free labor." In private, he expressed his hatred of blacks as well as the southern plantation owners more bluntly: "By God, sir, men born and nursed of white women are not going to be ruled by men who were brought up on the milk of some damn Negro wench!"[135] In fact, one Oregon election suggests frontier whites may have been more concerned with restricting the spread of free blacks than with restricting the spread of slavery. In the 1857 referendum on their new state constitution, only 74 percent of white Oregonians rejected slavery, but 89 percent supported excluding blacks from the state entirely![136]

This melding of racism and opposition to slavery's expansion characterized many in the new Republican party, which increasingly came to dominate northern politics in the 1850s. Prior to the Civil War, the Republican party opposed only the further extension of slavery into the territories. Although Lincoln always insisted that the nation should put slavery on the path of eventual extinction, neither he nor his party urged abolishing slavery where it already existed at any time in the foreseeable future, nor did they call for full equality for blacks, whether slave or free. In 1859, Republican senator Lyman Trumbull of Illinois declared, "We, the Republican party, are the white man's party. We are for the free white man, and for making white labor acceptable and honorable, which it can never be when negro slave labor is brought into competition with it." One party newspaper claimed that the Republican stand against the extension of slavery was not to help blacks but to protect whites from "the pestilential presence of the black man." Iowa Republicans summed it up more directly with the slogan WE ARE FOR LAND FOR THE LANDLESS, NOT NIGGERS FOR THE NIGGERLESS.[137]

And although Lincoln never quite endorsed beliefs in white supremacy as anything more than "feelings" or "prejudices," he was also careful never to propose genuine racial equality. He favored colonization; but that failing, he declared during one of his 1858 debates with Stephen Douglas:

> . . . I am not, nor ever have been in favor of bringing about in any way the social and political equality of the white and black races, [applause]—that I am not nor ever have been in favor of making voters or jurors of negroes, nor of qualifying them to hold

public office, nor to intermarry with white people; and I will say that in addition to this that there is a physical difference between the white and black races which I believe will for ever forbid the two races living together on terms of social and political equality. An inasmuch as they cannot so live, while they do remain together there must be the position of the superior and inferior, and I as much as any other man am in favor of having the superior position assigned to the white race.[138]

With even Republicans like Abraham Lincoln unwilling to speak in favor of racial equality, the 1850s saw further erosion of the rights of blacks. In 1850, Congress passed a new Fugitive Slave Act. Even more than the 1793 Fugitive Slave Act, the new law vastly expanded the scope of federal power and placed it in the service of slaveowners. United States marshals had to help slaveowners recapture their fugitives, the cost for which was borne by the government, not the slaveholders. The law also took the adjudication of slaveholders' claims against runaways out of the northern state courts by appointing hundreds of new federal commissioners to hear fugitive slave cases. In these cases, the alleged fugitives were denied due process and jury trials. The law even stated, "In no trial or hearing under this act shall the testimony of such alleged fugitive be admitted in evidence."[139] It also provided that a commissioner receive $10 in cases where he sided with a slaveowner, but only $5 when he ruled in favor of an alleged runaway. The bill's authors claimed that the difference was needed to compensate for the extra paperwork involved when a slave had to be returned. But obviously, the provision created a strong financial incentive to rule in favor of slaveowners. Given such advantages for slaveowners, it is no surprise that during the 1850s, 332 slaves were returned to their alleged masters under the act and only eleven maintained their freedom.[140]

The Fugitive Slave Act greatly endangered northern blacks. The law had no statute of limitations, so runaway slaves who had come North years before could still be dragged back into slavery. Furthermore, the law was so weighted against alleged fugitives that even free blacks risked being kidnapped into slavery. Rather than risk returning to slavery, many northern blacks chose to flee to Canada. The exact number who succeeded is impossible to determine, but evidence suggests that it was large. One estimate suggests that three thousand blacks ran off to Canada in the last three months of 1850 alone.[141] One black newspaper claimed that 40 percent of Boston's

blacks emigrated to Canada within twenty-four hours of the law's
passage. In Rochester, New York, 102 of the 114 members of one
black church ran off to Canada.[142]

The attack on black rights reached its culmination in 1857 with
the Supreme Court's decision in *Dred Scott v. Sanford.* Scott, a black
slave residing in Missouri, claimed that his travels into the free state
of Illinois and the free Wisconsin territory with his master had made
him free. The Court, in a 7–2 decision, denied Scott his freedom.
Chief Justice Roger Taney used the case to deliver "a sweeping proslavery polemic."[143] Denying the egalitarian spirit of the Revolutionary age and focusing on the accompanying patterns of continued
black oppression, Taney asserted that blacks had been considered
outside the scope of the Declaration of Independence and the Constitution, "a subordinate and inferior class of beings, who had been
subjugated by the dominant race, and whether emancipated or
not, yet remained subject to their authority."[144] Consequently, blacks
then, and blacks in 1857, had "no rights which the white man was
bound to respect."[145]

As Taney's opinion shows, the nation had completed its long march
away from the egalitarian ideals of the Declaration of Independence.
When that march began in 1789, the nation seemed guided by the
egalitarian spirit of the Declaration and the Revolution. Slavery had
been or was on its way to being abolished throughout the North
and greatly weakened in many areas of the South. Furthermore, free
blacks, in parts of both the North and the South, had been granted
a number of political and legal rights, including in some areas the
right to vote. Finally, few Americans, Southerners included, were
willing to defend slavery as a positive good, though they may have
disagreed over the wisdom of immediate abolition.

By 1860, however, America had become a very different place. In
the words of Horace Greeley, "the 'Color Phobia,' which prevails so
extensively . . . and causes such fearful spasms on those effected [sic]
by it, contrasts singularly enough with the politeness to Negroes
often exhibited by the Fathers of the Revolution."[146] The Declaration
of Independence was now seen as an irrelevant example of rhetorical excess, and its proposition that "all men are created equal" was
self-evidently limited to white men. Theories of racial hierarchy,
both scientific and religious, held sway among all classes of citizens.
In the South, slavery was vigorously defended as a positive good for
both whites and blacks. Law and custom protected the institution
from even the slightest of threats. In both the North and the South,

whites viewed free blacks as a dangerous and undesirable element to be segregated, excluded, and stripped of what few rights they had possessed at the outset of the century. Even among those opposed to slavery, few desired to do more than check its spread, and fewer yet sought to provide blacks with minimum guarantees of equal citizenship. Each of the two main political parties competed with one another to prove that they could best serve the interests of the white race.

Against this backdrop of retreat, there were only a few advances. In Massachusetts, blacks and their white allies were able to convince the state legislature to abolish segregated schools. In New York City, blacks achieved limited success in desegregating public transportation.[147] Throughout the North, a small but growing number of abolitionists began to attack slavery altogether and to question the nation's racial hierarchies in other areas.

Despite these achievements, the overall status of black Americans declined markedly in the 70 years prior to 1860. Abraham Lincoln saw this when he criticized Chief Justice Roger Taney's assumption in the *Dred Scott* decision "that the public estimate of the black man is more favorable *now* than it was in the days of the Revolution." According to Lincoln, "This assumption is a mistake. In some trifling particulars, the condition of that race has been ameliorated; but, as a whole, in this country, the change between then and now is decidedly the other way; and their ultimate destiny has never appeared so hopeless as in the last three or four years." Lincoln then went into particulars:

In two of the five States—New Jersey and North Carolina—that then gave the free negro the right of voting, the right has since been taken away; and in a third—New York—it has been greatly abridged. . . . In those days, as I understand, masters could, at their own pleasure, emancipate their slaves; but since then, such legal restraints have been made upon emancipation, as to amount almost to prohibition. In those days, Legislatures held the unquestioned power to abolish slavery in their respective States; but now it is becoming quite fashionable for State Constitutions to withhold that power from the Legislatures. . . . In those days the Declaration of Independence was held sacred by all, and thought to include all; but now, to aid in making the bondage of the negro universal and eternal, it is assailed, and sneered at, and construed, and hawked at, and torn, till, if its framers could rise from their graves, they could not at all recognize it.

After relating this pitiful history, Lincoln concluded:

> All the powers of earth seem rapidly combining against [black Americans]. Mammon is after him; ambition follows, and philosophy follows, and the Theology of the day is fast joining the cry. They have him in his prisonhouse; they have searched his person, and left no prying instrument with him. One after another they have closed the heavy iron doors upon him; and now they have him, as it were, bolted with the lock of a hundred keys, which can never be unlocked without the concurrence of every key— the keys in the hands of hundred different men, and they scattered to a hundred different and distant places; and they stand musing as to what invention, in all the dominions of the mind and matter, can be produced to make the impossibility of his escape more complete than it is.[148]

As Lincoln would soon find out, only the awesome violence and devastation of the Civil War would break this lock and allow black Americans to emerge from the prison that had been created for them.

TWO

"Thenceforward, and Forever Free"

The Civil War, 1860–1865

A s the year 1860 ended, the famed New York lithographic firm of Currier and Ives published a cartoon featuring the Republican president-elect, Abraham Lincoln. It portrayed him inviting a herd of supporters to "ask what you will and it shall be granted." A shrew-faced woman in the crowd was shown responding, "I want womans rights enforced, and man reduced in subjection to her authority." One vagrant demanded that "everybody have a share of everybody elses property." Another wanted "a hotel established by government, where people that aint inclined to work can board free of expense, and be found in rum and tobacco," and yet another, Irish-looking one wanted the police "stations houses burned up" so that "the bohoys" could "have a muss when they please." And a thick-lipped, flamboyantly dressed black man announced, "De white man hab no rights dat cullud pussons am bound to spect. I want dat understood." The caption was, "The Republican Party Going to the Right House"—as Lincoln was being carried on a rail into a brick building labeled "Lunatic Asylum."[1]

In short, even in the North, even after his recent election, the president who would eventually be revered as a symbol of America's profound commitment to racial justice was being depicted as a champion of every wild and lawless radical cause "respectable" people could imagine. At the time, that was not surprising. The election had by no means produced a mandate even for the limited changes Lincoln proposed, and in its wake the country threatened literally to come apart. By late February 1861, the not-so-United States of America was in full-blown crisis. Outraged over the election of Lincoln as president in November, seven southern states—South Caro-

lina, Mississippi, Florida, Alabama, Georgia, Louisiana, and Texas—
had voted to secede from the Union and had established a provi-
sional government for the Confederate States of America. Throughout these states, rebel authorities seized federal property and U.S.
army installations. Antagonisms were so intense that rumors of an
assassination plot forced president-elect Lincoln to travel secretly
through Baltimore on his way to Washington, D.C. for his inaugura-
tion. Disunion and even civil war seemed increasingly likely.

On February 28, 1861, the members of the lame-duck Thirty-sixth
Congress met in a desperate last-ditch attempt to find some compromise that might defuse the crisis. Republican congressman Thomas
Corwin of Ohio, supported by the president-elect, proposed a constitutional amendment that stated, "No amendment shall be made
to the Constitution which will authorize or give to Congress the
power to abolish or interfere, within any State, with the domestic
institutions thereof, including that of persons held to labor or service
by the laws of said State."[2] Corwin hoped that this unamendable
amendment, by giving perpetual constitutional protection to slavery
in those areas where it already existed, would keep the Union together by mollifying southern fears that the North sought to abolish
slavery.

When the amendment passed the next day by a vote of 133 to
65, the result was reportedly "received with loud and prolonged applause, both on the floor and in the galleries."[3] The amendment
gained bipartisan support, with 64 of 132 Republicans joining with
all but one Democrat. Then in the Senate, legislative maneuvering
and alcohol-fueled debate delayed a vote on the amendment until
March 3, when it narrowly passed by a vote of 24 to 12. Among
those voting for it were such ardent antislavery Republicans as Senator William Seward of New York, soon to be Lincoln's secretary of
state, and Representative Charles Francis Adams Sr. of Massachusetts.[4] Out-going President James Buchanan then took the unprecedented and unnecessary step of signing the amendment. The following day, Abraham Lincoln publicly endorsed the new amendment
in his inaugural address, declaring that the substance of the amendment was "implied constitutional law," and that he had "no objection to its being made express and irrevocable." Although Lincoln
hoped and anticipated that slavery would eventually die out in the
South if the rest of the country were free, he had repeatedly pledged
to repudiate any federal effort to eliminate it there.[5]

It is understandable that such an amendment could pass Congress
in 1861, for the election of 1860 had in fact abundantly demonstrated

the white electorate's commitment to slavery, not to its demise. None of the major candidates in that election ran on a true abolitionist platform. Lincoln's advocacy of a ban on slavery in the territories represented the only antislavery sentiment among the leading contenders; the others all supported greater leeway for slavery's spread. The Republican platform of 1860 did not contradict Lincoln's views in regard to the territories, but it stressed its support for "the right of each state to order and control its own domestic institutions according to its own judgment exclusively."[6] Furthermore, in response to opponents' charges that they favored "African amalgamation with the fair daughters of the Anglo Saxon, Celtic, and Teutonic races," many Republicans countered that they were the true "white man's party" since they advocated limiting the territories to whites only.[7] In reaction, many abolitionists criticized the party and its candidate. William Lloyd Garrison argued that "the Republican party means to do nothing, can do nothing, for the abolition of slavery in the slave states." Wendell Phillips labeled Lincoln "the Slave Hound of Illinois" for his support of the 1850 Fugitive Slave Act.[8]

Yet as the Currier and Ives cartoon suggested, even the very limited antislavery sentiment of the Lincoln Republicans made much of the electorate hysterical. Over 60 percent of the national vote went to the three candidates, Democrat Stephen A. Douglas, Southern Democrat John C. Breckenridge, and Constitutional Unionist John Bell, who advocated not only the maintenance of slavery but, in one form or another, its expansion. It was only this three-way split in the pro-expansion vote that allowed Lincoln to squeak through to the White House. Even so, he won with less than 40 percent of the popular vote—the lowest percentage for any winning presidential candidate in American history before or since.

After the election, the secession crisis only seemed to harden white attitudes toward blacks. In a widely reprinted editorial, a Providence, Rhode Island newspaper declared, "The everlasting Negro is the rock upon which the Ship of State must split. Will the people stand for this much longer? Will they make the Negro their god . . . ?"[9] The *Chicago Times* blamed the crisis on abolitionists, pleading, "Kill the vile cause of disunion, and disunion itself will perish for *lack of food*. ABOLITION IS DISUNION. It is the 'vile cause and most cursed effect.' It is the Alpha and Omega of our National woes. STRANGLE IT!" Urged on by such rhetoric, mobs in several northern cities during the winter of 1860–1861 unleashed the worst wave of antiblack and antiabolitionist violence since the 1830s.[10]

Following its passage by Congress, the proposed Thirteenth

Amendment was sent to the states for ratification, where approval seemed likely. Within the next year, Ohio, Maryland, and Illinois approved it, but the measure was too little and too late to avert the war that its proponents had sought to avoid. With the outbreak of hostilities, the amendment was soon forgotten.[11]

Four years later, in January 1865, many northern cartoons depicted Lincoln as a giant among men or as "Father Abraham," a venerable Biblical patriarch. Another lame-duck Congress, the thirty-eighth, found itself confronting a new and very different Thirteenth Amendment. Where the original had provided constitutional protection to slavery, the new Thirteenth Amendment abolished the institution, declaring, "Neither slavery nor involuntary servitude, except as punishment for crime whereof the party shall have been duly convicted, shall exist within the United States, or any place subject to their jurisdiction." This amendment had passed the Senate the previous April but had failed to secure the necessary two-thirds vote in the House. Since then, however, events had changed dramatically. On the battlefield, the end of the Civil War was in sight as the Union armies, aided in large measure by the contributions of tens of thousands of former slaves now serving in its ranks, had begun to tighten a noose around the Confederacy. In November, President Lincoln and the Republicans, running on a platform that expressly advocated a constitutional amendment that would abolish the "gigantic evil" of slavery, had swept to victory, guaranteeing at least a two-thirds majority in both houses of the next Congress.[12]

President Lincoln hoped to pass the amendment as soon as possible, however, and the new Thirty-ninth Congress would not meet until the following December. In addition, he hoped for at least some Democratic support (only four House Democrats had voted for the measure in June) in order to prevent the amendment from being seen as purely a partisan Republican measure. For this reason, Lincoln asked the lame-duck House to reconsider the amendment before it adjourned, declaring, "In a great national crisis, like ours, unanimity of action . . . is very desirable—almost indispensable." Claiming a mandate from the election, he called on opponents of the measure to heed "the voice of the people" and pass the amendment.[13]

Facing such a popular mandate and recognizing that passage of the amendment was assured in the next Congress, some Democrats sought to "cut loose from the dead carcass of negro slavery."[14] Other Democrats were persuaded by Lincoln's use of patronage and log-rolling. In total, sixteen Democrats voted for the amendment while eight others absented themselves, allowing the measure to pass, on January 31, 1865, by a margin of two votes, 119 to 58.[15]

After the votes were counted, a spectacular scene unfolded in the House. Congressman James G. Blaine of Maine witnessed the event: "When the announcement was made, the Speaker became powerless to preserve order. The members upon the Republican side sprang upon their seats cheering, shouting, and waving hands, hats, and canes, while the spectators upon the floor and in the galleries joined heartily in the demonstrations."[16] Another congressman, George Julian of Indiana, stated, "Members joined in the shouting and kept it up for some minutes. Some embraced one another, others wept like children. I have felt, ever since the vote, as if I were in a new country." The House then voted by acclamation to adjourn "in honor of this immortal and sublime event."[17] Outside, cannon boomed a hundred times in salute.[18]

Despite these celebrations, the amendment faced difficult going in the states. While most northern states quickly ratified it, the border slave states of Kentucky and Maryland refused to go along. Consequently, the amendment became law only after several southern states reluctantly approved it as a condition of readmission to the Union.

The story of these two amendments, like the story of Lincoln's evolution in editorial cartoons from magnet for crazy radicals to national saint, tells volumes about the dynamics of racial equality in America during the Civil War. In 1861, most of the nation stood ready to guarantee slavery in perpetuity in order to save the Union and avoid a civil war. By 1865, the nation abolished slavery in order to achieve peace and restore the Union. Neither before nor since has America moved so quickly or so far to dismantle its racial hierarchy. But as the difficulty in passing and ratifying the Thirteenth Amendment suggests, this movement toward equality was limited and resulted only from the extraordinary pressure of the Civil War. In the words of abolitionist senator Henry Wilson, "They accepted emancipation not so much from any heartfelt conversion to the doctrine of anti-slavery as from the conviction that the removal of slavery had become a military, if not a political necessity."[19]

When the Civil War began with the first shots at Fort Sumter in April 1861, few Americans, north or south, believed or desired that it would lead to the destruction of slavery. Lincoln may have believed that it was necessary to wage war rather than to allow slavery to extend throughout the country indefinitely, and that the nation could not in the long run remain a "House Divided." Most of his supporters, however, embraced only that part of his vision that insisted the Union must stand inviolate. In a statement typical of northern views toward the war, the *New York Tribune* editorialized on May 14 that "this War is in truth a War for the preservation of the Union, not for the destruction of Slavery; and it would alienate many ardent Unionists to pervert it into a War against Slavery. . . . We believe that Slavery has nothing to fear from a Union triumph."[20] Whites throughout the North chanted as they went off to war:

> *To the flag we are pledged, all its foes we abhor,*
> *And we ain't for the nigger, but we are for the war.*[21]

Soon enough, however, being for the war meant being against slavery and for the "nigger," if not for humanitarian reasons, then out of military necessity. In fact, the forces that would destroy slavery, military necessity along with slave resistance and flight, were set in motion almost as soon as hostilities broke out. Ironically, the beginning of the end of slavery would come on the Virginia coast only a few miles from where, in 1619, the first Africans were brought to the American colonies. On the night of May 23, 1861, three fugitive slaves paddled across Chesapeake Bay and presented themselves to the soldiers defending the Union garrison at Fortress Monroe. Claiming that they had been employed by their masters in preparing the Confederate batteries facing the fort, the slaves were brought before the Union commander, General Benjamin F. Butler. He ordered them fed and put to work inside the garrison. Only a few months before, Butler had offered federal troops to aid Maryland in suppressing a rumored slave rebellion. The requirements of his new situation—a small fort ringed by superior Confederate forces and reinforced only by sea—seem to have caused Butler to have a change of heart regarding slavery. The next day, Confederate Major John B. Carey approached the fort and demanded that Butler surrender the slaves to their rightful owners under the Fugitive Slave Act. Butler refused. He argued that since they had been employed in support of rebellion, the fugitives were "contraband of war" (a form of property, not personhood) and, therefore, subject to confiscation by Union troops.

Word of Butler's action soon spread throughout the region, and fugitive slaves began fleeing to Fortress Monroe in greater and greater numbers. Within a matter of days, seventy slaves had made their way into the fort while others were picked up by Union ships off-shore. After two months, nearly a thousand fugitive slaves had fled to the fort. Once begun, the tide of fugitive blacks did not cease until the end of the war as thousands of slaves flooded into Union lines whenever and wherever the opportunity arose. In the words of one observer, it was "like thrusting a walking stick into an ant-hill."[22] In doing so, these slaves not only freed themselves but also helped to destroy slavery by undermining the southern economy and providing their labor to the Union forces.[23]

Although the federal government had initially declared its unwill-ingness to interfere with slavery, the growing number of fugitive slaves compelled it to act. When General Butler defended his actions by asking rhetorically, "Shall [the Confederates] be allowed the use of this property against the United States, and we not be allowed its use in aid of the United States?,"[24] few in the North were willing to answer in the negative. This was particularly true after the Union defeat at Bull Run in July of 1861, which dashed northern hopes for a quick and easy victory. As one abolitionist stated, the Union's defeat at Bull Run "was a fearful blow," but "I think it may prove the means of rousing this stupid country to the extent & difficulty of the work it has to do."[25] Another northerner claimed, "I went out to Bull's Run battlefield a Breckenridge Democrat, coming home I turned into a fighting Abolitionist."[26]

Other abolitionists pointed out forcefully that the destruction of slavery was now a military necessity for the North because slavery was vital to the southern war effort. Its abolition would hasten a Union victory. According to black abolitionist Frederick Douglass, "The very stomach of this rebellion is the negro in the form of a slave," he declared. "Arrest that hoe in the hands of the negro, and you smite the rebellion in the very seat of its life."[27] As a consequence, "[s]ound policy, not less than humanity, demands the instant libera-tion of every slave in the rebel states."[28]

Those slaves who managed to escape into Union lines quickly proved their value. The growing number of contrabands soon pro-vided much of the Union army's civilian manpower. During the course of the war, over two hundred thousand civilian blacks, most of them former slaves, served as laborers for the Union army. As black historian and Civil War veteran, George Washington Williams, pointed out, "Whenever a Negro appeared with a shovel in his hands, a white soldier took his gun and returned to the ranks."[29] Other former slaves, possessing knowledge of local geography and the abil-ity to move behind Confederate lines without arousing suspicion, proved invaluable as guides and spies for the Union army. Historian Herbert Aptheker claims that "the greatest single source of military and naval intelligence, particularly at the tactical level, for the Federal government during the war was the Negro."[30]

Perhaps more than any other fugitive slave, Robert Smalls demonstrated both the bravery of the contrabands and their willingness to assist the Union cause. In May 1862, Smalls, pilot of the Confederate naval vessel *Planter,* waited until the white crew members had gone ashore and then, along with fifteen other fugitives, sneaked the ship out of Charleston harbor. Once past the Confederate harbor defenses, Smalls made for the Union blockade ships offshore. There he turned over his vessel to Union commander, saying, "I thought the *Planter* might be of some use to Uncle Abe." In addition, Smalls gave the Union navy valuable intelligence regarding Confederate shore defenses all along the coast. Details of the daring escape made great copy in northern newspapers and Smalls became a hero in the North.[31]

The exploits of Smalls and other contrabands helped to show the potential contribution that freed slaves might make to the Union cause. Mindful of this fact, Congress passed the Confiscation Act of 1861 on August 6. The act declared that any property used to aid the rebellion was subject to capture by Union forces and in cases where the property was slaves, they would be freed—made persons, not property.[32]

While the passage of the Confiscation Act signaled how far the Congress and northern sentiment had shifted against slavery in a few short months, President Lincoln still would not risk turning the war into an abolitionist crusade. On August 30, 1861, following a series of reverses at the hands of the Confederates, General John C. Frémont, the Union military commander in Missouri and Republican presidential candidate in 1856, declared martial law in that state and ordered the freeing of all slaves belonging to Confederate supporters. Lincoln, fearful that he would lose the support of loyal slaveholders in the border states, quickly countermanded Frémont. In justifying his decision, Lincoln wrote that allowing Frémont's order would have resulted in Kentucky's secession from the Union and, in such case, "[w]e would as well consent to separation at once, including the surrender of this capitol."[33]

Whatever the wisdom of Lincoln's caution at the time, the course of the war made it clear to other Union officers the action proposed by Frémont might eventually prove necessary. In November 1861, General Ulysses S. Grant wrote his father that if the rebellion "cannot be whipped in any other way than through a war against slavery, let it come to that legitimately. If it is necessary that slavery should fall that the Republic may continue its existence, let slavery go."[34]

As early as September 1861, the federal government began to recognize the usefulness of blacks to the war effort. That month, Secretary of the Navy Gideon Welles authorized the enlistment of former slaves in the navy. While an important step forward, Welles's action was relatively uncontroversial, since free blacks had a long record of service in the navy, albeit in menial positions. The use of freed slaves in the navy was also less visible and less consequential than their service in the army.[35] Eventually, more than twenty-nine thousand blacks would serve in the Union navy during the Civil War. In fact, blacks were so important to the navy's manpower needs that by June 1863, Welles would write in his diary that "all of our increased military strength now comes from Negroes."[36]

One month after Welles's decision, the federal government began to take the first limited steps to use freed slaves in the army. On October 14, the War Department issued orders to General Thomas W. Sherman, the commander of the Union expedition charged with occupying the coastal islands of South Carolina and Georgia. The expedition was severely undermanned and, thus, a serious gamble. Recognizing this, Sherman's orders authorized him to use contraband slaves, "if special circumstances seem to require it, in any other capacity, with such organization (in squads, companies, or otherwise) as you may deem most beneficial to the service. . . ." Sherman's authority to arm slaves was limited, since the orders forbad, at Lincoln's insistence, "a general arming of them for military service."[37] And Sherman did not believe that such "special circumstances" existed during his command; he never sought to enlist any blacks. Yet the orders given to him were important, for they signified that even before the war was a year old, the federal government, including President Lincoln, was willing to enlist freed slaves in the Union army when military necessity so dictated.[38]

In the meantime, Lincoln's understandable fears that northern whites would not yet support a war of general emancipation led him to stifle any official suggestions that this was or should be the aim of the war. In December, when Secretary of War Simon Cameron made public a report declaring, "Those who make war against the Government justly forfeit all rights of property . . . . It is as clearly a right of the Government to arm slaves, when it may become necessary, as it is to use gun-powder taken from the enemy," Lincoln ordered the report recalled and the passage deleted.[39]

But as 1861 faded into 1862 without hope for a quick Union victory in sight, more and more northern whites began to reassess the relationship of slavery to the war. Aiding them were abolitionists who increasingly tied the war to the egalitarian ideals of the American Revolution. Moncure Conway declared that the Confederate secession was "not a revolution but a revolution against the noblest of revolutions." Another abolitionist urged making the war into a "glorious second American Revolution" by linking it to the cause of freedom.[40]

Republicans in Congress reflected this growing antislavery sentiment. In December 1861, they refused to reaffirm the Crittenden-Johnson resolution of the previous July, which stated that the federal government would not interfere with slavery while suppressing the rebellion. In March 1862, Congress enacted a law forbidding Union officers from returning fugitive slaves to their masters. The following month it passed a bill allowing for the compensated abolition of slavery in the District of Columbia. In June it fulfilled Lincoln's 1860 goal by passing legislation barring slavery in the territories.[41]

At the same time, Union military commanders also began to recognize that the use of black manpower was crucial for the success of their forces. In April 1862, General David Hunter, Thomas Sherman's successor, organized the First South Carolina Volunteer Regiment, made up of 150 former slaves. Hunter justified his action by pointing to Sherman's orders. In May, Hunter went a step further. He declared martial law and freed all slaves residing in his Department of the South (South Carolina, Georgian, and Florida). Once more, Lincoln reversed Hunter's declaration of martial law; but this time he suggested that such an order *might* prove necessary, though he reserved the decision to himself. The War Department thus refused to respond to Hunter's request for pay for the unit's men and commissions for its officers, forcing him to disband the unit in August.[42]

Although Hunter's emancipation order may have moved too quickly ahead of northern opinion, it was not by much. Made molten by the searing pressures of war, especially the Union's declining military position, attitudes on the issue shifted weekly. In May, most believed that the war would soon be over. Union forces under General George B. McClellan were only a few miles from Richmond. But in June, the new Confederate commander, General Robert E. Lee, decisively defeated the boastful but battle-wary McClellan, whose retreat from Richmond dashed any hopes that the war might end that year or that it might be relatively costless.

In addition to the Union's military reverses, diplomatic considerations also pushed the government toward emancipation. During the summer of 1862, Great Britain edged toward diplomatic recognition of the Confederacy, a move that would have given both legitimacy and economic support to the South. The Union blockade of southern ports had cut off the supply of cotton, causing high unemployment among English textile workers. Furthermore, as long as the North refused to attack slavery, most in Britain could see little moral difference between the two sides. According to Thomas Carlyle, the Americans were "cutting each other's throats because one-half of them prefer hiring their servants for life, and the other by the hour."[43] Emancipation held out the promise of swinging English public opinion around to the North and against recognition of the Confederacy.[44]

These new realities led Congress to act. In July 1862, declaring that "the time has arrived when . . . military authorities should be compelled to use all the physical force of this country to put down the rebellion," and that the time of "white kid-glove warfare" had passed, congressional Republicans passed the Confiscation Act of 1862.[45] The law declared that after sixty days, the slaves of all supporters of the rebellion would be declared "forever free of their servitude, and not again held as slaves."[46]

Changing military and diplomatic developments also caused President Lincoln to consider measures he had previously rejected as too extreme. Recognizing that slavery was the root cause of the war, in the spring of 1862 he had offered the border states a plan for compensated emancipation. They rejected it, but the declining military situation soon led Lincoln to look to more radical action. He later explained, "Things had gone on from bad to worse, until I felt that we had reached the end of our rope on the plan of operations we had been pursuing, that we had about played our last card, and must change our tactics, or lose the game!"[47]

Rather than lose, on July 13 Lincoln informed Secretary of State Seward and Secretary of the Navy Welles of his intention to issue an emancipation order. According to Welles, Lincoln told him that emancipation was "a military necessity, absolutely essential to the preservation of the Union. We must free the slaves or be ourselves subdued. The slaves were undeniably an element of strength to those who had their service, and we must decide whether that element should be with us or against us. . . . We wanted the army to strike more vigorous blows. The Administration must set an example, and strike at the heart of the rebellion."[48]

On July 22, Lincoln announced to his cabinet that he had decided to issue an emancipation proclamation. Only the postmaster general, Montgomery Blair, thought the proclamation unwise, since he believed that it would prove extremely unpopular in the upcoming midterm elections. Seward advised the president to wait for a Union victory, lest the proclamation be seen as the "last measure of an exhausted government, a cry for help, the government stretching forth its hands to the Ethiopia, instead of Ethiopia stretching forth her hands to the government."[49] Despite the fact that his action was indeed a cry for help, Lincoln concurred with Seward and decided to postpone announcing the proclamation until after a Union victory.

While Lincoln waited for the appropriate moment to announce his decision, the North edged toward the complementary step of enlisting blacks, slave and free, into the Union armies. Once again military necessity created the conditions for such a move. Hopeful of an early victory, the North had closed its recruiting offices in April 1862. The failure of McClellan's spring campaign then made it clear that Union manpower needs would be much greater than expected. On July 2, the president asked the states for three hundred thousand new three-year volunteers to bring the war "to a speedy and satisfactory conclusion." The following month, the War Department called on the states for an additional three hundred thousand nine-month militia volunteers. Growing casualty lists and the prospect of a long war had, however, considerably dimmed the enthusiasm of potential recruits. In some places drafts had to be imposed to meet the quotas, but these steps were extremely unpopular. Anti-draft riots broke out in several areas, requiring suspension of the writ of habeas corpus and federal troops to keep order.[50]

Faced with growing manpower shortages and resistance to the draft, northern opinion began to shift in favor of enlisting blacks. According to W. E. B. Du Bois, "Either the Negro was to be allowed to fight, or the draft itself would not bring enough white men into the army to keep up the war."[51] Leading the way were several northern Republican governors who had to bear the burden of raising troops from a reluctant white population. In July, Governor Richard Yates of Illinois wrote President Lincoln, "Summon to the standard of the Republic all willing to fight for the Union. Let loyalty, and that alone, be the dividing line between the nation and its foes. . . . Shall we sit supinely by and see the war sweep off the youth and strength of the land and refuse aid from that class of men who are at least worthy foes of traitors . . . [?]"[52] Later that month, New Hampshire governor Nathaniel S. Berry wrote the president questioning the use of white soldiers for "digging trenches, piling fortifications and the like, while strong and willing hands await only to be invited to do this laborious service, that they may show their appreciation of the glorious boon of freedom."[53]

Others were more crass in their desire to see blacks serve in the Union army. In August 1862, Iowa governor Samuel Kirkwood wrote to General Henry Halleck, "When this war is over & we have summed up the entire loss of life it has imposed on the country I shall not have any regrets if it is found that part of the dead are niggers and all are not white men."[54] Union general John Logan stated, "I had rather six niggers . . . be killed than of [my] brave boys." One officer stated that "You can't replace these [white] men, but if a nigger dies, all you have to do is send out and get another one."[55] Rank and file soldiers shared a similar sentiment, as reflected in the popular song, "Sambo's Right to Be Kilt":

> Some say it is a burnin' shame
> To make the naygus fight,
> An' that the thrade o' bein kilt
> Belongs but to the white.
>
> But as for me 'upon my sowl'
> So liberal are we here,
> I'll let Sambo be murthered in place o' meself
> On every day in the year.[56]

Recognizing the Union's manpower difficulties, Congress passed the Militia Act of 1862 on July 17. In addition to empowering the president to call up three hundred thousand more men from the state militias, it authorized the states to use blacks to meet their militia quotas and for the president to use "persons of African descent" for "any war service for which they may be found competent."[57] The motivations behind this bill were clear. Representative James King of New York spoke of "the mangled corpses of thousands of our young men sunk in the marshes of the Chickahominy and other localities in the Southern States . . . as a reason why white men should be relieved from the diseases and death which have fallen upon them" by the enlistment of blacks.[58]

The Militia Act of 1862 also had a significance beyond black service in the Union army. Since the colonial era, American governments had treated militia service, especially, as a badge of citizenship that was restricted almost exclusively to whites. According to historian Mary Frances Berry, "arming blacks under the Militia Act, when traditionally only citizens served in the militia, could mean taking a giant step along the road away from *Dred Scott* and toward abolition and citizenship status."[59]

Still, despite growing opinion in its favor, President Lincoln remained opposed to black soldiers. Although he had no problem using free blacks and contrabands as military laborers, he stopped short of putting rifles into their hands. He believed that such a move "would turn 50,000 bayonets from the loyal Border States against us that were for us."[60] Lincoln also doubted whether blacks had the capacity to serve as soldiers. "If we were to arm them," he worried, "I fear that in a few weeks the arms would be in the hands of the rebels."[61]

The president's opposition to black enlistments did not keep Union commanders from taking matters into their own hands. On August 6, James H. Lane, the U.S. senator from Kansas and a general in the Union army, wired Secretary of War Stanton, "I am receiving negroes under the late act of Congress [the Militia Act of 1862]. Is there any objection? Answer by telegraph. Soon have an army."[62] Stanton did object, but this hardly mattered to Lane, a staunch abolitionist and disciple of John Brown who had fought against slavery since the days of "bloody Kansas." By the end of October, if Lane did not have the army he had promised, he did have two regiments of black soldiers organized, trained, and already put into action.[63]

At nearly the same time as Lane was organizing black regiments in Kansas, General Benjamin Butler, now the Union commander in New Orleans, sent a letter to Secretary of War Stanton stating that his outnumbered forces were threatened with attack and that "I shall call on Africa to intervene, and I do not think I shall call in vain."[64] Butler thereupon asked the free black militia of New Orleans, which only a few months before had served in the Confederate army, to join the Union army. The reply was positive. The next month, the First Regiment Louisiana Native Guards became the first official black unit in the Union army.[65] Though officially restricted to free blacks, Butler's recruiters were none too thorough in examining the backgrounds of black enlistees and the unit soon enrolled a large number of fugitive slaves.

Both Lane and Butler had enlisted blacks under their own initiative, but within days of their actions the War Department directed General Rufus Saxton, General Hunter's successor in the Department of the South, to "receive into the services of the United States such number of volunteers of African descent as you may deem expedient, not exceeding five thousand. . . ."[66] Ironically, this move came only a few weeks after Hunter had been forced to disband his black unit for lack of War Department support. Still, this was the first official move toward enlisting freed slaves as soldiers in the Union cause.

The battle of Antietam on September 17 of 1862 then gave President Lincoln the victory for which he had been waiting. On September 22, he issued a preliminary Emancipation Proclamation. Invoking his authority as commander in chief of the military and that of the Confiscation Act of 1862, Lincoln declared that on January 1, 1863 all persons held as slaves in rebel areas would be "forever free."

The announcement of the preliminary Emancipation Proclamation met with a mixed response. Abolitionists and most Republicans hailed the decision, but many in the general public displayed great hostility. By making emancipation one of the war's aims, Lincoln had opened himself to racist attacks that white boys were being killed to free blacks. Furthermore, northern white workers worried that emancipation would open the floodgates to a migration of southern blacks who would compete for their jobs.

These fears gave the opposition Democrats plenty of ammunition in the fall campaign. In Ohio, the Democratic slogan, "The Constitution as it is, the Union as it was," was amended to include, "and the Niggers where they are."[67] In Lincoln's Illinois, racism dominated the fall campaign. Democrats promised to "send men to the legislature who will take the means to prevent the State from being overrun by free niggers, and the labor of white men being reduced to free nigger prices."[68]

Appeals to the racism of northern whites along with criticism of the administration's inept handling of the war and suspension of civil liberties led to Democratic gains at the ballot box in November 1862. Democratic gains were strongest in the lower Midwest, where antiblack sentiment had been strongest before the war, and in New York and New Jersey, where immigrant workers most feared black economic competition. In the upper Midwest and in New England, abolitionism was strongest, blacks were less numerous, and the Republicans held their own.[69]

Though shaken by the election results, Lincoln remained steadfast in his desire to follow through with emancipation. In addition, the president altered his opposition to black enlistments. Several reasons for this change are possible. First, the military situation had not improved since the summer, especially in the aftermath of the Union's defeat at Fredericksburg in December, further reinforcing the need for black soldiers. Second, the fact that the limited use of black troops in Kansas, Louisiana, and South Carolina had gone well may have helped move the president's mind.[70] Finally, Lincoln seems to have had a change of heart after Massachusetts senator Charles Sumner gave him a copy of George Livermore's pamphlet, "An Historical Research: Opinions of the Founders of the Republic on Negroes as Slaves, as Citizens, and as Soldiers." It documented the contribution of blacks, slave and free, in the Revolutionary War and helped to convince Lincoln of the contribution that blacks might make in the current crisis.[71]

On January 1, 1863, saying, "I never, in my life, felt more certain that I was doing right than I do in signing this paper," Lincoln affixed his signature to the Emancipation Proclamation. In doing so, he declared that all slaves in rebellious areas "shall be then, thenceforward, and forever free." That such a step resulted from the pressure of the war is evident in the document itself. In it, the President justified his action as "a fit and necessary war measure for suppressing said rebellion" and "warranted . . . upon military necessity." Additionally, the Proclamation went beyond the preliminary version issued in September by authorizing the enlistment of blacks "into the armed services of the United States."[72]

Word of the Proclamation spread quickly among slaves in the South by way of the "grapevine" telegraph, further encouraging their flight and resistance and thereby placing additional burdens on the Confederate economy and war effort. The Proclamation also altered the diplomatic context of the war by turning European public opinion in favor of the Union and destroying southern hopes for diplomatic recognition of the Confederacy.[73]

Perhaps the most important aspect of the Emancipation Proclamation was the authorization of black enlistments into the Union army. The half-measures and trial balloons of the previous year gave way to an intensive effort at enlisting as many blacks as possible, north and south, slave and free, into the Union blue. In March 1863, the War Department sent General Lorenzo Thomas, adjutant general of the army, to the lower Mississippi Valley on a recruiting mission. "Thomas's appointment signaled a shift from the haphazard recruitment of blacks by interested parties and independent commanders to a centrally coordinated effort under War Department auspices."[74] Blacks, both free and slave, proved eager to join up. According to historian Joseph T. Glatthaar, "The Union Army offered freedom to all blacks who enlisted, as well as the opportunity to fight for the termination of slavery, and this was enough incentive to entice thousands to risk the hazards of running away to Federal lines for sanctuary."[75] By the end of 1863, over fifty thousand black soldiers were a part of the Union army.[76]

The army also needed to find white officers to lead its black units, since few would yet countenance the idea of black officers. Fortunately for the army, there was no shortage of whites volunteering to lead black units. Most prominent among these were sons of northern abolitionists who jumped at the chance to help turn the war into a fight against slavery. As one wrote, "Perhaps I shall be permitted to carry out the day dreams and night dreams of my youth, when I was devising ways and means for marching at the head of an army of blacks, proclaiming liberty, and rallying the slaves to my standard."[77] Others, to be sure, joined only at the prospect of obtaining a commission and an increase in pay. "I would drill a company of alligators for a hundred and twenty a month," was the comment of one soldier seeking a commission.[78] Much like the nation at large during the war, these whites were willing to bracket whatever racist sentiments they possessed and to tolerate emancipation and black military service when self-interest and the Union cause so required.

But despite the able service of blacks in previous wars, many northern whites believed that black soldiers would prove ineffective. Hence it mattered greatly that blacks quickly proved to all fair-minded observers that they could fight and die as well as whites. The first major engagement with black troops took place at Port Hudson, Louisiana in May 1863. Here the Louisiana Native Guards helped assault a heavily fortified Confederate position. Although the attack failed, those who witnessed the battle praised the skill and bravery of the black units. One white officer wrote, "You have no idea how my prejudices with regard to the negro troops have been dispelled by the battle the other day. The brigade of negroes behaved magnificently and fought splendidly; could not have done better. They are far superior in discipline to the white troops and just as brave."[79] Further engagements at Milliken's Bend, Louisiana and Fort Wagner, South Carolina (portrayed in the film *Glory*) further proved the point. Joseph Holt, judge advocate general and former secretary of war, wrote, "In view of the loyalty of the race and of the obstinate courage which they have shown themselves to possess, they certainly constitute, at this crisis in our history, a most powerful and reliable arm of the public defense."[80] Other were more direct. "I never believed in niggers before," stated one white soldier, "but by Jasus, they are hell for fighting."[81]

In addition to exploding white stereotypes, black military service also helped to transform the attitudes of many black soldiers. Early in the war, Frederick Douglass had declared, "Once let the black man get upon his person the brass letters, *U.S.;* let him get an eagle on his button, and a musket on his shoulder and bullets in his pocket, and there is no power on earth which can deny that he has earned the right to citizenship in the United States."[82] Douglass's prediction proved true. For many black soldiers, military service proved to be a radicalizing experience, transforming them into a vanguard in the fight for racial equality. As one former slave recalled, "I felt freedom in my bones."[83]

Evidence of the radicalization of military service can be seen in the fight for equal pay for black soldiers. Despite the fact that several northern black units were recruited with the promise of equal pay, the Militia Act of 1862 authorized that black soldiers be paid only $10 per month, minus a clothing allowance of $3, in contrast to white enlistees who were paid $13 a month plus a clothing allowance of $3.50. In short, white soldiers received more than twice the pay ($16.50 vs. $7.00) of black soldiers. This differential affronted black soldiers, suggesting as it did that their sacrifices were worth less than half that of whites. In fact, many refused to take any pay rather than submit to such discrimination. As one soldier of the fabled Massachusetts 55th wrote, "We did not come to fight for money, for if we did, we might just as well have accepted the money that was offered us; we came not only to make men of ourselves, but of our colored brothers at home."[84]

Throughout 1863 and 1864, Congress dithered over the pay issue, with Democrats and conservative Republicans declaring that equal pay would insult white soldiers. Black soldiers became even more restive. Several units threatened to lay down their arms unless pay was equalized. In a few units, black soldiers were court-martialed and executed for mutinous activity, though in many cases these punishments were due to the overreactions and prejudices of white officers.[85] Recognizing the trouble brewing in the black ranks and fearful that several black units would have to be mustered out because their terms of enlistment had been violated, Congress in June 1864 finally enacted equal pay legislation.[86]

Along with equal pay, black soldiers also fought for equal rights. In their minds, military service had proven their manhood and their rights as citizens, and the nation ought to reward them. In the words of Sergeant Henry Maxwell, "We want two more boxes besides the cartridge box—the ballot box and the jury box."[87] Veterans of the 60th U.S. Colored Infantry organized in Davenport, Iowa in November 1865 to demand the vote. In their resolution, they declared "that he who is worthy to be trusted with the musket can and ought to be trusted with the ballot."[88]

The war and the example set by black soldiers had a major impact on the attitudes of many northern whites. As the conflict grew longer and bloodier, the cause of preserving the Union, previously stressed by most whites, seemed by itself inadequate justification for such sacrifices. Consequently, northerners increasingly saw the war as a conflict to defend and reaffirm the nation's sacred egalitarian ideals. The Emancipation Proclamation helped to further this shift. To some extent, this was making a virtue of necessity, given that the Proclamation resulted more from military duress than ideological principle. Still, it is clear that by 1863 many in the North were convinced that the war had become a test of democracy, equal rights, and freedom. As abolitionist editor Theodore Tilton wrote, "This war is not of geographical sections, nor political factions, but of principles and systems. Our war against this rebellion is . . . a war for social equality, for rights, for justice, for freedom."[89]

This interpretation of the war found its most eloquent expression in Lincoln's brilliant oratory. Lincoln first linked the war to America's egalitarian ideals in July 1863, following the Union victories at Vicksburg and Gettysburg. Lincoln told a group of serenaders that it was fitting that these victories came on the Fourth of July, since the rebellion was "an effort to overthrow the principle that all men are created equal."[90] Five months later, Lincoln expanded upon this theme in his Gettysburg Address and in 272 words, according to historian David Donald, "succeeded in broadening the aims of the war from Union to Equality and Union."[91] His opening "Four score and seven years ago" implicitly rejected the notion that the war was fought to restore the Union created by the Constitution—a document that tolerated slavery. Lincoln instead tied the true origins of the nation, and the aims of the war to preserve it, to the Declaration of Independence and "the proposition that all men are created equal." The task was now to ensure "a new birth of freedom" so "that government of the people, by the people, for the people, shall not perish from the earth."

This "new birth of freedom" was not merely rhetorical. In many areas of the North the cause of black rights moved forward significantly. During the war, Congress removed the ban on blacks' carrying the U.S. mail and gave blacks equal rights in the federal courts, while several northern cities and states also repealed discriminatory legislation. In these instances, the example of black soldiers provided powerful ammunition for those attacking northern Jim Crow. After the widow of a black sergeant was ejected from a New York City streetcar, the *New York Tribune* declared, "It is quite time to settle the question whether the wives and children of the men who are laying down their lives for their country . . . are to be treated like dogs."[92]

Others went further, arguing that by serving the Union, blacks had earned their rights as citizens, including the right to vote. As early as 1862, Ulysses S. Grant remarked that once black contrabands began to work for the Union armies, "it would be very easy to put a musket in his hands and make a soldier of him, and if he fought well, eventually to put the ballot in his hand and make him a citizen."[93] In early 1864, Abraham Lincoln proposed privately that suffrage be granted to blacks "on the basis of intelligence and military service," a position he came to endorse publicly after his reelection.[94] In calling for the extension of suffrage to blacks in 1866, Governor William Stone of Iowa asked, "Have we that degree of moral courage which will enable us to recognize the services of these black veterans and do them justice?"[95]

We should not, however, overstate the changes that occurred during these years. Despite the war's impact, many Americans were not originally and did not become dedicated to the proposition of human equality. In fact, most northern whites remained deeply racist. Almost everything in their experience had taught them that blacks were a degraded race. Most therefore believed that their own superior status was somehow natural and right. Hence the shift in the war's purpose touched off a powerful reaction among many whites.

Even before Lincoln acted, many white Union soldiers expressed their strong dislike of the prospect of emancipation and black military service. One Indiana soldier wrote, "No one who has ever seen the nigger in all his glory on the southern plantations will ever vote for emancipation. If emancipation is to be the policy of this war . . . I do not care how quick the country goes to pot." Sentiments such as this led to a crisis in morale. Many white soldiers resisted fighting a "nigger war," causing a wave of Union army desertions during the winter of 1862–1863.[96] To them, emancipation not only meant fighting and, perhaps, dying for the hated and unworthy black man. Freeing the slaves also might increase economic competition for lower class white workers.

Others, using oft-repeated arguments, claimed that free blacks would refuse to work and would revel in lives of lazy self-indulgence and vicious crime, aided by the tax dollars of white workers all the while. The New York proslavery physician and editor John Van Evrie, for example, charged that free blacks "are engaged in no *productive* employments; they furnish a large proportion of our criminals; they fill our alms-houses; and hence are a constant tax upon white labor." "Free Negroism," charged Van Evrie, "destroys the negro, drags down white men, burdens them with taxes, and must inevitably end . . . in social convulsions and a horrible and revolting war of races."[97]

With these racial and economic anxieties being trumpeted, it is not surprising that many poor whites increasingly resented a war in which they believed they were being required to bear an unfair share of the burden. The new conscription system allowed the wealthy to avoid military service by hiring a substitute or by paying a three hundred dollar commutation fee. Copperhead Democrats whipped up these resentments during early 1863, declaring "we will not render support to the present Administration in its wicked Abolition crusade [and] we will *resist* to the *death* all attempts to draft any of our citizens into the army."[98]

These antagonisms fueled the wave of antiblack violence that began in the fall of 1862 and peaked in the New York City Draft Riot. That a riot took place in New York City is no mystery, as historian James McPherson has pointed out: "Crowded into noisome tenements in a city with the worst disease mortality and highest crime rate in the Western world, working in low-skill jobs for marginal wages, fearful of competition from black workers, hostile toward the Protestant middle and upper classes who often disdained or exploited them, the Irish were ripe for revolt against this war waged by Yankee Protestants for black freedom."[99] The riot began on July 13, after the names of the first conscripts were listed. Displaying the savagery that they accused blacks of possessing, mobs of whites attacked draft offices, federal buildings, Republican newspaper offices, and, especially, blacks. According to one contemporary account, blacks "were literally hunted down like wild beasts. They fled for their lives. When caught, they were shot down in cold blood, or stoned to death, or hung to the trees or the lamp-posts. Their homes were pillaged; the asylum which Christian charity had provided for their orphaned children was burned; and there was no limit to the persecution but in the physical impossibility of finding further material on which the mob could wreak its ruthless hate."[100] The violence went on for four days. Order was restored only by rushing into the city soldiers who had recently fought at Gettysburg. In the end, 105 people died, making it the deadliest riot in American history ever.[101]

Most northern whites abhorred the New York riot. Even so, many believed that by changing the aim of the war from the restoration of the Union to the abolition of slavery, Lincoln and the Republicans had prolonged the conflict by precluding a negotiated settlement and forcing the Confederates to fight to the last man. Capitalizing on such sentiments, in 1864 the Democrats nominated Lincoln's old nemesis, former General George McClellan, and ran on a platform promising to roll back emancipation and preserve "the rights of the States unimpaired," including the right to slavery.[102] Out on the stump, Democratic orators relied heavily on racist attacks to damn their Republican opponents. It was during this campaign that Democratic propagandists popularized the term *miscegenation* via a race-baiting hoax. They published what purported to be an abolitionist pamphlet entitled, "Miscegenation: The Theory of the Blending of the Races, Applied to the American White Man and Negro." It advocated "the blending of the white and the black."[103] Other Democrats claimed that the real Republican platform was

Subjugation
Emancipation
Confiscation
Domination
Annihilation
Destruction, in order to produce
Miscegenation![104]

Republicans responded by defending emancipation as a military necessity. President Lincoln wrote that the war was being fought "for the sole purpose of restoring the Union. But no human power can subdue this rebellion without using the Emancipation lever as I have done." To turn back now "would ruin the Union cause itself. All recruiting of colored men would instantly cease, and all colored men now in our service would instantly desert us. And rightfully too. Why should they give their lives for us, with full notice of our purpose to betray them?"[105] Elsewhere he wrote, "Take from us, and give to the enemy, the hundred and thirty, forty or fifty thousand colored persons now serving us as soldiers, seamen, and laborers, and we can no longer maintain the contest."[106]

Lincoln's argument prevailed in November, as he defeated McClellan with 55 percent of the vote and Republicans won overwhelming majorities in both houses of Congress. Still, it is important to remember that, even though the electorate did not include most of

the white Southerners who had voted in 1860, this victory and the
ratification of Lincoln's policy of emancipation and black enlistments
were not foregone conclusions. During the summer of 1864, most
in the North, Lincoln included, expected that he would lose the
election.[107] Only General William T. Sherman's capture of Atlanta
in September, which signaled that a Union victory was but a matter
of time and that the administration's policy was working, turned
the tide in favor of the president and the Republicans. Although
it is only speculation, it seems reasonable to suggest that without
Sherman's success the North might have elected McClellan and
turned its back on emancipation, allowing slavery to continue indefinitely.

In addition to helping ensure Lincoln's victory, Sherman's capture
of Atlanta and the Confederacy's declining military position also
forced the South to consider what until then had been the unthinkable measure of recruiting black soldiers. Such ideas had been around
since the start of the war. As early as May 1861, a white Georgian
wrote the Confederate secretary of war suggesting that black slaves
be "incorporated into our armies" and "that if they distinguished
themselves by good conduct in battle, they should be rewarded."[108]
Similar appeals were made throughout the war; but not until after
the fall of Atlanta did the Confederacy begin to consider the question
seriously. In October 1864, the governors of North Carolina, South
Carolina, Georgia, Alabama, and Mississippi passed a resolution calling for the use of slaves as soldiers. The following month, Confederate president Jefferson Davis called for the enlisting of forty thousand
slaves into the rebel army as laborers in exchange for their freedom
when the war was over.[109] Davis added that while he currently opposed the general arming of slaves, "should the alternative ever be
presented of subjugation or of the employment of the slave as a
soldier, there seems no reason to doubt what should then be our
decision."[110] The turning point came the following February, when
General Robert E. Lee stated in a letter that was made public, "I
think, therefore, we must decide whether slavery shall be extinguished by our enemies and the slaves used against us, or use them
ourselves at the risk of effects which may be produced on our social
institutions. My own opinion is that we should employ them without delay."[111]

Lee's views were shared by many in the Confederate army. Several
units passed resolutions or offered petitions calling for the recruitment of slaves. Some of these documents offer evidence of the ability
to put aside deeply held racist beliefs when necessity demands. For

example, the 56th Virginia Regiment passed a resolution declaring that although "slavery is the normal condition of the negro . . . if the public exigencies require that any number of our male slaves be enlisted in the military service in order to the successful resistance to our enemies, and to the maintenance of the integrity of our Government, we are willing to make concessions to their false and unenlightened notions of the blessings of liberty, and to offer to those, and those only who fight in our cause, perpetual freedom. . . ."[112]

Persuaded by such arguments, on March 13, 1865, the Confederate Congress passed a bill allowing the enlistment of slaves. "We shall have a negro army," wrote one observer. "It is the desperate remedy for the very desperate."[113] The Confederate army in Richmond quickly mustered together two companies of free blacks and slaves and sent them into the lines around Petersburg.[114] These moves were too little and too late to stave off what was now inevitable defeat. Still, the episode is quite remarkable, since it illustrates how military necessity helped to undo even the most entrenched of racial hierarchies.

On Monday, April 3, 1865, Union troops entered Richmond, signaling that four years of war were all but over. Among the first units entering the city was the Massachusetts Fifth Cavalry, a regiment of black soldiers. The symbolism of this event was not lost. According to the *Chicago Tribune*, "This war has been full of marked coincidence, and that by which the representatives of an enslaved race bore the banner of freedom into the birthplace and also the capital of the Rebellion, is not the least of the historical compensations of the war."[115]

The service rendered by black soldiers in the Civil War is indisputable. By the end of the war, approximately 180,000 blacks had served in the Union army.[116] Many believe these black soldiers provided the Union's margin of victory. According to historian Joseph T. Glatthaar, "During those key months in the late spring and summer [of 1864], when the picture for the Lincoln administration looked bleakest and the Union desperately struggled to maintain its uniform strength, more than 100,000 blacks were serving in the Union army and thousands more were in the Federal navy. In fact, there were more blacks in Union blue than either Grant commanded outside Petersburg or Sherman directed around Atlanta. Their absence would have foiled Grant's strategy and quite possibly doomed efforts at reunion; their presence enabled Grant to embark on a course that promised the greatest hope of Federal victory."[117] By the end of the war, one in every eight soldiers in Grant's army was black.[118] In the words of W. E. B. Du Bois, "the Emancipation Proclamation meant the Negro soldier, and the Negro soldier meant the end of the war."[119]

In addition to securing victory for the Union, black soldiers helped to compel the creation of a more egalitarian nation. Slavery was ended and the stage was set for black citizenship and suffrage. The nation, in the words of Abraham Lincoln, had been given "a new birth of freedom." As important as these achievements were, they did not result from a wholesale embrace of racial equality by white Americans. The New York City Draft Riot, the contingent nature of the election of 1864, and the reluctant approval of the Thirteenth Amendment indicate that the reaction of many white Americans to the changes wrought by the war ranged from grudging approval to violent opposition. What would happen now that the catalyst of the war was gone remained to be seen. As one abolitionist soldier wrote of his comrades, "Though these men wish to abolish slavery, it is not from any motive outside of their own selfishness; and is there not a possibility that at some not very distant day, these rank old prejudices, that are now lulled to sleep by selfish motives, may again possess these men and work evil?"[120]

THREE

"The Negro Has Got as Much as He Ought to Have"

Reconstruction and the Second Retreat, 1865–1908

On the evening of Saturday, October 24, 1908, Charles Francis Adams Jr. rose to address a distinguished audience gathered at the Academy of Music in Richmond, Virginia. His topic was the "Afro-American Race Problem" and the wisdom of Virginia's policies toward it. In this regard, Adams and Richmond had a special historical connection. He had entered the city as it lay in flames on April 3, 1865. That was the day after "the night they drove old Dixie down," when the Union army forced General Robert E. Lee and President Jefferson Davis to abandon the capital of their Confederate States of America. Adams had been Colonel Charles Francis Adams then—the officer in command of the black troops comprising the Massachusetts Fifth Cavalry Regiment. They helped extinguish the fires set by retreating southern whites, then joined the city's freedmen in jubilant celebrations that peaked with the arrival of Abraham Lincoln himself the next day. Adams later called his Richmond entry "the one event which I should most have desired as the culmination of my life in the Army."[1]

His desire was understandable. Adams was, as he told his Richmond audience forty-three years later, "an anti-slavery man from my birth." He was the great-grandson of John Adams, who signed the Declaration of Independence; grandson of John Quincy Adams, who valiantly defeated the House of Representatives' proslavery gag rule and defended the *Amistad* slaves before the Supreme Court; son of Charles Francis Adams Sr., the U.S. ambassador who persuaded the British not to side with the Confederacy during the war. But as he often did in his later years, in 1908 this Adams rose not to praise but to repudiate "the hateful memory of what is known as the Reconstruction period." The Yankee policies of those years, promoting African American enfranchisement and equal citizenship, had been, he announced, "worse than a crime." Henceforth, any solution to "the Afro-American race problem" must be "worked out in the South," without "external intervention." Blacks must not "ask to be held up, or protected from outside," in that process.[2]

Everyone knew what Adams meant: the well-advanced process of defeating Reconstruction in the South by disfranchising blacks and subjecting them to Jim Crow segregation laws should be accepted by the North, by all Americans. And though Adams said he spoke only for himself, he expressed confidence that the "mind of the North is rapidly crystallizing" in a "large and growing, and in the end most influential" consensus in favor of the views he advanced. A "great change" in public opinion and feeling, which he himself had experienced, had been "steadily going on for many years." The "glittering" beliefs in "the equality of men" that had characterized Reconstruction had come to seem to most Americans "strangely remote, archaic even."[3] In this Adams was right. The United States by 1908 was already well advanced in a rebuilding of legal, political, economic, educational, cultural and social systems of white suprem-acy that would on the whole endure until the 1960s. The results of this second great retreat from racial equality are known as the "Jim Crow" system, but they might well be called "White Reconstruc-tion."

What had happened between the spring morning of 1865 and the autumn evening of 1908 to produce this dramatic shift in the political sentiments of a Yankee antislavery warrior? Startling as this contrast was, the pattern was much like what has happened in the United States after each of the two other periods of major racial reforms, the Revolutionary era and the modern World War II–Cold War de-cades. The Civil War's transformations in favor of racial equality had come only under the impetus of the three great sources of racial progress in America. There had been a massive war requiring black assistance, against an enemy that led U.S. elites to stress their more egalitarian principles, reinforced by internal pressures to live up to those principles brought by antislavery groups. But as Reconstruc-tion proceeded, all those elements expired. The war was over; slavery was abolished; peace was at hand and could be sustained without black men in arms; and former antislavery advocates like William Lloyd Garrison, Frederick Douglass, and Elizabeth Cady Stanton di-vided bitterly over what the future reform agenda should be.

Most importantly, to many white Americans the main threats to a peaceful and prosperous nation now seemed to come not from pseudo-aristocratic white Southerners but from "extremist" radical Republicans and aspiring blacks. Many northern whites had hoped ending slavery's spread would mean they could avoid having to be exposed to blacks rather than having to embrace them as fully equal citizens. To preserve long-familiar privileges in a changing world, to oppose what were perceived as the excessive transformational goals of the racial "radicals," many white Americans underwent the "great change" Adams described. They now found intellectual defenses of inequality far more appealing than the once-sublime sentiments of sacred duty and egalitarian moral purpose that had been so movingly hymned and so painfully wrought out as basic American constitutional principles during the war and early Reconstruction.

Adams's life illustrates well the dynamics that led many northern whites both to fight for those principles during the war and to support their erosion in its aftermath. If not for the war, it is unlikely that Adams would ever have found himself working so closely with African Americans in a common cause. True, he had been "brought up in the faith" of the Declaration of Independence's proclamation of "the equality of men." But Adams, like most Northerners, was always far more firmly opposed to slavery than to white supremacy. The latter accorded with the great bulk of his everyday experiences amid the pervasive racial hierarchies of nineteenth-century America. Just as it was only the military exigencies of the war that compelled his government to employ African American troops, it was also the political and moral exigencies of justifying the war that made Adams think it personally important to lead those troops into action.

Adams aptly described these years as a "scriptural" period or "theological stage" in U.S. history and in his own life. Good northern Christians like himself told each other that the "African" was a "brother" to them, descended through Ham from Noah. But they viewed blacks as stunted members of the human family: in comparison with Noah's white descendants, blacks had "only partially developed under unfavorable fortuitous circumstances." Hence they not only seemed but actually were inferior now, though they need not be so in the future. This religious view strongly supported magnanimous efforts to uplift blacks. It could, amid the war-fired sense of purpose among Northerners in the mid-1860s, justify expansions of black opportunities. Even so, it was still far removed from genuine acceptance of racial equality.

Filled with this spirit, in 1865 Adams passionately wanted to dramatize the utter defeat of the sinful South he had been fighting for three years. Arriving in its capital with black troops seemed the perfect way to do so. He was, however, also curious to see if making soldiers of former slaves really produced the "regeneration of the African race" his religion promised. At that point Adams probably did want to believe that such beliefs in racial brotherhood might be fully vindicated.[4] A few months prior to his entry into Richmond, he assessed the performance of black troops at the battle of Petersburg, saying, "They seem to have behaved just as well and as badly as the rest and to have suffered more severely." Yet he was in truth deeply ambivalent about whether blacks were really his equals. And as his wartime experiences exerted less and less influence, he later claimed that "the only result" of leading black troops was "to afford myself convincing proof" of what he already half-believed. He maintained "the negro was wholly unfit for cavalry service, lacking absolutely the essential qualities of alertness, individuality, reliability, and self-reliance."[5]

By the time he wrote those ugly words, Adams was, by his own report, "a changed intellectual and moral being." His reservations about black equality had been enormously strengthened by his conversion to what he called the new late-nineteenth-century "scientific" worldview, massively influenced by Darwin's *On the Origin of Species* and his *The Descent of Man,* published in 1871. This science had "broken down" the theory of racial equality, Adams said. In its place stood the hard lesson that, due to "absolutely fundamental racial characteristics," African Americans could "only partially assimilate" and could not "be absorbed" into the white community on an equal basis. Those conclusions were reinforced, he contended, by examples of black misconduct in "Hayti and Jamaica," as well as by sad experience with the "promiscuous conferring of the ballot" in the United States. Adams was "glad to remember" that he had left the Republican Party when it supported disfranchisement of men like Robert E. Lee and enfranchisement of blacks.[6]

Adams presented that departure as proof of his own prescience. It is more likely that he felt deeply threatened by a new regime in which men of his distinguished lineage would not necessarily have political pride of place but would share power with those they had long regarded as comparative children. Adams's unhappiness over black rights was, moreover, part of his general sense of unease about his place in the industrializing, urbanizing, and increasingly demographically diverse United States of the Gilded Age. Although he drove himself to become a pioneering railroad analyst, regulator, and eventually businessman, Adams was never wholly comfortable

with the world of big corporations. He was positively opposed, moreover, to expansive readings of the Constitution and the "centralization of power and governmental control," whether these were used
as instruments of promoting racial equality or as "big government"
devices to make big business serve the public good. His nostalgia for
Jeffersonian traditions of minimalist central government and state's
rights, however peculiar for a descendant of John and John Quincy
Adams, characterized many opponents of national efforts to protect
the rights of the freedmen.[7]

Adams's long-standing attachment to practices of white supremacy despite his equally long-standing and sometimes impassioned
antislavery views; his anxieties about his place in postwar America;
his aversion to strong and coercive national government; his attraction to new scientific doctrines of racial inequality as justifica-
tions for abandoning the "theological" egalitarian views of the war
years—all captured in miniature the features of the late nineteenth
century that led to the fall of Reconstruction and the rise of Jim
Crow. The process began in earnest not long after Adams marched
into Richmond in 1865, though it would not be complete until
the end of the century. To grasp the transitions in these years
from the Civil War reform spirit to Jim Crow, from "Black" to
"White" Reconstruction, it is useful to think of the first Reconstruction as involving four stages. They may be termed the "preliminary,"
"obstructed," "congressional," and "remnant" phases of Reconstruction.[8]

The initial, "preliminary" stage was from 1862 to 1865, during
which time President Abraham Lincoln adopted tentative plans for
reconstituting recaptured states, usually by restoring all but the most
militant Confederates to full civic privileges if they would promise
henceforth to uphold the Union. Those proposals were too conservative for more radical congressional Republicans like Representative
Thaddeus Stevens of Pennsylvania and Senator Charles Sumner of
Massachusetts, but Lincoln slowly moved in the direction of their
proposals insofar as it seemed politically feasible to do so. Indeed,
he moved further than proved safe. Just one week after his visit to
Richmond, in a carefully crafted speech from the White House balcony, Lincoln for the first time publicly suggested that reconstructed
southern governments should include literate blacks and black veterans as voters. An angry southern actor in the crowd, John Wilkes
Booth, exclaimed "That means nigger citizenship!" Booth vowed
that Lincoln would never make another speech. Three nights later,
on Good Friday, April 14, 1865, he redeemed his grim pledge.[9]

Though no one can say what would have happened had Lincoln lived, there can be little doubt that his assassination catapulted into the White House a man, Andrew Johnson, who adamantly opposed any meaningful efforts to advance racial equality. The result, from late May 1865 through 1867, was the second, "obstructed" stage of Reconstruction. Just before it began, Congress had created the Bureau of Refugees, Freedmen, and Abandoned Lands (the Freedmen's Bureau) on March 3, 1865. It was the first of several measures designed to assist the former slaves in becoming self-supporting citizens, especially by helping them acquire farmland as well as education and legal protection. Black military service during the Civil War proved to be a powerful motivation for these efforts. As the *New York Times* editorialized, "This race has rendered an assistance to the government in times of danger that entitles them to its benign care. The government cannot, without the worst dishonor, permit the bondage of the black man to be continued in any form. It is bound by every moral principle, as well as prudential consideration, not to remit him to the tender mercies of an enemy."[10]

President Johnson, however, firmly believed that "[w]hite men alone must manage the South," and did all he could to thwart Congress's Reconstruction plans.[11] First he recognized a reconstructed Virginia government that offered few guarantees for black rights. Then on May 29, 1865, he granted amnesty to all but the most prominent and wealthy Confederates, promising them that their confiscated lands would be restored. Even rebel leaders, moreover, could obtain presidential pardons, a policy useful for turning them into Johnson allies. Johnson went on to remove all Freedmen's Bureau officials who took their mission of assisting blacks seriously. He also successfully vetoed Senate Bill 60 in 1866, which would have made the bureau permanent and enhanced its authority and resources. According to Johnson, the bill was unjust since Congress had never provided such assistance to "our own people" (whites). Moreover, in an early version of welfare dependency arguments, he asserted that such assistance would damage the "character" and "prospects" of the newly freed blacks by allowing them to think they would not have to work for a living.[12]

Not only did Johnson's actions hamper these key measures significantly, they also breathed a new spirit of resistance into many of the white Southerners who felt thoroughly defeated and demoralized when Richmond fell. In late 1865, unreconstructed Mississippi and South Carolina whites initiated new "Black Codes," laws that virtually restored slavery by requiring blacks either to work for their

old owners on the latter's terms or risk arrest for vagrancy, leading
to long sentences of forced hard labor. Other southern states soon
followed. According to one observer at the time, the Louisiana "codes
were simply the old black code of the state, with the word 'slave'
expunged, and 'Negro' substituted."[13]

Congress invalidated those codes via the 1866 Civil Rights Act and
the Fourteenth Amendment, both of which Johnson unsuccessfully
opposed. Section 1 of that amendment is particularly important for
its conferral of both U.S. and state citizenship on all native-born and
naturalized persons, including all African Americans, residing in the
United States, and for its guarantees of equal protection for their
due process rights and civic privileges and immunities. This measure
more than any other established a firm constitutional footing for
racial equality in a society that had never approached such a system,
despite a long history of egalitarian rhetoric.

Nonetheless, racial equality remained a distant and controversial
goal. Johnson remained adamantly opposed to congressional Reconstruction and denounced it at every opportunity, often in highly
racist terms. In 1867, he vetoed a supplementary Reconstruction bill,
saying: "The object of this bill . . . is to put the Southern states . . .
in the hands of the Negroes. They are wholly incompetent to administer such a trust. . . . It is vain to deny that they are an inferior
race—very far inferior to the European variety. They have learned
in slavery all that they know in civilization. When first brought from
the country of their origin they were naked savages and where they
have been left to their own devices or escaped the control of the
white race they have relapsed, to a greater or lesser degree into bar-
barism."[14]

Statements such as this along with Johnson's efforts to block Congress's Reconstruction measures gave great hope to white Southerners, emboldening them to further resistance. Consequently, racially
egalitarian reforms had to be pursued by extensive, ongoing confrontation and military coercion. Reconstruction then became vastly
more costly and controversial for Northerners, and more ultimately
unsuccessful, than it might have been.[15]

That fate would only become clear in later years. In 1866 the forces
prompting transformations toward greater racial justice remained
strong. Many northern white voters, converted by war to fervent
support for the antislavery cause, shared the outrage of African
Americans over the Black Codes and Johnson's obstructionism. For
them, the Black Codes seemed to signal that the white South intended to subvert the outcome of the war. The *Chicago Tribune*

warned, "We tell the white men in Mississippi that the men of the North will convert [their] state into a frog pond before they will allow such laws to disgrace one foot of soil in which the bones of our soldiers sleep and over which the flag of freedom waves."[16]

In addition, instrumental reasons led many Northerners to support a more radical Reconstruction policy. The Black Codes and Johnson's lenient policies promised not only to restore but to extend the South's power in national politics. With the abolition of slavery, blacks now counted as full rather than three-fifths of persons in the apportionment of House seats and electoral votes. Yet, the Black Codes ensured that this increased political power would be wielded not by the freedmen but by the whites who had led the rebellion. Republican political leaders saw the handwriting on the wall. An enlarged and solidly Democratic South combined with the still substantial Democratic Party in the North meant that the GOP would soon be the minority party in the House and in presidential elections. This prospect also concerned northern business leaders, since Democratic control of the federal government raised fears of tariff reductions, repudiation of the national debt, and state regulation of industry. Charles Sumner reflected this mix of motivations. While "Reason, humanity, and justice," all required equal rights for blacks, he added that "[o]nly through [the freedmen] can you redress the balance of our political system and assure the safety of patriot citizens. Only through him can you save the national debt from the inevitable repudiation which awaits it when recent rebels in conjunction with Northern allies once more bear sway."[17]

As a result of these concerns, anti-Johnson Republicans did well in the off-year elections of 1866, overcoming the president's hostile campaigning and securing veto-proof majorities in both houses. Thus emboldened, congressional Republicans sought to seize control of national policies. In so doing they established a third, "congressional" phase of Reconstruction from 1867 through 1876. Overriding Johnson's vetoes, they gave the vote to black citizens residing in the federal territories and the District of Columbia, and in March 1867 they passed a Military Reconstruction Act that established military rule over the southern state governments. Army officers were to ensure that each state held a constitutional convention in which blacks but not past rebels could vote on delegates. Those assemblies were to write constitutions that enfranchised citizens without regard to race, and the new legislatures then had to ratify the Fourteenth Amendment before their representatives could be seated in the U.S. Congress. In short, at this point radical Republicans were determined to establish black political equality and the broader guarantees of the Fourteenth Amendment everywhere they had the power to do so, and by military means if necessary.[18]

But these initiatives caused friction in Republican and reformer ranks. Women like Elizabeth Cady Stanton and Susan B. Anthony who had faithfully served the abolitionist cause complained that their rights were left out of the Fourteenth Amendment, rendering the new American Equal Rights Association virtually stillborn. More conservative Republicans feared instead that the party was going too far.

Amidst these divisions, more radical Republicans fared poorly at the polls in 1867. In Connecticut (one of a few states that elected its House members in odd-numbered years) the Republicans went from winning over 57 percent of the vote and all four of the state's House seats in 1865 to securing 49 percent of the vote and only one seat.[19] Further west, Kansas, Minnesota, and Ohio rejected establishing black suffrage by referenda. Republican senator John Sherman of Ohio summed up the results, saying, "The chief trouble is the [black] suffrage question."[20] Although the elections did not seriously effect the partisan balance in the Congress, they did signal that northern support for congressional Reconstruction had begun to reach its limits.

The following year, Republican Ulysses S. Grant won the presidency, but the Democrats, running on a platform that twice denounced "negro supremacy," made gains in the South and among northern white voters tired of the difficult struggles to win rights for southern blacks.[21] Despite Grant's status as war hero, he managed only a thin margin of victory, 52 to 47 percent. In fact, a switch of only 30,000 votes (about 0.5 percent of the votes cast) in Alabama, California, Connecticut, Indiana, Pennsylvania, and North Carolina would have resulted in a 147–147 tie in the electoral college. Furthermore, Grant's popular vote margin most likely rested upon the votes of southern blacks. A majority of whites had voted for his Democratic opponent.

At first, Republicans responded by trying to expand the black electorate. In 1869, the lame-duck Republican Congress passed the Fifteenth Amendment, banning racial discrimination in voting throughout the land, partly out of hopes of adding black votes to compensate for the white ones they were losing. As Republican congressman William D. Kelley put it, "party expediency and exact justice coincide for once." Passage of the amendment, however, entailed the inclusion of several weakening compromises. Among these were the deletion of provisions banning property qualifications and literacy tests, and the establishment of federal authority over voter qualifications.[22]

Even so, many still criticized the amendment. Activist women bitterly condemned their exclusion from its protections. Conservatives fought ratification hard even despite that concession. Virginia, Mississippi, Georgia, and Texas supported the Fifteenth Amendment only because their congressmen would not be seated if they did not do so, while border states like Maryland, Kentucky, Tennessee, and (initially) Delaware rejected it outright. In the North, passage required arm twisting by Republican politicians and liberal use of patronage by the Grant administration.[23]

As those battles raged, congressional Republicans also addressed the vicious tactics used by many southern whites, especially the hooded night riders of the Ku Klux Klan, to prevent blacks from voting or claiming any basic rights. In 1870 and 1871, Congress passed a set of bills setting penalties for violations of the Fifteenth Amendment, establishing national supervision of congressional elections to prevent discrimination, and punishing conspiracies to hamper state protection of constitutional rights, via the 1871 "Ku Klux Klan Act."[24]

These enforcement acts, however, were far weaker than they appeared. During the early 1870s, Congress appropriated only $2 million each year for federal courts and U.S. marshals throughout the nation. As historian William Gillette pointed out, this amount "could hardly keep the bureaucracy efficiently operating, much less support an ambitious and energetic program of enforcement." Not only did these efforts suffer from a lack of funds, but they also lacked sufficient protection from the military authorities charged with controlling the terror campaign mounted by the Klan and other paramilitary groups in the South. In 1868, twelve thousand U.S. soldiers were stationed in the South, but the following year this number was halved, and in 1870 it was reduced again to four thousand. By 1872, only about 3,400 troops remained in the South. And because most of these troops were infantry units, rather than cavalry, they were too slow-moving to be of much use in an emergency. All of this led one southern Republican to argue, "Reconstruction was and is a political mistake, not because of any defect in principles enunciated, but because it is *not enforced*."[25]

These rather frail enforcement measures in the South call into question the vigor of federal commitments to protecting black voting rights, especially when one examines voting enforcement efforts in the North during this period. Under the various enforcement acts passed by Congress, most power was given to election supervisors in cities with a population of twenty thousand and larger. Only five of the sixty-eight cities of this size were in the South. Furthermore, most funds allocated for enforcement were spent in the North, not in the South. In fact, as William Gillette pointed out, "half of the total expenditures between 1871 and 1894 for federal election officers had gone to New York state, and a quarter of the national outlay to New York City alone."[26]

Yet the unpopularity of even these mild measures, strenuously denounced by Democrats as "Force Bills," made yet more Republicans fretful about the political costs of supporting racial equality, especially those like Adams who had no strong belief in it anyway. The problem was made more acute because many west coast white voters were becoming anxious about Chinese immigrants. Republican leaders there felt increasingly pressured to bow to the upsurge of racist sentiments thus triggered, and they then found it harder to champion racial egalitarianism in regard to blacks.[27]

In this critical period, Charles Darwin published *The Descent of Man*, to the great benefit of Reconstruction's opponents. Darwin respectfully cited scientific racists like Josiah Nott and held that there was "no doubt that the various races, when carefully compared and measured, differ much from each other," including differences in both their "emotional" and their "intellectual faculties." The English theorist Herbert Spencer's applications of notions of evolution to social questions were less intellectually prestigious but far more popular than Darwin's writings. Spencer argued even more firmly that modern science provided "abundant proofs that subjection to different modes of life, produces in the courses of ages permanent bodily and mental differences" in the races. Whether or not Spencer "was the single most influential Anglophone thinker of the late 19th century," as some scholars contend, his views on these issues expressed the most powerful intellectual currents of the day. Efforts to make equal citizenship available to all, African Americans and Chinese Americans as well as "white" Americans, now appeared not only politically foolhardy but intellectually soft-headed.[28]

Thus it was that in 1871, Charles Francis Adams Sr., Charles Francis Adams Jr., and others like them formed a renegade "Liberal Republican" movement that urged abandoning Reconstruction for a postwar agenda of economic development without national centralization or any aid to any special interests, including blacks. In 1872 they united with the Democrats to run *New York Tribune* editor Horace Greeley for president against Grant (the elder Adams was briefly the front-runner to be the movement's candidate, but a man deemed "the greatest iceberg in the northern hemisphere" was not thought to be a promising nominee). Though Greeley and the Liberal Republicans lost, their departure gave further pause to many who remained in Republican ranks. The Republican vote in the North scarcely increased over that registered in 1868, despite the addition of black voters under the Fifteenth Amendment and the luxury of running against one of the worst candidates in the history of American presidential elections. (When asked of his previous criticisms of his new party, Greeley responded, "I never said all Democrats were saloonkeepers. What I said was that all saloonkeepers were Democrats.")[29]

At that point federal judges began playing an important role. Although many were Republicans, they had all been schooled in the state's rights jurisprudence of the Jacksonian era. Most shared conventional white fears of both strong, centralized national government and black equality. The antiegalitarian political and intellectual climate of the early 1870s reinforced those concerns. Hence federal judges began inventing legal doctrines to limit the scope and impact of the Reconstruction amendments and statutes.

The initial blows came in 1873. In *Blyew et al. v. United States,* the U.S. Supreme Court considered a case involving whites accused of brutally murdering an African American woman, Lucy Armstrong. Kentucky law did not permit the blacks who had witnessed the event to testify at the trial, and the lower courts had held that this state discrimination permitted transfer of the case to the federal courts. But the Supreme Court reversed, holding that no African Americans were parties in the litigation, and so none could claim state discrimination against them. The case involved only the (presumptively white) State of Kentucky and the white defendants. The one African American undeniably involved, Lucy Armstrong, was, the Court proclaimed, "beyond" all mundane concerns. Because the state was not discriminating against any live party to the case, it could complete the trial as it saw fit, without black witnesses. That meant Lucy Armstrong's killers walked free.[30]

The most telling judicial blow to Reconstruction came in the complex but momentous *Slaughter-House Cases* of 1873. Scholars continue to debate why, amid the flood of litigation involving blacks in the South that was rushing up to the Supreme Court, the justices made this their first occasion for expounding the meaning of the postwar amendments. For this case involved no African Americans; it was a challenge by white butchers in New Orleans to a measure imposed by the army-backed Reconstruction government of Louisiana. Out of a professed concern for public sanitation, that government had required all slaughtering for the New Orleans market to be done in a facility located outside of town and owned by a state-incorporated but northern-controlled syndicate, the Crescent City Slaughter-House Company. Other butchers had to shut down their own slaughterhouses and pay Crescent City to use its facility. The butchers' lawyer was former Supreme Court Justice John Campbell, who had left the bench to side with the Confederacy. Campbell claimed that Louisiana's requirement imposed involuntary servitude on his butcher clients in violation of the Thirteenth Amendment. He particularly stressed that it also denied them the right to labor freely, a basic prerogative of U.S. citizenship, so that it violated the Fourteenth Amendment's privileges and immunities clause. He added that it also deprived his clients of their economic liberty for arbitrary reasons, in violation of the Fourteenth Amendment's due process clause, and treated them unequally in comparison with the Crescent City company, in violation of the amendment's equal protection clause.[31]

In a 5–4 decision, the Supreme Court rejected these contentions. Some of the arguments in Justice Samuel Miller's majority opinion were reasonable, if not necessarily persuasive. It was indeed a stretch to call payment of this fee "involuntary servitude" comparable to chattel slavery. The due process clause, moreover, did read like a constraint only on governmental procedures. Equal protection was a guarantee primarily aimed at racial discrimination, even if it was not confined to it. But Miller took an extraordinary tack to argue that the butchers' right to pursue their honest trade was not a privilege and immunity of U.S. citizenship. Miller acknowledged that rights to labor freely were fundamental, that indeed opposition to forced labor had become the main cause of the Union during the war. Yet he still insisted that this right, like virtually all basic rights of citizenship, was a right of state citizenship, properly subject to regulation by the state governments. Hence if Louisiana chose to restrict the butchers' economic freedoms, the federal courts could do nothing.[32]

Miller's argument rested on a denial that basic liberties could be rights of state citizenship and U.S. citizenship simultaneously, a denial for which he had little legal authority. Few Republicans criticized the decision, however, for it upheld the Republican-run Louisiana government. That was part of the genius of the ruling: it read the power of the federal government to protect the rights of citizens against hostile state governments very narrowly, but it did so while seeming to support both black rights generally and Louisiana's Reconstruction regime in particular. One did not have to look too hard, however, to see that those appearances were deceiving. In 1873, the justices must have known that this reasoning also prevented federal judicial protection for African American citizens against the growing number of "Redeemed" southern state governments, governments that were being recaptured by whites virulently opposed to racial equality. The *Slaughter-House* decision laid the groundwork for national acquiescence in their rebuilding of racial hierarchies. After this decision and others like it, the Grant administration lost most of its waning energy for restraining southern whites. It was clear that such efforts would get little support in court or at the polls.[33]

As in the early years of the Republic, a sense of exhaustion now pervaded the country after a decade of egalitarian crusades. By 1874, most northern whites had grown tired of the effort to achieve racial equality. As one reporter stated, whites were no longer persuaded by the "tinsel tattle of Radical orators, by appeals to the Declaration of Independence, and that muck-mammocky rot about liberty and equality."[34] One northern white wrote that the country was exhausted with "undue efforts to force civil rights at the expense of *all rights.*" He added that Americans now wanted "*rest,* stability, prosperity, and the *greatest individual liberty possible.*"[35] Dr. Wells Brown, a black Bostonian, summed up these sentiments: "There is a feeling all over this country that the negro has got as much as he ought to have."[36]

During that year's election campaign, Democrats proved adept at capitalizing on these sentiments. In particular, they used Republican efforts to pass a new civil rights bill barring discrimination in public accommodations to raise the specter of "social equality" on both sides of the Mason-Dixon line. One Democratic editor claimed that the bill would put the "nigger into our tea and coffee." Another pointed to provisions in the bill that would bar discrimination in graveyards and schools: "The graveyards you have selected, beautified, and adorned as a resting-place of those you have loved must be desecrated to satisfy the spite of those liberty lovers. . . . Your children at school must sit on the back seats and in the cold, whilst the negro's children sit near the stove and on the front seats, and enjoy in every instance the money you toil for, whilst Sambo is sleeping and stealing."[37] In response to shifting public attitudes and Democratic attacks, Republican party leaders began to articulate

more conservative views. One Republican candidate claimed, "Socially he [the black man] must take care of himself. . . . As a party
we wash our hands of Negro-ology."[38]

Despite (or perhaps because of) this Republican backsliding, the
elections were a runaway for the Democrats, who picked up ninety-
three House seats along with ten seats in the Senate. These results
gave Democrats control of the House for the first time since 1858.
Once the new Congress convened, any further legislative efforts at
Reconstruction were effectively dead.

Even so, the "congressional" phase of Reconstruction was not
quite over. Following the elections, the now lame-duck Republicans
used their last opportunity to pass the Civil Rights Act of 1875. Originally proposed by the recently deceased Charles Sumner, the bill
aimed to make equality for blacks in all public institutions more
secure. To get it through, however, supporters had to jettison a ban
on segregated schools Sumner had championed. The law did ban
racial discrimination in all places of public accommodation such as
inns, streetcars, theaters, and restaurants. It also outlawed discrimination in composing federal and state juries and gave the federal
courts exclusive jurisdiction to enforce its provisions. The measure
sparked a flicker of hope that progress toward racial equality would
continue, if only because some Republicans still thought black voters
might help them win.[39] Still, according to William Gillette, "the
widely understood assumption that the measure would never operate effectively was the reason the bill had passed."[40]

That same session, Congress refused to pass a new Enforcement
Act that would have given the president more powers against conspiracies to prevent voting, including authority to suspend habeas
corpus. Many Republicans thought the time for such directly coercive measures had gone. In the words of radical Republican Joseph
R. Hawley of Connecticut, "There is a social, and educational, and
moral reconstruction of the South needed that will never come from
any legislative halls, State or national; it must be the growth of time,
education, and of Christianity. . . . We cannot put justice, liberty,
and equality into the hearts of people by statutes alone." Other Republicans recognized that northern opinion no longer supported
such policies, making them a drag at the ballot box. Joseph Medill,
editor of the Republican *Chicago Tribune*, wrote to GOP leader James
G. Blaine complaining that the force bill would "do our party infinite
mischief and arm the Democrats with a club to knock out our
brains."[41] In a similar spirit, Congress simultaneously bowed to grow-

ing anti-Chinese racial and economic sentiments for the first time. It passed the Immigration Act of 1875, barring Chinese immigrants perceived as coolie laborers or prostitutes—the first step toward national race-based immigration policies.[42]

As congressional Reconstruction came to an end, Grant's executive branch also proved reluctant to ensure either racial equality or civil order. In Mississippi, whites organized militia units around the state with the intention to "vote blacks down or knock them down."[43] Unlike the Klan, these whites organized openly, indicating that the threat of federal intervention no longer seemed serious.[44] Even so, as a wave of antiblack violence swept the state that summer, the Republican governor requested federal intervention. After some vacillation, the administration failed to act, fearing that the dispatch of federal troops would hurt the Republicans in Ohio's gubernatorial race.[45] As President Grant wrote: "The whole public are tired out with these annual autumnal outbreaks in the South . . . [and] are ready now to condemn any interference on the part of the Government."[46] Meanwhile, in Mississippi, violence, intimidation, and fraud allowed the Democrats to regain control.

Then in 1876, the surging tides of opposition to racial justice finally overflowed the political and legal dams radical Republicans had desperately been trying to erect against them. In two landmark cases, *United States v. Cruikshank* and *United States v. Reese,* the Supreme Court effectively gutted the civil rights enforcement laws passed in 1870 and 1871. The circumstances of *Cruikshank* were most dramatic. When the 1872 Louisiana election results were disputed, blacks in Grant Parish occupied and fortified the courthouse in Colfax against Confederate veterans, now organized as Klansmen, who laid siege on them. After three weeks the ex-rebels gained the upper hand, and over fifty blacks offered to surrender. The "white knights of the Klan" responded by slaughtering them and over two hundred others. Federal officials then indicted nearly one hundred of the whites under the 1870 Enforcement Act for conspiring to deprive African American citizens of many constitutional rights, including rights to vote, assemble, and receive due process. But the local trials produced only three convictions, and those were successfully appealed first to the federal circuit court, then to the U.S. Supreme Court. There, Chief Justice Morrison Waite stressed, like Miller in the *Slaughter-House Cases,* that many of the rights claimed by the African American plaintiffs were properly regulated by the states, not the national government. He also insisted that the Thirteenth and Fifteenth Amendments applied only against violations of rights motivated by racism. That claim was dubious. Even more incredibly, Waite and the other justices managed not to find racism present in the Colfax massacre.[47]

The chief justice relied on even more tortured reasoning in *Reese* to overturn the indictment of two Kentucky municipal election inspectors who had refused to receive the necessary poll tax of William Garner, an African American citizen. The government indicted the inspectors under sections 3 and 4 of the 1870 Enforcement Act, but Waite voided those sections because they did not specify that denials of the vote must be motivated by race, color, or previous condition of servitude. Sections 1 and 2 of the act did specify that those motivations were required, but Waite refused to read those specifications as implicit in the next two sections. Hence he denied that the act was "appropriate legislation" to enforce the Fifteenth Amendment, even though it was applied here to precisely the sort of offense everyone knew the amendment aimed to prevent.[48]

It would not have been hard for Congress to pass new legislation too explicit to permit this particular evasion of its intent. Black champions of Reconstruction like Mississippi senator Blanche Bruce urged that course. He invoked the service of African Americans on "more than one historic field" of battle, "beginning in 1776 and coming down to this centennial year of the Republic," to insist that the government must assure to "colored voters" the "same protection" provided "other citizens by the Constitution." But the Court's willingness to invent ways to negate Reconstruction laws, and the fact that hostile Democrats now controlled the House, blocked any such efforts.[49]

As the election of 1876 approached, it had become clear that national support for egalitarian reforms had come to an end. That summer, Frederick Douglass asked the delegates to the Republican convention, "But what is your emancipation?—what is your enfranchisement? What does it amount to, if the black man, after having been made free by the letter of your law, is unable to exercise that freedom, and having been freed from the slaveholder's lash, he is to be subjected to the slaveholder's shot-gun?" The *New York Evening Post* responded with an accurate summary of what had come to be the attitude of most northern whites: "It is to be regretted that Frederick Douglass will not teach to colored people the lesson of self-dependence, instead of always demanding for them fresh guarantees, by proclamation, by statute, and by bayonet, of the rights which they must largely maintain for themselves."[50]

It was in this spirit that both candidates, Republican Rutherford

B. Hayes of Ohio and Democrat Samuel Tilden of New York, stressed the need for reunion and reconciliation. The conservative Hayes and the former Wall Street lawyer Tilden were indeed close on many issues, and so was the election. After a campaign marked by violence and intimidation, especially in the states where white Southerners had not yet regained control from Reconstruction forces, Hayes lost the popular vote to Tilden. But if Hayes could capture the contested Reconstruction-governed states of South Carolina, Florida, and Louisiana, he could still win in the electoral college. In January 1877, Congress created an Electoral Commission to resolve the election's voting disputes. With its members voting along partisan lines, the commission awarded the contested states and the election to Hayes. Historians have long debated whether white Southerners acquiesced in this result because Hayes had, as was then charged, made an "infamous bargain" to end Reconstruction in return for possession of the White House. But whether due to a specific agreement, a culmination of a long-term pattern, or his own preferences, Hayes went on to restrain the remaining northern troops in the South from interfering with white "local control." He thereby largely abandoned the cause of black rights and brought the more radical "congressional" phase of Reconstruction to a close.[51]

Yet under Hayes, qualms about using federal troops extended only to the protection of black rights. The following year, soldiers withdrawn from the South and under the command of General O. O. Howard, former head of the Freedmen's Bureau, forced the Nez Percé Indians from their homelands.[52] Federal troops also helped quell labor unrest and defend property rights during the Great Strike of 1877. The irony of this was not lost on former President Grant, who wrote: "During my two terms of office the whole Democratic press, and the morbidly honest and 'reformatory' portion of the Republican press, thought it horrible to keep U.S. troops stationed in the Southern States, and when they were called upon to protect the lives of the negroes—as much citizens under the Constitution as if their skins were white—the country was scarcely large enough to hold the sound of indignation that belched forth by them for some years. Now, however, there is no hesitation about exhausting the whole power of the government to suppress a strike on the slightest intimation that danger threatens." He went on to add that if blacks were ever to intimidate and deny the rights of whites, "there would be no division of sentiment as to the duty of the President."[53]

Indeed, shortly thereafter the Supreme Court made even more manifest that its support for national power was at its nadir when the protection of black rights was at issue. In the *Civil Rights Cases* of 1883, the justices invalidated the final legislative monument of Reconstruction, Sumner's 1875 Civil Rights Act. Justice Joseph Bradley, a dissenter in the *Slaughter-House Cases* and an erstwhile advocate of broad readings of national power under the Reconstruction amendments, now wrote for the Court to oppose such views, at least when they might benefit African Americans. Like so many white Republicans, Bradley had never been a wholehearted enthusiast for black rights. By the mid-1870s he had already concluded that congressional Reconstruction had gone too far and must be cut back. In the *Civil Rights Cases*, he denied that Congress had power under the Thirteenth or Fourteenth Amendments to ban racial discrimination in places of public accommodation, as the 1875 act purported to do. Such discrimination could not be viewed as "badges and incidents of slavery," punishable by Congress using its Thirteenth Amendment enforcement power, Bradley said, because northern nonslave states had often permitted racial discrimination prior to the Civil War. The fact that both slavery and racial discrimination rested on a shared foundation of white racism did not alarm him. He also contended that congressional power under the Fourteenth Amendment was confined to "state action" denying persons equal protection of the laws, and the businesses covered by the 1875 act were private firms, not "state actors."

Revealingly, Bradley added a passage that showed his reasoning, like that of many "Liberal" or "reform" Republicans, stemmed from his strong desire to abandon the Reconstruction project of securing equal rights for African Americans. He insisted that there must be a "stage in the progress" of the black man "when he takes the rank of mere citizen, and ceases to be a special favorite of the laws." For Bradley, that stage had come. Despite, or more probably because, of the mounting hostility toward blacks, it was time to leave the freedmen to their fate.[54]

With the federal government no longer willing to enforce Reconstruction strenuously, southern whites began to roll back most of the egalitarian gains of the previous decade. Some of their methods were obvious. Freed from the threat of federal intervention, violent intimidation of blacks continued and in some places increased. Throughout the 1880s and into the early 1890s, the number of blacks lynched climbed dramatically (see table 2), until the adoption of formal means of disenfranchisement and segregation removed black threats to the political and social hierarchies. In fact, between 1885

Table 2. Lynchings of Blacks, 1882–1905

1882	49	1894	134
1883	53	1895	113
1884	51	1896	78
1885	74	1897	123
1886	74	1898	101
1887	70	1899	85
1888	69	1900	106
1889	94	1901	105
1890	85	1902	85
1891	113	1903	84
1892	161	1904	76
1893	118	1905	57

Source: Daniel T. Williams, "Lynching, Whites and Negroes, 1882–1968," in *Eight Negro Bibliographies*, comp. Daniel T. Williams (New York: Kraus Reprint, 1970).

and 1907, there were more lynchings in the United States than legal executions.[55]

Other methods of resurrecting white control were less direct but no less effective. Rejecting overt racist appeals, the "New Departure" Democrats professed acceptance of Reconstruction and the changes it had wrought. In reality, their coded attacks on crime, corruption, high taxes, and big government were subtle methods of promising whites that something like the status quo ante could be restored, a task that meant undermining the steps toward racial equality Reconstruction had taken.

As in the earlier reaction against black rights during the 1790s and early 1800s, measures ostensibly aimed at curbing crime and violence went hand in hand with efforts to limit black equality. Soon after Democrats took control of the Mississippi legislature in 1876, they passed the Pig Law, which vastly expanded the number of crimes classified as grand larceny, thereby causing the number of prison convicts (mostly black) to skyrocket.[56] According to Adolph Reed Jr., "The post-Emancipation criminal code was thus established as a vehicle of racial subordination, a device for realizing the linked objectives of stabilizing a cheap, tractable labor supply and undercutting blacks' capacities for effective participation in civic life."[57]

Another familiar aspect of Redeemer rule (so-named because these states had been "redeemed" from Reconstruction) was the association between fiscal and racial conservatism. True, many Reconstruction governments were corrupt, though no more so than many northern political machines of the time or the southern white governments before and after them. Yet they instituted an impressive set of egalitarian social policies, such as free public education, land redistribution, public works projects, state-supported colleges and hospitals, and aid for the indigent. These policies were also financed by modernized and progressive systems of taxation. Once in power, however, white conservatives marching under the banners of fiscal integrity, limited government, personal responsibility, and lower taxes managed to eliminate or reduce many of these programs—thereby ensuring the persistence of social and economic inequalities between the races.[58]

For a time, to be sure, Republicans continued to make some efforts to shield black voters from resurgent white racism, at least when it seemed opportune to do so. This was the final "remnant" phase of Reconstruction during which President Hayes vetoed eight bills designed to weaken protection of blacks, making the retreat from Reconstruction he led appear less than fullscale. His successors—James Garfield, who would later be assassinated, and his vice president Chester A. Arthur—did strive to enforce the Fifteenth Amendment in certain strategic contexts, but their efforts were even less vigorous than those of the Justice Department under Grant in the early 1870s. The Supreme Court actually handed down one major decision favorable to protection of black voting rights, *Ex parte Yarbrough,* in 1884.[59] Even so, all three Republican presidents made strenuous efforts to distance themselves from racial egalitarianism in hopes of building a white Republican party in the South.[60]

Arthur nonetheless gave way to a Democrat, Grover Cleveland, in 1885, and the new president was less zealous than ever in protecting the voting rights of largely Republican blacks. Southerners like *Atlanta Constitution* editor Henry Grady began promising a "New South" in which whites would treat blacks fairly and beneficently without permitting political rights that might compel white citizens to "submit to the domination of an inferior race." Against these tides, the cause of racially inclusive voting had one last push in the nineteenth century. In 1890–1891, Republicans had regained control of both the White House and Congress with the election of Benjamin Harrison. Two legislators from Massachusetts, Henry Cabot Lodge in the House and George Hoar in the Senate, then proposed a new federal elections bill that would have reinvigorated federal enforcement efforts on behalf of black voters.

Democrats condemned it as a new "Force" bill, and Republicans divided over it. Supporters like Lodge recalled the service of black soldiers in the Civil War, who "took their muskets in their hands and went to the front by regiments. They died in the trenches and on the battle-field by hundreds for the Government which up to that time had only fastened their chains more securely upon them. . . . Such loyalty and fidelity as this demand some better reward from the people of this country . . . than the negro has ever received."[61] For others, pragmatic politics were central: blacks could be counted on to vote the right way.[62] Liberal Republicans, now known as "Mugwumps," denounced the measure, however. E. L. Godkin, editor of *The Nation,* claimed that by helping to restore black suffrage, the measure "put [southern white] civilization itself in some peril."[63] Other Republicans claimed the bill was bad for northern businesses; it would disrupt the South's stability and prosperity, harming northern investments in the region. To this George Hoar replied, "[R]ather than have Constitutional Government overthrown and be governed by minorities for the sake of protecting their Southern investments, the people of Massachusetts would prefer to have their factories burned and to live on codfish and 50 cents a day."[64]

The elections bill passed the House with nearly unanimous Republican support, but this unity was a function of party discipline rather than party enthusiasm. The House Republican caucus voted to report the bill by a margin of only one vote.[65] In the Senate, protariff Republicans delayed its consideration until after that fall's congressional elections. When the lame-duck Senate met again, the bill was killed by an alliance of southern Democrats and western prosilver Republicans. The defeat of the elections bill showed that memories of the Civil War had faded and that economic issues had replaced racial egalitarianism as the driving force of the Republican party. Democratic senator John T. Morgan of Alabama wrote, "Protectionists want markets and the silver men want free coinage, and these and other craving people want the help of the South against their own people, and they prefer to leave the negro to work out his own salvation, rather than lose money. Money, my dear friend, is the real power in American politics at this day. I am glad to have its shelter, just now, when it is the most efficient barrier to a new descent upon the South."[66]

In 1892, Cleveland and the Democrats returned to power, having successfully decried the Republicans' effort to pass a new "Force Bill." Democrats now controlled the White House and both houses of Congress for the first time since before the Civil War. Using this opportunity, the Democrats repealed several of the remaining sections of the 1870 and 1871 laws regulating elections and franchise offenses.

With those last impediments gone, the disfranchisement of Afri-

can Americans proceeded in a rushing and long-flowing stream.
Over too many decades, the devices would include grandfather
clauses, prejudicially applied literacy tests, poll taxes, Constitution
tests, complex registration requirements, white primaries, and
more.[67] Although lawmakers wrote these disfranchisement measures
in race-neutral language to evade constitutional challenges, their
intent was clear. As Carter Glass told his fellow delegates to the
Virginia constitutional convention, their task was "to discriminate
to the very extremity of permissible action under the limitations of
the Federal Constitution, with a view to the elimination of every
Negro voter who can be gotten rid of, legally, without materially
impairing the numerical strength of the white electorate."[68]

The two champions of the 1890 federal elections bill symbolize
well why disfranchisement succeeded. Lodge's support for the elections bill, the only major egalitarian reform he ever advocated, was
at core purely the strategic tactic of an ambitious young man. The
political motives of Lodge and most other Republicans was accurately summed up when House Speaker Thomas B. Reed asked rhetorically, "Why should they [Democrats] be allowed to poll their
ignorance, and we not poll ours."[69]

Hoar, in contrast, had served in Congress since Reconstruction
was at its height, and he had been an outspoken champion of wom-
en's rights, national aid to public education, and other reforms more
radical than many Republicans would ever support. He revered the
legacy of his friend and Senate predecessor Charles Sumner, and
he steadfastly resisted the rising tide of renewed racist beliefs and
policies through the late nineteenth century. In 1882, he led the
unsuccessful opposition to the first Chinese Exclusion Act, attacking
the new evolutionary doctrines of racial inferiority on which the
act's proponents heavily relied. Hoar invoked the Declaration of
Independence and insisted that claims that "free institutions are a
monopoly of the favored races" stemmed from false theories "of
quite recent origin." He pointed out that charges of civic unfitness
had also been made against blacks, and against the prevailing zeit-
geist, he contended that those claims had been utterly falsified. Yet
the bill passed. In signing it, Republican President Chester A. Arthur
contended it was time to end the "experiment" of permitting new-
comers with "race idiosyncrasies" like those of the Chinese. This law
initiated a series of acts that would render most Chinese ineligible
for immigration through 1965. It also helped more generally to reha-
bilitate policies restricting opportunities on the basis of alleged racial
deficiencies.[70]

The nation's "experiment" with honoring its commitment to egalitarianism rapidly gave way in the late 1800s to proposals to reestablish white supremacy in myriad forms, even from those who claimed to venerate Lincoln's legacy. In 1885, for example, Rev. Josiah Strong published a widely read tract for the American Home Missionary Society entitled *Our Country* that added a powerful religious endorsement to scientific doctrines of racial inequality and immigration restriction. Strong was an ardent Lincoln Republican and an architect of the theologically and politically liberal Social Gospel movement, which sought to aid those harmed by industrialization and its attendant safety risks and economic inequalities. He was also, however, a firm believer that the United States, as the most favored representative of the "mighty Anglo-Saxon race," the best part of "the great German family," had been "divinely commissioned" by the Protestant God to lead the rest of the world to Christian civilization. Strong was desperately fearful that this mission was being endangered by Catholic and atheistic immigrants. He thought such immigrants, and all non-Anglo-Saxons, should be excluded by new immigration laws. He also envisioned Anglo-Saxon America spreading its rule "down upon Mexico, down upon Central and South America, out upon the islands of the sea, over upon Africa and beyond," until it had buried the "feebler and more abject races" in a "*final competition of the races.*" Though he wrote nothing about African Americans, racial equality in any form clearly had little place in this vision of race-based immigration exclusion and global imperialism.[71]

By the end of the nineteenth century, that vision would be America's dominant policy at home and abroad. It was reinforced not only by Spencer's version of evolutionary theory but by the dominance of the "Teutonic" school of historical and political research in the new graduate programs in history and political science being established by American academicians trained in Germany. They were busily converting leading American colleges to universities on the German model and creating new academic professions in the United States. Men like the historian Herbert Baxter Adams at Johns Hopkins, who trained Woodrow Wilson, and the political scientist John W. Burgess at Columbia, who taught Theodore Roosevelt, used historical research to show that American republican institutions were descended from ancient, freedom-loving Teutonic tribes via the Anglo-Saxons. Other peoples supposedly lacked the aptitudes for self-governance displayed in this superior lineage. Similar teachings prevailed at Harvard, advanced for a time by Charles Francis Adams' brother Henry, though he would later renounce this "Teutonic

germ" theory of American origins. By then, he had already helped
inculcate those ideas into the mind of the first holder of a Harvard
Ph.D. in political science and history, Hoar's 1890 ally, Henry Cabot
Lodge (of whom it was said that his mind was like New England's
soil, "intrinsically barren but highly cultivated").[72]

Lodge was a member of a highly influential circle of wealthy
northeastern Republicans who would do much to inter the cause
of racial justice with which their party had once been identified.
Some joined with Lodge in the Boston-based Immigration Restriction League. Others shared his interest in imperial foreign policy.
The set included men like Charles Francis Adams; Francis Walker,
president of the Massachusetts Institute of Technology, and other
leading American academicians; naval strategist Alfred Thayer Ma-
han; and, most importantly, Theodore Roosevelt. Unlike Adams,
the patrician scholar-politician Lodge and most of the other younger
members of this circle never had to be converted to the new evolutionary and historical theories of Anglo-Saxon superiority. They all
grew up steeped in them. As the new century dawned they zealously
propagated these views, favoring both racial immigration restriction and racially justified imperialism. Later, under Woodrow Wilson,
many concluded that American racial and cultural purity could be
better served by isolationism, the policy that Adams himself always
favored; but their version of Americanism was white supremacist
throughout.

Hence, even though for a time Lodge favored the expansion of
American rule over "inferior" peoples, he nonetheless steadfastly
opposed their corrupting presence within the United States. Indeed,
he made immigration control his most abiding political goal. Lodge
had long been disturbed by what he perceived to be the character
of the immigrants who were flooding into Boston and New York,
but it was his reading of Gustave Le Bon's recently published *The
Psychology of Peoples* in the summer of 1895 that galvanized his racialist
ideology. Le Bon saw each race as having acquired through evolution
a distinct "soul" that determined its moral character in ways nothing could alter. In 1896, Lodge invoked these teachings of "modern
science" as well as the Teutonism of "modern history," to endorse
a literacy qualification for new immigrants. Titularly a measure of
intellectual achievement, Lodge openly presented this literacy test
as aimed at "something deeper and more fundamental than anything which concerns the intellect." It sought to weed out "lower"
races with inferior "moral characteristics" that were the "accumula-
tion of centuries of toil and conflict." Lodge thought the test would

be particularly useful in excluding "the Italian, Russians, Poles, Hungarians, Greeks, and Asiatics" (among whom he counted Jews). Only in this way could "the quality of our race and citizenship" be preserved. Theodore Roosevelt applauded Lodge's speech and eagerly requested Le Bon's writings, judging their racial arguments to be "very fine and true." The literacy test passed Congress but was vetoed by Cleveland, whose party profited from immigrant votes. The test nonetheless remained on the Republican agenda until it was passed during World War I, and then superseded by the even more explicitly racist national origins quota system for immigration.[73]

Significant as Lodge's race-based endorsement of the literacy test was, however, its role in U.S. race relations was only a stiff breeze in comparison with the whirlwind of excitement stirred by a speech prepared while Lodge was reading Le Bon. On September 18, 1895, less than seven months after the black lion of abolitionism and equal rights, Frederick Douglass, died at last, proponents of Henry Grady's "New South" convened the Atlanta Exposition. This grand commercial fair sought to showcase the region's potential to be an equal participant in the new industrial economy. After much controversy, its organizers decided to allow a suitable "representative of Negro enterprise and Negro civilization" to address the huge, prestigious, predominantly white audience at the opening ceremonies. Many whites froze in silence as Booker T. Washington, founder and head of the Tuskegee Institute, the South's premiere normal and vocational school for blacks, rose to speak, cheered on chiefly by the Jim Crow section of the crowd. But as Washington courted his listeners with practiced ease and two well-honed metaphors, he stirred first interest, then admiration, then delirious enthusiasm throughout the vast throng. At the speech's crucial passage, the entire audience leapt up to thunder their ecstatic approval for minutes on end. In that instant Booker T. Washington became a national figure, designated by whites as the leader of all African Americans, a position he would hold until his death twenty years later.[74]

Although he was by this time in his life a skilled public speaker, Washington's smashing success did not come from his oratorical talents alone. White responses to the printed speech were equally enthusiastic. The magic was in his message. Here was a prominent black man offering a vision of progress for his race on terms that did not threaten whites, a vision similar to the one Charles Francis Adams would endorse in Virginia thirteen years later. Indeed, Washington's mentor, General Samuel Chapman Armstrong, founder of a famed Reconstruction school for blacks, Virginia's Hampton Institute, was a man much like Adams. His religion led him to believe he should strive to assist African Americans; but he always regard "the Negro" as a "primitive man" belonging to "the early stages of civilization" who should be trained in basic vocational skills, higher learning being as yet beyond most members of the race. Armstrong easily acquiesced in the end of Reconstruction, for he never embraced its more radically egalitarian strains. Washington, his prize Hampton student, then won acclaim by defining for white America the racial agenda that should replace Reconstruction.

In Atlanta in 1895, Washington first complimented the white organizers for generously including a "Negro Building" of exhibits. He then counseled his fellow African Americans to eschew political agitation and full civic equality through his famous exhortation, "Cast down your bucket where you are!" Blacks should not resist disfranchisement but instead should concentrate on improving their economic position through hard work at the lower occupations for which they were at present best suited. Then in his climax, Washington offered whites the reassuring metaphor that brought them roaring out of their chairs: "In all things that are purely social we can be as separate as the fingers, yet one as the hand in all things essential to mutual progress." Nothing could possibly have pleased whites more than to hear a black leader telling them that the spread of Jim Crow laws was not a moral betrayal but rather the right thing to do.[75]

Washington's own agenda was in fact more complex. Secretly, he aided lawsuits to combat the very segregation and disfranchisement that he publicly urged blacks to accept. He was convinced, however, that blacks in general, and he personally, could do more to improve their lot in the late nineteenth century through the accommodationist position of what became known as the "Atlanta Compromise Address" rather than through strident demands for equality. Because, for a time, Washington's message seemed more positive and promising than apparently futile head-on resistance to the swelling forces of white reaction, and because Washington was undeniably gaining recognition afforded few other blacks, many African Americans also initially embraced his message. Within a few years, however, it became evident to more militant black leaders that Washington's strategy worked well for him but was disastrous for most other African Americans. The popularity of Washington's "compromise" among white voters, along with Republicans' new endorsements of racial immigration exclusions, made it harder for any politician to oppose the racism that undergirded the rise of Jim Crow as an alternative structure of white supremacy in the place of slavery.[76]

Indeed, it was yet another Massachusetts-bred Republican (and a member of the American Social Science Association), Justice Henry Billings Brown, who wrote for the Supreme Court a few months later in 1896, sustaining state-imposed segregation of railroads in the infamous case of *Plessy v. Ferguson.* Louisiana's law requiring blacks and whites to occupy "separate but equal" railroad cars was constitutional, Brown ruled, because on its face it did not disadvantage one race more than the other. It also was reasonable for the state to recognize that "racial instincts" might produce violence if people were allowed to mix indiscriminately. Brown's belief in the natural reality of human "races" and racial animosities was a central tenet of the new scientific doctrine of racial differences. It was also central to his reasoning as to why Jim Crow segregation was desirable even though, as former slaveholder Justice John Marshall Harlan pointed out in his noble but lonely dissent, everyone knew segregation was in fact a means to preserve white social, economic, and political supremacy.[77]

Thus with the 1890 federal elections bill defeated, with Democratic successes in denying black voting rights federal protection against mounting state disfranchising measures, with black leaders like Washington preaching accommodation and compromise, and with the Republicans' own rising attraction to doctrines of Anglo-Saxon superiority, the GOP had little political, intellectual, or moral incentive to attack Jim Crow. The small amount they did have was finally obliterated when the forces of war once again reshaped U.S. politics—even if the conflict in question, the Spanish-American War of 1898, was only a "splendid little war," as Republican Secretary of State John Hay (another member of the Lodge/Roosevelt circle) proclaimed. Little it may have seemed, but it was also a war that greatly strengthened political support for systems of racial hierarchy in the United States.

It did so because the Spanish-American War was not a war triggered by any pressing military, diplomatic, or economic necessity. Rather, it was conducted to make the U.S. an imperial power in a world increasingly dominated by great empires. In the roughly three decades from the end of congressional Reconstruction to World War I, one quarter of the world fell under the control of European imperialism, with Britain adding the four million square miles of empire on which the sun never set. American leaders claimed a long-term need, and felt pressing immediate desires, to share in this empire-building. Like their northern European counterparts, though with the requisite adjustments for their own national glorification, they defended their conquests by contending that their opponents, Spain and its Caribbean and Pacific colonial subjects, were their racial infe-riors, unfit for self-government. Americans were doing them a favor by conquering them.

The arguments were not new; the stereotypes of slavish Latino and Asian peoples traced back to the Mexican-American War as well as the Chinese Exclusion debates. But in the late 1890s many white Americans—disappointed by Reconstruction, worried by industrial-ization, urbanization, and immigration, threatened morally and in-tellectually by the new scientific worldviews, and envious of the expanding European powers—became intoxicated by the promise that a new empire would solve all their problems. Casting aside the gloom, anxieties, and divisions of Reconstruction and the Gilded Age, the United States could, many believed, prove that true Ameri-cans were what the feisty Theodore Roosevelt assured them they were: one of "the great masterful races," a "fighting" race, destined to rule, and nobly uplift lower races as far as such primitives could be improved. Rudyard Kipling challenged the United States in his poem "The White Man's Burden" to do just that in the Philippines. Americans responded, believing that the result would be greater wealth and prestige for the United States and also a more secure and even morally commendable racial hierarchy in the world and within the American domain. (The excitement also helped William Randolph Hearst and Joseph Pulitzer sell newspapers, so they fed it.) On the crest of such motives, Americans seized on the U.S.S. *Maine*'s explosion, probably due to a shipboard accident, as a pretext for launching the war that culminated in the nation's acquisition of Puerto Rico, the Philippines, and Guam, along with the effective domination of Cuba, at the same time that the United States annexed Hawaii.[78]

In this American war, as in every other, African Americans joined in fighting for their homeland; and in the wake of their sacrifices, as after every other war, black leaders insisted their efforts had earned them better treatment. Even Booker T. Washington made an un-characteristically bold statement of this position, and in a highly public setting. At the Chicago Peace Jubilee in October 1898, Wash-ington spoke before President William McKinley and a packed audi-torium audience of sixteen thousand. The "Atlanta Compromiser" now forthrightly insisted that the black American who had proven his willingness to serve and die despite "the laws and customs that discriminate against him in his own country" should receive "the highest opportunity to live" for his country. The war's settlement should be "the eternal burial place of all that which separates us in our business and civil relations." Otherwise, Washington warned, American would find itself with "a cancer gnawing at the heart of the Republic, that shall one day prove as dangerous as an attack from an army without or within."

This speech did not win anything like the exhilarated approval of his earlier Atlanta address. Instead, Washington soon felt compelled to clarify that he had not departed from his "separate as the fingers" formula, and that the phrase "civil relations" was not meant to include equal, intermingled social relations. Washington thereafter abandoned the militant tone of his Chicago speech in his public addresses. Given the relatively small scale and brief duration of the war, the racist sentiments used to stir up public opinion to support it, and the failure of the most influential black leader to push strenuously for greater equality for African American veterans, it is not surprising that the Spanish-American conflict did not catalyze any egalitarian reforms in American race relations.[79]

Instead, the highly inegalitarian racial vision that both helped urge the acquisition of the Spanish-American War colonies and then shaped how they, and the domestic United States, would be governed was well defined two years later by a young Republican senator from Indiana, Albert Beveridge, yet another ally of Roosevelt. In a speech that proved far more popular than Washington's Jubilee address, Beveridge insisted that the issue of U.S. imperial growth was "deeper than any question of party politics," or even national "policy" or "constitutional power." It was "racial." In words that foreshadowed the Berlin of the 1930s, Beveridge proclaimed:

God has not been preparing the English-speaking and Teutonic peoples for a thousand years for nothing but vain and idle self-contemplation and self-admiration. No! He has made us the master organizers of the world to establish system where chaos reigns. He has given us the spirit of progress to overwhelm the forces of reaction throughout the earth. He has made us adepts in government that we may administer government among savage and senile races. . . . And of all our race He has marked the American people as His chosen nation to finally lead in the regeneration of the world. This is the divine mission of America, and it holds all the profit, all the glory, all the happiness possible to man. We are trustees of the world's progress, guardians of its righteous peace. The judgment of the Master is upon us: "Ye have been faithful over a few things; I will make you ruler over many things."[80]

The audience in the Senate galleries responded with resounding applause. Headlines made Beveridge a national figure, and Henry Cabot Lodge accepted him as a junior ally on the Senate committee to determine the fate of the new colonial possessions. Doubts that the Constitution permitted the United States, founded on the principles of republican self-governance and human rights, to hold colonies were laid to rest by the Supreme Court. It eventually accepted a doctrine proposed by political scientist A. Lawrence Lowell, then a professor and later president of Harvard, that the "theory that all men are equal politically" had peaked in America during Reconstruction. Like Adams a few years later, Lowell argued that acceptance of that theory had since declined due to recognition that it applied "rigorously only to our own race, and to those people whom we can assimilate rapidly." The "Spanish" race did not qualify; so the residents of the new Spanish-contaminated colonies should be seen as dwelling in "unincorporated" territories, to which the Constitution did not fully apply.[81]

There were, however, a few other voices raised against these policies. In 1899, as U.S. troops attempted to pacify the Philippines, many Northerners were shocked by reports of the lynching, torture, and dismemberment of a black man, Sam Hose, in Newnan, Georgia. In response, Albert E. Pillsbury, former Massachusetts attorney general, asked, "Do you really think that we have any civilization to spare for the Philippines? And do you know of any better use we can make of our armies than to recall them from the islands . . . and see if they can suppress this rebellion against humanity?"[82]

Complaints such as this, however, were ignored. With the Republicans now firmly committed to "tutelary" imperial rule over peoples of color abroad and exclusion of "inferior" races from entry into the United States, they simply had no grounds left to object to Jim Crow policies of segregation and disfranchisement at home, however much they might still want black votes. If only Anglo-Saxons were fit for self-rule, at least at present, who could object to the white South's "tutelary" subordination of African Americans? After all, Republicans like Roosevelt's governor of the Philippines, William Howard Taft, and his Indian commissioner, Francis Leupp, provided training for Filipinos and Native Americans modeled on the segregated, vocationally oriented schooling provided at Hampton, Tuskegee, and other traditionally black institutions. (General Armstrong had modeled Hampton, in turn, on the missionary school his father had established for the "weak tropical races" in Hawaii during the antebellum era.)

Southerners pressed these analogies in Congress, and northern Republicans did not resist them. Like most Americans, they were reading the vivid novels of Thomas Dixon, another friend of Roosevelt (and a former classmate of Woodrow Wilson). In self-described "romances" like *The Leopard's Spots: A Romance of the White Man's Burden, 1865–1900* (1902), *The Clansman: An Historical Romance of the Ku Klux Klan* (1905), and *The Traitor: A Story of the Fall of the Invisible Empire* (1907), Dixon retold the story of race in America in ways that made Reconstruction's egalitarian ideals seem vile. *The Traitor* ultimately sold over a million copies. Further down the list of widely selling books was Booker T. Washington's reassuring self-help story, *Up From Slavery*, as well as a cruder but more popular ghost-written account of Washington's life. By that time, more radical northern black intellectuals like W. E. B. Du Bois and William Monroe Trotter had launched the Niagara Movement, challenging Washington's leadership and insisting on greater political power for blacks. It would be followed by the ideologically similar National Association for the Advancement of Colored People (NAACP) in 1909. But Washington fought against both associations tooth and nail; through the Progressive era, their influence remained marginal compared to his; and his books and speeches continued to do more to assist than to oppose the segregationist spirit of the day.[83]

Similarly, the Supreme Court, with ex-Klansmen Edward White an increasingly influential presence upon it, went to extraordinary lengths to turn its eyes away from even the most blatant and horrendous exclusions of black voters. From Booker T. Washington's home state, for example, came two challenges to egregious denials of black rights to register to vote. Jackson W. Giles, president of the Colored Men's Suffrage Association of Alabama, served as plaintiff in the cases because he had a relatively safe federal job as a mailman. Even so, his involvement eventually caused him to lose that position, and the cases for which he sacrificed so much came to naught. (He did not sacrifice alone. The "Wizard of Tuskegee" supported him, but very secretly: apparently not even Giles realized that Booker Washington paid the association's lawyer additional fees to litigate the cases).

The Supreme Court's stony responses were authored by another

Massachusetts Republican, Oliver Wendell Holmes Jr. He wrote that even if the state's registration practices and voting rules amounted to a "fraud upon the Constitution," the Court could not insist that any black plaintiff be enfranchised. Doing so would only make the Court "a party to the unlawful scheme." And if nothing unlawful had been done, then of course there was also no need for any judicial remedy. When it came to constitutionally damning electoral fraud, southern whites were pardoned if they did and pardoned if they didn't.

The consequences of this federal indulgence of black disfranchisement were dramatic. As late as 1896, over 130,000 African Americans voted in Louisiana; by 1904, the total was only 1,342. Alabama and North Carolina also saw black voting turnout reduced by over 90 percent during these years, and reductions exceeded two-thirds in Arkansas, Mississippi, and Tennessee. This was the context that resulted in the disappearance of tenacious southern black political leaders from the halls of power in the United States, not to return until their absence became a liability during the Cold War.[84] In 1901, the country's only remaining African American congressman, George H. White of North Carolina, served out his term, aware that electoral rigging in the service of white rule gave him no hope of reelection. On January 29, White defiantly told the House that his departure was "perhaps the Negroes' temporary farewell to the American Congress; but we say, Phoenix-like he will rise up some day to come again." Most white Americans envisioned a different future. On March 4, 1901, as White's tenure officially expired, members in both houses of the North Carolina legislature offered speeches of thanksgiving to God that their state would no longer be represented in Congress by a black man.[85]

The same year as White's departure saw Theodore Roosevelt ascend to the presidency after the assassination of William McKinley. Roosevelt always professed allegiance to Lincoln's legacy as he strove to fuse "progressivism" and "Republicanism" during the first two decades of the twentieth century. He was willing to appoint exceptionally accomplished African Americans to office; he fervently denounced the burgeoning numbers of racist lynchings, though he ultimately blamed them on black rapists; and he regularly spoke in favor of securing "to each man, whatever his color, equality of opportunity, equality of treatment before the law." He even invited Booker T. Washington for dinner at the White House, but only once, because southern reactions persuaded him he had made a political error. And while Roosevelt regarded certain blacks as exceptional, he remained utterly convinced that African Americans were a "back-ward race" that had to "be trained so that it may enter into the possession of true freedom." Elite individual blacks, like Washington, might prove capable of high responsibilities under conditions of equal opportunity, but policies should still recognize that "the prime requisite of the race is moral and industrial uplifting" of a sort whites did not require and in fact must supply. This view meant that the problems blacks faced were really traceable to their own deficiencies. Black traits of "laziness and shiftlessness" and "vice and criminality of every kind" did more "harm to the black race than all acts of oppression of white men put together." Furthermore, given black backwardness, "race purity must be maintained."

Those attitudes permitted Roosevelt to acquiesce in the segre-gated, subordinated, "tutelary" status white Southerners imposed on most African American citizens, even as he talked of equal opportu-nity. By either appointing whites to posts once held by blacks or by abolishing positions, his administration reduced rather than in-creased the number of African American officeholders. And when racial violence broke out in Brownsville, Texas in 1906, he imposed dishonorable discharges on three companies of black troops without any trial to establish their guilt—thereby proving to many African Americans that TR had no real commitment to justice for all. Even-tually, as the Progressive Party's leader, Roosevelt would bid to re-turn to power by explicitly endorsing black disfranchisement.[86]

But in these regards Roosevelt, like his friend Charles Francis Adams Jr., accurately represented the opinion of most American whites. By the height of the Progressive Era, the commitments to racial equality forged during the Civil War had been all but effaced. In the three decades following Adams's 1908 speech, America would be what in one way or another it had almost always been—a regime elaborately committed to white supremacy.

FOUR

"The Color Line"

Jim Crow America, 1908–1938

In August of 1908, two months before Charles Francis Adams Jr. reassured white Southerners about the propriety of Jim Crow, matters were far less harmonious in Springfield, Illinois, the home town of Adams's former commander in chief, Abraham Lincoln. Although the city was celebrating the centennial of Lincoln's birth, events there made it clear that race relations, north and south, were no longer guided by the spirit of the Great Emancipator.

Located on flat, sun-beaten farmland near the geographic center of a state that stretched from farther north than New York City to farther south than Richmond, Virginia, Springfield had always been a crossroads for New England Yankees migrating from the east and poor whites moving up from the south. Among the latter group was Lincoln himself. But Southerners more typical in their racial outlooks had always predominated in Springfield: in each of his two races for the presidency, Lincoln failed to carry his home county. Even so, in the first decade of the twentieth century, Springfield had a rapidly growing population of blacks who had come north to the Land of Lincoln to avoid the spreading Jim Crow system, little suspecting the divided and resentful white citizenry that met them there. The result in 1908 was an increasingly volatile racial mix that, heated by the sweltering temperatures and humidity of the central Illinois summer, finally boiled over.

The catalyst was an attractive twenty-one-year-old white woman, Nellie Hallam, married for four years to a streetcar conductor who worked late. On August 14, Hallam claimed she had been raped the night before by a local black workman, George Richardson, a sober citizen without any arrest record. Soon she recanted, saying she had been assaulted by a white man she refused to name. But a white mob nonetheless formed, aiming to lynch Richardson; and when local officials succeeded in spiriting him and another black defendant out of town, the frustrated mob began raiding stores, seizing weapons, and destroying black businesses and homes. Shouts of "Curse the day that Lincoln freed the nigger" and "Abe Lincoln brought them to Springfield and we will drive them out" fired up the crowd. They burned a barber shop, shooting Scott Burton, its black proprietor, when he fired into the assaulting mob. The rioters then triumphantly dragged his body over the town's red-brick streets. Then frenzied whites seized a sleeping eighty-four-year-old black man, William Donegan, who had been married to a white woman for over thirty years, and lynched him. When he did not die quickly enough, they cut the rope around his neck, slicing his throat, and then hacked his body with knives. The slaughter occurred within a block of the Old State Capitol, the same building where fifty years before, Lincoln had delivered his famous speech insisting that a house divided against itself cannot stand, that a nation could not survive only half free.

The violence did not end until roughly four thousand militia men were called out, four white men were killed, more than seventy people were wounded, and over a hundred were arrested, though the leaders of the mob escaped punishment. In its wake, the Springfield paper, the *Illinois State Journal,* editorialized that the root cause was "the negroes' own misconduct, general inferiority, or unfitness for free institutions." A number of employers fired their black workers and many local shopkeepers refused any longer to serve them. As a result, two thousand blacks fled the city, only to be refused entry into the central Illinois towns of Jacksonville and Peoria. The last death stemming from the riot was that of a black infant who died of exposure near Pittsfield, Illinois as her mother sought refuge from the carnage.[1]

Shocked, the journalist William English Walling visited Springfield and wrote of the "Race War in the North." As a nation reeled at the atrocities he documented, a biracial group of distinguished social activists began organizing. Walling, William Lloyd Garrison's grandson Oswald Garrison Villard, social workers Mary White Ovington and Jane Addams, democratic philosopher John Dewey, and great African American leaders including the antilynching organizer Ida B. Wells, the brilliant scholar W. E. B. Du Bois, and religious leaders Bishop Alexander Walters and Reverend William Henry Brooks joined in forming what became the National Association for the Advancement of Colored People (NAACP).[2]

Despite its impressive array of founders, however, the NAACP was far in advance of even most liberal white outlooks of the time. In May of 1908, journalist Ray Stannard Baker published *Following the Colour Line,* a collection of articles that he had written over the previous two years detailing nearly every aspect of contemporary American race relations. Perhaps the most prominent of the "muckraking" journalists of the Progressive Era, Baker was described as "America's #1 reporter." Not surprisingly given his fame, Baker's book was an immediate sensation, achieving high sales and nearly universal acclaim on both sides of the Mason-Dixon line. A review in the *American Journal of Sociology* cited it as "remarkable for its objectivity and psychological insight." Even Villard and Du Bois complimented the book.[3]

Following the Colour Line still stands as an important and critical account of the racial hierarchy that had emerged in the aftermath of Reconstruction. Baker ably recounts how most southern blacks led lives of oppression and destitution, interspersed with the terror of white violence. He even recounts how racism increasingly restricted the lives and opportunities of the growing number of blacks in the North—a fact made painfully evident by the Springfield riot. Nonetheless, Baker reached typical mainstream Progressive—and anti-black—conclusions. He contended that "the vast majority of Negroes . . . are still densely ignorant, and have little or no appreciation of the duties of citizenship." He added, "Negroes as a class are today far inferior in education, intelligence, and efficiency to the white people as a class." Blacks, therefore, must accommodate themselves to a subservient and tutelary position in American society. "Here and there an able Negro will develop superior abilities; but the mass of Negroes for years to come must find their activities mostly in physical and more or less menial labour. Like any race, they must first prove themselves in these simple lines of work before they can expect larger opportunities." Given such conditions, egalitarian reforms like the Fifteenth Amendment were of no avail since the amendment "could not really enfranchise the Negro slaves. Men must enfranchise themselves." In the end, Baker could only advocate the conservative trinity of solutions to social problems: time, education, and patience. He wrote, "All such relationships will work themselves out gradually, naturally, quietly, in the long course of the years: and the less they are talked about the better."[4]

Looking back, the title of Baker's book can be read in two ways. Baker certainly "followed" the color line by traveling throughout the country in his research. But, as the book's warm reception indicates, he also followed the color "line" in his espousal of the racial prejudice of the day. Precisely because Baker was no conservative, because he and other Progressives advocated sweeping reforms to remedy the nation's ills, his laissez faire attitude toward racial inequality suggests how pervasively racist assumptions characterized the minds of most white Americans in this era. In fact, over the next three decades, the color line described by Baker would become even more rigid, despite the efforts of the NAACP. Black Americans would remain impoverished, segregated, and stigmatized. On the other side of the line, white supremacy of one sort or another would dominate the thinking of most white Americans, from presidents and respected intellectuals to average citizens, and across the political spectrum from conservative to liberals like Baker. Although often courageous and resourceful, those who would call out for racial equality were few in number and virtually ignored in the corridors of power. Even though the nation would undergo significant change and reform during the Progressive Era, World War I, and the New Deal, these developments would leave the color line largely undisturbed and in some ways enhanced.

If Theodore Roosevelt was no true advocate of racial equality, as we have seen, Republican treatment of blacks grew worse yet under Roosevelt's successor, William Howard Taft, elected in the racial gloom of 1908. Taft did not believe blacks should be appointed to office anywhere whites might object, which meant just about everywhere in America. In any case, Taft explained to a black audience, "Your race is adapted to be a race of farmers, first, last and for all time."[5] He also reassured southern whites that the Fifteenth Amendment did not bar their efforts to prevent "domination by an ignorant electorate."[6]

Yet even though Taft and other northern Republicans played lead roles in colonial expansion and, eventually, immigration restriction, they still only grudgingly acquiesced in, rather than sponsored, the development of Jim Crow. That was chiefly the work of southern Democrats. Correspondingly, segregation gained the most support at the federal level when a southern Democrat turned northeastern "progressive," Woodrow Wilson, gained the White House due to the Roosevelt-Taft split in 1912.

Wilson, the son of a Confederate sympathizer, defended southern secession as a college freshman before going on to his graduate studies in the racist "Teutonic germ" school of U.S. history. Although Wilson eventually came to identify retroactively with the cause of national union against the South, throughout his life his scholarly writings still interpreted that union as the product of the "progress in civilization" made by the "stronger and nobler races," "principally" those of "Aryan" origins. Few southern whites disagreed.[7]

In regard to blacks, Wilson was probably the most racist president of this century. In his *A History of the American People,* Wilson offered up the then typical portrayal of Reconstruction as "the veritable overthrow of civilization in the South." "Mere instinct of self-preservation" led whites to form vigilante groups like the Ku Klux Klan to free themselves from rule of "ignorant negroes" and stamp out the "incubus" of black voting.[8] Later, as president of Princeton University, Wilson barred the entry of black students. In the White House, he enjoyed telling "darky stories," sometimes in dialect, to his Cabinet.[9] In 1915, Wilson arranged for a White House screening of D. W. Griffith's film *Birth of a Nation,* based on the novel *The Clansman* by his Johns Hopkins classmate, Thomas Dixon. After seeing the film, the president (whose aforementioned description of Reconstruction's evils had been used in the film's title cards), praised it as "History written with lightning," adding, "my only regret is that it is all so terribly true."[10] When Dixon wrote him to express concern that black employees of the federal government might be able to "boss white girls," Wilson replied reassuringly that the administration was "handling the force of colored people . . . in just the way they ought to be handled."[11]

And what a way it was. Wilson's cabinet officers, disproportionately composed of white Southerners, greatly expanded segregation practices in federal agencies and kept African Americans in inferior jobs, despite rhetorical commitments to civil service "meritocratic" standards. On July 5, 1913, only one day after Wilson spoke at the fiftieth anniversary of the battle of Gettysburg, the Post Office began to segregate its black clerks. One week later, the Treasury Department established segregated toilets for its employees.[12] The following year, the Civil Service Commission began requiring applicants for posts to provide photographs, and job acceptances and assignments soon generally followed inegalitarian racial lines. Wilson himself explicitly endorsed "the segregation that is being attempted in several of the departments" as "distinctly to the advantage of the colored people themselves," while denying that the system posed any barriers to their advancement. Although the Wilson administration moderated some abuses in response to criticism from the NAACP and others, before white southern audiences Wilson continued to identify himself as a like-minded "Southern man." He assured them that he knew white segregationists were working for "the good of the Negro

. . . on all sound and sensible lines." He also knew that those lines involved ongoing white domination of blacks.[13]

Although Wilson won another term in 1916 on the campaign slogan, "He Kept Us Out of War," America found itself at war within six months of the election. The conflict, however, held out the possibility that war might once again serve as a catalyst for greater racial equality. As in the Revolution and the Civil War, America's involvement in World War I was suffused with liberal principles. Describing it as a war to make the world safe for democracy, President Wilson repeatedly invoked principles of human rights, especially the rights of subject minorities, to justify America's intervention. In addition to the war's ideological nature, it also required the type of intensive mobilization and sacrifice from African Americans that had previously been used as a means to leverage white America for greater racial equality. Almost four hundred thousand African Americans performed military service during the war, and black civilians contributed over $250 million during five Liberty Loan drives.[14] Military leaders were well aware of these circumstances. A report by the General Staff stated, "[T]he government is asking the entire colored population to take a full share in the war. Their men, their money, and their devotion are needed to the greatest possible extent."[15]

Yet despite these conditions, World War I led to no great advance for black rights. Throughout the war, both the military and the nation at large remained intensely racist. Following the war, a wave of antiblack violence swept the country. If anything, World War I, rather than ameliorating American racism, further contributed to it.

Two reasons explain the lack of racial progress in World War I. First, while it entailed broad mobilization—4.8 million men served in the military during the war—America's commitment to the war was very brief, lasting a total of only twenty months from April 1917 to November 1918. Furthermore, Americans' involvement in combat was even shorter. American divisions first entered combat only in April of 1918, and American casualties were concentrated in the last few weeks of the war. Approximately 68 percent of American battle deaths occurred in the final twelve weeks, with 57 percent occurring in the final eight. As a consequence, America in World War I never reached a point where national political leaders consciously saw the military role of blacks as crucial to the success of their cause, as Washington and Lincoln had done during the Revolution and the Civil War.[16]

World War I also differed from those crises because it lacked the presence of strong egalitarian movements that used the war as lev-

erage to compel greater inclusion. At that time most white liberals had little or no interest in the cause of racial equality. Furthermore, they quickly became caught up in the wave of nationalistic
fervor that swept the nation after America's entry into the war, putting their reformist zeal aside for the duration. Farther left on the
spectrum, most socialists chose to remain true to their principles by
opposing the war. But doing so merely brought them into greater
disrepute, precluding their ability to use the war as a means to obtain
greater equality for blacks.[17]

Yet perhaps the most important factor in limiting the cause of
racial equality in World War I was the conservative stance taken by
most black leaders during the war. To be sure, not all blacks supported the war absent a quid pro quo of greater civil rights. In July
1917, five thousand blacks marched silently down New York's Fifth
Avenue, protesting a race riot in East St. Louis, Illinois and carrying
banners asking, "Mr. President, Why Not Make AMERICA Safe for Democracy?"[18] Nonetheless, most black leaders still supported the war
effort. Even after Booker T. Washington's death in 1915, his legacy
carried considerable influence among black elites. Reluctant to push
hard for civil and political rights in peacetime, these leaders were
even less likely to do so during the war. Emmett Scott, Washington's
former secretary, was the most visible black in government during
the war, serving the secretary of war as Special Assistant for Negro
Affairs. "This is not the time to discuss race problems," claimed Scott.
"Our first duty is to fight. . . . Then we can adjust the problems
that remain in the life of the colored man." Though he seems to
have been deeply disturbed by the mistreatment of blacks in the
military, Scott failed to speak out publicly and his private protests
were dismissed by his white superiors.[19]

Such a stance from Washingtonites like Scott was predictable; but
even more radical black leaders took a similar position during World
War I. NAACP officials like W. E. B. Du Bois supported the establishment of a segregated training camp for black officers. In his most
famous statement on the war, Du Bois editorialized in the NAACP
journal *Crisis,* "Let us not hesitate. Let us, while this war lasts, forget
our special grievances and close ranks shoulder to shoulder with
our white fellow citizens and the allied nations that are fighting for
democracy."[20] More directly, he wrote, "First your country, then
your Rights!"[21]

Prompted by such statements, most black Americans did close
ranks during the war. As one historian pointed out, "Black clergymen led bond drives and urged eligible men in their congregations

to join the armed forces. Black colleges threw themselves into the war effort. Howard University did away with German language courses. Blacks purchased hundreds of millions of dollars' worth of Liberty Bonds and stamps and took hundreds of thousands of war jobs and staged loyalty parades. . . . The vast majority of African-American newspapers spoke favorably of America's part in the war," even as hundreds of thousands left home and risked their lives.[22]

Black patriotism and sacrifice was not repaid during the war. Far from it. Throughout the war the military remained rigidly segregated, and the Marine Corps prohibited black enlistments entirely. Black sailors and soldiers were, for the most part, assigned to menial service and labor units. Only a tenth of those in the armed forces drew combat duty. The few black combat units were poorly trained and equipped and mostly led by incompetent and racist officers. When some therefore did not perform well, white officers interpreted their poor combat performance as new evidence of blacks' incapacity for military service. These officers conveniently overlooked the achievements of the black units of the U.S. army that had been assigned to the French army, including the 15th New York and the 8th Illinois Infantry. There they received adequate training and were led by competent and sympathetic officers, and these units consequently performed valiantly. The black 92nd Division was the only U.S. unit to receive little training until it arrived overseas, but it fought so well in the last two months of the war that the French high command cited a whole battalion for bravery and awarded it the *Croix de Guerre.* American military leaders were far more grudging in their recognition of black contributions.[23]

The U.S. army in World War I also contributed to American racism in another way. Throughout the war, army recruits were given intelligence tests. Not surprisingly, given the racial biases of the scientific community at the time, the low levels of education and language skills among most blacks and recent immigrants, and the exams' shoddy methodology, these tests provided a mountain of data that purportedly proved the mental deficiencies of blacks and various white ethnic groups. The most famous analysis of this data was *A Study of American Intelligence,* published by a Princeton assistant professor of psychology, Carl Campbell Brigham, in 1923. Brigham contended his results vindicated the 1916 claims of Madison Grant, the patrician founder of the New York Zoological Society, on behalf of the intellectual superiority of "Nordic" peoples over all others. Like Grant, Brigham ended his book by bemoaning the "alarming" rise of the "negro" and mulatto populations in the United States as well as the introduction into it of other "defective strains," such as the "Alpine Slav" and "the degenerate hybrid Mediterranean," via immigration. The next year, Brigham became the first head of the new Princeton-based Educational Testing Service, where he helped develop the Scholastic Aptitude Test (SAT) still used in college admission processes. In the course of that work, he eventually came to renounce his earlier racist research as incompetent. But before then, racists and nativists were able to use books like Brigham's and Grant's not only to defend Jim Crow but also to support passage of the Immigration Restriction Act of 1924. It used a "national origins quota" system to admit immigrants in ratios replicating the nation's ethnic composition at the turn of the century, an approach that greatly limited the flow of persons from central, southern, and eastern Europe.[24]

Even though many whites were reading the lessons of the war experience concerning blacks so negatively, many blacks still hoped after the armistice that their wartime patriotism would be rewarded. *Crisis* editor Du Bois now wrote:

> *We* return. *We* return from fighting. We return fighting.
> *Make way for Democracy! We saved it in France, and by the Great Jehovah,*
> *we will save it in the U.S.A., or know the reason why.*[25]

The reason why, as it turned out, was that many if not most white Americans entered the postwar era in a profoundly reactionary mood. Desiring "normalcy" and fearful of change, they lashed out at those elements—blacks, leftists, unionists, and foreigners—that they believed threatened the old order. Far from accepting that black military service justified more equal treatment for African Americans, many white Americans agreed with the *Houston Chronicle* when it editorialized that the army had foolishly given blacks "an unprecedented degree of protection and consideration while huge wages and allotments have tended to make them shiftless and irresponsible." It was in this climate that the Ku Klux Klan underwent a resurgence. Promising to unite "native-born white Christians for concerted action in the preservation of American institutions and the supremacy of the white race," the Klan soon attracted over one hundred thousand members throughout the nation.[26]

Black expectations and white fears collided in the "Red Summer" of 1919, one of the worst periods of interracial violence in American history. The mixing of three combustible factors produced its destructive conflagrations. First, the war greatly accelerated the "First

Great Migration" of southern blacks to the north and west that had begun with the triumphs of Jim Crow in the late nineteenth century. The war's enormous industrial demand for unskilled labor prompted northern employers to offer blacks unprecedented economic opportunities, and from 1916 through 1919 nearly four hundred thousand blacks moved north to take advantage of them. New York's black population rose from 91,709 in 1910 to 152,467 in 1920, but most of the growth came in the upper Midwest. Detroit's 1910 black community of a mere 5,741 burgeoned to 40,838 by the next census. In Chicago, blacks increased from about 44,000 to nearly 110,000 from 1910 to 1920, while the white population rose much more slowly. The shift of blacks to the north would continue through the 1920s, when up to another million would come "out of Egypt"; but the war years represented a historic peak of intensity.[27]

Second, after the war ended, those blacks were reinforced by returning black veterans, many of whom had experienced more equal treatment in France. Filled with belief in their rights and pride in their fighting abilities, they were unwilling to submit to the many constraints and indignities of the nation's racial hierarchies and exclusions. Finally, after the armistice, the nation's booming war industries collapsed, and northern whites and blacks alike faced a severe shortage of jobs and affordable housing during the recession of 1919. These economic troubles hardened the determination of many whites to drive blacks back out of northern cities and occupations, even as blacks determined that they would not be driven out. As black poet Claude McKay wrote:

> Like men we'll face the murderous, cowardly pack,
> Pressed to the wall, dying but fighting back![28]

The result was incredibly widespread violence. As the 1908 Springfield riot had foreshadowed, whites tried to recreate the repression of southern blacks achieved in part through lynchings by sending murderous mobs into black neighborhoods whenever racial tensions flared. From 1917 on, lynchings began rising rapidly once again and attacks on blacks mounted in the cities. Then, from June to December of the terrifying year of 1919, up to twenty-five race riots broke out in various cities and towns around the country. The worst was in Chicago, where since 1917 whites had regularly bombed the homes of new black residents (from 1917 to 1921, 58 black homes were bombed in Chicago, an average of one every three weeks). In this tinderbox, when reports spread that whites had attacked a black swimmer at a Lake Michigan beach who had drifted into the "white" section of the water, the city exploded. Blacks and whites fought in the streets for nearly two weeks. Before the violence ended, thirty-eight people, mostly blacks, had been killed and another 537 were injured. Close to a thousand black families lost their homes. Violence such as this made it very clear that while America's participation in World War I might have made the world safe for democracy, it did little to make it safe in America.[29]

The battles of 1919 were momentous and their results were not entirely negative for African Americans. The strenuous resistance to white assaults mounted by northern blacks, especially the returned veterans, meant that whites failed to expel blacks from northern cities and towns. And from this point on in U.S. history, whites rarely felt able to resort to open mass violence against blacks in order to maintain their racial prerogatives. Over time, American governments would instead make it easier for whites to move to well-guarded suburbs, often taking many of the good jobs with them. Violence toward individual blacks and protesting black groups would certainly not end. But henceforth, public and private policies of omission and avoidance of blacks and their interests, rather than overt brutality, would do most of the work of sustaining white supremacy.

Those policies worked in part because, understandably, many blacks responded to the white violence that greeted the First Great Migration by acquiescing in a northern, de facto version of Jim Crow: pervasive racial residential segregation. In the nineteenth century, blacks rarely formed more than 30 percent of any residential area in any northern city, and not only because their numbers were low. Black residents were then relatively interspersed with whites. From early on in the twentieth century, those patterns changed. As whites began viciously opposing black entry into white neighborhoods, many blacks found it preferable to accept the designation of some turf as their own, even if the location and borders of the new black neighborhoods were constantly in dispute.

The result was the creation of the urban ghettoes. In 1860, less than a third of the nation's urban blacks lived in sharply segregated city neighborhoods. By 1910, nearly 40 percent did. The white violence that resisted would-be black homeowners in northern cities after World War I then accelerated that segregating trend. By 1940, it would engulf over 80 percent of urban blacks, a level of ugly "hyper-segregation" that the nation has since essentially maintained. And as residential segregation grew, so did other forms of white avoidance of blacks. Although no formal Jim Crow laws were enacted in the north, white parents increasingly removed their children from schools that included blacks. And, to both their economic and political disadvantage, the small but important class of black professionals, lawyers, clergymen, doctors, dentists, teachers, businessmen, and others now found it difficult to retain white clients, professional associates, or friends.[30]

Unsurprisingly, the post–World War I conflicts left most blacks profoundly embittered about their unrewarded war efforts and about their prospects for full and equal citizenship in the United States. While some gave up on residential integration, many also began to doubt the value of pushing strenuously for full political equality in the United States. Instead blacks responded to a different call. It rang out strong and clear at Madison Square Garden on August 2, 1920, when a charismatic Jamaican immigrant, Marcus Garvey, addressed a huge gathering of twenty-five thousand African Americans from around the United States and the world. They were delegates to the annual conference of the wildly burgeoning organization he had founded, the Universal Negro Improvement Association (UNIA). Garvey told this historically unprecedented throng:

> We New Negroes, we men who have returned from World War I, we will dispute every inch of the way until we win. We will begin by framing a Bill of Rights for the Negro race. . . . The Constitution of the United States means that every white American should shed his blood to defend that Constitution. The Constitution of the Negro race will mean that every Negro will shed his blood to defend his Constitution. If Europe is for the European, then Africa shall be for the black people of the world. We say it; we mean it. . . . we are going home after a long vacation and are giving notice to the tenant. If he doesn't get out there is such a thing as forcible eviction.

The message was unmistakable. Although blacks in America and elsewhere should not for a minute accept racial discriminations and exclusions as just, they should focus their efforts on separatist, not integrationist, strategies. They should not stress gaining equal rights as U.S. citizens so much as gaining independent power bases for blacks, a program that included building up black businesses in the United States, liberating Africa from white colonial powers, and establishing it as a self-governing black home continent.[31]

In the acrid atmosphere of disillusionment, anger, and economic suffering that prevailed among African Americans in the wake of the First World War, this message had staggering appeal. Garvey had arrived in the United States in 1916 with few acquaintances and only a rudimentary UNIA organization in Jamaica behind him. Yet during the war years, he proved able and willing to speak directly to the great mass of African Americans as none of the established black leadership groups really tried to do. They responded by flocking to his banner. The war also awakened many American blacks to their linked histories with African-descended peoples oppressed by colonial powers and by whites within former colonies around the globe, even as it led them to despair of their prospects within the United States. Hence they were willing to embrace the boundary-crossing black racial nationalism Garvey espoused in place of the visions of racial integration within the American mainstream offered by many NAACP leaders, or the prospect of a united white and black proletariat advanced by socialist leaders. The 1919 race wars enabled Garvey's movement to enroll hundreds of thousand of blacks; at the year's end he claimed that the UNIA had 2 million members. Although many criticize that figure as exaggerated, most historians accept that at its peak in the early 1920s the association certainly had 250,000 working members and at least a million more occasional participants in more than four hundred U.S. divisions. As such, the UNIA was the largest black political organization that ever existed in the United States, before or since.[32]

The fact that black Americans gave such tremendous support to a leader and organization campaigning for a pluralistic society in which blacks would develop separately from whites, if they did not go "back" to Africa, had consequences. It meant that white Americans felt under relatively little pressure to end Jim Crow segregation in the 1920s. That egalitarian aim was thus almost invisible on the American national political scene during the decade.

To be sure, at its outset, the hopes of some civil rights advocates were stirred when Republican presidential candidate Warren G. Harding declared in the 1920 campaign that "the Federal government should stamp out lynching." He also averred that "Negro citizens of American should be guaranteed the enjoyment of all their rights, that they have earned their full measure of citizenship bestowed, that their sacrifices in blood on the battlefields of the republic have entitled them to all of freedom of opportunity, all of sympathy and aid that the American spirit of fairness and justice demands." In private, Harding told James Weldon Johnson, a leading black poet and playwright and the secretary of the NAACP, that he supported a new national elections bill to secure black voting rights and that, if elected, he would overturn Wilson's segregation of the federal government by executive order.[33]

Some blacks were also encouraged by the fact that Harding was rumored to be of African American ancestry. These charges originated with Democratic propagandists and the issue roiled the campaign, indicating how important questions of "racial purity" were to white Americans of the time. The *New York Times* even published a genealogical history of the Harding family. Such rumors had followed the Harding family for years and, according to Harding's major biographer, constituted a "shadow" over his hometown of Blooming Grove, Ohio. "How do I know Jim," Harding once told a friend, "One of my ancestors may have jumped the fence." Publicly, he was considerably less willing to question his forebears. Harding's campaign manager averred, "No family in the state has a clearer or more honorable record than the Hardings, a blue-eyed stock from New England and Pennsylvania, the finest pioneer blood, Anglo-Saxon, German, Scotch-Irish, and Dutch."[34]

Whatever his roots, once in office Harding gave little sympathy to black rights. In October 1921, he resoundingly endorsed racial separatism in a speech to a racially mixed audience in Birmingham, Alabama. "Men of both races," he said, "may well stand uncompromisingly against every suggestion of social equality. . . . Racial amalgamation there cannot be." This was "a question of recognizing a fundamental, eternal, and inescapable difference." On behalf of these propositions, he quoted another widely selling racist tract, Lothrop Stoddard's *The Rising Tide of Color against White World Supremacy.* Although Harding insisted social segregation was good for all, there could be little doubt where he would stand in the apocalyptic conflict Stoddard depicted. Yet Marcus Garvey telegraphed congratulations and "the heartfelt thanks of four hundred million Negros of the world" for the "splendid interpretation" Harding had given the "race problem," since the president recognized that "all races should develop on their own social lines." Such support could only have strengthened the president in that course. Formally complying with his campaign promises, Harding did call on Congress to enact antilynching legislation and to establish a commission to study American race relations, but his actual efforts on these matters were minimal. After the House passed an antilynching bill in 1922, Harding ignored pleas from the NAACP and did nothing to dissuade Senate Republicans from abandoning the bill in the face of a Democratic filibuster.[35]

But Garvey did not stop at lending credence to the white racism of mere conservatives like Harding. The UNIA chief shocked many northern black leaders and ultimately damaged his own credibility by repeatedly applauding the calls for racial purity issued by the KKK, John Powell's Anglo-Saxon Clubs, and similar white supremacist organizations. Garvey, to be sure, never accepted white supremacist claims, and the UNIA officially opposed racial discrimination and Klan violence. But in many respects the Klan's program did mesh with Garvey's own ideals of racial purity and separatism, and he did not hesitate to affirm that fact. Instead, he met with Klan leaders in Atlanta in 1922 in order to persuade them that the UNIA and the Klan had no reason to fight each other. When Du Bois and other prominent blacks expressed their outrage, Garvey responded that "the Klan, the Anglo-Saxon Clubs and White American societies" were "better friends of the race than all other groups of hypocritical whites put together. I like honesty and fair play. You may call me a Klansman if you will, but, potentially every white man is a Klansman, as far as the Negro in competition with whites socially, economically and politically is concerned, and there is no use lying about it." Garvey's position provoked severe dissension even within UNIA ranks, and discontents were already brewing due to problems with the organization's financial ventures, especially its highly publicized Black Star Steamship Line. Soon thereafter, the U.S. government successfully prosecuted Garvey for allegedly fraudulent stock advertising, though he was far more guilty of naive optimism than deliberate deception in his business dealings. In the wake of these troubles, Garvey's personal following and that of his organization faded rapidly in the mid-1920s. But by then, the opportunity to use the nation's World War I rhetoric of human rights against Jim Crow had also receded. The war already seemed long ago.[36]

In fact, with the Democrats well established as the party of the Solid South and Jim Crow, with a resurgent Klan, and with the Republicans and the nation's largest black organization all also endorsing racial separatism, prominent champions for ideals of equal rights for all within an integrated nation were as hard to find in the early 1920s as at any point in U.S. history. Even among reform-minded American intellectuals who opposed many aspects of the era's resurgent racism, acquiescence in segregation was commonplace. As a telling example, no one opposed the rise of ethnically based immigration restrictions more vigorously than the Columbia University philosopher Horace Kallen. Although he was never the famed figure his colleague John Dewey became, Kallen's writings on American identity were influential in his own day. They have since been widely recognized as seminal forerunners of today's "multiculturalism," the vision of America as, properly, a democratic but culturally pluralistic society. In his 1924 essay collection, *Culture and Democracy in the United States*, Kallen produced the leading attack on the national origins quota system, contending that the nation faced a choice between pursuing a "Kultur Klux Klan" policy of Nordic immigration or a more inclusive, egalitarian "cultural pluralism." Yet even he refused to argue that blacks should have an equal place in the pluralistic society he envisioned.[37]

In truth, Kallen shared many of the premises of the immigration restrictionists he opposed. Although he wanted the United States to be a democratic federation of different ethnic groups who would treat others with respect, his position accepted the notion that these racial and ethnic groups were ineradicably distinct in ways that made substantial social segregation appropriate. When John Dewey pointed out to him that Kallen's views had segregationist potential, Kallen did not protest. As his critics noted, it was hardly a wrenching further step to suggest that nationalities that were too sharply distinct from older American stocks should not be admitted. And in regard to African Americans, Kallen would only say in his 1924 book that "the negro" requires "separate analysis." As a young man, he had written more candidly in a private letter that he had "neither respect nor liking" for blacks, with the exception of a few like his former Harvard tutee, the brilliant black writer Alain Locke. For Kallen, most blacks indeed seemed too "different" to be accorded equal respect with other nationalities.[38]

In a time when even prominent, left-leaning intellectual champions of democracy and minority rights thus accepted racial separatism and inequality, the question may well be asked, who did speak for equal rights and integration? There were two notable groups, but neither exercised any great political clout. The first were those educated black elites who rejected Garveyism and thought it crucial to assault the Jim Crow system; W. E. B. Du Bois and most of the African Americans among the NAACP leadership can be counted among this group.. The second were members of the white progressive left like John Dewey, who rejected both Roosevelt's assimilationist view of Americanism and Kallen's acceptance of ineradicable racial and ethnic differences.

Of these, the black leaders clearly did more to keep alive the Reconstruction spirit of genuine human moral equality and common citizenship for all races in the United States. Throughout the 1920s, Du Bois's *Crisis* editorials vituperatively denounced Garvey's radical black nationalism as well as Klan lynchings and disfranchisement, insisting that African Americans must still seek "equal rights and opportunities for all" in all American institutions. Led by its first president Moorfield Story, a former president of the American Bar Association, the NAACP also turned increasingly to what became its central strategy for change: appealing to the egalitarian, inclusive Reconstruction amendments and statutes in court cases in order to curb racial discrimination by judicial orders. Those efforts by black and white NAACP lawyers produced some important victories, including the Supreme Court's invalidation of laws requiring residential racial segregation and disfranchising blacks via grandfather clauses.[39]

Yet significant as those successes were, they did not alter the still-rising patterns of sharp residential segregation and effective bans on black voting achieved by other means. As long as racial discrimination was clearly performed by private parties, or at least not too blatantly performed by governmental officials, the courts still tended to sustain challenged practices.[40] Indeed, in these years the NAACP lawyers won cases against Jim Crow arrangements only by showing that various sorts of separate facilities were not genuinely equal—a rationale that left the basic constitutionality of segregation unimpaired, even unchallenged. These legal triumphs also did not alter the fact that the NAACP was largely an organization of black and white elites that lacked a mass following that could bring pressure to bear in legislatures, in boardrooms, and in the streets, as well as in court. The results of this litigative approach were so limited that by the early 1930s, Du Bois himself would conclude that it was more practical for the time being to concentrate on building up separate black economic and educational institutions, as moderate black nationalists had long argued. His new position was fiercely controversial within the NAACP, and he finally left the organization. Few could deny, however, that during the 1920s the NAACP program of "equal rights in the public schools, in the voting booths, on the railroads, and on juries" was only a small eddy against a churning tide of white racism.[41]

Still, the NAACP legal victories helped bolster the conscience of that small number of white reformers who had never abandoned the egalitarian ideals of Reconstruction. They found the allegedly scientific racism of men like Madison Grant and Carl Campbell Brigham far less persuasive than newer, more egalitarian views then being advanced by scholars like the anthropologists Franz Boas and Ruth Benedict. By the 1920s, John Dewey's long career as a philosophical and educational innovator, his many celebrated scholarly works, and his more popular writings in journals like the *New Republic* had made him the nation's most prominent public intellectual. And though he had been reluctant to criticize American jingoism during World War I, Dewey consistently decried Americanization rhetoric as a cult of intolerant "Anglo-saxondom." In its place, through the late teens and the early twenties, Dewey repeatedly advocated the almost unheard-of ideals of genuine "internationalism and inter-racialism." He insisted that democratic institutions and associations, in the United States and throughout the world, should serve to "de-velop the capacities of human individuals without respect to race, sex, class or economic status."[42]

Yet even though he provided an important new articulation of the ideals of democracy, human rights, equal opportunities, and an end to racial barriers that had been advanced in previous periods of egalitarian reform in America, Dewey did not find the 1920s a propi-tious time to press hard for all those goals. Instead, he minimized racial issues while answering charges that democratic ideals made little sense even for whites. At times even he seemed to underwrite the propriety of Tuskegee-style purely vocational education for blacks. His writings, like the NAACP legal victories, at best planted seeds that would only flourish in a very different political climate formed by yet another, and even vaster, world war.[43]

Until then, racial liberalism remained at the margins of American political life. When Harding died in office in 1923, Vice President Calvin Coolidge ascended to the Oval Office. True to form, "Silent Cal" let the business of America be business as he said little and did less when it came to equal rights. Coolidge's most damning silence was his failure to denounce the Ku Klux Klan during the 1924 presi-dential campaign, even though his opponents, Democrat John W. Davis and Progressive Robert LaFollette, had done so. (Davis would later defend racial segregation of public schools before the Supreme Court in *Brown v. Board of Education*). In 1925, the president kept coolly silent as forty thousand costumed Klansmen paraded through the streets of Washington, D.C. Still, there were benefits to Coolidge's reticence; many of his utterances, such as when he declared, "Biolog-ical laws shows us that Nordics deteriorate when mixed with other races," hardly helped the cause of equal rights.[44]

During the election of 1928, black disappointment with the Re-publicans only deepened. The party's nominee, Herbert Hoover sought "to break up the solid south and to drive the negroes out of Republican politics" by supporting "Lily-White" Republicans organizations in those states, according to a none too radical observer, Chief Justice William Howard Taft.[45] Many blacks also claimed that as director of the federal government's relief efforts during the Great Mississippi Flood of 1927, Hoover had been insensitive to the plight of black sharecroppers and their abuse by local whites during the crisis.[46]

For those blacks who saw voting for the party of Lincoln as an empty gesture, the Democratic candidate, Governor Al Smith of New York, a Roman Catholic and son of immigrants, brought a glimmer of hope. Smith's nomination signaled the declining power of the south in party councils and the rise of a more inclusive and pluralistic Democratic party based in the urban north. The failure of whites to repel blacks from northern cities after the war raised the possibility of, instead, trying to incorporate them as political supporters, and some northern Democrats as well as Republicans gave that prospect serious consideration. In fact, Smith toyed with the idea of campaigning actively for black votes. He was, after all, a product of the New York City that had undergone the Harlem Renaissance during the 1920s, when whites as well as blacks in the nation's greatest metropolis reveled in the new cultural contributions to poetry, music, art, and literature produced by the city's African Americans. But the rest of the nation was clearly not New York; and by the time the Democratic convention met in Houston (only days after a lynching there), Smith backed away from these plans. To appease southern Democrats, he chose Arkansas senator Joseph Robinson as his running mate. Inside the convention hall, black visitors were segregated within a chicken wire cage.[47]

Even with these affronts, Smith managed to increase his party's share of the black vote. Nonetheless, Hoover won in a walk and became the first Republican candidate since Reconstruction to crack the Solid South, winning Florida, North Carolina, Tennessee, Texas, and Virginia. To many Republicans, these southern victories suggested that they no longer needed to rely on black votes. Hoover's actions, once in office, similarly indicated that he took black interests even less seriously than his predecessors. Not only did he continue efforts at building up lily-white Republicanism in the South, but in his first year in office, Hoover made no significant black appointments.[48]

The Hoover administration's most controversial move came in 1930. The previous year, Congress had passed a law providing for the government to arrange for "Gold Star" mothers and wives of deceased World War I servicemen to travel to France to visit the grave sites of their sons and husbands. In organizing the trip, the War Department chose to send black mothers and wives on separate ships from their white counterparts. According to the secretary of war, "It would seem natural to assume that these mothers and widows would prefer to seek solace in their grief from companions of their own people." "Surely there was no time in the history of our country when segregation was less necessary and more cruel," wrote the *Nation*.[49]

After the stock market crash of 1929 and the onset of the Great Depression, the economic status of most black Americans went from bad to worse. Always "last hired and first fired," blacks suffered the brunt of the nation's economic collapse. By 1932, black unemployment in many cities ran as high as 40 or 50 percent, sometimes more. Falling crop prices forced many rural blacks to the brink of starvation. And as whites also became economically more desperate, they lashed out at blacks, declaring, "No Jobs for Niggers Until Every White Man Has a Job!" These conditions led T. Arnold Hill of the Urban League to declare in 1931 that "[a]t no time in the history of the Negro since slavery has his economic and social outlook seemed so discouraging."[50]

As the 1932 election approached, blacks' political choices seemed almost as dismal as their economic condition. Hoover had proven a major disappointment on civil rights issues, and his inaction in the face of the depression compounded black disenchantment. The president's eleventh-hour attempts to regain black support with a few symbolic gestures during the campaign (he even allowed himself to be photographed with blacks for the first time in his presidency) did little to change this impression.[51]

Any thoughts of defecting to the Democrats, however, were tempered by that party's history of racism and the character of its nominee, New York governor Franklin Roosevelt. To be sure, the Democrats had some attractions. In those desperate days, the Dewey-style "new liberalism" that called for greater governmental efforts to relieve poverty began to be taken more seriously. This was especially so among leaders of the Democratic Party, who had, after all, long been losing national elections and needed a new theme. FDR would in fact prove to be the politician most responsible for making the term *liberalism* a staple of American political discourse, and for a generation, a popular one. In 1932, however, he still ran as a balanced budget fiscal conservative, with only a few contrary indications. Yet even if voters thus had some reason to think Roosevelt and other Democrats might embrace a new economic "liberalism" involving egalitarian governmental initiatives, there were still no signs of much racial liberalism. FDR had shown no sympathy toward blacks during his political career. As assistant secretary of the navy during the Wilson administration, he helped bring about segregation of toilets in the State, War, and Navy Department Building. Running as the Democratic candidate for vice president in 1920, Roosevelt labeled Republican efforts to court black voters as an appeal to racial hate and prejudice. In his campaign for the Democratic nomination in 1932, Roosevelt sought favor with southern Democrats by playing up his status as an adopted son of Georgia, where he had a second home in Warm Springs. Finally, his selection of House Speaker John Nance Garner of Texas for his running mate was anathema to most civil rights advocates.[52]

Despite his prior record, after his election Roosevelt did immediately turn to economic liberalism, and his "New Deal" provided blacks with desperately needed economic relief. The most important New Deal jobs program, the Works Progress Administration (WPA), gave work to over 1 million blacks by 1939. Assistance from the WPA and other New Deal measures often meant the difference between survival and starvation for many, particularly for blacks who had been most hard-hit by the Depression. For this help, blacks responded with gratitude. As one woman wrote, "Me and my people have been able to live through the depression with food shoes clothing and fuel all through the kindheartedness thoughtfulness and sane leadership of Roosevelt." More broadly, blacks reacted to the New Deal by shifting their allegiance from the party of Lincoln to the party of Roosevelt. In the presidential election of 1936, blacks gave a majority of their votes to the Democratic candidate for the first time ever. According to polls, Roosevelt won 76 percent of the northern black vote that year.[53]

Nonetheless, this overwhelming shift of black voters to the Democrats came about despite, not because of, the racial policies of the New Deal. Jim Crow was a prominent feature in many New Deal programs. Civilian Conservation Corps (CCC) camps and the planned communities established by the Tennessee Valley Authority (TVA) were strictly segregated. Other New Deal programs had non-discrimination guidelines, but state and local administrators often ignored them, particularly in the South. Blacks were often excluded from relief or jobs in favor of whites. When blacks did receive benefits, they were often at lower levels. In 1935, blacks on relief in Atlanta received an average of $19.29 a month versus $32.66 for whites.[54]

Some New Deal programs even added to the plight of blacks. In the Agricultural Adjustment Administration (AAA), federal officials turned a blind eye as white landlords kept for themselves crop support payments intended for black sharecroppers. In other cases, landlords simply evicted tenants from the land. The wage codes set up by the National Recovery Administration (NRA) entailed lower pay for most industries and jobs where blacks had traditionally been employed. When informed of this, President Roosevelt responded, "It is not the purpose of this Administration to impair Southern industry by refusing to recognize traditional differentials." When NRA codes did mandate equal pay for blacks and whites, employers often fired their black workers. Consequently, for many blacks, NRA stood for "Negro Run Around."[55]

Other New Deal programs, while providing some aid to blacks, were structured in such a way as to reflect the racial inequality in American society and, therefore, to reinforce it. The Wagner Act, for example, gave legal protection to labor unions and made possible their emergence as a powerful force in the American economy. But despite black protests, the act did nothing to end the tradition of racial discrimination in many unions, nor did it extend to agricultural or domestic employment, where most black workers were found. Hence it left blacks largely outside the most effective organizations for advancing the economic interests of working class Americans.

Federal housing programs also contributed to racial stratification since, according to historian Kenneth T. Jackson, they "embraced the discriminatory attitudes of the marketplace" and "exhorted segregation and enshrined it as public policy." Not only were local authorities allowed to segregate public housing projects built with federal money but, more importantly, federal aid to private homeowners actually assisted residential segregation. The Federal Housing Administration (FHA) refused to provide loans to blacks moving into predominately white areas. Appraisal maps developed by the Homeowners Loan Corporation (HOLC) classified black areas as high risk, thereby dissuading private mortgages and new developments in such areas. These policies further segregated America's cities and suburbs, concentrated public housing in predominantly black areas, kept blacks in the most crowded and run-down residential areas, and limited the ability of blacks to accumulate wealth through home ownership. Their impact is still being felt today.[56]

The Social Security Act of 1935 was also discriminatory, despite its race-neutral language. This legislation established the first national social welfare system through the creation of Old-Age Insur-

ance (OAI), Unemployment Insurance (UI), and Aid to Dependent
Children (ADC). Old-Age Insurance and Unemployment Insurance,
however, excluded agricultural and domestic workers. Other nations, to be sure, also made such exclusions in the early stages of
their social insurance programs. But in the United States, unlike in
other countries, the economic sectors excluded from these programs
were dominated by blacks and other racial minorities. Whether or
not these programs were designed to protect and deepen American
racial inequalities, in many ways they did so. And in the United
States, these exclusions formed part of a pattern in which many New
Deal programs were structured to placate southern congressmen,
some of whom explicitly raised concerns about disrupting existing
racial hierarchies. In the case of Social Security, the act's main social
insurance provisions covered only half of black workers but nearly
three-quarters of whites. As Charles H. Houston of the NAACP
pointed out to the Senate Finance Committee at the time, the program was "a sieve with the holes just big enough for the majority
of Negroes to fall through." Furthermore, since benefit levels in both
programs were tied to earnings, blacks, who suffered disproportionately from unemployment, underemployment, and low wages,
generally received lower benefit levels than whites even when they
qualified.[57]

While the ADC program did theoretically apply to blacks, southern members of Congress made sure that state and local governments would have responsibility for administering the program and
determining benefit levels. As a result, the program was often rife
with discrimination and the low benefit levels in the South ensured
that the program would not interfere with that region's supply of
cheap black labor. Finally, by distinguishing between "earned" programs like OAI, which primarily benefited whites, and "unearned"
programs like ADC, which had many more black recipients, the
Social Security Act helped to reinforce stereotypes of blacks as lazy
and indolent and to stigmatize welfare programs as "handouts" to
blacks.[58]

Thus, while the New Deal did provide much needed economic
assistance to blacks in the short run, it often did so in a discriminatory way. In the long run, the New Deal did little to help break
down economic inequality between blacks and whites and, in some
important ways, helped to sustain and advance it. One indicator of
the declining relative economic position of blacks during the depression is seen in the percentage of blacks employed in manufacturing.
From 1910 to 1930, this percentage grew from 6.2 to 7.3, but by 1940

it had fallen to just 5.1 percent. The only employment gains made by blacks were in domestic service. These and other developments led black political scientist Ralph Bunche to write in 1939, "The New Deal has done much to help, unquestionably, but it has fallen far short of meeting adequately the minimal needs of the Negro. It has gotten off on the wrong foot in some instance, gone up blind alleys in others, and has often run afoul of race prejudice."[59]

Whatever economic aid the New Deal provided for black Americans, little or nothing was done to help their political and social problems. The racial and ethnic violence sparked by World War I had made New Dealers wary of addressing civil rights issues directly, since doing so might only trigger a racist backlash.[60] As historian Peter Kellogg pointed out, "The most important social categories to [white liberals in the 1930s] were class divisions and the most important issues were conflicts of economic interests. From that perspective race was not so much a problem to be solved as a diversion to be avoided. When they noticed the plight of black people at all, they tended to picture them not as victims of the exclusions of caste but as the archetype of the dispossessed Southern poor. Attention to racial identity could in fact be dangerous for it provided conservatives with a weapon to divide the South's poor and frustrate the liberalization of that semi-feudal and exploited region."[61]

Fear of introducing racial issues into the New Deal haunted white liberals. Henry Wallace once asked one of his assistants, "Will, don't you think the New Deal is undertaking too much for the negroes?" A major reason for this attitude was the power of southern Democrats in Congress. When pressed to come out in support of anti-lynching legislation, President Roosevelt told Walter White of the NAACP, "I did not choose the tools with which I must work. Had I been permitted to choose them I would have selected quite different ones. But I've got to get legislation passed by Congress to save America. The Southerners by reason of the seniority rule in Congress are chairmen or occupy strategic places on most of the Senate and House committees. If I come out for that anti-lynching bill now, they will block every bill I ask Congress to pass to keep America from collapsing. I just can't take that risk."[62]

Even when New Dealers did pay attention to race, they did so only within carefully circumscribed limits. In general, white liberal comments were limited to particular racial "outrages," such as lynchings. Even then, liberals often cited the impact of these injustices on whites. Proponents of antilynching legislation saw it as a means to protect labor organizers in the South, while critics of the poll tax usually spoke of how it disfranchised poor whites to the benefit of Southern Bourbons and economic elites. In one of his few statements against the poll tax, President Roosevelt made it clear that its abolition was to be for whites only, since blacks "were a problem to be handled separately."[63]

Perhaps the most celebrated response of white liberals to a racial outrage came in 1939 after the Daughters of the American Revolution (DAR) barred Marian Anderson, the gifted African American contralto, from singing in Washington D.C.'s Constitution Hall. In reaction, Eleanor Roosevelt publicly resigned her membership in the DAR and the NAACP obtained approval from Interior Secretary Harold Ickes to have an outdoor concert at the Lincoln Memorial. The concert took place on Easter Sunday before a large crowd of blacks and whites, public officials and ordinary Americans. Thousands more listened at home through a nationwide radio broadcast. After Secretary Ickes introduced her, saying, "Genius, like justice, is blind. . . . Genius draws no color line," Anderson electrified the crowd by singing, "America."[64]

The concert was an emotionally moving event, but it also represents the New Deal's conservative approach to racial issues. As historian Nancy Weiss stated, the concert "was different from an issue such as antilynching legislation in that it in no way threatened the established system of race relations in the South; it involved no federal encroachment on state rights; and it entailed no congressional action, hence no need to risk votes that the administration needed for other measures."[65]

Although liberals responded to particularly egregious examples of segregation like that against Marian Anderson, even the most prominent racial liberals in the New Deal did not dare to criticize Jim Crow generally. As Harold Ickes confided in his diary, "As a matter of fact, I think it is up to the states to work out their social problems if possible, and while I have always been interested in seeing that the Negro has a square deal, I have never dissipated my strength against the particular stone wall of segregation. I believe that wall will crumble when the Negro has brought himself to a high educational and economic status. After all, we can't force people on each other who do not like each other, even when no question of color is involved. Moreover, while there are no segregation laws in the North, there is segregation in fact and we might as well recognize this."[66] Thus, while Ickes thought segregation inappropriate for a genius like Marian Anderson, it was perfectly acceptable for the vast majority of less gifted black Americans.

The most visible New Dealer on race issues was Eleanor Roosevelt. Throughout her husband's administration, she met frequently with black groups and served as their intermediary to the president. But even she was unwilling to speak out against Jim Crow. The most famous example of her reticence came at the first meeting of the Southern Conference on Human Welfare in Birmingham, Alabama in 1938. The First Lady arrived after the local police, headed by Public Safety Commissioner Eugene "Bull" Connor, informed the assembly that they would have to conform to the city's Jim Crow regulations and segregate black and white attendees. Contrary to most accounts, Mrs. Roosevelt did not defy the Jim Crow seating policy by placing her chair on the line between the white and black sections. In fact, she merely asked that her group's chairs be placed with the speakers, facing the entire gathering. As John Egerton pointed out, Mrs. Roosevelt "didn't seize upon the opportunity to make an issue of local laws and customs; in general, it was not her inclination to challenge segregation directly." In fact, when asked, "What do I think of the segregation of white and Negro here tonight?," she responded, "Well, I could no more tell people in another state what they should do than they can tell another country what to do. I think that one must follow the customs of the district. The answer to that question is not up to me but to the people of Alabama."[67]

Even the rather diluted racial liberalism of Ickes and Mrs. Roosevelt was a scarce commodity during the 1930s. Throughout the decade, civil rights advocates failed to achieve their most important substantive goals, from antilynching legislation to abolition of the poll tax to full inclusion of blacks in various New Deal programs. In fact, rather than abating during the decade, historian C. Vann Woodward suggests that Jim Crow became even more elaborate:

An Atlanta ordinance of June 1940 made the single exception of its park segregation "so much of Grant park as is occupied by the zoo." Only in the presence of the lower anthropoids could law-abiding Atlantans of different races consort together. The same city in 1932 prohibited amateur baseball clubs of different races from playing within two blocks of each other. In 1933 Texas prohibited "Caucasians" and "Africans" from boxing and wrestling together. . . . An Arkansas law of 1937 required segregation at all race tracks and gaming establishments "in seating, betting, and all other accommodations." In 1935 Oklahoma extended the white man's law to separate the races while fishing or boating. A Birmingham ordinance struck at another pestilent nest of racial intermingling in

1930 by making it "unlawful for a Negro and a white person to play together or in the company with each other" at dominoes or checkers.[68]

Despite the failure of the New Deal to address or ameliorate racial inequality, some historians still suggest that through symbolic victories like Marian Anderson's concert, the rise of the so-called Black Cabinet of federal advisors, or the growth of such interracial groups as the Southern Tenant Farmers Union (STFU) and the Southern Conference on Human Welfare (SCHW), the New Deal signaled a small but significant shift toward greater racial tolerance and inclusion.[69] Significance is to some degree in the eye of the beholder, but the shift was undeniably small. The problem of racial inequality was far down the national agenda and racially liberal individuals and organizations remained largely powerless. Furthermore, any upswing in racial liberalism in the latter part of the 1930s was counterbalanced by a growing conservative backlash during these years. These resentments were summed up in a popular ditty of the time in which the president tells Eleanor:

> *You kiss the niggers,*
> *I'll kiss the Jews*
> *And we'll stay in the White House*
> *As long as we choose!*

Some racial conservatives, like South Carolina senator "Cotton" Ed Smith, instantly denounced anything that violated the strictest norms of white supremacy and then boasted of their actions for later political advantage. As Smith often told white audiences, during the 1936 Democratic convention in Philadelphia he walked out during an invocation by a black minister, declaring as he bolted from the hall, "By God, he's as black as melted midnight! Get outa my way. This mongrel meeting ain't no place for a white man!"[70] Other racial conservatives like Virginia senator Carter Glass stressed that the New Deal's centralizing tendencies threatened "states' rights" racial prerogatives. But whatever their rhetoric, during the latter half of the 1930s, racial conservatives began organizing to protect the status quo.

The first effort came in January 1936. Georgia governor Eugene Talmadge allied himself with the Reverend Gerald L. K. Smith, a protégé of and self-appointed race-baiting successor to the late demagogical leader of Louisiana, Huey Long, and novelist Thomas Dixon, who now saw Communists, New Dealers, and blacks all working hand in hand to destroy the country. The trio organized a "Grass

Roots" convention of New Deal opponents in Macon, Georgia. Although the convention was bankrolled by industrialists like John J. Raskob and Pierre S. du Pont, who opposed the New Deal chiefly on economic grounds, the Talmadge movement was "united to oppose Negroes, the New Deal and . . . Karl Marx." Its leaders set out to "Stop—and stop quickly—THE EFFORTS OF THE DEMOCRATIC PARTY TO FOIST THE NEGRO AND SOCIAL EQUALITY UPON THE WHITE PEOPLE OF THE SOUTH."[71]

Although Talmadge could not slow the Roosevelt steamroller in 1936, the conservative backlash gained momentum the following year after the president put forward his plan to "pack" the Supreme Court. Southern Democrats like Carter Glass declared that the plan foreshadowed "another tragic era of reconstruction for the South." The more liberal Court Roosevelt sought to create would reverse the anti-Reconstruction rulings "that saved the civilization of the South." After the opponents of the Court plan prevailed, southern leaders made further efforts to forge a "Conservative Coalition" of Republicans and southern Democrats with a "Conservative Manifesto" that stressed opposition to the New Deal and support for "states' rights." Although the effort failed, it laid the foundations on which others would build in later years as the popularity of New Deal liberalism waned.[72]

In 1938, the split between southern conservatives and the New Deal widened. That year, southern Democrats in the Senate filibustered an antilynching bill to death. South Carolina's James Byrnes claimed that the bill was but a first step, and asked whether next would come "legislation to punish officials of a State who fail to protect Negroes in the right to stop at hotels where white persons are entertained . . . ?" Theodore "The Man" Bilbo of Mississippi spewed forth an example of the oratory that earned him the label the "Bilbonic plague." According to him, the bill would "open the floodgates of hell in the South." To those supporting the legislation, he warned that "upon your garments . . . will be the blood of the raped and outraged daughters of Dixie, as well as the blood of the perpetrators of these crimes that the red-blooded Anglo-Saxon white southern men will not tolerate." He taunted that since white liberals believed in equal rights, they should not "object if one of the nice daughters from one of the aristocratic homes marries some 'buck nigger' from Kalamazoo." Bilbo went on to propose sending all blacks to Africa, dead ones excepted, since "their days of amalgamation are over."[73]

Although most northern Democratic senators supported the bill, they were unwilling to sacrifice party unity for it and made only half-hearted attempts to break the filibuster. A vote to invoke cloture and cut off debate failed by a vote of 46 to 42. Even more importantly, GOP senators gave notice that their old commitment to black rights was now expendable in their desire to unite with the South against the New Deal—no Republicans signed the cloture petition and only two of twelve Republicans voted for it on the floor.[74]

Meanwhile, in the House, Texas representative Martin Dies used his position as chair of the newly created House Committee on Un-American Activities to investigate subversion of all sorts, including attempts to upset the racial status quo. According to Dies, Communist influence was the source of any complaints blacks might have with America. Communist agents sought to give blacks "a taste of 'social equality' " by sponsoring interracial dances. In fact, Dies warned, "communist girls have been sent among Negroes to practice 'social equality.' "[75]

The growing animosity between southern conservatives and the New Deal culminated in President Roosevelt's attempt to purge the former from the Democratic party during the 1938 primary season. The president carefully avoided racial issues and stressed economics, but the targets of his purge, South Carolina's "Cotton" Ed Smith and Georgia senator Walter George, were quick to play the race card in response. George termed Roosevelt's opposition to him a "second march through Georgia" while Smith made sure to regale primary voters with tales of his walkout in "Philly-delphy." At one campaign stop, Smith said that as he walked out of the convention "it seemed to me that old John Calhoun leaned down from his mansion in the sky and whispered in my ear, 'You did right, Ed.'" He then closed by saying, "Outside forces are seeking to defeat me because of my stand for White Supremacy." Conservatives like Smith and George weren't the only ones to denounce the purge. The relatively liberal *Atlanta Constitution* editorialized that the purge was part of Roosevelt's effort to pass "the vicious, dangerous and cruel anti-lynching bill. A bill that would forever make the sovereign states but chattels of the central government."[76]

Both George and Smith won their primaries easily; and that fall, Roosevelt and the New Deal suffered an even greater blow. Republicans gained six seats in the Senate and eighty in the House. From now on, a conservative coalition of southern Democrats and Republicans could control the nation's domestic agenda. Not only was the New Deal dead, but so was whatever hope had existed for legislation to help the plight of black Americans. After six years of New Deal reform, Gunnar Myrdal later wrote, "Negroes had relief, but no jobs; and there was no significant improvement in their position on any other front."[77]

As the New Deal drew to a close, the color line that had been drawn between black and white America over three decades earlier remained intact. Although some elements of the New Deal had alleviated the crushing poverty in which the vast majority of blacks lived, few had been enabled to escape that poverty. The structures of economic inequality that kept them down remained largely in place, in some ways even embellished. Jim Crow still ruled the South, having successfully fought off the rather weak challenges presented to it by the New Deal, while de facto segregation increasingly isolated northern blacks. Black political power was nonexistent in the South and largely ineffectual in the North. Yet, just as matters seemed their worst, the growing challenge of fascism and the rise of black militance would put new and increasing pressure on America's racial hierarchies.

FIVE

"Deutschland and Dixieland"

Antifascism and the Emergence of Civil Rights, 1938–1941

In June 1936, America's most promising heavyweight contender, a quiet young fighter out of Detroit with thunderous fists and the heart of a lion, suffered his first professional defeat. It came at the hands of German boxer Max Schmeling. Strikingly, many otherwise patriotic Americans jubilantly celebrated Schmeling's victory. The opponent Schmeling defeated, Joe Louis, was a black man threatening to win the most prestigious title in sports, the world heavyweight boxing championship. Many whites therefore acclaimed Schmeling as the new "Great White Hope." Hundreds of them even sent him congratulatory telegrams. One sports reporter wrote that the black "reign of terror in heavyweight boxing was ended by Schmeling. The big bad wolf had been chased from the door. It took the black Uhlan [Schmeling] to prove that the black terror is just another fragile human being." Perhaps most telling was a wire service report that "[c]heers for Max Schmeling's startling knockout of Joe Louis stopped transaction of important business in the Senate." The report identified southern senators as those doing the cheering.[1]

But like so many great champions of all backgrounds, and like so many ordinary African Americans throughout U.S. history, Louis did not succumb to defeat. He came back from his loss to Schmeling and in 1937 he won the world heavyweight championship from James J. Braddock. His greatest test then came in 1938, when Louis and Schmeling met for a rematch in New York City. But something had changed; as this fight began, most of the huge throng in attendance and the millions more Americans listening on radio now fervently cheered on their "Brown Bomber." The reasons for this extraordinary turn of events tell much about the most powerful forces working for racial change in U.S. history. For in 1938, the specter of war with Germany loomed larger than the shadow of Jim Crow. Hence Max Schmeling was no longer first and foremost a white man fighting a black man. Schmeling was the symbolic representative of Nazism, and soft-spoken Joe Louis had become the standard bearer for the whole United States of America, and for the grand cause of democracy itself.

Given that the New Deal was largely ineffective in forcing the nation to confront Jim Crow, it is hard to escape the conclusion that it was instead the emergence of fascism and Nazism in the 1930s that most set the stage for real transformations. The Nazi menace forced at least some white Americans to begin to reexamine the racial inequalities in their midst. As historian John Higham wrote, notions of white supremacy began to wane in intellectual circles as "Hitler's demonstration of the fruits of racism inflicted a moral shock on every sensitive mind."[2]

That shock led to an intellectual battle in 1938 that was less publicized but in some respects as significant as Joe Louis's second clash with Schmeling. That year the American Anthropological Association, the leading organization in a profession that had done so much to legitimate notions of natural racial hierarchies in the late nineteenth century, considered a resolution denouncing racism. Anthropologists and scholars in the related disciplines of psychology and sociology had been debating race differences intensely through the 1920s and 1930s, but by the late thirties the conflict was one-sided. The resolution passed unanimously. It was a resounding triumph for the longstanding campaign of anthropologist Franz Boas, his student Ruth Benedict, his admirer psychologist Otto Kleinberg, and others to establish that apparent racial differences were fundamentally matters of environmental influences, not biology.

Despite tireless efforts by egalitarian-minded social scientists in the journal wars of the 1920s and 1930s, sadly that triumph cannot be traced to the discovery of decisive scientific evidence sustaining Boas's view. Instead, as the resolution indicated, the results of volumes of research were inconclusive: significant differences between the races "have not been ascertained by science," but neither had they been disproved. Instead, more and more social scientists had simply decided in the face of continued uncertainty to presume that the races, if they existed at all as biological categories, were essentially equal in genetic endowments rather than hierarchically arranged. Social scientists had done so in part because the notion that differences among the races were environmental suggested that social scientists might play a vital role in redesigning environmental conditions to promote human flourishing. They did so, also, because many more were now themselves of immigrant origins and inclined to oppose racially and ethnically based immigration restrictions. Some were impressed by the cultural accomplishments of blacks during the Harlem Renaissance. Some were moved by black suffering in America.

But American scholars adopted premises of racial equality most of all, the historian Carl Degler has concluded, as a result of "the impact Nazi practices had on American scholarly thinking about race and biology in human affairs." Even a formerly ardent eugenicist and defender of Nazi science, Paul Popenoe, later said "the major factor" in the declining popularity of his views "was undoubtedly Hitlerism." Degler contends this "impact can hardly be overestimated in explaining why during the 1930s and 1940s concepts and terms like 'heredity,' 'biological differences,' and 'instinct' dropped below the horizon in social science."[3]

The impact was, moreover, increasingly not confined to academic discussions of race. "The terrifying popularity of Nazi racist doctrines," wrote Gary Gerstle, "forced American liberals to reconsider their 'hands-off' approach to problems of . . . racial hatred. . . . Racism and prejudice had to be subjects of political commentary and targets of social action." As many white Americans gradually awakened to the ideological and military threats posed by Hitler, they realized that meeting these threats was especially difficult when America tolerated similar racist and undemocratic practices at home. As early as 1933, socialist leader Norman Thomas asked, "How can we either protest Hitlerism with good grace or hope to escape similar ills in America when we chronically carry out a more thoroughgoing discrimination against our colored fellow citizens than he has yet imposed upon the Jews?" Later, *Atlanta Constitution* editor Ralph McGill pointed out, "We can't do much pointing of the accusing finger at Adolph Hitler or ell Doochey for trying to give their people an exaggerated idea of the supremacy of their blood. We have the Klan."[4]

As the need to confront fascism abroad meant facing up to Jim Crow at home, liberals increasingly made the connection between "Deutschland and Dixieland." In 1935, Senator Edward P. Costigan of Colorado, cosponser of an antilynching bill, told his colleagues that the legislation presented America with a "choice between Hitler and Mussolini on the one side, and Washington, Jefferson, Lincoln, Henry Grady, Woodrow Wilson, and Franklin Delano Roosevelt on the other." In order to drum up support for their efforts to organize black and white sharecroppers, the Southern Tenant Farmers Union proclaimed, "Hitler stalks the cotton fields of the South," and "Hitler over the plantations." Liberal journalists dubbed Theodore Bilbo the "Mussolini of Mississippi," and Eugene Talmadge the "Fuehrer of Sugar Creek." Bilbo merited the label. In 1938, he offered an amendment that would deport all black Americans to Liberia, telling the Senate, "Race consciousness is developing in all parts of the world. Consider Italy, consider Germany. It is beginning to be recognized by the thoughtful minds of our age that the conservation of racial values is the only hope for the future of civilization. . . . The Germans appreciate the importance of racial values." Eventually, the association between Jim Crow and fascism was so strong that one southern conservative complained, "Is there any sanity in the view now often stated that no one but a Fascist or a Nazi can believe one people or race superior to another?"[5]

Next to political and academic debates, the comparatively genteel world of sport best dramatizes how the developing struggle against fascism had implications for American race relations in the 1930s. After the Civil War, blacks had participated in organized athletics, but as the rest of American society became increasingly segregated after the 1880s, so did sports. In 1887, Cap Anson refused to allow his famed Chicago White Stockings to play against teams with black players. Many agreed with Anson and soon all of professional baseball was limited to whites. By the 1930s, nearly every professional sport, from horse racing to football, was closed to blacks. America's sports heroes—from Babe Ruth to Red Grange to Jack Dempsey—were all white men. But during the middle 1930s, this pattern began to change. A few black athletes gained broad acceptance by defeating the nation's ideological foes in what George Orwell termed "war without the shooting"—sports.[6]

One example was Jesse Owens, the first black sportsman to gain widespread fame among white Americans. In 1932, another black man, Eddie Tolan, had won gold medals in the 100- and 200-meter dashes at the Los Angeles Olympics, but he was ignored by the white public. Owens, however, competed at the Berlin Olympics of 1936, which were elaborately staged by Hitler to show the purported success of his regime and the athletic superiority of the Aryan race. Owens destroyed this symbolic challenge to the democratic and egalitarian strains in American ideals by winning gold medals in the 100 meters, 200 meters (in Olympic record time), the 100-meter relay (in world record time along with Ralph Metcalfe, another black

American), and the long jump (where he set yet another Olympic record and triumphed over Germany's blond and blue-eyed Luz Long). The American press exulted over Owens's victories, declaring that they showed the triumph of America over Germany and the fallacy of Hitler's racial theories. When Owens returned from Berlin, he was greeted with ticker-tape parades in New York and his home-town of Cleveland—a reception heretofore unheard of for a black athlete. Even the southern press celebrated Owens's triumph as a vindication of American democracy over German fascism.[7]

It was, however, stoic Joe Louis who most came to embody the significance of the struggle against fascism for the racial attitudes of white Americans. Louis was the most prominent black boxer since Jack Johnson, who two decades earlier had been the first black heavy-weight champion. Johnson had been hated by most whites. Not only was he black, but he gloated over his defeated white opponents. Flamboyant and arrogant, Johnson openly flouted racial conven-tions, marrying two white women in succession and publicly con-sorting with others at a time when blacks were frequently lynched just for the suspicion of touching a white woman. When Johnson successfully defended his title in 1910 against former champion Jim Jeffries, angry whites in several cities lashed out at blacks in violent attacks. White anger against Johnson was so great that Congress passed a law banning fight films from interstate commerce to pre-vent people (especially blacks) from seeing his victories. Federal au-thorities also tried to jail the boxer on trumped up charges of vio-lating the Mann Act, which forbad the transportation of women across state lines for "illicit purposes," by traveling with his white female companions. He was convicted but fled the country. The uproar over Johnson contributed to the flurry of proposals for state and federal antimiscegenation laws in 1912–1913.[8] White boxing fans exulted in 1915 after Jess Willard, the "Great White Hope," finally defeated Johnson. Over the next two decades, the boxing world kept the heavyweight ring segregated by refusing to give black contenders title shots and because several states barred interracial matches.[9]

In contrast to Johnson, Joe Louis's managers did everything they could to make him acceptable to whites. They instructed him to be quiet, clean-cut, modest, and "for God's sake, after you beat a white opponent, don't *smile!*" These measures worked well enough for Louis to be considered "a credit to his race" or "a good nigger" by many whites and allowed to become a title contender. Even so, Louis was unable to escape racial stereotypes. Most press accounts made reference to his color, usually in alliterative terms. Louis was always the "Brown Bomber," the "Dusky Destroyer," or the "Sepia Slugger." Even less flattering, many stories described Louis as a savage "jungle killer" in the ring, but a typical "lazy negro" who loved to sleep and eat fried chicken out of the ring.[10]

As these descriptions suggest, racism was rife in American sporting life. Even as his fame grew, many white fans still considered Louis a black interloper and a threat to white supremacy. That is why so many rooted for Schmeling in 1936. But in the fight's aftermath, the play German propagandists gave Louis's defeat, combined with mounting fears about the German government in other regards, changed many American minds. Before the first Louis-Schmeling bout, the Nazi leadership had been cool to Schmeling, who already had been knocked out by a Jew (Max Baer). Many feared he might further embarrass Germany by losing to another member of an "inferior" race. After his victory, however, the Nazi leadership quickly embraced Schmeling, declaring that he had won a "great Aryan victory." Hitler wired congratulations after the fight. Propaganda Minister Joseph Goebbels told the fighter that he had "saved the prestige of the white race" and "I know you have fought for Germany. Your victory is a German victory. We are proud of you." Geobbels's minions then turned a film of the fight into a full-length motion picture, entitled *Max Schmeling's Victory, A German Victory,* which played to packed theaters throughout Germany. The highlight of the film was a closeup of Schmeling's gloved white fist smashing into Louis's black jaw.[11]

Even more importantly, between the first fight in 1936 and the rematch in 1938, the threat posed by Nazi Germany became far more apparent. In 1936, Hitler abrogated the Treaty of Versailles, rearmed the Rhineland, and began openly building up his war machine. That same year, Germany and Italy, now allied in the "Pact of Steel," intervened on the side of rebel leader General Francisco Franco in the Spanish Civil War. German "volunteers" flying for Franco's forces outraged the world the following year when they destroyed the village of Guernica by aerial bombing. Germany then swallowed up Austria in the Anschluss of March 1938. In May, one month before the second Louis-Schmeling bout, Hitler began making threats against Czechoslovakia, thereby setting in motion the chain of events that would lead to the Munich Crisis of October. Just two weeks before the fight, the U.S. government announced indictments of eighteen people charged with spying for Nazi Germany. As Louis's biographer wrote, "America joined the general alarm about Hitler's ambitions. In addition, Americans were repelled by news of increased persecution of Jews and suppression of civil liberties in Germany. World events made it increasingly difficult for Americans to disassociate Max Schmeling from his Nazi homeland."[12]

In the weeks leading up to the fight, the symbolism of the match intensified. Nazi publicists put words in Schmeling's mouth, claiming he said, "I would not take this fight if I did not believe that I, a white man, can beat a Negro." And, "The Negro . . . the black amateur . . . the dumb animal . . . will always be afraid of me." American reporters also hyped the political aspects of the fight, falsely claiming that Schmeling was "a Nazi commodity" and a "close friend" of Hitler. A newspaper cartoon showed Louis and Schmeling in a boxing ring illuminated by a searchlight labeled "politics." Above Schmeling was a menacing figure holding a scroll with "Nordic Supremacy" written on it. Above Louis was Abraham Lincoln and scroll reading, "That All Men Are Created Equal." President Roosevelt even got into the act by inviting Louis to the White House. There FDR told him, "Joe, we need muscles like yours to beat Germany." The press, however, reported that Roosevelt had said, "Joe, beat Schmeling to prove we can beat the Germans." In a syndicated newspaper article that had been ghostwritten for him, Louis declared, "Tonight I not only fight the battle of my life to revenge the lone blot on my record, but I fight for America against the challenge of a foreign invader, Max Schmeling. This isn't just one man against another or Joe Louis boxing Max Schmeling; it is the good old U.S.A. versus Germany." One commentator wrote later, "Louis-Schmeling II was no longer just a championship boxing match. It was a prelude to World War II."[13]

With such a buildup, excitement over the fight was intense. That night, the capacity crowd of 70,000 at Yankee Stadium included six mayors, several governors, and assorted celebrities. The bout was also broadcast throughout America and around the world. Nationwide, 64 percent of radio owners listened to the fight, a figure topped that year only by two presidential speeches. In New York City, 97 percent of the radios were tuned in to it.[14]

Virtually as one-sided as the contest over the American Anthropological Association's antiracism resolution, the much-ballyhooed second Louis-Schmeling fight was over almost as soon as it began. Less that a minute after the opening bell, Louis delivered a series of punches that put Schmeling on the ropes. Another hit to the back of the ribs fractured one of Schmeling's vertebrae and drove it against his kidney, causing him to scream in pain. The referee waived Louis off and Schmeling staggered back to center ring. Louis met him with more blows, one of which dropped Schmeling to the canvas. He got

up, but Louis quickly knocked him down again. Schmeling rose to
his feet once more, but Louis then landed two punches that flattened
him for good. The referee called the fight after only two minutes
and four seconds.[15]

Louis's victory set off wild celebrations, particularly among blacks.
But unlike the first match with Schmeling in 1936, most whites were
also full of praise for Louis, a rare thing indeed for a black man in
1938. The *Chicago Daily News* ran a cartoon of a plane labeled the
"Brown Bomber" dropping its payload of explosives on a discouraged
caricature of Hitler. One columnist wrote that "the Brown Bomber
may have done something which the world's diplomats have been
unable to accomplish: bring Herr Goebbels, Nazi Minister of Propaganda, to his senses." Elation over Louis's triumph was even evident
among ordinary whites in unlikely places. One woman who listened
to the fight in a hotel lobby in Vicksburg, Mississippi recounted that
when Louis won, "white patrons and colored bellhops hugged each
other in joy."[16]

Appreciation for what Louis had done led many in the press to
see past his color, shed their racist descriptions of him, and focus
on his stunning achievement. A reporter for the *New York Daily Mirror*
wrote, "Louis has finally come into his full estate as a great world's
champion. If any one doubts his greatness after his masterful job
last night, he's plain plumb prejudiced." According to Louis's son,
"What my father did was enable white America to think of him as
an American, not as a black. . . . By winning he became white America's first black hero."[17]

Not only did Louis's victory allow him to gain acceptance among
whites, he also helped to spur at least some whites to question the
inequality facing the rest of black America. Hugh S. Johnson, former
head of the New Deal's National Recovery Administration (NRA),
wrote in his syndicated column that Schmeling's defeat was "nothing for us to weep about and seek white hopes. These black boys
are Americans. . . . There should be just as much pride in their
progress and prowess under our system as in the triumph of any
other American. For all their misfortunes and shortcomings they
are our people—Negroes, yes, but our Negroes." Less condescend-
ingly, the *Boston Globe* editorialized that "brown Joe was accepted by
multitudes as the representative of world democracy . . . [which]
is strange when the undemocratic treatment of Negroes by many
who boast of their own attitude toward freedom and equality is recalled."[18]

Joe Louis was not the only black American fighting against racism, symbolically or otherwise. The highly charged political atmosphere of the late 1930s saw a tremendous increase in political awareness and activism among African Americans. One indicator in this regard was the growth of black newspapers. Between 1933 and 1940, the average weekly circulation of black newspapers doubled, from approximately 600,000 to 1,276,000.[19] Blacks also became more politically active during these years, as seen by the increased membership in the National Association for the Advancement of Colored People (NAACP), which went from 21,000 in 1929 to 54,000 in 1939.[20]

Perhaps even more important than the rise in black political activism in the 1930s was the militant turn that activism took. Decades of political abandoment or outright hostility by the major parties; the failure of accomodationist, self-help efforts like those espoused by Booker T. Washington; the impracticability of Garvey's black nationalism; the inability of interest groups like the NAACP to achieve any truly transformative victories against Jim Crow; years of economic destitution—these factors led many blacks to seek more radical means to alleviate their dire conditions. In the words of Mary McLeod Bethune: "The spirit of democracy is being galvanized into realistic action."[21]

Undergirding this new militance was a belief that although white liberals could be crucial allies, the success of the civil rights struggle depended upon the actions of blacks themselves. In the words of A. Philip Randolph, the head of the Brotherhood of Sleeping Car Porters: "[I]t is more and more becoming correctly understood that the task of realizing full citizenship for the Negro people is largely in the hands of the Negro people themselves. . . . Freedom is never given; it is won. And the Negro people must win their freedom. They must achieve justice. This involves struggle, continuous struggle." Moreover, Randolph added, this new effort must be mass based and representative of all sectors of black life. "True liberation can be acquired and maintained only when the Negro people possess power; and power is the product and flower of organization—organization of the masses, the masses in the mills and the mines, on the farms, in the factories, in the churches, in the fraternal organizations, in homes, colleges, women's clubs, student groups, trade unions, tenants' leagues, in cooperative guilds, political organizations and civil rights associations."[22]

The new militance and organization Randolph spoke of was evident in a variety of areas. Throughout the Great Depression, blacks in many northern cities organized "Don't Buy Where You Can't Work" campaigns to force white-owned stores and business to integrate their work forces. Groups like the National Negro Congress (NNC) organized blacks at the national and local levels to fight back against discrimination and economic injustice. The NNC and other radical groups also aligned with Communist-affiliated organizations and left-led unions of the newly established Congress of Industrial Organizations (CIO) to achieve common goals.[23]

What made this activism unique was its reliance on more militant direct action tactics such as protests, pickets, and boycotts. As historians August Meier and Elliot Rudwick observed, "[D]irect action during the Depression contrasted sharply both quantitatively and qualitatively with the history of such tactics during the entire preceding century." This change in tactics stood out at the time. In 1939, black political scientist Ralph Bunche declared, "Never before have Negroes had so much experience with picket lines, and it may be a lesson that will sink in."[24]

Black militance also took more aggressive forms than picket lines. Despite some successes from a local "Don't Buy Where You Can't Work" campaign, Harlem blacks still seethed from persistent discrimination and poverty. These complaints finally boiled over on March 19, 1935. That afternoon a fight broke out between Lino Rivera, a sixteen-year-old Puerto Rican black, and white employees of a Harlem five-and-dime store who claimed he had tried to steal a ten-cent penknife. Although Rivera was unhurt and released after the police arrived, rumors that he had been beaten and killed spread quickly throughout the neighborhood. Members of local Communist and radical black organizations spread leaflets denouncing the alleged beating. Soon, a crowd of thousands had gathered and began breaking windows and looting white-owned stores. When the violence ended the next day, three blacks had been killed, and fifty-seven civilians and seven policemen had been injured. In addition, rioters broke more than six hundred windows and did over $2 million in damage.[25]

The Harlem riot was a watershed. Unlike previous race riots, which usually consisted of whites attacking blacks, for the first time blacks were the instigators and their targets were the symbols of white racism. After the riot, Mayor Fiorello La Guardia appointed a commission to look into the cause of the disorder. Led by E. Franklin Frazier, the eminent black sociologist, the commission declared that the riot arose from "resentments against racial discrimination and poverty in the midst of plenty." It had, moreover, demonstrated to blacks "the power of their organized number . . . strengthening the belief that the solution to their problems lies in organized action."

In fact, the riot was very effective in forcing New York's white power structure to recognize and accommodate black demands. As historian Cheryl Greenberg pointed out, "[T]he potential for future radical action suggested by the riot helped convince La Guardia that he must act forcefully to address the issues raised by the riot." La Guardia appointed an Advisory Council on Negro Problems to the city relief commission and had the commission hire more black supervisors. The city also began to direct more funds and public works projects into Harlem, including new health facilities, several new schools, and a public housing project. White store owners, "undoubtedly with the memory of the riot in mind," also agreed to hire more blacks.[26]

Rising black militance was also evident in the arts. Although not without social criticism, the dominant theme of the Harlem Renaissance of the 1920s was the development of authentic black cultural voices. In the latter part of the 1930s, however, the work of black artists, particularly writers, became increasingly politicized and militant. "The interests of the writers of the Harlem Renaissance stood in sharp contrast to the social realism of the thirties," wrote historian Harvard Sitkoff. "Strike meetings replaced sultry jungle nights for background and atmosphere; the leading characters became embattled croppers and proletarian workers rather than quaint and religious black folk peasants; the problems of economic necessity and survival in a racist culture took precedence over those of 'passing' and black identity. All separatist themes were subordinated to those of interracial unity and the struggle for civil rights." The work of writer Langston Hughes reflected this shift. During the 1920s, he had been a proponent of black nationalism, but by the mid-1930s he was calling on black writers to quit writing about the "soul world" and instead offer writings that would "explain and illuminate the Negro condition in America."[27]

Hughes's own worked reflected this new militance, such as in the poem "Tired" (1931):

> *I am so tired of waiting,*
> *Aren't you,*
> *For the world to become good*
> *And beautiful and kind?*
> *Let us take a knife*
> *And cut the world in two—*
> *And see what worms are eating*
> *At the rind.*[28]

The new emphasis among black authors on protest and social realism was perhaps expressed most powerfully in Richard Wright's classic novel *Native Son* (1940). There Wright offered readers a bleak and graphic depiction of the alienation and oppression of black Americans by white society. His portrayal of the novel's protagonist, Bigger Thomas, showed that black silence did not mean consent.

Singer and actor Paul Robeson was another who fused his art with politics. During the late 1930s, Robeson claimed that his songs were for civil rights in America and for "those seeking freedom from the dungeons of fascism in Europe today." Robeson's most popular song in the late 1930s was "Ballad for Americans." It extolled an inclusive American identity and claimed that "Man in white skin can never be free/while his black brother is in slavery."[29]

The rising currents of antifascism and black activism gained new strength in the fall of 1939. On September 1, German armies rolled into Poland and commenced World War II. Poland fell in a matter of weeks. Within a year, Hitler's blitzkrieg also overran Denmark, Norway, Luxembourg, the Netherlands, Belgium, and France. By the summer of 1940, only Great Britain still held out against the Nazi onslaught, but, battered by German bombers and increasingly isolated by U-boats, its eventual collapse seemed inevitable. Across the Pacific, Germany's ally, Japan, continued its conquest of China and began to threaten southeast Asia.

Although the United States remained officially neutral, President Roosevelt expressed the feelings of most of the nation when he said, "I cannot ask that every American remain neutral in thought as well. Even a neutral has a right to take account of facts. Even a neutral cannot be asked to close his mind or his conscience."[30] Indeed, few Americans were neutral in thought, with over 80 percent hoping for Germany's defeat.[31] Furthermore, Germany's staggering victories and Japanese expansionism made Americans increasingly aware of the military threat confronting them. With the rise of air power, America itself seemed vulnerable to foreign attack for the first time since the War of 1812. Consequently, as historian Robert Divine pointed out, "By the end of the first year of the war, American foreign policy had undergone a startling transformation. The nation that had attempted to insulate itself from war was now committed to all possible aid to England and to economic pressure to restrain Japanese aggression in the Far East." To further these policies, America began to rearm and transform itself into the "arsenal of democracy." In 1939, the federal government spent only $1.1 billion on national defense, but by 1941 that figure had increased to over $6 billion. In 1940, the country also instituted the first peacetime military draft in its history.[32]

The coming of war also led Americans to an ideological rearmament. As President Roosevelt told the nation as the German panzers rolled through France, "While our navy and our airplanes and our guns may be our first line of defense, it is still clear that way down at the bottom, underlying them all, giving them their strength, sustenance and power, are the spirit and morale of a free people."[33] Accounts of Hitler's Nazi ideology, his brutal treatment of occupied Europe, and of Japanese atrocities in China caused Americans to increasingly contrast their values of democracy and equality with those of fascism and militarism. The war, President Roosevelt proclaimed, was intended to establish "Four Freedoms": freedom of speech, freedom of religion, freedom from want, and freedom from fear. He went on to insist, against the realities of history but in line with the war's ideological imperatives, that unlike the Nazis' racist nationalism, Americanism was a "matter of mind and heart." It "is not and never was, a matter of race and ancestry."[34] According to black philosopher Alain Locke, "Democracy has encountered a fighting antithesis, and has awakened from considerable lethargy and decadence to a sharpened realization of its own basic values." A newly organized Council for Democracy sought to "crystallize and instill in the minds of Americans the meaning, value, and workability of democracy as a dynamic, vital creed."[35]

Paeans to America's democratic virtues, however, still rang hollow for many black Americans. Rather than the Four Freedoms, black sociologist Ira Reid claimed that blacks had four fears: "fear of physical violence (lynchings and race riots), fear of further discrimination, fear of appeasement (the granting of minor racial concessions to forestall major adjustments), and fear of revolution from the right that would destroy democratic rights now held."[36] The NAACP's *Crisis* editorialized that it was "sorry for brutality, blood, and death among the peoples of Europe, just as we were sorry for China and Ethiopia. But the hysterical cries of the preachers of democracy for Europe leave us cold. We want democracy in Alabama, Arkansas, in Mississippi and Michigan, in the District of Columbia—in the *Senate of the United States*."[37] The *Pittsburgh Courier*'s George Schuyler wrote, "Our war is not against Hitler in Europe, but against Hitler in America. Our war is not to defend democracy, but to get a democracy we never had."[38]

In fact, the defense buildup further highlighted the second-class nature of black citizenship. In the U.S. military, attitudes toward blacks often seemed more in keeping with Hitler's Wehrmacht. According to an Army War College report, "In the process of evolution, the American negro has not progressed as far as other sub species of the human family. . . . The cranial cavity of the negro is smaller than whites. . . . The psychology of the negro, based on heredity derived from mediocre African ancestors, cultivated by generations of slavery, is one from which we cannot expect to draw leadership material. . . . In physical courage [he] falls well back of whites. . . . He cannot control himself in fear of danger. . . . He is a rank coward in the dark."[39]

Shocking as that description may now seem, the War College report merely expressed what was still the conventional wisdom of the times. Its language closely resembled the advice offered to America's children in 1939 in a Quaker Oats advertising pamphlet, "Dick Tracy's Secret Detective Methods and Magic Tricks." There, young would-be crimefighters, like would-be soldiers, learned that "ethnology," the "study of races," had found that "negroes are a simple, happy folk." The criminals among them "commit crimes in blundering fashion" using "brute force. . . . When cornered, they generally give up."[40]

Amid such judgments, Jim Crow ruled within the ranks. Of the nearly five hundred thousand men in the army in 1940, only forty-seven hundred were black, all of whom served in segregated units. Black army officers could be counted on one hand—three chaplains, a colonel, and a captain. Even worse racism prevailed in the other branches. The navy allowed blacks to enlist only as messmen. The marines and the air corps excluded blacks completely.[41] Segregation in the military extended even to the blood stored for wounded soldiers. The surgeon general of the army explained, "For reasons not biologically convincing but which are commonly recognized as psychologically important in America, it is not deemed advisable to collect and mix caucasian and negro blood."[42]

Racism also pervaded the defense industry. Such discrimination was evident in all sectors of the country. A federal government survey of employers found that of 17,435 defense jobs in Texas, only 9,117 (52 percent) were closed to blacks; but in Michigan, 22,042 of 26,904 (82 percent) were reserved for whites.[43]

Black job seekers faced the most resistance in the rapidly growing aircraft industries where much of the work was relatively clean, light, and classified as skilled or semi-skilled—traditionally the province of whites only. One aircraft industry executive responded to a civil rights group's survey on black employment by saying, "I regret

. . . that it is not the policy of this company to employ people other than of the Caucasian race, consequently, we are not in a position to offer your people employment at this time." Attitudes like this explain why in 1940 only 240 blacks (0.1 percent of all aircraft workers) were employed in the entire aviation industry.[44]

Although increased military spending finally began lifting the country from the depression by 1940, discrimination by the defense industry kept blacks from enjoying the economic benefits. Between April and October 1940, white unemployment fell from 17.7 to 13 percent, but black unemployment remained at 22 percent. Moreover, now that most whites were returning to work, Congress began slashing funding for New Deal job and relief programs even though many blacks still relied on them for support.[45]

The government did take some steps to prevent such discrimination. In June 1940, the National Defense Advisory Commission, the first government agency charged with coordinating the nation's military buildup, appointed black economist Robert C. Weaver to its Labor Division to help ensure more participation by blacks in the defense industry. In August, the commission directed defense contractors that "workers should not be discriminated against because of age, sex, race, or color."[46] In October, Congress passed a defense training appropriation that included a nondiscrimination clause.[47] Nonetheless, as with other government efforts at stamping out discrimination, these statements meant little and accomplished less absent affirmative steps by the government to enforce them. As Weaver later pointed out, "[M]anagement paid only slight attention to any of the federal policies for labor supply; it paid even less attention to statements that minorities *should not* be discriminated against on defense work."[48] In fact, governmental policies often worsened the situation. The U.S. Employment Service, which helped direct labor to defense industries, allowed employers to classify jobs as being "for whites only," and consistently classified black applicants as unskilled laborers regardless of their qualifications.[49]

Further adding to black criticism of the defense buildup were the bitter memories of World War I, when black service had been repaid not with equal rights but with segregation and violence. The *Chicago Defender* asked, "What democracy have we enjoyed since the last World War? Are our people not segregated? Are they not Jim-Crowed and lynched? Are their civil and constitutional rights respected?"[50] Several black newspapers ran articles by black World War I veterans who recounted their experiences in the military. One was these was Charles H. Houston, the noted civil rights lawyer, who warned of discrimination that he faced as an officer in World War I so that "this generation of Negro boys may have their eyes opened to what is ahead of them."[51] In contrast to the "close ranks" sentiment of World War I, blacks vowed that this time the nation could expect black support for defense only in return for greater civil rights. In a letter to the president, Houston warned that blacks "will not again silently endure the insults and discriminations imposed on its soldiers and sailors in the course of the last war."[52]

Even before the war began, blacks began mobilizing to press the case for more equal treatment in national defense. In 1939, *Pittsburgh Courier* publisher Robert Vann pointed out that white spies and traitors could enter the military more easily than loyal blacks. To rectify the situation, he organized the Committee for the Participation of Negroes in the National Defense Program (CPNNDP). Headed by black historian and World War I veteran, Rayford W. Logan, the group sought to obtain a "fair share" for blacks in national defense. The CPNNDP, in conjunction with several black fraternal and professional organizations, established chapters in twenty-five states and the District of Columbia. Existing black organizations like the NAACP and the Urban League also pushed for more equal treatment in the defense effort.[53]

The CPNNDP and its allies won a victory of sorts on September 14, 1940, when Congress passed an amendment to the Selective Service Act sponsored by Representative Hamilton Fish of New York, who had commanded black troops in World War I. It barred racial discrimination in military selection and training. Important as this step was, the amendment merely assured blacks that their still separate place in the military would become more equal. The amendment was also vague and the War Department and military commanders had often ignored previous antidiscrimination mandates.[54]

To clarify the issue, black leaders Walter White of the NAACP, A. Philip Randolph of the Brotherhood of Sleeping Car Porters, and T. Arnold Hill of the National Urban League met with President Roosevelt, Assistant Secretary of War Robert P. Patterson, and Navy Secretary Frank Knox on September 27. The civil rights leaders presented Roosevelt with a seven-point program to end discrimination in the nation's defense effort, including ordering the military "to accept and select officers and enlisted personnel without regard to race."[55] Randolph then told the president, "I thought I might say on the part of the Negro people, they feel they are not wanted in the armed forces of the country, and they feel they have earned their rights to participate in every phase of the government by virtue of their record in past wars since the Revolution."[56]

Roosevelt seemed receptive to his visitors' request, telling them that although integration of army units would need to proceed slowly, he was not opposed to integrating units through their replacements gradually: "Now, suppose you have a Negro regiment . . . here, and right over here on my right in line, would be a white regiment. . . . Now what happens after a while, in case of war? Those people would get shifted from one to the other. The thing gets sort of backed into . . . gradually working in the field together, you may back into it. . . ."[57]

Somewhat contradictorily, Secretary Knox stated that "an army fighting allegedly for democracy should be the last place in which to practice undemocratic segregation," but then rejected the idea for the navy since "these men live aboard ship."[58] Knox added, falsely, "And in our history we don't take Negroes into a ship's company. . . ." (A few weeks later, Roosevelt suggested to Knox that the navy might start integrating its ships by putting "a colored band on some of these ships because they're *darned good at it*. . . . Look, to increase the opportunity, that's what we're after.")[59]

White, Randolph, and Hill left the meeting upbeat, believing that they had convinced the president to ease some of the military's Jim Crow restrictions. Military officials, however, quickly vetoed the idea. Army Chief of Staff General George Marshall argued that now was not the time "for critical experiments which would have a highly destructive effect on morale." Secretary of War Henry Stimson was also vigorously opposed, telling his diary, "I saw the same thing happen 23 years ago when Woodrow Wilson yielded to the same sort of demand and appointed colored officers to several of the Divisions that went over to France, and the poor fellows made perfect fools of themselves. . . . Leadership is not embedded in the Negro race yet . . . . Colored troops do very well under white officers but every time we try to lift them a little beyond where they can go, disaster and confusion follow. . . . I hope for heaven's sake they won't mix the white and colored troops together in the same units for then we shall certainly have trouble."[60]

On October 9, the White House issued a statement regarding the meeting that, while offering vague promises of equal treatment, declared, "The policy of the War Department is not to intermingle colored and white enlisted personnel. . . . This policy has proven satisfactory over a long period of years, and to make changes would produce situations destructive to morale and detrimental to the preparation for national defense." The statement implied that the policy had been agreed to by White, Randolph, and Hill at the September 27 meeting.[61]

Reactions came fast and furious. White, Randolph, and Hill denied that they had agreed to such a policy and denounced it, stating, "We are inexpressibly shocked that a President of the United States at a time of national peril should surrender so completely to enemies of democracy who would destroy national unity by advocating segregation. Official approval by the Commander-in-Chief of the Army and Navy of such discrimination and segregation is a stab in the back of democracy."[62] A mass protest meeting in Harlem drew thousands of blacks.[63] Liberal whites also objected to the statement. The *Nation* described it as "discrimination of the most flagrant kind," while the Catholic magazine *America* ran an editorial entitled, "Our Jim Crow Army," stating that "what the country needs today is not separation, but unity."[64]

Coming just weeks before election day, the controversy over the White House statement became an issue in the 1940 presidential campaign. The election seemed relatively close and the Republicans and their candidate Wendell Willkie were actively pursuing black voters, who they felt were important to the outcome in several big northern states. The Republicans pointed to their platform which, after keeping silent on the issue in 1936, took a relatively strong stand on civil rights, declaring, "Discrimination in the civil service, the army, navy, and all other branches of the Government must cease."[65] They also ran full-page ads in black newspapers declaring, "Roosevelt, as Commander-in-Chief, permits Jim Crow in the U.S. Navy."[66]

Matters got worse after White House press secretary Stephen Early kicked a black policeman assigned to protect the president during a campaign stop. The Roosevelt campaign responded frantically. "The Negro situation," warned one aide to the president, "has become more difficult." Unsure of how to respond, presidential advisor Harry Hopkins sought the advice of Will Alexander of the Farm Security Administration, a prominent southern white liberal. "It looks as though they are all going against him," Hopkins said, "tell me what to do."[67] Walter White recalled in his memoirs, "My telephone rang night and day with calls from friends of the President . . . who asked what could be done to repair the damage. . . ."[68]

To stop black defections to Willkie, the White House quickly backtracked. It admitted that the policy on blacks in the military had not received the blessing of White, Randolph, and Hill. Furthermore, the military's segregation policy, said the president, applied "at this

time and this time only." He had "no fixed policy" for the future.
More importantly, Roosevelt promoted U.S. army colonel Benjamin
O. Davis Sr., making him the first black to obtain the rank of general.
The president also appointed William Hastie, Dean of the Howard
University Law School and formerly the first black appointed to the
federal bench, as Civilian Advisor to the Secretary of War.[69] Even
though they were largely symbolic, these appointments won approval. Walter White thanked the president "for all you did to insure
a square deal for Negroes in the defense of our country," and the
Pittsburgh Courier described the appointments as a victory "in the fight
for equitable participation of colored people in the national defense
program."[70] On election day, Roosevelt won comfortably. Black support for the president was equal to or higher than in 1936.[71]

Although most blacks welcomed the Davis and Hastie appointments, they saw them as only a start. Moreover, the fruitlessness of
White, Randolph, and Hill's meeting with the president showed that
the usual tactics of personal entreaties and quiet pressure were not
enough to achieve significant changes in government policies. "The
masses of Negroes are getting fed up on these frauds," wrote George
Schuyler, calling for "some technique of fighting other than sending
letters and telegrams of protest."[72] Within the NAACP, Assistant Executive Director Roy Wilkins complained that the organization was
too focused "on individual lobbying in Washington with politicians
rather than on beating the tom tom of public opinion over the country."[73] Frustration soon led to militance, as blacks around the country began demanding action. In December 1940, the CPNNDP called
on blacks to "hold huge defense mass meetings in their cities and
towns to which their congressmen and senators would be invited."
In Kansas City, over five thousand persons gathered to protest discrimination in local defense plants. Similar protests took place in
several cities over the next two months.[74]

A. Philip Randolph decided to take these protests a step further.
He saw the traditional methods of civil rights organizations as but
"chloroform for the masses. When the chloroform wears off, the
passions of the beast of race prejudice flare up again."[75] Preferring
to take the beast head on, Randolph boldly proposed a mass march
by blacks on Washington, D.C. to protest against discrimination in
the nation's defense effort. Randolph first broached the idea to his
associate Milton Webster, telling him, "You know, Web, calling on
the President and holding those conferences are not going to get us
anywhere. We are going to have to do something about it." Randolph was silent for a moment and then said, "I think we ought to

get 10,000 Negroes to march on Washington in protest, march down Pennsylvania Avenue. What do you think of that?" Webster agreed with the idea, but asked Randolph, "Where are you going to get 10,000 negroes?" "I think we can get them," he replied.[76]

Randolph believed the need for such a tactic was clear. "Only power can effect the enforcement and adoption of a given policy, however meritorious it may be. . . . Power and pressure are at the foundation of the march of social justice and reform . . . power and pressure do not reside in the few . . . they lie in and flow from the masses. . . . Hence, Negro America must bring its power and pressure to bear upon the . . . Federal Government to exact their rights in National Defense employment and the armed forces of the country."[77] As he tested the idea before groups of blacks, Randolph received enthusiastic responses. In meeting after meeting, the "forgotten black man" rose and told "about jobs he had sought but never got, about the business agent of the union giving him the brush-off, how he had gone to the gates of the defense plants only to be kept out while white workers walked in, how he cooled his heels in an office and finally was told with a cold stare 'no more workers wanted.' "[78]

On January 15, 1941, Randolph announced his idea publicly: "I suggest that TEN THOUSAND Negroes march on Washington, D.C. . . . with the slogan: WE LOYAL NEGRO AMERICAN CITIZENS DEMAND THE RIGHT TO WORK AND FIGHT FOR OUR COUNTRY. . . . [T]here can be no national unity where one tenth of the population are denied their basic rights as American citizens. . . . One thing is certain and that is if Negroes are going to get anything out of this national defense . . . WE MUST FIGHT FOR IT AND FIGHT FOR IT WITH GLOVES OFF."[79]

Despite or perhaps because of its militant tone, Randolph's statement touched a nerve with blacks throughout the country. As one of Randolph's aides later recalled, support for the march "grew like Topsy. . . . It got out of hand almost overnight. People began writing us, 'What can we do?' How could they go about getting groups together?"[80] "This is the time, the place, the issue and the method," wrote the *Chicago Defender,* summing up the attitudes of many blacks.[81] Using the Brotherhood of Sleeping Car Porters as its nucleus, Randolph established the March on Washington Committee with both a national headquarters and branches in cities and states around the country. Although somewhat uncomfortable with such militant action, both the NAACP and the National Urban League supported the march and lent Randolph assistance in organizing it.

Perhaps the most controversial aspect of Randolph's proposal for the march was that it be undertaken exclusively by blacks. Randolph cited two reasons for this. First, he feared that the march might be taken over by Communists, who Randolph believed were more interested in advancing the foreign policy of the Soviet Union than the interests of American blacks. Furthermore, if Communists were seen as playing a significant role in the march, it would lose legitimacy in the eyes of many whites and government officials. The second and more important reason for restricting the march to blacks was that Randolph believed it was important for blacks to show themselves as well as white Americans that they could organize and execute such an important endeavor. As he put it, "The essential value of an all-Negro movement such as the March on Washington is that it helps to create faith by Negroes in Negroes. It develops a sense of self-reliance with Negroes depending on Negroes in vital matters. It helps to break down the slave psychology and inferiority-complex in Negroes which comes and is nourished with Negroes relying on white people for direction and support."[82]

These explanations did not satisfy some of Randolph's black critics. Charles H. Houston thought that blacks alone could not win the battle against Jim Crow, thus making an alliance with liberal whites necessary. Houston and Roy Wilkins also claimed that excluding whites was Jim Crow in reverse. "In one breath, they call for integration of the Negro into American life and in the next breath they refuse membership to persons who want to further that integration simply because those persons happen to be white," wrote Wilkins.[83]

Even so, the all-black nature of the march probably added to its popularity among most ordinary blacks. Although Randolph had opposed Marcus Garvey, he was well aware that Garvey's appeals to racial identity had allowed him to create the only mass movement among American blacks. Hence, Randolph was willing to use Garvey's emphasis on racial exclusiveness as a means to achieve his own distinctly un-Garveyite goal of "full integration of Negro citizens into all phases of American life."[84]

On May 1, Randolph issued the official call for the march:

Dear fellow Negro Americans, be not dismayed in these terrible times. You possess power, great power. Our problem is to hitch it up for action on the broadest, daring and most gigantic scale.

In this period of power politics, nothing counts but pressure, more pressure, and still more pressure, through the tactic and strategy of broad organized, aggressive mass action behind the vital and important issues of the Negro. To this end we propose that ten thousand Negroes MARCH ON WASHINGTON FOR JOBS IN NATIONAL DEFENSE AND EQUAL INTEGRATION IN THE FIGHTING FORCES OF THE UNITED STATES.

> An "all out" thundering march on Washington, ending in a monster and huge demonstration at Lincoln's Monument will shake up white America.
> It will shake up official Washington.
> It will give encouragement to our white friends to fight all the harder by our side, with us, for our righteous cause.
> It will gain respect for the Negro people.
> It will create a new sense of self-respect among Negroes. . . .
> [I]f American democracy will not defend its defenders; if American democracy will not protect its protectors; if American democracy will not give jobs to its toilers because of race or color; if American democracy will not insure equality of opportunity, freedom and justice to its citizens, black and white, it is a hollow mockery and belies the principles for which it is supposed to stand.[85]

The enthusiastic response soon led Randolph to predict not ten thousand marchers, but one hundred thousand. Whatever the likely turnout may have been, the federal government was becoming increasingly worried about Randolph's plans. Even if only ten thousand blacks marched, it would profoundly embarrass an administration and a nation devoted to the defense of freedom. Further adding to the worries of the White House was the potential for violence, a very real possibility in so thoroughly segregated a city as Washington, D.C. If violence did occur, it would provide ample propaganda for America's enemies.

Thus the administration attempted to persuade Randolph to call off the march. Eleanor Roosevelt tried first, writing Randolph in June to say that it was "a very grave mistake" to allow the march to take place. Doing so would "set back the progress which is being made . . . towards better opportunities and less segregation. I feel if any incident occurs as a result of this, it may engender so much bitterness that it will create in Congress even more solid opposition from certain groups than we have had in the past. . . . You know that I am deeply concerned about the rights of Negro people, but I think one must face situations as they are and not as one wishes them to be."[86]

Mrs. Roosevelt's appeal was in vain. Randolph refused to call off the march unless the president issued an executive order abolishing discrimination in the military and defense industries. The president then had his wife and New York Mayor Fiorello La Guardia meet with Randolph and Walter White on June 13. According to Randolph, Mrs. Roosevelt reiterated her sympathy with his goals but complained that the march was ill-advised. "Where would all those thousands of people eat and sleep in Jim Crow Washington?" she asked. Randolph replied calmly that they "would simply march into hotels and restaurants, and order food and shelter." Mrs. Roosevelt responded that doing so would lead to violence. Randolph shot back that "there would be no violence unless her husband ordered the police to crack black heads." La Guardia added, "Phil, I'll tell you. [Calling off the march] will be one of the greatest services you've ever given your country, and given Negroes, too, for that matter. . . . *You are going to get Negroes slaughtered!* . . . It just can't come off without trouble."[87] Again, Randolph stated that only an executive order could convince him to call off the march.[88]

Mrs. Roosevelt and La Guardia told the president that the only hope for heading off the march was for him to meet with Randolph and White. Roosevelt quickly agreed to do so, and on June 18 Randolph and White met with the president, La Guardia, and several administration officials. Roosevelt opened the meeting with casual small talk and political anecdotes. Finally, Randolph broke in, "Mr. President, time is running on. You are quite busy, I know. But what we want to talk with you about is the problem of jobs for Negroes in defense industries. . . . Now, what are you going to do about it?"

"Well, Phil," asked the president, "what do you want me to do?"

"Mr. President, we want you to do something that will enable Negro workers to get in these plants."

Roosevelt suggested that he call up the heads of various defense industries and "see to it that Negroes are given the same opportunity to work in defense plants as any other citizen in the country." Randolph knew that such a vague promise was of little help. "We want you to do more than that. We want something concrete, something tangible, definite, positive, and affirmative."

"What do you mean?"

"Mr. President, we want you to issue an executive order making it mandatory that Negroes be permitted to work in these plants."

"Well, Phil," answered the president, "you know I can't do that. If I issue an executive order for you, then there'll be no end to other groups coming in here and asking me to issue executive orders for them, too. In any event, I couldn't do anything unless you called off this march of yours. Questions like this can't be settled with a sledge hammer."

"I'm sorry, Mr. President, the march cannot be called off," Randolph responded steadfastly.

"How many people do you plan to bring?" asked Roosevelt.

"One hundred thousand, Mr. President," answered Randolph.

Sensing a bluff, Roosevelt asked Walter White how many people really planned to march. Unhesitatingly, White replied, "One hundred thousand, Mr. President."

Whether Randolph and White were bluffing, no one can say for sure. What is known is that the president seemed alarmed at the prospect. "You can't bring 100,000 Negroes to Washington," he said. "Somebody might get killed."

Randolph replied that violence was unlikely if the president spoke to the marchers. Roosevelt responded impatiently, "Call it off and we'll talk again."[89]

La Guardia then suggested that a compromise might be worked out if Randolph and White met separately with various administration officials. This they did, but the officials still balked at issuing an executive order, arguing that informal pressure on defense contractors by the administration would prove sufficient. Randolph replied that similar efforts had thus far yielded nothing. Finally, the officials relented and agreed to draw up an executive order for the president to sign. After he rejected several initial drafts as too weak, the White House finally came up with an executive order that met Randolph's approval. On June 25, 1941, President Roosevelt signed Executive Order 8802. The order mandated that "there shall be no discrimination in the employment of workers in defense industries or government because of race, creed, color, or national origin." Furthermore, it was "the duty of employers and of labor organizations . . . to provide for the full and equitable participation of all workers in defense industries." Most importantly, the order established a Fair Employment Practices Committee (FEPC) to "receive and investigate complaints of discrimination" and to take "appropriate steps to redress grievances."[90] Holding up his end of the bargain, Randolph agreed to cancel the march.

The great majority of blacks saw the executive order and the creation of the FEPC as an immense achievement, with some even going so far as to compare it to the Emancipation Proclamation.[91] This vastly overstated the case, especially since the FEPC lacked real enforcement power and so proved to be less effective than it might have been in ending discrimination in the defense industry. Furthermore, the order said nothing about Randolph's original demand to end discrimination in the military. Nonetheless, Executive Order 8802 was truly historic. For the first time since the Civil Rights Act of 1875, the federal government took concrete action to protect the civil rights of black Americans.

After decades of disappointment, what had made this achievement in black rights possible? First, the ideological demands of fighting an enemy who espoused racial hierarchies made more white Americans sensitive to the presence of racial discrimination in America. The vision of blacks marching to claim their rights contradicted the image of America as the defender of democracy. Second, though America had not yet entered the war, the nation's defense buildup was of crucial importance since Hitler seemed unstoppable. Marches and protests threatened to disrupt this buildup. Adding urgency to this was the German invasion of the U.S.S.R. on June 22, 1941, just days before the president issued his executive order. Roosevelt's military advisors believed that the Soviet Union would collapse before the onslaught, further enhancing Hitler's power.[92] Finally, and most importantly, blacks actively took advantage of the first two factors to press a still-reluctant government for greater equality. As Randolph had predicted and has proven true throughout American history, only "pressure, more pressure, and still more pressure" had forced this first important achievement in the modern struggle for civil rights.[93]

SIX

"Double V: Victory Abroad, Victory at Home"

World War II

At 7:55 A.M., on Sunday, December 7, 1941, Japanese warplanes struck at Pearl Harbor. Completely surprised, the ill-prepared American naval and air forces offered little resistance. One of the few heroes on this day of "infamy" was Doris (Dorie) Miller, a crew member on the battleship *West Virginia*. Miller first helped carry his mortally wounded captain from the ship's burning bridge. Later, though untrained in the weapon, he manned a machine gun and began "blazing away as though he had fired one all his life," reported one eyewitness. Miller shot down two enemy aircraft before flames forced him from the gun. (Some unofficial accounts claimed he had shot down six planes.) He then helped pull wounded men from the water, "thereby, unquestionably saving the lives of a number of people who might otherwise have been lost."[1]

Miller's heroism was exceeded only by its irony. Miller was black, the son of Texas sharecroppers, and, like all blacks then serving in the navy, a messman. Although black sailors had served ably since the Revolutionary War, in the 1920s the navy began restricting blacks to work in the galleys, claiming that they lacked courage, skill, and initiative.[2] The destruction and confusion of the Japanese attack momentarily erased the navy's color line. After the attack, however, the navy refused to release Miller's name, referring to him only as "an unidentified Negro messman." Some writers contend that it did not want the first hero of the war to be a black man.[3]

Black newspapers and civil rights organizations uncovered Miller's name and publicized the incident in the hopes of forcing the navy to recognize his exploits and to open its ranks to blacks. The *Pittsburgh Courier* editorialized, "Is it fair, honest or sensible that this country, with its fate in the balance, should continue to bar Negroes from service except in the mess department of the Navy, when at the first sign of danger they so dramatically show their willingness to face death in defense of the Stars and Stripes?"[4] Black columnist George Schuyler pointed out that the navy's racism "must be comforting to Hitler, Mussolini, and the Japanese" since it reinforced their undemocratic ideas.[5] Among ordinary blacks, Miller became a folk hero, and his exploits were the subject of a gospel recording.[6]

Miller's bravery resonated among whites as well. Hollywood, ever sensitive to the public taste, included a Dorie Miller–like character in the war movie *Crash Dive* (1943).[7] Among the whites touched by Miller's story was Ronald Reagan. Decades later, President Reagan would tell of "a Negro sailor whose total duties involved kitchen-type duties. . . . He cradled a machine gun in his arms . . . and stood on the end of a pier blazing away at Japanese airplanes that were coming down and strafing him and that [segregation] was all changed."[8]

Typically, Reagan's zest for a good story exceeded his knowledge of the facts. Miller's bravery was indeed impressive, but that alone was not nearly enough to force a change in military policy. The wave of protests by blacks was far more important in forcing the navy to begin dismantling its Jim Crow policy. In April 1942, the Department of the Navy announced that it would begin accepting blacks for general service in the navy, the marine corps, and the coast guard. But blacks would still train and serve in segregated units.[9] Such a halfway step also characterized the navy's treatment of Miller. In May, 1942, it awarded him the Navy Cross, that service's highest decoration. Yet Miller's "distinguished devotion to duty, extraordinary courage, and disregard for his own personal safety" brought him only a promotion from Mess Attendant 2nd Class to Mess Attendant 1st Class. Thus, on Thanksgiving Day 1943, when Miller went down at sea aboard the aircraft carrier *Liscombe Bay*, he was still waiting on white officers.[10]

In some ways, the story of Dorie Miller symbolizes the experience of American race relations in World War II. During that war, the interaction of pressing requirements of national security, the service and heroism of blacks in uniform, protest by black civilians, and the need to set America apart from its undemocratic and racist opponents put great strain on the nation's Jim Crow system. Although white Americans often responded grudgingly and halfheartedly, the nation nonetheless began to take the first significant steps toward racial equality in nearly a century—greater equality, that is, for "races" seen as resources for the American cause, including whites, blacks, and also the nation's wartime allies, the Chinese.[11] At the same time, the war against Japan fed white racism against all persons of Japanese descent. The federal government adopted coercive policies toward all Japanese Americans that were explicitly urged on the basis of that group's allegedly suspect "racial" traits.

The relative progress of blacks was still hard won. Advocates of civil rights were by no means satisfied with their partial victory over the navy. In fact, in the year following Pearl Harbor, blacks became even more embittered at the irony of defending freedom while enduring Jim Crow at home. A small minority of blacks were so opposed to what they saw as a white man's war that they openly supported the Japanese and were prosecuted for sedition.[12]

The vast majority of blacks rejected such radical anti-Americanism, but many took vicarious pleasure in the victories of the "colored" Japanese. After the Japanese sunk the British warships *Repulse* and *Prince of Wales,* two black messengers in the War Department called out to each other, "We just got the 'Repulse' and the 'Prince of Wales.' Good hunting, eh?"[13] This mood was best summed up by the feelings of one black, who told sociologists St. Clair Drake and Horace Cayton:

> I was really ashamed of myself the day Pearl Harbor was hit. When I heard the news I jumped up and laughed. "Well, sir," I said, "I don't guess the white folks will say colored people can't fly airplanes from now on. They sure slammed hell outa Pearl Harbor." Then I caught myself. I know the Japanese are a bunch of fascists. . . . I know this isn't a race war. I shouldn't have been pleased at anything the Japs did. But I suppose I see it this way— we're bound to win this war in the long run, and a few tactical defeats like Singapore and Pearl Harbor, in the framework of a strategy for total victory, may help democracy in the long run. They may make the white man wake up to the fact that he can't shove darker people around forever.[14]

Other blacks refused induction into a Jim Crow military. Although small in number, these draft resisters received publicity and support from civil rights organizations and black newspapers. One of them, Winfred Lynn, wrote his draft board in June 1942, "Please be informed that I am ready to serve in any unit of the armed forces of my country which is not segregated by race. Unless I am assured that I can serve in a mixed regiment and that I will not be compelled to serve in a unit undemocratically selected as a Negro group, I will refuse to report for induction." Lynn took his case all the way to the Supreme Court, but the justices refused to hear it on a legal technicality.[15]

Most blacks supported the war, but only with reservations. Shortly after Pearl Harbor, the National Association for the Advancement of Colored People (NAACP) and the Urban League sponsored a conference of sixty prominent black leaders to discuss blacks and the war. The group passed, with only five dissents, a resolution declaring that "the colored people are not wholeheartedly and reservedly all out in support of the present war effort."[16] This ambivalence was expressed by James G. Thompson, a cafeteria worker in a Kansas aircraft factory, in a January 1942 letter to the *Pittsburgh Courier*: "I suggest that while we keep defense and victory in the forefront that we don't lose sight of our fight for true democracy at home." Thompson suggested that since the "V" sign had come to symbolize victory over the Axis, "then let we colored Americans adopt the double VV for a double victory. The first V for victory over our enemies from without, the second V for victory over our enemies from within. For surely those who perpetuate these ugly prejudices here are seeking to destroy our democratic form of government just as surely as the Axis forces." Thompson's idea quickly took hold as the *Courier* displayed the logo "VV" and announced a "Double V campaign" to "fight for the right to fight." The "Double V" slogan was soon adopted by most of the black press and became the wartime slogan of most black Americans.[17]

Underlying the Double V campaign was the belief that although the war would entail profound sacrifices, it also presented black Americans with an unprecedented opportunity to leverage the government and society for greater rights. Historian Rayford Logan commented that "the white man's distress is the black man's gain."[18] The *Pittsburgh Courier* wrote early in the war, "What an opportunity this crisis has been . . . for one to persuade, embarrass, compel and shame our government and our nation . . . into a more enlightened attitude toward a tenth of its people!"[19] Any gain, however, could only come from active and continuous pressure from blacks. Waiting until the war was over to press for equal rights would be foolish and futile, as the experience of World War I had shown. Consequently, blacks kept up the attempts that had begun before the war to secure their rights.

This growing militancy was found in many areas, such as A. Philip

Randolph's decision to turn the March on Washington Movement (MOWM) into a permanent organization. It would press for greater equality not only in national defense but also "in education, in housing, in transportation, and in every other social, economic and political privilege." "We want the full works of citizenship with no reservations," declared Randolph. "We will accept nothing less."[20] Ruling out the possibility of a march on Washington in the middle of a war, Randolph instead sponsored mass meeting in various cities. On the night of the New York rally in Madison Square Garden, the MOWM sponsored a "blackout" in Harlem. Businesses and private homes extinguished or blinded their lights during the rally to "dramatize the economic and political blackout" of black Americans. The event was very effective, with one observer commenting that "Harlem was like a deserted village. Every man, woman, and child who had carfare was in Madison Square Garden."[21] Over twenty thousand people attended. A similar rally in Chicago proved equally successful.[22]

The war also saw the creation of a new civil rights group, the Congress of Racial Equality (CORE). Established in Chicago in June of 1942, CORE's interracial founders were "intensely committed to applying Gandhian techniques of *Satyagraha,* or nonviolent direct action, to the resolution of racial and industrial conflict in America." Using sit-ins and protests, the group sought to integrate Jim Crow restaurants, neighborhoods, theaters, and public facilities. CORE chapters spread to other northern cities during the war and though the organization remained small, its direct action tactics did achieve some successes and provided an important example for civil rights activists in coming years.[23]

Still, there were important limitations on black militancy during World War II. Population movements, fear of federal sedition charges, the enlistment of thousands of young black men, the increased demands of war-related work, and the general atmosphere of patriotism and loyalty all limited what organizations like MOWM and CORE could accomplish.[24] In fact, by 1943 MOWM had all but withered away. Nonetheless, World War II still represented a significant upsurge in black political activism, especially in contrast with World War I. Traditional civil rights groups such as the NAACP became more militant. As Roy Wilkins wrote to Walter White in 1942, "it is a plain fact that no Negro leader with a constituency can face his members today and ask for full support for the war in light of the atmosphere the government has created."[25] In response, the NAACP declared, "We shall not abate one iota our struggle for full citizenship rights here in the United States."[26] Most importantly, ordinary blacks increasingly became part of the NAACP's struggle; between 1939 and 1945, NAACP membership grew nearly tenfold from fifty-four thousand to more than five hundred thousand, giving the organization its first mass base.[27]

Another sign of heightened black militancy during the war was that displayed by blacks in uniform. Although unorganized and forced to operate within the restrictive environment of military discipline, black soldiers throughout the war engaged in protest and resistance. As Drake and Cayton pointed out, blacks in the military "were aware, however vaguely in some cases, that they were participating in a titanic struggle under the banner of the Four Freedoms. They were liberating people from Fascism abroad and they were expecting to be liberated from Jim-Crow at home. For them this was a Fifth Freedom as precious as the other four."[28]

Even though all branches of the service had been opened to them by the summer of 1942 (the army's air corps began training blacks in January of 1941), blacks were still segregated and assigned mostly to service or labor units. Base facilities, such as post exchanges, USO clubs, theaters, and hospitals, were often denied to them or provided on a separate and distinctly unequal basis. On one base the schedule of religious services read, "Catholics, Jews, Protestants, and Negroes."[29] Off base, the situation was usually worse because many camps were located in the South, which cared more about the color of a man's skin than of his uniform.[30] Furthermore, these black servicemen were often commanded by racist officers who frequently used military police to help enforce local racial customs.

Northern blacks found racism in the military particularly galling. Many had never been forced to sit in the back of the bus, drink from "colored" water fountains, and observe all the standards of obsequiousness to whites demanded by the Jim Crow South. Furthermore, as Drake and Cayton observed, "The Negroes who went to fight in the Second World War, unlike those who fought in the First, were not masses of illiterate cotton-field hands dragooned into battle, never asking, 'Why?' At least half of the Negro soldiers . . . were city people who had lived through a Depression in America's Black Ghettoes, and who had been exposed to unions, the Communist movement, and to the moods of 'racial radicalism' that occasionally swept American cities. Even the rural southern Negroes were different this time—for the thirty years between the First and Second World Wars had seen a great expansion of school facilities in the South and the wide distribution of newspapers and radios."[31] And in some ways, their military training made black servicemen even more prone to resist Jim Crow. As William Hastie pointed out, "it is impossible to create a dual personality which will be on the one hand a fighting man toward the foreign enemy, and on the other, a craven who will accept treatment as less than a man at home."[32] One black soldier warned in letter to the *Baltimore Afro-American*, "If this is Uncle Sam's Army, then treat us like soldiers not animals or else Uncle Sam might find a new axis to fight."[33]

When Uncle Sam remained slow to improve their treatment, many black soldiers did fight back. According to one black veteran, they "felt dying stateside was just as good, if not preferable, to dying on foreign soil. Moreover, they didn't give a damn about a military career. It boiled down to this: all they had to lose was their lives."[34] As a result, according to political scientist Dan Kryder, "[o]f nineteen cases of urban, collective racial violence in 1941, seventeen involved soldiers."[35] The most publicized incident was in August 1941, when white MP's began using nightsticks to subdue unruly black soldiers on a bus in Fayetteville, North Carolina. One of the black soldiers, Private Ned Turman, grabbed a pistol from one of the MPs and shot and killed him. In the ensuing gun fight, Turman was killed, along with two MPs and seven black soldiers.[36] Among blacks, Turman was seen as a hero and memorialized in poem:

> They say this is a war
> For Freedom Over There
> Say, Mr. F D R
> How 'bout som Freedom Here?
> 'T was a Fort Bragg M.P. shot him down
> One Evening when he was leaving town.[37]

Racial incidents at military facilities worsened the following year. In 1942, Kryder found 59 separate instances of confrontations between black soldiers and military and civilian authorities.[38] In one of these, MPs attempting to arrest a black soldier in Alexandria, Louisiana triggered a race riot in which twenty-eight blacks were shot and nearly three thousand arrested.[39] One of those arrested later wrote, "I would almost rather desert and be placed before a firing squad and shot down before fighting for America."[40]

Along with blacks, the war prompted a growing number of white liberals to step up their civil rights efforts. In 1942, the *New Republic* claimed that racial discrimination in America made "a mockery of the theory that we are fighting for democracy, and we are giving aid and comfort to the enemy thereby."[41] In addition, American racism hampered the war effort by damaging the morale of blacks. United States representative Martin L. Sweeney of Ohio told his colleagues, "I hesitate to say what the morale of the colored boy in the Army will be when he contemplates the fact that his brother, his father, and his sister back home cannot receive Army work in the defense industries because of their color."[42] Racial outrages at home, liberals noted, provided grist for German and Japanese propaganda mills. In response to the outbreak of racial violence in Detroit in early 1942, the editors of the *New Republic* wrote that rioting whites "were assuredly doing Hitler's work. We don't doubt that the story of that riot was told all over Asia, with Nazi trimmings."[43]

White liberals were far less perceptive in formulating racial solutions. Since, as the *Nation* claimed, "[i]t is obvious that the white majority is not yet ready to abandon the disastrous policy of segregation," white liberals, especially partisan leaders, resorted to merely symbolic statements of America's democratic ideals (in contrast to its racist traditions) and counseled blacks to be patient. In 1942, Eleanor Roosevelt wrote in the *New Republic,* "It seems trite to say to the Negro, you must have patience, when he has had patience for so long. . . . Nevertheless, that is what we must continue to say in the interests of our government as a whole and of the Negro people."[44]

As limited as this approach was, it was still far in advance of most whites, who endorsed the racial status quo. In 1942, polls showed approximately 60 percent of whites believed that blacks were getting all the opportunity that they deserved.[45] This was particularly true in the South, where, as John Egerton has pointed out, the "Ku Klux Klan, the German American Bund, and the shirted factions of fascism had more standing in the average Southern community than any outspoken integrationist."[46] Wartime threats to Jim Crow only made many southern whites even more adamant in its defense. In 1942, the South Carolina House of Representatives declared "our belief in and our allegiance to established white supremacy as now prevailing in the South." The legislators went on to offer "our lives and our sacred honor to maintain it, whatever the cost, in war and in peace."[47] One white Southerner told a northern journalist, "There's no white man down here going to let his daughter sleep with a nigger, or sit at the same table with a nigger, or go walking with a nigger. The war can go to hell, the world can go to hell, but he ain't going to do it."[48]

Even mild unsettling of the racial status quo triggered a wave of rumors throughout the white South. One had black men telling each other, "Aren't we going to have a time with these white women, when all these white men go off to war!" Another claimed that blacks were arming themselves with ice picks and other weapons for a prearranged uprising against whites. The most popular rumor declared that black domestics, their expectations raised by the egalitarian rhetoric of the First Lady, were forming "Eleanor Clubs" to organize strikes and walkouts. The motto of these clubs was "A white woman in every kitchen by 1943."[49]

As the "Eleanor Club" rumor suggests, most southern whites believed that the rise in black discontent resulted from the work of "outside agitators." The South Carolina legislature stated that "we firmly and unequivocally demand that henceforth the damned agitators of the North leave the South alone."[50] To back up the point, Governor Olin Johnston, told the state's national guard, "If any outsiders come into our state and agitate social equality among the races, I shall deem it my duty to call upon you men to help expel them."[51] Representative Martin Dies of Texas, the ever-vigilant head of the House Un-American Activities Committee, warned that "subversive elements are attempting to convince the Negro that he should be placed on social equality with white people; that now is the time for him to assert his rights."[52] Dies's colleague from Mississippi, John Rankin, saw "Japanese fifth columnists" as the force "behind this drive to try to stir up trouble between the whites and the Negroes." Blacks would be perfectly happy, Rankin added, "if these fifth columnists and the flannel-mouthed agitators throughout the country will let them alone."[53]

Most disturbing for many white Southerners was that the federal government, in the form of the Fair Employment Practices Committee (FEPC), now stood among the "outside agitators." When the committee opened hearings in Birmingham, Alabama in June 1942, committee chairman Mark Ethridge tried to reassure local whites by declaring that "there is no power in the world—not even all the mechanized armies of the earth, Allied and Axis—which could now force the Southern white people to the abandonment of the principle of social segregation"[54] Many whites were not mollified. A local magazine described the hearings as "the gravest threat yet to the time-honored right of Southerners to direct the social development of their own region."[55] Alabama governor Frank Dixon (nephew of *Clansman* author Thomas Dixon) accused the committee of "operating a kangaroo court obviously dedicated to the abolition of segregation."[56] Dixon also publicly refused to sign a contract with the federal government to sell cloth produced in the state prisons because it contained an antidiscrimination clause. According to him, "The war emergency should not be used as a pretext to bring about abolition of the color line in the South."[57] Birmingham's Commissioner of Public Safety Eugene "Bull" Connor wrote President Roosevelt, telling him "that federal agencies have adopted policies to break down and destroy the segregation laws of the . . . entire South. Unless something is done by you, we are going to . . . witness the Annihilation of the Democratic Party in this section of the Nation, and see a revival of organizations which will . . . destroy the progress made by law abiding white people." Connor added that venereal disease, not the lack of "Social Equality," was the principal problem facing blacks, but the FEPC was stirring up blacks, making them "impudent, unruly, arrogant, law breaking, violent and insolent."[58]

Extreme conservatives like Dixon and Connor were not the only ones worried about threats to Jim Crow. As the war led to increased demands by blacks, many white southern liberals began to shift rightward in their thinking. Journalist Virginius Dabney, editor of the *Richmond Times-Dispatch,* was one such person. In the 1930s, Dabney had been a strong supporter of the New Deal and antilynching legislation. But in the 1940s, he began lashing out at "Negro agitators" who were "demanding an overnight revolution in race relations." He singled out the "radical element of the Negro press" for "stirring up racial hate." He warned that "it is a foregone conclusion that if an attempt is made forcibly to abolish segregation throughout the South, violence and bloodshed will result."[59]

Racial fears played a prominent part in southern election campaigns in 1942. Historian Patricia Sullivan describes these campaigns as "reminiscent of the campaigns that had accompanied the wave of disenfranchisement and segregation laws at the turn of the century." In Louisiana, a U.S. Senate candidate warned white voters that "unless we do something about this menace, social equality will be forced down the throats of white people in the South."[60] On election day, Louisiana police arrested blacks who were trying to vote and charged them with disturbing the peace. In Georgia, Governor Eugene Talmadge put the state Home Guard on riot alert and warned that it was unsafe for white women to travel alone. The head of the state highway patrol ordered his men to stop all blacks traveling after 9 P.M. and advised, "Use your black jack on them whenever you can."[61] Although Talmadge then lost to Ellis Arnall, the differences between the two candidates on race was of microscopic proportions. During the campaign Arnall declared, "If a nigger ever tried to get into a white school in my part of the state the sun would never set on his head, and we wouldn't be running to the Governor or the State Guard to get things done either."[62]

In this climate, lynchings resurged, though often more covertly.[63] In 1942, there were three lynchings in Mississippi within the span of a week. Among the victims were Charles Lang and Ernest Green, two fourteen-year-old boys who were mutilated and hung from a bridge because they allegedly frightened a white girl.[64]

Many southern whites saw any uniformed black man as "a nigger who doesn't know his place," and they often singled out black soldiers for violence. In April 1941, Private Felix Hall was found in uniform hanging from a tree at Fort Benning, Georgia. Although Hall's hands and feet were bound, the War Department would not rule out suicide as the cause of death. Throughout 1942, black soldiers were beaten or shot by southern whites on numerous occasions. Treatment of black servicemen in the South was so bad, according to writer James Baldwin, that their families "felt, mainly, a peculiar kind of relief when they knew their boys were being shipped out of the South to do battle overseas. It was, perhaps, like feeling that the most dangerous part of the journey had been passed and that now, even if death should come, it would come with honor and without the complicity of their countrymen."[65]

White resistance also surfaced in the North, where in 1942 a majority of whites supported segregated schools, restaurants, and neighborhoods.[66] Here too, wartime changes eroded the color line. Tight labor markets, pressure from the FEPC, and growing black demands increasingly opened up jobs to blacks. Many white workers were less than happy about such changes. As one union official at Boeing Aircraft said, "Labor has been asked to make many sacrifices in the war and has made them gladly, but this sacrifice [having to work alongside blacks] is too great."[67] Despite opposition from both company and union officials, white workers undertook numerous "hate strikes" to protest the introduction of blacks into the workplace.[68] One of the worst of these occurred in October 1941 at the Packard Motor Company in Detroit after two blacks were shifted into a previously all-white department. In response, 600 whites staged a sit-down strike and the black workers were removed. Only after six months of negotiations between union, company, and FEPC officials were blacks reintroduced into the department.[69]

White racism similarly flared with the influx of thousands of southern blacks into the North seeking defense jobs. Just as in World War I, the black population in cities like New York, Detroit, Los Angeles, and Chicago grew rapidly; Chicago's black population grew by sixty thousand between 1940 and 1944.[70] The sudden flood of new-comers strained crowded public transportation, theaters, and places of amusement. Racial factors exacerbated these tensions as whites complained that blacks were forming "bump clubs" to push and shove whites on packed streets and buses.[71]

Since little or no new housing was built during the war, the swelling black migration began moving beyond the already overcrowded black ghettoes into previously all-white neighborhoods. Whites often bitterly resisted the newcomers. In February 1942 in Detroit, rioting whites prevented black families from entering the just-completed Sojourner Truth housing project in a white neighborhood. A two-day racial street battle ensued, injuring forty people. Two months later, fourteen black families finally moved into the project, but only behind a protective wall of nearly seventeen hundred Michigan national guardsmen and fourteen hundred state and city police.[72]

Conservative fringe groups flourished in these hothouse conditions. In Detroit, the local Ku Klux Klan, renamed the United Sons of America, played a prominent role in several union locals where it encouraged resistance to workplace integration.[73] Detroit was also the new home of the Reverend Gerald L. K. Smith, erstwhile protégé of the late Huey Long. Smith's racist and antisemitic diatribes found a receptive audience among many local whites. In September 1942, he received 31 percent of the vote in Michigan's Republican U.S. Senate primary.[74]

Between the rising expectations of blacks and the increasing intransigence of whites stood the federal government. Focused single-mindedly on the task of winning the war, the government sought to raise black morale, but without triggering an even greater white backlash that would also harm the war effort. Consequently, the federal government's response to increasing racial friction in 1942 was reactive, temporizing, and often contradictory. In 1942, the government wartime propaganda agency, the Office of Facts and Figures (later renamed the Office of War Information (OWI)) conducted a survey of New York blacks on the war effort and found a rich reservoir of resentment. Many blacks felt that they were worse off since the start of the war. Fully 38 percent said that country should concentrate on spreading democracy at home rather than defeating the Axis (only 5 percent of poor whites felt the same). Most of those surveyed viewed the army and the navy as unfair in their treatment of blacks. Shockingly, nearly half of the blacks interviewed thought that they would be treated the same or better by the Japanese than by white Americans. Similarly, the survey found that in games, black children showed "a pronounced inclination" to play the Japanese, since "they are fond of imagining that they are in a position to avenge themselves against white oppressors." The report concluded that there was "formidable evidence of the degree to which racial grievances have kept Negroes from an all-out participation in the war effort."[75]

In response to this crisis in black morale, the federal government made some efforts during the war's first year to back up its rhetoric and to protect and extend the rights of blacks. One example was the Department of Justice's investigation of the lynching of Cleo Wright in Sikeston, Missouri in January 1942. Wright, arrested for suspicion of attempting to rape a white woman, had been shot in an ensuing scuffle with the police officers. Hearing that Wright had confessed to his employer, Milan Limbaugh, a mob of local whites assembled outside of the jail. As Wright lay dying, the mob demanded more direct and immediate vengeance. They stormed the jail, removed the mortally wounded prisoner, tied him behind a car and dragged him through the black section of town. After stopping to force Wright's wife to view him, the lynchers set Wright's body ablaze in view of two congregations of black churchgoers.[76]

As historian Dominic Capeci pointed out, of the "3,842 lynchings that occurred between 1889 and 1941" this was the first time that the Department of Justice became directly involved. Previously, the department had claimed that lynching was simply not a federal crime, but the coming of war required a change in policy. Occurring shortly after Pearl Harbor, Axis propagandists broadcast details of the incident around the world. In particular, the Japanese used the incident to warn Asians of how Western "democracies" treated nonwhites.[77]

Black Americans seized upon the incident as proof of America's wartime hypocrisy. One wrote President Roosevelt, asking, "Is this Democracy that our Missouri Americans have shown the world?" Several black newspapers told their readers to "Remember Pearl Harbor . . . and Sikeston, Missouri."[78] The *Baltimore Afro-American* showed a cartoon in which a smiling Hitler and a Japanese soldier viewed the Wright lynching from across the ocean. The caption read, "Defending America Our Way."[79] Many whites agreed; one wrote to Missouri's governor that the lynchers were "more fanatic, cannibalistic, uncivilized and barbaric than Hitler."[80]

In response to the "flocks of telegrams" he received regarding the case and "considerably distressed" about Axis propaganda, U.S. Attorney General Francis Biddle ordered the Department's Civil

Rights Section (CRS) and the FBI to investigate. Relying on reinvigorated interpretations of old Reconstruction statutes, the CRS lawyers
sought indictments for several of the lynchers and of the local police
who failed to protect Wright. Although the federal grand jury denounced the lynching and the conduct of the local police, it declared
that no violation of federal law had occurred. Even so, the case signaled that the federal government no longer considered lynching
a purely state matter. That July, President Roosevelt ordered the
Justice Department to investigate all suspected lynchings. Thus, according to Capeci, the case "brought the federal government more
directly into the protection of blacks and the struggle for racial
equality than at any time since Reconstruction."[81]

Perhaps the most important step that the federal government
took in this period was in the area of voting rights. Beginning in
the late 1930s, congressional liberals had tried to pass legislation barring poll taxes in federal elections. Although poll tax opponents usually stressed their impact on whites or their potential for corruption,
it was clear that repeal would provide a first step in dismantling
the system of racial exclusion in southern elections. Many white
Southerners certainly saw it that way. As one southern conservative
in Congress claimed, abolishing the poll tax represented an assault
on "our southern way of life and on white supremacy."[82]

Before Pearl Harbor, efforts at banning poll taxes had gone no-
where. Southern conservatives had kept the bills bottled up in the
House Judiciary Committee. The advent of the war, however, provided poll tax critics with new ammunition. In the summer of 1942,
Congress took up the Soldier Vote Act, which sought to provide
absentee ballots to those in the military. The bill also included an
amendment that waived the payment of poll taxes for those on active duty. Supporters of the amendment argued if a soldier was
"qualified, without paying tribute, to fight under the flag, he is qualified without paying tribute, to vote under the flag."[83] In addition,
Senator Claude Pepper of Florida declared that eliminating the poll
tax for soldiers "would ring around the world that America was
carrying out its professions of democracy" and that "all men everywhere with confidence may look to the United States of America
to liberate them from every slavery and subjugation and form of
oppression, whatever might chance to be its odious name."[84] Despite
their objection to the bill, according to historian Steven Lawson,
southern conservatives did not "filibuster [it] because they found it
difficult to justify the deprivation of the right to vote to men fighting
for their country."[85] Hence the bill became law that September. Just

as in the Revolution and the Civil War, black military service had proven instrumental for attaining black political rights. Even though it was extremely narrow in scope, the law provided the first legislative expansion of black voting rights since the 1870s.

That same year, Congress also considered a bill to eliminate all poll taxes in federal elections. Once again, the bill's supporters invoked the military and ideological imperatives of the war. In a fiery speech to the House, Representative Emanuel Celler of New York declared:

> We guarantee the four freedoms, including freedom from fear, to far-flung peoples [around the world], but the opponents of this bill deny freedom from fear to southern impoverished people . . . both Negro and white alike. In a sense those who cannot pay poll taxes are, in the language of Hitler, slavenvolk who fear their masters, the herrenvolk. . . . Suffrage is the greatest weapon of democracy. Insistence on the payment of the poll tax . . . so blunts the edge of democracy as to make it ineffectual. . . . The time has come in this country when men of all shades of color and men of all faiths should have equal rights. We have paid for this in days gone by in another war. Today men of all faiths, of all creeds and colors, are standing shoulder to shoulder and step to step to insure the continuation of democracy. But there can be no democracy if those who are underprivileged . . . are deprived of the principal weapon of democracy, the power of the vote.[86]

Celler's argument carried the bill in the House by an overwhelming majority. In the Senate, however, southern conservatives launched a vigorous filibuster. It killed the bill, though Majority Leader Alben Barkley of Kentucky claimed, "I know of no more opportune time to try to spread democracy in our country than at a time when we are trying to spread it in other countries and throughout the world."[87] Despite this, not since the Lodge Elections Bill of 1890 had even one house of Congress stood in favor of such a major protection of the right to vote.[88]

Still, the Justice Department's investigation of lynchings and the limited expansion of voting rights in the Soldier Vote Act were not nearly enough to meet the heightened expectations of blacks. In general, the Roosevelt administration was focused on winning the war, often at the expense of racial issues. In February 1942, President Roosevelt met with Edwin Embree, head of the Julius Rosenwald Fund, a prominent racial philanthropy founded by a businessman from Lincoln's hometown of Springfield, Illinois. Embree suggested that the president create a commission of race relations experts to advise him on the topic. Roosevelt demurred, claiming that any such considerations had to be put off until after the war: "I am not convinced that we can be realists about the war and planners for the future at this critical time."[89]

In truth, the Roosevelt administration was at a loss as to how to handle racial issues. Jonathan Daniels, one of the president's closest advisors on race matters, typified this quandary. In August 1942, he mused that he was extremely "disturbed about the state of Negro-white relationships" because he saw the "rising insistence of Negroes on their rights now" conflicting with the "rising tide of white feeling against Negroes." Although black demands were "logically strong," meeting them would leave the country "so divided in home angers that we would lack the strength for victory over our Fascist enemies."[90]

Plagued by such uncertainty, when the federal government did respond to black complaints, it usually avoided substantive measures likely to stir white resistance and relied instead on the less divisive methods of symbolism and rhetoric. In response to its survey on black morale, the OWI did call for a strong federal effort to expand economic opportunities for blacks, integration of military units, and "unqualified firmness in test cases" such as in the Sojourner Truth riot in Detroit. But, as historians Clayton Koppes and Gregory Black remarked, "This program, at best a modest start toward racial justice, proved too ambitious for wartime." Instead, the federal government began what it called "a direct and powerful Negro propaganda effort as distinct from a crusade for Negro rights," the purpose of which was to "lower hostility on the part of whites and reduce militance on the part of blacks."[91]

This propaganda effort took several forms. Most obvious was official "jawboning" against discrimination. The president set the tone in his January 1942 State of the Union Address, saying, "We must be particularly vigilant against racial discrimination in any of its ugly forms."[92] A nation fighting for the Four Freedoms could hardly be seen as denying them to its own citizens, especially when it needed the help of nonwhites around the world. In addition, discrimination impeded the nation's total mobilization for war. "In some communities," remarked the president, "employers . . . are reluctant to hire Negroes. We can no longer afford to indulge such prejudice."[93]

The OWI published and distributed 2.5 million copies of the pamphlet *Negroes and the War*. It aimed to bolster black morale by showing that though America did have racial problems, they were not pervasive and had been steadily decreasing, especially since 1933. The pamphlet also stressed that blacks would be far worse off under Hitler. Though rather innocuous, *Negroes and the War* met with an overwhelmingly negative response. Blacks characterized it as "just a bunch of baloney" while white southern conservatives accused the OWI of fomenting racial animosity.[94] Less overtly, the OWI also attempted to improve black morale and lessen white racism by persuading Hollywood studios to begin portraying blacks and racial equality in a more sympathetic light.[95]

The government often used boxer Joe Louis as both a symbol and a spokesperson to improve black morale and lessen white racism. Louis, who had enlisted in the army shortly after Pearl Harbor, was touted as the "first American to kayo a Nazi" and was featured in recruiting posters and propaganda films. The military hoped that Louis's military service and his claim that "We are going to do our part, and we will win, because we are on God's side," would help motivate blacks to support the war effort. In addition, by publicizing Louis's quiet demeanor and work for military charities, the military sought to create a more positive white image of blacks.[96]

Not all of the federal government's responses to black morale were so benign. In fact, many in the government believed that black criticisms of the war effort stemmed not from real grievances but from outside agitation. Concerned that foreign agents were stirring up black discontent, the Roosevelt administration ordered FBI surveillance of civil rights groups. These efforts began in 1941 when the FBI installed wiretaps in the headquarters of the March on Washington Committee and placed informants in the organization. The program expanded the following year to include groups ranging from the National Negro Congress to the NAACP and continued throughout the war.[97]

Of still greater concern to the federal government was the black press, with its constant publicizing of racial incidents and calls for victory at home as well as abroad. According to an OWI memorandum, "The Negro press is flagrantly abusing the privilege [of freedom of the press] everyday. Much of the present unrest among the Negro population is due to the inflammatory and extremist tenor of the Negro papers. . . . As long as the Negro press is permitted to continue its present practices with impunity, we can expect very little improvement in morale of the Negro population."[98] The OWI tried to get black newspapers to tone down their reporting, and it also recommended that the Attorney General Biddle investigate several papers for possible sedition. Biddle, a strong civil libertarian (except when in came to interning Japanese Americans), refused to bring any sedition charges against the black press, though he did complain to black editors about their coverage.[99] The army had fewer concerns about civil liberties; black newspapers were banned on several posts.[100]

The Roosevelt administration's efforts to maintain racial peace during the war cut both ways. Just as it was willing to make concessions to blacks to advance its political agenda and help the war effort, it was also willing to make concessions to whites for the same reasons. In fact, these concerns led the White House to rein in the FEPC's already limited power. Attacks on the FEPC following the Birmingham hearings made the White House fearful of losing southern votes in the upcoming congressional elections and in the 1944 presidential contest. Shortly before the November 1942 elections, Gessner McCorvey, chair of the Alabama Democratic party warned the Democratic National Committee (DNC) of a "rising tide of indignation" that was "sweeping over the South as a result of the orders and regulations coming out of Washington dealing with the Negro questions down here."[101] On election day, the Democrats suffered a severe drubbing nationally and almost lost their congressional majorities. Afterwards, DNC surveys found criticism of Roosevelt and the New Deal strongest in the South.[102] Early the following year, governors Frank Dixon of Alabama and Sam Jones of Louisiana began threatening to form a third party.[103]

Southern conservatives were not the only ones criticizing the FEPC. The State Department claimed that the FEPC's exposure of discrimination was providing material for Axis propaganda.[104] Even administration liberals condemned the commission. Victor Rotnem, head of the Justice Department's Civil Rights Section, called the FEPC a "political mistake" that was "liable to explode at any moment" and do "infinite harm to the political interests of the administration" by catering to the "professional Negro" and providing new "ammunition" to the "Southern rebellion."[105]

In June 1942, these pressures led President Roosevelt to reassign the FEPC to the War Manpower Commission (WMC), where it could be kept under tighter control. That control was most apparent in January 1943 when WMC Chairman Paul McNutt announced that he had "indefinitely postponed" proposed FEPC hearings into discriminatory practices by southern railroads.[106] That same month, frustrated by his inability to convince or shame the military into lessening its Jim Crow policies, William Hastie resigned as civilian advisor to the secretary of war. In his letter of resignation, he declared the military's handling "of racial issues has been reactionary and unsatisfactory from the outset."[107]

If that was the case for African Americans, it was vastly more so in the case of all Americans with ancestral links to the nation's Pacific enemy. In regard to Japanese Americans, the propensities of military and civilian government officials, the press, and popular opinion to treat various people of color as potential subversives not only went unchecked; the war fired anti-Japanese sentiments to an unprecedented intensity. On February 19, 1942, President Roosevelt issued Executive Order 9066, permitting the secretary of war and his military subordinates to designate military zones "from which any or all persons may be excluded." By the end of 1942, Lieutenant General John L. DeWitt, operating out of his imposing Fourth Army headquarters at the Presidio in San Francisco, had ordered the internment of all but a handful of west coast Japanese Americans into ten "relocation centers" (originally termed "concentration camps"). Many would remain there until 1946. His reasons were given in a "final recommendation" the general had signed and sent to Assistant Secretary of War John J. McCloy in February. It explained that the "Japanese race is an enemy race," that "racial affinities are not severed by migration," and that even among "third generation Japanese born in the United States," the "racial strains are undiluted." Hence even citizenship should provide no protection against relocation. Meanwhile, the media were vilifying all people of Japanese origins, often with grotesque racist stereotypes. A San Francisco columnist expressed the dominant mood, saying, "I hate the Japanese. And that goes for all of them."[108]

With the federal government actively locking up Japanese Americans as an "enemy race" and timidly temporizing on discrimination against blacks, few African Americans were content with prevailing policies. An OWI survey of white and black attitudes in March 1943 showed a vast chasm between blacks and whites. The great majority of blacks were dissatisfied with their treatment during the war. Approximately 70 percent felt that they were denied the chance to participate equally in the war effort. Blacks were almost equally split on whether the country should focus on winning the war or making democracy work at home first. On the other hand, both southern and northern whites overwhelmingly endorsed segregation—less than one-half of 1 percent of whites were willing to give blacks the "chance to the go to the same places" and 90 percent endorsed segregation in military units. Whites and blacks also divided drastically on the role of the federal government in race relations (see table

Table 3. Black and White Opinions of Government Efforts for Blacks,
March 1943

	Whites	Blacks
Doing too much	17%	0%
About right	46	18
Should do more	9	73
Don't know	28	9

Source: Morris J. MacGregor and Bernard C. Nalty, *Black Soldiers in World War II*, vol. 5 *of Blacks in the United States Armed Forces: Basic Documents* (Wilmington, Del.: Scholarly Resources, 1977), p. 187.

3). As the OWI report concluded, whites lacked the "disposition to make any fundamental concessions to black demands."[109]

These racial animosities soon ignited into violence. Like a string of firecrackers, race riots exploded in quick succession across the country. The first came on May 25 in Mobile, Alabama when the Alabama Dry Dock and Ship Building Company promoted several black workers to the job of welders in compliance with an FEPC directive. Shouting, "No nigger is goin' to join iron in these yards," whites there began attacking blacks. Order was restored only after 350 state guardsmen and federal troops were sent into the yard and the company reassigned the black welders.[110] Less than two weeks later, on June 3, mobs of white sailors, soldiers, and some civilians in Los Angeles staged a pogrom against "zoot-suited" Chicano and black youths. Egged on by local newspapers that blamed the violence on the "zoot-suiters," the riot went on for five days.[111] Two days later, on June 9, whites in Beaumont, Texas rioted after hearing reports that a black man had raped a white woman. After being told that the black suspect had been taken to another jail, a white mob ran loose in the city's black section, dragging blacks from their homes and cars and beating them. Two blacks were killed and seventy-three were wounded.[112]

The worst violence occurred in Detroit. The previous August's issue of *Life* magazine had declared "Detroit is Dynamite" and had claimed that, because of the city's racial friction, it "can either blow up Hitler or it can blow up the U.S."[113] Since then, tensions had only mounted. In early June 1943, a hate strike at Packard Motors idled twenty-five thousand workers and halted 95 percent of the plant's production of bomber engines after whites walked out to protest the upgrading of three blacks.[114] One white worker proclaimed, "I'd rather see Hitler and Hirohito win than work next to a nigger."[115] Throughout June, a series of small-scale racial clashes took place in and around the city. After the riot, Detroit Mayor Edward Jeffries would comment that he "was taken by surprise only by the day it happened."[116]

That day was Sunday, June 20. As the temperature topped 90 degrees, thousands of blacks and whites crowded into the park on Detroit's Belle Isle. Throughout the day, several fights broke out between blacks and whites. By 10 P.M., a full-scale riot had broken out on the bridge linking the island to the mainland. It soon spread into the city. In several areas, blacks attacked innocent whites, but most of the violence was by whites, often aided by the police, against blacks. By the next day, as many as ten thousand whites were on a rampage against Detroit's blacks; 75 percent of the city's police precincts reported riot activity. Those injured in the violence were entering city hospitals at the rate of one every minute. That morning, Mayor Jeffries and Michigan governor Harry Kelly requested federal troops be sent in to put down the riots. Miscommunications and an uncertain chain of command meant that the first soldiers were not deployed for another twelve hours, however, and it was not until Thursday that the city was back to something approaching normal. By then, twenty-five blacks and nine whites had been killed, with hundreds more injured.[117]

Although it was the worst riot that year, Detroit's was not the last. In August, Harlem exploded after a white policeman shot a black solider. In total, Fisk University's Social Science Institute counted 242 incidents of racial violence in forty-seven cities in 1943. Nor was the unrest limited to cities. Military bases also saw an increase in racial violence as black soldiers continued to suffer under Jim Crow. Perhaps most galling was the sight of white German prisoners of war receiving better treatment than they were given. As poet Wittner Bynner wrote:

> On a train in Texas German prisoners eat
> With white American soldiers, seat by seat,
> While black American soldiers sit apart—
> The white men eating meat, the black men heart.[118]

Unlike the violence of the previous two years, the incidents at military bases in 1943 were more likely to occur in the camps themselves than in nearby towns, were more likely to have been organized beforehand, and the black soldiers were more likely to have been aggressors than victims.[119] The first major incident came in May at Camp Van Dorn in Mississippi after Private William Walker, a black soldier, was shot during a fight with white MPs and local law enforcement officers. Walker's comrades seized a cache of rifles and attempted to leave the camp in search of the killers. A squad of black MPs opened fire on them, wounding one. Only quick action by the unit's white commander and the regimental chaplain prevented more violence.[120] A similar mutiny took place at Camp Stewart near Savannah, Georgia in June. The following month, black soldiers from Camp McCain in Mississippi retaliated against local whites by firing on the hamlet of Duck Hill. No one was hurt, but the incident led to the court-martialing of six soldiers.[121] Violent incidents took place at in at least ten other camps around the country.[122] The following year, violence on military bases declined, but this did not signal black satisfaction. Rather, as Daniel Kryder has shown, black soldiers were now likely to respond to discrimination more through organized protests rather than brawls.[123]

This latest wave of violence prompted a significant change in the attitudes of many whites. If not convinced of the morality of racial equality, many now saw that racial friction and violence were serious impediments to the war effort. Every soldier needed to keep the peace in Beaumont or Detroit was a soldier kept from fighting the war in Europe or the Pacific. In just three months from March 1 to May 31, 1943, hate strikes over the upgrading of black workers resulted in the loss of nearly 2.5 million man hours of war production.[124] The Detroit riot caused the loss of an additional 1 million man hours of war production, a total greater than that lost due to labor disputes during the first two months of the year.[125] Racial violence and Jim Crow also continued to hurt America in the battle for hearts and minds. As Radio Tokyo broadcast to Asia, "It is a singular fact that supposedly civilized Americans in these time deny the Negroes the opportunity to engage in respectable jobs, the right of access to restaurants, theaters or the same train accommodations as themselves, and periodically will run amuck to lynch Negroes individually or to slaughter them wholesale—old men, women, and children alike—in race wars like the present one."[126] White Americans recognized that such propaganda was effective because it was essentially true.

Hence the war made civil rights an important feature of American discourse for the first time since Reconstruction. Over the next year, more than two hundred local, state, and national committees were established "to promote better race relations," including twenty in Chicago alone. Most of these committees accomplished little, but their creation suggests an important shift in white attitudes.[127] One pamphlet designed to help these groups avoid race riots declared, "Racism warps personalities in unlovely and hateful directions. It continues Hitler's work in this live, free land." The pamphlet also contained a quiz that allowed readers to determine, "How good a citizen of a democracy are you?" One question asked, "Do you believe in 'white supremacy,' that 'international bankers' are all Jews, that colored groups are made up of people who are all 'childish, irresponsible, and lazy'?" Those who responded, "No. Besides being untrue, these catch phrases endanger democracy," received ten points. The response, "I'm not quite sure," was worth only five points, while those who answered, "Of course I do!" scored zero points.[128]

At the same time, white liberals produced a flood of books arguing for greater racial equality. Journalist Selden Menefee in *Assignment: U.S.A.* called race "the weakest point in our domestic battle-front. . . . If we want to produce and fight efficiently and to command the respect and affection of our Allies in Asia and Latin America, we must show our good will by fair treatment of our racial minorities."[129] In *Brothers Under the Skin,* Carey McWilliams declared that "[r]acial segregation, like slavery itself, is a malignant growth in a democracy. Biracialism is stultifying, costly, stupid, and self-perpetuating."[130] Former GOP presidential candidate Wendell Willkie in his book *One World,* which sold 1 million copies in two months, denounced what he called "race imperialism" by white Americans. He warned, "When we talk of freedom and opportunity for all nations, the mocking paradoxes in our own society become so clear they can no longer be ignored. If we want to talk about freedom, we must mean freedom for others as well as ourselves, and we must mean freedom for everyone inside our frontier as well as outside. During a war, this is especially important."[131]

Easily the most influential statement on American race relations in this period (or perhaps in any other) was Gunnar Myrdal's *An American Dilemma,* published in January 1944. Although Myrdal, a Swedish economist, began the project in 1938, the war greatly influenced his conclusions. Myrdal saw America as the champion of liberal, democratic ideals in the global struggle against fascism and dictatorship. Racism and inequality, however, contradicted what Myrdal labeled America's democratic "creed" and thus weakened it militarily and ideologically in that struggle.[132] Moreover, Myrdal biographer Walter Jackson asserted that most scholars viewed Myrdal's project "as if it were part of the war effort—a large, collaborative enterprise to produce a report for the general public on a sensitive issue bound up with the morale of American troops, the productivity of the war industries, and the ideology of the war against fascism."[133]

In the book, Myrdal presented a radical reformulation of America's racial problems. The "Negro problem" was in fact a "white man's problem." Race, as a biological construct, according to Myrdal, accounted for little when examining blacks' unequal status in American society. Instead, white racism and not innate inferiority determined black inequality. This racism directly contradicted whites' own "American creed" of "liberty, equality, justice, and fair opportunity for everybody." Myrdal was aware that through much of U.S. history white supremacy had been a rival American "creed," but he confidently dismissed such views as discredited prejudices.[134] As Stephan and Abigail Thernstrom have written, *An American Dilemma* "concocted an American moral tradition by reading the past selectively, emphasizing things that fit with contemporary racial liberalism and ignoring those that did not." But this "fictitious history" served the goal of arguing that "the federal government should do more to combat" racial discrimination.[135] Myrdal rejected both fatalism and gradualism, declaring that through a conscious program of legal and educational social engineering, America could solve its dilemma. "America," he wrote, "is free to choose whether the Negro shall remain her liability or become her opportunity."[136]

At the time, Myrdal's now-familiar conclusions were revolutionary. Before the war nearly all white Americans believed that blacks were in some ways their inferiors and even among the most committed of liberals, only a few believe that much could be done about racism and racial inequality in the near term. Even so, in newspapers, magazines, and academic journals, white Americans responded to *An American Dilemma* with almost universal acclaim. Even *Time* and *Life* magazines, the twin embodiments of middle-class white attitudes and values of the day, praised it lavishly. Declaring racial conflict to be "America's No. 1 social problem," *Life*'s editors cited the book as "timely expert advice." *Time* compared Myrdal to Alexis de Tocqueville and Lord Bryce in his perceptive analysis of America. If the book had appeared only a decade earlier, reactions would likely have been sharply different; but the catalyst of war had fundamentally altered racial attitudes, making white Americans receptive to Myrdal's thesis, at least temporarily. Tellingly, *Time* reviewed *An American Dilemma* under the heading, "U.S. At War."[137]

Racial concerns were not limited to works of nonfiction. In 1944, the novel *Strange Fruit*, Lillian Smith's tale of an interracial affair, climbed the best-seller lists and eventually sold 3 million copies. Smith, a white southern liberal, bluntly claimed that fighting for democracy while defending Jim Crow was like "trying to buy a new world with old Confederate bills."[138] Richard Wright's *Black Boy*, a searing autobiographical account of growing up black in Mississippi, was one of the most acclaimed and popular books of 1945.[139]

The movies also showed the growth of racial liberalism. Prior to World War II, Hollywood cast blacks almost exclusively in demeaning and stereotyped roles. In the words of screenwriter Dalton Trumbo, the movies made "tarts of the Negro's daughters, crap shooters of his sons, obsequious Uncle Toms of his fathers, superstitious and grotesque crones of his mothers, strutting peacocks of his successful men, psalm-singing mountebanks of his priests, and Barnum and Bailey side-shows of his religion."[140] Although films still had more than their share of mammies and Stepin Fetchits during the war, black roles showed a noticeable improvement. The appearance of strong, important, and nontraditional black characters suggested that white audiences were willing to consider blacks in a new, more positive light.

One of the first and best films to reflect this change was *Casablanca* (1943), which portrayed the black character of Sam (Dooley Wilson) as the friend, business partner, and relative equal of the white protagonist, Rick (Humphrey Bogart). Even though Sam was still in the stereotypical black role of musician, the film cleverly attempted to explode that stereotype as well as others. When Ilsa (Ingrid Bergman) praises Sam's natural ability as a musician, he replies that his talent comes from twelve years of training at Juilliard rather than from any innate ability. "Well," responds Ilsa, "all the best theories are going under these days."[141]

In *Bataan* (1943) and *Sahara* (1943), Kenneth Spencer and Rex Ingram, respectively, played competent and heroic black soldiers, even though their real-life counterparts were still largely restricted from combat.[142] Thomas Cripps pointed out that in *Bataan*, Spencer's character Epps "was calculatedly centered in the frame, given a military skill, a place in the action, and a civilian calling, all unthinkable attributes before the war that inspired them."[143] Hollywood also took on the race-laden issue of lynching in *The Ox-Bow Incident* (1943). Although the victims in the story are white, the racial angle was still evident. Leigh Whipper played a black preacher who sought unsuccessfully to prevent the lynching. In addition, at head of the lynch mob was a former Confederate officer—though eventually his rank was revealed to be a sham.[144]

From books to magazines to movies, it is clear that in the years 1943 to 1944 civil rights was emerging as an important national issue.[145] This was particularly true for liberals; and their thinking about possible solutions was changing. As historian Alan Brinkley pointed out, liberals began moving "from a preoccupation with 'reform' (with a set of essentially class-based issues centering around confronting the problem of monopoly and economic disorder) and toward a preoccupation with 'rights' (a commitment to the liberation of oppressed peoples and groups)."[146]

In this climate of shifting attitudes and domestic political pressures, the problems of racial violence, and especially the severe needs of the war, federal officials found it increasingly difficult to delay addressing racial inequalities. Until now the military had been the branch of government most resistant to change, but worries over discipline and adequate manpower compelled it to take the lead in starting to dismantle Jim Crow. The wave of violence at military installations in the summer of 1943 convinced the army's high command that black morale problems could no longer be ignored. "My God! My God! . . . I don't know what to do about this race question in the army," General Marshall told one reporter. "I tell you frankly, it is the worst thing we have to deal with. . . . We are getting a situation on our hands that may explode right in our faces."[147]

On July 3, Marshall issued an order calling for "continuous and vigorous action to prevent incidents of discrimination."[148] The War Department's new Advisory Committee on Negro Troop Policies, established the previous year under Assistant Secretary of War John J. McCloy, successfully urged further steps. One was to increase transportation on and off bases for blacks, a source of much friction. In 1944, the McCloy committee won an order for the desegregation of all facilities on military bases and military-operated transport. This order was certainly significant, but it did not end military Jim Crow practices; segregation on the basis of units was still allowed, and most blacks were assigned to separate units.[149]

The military also began an extensive educational program to strengthen black morale and lessen white racism. In February 1944, the army issued a new pamphlet for its officers, *The Command of Negro Troops.* Directly contravening prewar conventional wisdom, the pamphlet explained differences between white and black soldiers in terms of differing levels of education, not inherent abilities. It also explicitly linked racism with Nazism, declaring that "effective command cannot be based on racial theories. The Germans have a theory that they are a race of supermen born to conquer all peoples of inferior blood. This is nonsense, the like of which has no place in the Army of the United States—the Army of a Nation which has become great through the common effort of all people."[150] The pamphlet is all the more remarkable when one compares it to the army's prewar statements regarding blacks' limited cranial capacities and their inherited mental deficiencies.

For enlisted men, the army produced *The Negro Soldier*, a documentary film that extolled the virtues of black military service in American history and showed how important blacks were to the current war effort. Although rather heavy-handed in its message, the film was extremely popular with both black and white audiences. One army survey of viewers found that 90 percent of blacks and 80 percent of whites believed that it should be shown to all new soldiers. This the army soon did, making it mandatory viewing in all U.S. training centers and releasing it for civilian distribution where it was widely seen. In doing so, Thomas Cripps pointed out, "the army had joined with black activists and white social engineers in tutoring its troops [and many civilians] in an NAACP social goal that had all but become a war aim—'racial tolerance.' "[151]

Manpower shortages played an even more important role in altering the military's racial practices. The popular conception of World War II suggests that America possessed nearly limitless amounts of both men and material. Even though the nation did have an abundance of material, wars are fought and won by soldiers, and these America had only in short supply. One reason was the military's initial unwillingness to accept a proportionate share of blacks. By 1943, three hundred thousand eligible blacks had been passed over in draft calls. A government official pointed out the potential for trouble "as the single white registrants disappear and husbands and fathers become the white inductees, while single Negro registrants who are physically fit remain uninducted."[152] In response, in 1943 the Selective Service ended its practice of having separate calls for black and white draftees. As manpower shortages worsened, the military began lowering its strict literacy requirements, a standard instituted to limit the number of black soldiers. The services also began special remedial education programs for both black and white illiterates that eventually trained an additional 136,000 blacks.[153]

Manpower needs and pressure from the black press and civil rights groups also forced the military to begin sending black units into combat. Until then, worries about the abilities of black troops under fire had largely kept blacks off the front lines. One of the few black combat units put into action was the 99th Pursuit Squadron, the famed "Tuskegee Airmen." Although the air corps had planned to assign them to noncombat duties, pressure from black groups and, most importantly, the shortage of fighter units in North Africa in 1943 at last compelled their combat use.[154] After a rocky start, due mainly to segregation policies that kept the black pilots from gaining experience by flying with veteran (white) units, the squadron eventually proved itself in combat over Sicily and Italy. The performance of the 99th convinced the air corps to add three more black squadrons. The four black squadrons, designated the 332nd Fighter Group, ended the war among the most decorated units in the air corps. The men of the 332nd shot down 111 enemy planes and earned 865 Legion of Merit, 95 Distinguished Flying Crosses, 1 Silver Star, 14 Bronze Stars, 744 Air Medals, 8 Purple Hearts, and a Presidential Citation for the Group. In addition, the unit never lost a bomber under its escort to enemy planes.[155]

Despite the heroism of the Tuskegee airmen, the army still proved reluctant to use blacks in ground combat and began converting several black combat units to service units. The *Pittsburgh Courier* editorialized against this policy, "The tactics appear to disclose a determination to prohibit Negroes . . . from reaching any of the front lines where they might gain glory and prestige for themselves and their race." General Benjamin O. Davis warned the War Department that as a result of refusing to use them in combat, the "colored soldier has lost confidence in the fairness of the Army to Negro troops."[156] Representative Hamilton Fish recalled the bravery of the black soldiers that he had led in World War I. He told the House of Representatives, "Fourteen millions of loyal Americans have the right to expect that in a war for the advancement of the 'four freedoms' that their sons be given the same right as any other American to train, to serve, and to fight in combat units in defense of the United States in this the greatest war in its history."[157]

In response to these concerns, both military and political, the War Department agreed in early 1944 to begin committing black combat units. The first to see action were two battalions of infantry on the island of Bougainville in the South Pacific. Although they performed competently, these and other black units in the Pacific were later used mostly for garrison and mopping-up operations. The first black division to enter combat was the 92nd Infantry Division, sent to Italy in June 1944. Its record was mixed, but the unit was clearly hampered by poor training and officers who were often less than competent and/or racist. Other blacks units performed well, especially those that received better training and leadership because they were more closely integrated into larger white units.[158]

After the invasion of France in June 1944, manpower concerns grew yet more acute. By that fall, American forces in Europe faced a growing shortage of infantry riflemen, the most important element in any army. The crisis came in December when the Germans launched a major counter-offensive in the Ardennes Forest. The resulting Battle of the Bulge was the largest military engagement ever fought by America and it placed great strains on army manpower. Already seriously undermanned, American forces suffered over fifty thousand casualties (almost all in the infantry) in the first week of the battle.[159]

Just as in the Civil War, the army turned to blacks to fill its depleted ranks in time of need. General John C. H. Lee, the commander responsible for logistics in Europe, issued an order on December 26 calling for black volunteers for combat infantry units, promising them that they would be assigned "without regard to color or race to the units where assistance is most needed, and give you the opportunity of fighting shoulder to shoulder to bring about victory."[160] This went a bit too far for General Dwight D. Eisenhower, the Supreme Commander of Allied Forces in Europe. Ike rewrote the order two weeks later, withdrawing the promise of service in integrated units and saying instead that if black volunteers could not be used in existing black units, "these men will be suitably incorporated in other organizations so that their service and fighting spirit may be efficiently utilized."[161]

Nonetheless, thousands of black soldiers responded with enthusiasm, so many in fact that over three thousand had to be turned away. Since only privates were wanted, many higher ranking blacks took demotions for the chance to prove themselves on the front lines. In one black unit, 171 of 186 men volunteered.[162] Black volunteers were organized into platoons or companies and mixed in with white units. Although blacks and whites were not yet fighting "shoulder to shoulder," this was the most advanced integration of the U.S. army since the Revolutionary War.[163]

Despite any fears that the army might have had, *Stars and Stripes* (the army's newspaper) reported in April 1945 that "[i]f comments of white personnel of these divisions are any indication, the plan of mixing white and colored troops in fighting units, a departure from previous United States Army practice, is operating successfully."[164] An army survey of white officers and noncommissioned officers

(NCOs) who fought with black units offers convincing proof for this assertion. Although most whites initially felt unfavorable toward working with black troops, the experience left them open to integration. Perhaps the most striking findings are that none of the whites surveyed felt less favorable about serving with black units after having done so and the near-unanimous opinion that black units had performed well in combat (see table 4).

Anecdotal sources back up these survey results. One white officer rated black soldiers as "aggressive fighters. The only trouble is getting them to stop. They just keep on pushing." According to a platoon sergeant from South Carolina, "When I heard about it I said I'd be damned if I'd wear the same patch they did. After that first day when we saw how they fought I changed my mind. They're just like any of the other boys to us."[165] Another white South Carolinian said, "I don't give a damn what color a man is as long as he's up here helping to win this war."[166]

After blacks rioted over segregation at a navy base during the summer of 1943, that service also moved to ease tensions and established a Special Programs Unit. The unit convinced the navy to begin training black officers and, as an experiment, to allow an all-black crew, under white officers, to man a handful of ships. These segregated crews performed well, but the navy ended the experiment in 1944. The new secretary of the navy, James Forrestal, was a strong civil rights advocate who believed that the most efficient use of black

Table 4. Attitudes of White Soldiers toward Serving with Black Units

	White Officers (%)	White NCOs (%)
Initial feelings about serving with black units		
Relatively unfavorable	64	64
Relatively favorable	33	35
No answer	3	1
Feelings after serving with black units		
Still the same	16	21
More favorable	77	77
Less favorable	0	0
No answer	7	2
Opinions of black combat performance		
Not well at all	0	0
No so well	0	1
Fairly well	16	17
Very well	84	81
Undecided	0	1

Source: Morris J. MacGregor and Bernard C. Nalty, *Black Soldiers in World War II*, vol. 5 of *Blacks in the United States Armed Forces: Basic Documents* (Wilmington, Del.: Scholarly Resources, 1977), pp. 514–5.

sailors was in integrated units. According to him, "[t]he Negroes resent the fact that they are not assigned to general service billets and white personnel resent the fact that Negroes have been given less hazardous assignment ashore."[167] In the summer of 1944, Forrestal began integrating the crews of twenty-five auxiliary ships, aiming eventually to integrate the rest of the navy's vessels. His initial efforts succeeded, and integration of additional ships continued until the end of the war.[168]

Blacks also made important strides in civilian war-related employment. Between January 1942 and January 1944, the percentage of black workers in the defense industries grew from 3 to 8.3 percent.[169] Blacks also increased the quality of the jobs they held. In 1940, only 4.4 percent of all black males held skilled jobs, but by 1944 the figure had grown to 7.3 percent. Consequently, the black percentage of skilled workers rose from 2.6 to 3.6 percent during this period.[170] "These changes," according to Robert Weaver, resulted in "more industrial and occupational diversification for negroes than had occurred in the 75 preceding years."[171]

Although much of this increase was due to wartime labor shortages, the federal government also played a significant part in expanding black employment opportunities. In 1943, the War Labor Board banned racial differentials in wages, the U.S. Employment Service forbad race-specific job listings, and the National Labor Relations Board ruled that it would no longer certify unions that barred minority members.[172] Most importantly, protests by civil rights organizations forced the Roosevelt administration in May 1943 to restore the FEPC as an independent agency and to increase its staff and budget. Even though still limited in its mission and resources and constantly harried by southern members of Congress, the FEPC persisted in its efforts to achieve greater black participation in defense industries.

Perhaps the most crucial moment in the FEPC's history came in 1944 during the Philadelphia transit strike. After the FEPC ordered the Philadelphia Transportation Company to accept blacks for jobs as motormen and conductors on its streetcars, white employers staged a strike that shut down the city's transit system on August 1. To a cheering crowd of white workers, one strike leader declared, "We don't want Negroes and we won't work with Negroes. This is a white man's job. Put the Negroes back where they belong."[173] The strike's impact was significant; Philadelphia was the nation's second largest war production center and the strike prevented thousands of workers from going to work.[174] The Philadelphia Navy Yard reported 72 percent of its workers were absent during the strike.[175] Furthermore, fears ran high that the strike might lead to a race riot like that in Detroit the previous summer.[176]

Faced with similar white resistance and concerns over disruptions in war production, the FEPC had backed away from its antidiscrimination order in the Mobile shipyards the previous year. This time it held firm. Even more importantly, President Roosevelt decided to back up the agency; so for the first time since Reconstruction, the federal government used the military to enforce a civil rights measure. On August 3, the president ordered the army to take over the transit system. Two days later, five thousand soldiers entered the city and began operating the streetcars.[177] The Justice Department arrested the strike's ringleaders and the Selective Service announced that it would begin drafting any transit workers who failed to report to their jobs. Consequently, the strike collapsed, the streetcars began running again, and black motormen and conductors soon became a permanent presence on Philadelphia's transit system.

The FEPC's success in the Philadelphia transit strike helped it to desegregate the transit system in Los Angeles and greatly enhanced its influence in other cases.[178] Even if labor shortages were paramount in increasing black employment, these FEPC efforts still mattered. According to the most recent and thorough survey of the FEPC, the Committee's "stress on qualifications and quality was a startling idea whose time had not come as far as the vast majority of white war workers and their employers were concerned. . . . That market forces alone, in the absence of an FEPC, could have overcome prejudice and produced a similar emphasis on quality is doubtful."[179] Furthermore, the success of the FEPC in the Philadelphia transit strike showed that with sufficient will, the federal government had the capacity to enforce civil rights.

The FEPC also played a crucial role in opening up federal employment to blacks during the war. In 1938, blacks comprised 9.8 percent of the federal workforce. By 1944, the number had risen to 12 percent. In addition, blacks on the federal payroll increasingly won positions requiring more skills and responsibility. In 1938, approximately 90 percent of all blacks working for the federal government were custodians, 9.5 percent clerical-administrative, and 0.5 percent subprofessional or professional. In 1944, only 39.6 percent were classified as custodial or crafts-protective, while 49 percent were in clerical-administrative and fiscal jobs, 9.9 percent clerical-mechanical, and 1.1 percent subprofessional or professional.[180]

The most important wartime step taken by the federal government to advance black equality came in 1944, when the Supreme Court struck down the "white primary" in *Smith v. Allwright*.[181] Barring blacks from voting in Democratic primaries, the only real electoral contests in the solidly Democratic South, the white primary was described by political scientist Ralph Bunche as "the most effective device for the exclusion of Negroes from the polls in the South and, therefore, the most effective political instrument for the preservation of white supremacy."[182] Less than a decade earlier in *Grovey v. Townsend*, the Supreme Court had unanimously upheld the white primary, claiming that political parties were private associations, not agents of the state government and hence not covered by the Fifteenth Amendment's protection against racial discrimination in voting.[183] In the *Smith* decision, however, the Court reversed its earlier decision and ruled 8-1 that primaries were an integral part of the election process. Whether delegated or not, the power to control primary elections was under the authority of the state and therefore protected by the Fifteenth Amendment.[184]

The Court's decision in *Smith* reflected its emerging stress on the protection of civil and political rights, an emphasis influenced by the changing global context. One of the first and most important statements of this doctrine was by Justice Harlan Fiske Stone in *United States v. Carolene Products*, where he declared that the Court would apply a more rigorous test of constitutionality to legislation that violated the guarantees of the Bill of Rights or discriminated against "discrete and insular minorities."[185] The day after delivering that decision, Stone wrote to a friend, "I have been deeply concerned about the increasing racial and religious intolerance which seems to bedevil the world, and which I greatly fear may be augmented in this country."[186] Stone would later author the Court's opinion in *United States v. Classic*, which paved the way for *Smith* by declaring primaries to be an integral part of the election process.[187]

Although Justice Stanley Reed made no mention of the war in his opinion in *Smith*, to at least one observer at the time, the connection was clear. Arthur Krock, the Washington correspondent for the *New York Times*, wrote, "Neither [Reed] nor [Justice Owen Roberts, the sole dissenter] mentioned the real reason for the overturn [of *Grovey*]. It is that the common sacrifices of wartime have turned public opinion and the Court against previously sustained devices to exclude minorities."[188] More recently, historian Darlene Clark Hine wrote, "The white primary was one of the casualties of World War II."[189]

The sacrifices of wartime also, however, impelled public opinion and the Court toward much harsher treatment of one minority,

Japanese Americans, as shown by another landmark 1944 case, *Korematsu v. United States*. In this decision the majority of the Court delivered the most important of several rulings upholding the curfews and forced internments imposed by General De Witt on the west coast Japanese. Justice Hugo Black's opinion for the majority reflected the Court's new emphasis on civil rights generally by insisting that "legal restrictions which curtail the civil rights of a single racial group are immediately suspect." Yet even so, he concluded that, given the difficulty of telling "the disloyal from the loyal" among persons of Japanese descent, De Witt's measures had been legitimate products of a "military imperative" born of "real military dangers," not expressions of "racial prejudice." Justice Frank Murphy in dissent acknowledged the military situation on the west coast in 1942, but he argued powerfully that it did not explain or justify the government's actions. Instead, he pointed to the racial reasoning used to advocate internment—the fact that German Americans and Italian Americans received individualized judgments of whether they were security threats or not, unlike Japanese Americans; the fact that the British had rapidly made individualized assessments of all the persons they deemed security risks, regardless of race; and the fact that no Japanese Americans had ever actually been found guilty of subversion—to conclude that the Court's decision upholding Fred Korematsu's internment amounted to a "legalization of racism."[190]

The *Korematsu* ruling is compelling evidence of how crucial World War II, and wars generally, have been in shaping America's racial destiny. Even as wartime imperatives generally drove the U.S. government toward greater realization of American ideals of racial equality, especially for blacks, the same imperatives drove the same executive and judicial branch officers to endorse policies that reflected and reinforced America's "Yellow Peril" racist traditions. Ward W. Y. Elliott later wrote, "The war surely limited the power of the Court in some race questions, like those involved in the Japanese internment cases, but it strengthened the Court's hand immeasurably for intervening against white primaries because of national sympathy for the fighting man, including the black fighting man. It would be surprising if [the Court] had not been disposed to help the blacks vote in primaries if a way could be found."[191] By the same token, it would have been surprising if the Court had not sustained Japanese American internment. The nation's conflicted racial past, and the temptation to respond to pressing emergencies in whatever way seems most immediately effective, made that route all too convenient.

Yet even though the white primary rulings expressed wartime concerns fully as much as *Korematsu,* the *Smith* decision still stunned and angered the white South. South Carolina senator "Cotton" Ed Smith avowed that "all those who love South Carolina and the white man's rule will rally in this hour of her great Gethsemane to save her from a disastrous fate."[192] Even Senator Claude Pepper, a determined foe of the poll tax denounced the decision and declared that "the South will allow nothing to impair white supremacy."[193] Several states quickly passed laws to evade the decision. One of these was South Carolina, which sought to make primaries strictly private affairs by repealing all such laws regarding elections.[194] The plan failed. The federal courts overturned these newly constituted white primaries.

These court decisions came from an unlikely pair of judges. The first was federal district court judge J. Waties Waring. Nominated for the bench by "Cotton" Ed himself, Waring's views on race underwent a remarkable transformation during the war. In particular, his reading of Myrdal's *An American Dilemma* proved crucial to his emerging racial liberalism. Waring struck down South Carolina's attempt to nullify the *Smith* decision, dismissing the state's reasoning as "pure sophistry." In addition, he cited the importance of racial equality for America's international position and called on South Carolina to "rejoin the Union."[195] The case then went to the U.S. Court of Appeals and Judge John J. Parker, who in 1930 had been rejected by the Senate for nomination to the Supreme Court in part because of opposition by the NAACP, who criticized earlier statements by him in favor of black disfranchisement. This time, Parker could not have pleased the NAACP more, declaring that "no election machinery can be upheld if its purpose or effect is to deny to the Negro . . . any effective voice in the government."[196]

The abolition of the white primary was the first serious boost to black voting in decades. According to one analysis of black voting, "Once the white primary had been killed, the number and proportion of Negroes registered to vote in the southern states increased with startling speed." In 1940, only 250,000 southern blacks were registered to vote. By 1947, however, the number had risen to 595,000 and by 1952 (after various efforts to evade the decision had been struck down) it was over 1 million (see tables 5 and 6). Moreover, these blacks were no longer limited to voting in meaningless general elections and could now more often participate in the all-important Democratic primaries, though many obstacles to full black electoral equality remained.[197]

The *Smith* decision was also an important achievement for civil rights organizations. It was the first significant victory before the Supreme Court for the NAACP's legal defense fund and its leader Thurgood Marshall, encouraging them to redouble their efforts against Jim Crow. "We must not be delayed by people who say, 'The time is not ripe,' nor should we proceed with caution for fear of destroying the status quo," Marshall told the NAACP's national conference. "People who deny us our rights should be brought to justice now."[198]

Congress also continued to deal with the issue of voting rights, though less successfully than the Supreme Court. In 1943 and again in 1945, the House passed legislation to overturn the poll tax. In both instances, the importance of translating America's democratic ideals into reality was a constant theme. During the 1943 debate over the legislation, Evan Owen Jones, a white sailor, stood up in the gallery of the House and shouted, "If a man doesn't have to pay to fight, why should he have to pay a tax to vote? You're fighting the Civil War all over again."[199] While the House was swayed by such arguments, southern filibusters blocked the legislation's passage in

Table 5. Southern Black Voter Registration, 1940–1952

Year	Estimated Number	Percentage of Eligible Blacks
1940	250,000	5
1947	595,000	12
1952	1,008,614	20

Source: Donald R. Matthews and James W. Prothro, *Negroes and the New Southern Politics* (New York: Harcourt, Brace, and World, 1966), p. 17.

Table 6. Southern Black Voter Registration (%) by State, 1940–1952

State	1940	1947	1952
Alabama	*	1	5
Arkansas	3	21	27
Florida[a]	3	13	33
Georgia	2	20	23
Louisiana	*	2	25
Mississippi	*	1	4
North Carolina[a]	10	14	18
South Carolina	*	13	20
Tennessee[a]	16	25	27
Texas	9	17	31
Virginia[a]	5	11	16

Source: Donald R. Matthews and James W. Prothro, Negroes and *the New Southern Politics* (New York: Harcourt, Brace, and World, 1966), p. 148.

* Less than 0.5 percent.

[a] States without white primary rules.

the Senate. In 1945, however, for the first time a majority of senators (but not the required two-thirds) voted to impose cloture on the filibusterers, signaling the growing sentiment in favor of poll tax repeal.[200] Those advocating a broadened franchise suffered another defeat in 1944, when southern conservatives blocked an attempt to provide federal ballots to soldiers on active duty. Even though poll taxes were again waived, responsibility for ballot distribution and voter qualifications was kept in the hands of the states.[201]

Although tentatively and incompletely, the Supreme Court, the FEPC, Congress, and even the military all showed signs of moving to tear down the nation's racial hierarchies. The same cannot be said of President Roosevelt. Despite the urgings of many of his advisors, the president, except during the Philadelphia transit strike, refused to act in favor of civil rights. After the Detroit riots, he rejected proposals by Interior Secretary Harold Ickes and others to appoint a national commission on race relations. The most Roosevelt could manage was a statement to the annual meeting of the Urban League saying, "We cannot stand before the world as a champion of oppressed peoples unless we practice as well as preach the principles of democracy for all men." He also cautioned militant blacks, instructing them as to "the responsibilities that go with democratic privileges."[202] To promote such responsibility, the president stepped up government surveillance of civil rights groups. He also sent his controversial wife on a good-will mission to New Zealand until things cooled off.[203]

Roosevelt's unwillingness to speak out in favor of civil rights stemmed from his almost single-minded devotion to the war effort and his fears of triggering a southern revolt in the Democratic party. Such fears were not groundless as the 1944 presidential election approached. The political revolt that began in 1942 continued in the months leading up to the Democrats' convention. A DNC survey of county chairman found increasing criticism in the South of the party's perceived racial liberalism. One South Carolina party official wrote that "the South will stand for almost any kind of treatment from the party except on the race question. I believe that the National Democratic Party will have to choose between the South and the negroes of the North."[204] Throughout the South, conservative, anti-New Deal factions were challenging party regulars for control of the delegations being sent to the national convention. In Texas, after conservative "Regulars" took control of the state convention in May, they proceeded to pass a series of resolutions demanding that the party platform include "a condemnation of the *Smith v. Allwright* decision, together with a promise that the federal government would not interfere in elections; denunciations of strikes, bureaucracy, and 'social equality'; and readoption of the two-thirds rule." Conservatives, warning of "the dangers of racial intermarriage and miscegenation," also took over the Mississippi delegation.[205]

Southern whites were not the only ones causing problems for the Democratic party. In South Carolina, after the state tried to defy the Supreme Court's ruling against the white primary, blacks organized the South Carolina Progressive Democratic Party (PDP) to protest their exclusion. The PDP organized forty-five thousand members and elected its own slate of delegates to the Democratic national convention. The DNC, however, refused to seat any of the PDP delegates.[206] Despite its failure, the PDP demonstrated the growing activism of southern blacks and their increasing willingness to challenge the status quo.

Discontent among southern white conservatives and militant blacks were far too limited to derail Roosevelt's nomination in 1944, which he won 1,068 to 89 over Senator Harry Byrd of Virginia, the candidate of the Dixie conservatives. Instead, southern conservatives focused their energies on keeping Vice President Henry Wallace off the ticket. Wallace, a dedicated liberal on economic issues (and a recent convert on racial ones), represented the growing power of northern liberals, unions, and blacks in party circles. Thus, his defeat would demonstrate the South's continued influence in the party. In addition, with Roosevelt's health failing noticeably, the person selected for the vice presidential slot seemed almost certain of becoming president during the next four years. Fearing a split in the party, Roosevelt gave in to these demands by dumping Wallace in favor of Senator Harry Truman. Truman's support for organized labor and the New Deal and his good relations with blacks made him tolerable to the party's more liberal elements. In addition, coming from a border state and his friendships with southern congressional leaders made him acceptable to the South.[207] Only in time would southern conservatives come to realize the error of this judgment.

During the campaign, Roosevelt kept race issues on the back burner. His advisors urged him that doing otherwise "at this time might be the fact which would translate impotent rumblings against the New Deal into actual revolt at the polls."[208] His boldest statement on race came in a radio address late in the campaign when he stated his belief that the "right to vote must be open to our citizens irrespective of race, color, or creed—without tax or artificial restriction of any kind."[209]

In November 1944, Roosevelt won a fourth term over his Republican opponent, New York governor Thomas Dewey. Beneath the surface, however, racial issues were beginning to transform the party. Roosevelt's margin of victory relied heavily on the votes and efforts of blacks, organized labor, and northern liberals—groups for whom civil rights was increasingly a priority. On the other hand, though the South remained solid, a few hairline cracks were visible. Throughout the region, the Democratic vote decreased significantly and in Texas a slate of unpledged electors put on the ballot by the conservative "Regulars" won 12 percent of the popular vote. Overall, Roosevelt's vote in the South dropped 6.6 percent from 1940, but outside of the South it was largely unchanged, falling only 0.9 percent, and in several large industrial states (with sizeable and growing black populations) like New York, Illinois, and Michigan his vote actually increased slightly. While race was not the only reason for this decline in the southern Democratic vote, it was surely one of the most important.[210]

Roosevelt's unwillingness to take a stronger stand on racial issues was, in hindsight, regrettable and costly. True, white Southerners were becoming more restive, but it seems clear that in the context of the war, nationally public attitudes on race had shifted enough that he could have been more outspoken for reform. Had he been willing to lend his popularity as president and his prestige as commander in chief during wartime for the cause of equal rights, as Lincoln had done, Roosevelt could have further advanced that cause. Those looking to the White House for leadership on civil rights would have to wait, but not for long.

Changing racial attitudes were also found outside of Washington. Prodded by the war and black protests, several states and cities began taking their own steps to ensure racial equality, producing the greatest burst of civil rights laws in nearly seventy years. In response to a series of sit-in demonstrations, St. Louis passed an ordinance integrating municipal cafeterias in May 1944.[211] In Alaska, Native Americans were victimized by segregation nearly as bad as that in the Jim Crow South until the territorial legislature banned such practices in February 1945.[212] Perhaps the most significant state-level action occurred in New York. In 1941, Governor Herbert Lehman termed discrimination in defense jobs "unpardonable defeatism" and established a state FEPC, the Governor's Committee on Discrimination in Employment.[213] Four years later, with the strong support of Governor Dewey, the state legislature passed the Ives-Quinn Act. It set up a permanant fair employment practices committee and made employment discrimination a misdemeanor, punishable by a $500 fine or up to a year in jail.[214] By the end of the year, New Jersey and twenty-eight cities from Phoenix to Chicago followed New York's example and passed fair employment laws.[215]

When World War II ended in August 1945, the conflict had substantially altered the racial status quo. Most importantly, the war had eroded the moral and intellectual respectability of claims for racial supremacy. In 1945 scenes from Nazi concentration camps had shown in graphic and horrifying detail the ultimate implications of such thinking.

Black military service also contributed to changing white attitudes. One example of this came in the summer of 1945. Senator James Eastland, Theodore Bilbo's junior but equally racist Mississippi colleague, held forth in the Senate, claiming that "numerous high-ranking generals" had told him that the "Negro soldier was an utter and dismal failure in combat in Europe." Blacks in service units "were lazy; . . . they would not work," while blacks on the front line "would desert their posts of duty, without cause." On several occasions, black units were disarmed after they "criminally assaulted" white women. "I state that the conduct of the Negro soldier in Normandy, as well as all over Europe, was disgraceful, and that Negro soldiers have disgraced the flag of their country," declared Eastland. Furthermore, "the white soldier from New York, feels about the racial question today just as does the veteran from Mississippi or Georgia or South Carolina or Tennessee."[216]

Although Eastland may have been correct that white soldiers across the country agreed about black soldiers, he was greatly mistaken in believing they agreed with him. One white soldier, Lieutenant Van T. Barfoot of Carthage, Mississippi, winner of Bronze and Silver Stars and the Congressional Medal of Honor, told Eastland, "I found out after I did some fighting in this war that the colored boys fight just as good as the white boys." "I've changed my ideas a lot about colored people since I got into this war," the soldier added, "and so have a lot of other boys from the South." He asked, "I've fought with colored men—why shouldn't I eat with them?"[217]

Many other soldiers agreed with Barfoot. At the war's end, *Yank* magazine asked its readers, "What changes would you like to see made in post-war America?" According to the editor, the respondents "mentioned, above everything else, the need for wiping out racial and religious discrimination."[218]

Outside of the military, the same was true. Although public opinion polling had yet to pay much attention to racial attitudes, one series of surveys provides some insight into the liberalization of white racial attitudes during the war. In 1939, the Roper Organization found that approximately 70 percent of Americans believed that blacks were less intelligent than whites. Though the survey did not give the results for the whites surveyed, the percentage would undoubtedly have been higher. In 1942, 1944, and 1946, the National Opinion Research Center asked whites a similar question. In 1942 and 1944, just under half of the whites surveyed thought that blacks and whites were equally intelligent, a significant shift since 1939. When asked again in 1946, that percentage had increased to 57 percent.[219]

The war also greatly altered the lives and attitudes of black Americans. Over a million blacks served in the military and millions more worked in defense jobs. This service not only increased the education and skills of many blacks, but also heightened their demands and expectations. Furthermore, the war had shown them that their protests and activism, such as in the MOWM or the NAACP's challenge to the white primary, could produce tangible and significant victories. Finally, the wartime rhetoric of democracy and freedom made blacks increasingly likely to demand the same for themselves. In the words of one black soldier, "I spent four years in the Army to free a bunch of Dutchmen and Frenchmen, and I'm hanged if I'm going to let the Alabama version of the Germans kick me around when I get home. No sirreee-bob! I went into the Army a nigger; I'm comin' out a *man.*"[220]

Thus, while poverty, segregation, discrimination, and disenfranchisement still dominated the lives of most black Americans in 1945, the war had undermined Jim Crow in important ways. Furthermore, the conflict had transformed black and white attitudes regarding race and the role of blacks in American democracy, even if it had for the time being inflamed anti-Japanese sentiments. While the second V of victory at home against racism might not yet have been won, the offensive was underway. In the words of poet Langston Hughes:

> *When Dorie Miller took gun in hand—*
> *Jim Crow started his last stand.*
> *Our battle yet is far from won*
> *But when it is, Jim Crow'll be done.*
> *We gonna bury that son-of-a-gun!*[221]

SEVEN

"Hearts and Minds"

The Cold War and Civil Rights, 1946–1954

On the morning of February 12, 1946, at Fort Gordon, Georgia, twenty-seven-year-old black army Sergeant Isaac Woodard Jr. ended four years of military service. For the previous fifteen months, Woodard had served in the Pacific, where he had seen action in combat. After receiving his honorable discharge papers, Woodard boarded a Greyhound bus that would take him first to North Carolina, where his wife would join him, and then to New York City to visit his parents. Like nearly all returning veterans, Woodard looked forward to reuniting with his family and starting a new life.

During a stop in South Carolina, the bus's white driver cursed and threatened Woodard for taking too long in the "colored" bathroom. Woodard must have felt outrage and humiliation. He was a combat veteran, still in his uniform, going home to his family after serving four years to protect his country and ensure freedom and democracy for people around the globe. All of this meant nothing; he was still a black man in the Jim Crow South. Perhaps because he was now a veteran warrior, Woodard protested. Soon a heated argument broke out between him and the bus driver.

At the next stop in Batesburg, South Carolina, the driver called the local police to report a drunk and disorderly passenger. Police chief Lynwood E. Shull and a deputy arrived on the scene and ordered Woodard off the bus. As he left the vehicle, the police officers grabbed and began beating him. The beating continued at the local jail, where the officers used the end of a night stick to gouge Woodard's eyes, blinding him permanently.[1]

The assault on Isaac Woodard is only one of the horrifying examples of violence against black veterans in the aftermath of World War II. As after World War I, throughout the South whites resorted to violence in an effort to "put blacks in their place" and to crush whatever aspirations they might have gained during the war. On August 25, 1945, less than two weeks after Japan's surrender, a mob in the ironically named town of Liberty, Mississippi lynched Eugene Bells, a black ex-serviceman who had the temerity to refuse to go back to work for his former white employer, going into business with his father-in-law instead.[2] Over the next year, another eight blacks would be lynched, the most in a decade.[3] And though not technically lynchings, several other blacks, often returning veterans who tried to vote or in some way antagonized local whites, were killed or attacked during this period.

Race riots also broke out. Two weeks after the assault on Isaac Woodard, a white mob in Columbia, Tennessee, thwarted in its effort to lynch a black suspect, began attacking local blacks. When black veterans, among others, attempted to defend their homes and stores, local and state police and National Guardsmen ransacked the black section of town. By the time order was restored, two blacks were dead and a hundred others were under arrest.[4] In Athens, Alabama, racial tensions exploded in a riot that injured between fifty and one hundred blacks after a biracial veterans organization tried unsuccessfully to win a local election. One local white complained, "It's got to the place white folks can't walk on the streets for the niggers. It's the nigger GIs that's getting out of their place."[5]

Many white southern politicians actively encouraged such racism. Recognizing that the demise of the white primary might allow southern blacks to vote in significant numbers for the first time since Reconstruction, they whipped up racial resentments to ensure the continuance of both white supremacy and their political careers. In Georgia, Eugene Talmadge won the governorship once again by campaigning under the slogan "The One Issue in this Race is White Supremacy."[6] In Mississippi, Senator Theodore Bilbo reached a new low, even for him, in racist vitriol, claiming that "the nigger is only 150 years from the jungles of Africa, where it is his great delight to cut him up some fried nigger steak for breakfast."[7] In response to the possibility of blacks voting, Bilbo all but urged white Mississippians to resort to violence, asking "every red-blooded Anglo-Saxon man in Mississippi to resort to any means to keep hundreds of Negroes from the polls. . . . And if you don't know what that means you are just not up on your persuasive measures."[8] For those who still didn't get it, Bilbo added, "But you know and I know what's the best way to keep the nigger from voting. You do it the night before the election.

I don't have to tell you any more than that."[9] (Both Talmadge and Bilbo died before they could take office. Bilbo died of complications resulting from cancer of the mouth).

Clearly, the outbreak of racial violence after World War II suggested a repeat of the Red Summer of 1919, when blacks' wartime aspirations were met with bloody rebuffs. Yet despite real similarities, 1946 was not 1919. In a letter written not long after the incident, President Harry S. Truman discussed Isaac Woodard's case in tones very different from the Democrat who had occupied the White House in 1919, Woodrow Wilson. Truman wrote, "When a mayor and a City Marshal can take a negro Sergeant off a bus in South Carolina, beat him up and put out one of his eyes, and nothing is done about it by the State Authorities, something is radically wrong with the system. . . . I can't approve of such goings on and I shall never approve of it, as long as I am here. . . . I am going to try to remedy it and if that ends up in my failure to be reelected, that failure will be in a good cause."[10]

Why did this Democratic president, like Wilson a descendant of Confederate sympathizers, react to racial oppression so differently? Certainly, Truman himself deserves real credit. But more broadly, both America and the world had changed greatly since 1919, making this most recent wave of racial violence less acceptable to many national leaders and most U.S. citizens. After nearly four years of hard-fought struggle against fascism and especially after learning of the enormous evils of the Holocaust, it became harder and harder for Americans to justify their own racial hierarchies. Instead of imposing new forms of racial subordination, the brutal treatment of Isaac Woodard and other African Americans in this era thus worked to heighten pressures for reform. As the *New York Times* editorialized in February 1946, "This is a particularly good year to campaign against the evil of bigotry, prejudice, and race hatred because we have witnessed the defeat of enemies who tried to found a mastery of the world upon such cruel and fallacious policy."[11]

It was a good year, and a good era, to oppose bigotry not only because of the exposure and defeat of Nazism, and not only because the sheer magnitude of the war effort had required the United States to rely on black contributions to an extraordinary extent. After all, the U.S. government had always relied on black soldiers to help win wars, and it then had often turned its back on them. This time, however, the American and Allied victory over Germany and Japan had also depended upon the cooperation of nonwhites around the world. And in its wake, U.S. leaders quickly recognized that Winston

Churchill was right; although the intensely hot war against European and Japanese fascism was over, they were embroiled in a comparably momentous "Cold War" against the emerging threat of Soviet Communism. It, too, demanded ongoing large-scale military mobilization of American manpower, so that alienating African Americans was more costly than ever before. And in this war, for the first time, the allegiance of nonwhite nations would be crucial. If America's leaders hoped to win the hearts and minds of the world, it could not ignore what discrimination was doing to the hearts and minds of black Americans at home. Because the United States had never before been such a prominent world power, never before had U.S. leaders given so much weight to international considerations; and never before had a war that triggered racial reforms been followed by an international context generating such strong imperatives to sustain and extend those reforms. Even so, as we shall see, it remained a gamble for national officials like Truman to voice support for those changes; so while the times were propitious for racial progress, it was far from inevitable.[12]

Thus the final indispensable element sustaining the momentum of reform was the aggressive activism of black Americans, inspired by their war experiences, to achieve truly equal rights within an inclusive society, not a segregated one. Again, most blacks had come back from World War I with similar demands, but then the hatred and brutality with which they were met led many instead to embrace the separatism of Marcus Garvey. This time, many black activists recognized that they faced a far more opportune moment, and so their efforts to prod the United States to live up to its recently professed egalitarian principles were stronger and more persistent than ever before. Furthermore, the war had contributed mightily to the Great Migration of blacks from the rural South to the urban, industrial North, where black access to greater education, economic opportunities, and, most importantly, the voting booth greatly strengthened their political possibilities. Although their quest remained daunting, these conditions allowed advocates of civil rights, black and white, to keep in motion the still-halting strides toward racial equality taken during World War II, instead of being overwhelmed once again by the forces of reaction.

As the wave of violence spread throughout the South in 1946, both black and white civil rights activists began pressuring the government to act. In August 1946, representatives from civil rights, labor, religious, and veterans organizations formed the National Emergency Committee Against Mob Violence to publicize violence against blacks and to push the administration "to throw the full force of the federal government behind our actions and sentiments in bringing before the bar of justice and convicting the lynchers." That same month saw large demonstrations in New York City and Washington, D.C. against the violence, including four hundred women from the National Association of Colored Women who picketed outside the White House for a week.[13] Hollywood's liberal community staged "It's Happening Here," a radio program that condemned the violence. Among the celebrities involved was Ronald Reagan, who called the lynchings a "capably organized systematic campaign of fascist violence."[14]

In contrast to the aftermath of World War I, many prominent white leaders listened to these appeals. The most important one who did was the man sitting where the buck stopped, President Harry Truman. Prior to his becoming president, Truman's racial views were decidedly mixed. As a senator, Truman had a relatively liberal record on civil rights; he actively sought and received black votes, and he supported antilynching bills and legislation to repeal poll taxes. Running for reelection in 1940, he told a white audience, "I believe in the brotherhood of man; not merely the brotherhood of white men, but the brotherhood of all men before the law. . . . In giving the Negroes the rights that are theirs, we are only acting in accord with ideas of a true democracy. If any class or race can be permanently set apart from, or pushed down below the rest in political and civil rights, so may any other class or race . . . and we may say farewell to the principles on which we count our safety."[15]

Privately, however, Truman shared the prejudices of most Missouri whites. The self-described "son of an unreconstructed rebel mother," he commonly referred to blacks as "niggers" and "coons." In 1940 he told a group of black Democrats that he opposed "social equality" and that the "highest types of Negro leaders say quite frankly that they prefer the society of their own people."[16] As for his support of antilynching legislation, he told one southern colleague, "You know I am against this bill, but if it comes to a vote, I'll have to vote for it. All my sympathies are with you but the Negro vote in Kansas City and St. Louis is too important."[17] Thus reassured, southern conservatives went along with his nomination as vice president in 1944. When President Roosevelt died the following April, South Carolina senator Burton Maybank told a friend, "Everything's going to be all right—the new President knows how to handle the niggers."[18]

Maybank, however, misread the new president and the changing context of American race relations. Along with powerful domestic and international political considerations, the experience of World War II and the recognition that as president he represented all Americans seem to have pushed Truman to act in accordance with his liberal instincts on racial issues. Soon after taking office, Truman sent a letter to Representative Adolph Sabath, chairman of the House Rules Committee, endorsing the creation of a permanent Fair Employment Practices Committee (FEPC) now that southern conservatives had successfully ended funding for the original wartime agency. The president reiterated this request in September when he sent Congress a twenty-one-point postwar reconversion program and again in his January 1946 State of the Union message.[19]

But though President Truman spoke out in favor of a permanent FEPC, he feared an open breach with the southern conservatives in Congress and did little to push the issue.[20] Then as 1946 wore on, both personal and political motivations impelled Truman toward a more active position on civil rights. First, Truman seems to have been genuinely shocked at the attacks on returning black veterans like Isaac Woodard. "My God!" Truman told a civil rights delegation that met with him to urge action against the racial violence, "I had no idea it was as terrible as that! We've got to do something!"[21] On another occasion he wrote, "[M]y very stomach turned over when I learned that Negro soldiers, just back from overseas, were being dumped out of army trucks in Mississippi and beaten. Whatever my inclinations as a native of Missouri might have been, as President I know this is bad. I shall fight to end evils like this."[22]

Such attacks were particularly galling following World War II, which Truman, like most Americans, saw as a struggle against the forces of tyranny and prejudice. In a September 1946 letter to the head of a liberal veterans organization, the president denounced discrimination in education, saying, "We have only recently completed a long and bitter war against intolerance and hatred in other lands. A cruel price in blood and suffering was paid by the American people in bringing that war to a successful conclusion. Yet, in this country today there exists disturbing evidence of intolerance and prejudice similar in kind, though perhaps not in degree, to that against which we fought the war."[23] That same month, Truman wrote Lester Granger of the Urban League, "To give the Bill of Rights its full meaning, we must work to preserve the same rights at home that we fought for so successfully abroad."[24]

International considerations were visibly reinforcing such feelings in the president and other national leaders. All knew that accounts

of racial violence in the South were widely communicated and condemned throughout the world. In Italy, one newspaper wrote that
"in the land of the Four Freedoms thirteen million Negroes struggle
against American racial discrimination." Other papers, from Bombay
to Baghdad to Buenos Aires carried similar stories.[25]

Americans might once have blithely ignored such criticisms. But
as the U.S. government assumed leadership of non-Communist nations against the Soviet regime that it increasingly equated with Nazi
totalitarianism, it could no longer afford to do so.[26] Already by early
1946, the wartime alliance of convenience between the United States
and the U.S.S.R. had ended and relations between the two nations
quickly became threatening. When Churchill warned in March during a speech in Truman's Missouri that an "iron curtain" had descended across Europe, dividing the free peoples of western Europe
from the Soviet Union and its puppet regimes in the east, he only put
a name to the reality that was already foremost in every international
leader's mind. In this confrontation, American racial practices were
even more a liability than in the propaganda wars against the Nazis.
Although the totalitarian character of the Soviet Union led the
United States again to stress its contrasting traditions of freedom and
democracy, the U.S.S.R. professed to be a more racially egalitarian
nation than America. Hence every episode of racial brutality in the
United States allowed Soviet leaders to boast of their own fairness
and to denounce their American counterparts as hypocritical oppressors of people of color. And the postwar United States generated
so many discriminatory episodes that American racism became a frequent and increasing theme of Soviet propaganda. In 1946, *Pravda*
editorialized that "the Constitution of the U.S. guarantees to all its
citizens equal rights before the law; however, the Negro population,
consisting of 13,000,000 people, actually does not have these rights.
Racial discrimination continues to exist in all its forms and in all
branches of the economy and culture of the country."[27] An analysis
of the Soviet newspaper *Izvestia* during the first six months of 1947
found that denial of rights for political and racial minorities was
the second most common theme in its description of the United
States.[28]

Much to their consternation, U.S. diplomats recognized that
on this topic *Pravda* was true. The U.S. embassy in Moscow cabled
the State Department, telling it that articles such as this "may por-
tend stronger emphasis on this theme as [a] Soviet propaganda
weapon."[29] Consequently, State Department officials began arguing
that civil rights were in the interests of U.S. foreign policy. In May

1946, acting Secretary of State Dean Acheson (hardly a misty-eyed idealist) wrote:

> The existence of discrimination against minority groups in this country has an adverse effect on our relations with other countries. We are reminded over and over by some foreign newspapers and spokesmen, that our treatment of various minorities leaves much to be desired. While sometimes these pronouncements are exaggerated and unjustified, they all too frequently point with accuracy to some form of discrimination because of race, creed, color, or national origin. Frequently we find it next to impossible to formulate a satisfactory answer to our critics in other countries; the gap between the things we stand for in principle and the facts of particular situation may be too wide to be bridged. An atmosphere of suspicion and resentment in a country over the way a minority is being treated in the United States is a formidable obstacle to the development of mutual understanding and trust between the two countries. We will have better international relations when these reasons for suspicion and resentment have been removed.
>
> I think it is quite obvious . . . that the existence of discriminations against minority groups in the United States is a handicap in our relations with other countries. The Department of State, therefore, has good reason to hope for the continued and increased effectiveness of public and private efforts to do away with these discriminations.[30]

Civil rights organizations quickly began to take self-conscious advantage of America's new global role. In August 1946, the National Negro Congress petitioned the United Nations to investigate and take action against violations of black Americans' human rights. The following year, the National Association for the Advancement of Colored People (NAACP) did likewise. In a petition drafted by W. E. B. Du Bois, the NAACP presented "a frank and earnest appeal to the world for elemental Justice against the treatment which the United States has visited upon us for three centuries. . . . It is to induce the nations of the world to persuade this nation to be just to its own people that we have prepared and now present to you this document."[31] The petition also declared, "It is not Russia that threatens the United States so much as Mississippi; not Stalin and Molotov but Bilbo and Rankin; internal injustice done to one's brothers is far more dangerous than the aggression of strangers from abroad."[32]

The NAACP's petition received great publicity, both in the United States and abroad, especially after the Soviet Union pressed the United Nations Commission on Human Rights to investigate the charges.[33] Though this effort failed, the episode was a foreign relations embarrassment for the United States. "I was humiliated," U.S. Attorney General Tom Clark told the National Association of Attorneys General, "as I know you must have been, to realize that in our America there could be the slightest foundation for such a petition. And that the [NAACP] could conclude that amongst all of our honorable institutions there was no tribunal to which such a petition could be presented with hope of redress."[34] In response, Clark said that he would act "with as great vigor and force as is permitted under the law where States through negligence, or for whatever reason, fail . . . to protect the life and liberties of the individual." To do this, he announced his intention to expand and strengthen the Civil Rights Section of the Justice Department.[35]

In addition to the struggle with the Soviet Union abroad, the Truman administration, and Clark in particular, increasingly feared Communist subversion at home. They knew well that a bitter, impoverished, and frustrated black community provided a fertile ground for such activities. In September 1946, Truman aide Clark Clifford warned the president that Communists had instigated "the recent anti-caste agitation."[36] Thus, support for civil rights was also seen as an important means of combating internal subversion and unrest.

Electoral considerations also helped to motivate Truman's emerging stand on civil rights. He did not wish to run strongly to the right on the issue, nor did it seem likely that he could do so effectively. But, looking ahead to 1948, the president realized that his chances of winning either the Democratic nomination or the general election were slim unless he acted to enhance his support among white liberals and African Americans. This was particularly true after he fired Secretary of Commerce and former Vice President Henry Wallace, who had openly criticized Truman's policy toward the Soviet Union. Wallace was still very popular with blacks and liberals, and if he ran (as seemed likely) as a third-party candidate, he would likely dash any hopes Truman might have of being elected. In addition, the probable Republican nominee, New York governor Thomas Dewey, had also taken a strong stand in favor of civil rights with his support of the Ives-Quinn law barring racial discrimination in employment in that state.

These factors seem to have prompted President Truman to become more outspoken on civil rights during the summer of 1946. On June 26, he sent a message to the NAACP's annual convention declaring, "The ballot is both a right and a privilege. The right to use it must be protected and its use by everyone encouraged. Lastly, every veteran and every citizen, whatever his origins, must be protected from all forms of organized terrorism.[37] Four days later he ordered the Justice Department to investigate incidents of racial violence in the South. In September he met with representatives of the National Emergency Committee Against Mob Violence and promised to appoint a presidential committee on civil rights—a step that President Roosevelt had refused to take. In December, he issued Executive Order 9008, creating the President's Committee on Civil Rights (PCCR). Declaring civil rights to be "essential to domestic tranquillity, national security, the general welfare, and the continued existence of our free institutions," he ordered the committee to make recommendations "to safeguard the civil rights of the people."[38]

Unlike most presidential commissions, the PCCR was not an effort to duck a controversial issue by offering boilerplate language and modest proposals. Pro–civil rights liberals dominated the body. Even the committee's two southern members, Frank Graham, president of the University of North Carolina, and Dorothy Tilly, an Atlanta philanthropist, were both prominent liberals. According to historian William Juhnke, "the Committee was without a doubt left-of-center and sympathetic to civil rights reform."[39]

Even more importantly, Truman seems to have hoped that the committee's work would help make public opinion more receptive to his civil rights proposals. Thus he urged its members to come up with a strong report. In fact, when the committee made an interim presentation of its work to him, the president "seemed elated with the Committee's progress, happy with its unanimity in favoring significant action in civil rights, and particularly encouraged by the Committee's interest in gearing the report for public consumption." In doing so, according to Juhnke, "Truman passed up an opportunity to emphasize political realism. He was not merely cooperative, he was enthusiastic." Emboldened by Truman's words, the committee vowed to be even more aggressive in its statements.[40]

Statements of State Department officials also strongly influenced the PCCR. Charles Fahy, the department's legal advisor, stressed the importance of the nation's obligations under the U.N. Charter and various human rights conventions. He then added, "Irrespective of what the U.S. obligation may eventually prove to be with regard to

human rights, it must be realized that as a leading member of the
international community, the eyes of the world will be upon the
United States." Assistant Secretary of State Dean Rusk wrote that
"the conduct of our foreign policy is handicapped by our record in
the field of civil rights and racial discrimination." Secretary of State
George C. Marshall (hardly a racial liberal as Army Chief of Staff
during World War II) backed up these views, telling the Committee:

> The foreign policy of a nation depends for most of its effective-
> ness, particularly a nation which does not rely upon possible mili-
> tary aggression as a dominant influence, on the moral influence
> which that nation exerts throughout the world. The moral influ-
> ence of the United States is weakened to the extent that the civil
> rights proclaimed by our Constitution are not fully confirmed in
> actual practice. The failure to secure the full and equal enjoyment
> of these civil rights has affected the conduct of our foreign rela-
> tions in two ways. On the one hand, isolated incidents have oc-
> curred which involved directly the nationals of other states. Per-
> haps even more damaging, however, have been the violations
> practiced against groups of our own citizens. These practices have
> been alluded to frequently in the foreign press. . . . Since it is a
> major objective of the foreign policy of the United States to pro-
> mote world-wide respect for and observance of civil rights, our
> failure to maintain the highest standards of performance in this
> field creates embarrassment out of proportion to the actual in-
> stances of violation.[41]

As his committee on civil rights prepared its report, President Truman continued to speak out strongly in favor of civil rights. In his
January 1947 State of the Union message, he denounced racial violence and declared that "the will to fight these crimes should be in
the heart of everyone of us." Revealing the contents of his own
heart, he asked Congress to consider additional legislation to allow
the federal government to prosecute such crimes and, declaring discrimination to be "repugnant to the principles of our democracy,"
he once again he urged the creation of a permanent FEPC.[42]

The following month, the president himself made the connection
between civil rights and American foreign policy in the postwar
world. While presenting several black newspapers with journalism
awards, he told the audience:

> We are living in a time of profound and swiftly moving
> change. We see colonial peoples moving toward their indepen-

dence. . . . We, as Americans, will want to supply guidance and help wherever we can. One way in which we can help is to set an example of a nation in which people with different backgrounds, with different origins work peacefully and successfully alongside one another. . . . More and more we are learning . . . how closely our democracy is under observation. We are learning what loud echoes both our successes and our failures have in every corner of the world. That is one of the pressing reasons why we cannot afford failures. When we fail to live together in peace, the failure touches not us, as Americans, alone, but the cause of democracy itself in the whole world. That we must never forget.[43]

Truman's most important statement on civil rights came in June 1947 when he appeared before the NAACP's annual convention. As the first president ever to speak in person before the NAACP, Truman was taking a highly controversial step. Some of the president's aides suggested that he devote only one paragraph at the end of the speech to civil rights. President Truman rejected this advice and delivered one of the most impassioned defenses of equal rights by any president.

The speech took place at the Lincoln Memorial and was broadcast live on all four radio networks, most independent stations, and short-wave broadcasts arranged by the State Department to the increasingly important audience of millions of people around the world.[44] The president told his audience, "Our immediate task is to remove the last remnants of the barriers which stand between millions of our citizens and their birthright. There is no justifiable reason for discrimination because of ancestry, or religion, or race, or color. . . . We cannot wait another decade or another generation to remedy these evils. We must work, as never before, to cure them now."[45]

President Truman also indicated the importance of World War II for the goal of civil rights, telling his audience that "the aftermath of the war and the desire to keep faith with our Nation's historic principles makes the need a pressing one."[46] He also laid out the emerging foreign policy concerns of the Cold War. "The support of desperate populations of battle ravaged countries must be won for the free way of life. We must have them as allies in our continuing struggle for the peaceful solution of the world's problems. Freedom is not an easy lesson to teach, nor an easy cause to sell, to peoples beset by every kind of privation. They may surrender to the false sense of security offered so temptingly by totalitarian regimes unless we can prove the superiority of democracy. Our case for democracy should be as strong as we can make it. It should rest on practical evidence that we have been able to put our own house in order."[47]

When he finished his speech, the president turned to NAACP leader Walter White, telling him, "I said what I did because I mean every word of it—and I am going to prove that I do mean it."[48]

The first proof of Truman's intentions came on October 29, when his civil rights committee issued its report. Entitled *To Secure These Rights,* the report strongly condemned racial violence, discrimination, and the denial of political and legal rights for minorities. It also criticized segregation, a major step that few white liberals had previously been willing to take. Mincing no words, the PCCR called "separate but equal" a "failure" and "the cornerstone of the elaborate structure of discrimination against some American citizens." Furthermore, "not even the most mathematically precise equality of segregated institutions can properly be considered equality under the law. No argument or rationalization can alter this basic fact: a law which forbids a group of American citizens to associate with other citizens in the ordinary course of daily living creates inequality by imposing a caste status on the minority group."[49] The committee then cited several examples, including the army's survey of white soldiers who had served alongside black units in World War II, suggesting that integration led to greater racial harmony and understanding.[50]

To Secure These Rights also rejected antiquated notions of federalism and the idea that "stateways can't change folkways" by advocating a sweeping federal policy agenda. Among its recommendations were the strengthening of the Civil Rights Section of the Justice Department, an antilynching law, abolition of the poll tax, statutes protecting the right to vote, integration of the military, denial of federal funds to institutions that discriminate, and federal laws against discrimination and segregation in employment, interstate commerce, and public accommodations.[51]

In addition to moral and economic reasons, *To Secure These Rights* relied heavily on foreign policy concerns to justify its calls for federal action. It stated, "A lynching in a rural American community is not a challenge to that community's conscience alone. The repercussions of such a crime are heard not only in the locality, or indeed only in our own nation. They echo from one end of the globe to the other. . . . Similarly, interference with the right of a qualified citizen to vote locally cannot today remain a local problem. An American diplomat cannot forcefully argue for free elections in foreign lands without meeting the challenge that in many sections of America qualified voters do not have free access to the polls. Can it be doubted that this is a right which the national government must make secure?"[52] The PCCR report went on to cite a press report that quoted British diplomats saying that recent lynchings "have played into the hands of Communist propagandists in Europe," and that "incidents of mob violence would provide excellent propaganda ammunition for Communist agents who have been decrying America's brand of 'freedom' and 'democracy.' "[53] The report then added ominously, *"The United States is not so strong, the final triumph of the democratic ideal is not so inevitable that we can ignore what the world thinks of us or our record."*[54] (Emphasis in the original.)

The PCCR also condemned the evacuation of Japanese Americans during World War II and called for compensation for their property losses. Once again, the changing international environment seems the reason for criticism of so recent a policy. With the war over, the Japanese were no longer the enemy. Instead, Japan was now an important bulwark against Communist expansionism in Asia. Consequently, making amends on this issue became desirable from a foreign policy point of view, though domestic politics would not support compensation until after four decades had passed.[55]

The reports of government commissions are usually carefully crafted documents, designed to determine and ratify the existing consensus, before being put away on a shelf to gather dust. *To Secure These Rights* instead took positions far in advance of public opinion. The document was even beyond what many civil rights organizations were urging. Roy Wilkins of the NAACP stated, "It is the greatest stimulant to our program," and in its wake, the NAACP's board of directors decided to take an even more aggressive stance, criticizing for the first time federal aid to segregated schools and vowing to mount a direct challenge to legal segregation.[56] The report was also given widespread coverage in the nation's press. The *Chicago Sun Times* called the report "the book of the year," while the *Washington Post* called it "monumental." Several national radio programs also discussed the report at length, including the Mutual Broadcasting System, which aired transcripts of the report.[57] *Senior Scholastic* also carried the report's message to thousands of school children.[58] The *New York Times Magazine* ran an article by committee member Robert Cushman restating the report under the title, "Our Civil Rights Become a World Issue."[59] Along with its press coverage, *To Secure These Rights* also became something of a best seller, with 1 million copies either sold or distributed free by the government, civic groups, and liberal organizations and newspapers over the next year.[60]

Although the document went beyond what he had called for, President Truman embraced it and used many of its proposals in his civil rights message to Congress on February 2, 1948. The president criticized the "serious gap between our ideals and some of our practices." To close this gap, he asked Congress for abolition of the poll tax, a permanent FEPC, antilynching legislation, home-rule and presidential election suffrage for Washington, D.C., a ban on segregation in interstate transportation facilities, and reform of immigration laws.[61] President Truman concluded his message, which was broadcast as the story of the day on Voice of America and distributed to all U.S. missions around the world, by stressing the role of civil rights in American foreign policy:

> The position of the United States in the world today makes it especially urgent that we adopt these measures to secure for all our people their essential rights. . . .
>
> To be effective in these efforts, we must protect our civil rights so that by providing all our people with the maximum enjoyment of personal freedom and personal opportunity we shall be a stronger nation—stronger in our leadership, stronger in our moral position, stronger in the deeper satisfactions of a united citizenry.
>
> We know that our democracy is not perfect. But we do know that it offers a fuller, freer, happier life to our people than any totalitarian nation has ever offered.
>
> If we wish to inspire the peoples of the world whose freedom is in jeopardy, if we wish to restore the hope to those who have already lost their civil liberties, if we wish to fulfill the promise that is ours, we must correct the remaining imperfections in our practice of democracy.
>
> We know the way. We need only the will.[62]

The Truman administration's response to civil rights was not limited to words. The day after the PCCR issued its report, the Justice Department announced its intention to file an *amicus curiae* brief with the Supreme Court supporting the NAACP's challenge to racially restrictive covenants. These covenants forbad the owners to sell their property to members of certain racial and religious groups, and were important barriers to blacks seeking to purchase homes in white areas. According to Richard Kluger, Cold War concerns weighed heavily in the Justice Department's decision. When the NAACP appealed to Attorney General Tom Clark to file a brief, "it was plain to Clark that the Cold War which had driven him to hound Communists in the name of patriotism obliged the President and his government to come to the aid of the Negro in the same name."[63]

In this case, *Shelley v. Kraemer,* the government for the first time ever intervened before the Supreme Court in favor of civil rights in a case between two private parties.[64] The government's *amicus* brief argued that judicial enforcement of restrictive covenants was an unconstitutional use of state power under the Fourteenth Amendment's guarantee of equal protection. In addition, the brief included a memo from the State Department, which argued "the United States has been embarrassed in the conduct of foreign relations by acts of discrimination taking place in this country." It stated that restrictive covenants violated various international agreements, including the U.N. Charter. The government also took the unprecedented step of publishing its brief as a pamphlet for public distribution.[65] In his oral argument before the Court, Solicitor General Philip Perlman again stressed that enforcement of restrictive covenants damaged the ability of the government in "the fields of public health, housing, home finance, and in the conduct of foreign affairs."[66]

Shelley v. Kraemer also showed the growing effectiveness of the NAACP's Legal Defense Fund. In preparing the case, the NAACP's lawyers, headed by Thurgood Marshall, developed sophisticated legal arguments, assembled mountains of sociological data, and recruited numerous private and governmental bodies to file *amicus* briefs on its behalf. Such tactics would be used with increasing effectiveness in coming years.[67]

Swayed by the arguments of the NAACP and the federal government, the Supreme Court in May 1948 ruled unanimously that judicial enforcement of restrictive covenants was unconstitutional. The Court's decision proved to be an important blow against the legal underpinnings of residential segregation, and its effects were soon evident. For example, in Chicago it was estimated that within four years, following the *Shelley* decision twenty-one thousand black families were able to purchase or rent homes in areas that had previously been limited to whites.[68]

Although President Truman willingly took a liberal stand on many racial issues, it often took pressure from civil rights activists to push him even further. For example, President Truman's order desegregating the military, easily the most important civil rights measure of his presidency and one for which he is usually given full credit, came about only through such pressure. Despite the fact that his civil rights committee had recommended desegregating the armed forces, in his February 1948 civil rights message to Congress, Truman merely stated that he would use his executive authority to stop discrimination in the military. He said nothing about ending segregation.[69] Most likely, the president thought that barring segregation in the military would only add to the growing rebellion of southern Democrats and, in addition, cause a backlash by the military.

Such caution, however, was unacceptable to blacks like Grant Reynolds. During the Second World War, Reynolds had served in the army as a chaplain and his experiences led to his "revulsion with the system" of military Jim Crow. According to him, "I made a promise to the men I contacted" in the military to do whatever was possible to change the system. By early 1944 he and other black veterans organized the Committee Against Jim Crow in Military Service and Training. The committee languished as mostly a paper organization until after the war when one day, Reynolds, who was now attending Columbia Law School, received a phone call from A. Philip Randolph. "I think we ought to get together to talk," he told Reynolds. Randolph had long been opposed to segregation in the military and by joining up with the committee he gave it the prestige and resources to begin mounting an active campaign against segregation in the military.[70]

Randolph and Reynolds both knew that political and foreign policy considerations made President Truman vulnerable to pressure on this issue. Not only did Truman need black votes, but in the spring of 1948, the Cold War took a chilling turn for the worse. Following a Communist coup in Czechoslovakia in February, war fears ran rampant. America's rapid demobilization after World War II also meant that it was unable to meet any serious military challenge from the Soviet Union, leading President Truman on March 17 to ask Congress to reinstate the draft.[71] Recognizing the leverage this action provided African Americans, on March 22 Randolph and other civil rights leaders met with President Truman. Randolph told Truman, "Mr. President, after making several trips around the country, I can tell you that the mood among Negroes of this country is that they will never bear arms again until all forms of bias and discrimination are abolished."

"I wish you hadn't made that statement. I don't like it at all," bristled Truman.

"I'm giving you the facts," replied Randolph. At that point, the president abruptly ended the meeting.[72]

Truman's icy response did not, however, deter Randolph and

Reynolds. Testifying before the Senate Armed Services Committee on March 31, both men vowed to organize a campaign of civil disobedience, urging young black men to resist induction into a Jim Crow military. "This time," Randolph warned the senators, "Negroes will not take a jim crow draft lying down. The conscience of the world will be shaken as by nothing else when thousands and thousands of us second-class Americans choose imprisonment in preference to permanent military slavery. . . . I personally will advise Negroes to refuse to fight as slaves for a democracy they cannot possess and cannot enjoy." When Senator Wayne Morse cautioned him that aiding and encouraging resistance to the draft in time of war was treason, Randolph stood firm. "I believe that is the price we have to pay for democracy that we want."[73] Later, Reynolds would write of their testimony, "I was convinced of the idea's effectiveness as soon as the testimony was concluded. We had sat in the Senate committee room all morning, and observed the cool and indifferent treatment that was given to representatives of the [NAACP] and other race-relations organizations whose proposals were couched in familiar legal and Constitutional terms. It wasn't until Mr. Randolph and I laid down the civil-disobedience 'ultimatum' that the Senators across the table . . . came to life and seemed to realize that here was something new to contend with. . . . For in that brief hour's testimony, we informed the nation and the world that segregation was reaching an unbearable point."[74]

Some black leaders were critical of Randolph and Reynolds's proposal, fearing that the last thing blacks needed was to have the label "treason" hung around their necks. But many others were open to the suggestion of resisting the draft. In April at a National Defense Conference on Negro Affairs organized by Secretary of Defense James Forrestal, the black leaders involved refused to go on record against Randolph and Reynolds. Other black leaders were enthusiastic, such as Congressman Adam Clayton Powell of New York, who declared, "We are not going to be frightened by the cry of 'Treason.' If the finger of treason can be pointed at anyone, it must be pointed at those of you who are traitors to our Constitution and to our Bill of Rights. There aren't enough jails in America to hold the colored people who will refuse to bear arms in a jim crow army."[75] (Ironically, both Randolph and Reynolds were hardly Powell's friends. Randolph and Powell had long been rivals in New York City black politics and Reynolds had run against Powell for Congress in 1946.)

Powell's warning about the lack of prison cells was no idle threat. A poll by the NAACP's Youth Division of black draft-age college students showed that 71 percent favored Reynolds and Randolph's proposal and only 15 percent opposed it. When asked if they would serve in the event of a war, 51 percent said they would serve only if segregation were abolished. Ten percent said they would not serve under any conditions. Although the poll did not survey a representative cross section of blacks, it did indicate that black draft resistance might be a serious problem.[76] Reynolds has maintained that it is "speculation" to guess how successful their campaign might have been, commenting, "Who knows what the FBI and J. Edgar Hoover would have done if we had gone through with it." Nonetheless, he has remarked that his speeches were "well received" by black audiences.[77]

Randolph and Reynolds also found support among some liberal whites. Columnist Max Lerner wrote, "The threat of civil disobedience undoubtedly weakens the military front we present to Russia; but what weakens us far more is the fact of racist discrimination. . . . World War III will be fought over the world as an ideological war. . . . And in such a struggle one of the real enemies within is Jim Crow. It is Jim Crow who will be committing treason, who has already committed treason."[78] *Time* and *Newsweek* treated Randolph and Reynold's testimony before Congress sympathetically. *Time* wrote, "In the bitter ideological war between Communism and democracy, too many Americans forget what the Communists never let others forget—that democracy in the U.S. is far from perfect. Last week those Americans got a jolting reminder from . . . A. Philip Randolph."[79] According to *Newsweek,* "To a self-conscious and edgy nation, mounting its third great mobilization, what had previously been an incidental fact of life was rapidly becoming a top-priority problem. Negro sentiment against segregation in the armed services had reached the boiling point."[80]

Throughout the spring of 1948, Randolph and Reynolds kept up the pressure, including picketing in front of the White House. As the two sought to influence the president, both international and domestic considerations worked to their advantage. At home, Henry Wallace's presidential campaign appeared to be drawing strong support, forcing Truman to do nothing that might further alienate black voters. Even more importantly, the war fears of the spring grew much worse on June 24, when the Soviet Union clamped a blockade on West Berlin. Two days later, Randolph announced that unless the president issued an executive order barring segregation in the military, when the draft resumed in August he would organize a League for Non-Violent Civil Disobedience Against Military Segregation to "work in the big east coast cities in behalf of a campaign of civil disobedience, non registration, and non induction."[81]

With war appearing imminent, President Truman could not run the risk of black opposition to the draft. "With a political campaign approaching and a crisis already at hand in Europe," wrote Truman biographer Robert Donovan, Randolph had "put Truman in a corner."[82] The president soon gave in. On July 26, 1948, he issued Executive Order 9981, calling for "equality of treatment and opportunity for all persons in the armed services without regard to race, color, religion, or national origin." Although the order made no direct mention of it, when a reporter asked Truman the next day if the directive required "eventually the end of segregation," the President responded unequivocally, "Yes." Satisfied, Randolph decided to call off his civil disobedience campaign.[83] Ironically, Randolph was able to achieve two of the most important civil rights measures in this century, the FEPC and integration of the military, via threats (and perhaps bluffs). If not the most widely known civil rights leader in American history, Randolph was surely one of the most important and most shrewd.

Civil rights advocates also played a key role in pushing the 1948 Democratic National Convention to adopt a civil rights platform plank that was significantly stronger than the president's proposal. Truman still hoped that he might avert growing threats of a southern bolt from the Democratic party. To do this, he proposed retaining the party's 1944 civil rights plank, which declared mildly, "We believe that racial and religious minorities have the right to live, develop and vote equally with all citizens and share the rights that are guaranteed by our Constitution. Congress should exert its full constitutional powers to protect those rights."[84] Northern Democratic liberals, however, saw several benefits in a stronger civil rights plank. The issue had come to hold a central place in their ideology, providing, according to Harvard Sitkoff, "a needed moral justification for their own anti-communist liberalism." Several pragmatic reasons also urged promotion of civil rights. Truman seemed certain to lose in November, with or without a southern bolt, but taking a strong stand on civil rights might rally the black vote in the North and help to salvage the election for Democrats running in state and local contests. In addition, if such a plank caused the South to defect, it would further enhance the power of northern liberals in party councils.[85]

Spearheaded by the newly formed Americans for Democratic Action (ADA), liberals pushed the convention to adopt a minority civil rights plank, one that in fact endorsed and reiterated the president's own civil rights proposals. Hubert Humphrey, the mayor of Minneapolis and Democratic candidate for the U.S. Senate that fall, made his first appearance on the national stage when he told the delegates the time for civil rights was now: "There are those who say to you— we are rushing this issue of civil rights. I say we are 172 years late. . . . [T]he time has arrived for the Democratic Party to get out of the shadow of states' rights and walk forthrightly into the bright sunshine of human rights." Humphrey later wrote, "Then I set [the speech] in the international scene. It was the practice in those post-war, early cold-war years to make these international comparisons." He told the delegates, "Every citizen in this country has a stake in the emergence of the United States as a leader of the free world. That world is being challenged by the world of slavery. For us to play our part effectively we must be in a morally sound position. We can't use a double standard. . . . Our demands for democratic practices in other lands will be no more effective than the guarantee of those practices in our own country." [86] Despite opposition from the South and from Truman loyalists, the convention took Humphrey's advice and adopted the minority plank. Whether he liked it or not, Truman would have to run as the candidate of civil rights. [87]

This civil rights plank finally set off the southern rebellion against the Democratic party that had been building for years. After it passed, the delegation from Mississippi and half that from Alabama walked out of the convention. (Among those who walked out was Birmingham Public Safety Commissioner Eugene "Bull" Connor. Among those who stayed was a young and as yet racial moderate George Wallace). [88] These and other dissident Southerners organized the States Rights party convention in Birmingham a few days later. The "Dixiecrats," as they were better known, nominated South Carolina governor J. Strom Thurmond as their candidate for president. Although Thurmond and other Dixiecrats tried to argue that they were motivated by the cause of states' rights, not white supremacy, this ploy was more a reflection of the nation's declining tolerance for overt racism rather than any genuine devotion to principle by the Dixiecrats. Racism was never far below the surface at the Birmingham convention and often bubbled over. The keynote speaker, former Alabama governor Frank Dixon (wrapping up a half century of Dixon family contributions to American racism), denounced civil rights as a diabolical plan "to reduce us to the status of a mongrel, inferior race, mixed in blood, our Anglo-Saxon heritage a mockery."[89] "That whole Dixiecrat thing in 1948 being about race, that's all wrong," Thurmond still avers. "It wasn't about race, it was about states' rights. Harry Truman wanted to be a dictator, just like Saddam Hussein." The judgment of one of his contemporaries, Clark Clifford, seems more accurate, "Men often try to change their image in response to the flow of history, and Thurmond . . . the senior serving United States Senator and a Republican for over thirty years, later worked hard to develop a different image—but in 1948 he led a political movement based openly and almost entirely upon racism."[90]

As Truman went about his seemingly hopeless fall campaign, he continued to champion civil rights rather than taking the milder approach he had assumed at the convention. In October, he became the first president and only the second presidential candidate to campaign in Harlem (the first was Wendell Willkie in 1940). Speaking on the first anniversary of his civil rights committee's report, he told his audience that he had created the PCCR "because racial and religious intolerance began to appear after World War II. They threatened the very freedoms we had fought to save." The president added that enacting the report's recommendations was crucial since "the democratic way of life is being challenged all over the world. Democracy's answer to the challenge of totalitarianism is its promise of equal rights and equal opportunity for all mankind."[91]

Truman went on to startle the nation by winning in November. In most analyses of the 1948 election, the votes of northern blacks are seen as crucial to Truman's victory. Hence many observers, both at the time and since, have credited his stand on civil rights to cynical political calculations. There is merit to this view. Harry Truman was, if nothing else, a politician and the November 1947 memorandum that set out his campaign strategy for 1948 was clear in its appraisal of the importance of black voters and a strong position on civil rights.[92]

Yet, important as they may well have been, Truman's support for civil rights was not solely the result of political calculations. As mentioned previously, personal and foreign policy considerations were at least as important as his desire to win election. In fact, an August 1948 memo from Clark Clifford argued that Truman "should stress the need for a federal Civil Rights program to cover every section of the United States, to prove to the world that the great benefits of American democracy are meant for all groups in the country."[93] This memo suggests that the Truman campaign's focus on civil rights was done as much for international reasons as for domestic politics.

Furthermore, as an electoral strategy, Truman's campaign represented a brave gamble. The president had other options. He might have held back on the issue of civil rights to appease southern conservatives and shore up the Solid South, while pressing New Deal economic issues to gather enough votes in the rest of the country to win. Such a strategy had, after all, worked well for Roosevelt. Not only did he win four elections but he still managed to carry a sizable percentage of the black vote. In contrast, even with his advocacy of civil rights, of the six northern states with the largest black populations, Truman lost four: New York, New Jersey, Pennsylvania, and Michigan. Truman's victories in the other two, Ohio and Illinois, probably had more to do with his strength in farm areas than with blacks. Going for the black vote was certainly not a sure route to victory for him, and it is unlikely that he thought it was.

Whatever the reasons for Truman's support for civil rights, much more significant is that it seemed to have succeeded. For the first time since the 1860s, support for black rights was seen as a net gain in presidential politics. Before 1948, presidential candidates had sought black votes, but almost always in careful, symbolic, and often covert ways, for fear of triggering a white backlash in the North as well as the South. Truman, on the other hand, openly and directly bid for black votes by promising substantive action on civil rights. In doing so, he signaled that enough white Americans, particularly in the North, had come to view at least some civil rights measures (those dealing with the South) with a measure of approval or at least tolerance.

And if black votes could shape presidential choices, it was because blacks themselves had made them matter. Not only had the Great Migration increased the number of black voters in the North, but the rising militancy of the previous decade had raised black expectations and demands. No longer would they be satisfied with the usual efforts to woo their votes, such as symbolic appointments to meaningless positions or token appearances by candidates with a few well chosen black representatives. Now, candidates would be judged on their promise to provide substantive benefits and their ability to deliver if elected. All in all, Truman's attempt to capture their votes in 1948 signals a significant breakthrough in the political position of black Americans.

Truman continued pushing for civil rights after the 1948 election, but to no avail. Although the Democrats had recaptured both houses of Congress, the president's civil rights proposals fared no better than under the Republicans. Throughout the rest of Truman's term in office, southern obstructionism prevented passage of any civil rights measures.

Nonetheless, civil rights supporters continued to use foreign policy arguments to make their case. During debates in 1950 over the creation of a permanent FEPC, Connecticut senator William Benton told his colleagues that as an official with the State Department and then the U.N., he "saw how our unsolved civil rights problems hampered our efforts and our prestige in reaching out—gropingly as it were—for the hearts and the minds of men."[94] (Benton, of course, knew a thing or two about reaching hearts and minds. Prior to his career in government, he and Chester Bowles—another liberal foreign policy official deeply concerned over the impact of Jim Crow abroad—had founded the Madison Avenue advertising firm of Benton and Bowles.)

That same year, Eleanor Roosevelt declared, "Racial discrimination is the weak spot in our democracy." More importantly, she abandoned the go-slow approach that she had advocated during the war and now advocated a bolder and speedier response to the problem: "Until now we have regarded it as our own domestic problem which would be settled in good time. We felt that we could afford to wait, but that day is past. Racial discrimination is now an international problem, and the way we treat our minorities is one of the major weapons used against us by our enemies. We must re-examine ourselves and work out a solution as quickly as possible."[95]

Blacks too made use of Cold War arguments to advance their cause. In 1950, Charles S. Johnson, president of Fisk University, spoke on the popular and influential national radio program *America's Town Meeting of the Air.* He told the audience that racial inequality was the "Achilles heel" of America's foreign policy. "We are before the bar of world opinion as the chief advocate of the right of individuals to live as free men, equal before the law," Johnson declared. "Unless we can solve our own racial problem we cannot hope to plead successfully the cause of freedom and equality for others."[96]

While they were becoming increasingly frequent, sentiments such as these were as yet unable to prevail in Congress. The best President Truman could accomplish during his second term was to veto an education bill requiring schools on federal property to follow the segregation dictates of the states in which they were located. In his veto message, Truman declared, "We have assumed a role of world leadership in seeking to unite people of great cultural and racial diversity for the purpose of resisting aggression, protecting their mutual security and advancing their own economic and political development. We should not impair our moral position by enacting a law that requires a discrimination based on race. Step by step we are discarding old discrimination; we must not adopt new ones."[97]

Many have suggested that President Truman failed to push hard enough for his civil rights measures.[98] Perhaps so; but we should keep in mind that if Truman got none of his civil rights proposals through Congress, the rest of his domestic agenda fared little better. It seems fair to suggest that Truman's failure to push civil rights through Congress came more from a lack of ability than from a lack of will.[99]

Despite the failure of its efforts in Congress, the Truman administration continued to press for civil rights in the courts. In 1949, the Justice Department filed an *amicus* brief with the Supreme Court in the case of *Henderson v. United States,* arguing against segregated dining cars on interstate trains. Even more than in its brief in the *Shelley* case, the department's brief in *Henderson* conspicuously cited the damage such Jim Crow practices did to U.S. interests abroad. It also contended that racial discrimination fed domestic radicalism and subversion: "The apparent hypocrisy of a society professing equality but practicing segregation and other forms of racial discrimination furnishes justification and reason for the latent urge to rebel, and frequently leads to lasting bitterness or total rejection of the American creed and system of government."[100]

With such views being advanced ever more widely, civil rights progress began to come on other fronts, if not in Congress. From 1946 to 1952, six states (Massachusetts, Connecticut, New Mexico, Oregon, Rhode Island, and Washington) passed fair employment practices legislation and six states (Connecticut, New Jersey, New York, Rhode Island, Massachusetts, and Oregon) passed laws barring discrimination in public accommodations. Similar measures were also passed by numerous local governments. Various state and local authorities also began enforcing Reconstruction-era antidiscrimination statutes that had lain dormant for over a half century.[101] Even at the state and local level, Cold War concerns played a role. In Illinois, Democratic governor Adlai Stevenson argued for greater state efforts to protect civil rights, claiming that "a democracy qualified by color" would damage American interests throughout the world.[102]

One of the most important changes in race relations in this period came not in the halls of government but on the fields of America's pastime, baseball. More than fifty years after Jackie Robinson first broke baseball's color line, most accounts of the event portray it as a triumph of individual spirit over adversity. Although Robinson's athletic prowess and indomitable character were magnificent, he was hardly the first black ballplayer capable of succeeding in the major leagues. Robinson's breakthrough was made possible by the same forces that had put civil rights on the nation's political agenda: World War II and the militancy of black and white civil rights advocates. In the words of historian Jules Tygiel, "The changes wrought by World War II and the dogged dedication of integration advocates had at last elevated the issue to the forefront of public attention and thereby hastened the end of Jim Crow in baseball."[103]

Beginning in the 1930s, rising revulsion at Nazi racial policies put pressure on all forms of Jim Crow, including major league baseball. In 1938, columnist Westbrook Pegler claimed that baseball treated "Negroes as Adolf Hitler treats the Jews."[104] With the outbreak of World War II, the service of black soldiers made baseball's exclusion of blacks all the more troubling. In 1945, major league commissioner A. B. "Happy" Chandler told a black sportswriter, "If a black boy can make it on Okinawa and Guadalcanal, hell, he can make it in baseball."[105] Just as in the army, the lack of manpower also put pressure on baseball to recruit blacks. As the draft depleted the ranks of top white athletes, teams had to sign players with lesser skills, including, in one case, a one-armed outfielder. Such examples led several owners to contemplate signing black ballplayers to replenish their talent.[106]

Political pressure also helped change the attitudes of the whites who ran baseball. Throughout the war, blacks and their white allies, particularly those in the Communist Party, persistently attacked baseball's Jim Crow policies. One black newspaper wrote mockingly, "Let the Negro have his name on the casualty lists of Pearl Harbor or Bataan or Midway. But, for heavensakes, let's keep his name out of the boxscores."[107] In 1943, singer, activist, and former college and professional football star Paul Robeson addressed the baseball owners to argue for integration of the major leagues.[108] On opening day in 1945, Communist protesters picketed Yankee Stadium with signs that read, "If We Can Stop Bullets, Why Not Balls?"[109] Later that year, Benjamin Davis, New York City's black Communist city councilman ran for reelection by passing out flyers that showed a dead black soldier and a black baseball players, and read, "Good enough to die for his country, but not good enough for organized baseball."[110] Less publicly, Mayor Fiorello La Guardia was working behind the scenes for integration of New York's teams. The passage of FEPC legislation in New York, the Ives-Quinn law, also put great pressure on the teams in that state to integrate.[111]

The end of baseball's color line began in October 1945, when the Brooklyn Dodgers signed Jackie Robinson to their minor-league farm team in Montreal. They thought Canada a safer place to begin their integration experiment. In many ways, Robinson himself embodied the changes in black America over the previous three decades. He was raised in Pasadena, California after his mother, like millions of other blacks, fled the South to escape its poverty and oppression. Robinson also represented the growing number of blacks with college educations, having been perhaps the greatest all-around athlete in the fabled history of UCLA. During the World War II, he served in the army and, like many other blacks in uniform, he railed against the military's Jim Crow policies. In 1944, the future American icon was nearly court-martialed after he refused to go along when a white bus driver told him to "get to the back of the bus where the colored people belong."[112]

The response to Robinson's signing strongly reflected the impact of World War II on American race relations. Indeed, those who supported Robinson's signing often referred to the war's egalitarian goals and the service of black soldiers. The *New York Times* editorialized, "If we are willing to let Negroes as soldiers fight wars on our team, we should not ask questions about color in the great American game."[113] A *Sporting News* columnist created an imaginary exchange between several whites discussing the Robinson signing. After one of the men claimed that baseball would soon become a minstrel show, another responded, "Wake up Willie, this is 1945. Negroes helped win the war."[114]

On April 15, 1947, Jackie Robinson made his major league debut, formally ending baseball's policy of racial segregation.[115] Despite often vicious opposition by opposing players and fans, Robinson soon showed himself to be one of the sport's great players. Over time, his skills won him the acceptance of teammates, opposing players, and fans. As Robinson biographer David Falkner pointed out, "In the end [Robinson] was accepted not because the Dodgers were more democratic than the rest of America but because they needed him." So it has been for blacks in America more generally.

Much like Joe Louis, Robinson's ability to achieve greatness despite his race made him a powerful symbol in America's contest against its ideological foes. In 1949, Robinson appeared before the House Committee on Un-American Activities to rebut Paul Robeson's re-

cent assertion that black Americans would never "go to war on behalf of those who have oppressed us . . . against a country [the Soviet
Union] which in one generation has raised our people to the full
dignity of mankind."[116] Robinson confirmed for the committee the
injustices facing black Americans, and he said he was "not fooled
because I've had a chance open to very few American Negroes." Still,
he explained that he had "too much invested for my wife and child
and myself in the future of this country, and I and other Americans
of many races and faiths have too much invested in our country's
welfare, for any of us to throw it away for a siren song sung in bass.
. . . We can win our fight without the Communists and we don't
want their help."[117] Robinson would later come to regret his criticism
of Robeson, for left unsaid was the help Communists and other
radicals, including Paul Robeson, had given in the fight to open the
major leagues to African Americans.

Other black baseball players soon traveled down the path that
Robinson had blazed, both as athletes and as symbols of America's
commitment to democracy and equal rights. In 1953, when the first
black player joined the minor league team in Columbia, South Carolina, the local newspaper wrote, "You will have a difficult time convincing Hank Aaron, a solid medium-size hunk of merchandise, that
America is anything other than the land of opportunity. The communists will be unhappy to hear that this 19-year-old colored boy
from Mobile, Alabama, is getting along nicely—and with a bright
future ahead." Aaron's life, however, showed that opportunity for
black Americans was not so simple and often met powerful resistance. In 1942, his father, Herbert Aaron, was one of the black workers who feared for his life at Mobile's Alabama Dry Dock and Ship
Building Company when white workers rioted over the upgrading
of black welders.[118] Later in his career, Aaron would be profoundly
embittered by the voluminous hate letters and death threats he received for having the temerity to challenge and surpass Babe Ruth's
lifetime home run record.

For despite the progress made by civil rights advocates in the late
1940s, racism was far from vanquished. Throughout the South, efforts to alter the racial status quo met stubborn resistance. Whether
organizing the Dixiecrat revolt in 1948 or heading off the threat of
blacks voting, most white Southerners began manning the barricades
of white supremacy. After the federal courts stopped white primaries,
southern states sought to keep blacks from voting through poll
taxes, literacy tests, and ultimately, violence, intimidation, and economic coercion. These efforts did not stop the rise in black voting,

but they slowed it significantly. In Washington, Southerners worked diligently to obstruct passage of all civil rights proposals. The Dixie-crat campaign of 1948 served notice that the South was willing to break its traditional bond with the Democratic party in the cause of white supremacy. Finally, the primary defeats of liberal Senators Claude Pepper of Florida and Frank Graham of North Carolina in 1950 showed southern whites' narrowing tolerance for even the mildest racial liberalism.

Nor were Southerners the only ones resisting civil rights. Al-though they might have tolerated attacks on Jim Crow in the South, most northern whites were unwilling to confront their own racial practices. Throughout the north, racial violence rose as blacks at-tempted to expand beyond the ghetto boundaries that confined them. Between January 1945 and July 1946, whites attacked forty-six black homes in Chicago. Four full-scale riots against blacks moving into white neighborhoods rocked the city between 1946 and 1949.[119] When Mayor Ed Kelly gave strong support to residential integration, affirming blacks' "right to live peaceably anywhere in Chicago," Chi-cago Democratic machine leaders, closely attuned to the growing racial animosities of their predominantly white ethnic constituents, ousted him in favor of the more conservative Martin Kennelly in 1947.[120]

Although Detroit was the home of the liberal United Auto Work-ers (UAW), the story was much the same there: concerns over blacks moving into white neighborhoods led to the defeat of liberal can-didates. In 1945, Mayor Edward Jeffries won reelection over UAW leader Richard Frankensteen by widely distributing bogus leaflets that read, "Negroes Can Live Anywhere With Frankensteen Mayor. Negroes—Do Your Duty Nov. 6." Four years later, similar fears of black encroachments on white neighborhoods led to the elec-tion of conservative businessman Albert Cobo over George Edwards, a staunch liberal and labor activist with strong support from the UAW.[121]

Although many observers have suggested that white Southerners and northern working class whites defected from the New Deal Democratic coalition in the late 1960s in response to the excesses of racial liberalism, urban riots, and black power rhetoric, the examples of the Dixiecrats and the racialized nature of politics in Chicago and Detroit suggest otherwise.[122] Already by the late 1940s, racial divides, albeit localized ones, were already beginning to appear throughout the Democratic coalition. White "backlash" against racial liberalism thus began long before there was much of anything at which to lash back. The emergence of these divides suggests that racial issues made the Democratic party's effort to construct a broad working class political coalition during the New Deal and after enormously difficult. As those issues began intruding onto the party's political agenda, leaders proved unwilling or unable to find ways to reassure whites that old racial hierarchies could be transformed to the benefit of all. Consequently, the New Deal coalition began to weaken and, ultimately, disintegrate.

And though on balance the Cold War helped precipitate racial progress, it also provided ammunition for some conservative rhetorical weapons. Opponents of racial change regularly tried to discredit civil rights activists as "Communists" and "subversives." These sorts of attacks were nothing new, but they gained added purchase during the paranoid years of the early Cold War. In particular, the anti-Communist backlash had a devastating effect on the left wing of the labor movement. In both the North and the South, several labor unions sought to build an alliance of white and black workers that would challenge the prevailing racial and economic order. Since many of these unions were in fact closely allied with Communists and other radicals, they were highly vulnerable to such attacks. Red-baiting by management, the banning of Communist members by the Taft-Hartley Act, and banishment of these unions from the CIO eventually destroyed them.[123]

The demise of these organizations limited the civil rights movement in several ways. First, many of these unions helped to mobilize working class blacks into the civil rights movement. With their decline, the movement lost much of the grassroots support and militancy that it had developed during World War II. For example, the alliance between UAW leftists and the Detroit NAACP during World War II helped make the latter the largest local branch in the country with twenty-five thousand members. When the Detroit NAACP began purging its leftist members, however, membership dropped to only 5,162 in 1952.[124] Nationally, the NAACP saw a similar decline in membership during the late 1940s and early 1950s for the same reasons.[125] In addition, as the civil rights movement lost its mass base of blue collar workers, it also lost much of its willingness and ability to speak to the economic problems confronting black America.[126]

Yet the rise of anti-Communism only limited the civil rights movement. It did not stop it. In this regard, the assessment of historian Michael Sherry seems accurate, "Scholars disagree on how much anti-communism curbed racial reform—most likely it pushed reform into narrower but faster-running channels—but national security certainly cut both ways."[127] These "narrower but faster-running channels" fostered a civil rights movement better able to take advantage of the instrumental nature of white support for formal black legal and political equality, though less able to push for sweeping egalitarian transformations. This moderate civil rights movement was based more on middle-class blacks and churches as well as legal, not economic, activism. It thus focused (perhaps naively) on reforming what it saw as one deviant and contradictory aspect of American society to make it conform to national ideals of democracy and individual equality, and not on a radical restructuring of the whole racial and economic status quo. It was a movement not of Paul Robeson and W. E. B. Du Bois, but of Martin Luther King Jr. and Thurgood Marshall. Consequently, it was a movement that garnered important allies among white governmental, business, educational, and religious elites, and proved far less vulnerable (though not immune) to anti-Communist fears.[128] (Even Du Bois, who, like Robeson was driven from the United States for his radical views, saw how the Cold War advantaged civil rights. He claimed that the Supreme Court decision in *Brown v. Board of Education* would not have happened "without the world pressure of communism led by the Soviet Union. It was simply impossible for the United States to continue to lead a 'Free World' with race segregation kept legal over a third of its territory.")[129]

Even as Red-baiting dampened some civil rights activism at home, a "hot" phase of the Cold War in Korea provided the impetus for completing the integration of the military. The air force and the navy had made great strides toward desegregating their branches since President Truman's desegregation order in 1948, but in the army bureaucratic inertia and resistance had resulted in only token integration. With the outbreak of the Korean War in June 1950, however, the army quickly acknowledged that continued segregation was inefficient. Heavy casualties left many white combat units seriously short on men, but black units, particularly service battalions, were often greatly overmanned. Several commanders thus began using black soldiers to fill the depleted ranks of white units. As one officer put it, "We had no replacements. . . . We would have been doing ourselves a disservice to permit [black] soldiers to lie around in rear areas at the expense of the still further weakening of our [white] rifle companies."[130] Furthermore, in contrast to the often weak combat performance of ill-trained all-black units, these integrated outfits held up well in their trial by fire. Encouraged by these unofficial experiments, the army in early 1951 authorized the formal integration of its units in Korea, followed soon by similar steps throughout the service. By October 1953, 95 percent of the army's black soldiers were serving in integrated units.[131] The following year the army disbanded its last all-black unit.[132] Although discrimination in the military would remain a problem, after decades of struggle, black Americans had finally won their "fight for the right to fight."

As its units integrated, the military became an important symbol of racial progress to audiences at home and abroad. To the world, an integrated military showed that America practiced what it preached about freedom and equality. President Truman stressed this in a speech at Howard University in June 1952. "From Tokyo and Heidelberg [desegregation] will make our fighting force a more perfect instrument of democratic defense." Furthermore, desegregation of the military had been "taken care of in a quiet and orderly way. The prophets of doom have been proved wrong. The civil rights program has not weakened our country—it has made our country stronger. It has not made us less united—it has made us more united."[133]

In December 1952, the *Saturday Evening Post* echoed Truman's claim. The magazine reported that integration of the military was "taking place in especially 'sensitive' areas, in lands whose people have been indoctrinated by noisy communist propaganda to believe that lynching is the standard method of treatment for Negroes in the United States. When Europeans see white and black American soldiers in casual comradeship in arms today, our moral prestige is raised."[134] Integration of the military also pointed to the possibility of successful integration of American civilian life. The same *Saturday Evening Post* article showed black and white soldiers working and relaxing together. Another photo showed a white officer and his wife socializing in the home of a black officer and his family. This was perhaps the first picture in the mainstream American media of such a scene. The article then asked, "[W]ill the effects of integration carry over into the lives of those exposed to it . . . ? Will it have a lasting impact on their thinking and the way they act when they get back to the United States?" In answer, the article quoted two whites from an integrated unit. The first, a corporal from Georgia, said, "I'll tell you rightly. I didn't much like it when they told us boy's they's bringing a lot of blacks into the command. But then they come in and I got kind of used to the idea." The article closed with the comment of a white officer from Chicago, who stated, "I'll be the first to admit I had my doubts about this whole project when they first loaded it on me. But it's working. I'd be very surprised if things didn't percolate back to the States and have an effect on us there too."[135] Military integration undoubtedly percolated back home. During the Cold War, millions of Americans served in the military, and it was here that many whites had their first experience of living, working, and often fighting and dying on an equal footing with blacks.

As military Jim Crow died on the battlefields of Korea, segregation was undergoing an equally vigorous assault in the courts. In 1950, the Supreme Court issued unanimous decisions in two cases that indicated the first serious cracks in the legal doctrine of separate but equal. In *McLaurin v. Oklahoma* and *Sweatt v. Texas,* the Court struck down segregation in graduate and law schools, and indicated that it was edging ever closer to declaring that *all* separate educational institutions were unconstitutional. In both cases, the Justice Department again filed *amicus* briefs that highlighted foreign policy concerns, declaring that it "is in the context of a world in which freedom and equality must become living realities, if the democratic way of life is to survive, that the issues of these cases should be viewed."[136]

Encouraged by its victories in *Sweatt* and *McLaurin,* the NAACP decided to mount a direct challenge to the separate but equal doctrine and to do so in the area where it mattered most—public schools. In 1952, the NAACP brought the case of *Brown v. Board of Education of Topeka* before the Supreme Court, arguing that segregation in public education was inherently unequal. In appealing for funds to mount their challenge, the NAACP sought to place the case in the context of the Cold War by asking for "CONTRIBUTIONS FROM CITIZENS WHO UNDERSTAND SIGNIFICANCE TO NATIONAL LIFE AND IMPACT UPON WORLD STRUGGLE."[137] In its brief to the Supreme Court, the NAACP's lawyers argued, "Twentieth century America, fighting racism at home and abroad, has rejected the race views of *Plessy v. Ferguson* because we have come to the realization that such views obviously tend to preserve not the strength but the weakness of our heritage."[138] They claimed that the "survival of our country in the present international situation is inevitably tied to resolution of this domestic issue."[139]

Once again, the Department of Justice entered the case on the side of the NAACP with an *amicus* brief. According to Richard Kluger, the brief was "a good deal more useful to the Justices than all ten briefs filed . . . by the litigants."[140] Even more than in its previous briefs, the Department of Justice stressed international concerns, claiming that desegregation of public schools was critical to the nation's foreign policy. In fact, foreign affairs was the principal justification for the government's position, with legal arguments offered as means to achieve the desired goal. As the brief stated:

> It is in the context of the present world struggle between freedom and tyranny that the problem of racial discrimination must be viewed. The United States is trying to prove to the people of the world, of every nationality, race, and color, the a free democracy is the most civilized and most secure form of government yet devised by man. We must set an example for others by showing firm determination to remove existing flaws in our democracy.
>
> The existence of discrimination against minority groups in the United States has an adverse effect upon our relations with the other countries. Racial discrimination furnishes grist for the Communist propaganda mills, and it raises doubts even among friendly nations as to the intensity of our devotion to the democratic faith.[141]

The brief then went on to add a statement from Secretary of State Dean Acheson. According to Acheson:

> During the past six years, the damage to our foreign relations attributable to [racial discrimination] has become progressively greater. The United States is under constant attack in the foreign press, over the foreign radio, and in such international bodies as the United Nations because of various practices of discrimination against minority groups in this country. As might be expected, Soviet spokesmen regularly exploit this situation in propaganda against the United States, both within the United Nations and through radio broadcasts and the press, which reaches all corners of the world. . . . [T]he undeniable existence of racial discrimination gives unfriendly governments the most effective kind of ammunition for their propaganda warfare. The hostile reaction among normally friendly peoples, many of whom are particularly sensitive in regard to the status of non-European races, is growing in alarming proportions. In such countries the view is expressed more and more vocally that the United States is hypocritical in claiming to be the champion of democracy while permitting practices of racial discrimination here in this country.
>
> The segregation of school children on a racial basis is one of the practices in the United States that has been singled out for hostile foreign comment in the United Nations and elsewhere. Other peoples cannot understand how such a practice can exist in a country which professes to be a staunch supporter of freedom,

justices, and democracy. The sincerity of the United States in this respect will be judged by its deeds as well as by its words.

Although progress is being made, the continuance of racial discrimination in the United States remains a source of constant embarrassment to this Government in the day-to-day conduct of its foreign relations; and it jeopardizes the effective maintenance of our moral leadership of the free and democratic nations of the world.[142]

The brief concluded by again reiterating foreign policy concerns:

> In these days, when the free world must conserve and fortify the moral as well as the material sources of its strength, it is especially important to affirm that the Constitution of the United States places no limitations, expressed or implied, on the principle of equality of all men before the law. . . . As the President has stated: "If we wish to inspire the people of the world whose freedom is in jeopardy, if we wish to restore hope to those who have already lost their civil liberties, if we wish to fulfill the promise that is ours, we must correct the remaining imperfections in our practice of democracy. We know the way. We need only the will."[143]

As the Court grappled with the question of school desegregation, the nation elected Dwight D. Eisenhower as president. Whatever his prior beliefs, as president, Truman developed a genuine commitment to equal rights. Eisenhower, raised in the same state that provided the lead case in *Brown v. Board of Education,* proved much less able or willing to shed his commitment to racist beliefs and habits. He would swap "nigger" jokes with his golfing buddies at Augusta, Georgia and always seemed to go out of his way to be sympathetic to white southern racial attitudes.[144] At a White House dinner in the spring of 1954, just as the Supreme Court was preparing its opinion in *Brown,* Eisenhower remarked to Chief Justice Earl Warren, "These [white Southerners] are not bad people. All they are concerned about is to see that their sweet little girls are not required to sit in school alongside some big overgrown Negroes."[145] Eisenhower's only notable pro–civil rights action prior to his presidency came only under pressure. As Supreme Commander in Europe in 1944, a severe shortage of infantrymen forced him to allow limited integration of combat units.

As president, Eisenhower displayed a similar pattern, acting in favor of civil rights only when necessity required. The foremost of these necessities was the Cold War. In 1948, General Eisenhower had opposed integration of the military, telling Congress that "if we attempt merely by passing a lot of laws to force someone to like someone else, we are just going to get into trouble."[146] But national security concerns soon made him more favorable to the idea. During the 1952 campaign, Eisenhower declared, "In a time when America needs all the brains, all the skills, all the spiritual strength and dedicated services of its 157 million people, discrimination is criminally stupid."[147] Upon taking office, Eisenhower's ambassador to the United Nations warned that racial discrimination was the "Achilles heel" of American foreign policy. Other advisors told him that integration of the military helped build U.S. support in the Third World since it "puts us on their side in their drive for national identity." Thus motivated, Eisenhower reversed his earlier opposition and moved to complete the process of desegregating the military begun by Truman.[148]

Cold War concerns also prompted President Eisenhower to desegregate public facilities in Washington, D.C. During the 1952 campaign, he had decried discrimination against nonwhite foreign visitors to the city as "a humiliation to this nation." Furthermore, he added, "This is the kind of loss we can ill afford in today's world" (perhaps because it did not cause global repercussions, he had nothing to say about less costly discriminations against American citizens).[149] Eisenhower was not the only one voicing such concerns. In February 1950, the *Woman's Home Companion* ran an article entitled "Washington—Disgrace to the Nation." The article quoted Senator Hubert Humphrey describing the city's slums as "an international disgrace." It also denounced segregation and lack of home rule in the nation's capital, asking, "How can we sell democracy if we don't dare open our sample case? How can we try to democratize the outside world until we have really democratized Washington, D.C.?"[150] In his first year in office, President Eisenhower signed an executive order integrating all federal facilities in Washington, D.C., since the city was "the Capital of our nation and a symbol of democracy in the eyes of the world."[151] In addition, Attorney General Herbert Brownell submitted an *amicus* brief in a Supreme Court case to support striking down segregation in Washington, D.C. restaurants. Finally, the president also worked behind the scenes to secure desegregation of District theaters and hotels.[152]

Eisenhower also established a Committee on Government Contracts that tried to use publicity and persuasion to achieve greater hiring of minorities in companies with government contracts. Headed by Vice President Richard Nixon, the committee saw its work within the context of America's Cold War foreign policy. In a 1953 report, it stated, "The United States has assumed leadership of the world in a crusade to extend the blessings of liberty and freedom to all men. This Nation was founded on the fundamental principle that all men are created equal. . . . [O]ut of these principles springs our national policy of equal treatment and opportunity. Our government, being a government 'of the people, by the people, and for the people,' can accept no less."[153]

Although purely unintentional, the Eisenhower administration's most important contribution to the struggle for civil rights was the appointment in 1953 of California governor Earl Warren as Chief Justice of the Supreme Court. Warren arrived just as a deeply divided Court was struggling with a decision in *Brown v. Board of Education*. Warren had no previous judicial experience, but his political savvy unified the Court into unanimous support for overturning the separate but equal doctrine and declaring segregation in public schools unconstitutional.[154]

If it lacked the soaring rhetoric of some of the Court's most eloquent opinions, Chief Justice Warren's opinion in *Brown* was notable for its power and clarity. He wrote that to separate black children "from others of similar age and qualifications solely because of their race generates a feeling of inferiority as to their status in the community that may affect their hearts and minds in a way unlikely ever to be undone. . . . We conclude that in the field of public education the doctrine of 'separate but equal' has no place. Separate education facilities are inherently unequal."[155]

The Court's opinion in *Brown v. Board of Education* did not directly address the topics of World War II and the Cold War, but these conflicts seem to have had an important influence nonetheless. As historian and legal scholar Mary Dudziak wrote, "[M]embers of the Court were a particularly receptive audience for the Justice Department's Cold War arguments."[156] In a memo to his brethren, Justice Robert Jackson (who had taken a leave from the Court after the war to serve as the chief prosecutor in the Nuremberg trials) supported striking down segregation in schools by noting the "profound change" in public opinion caused by "the awful consequences of racial prejudice revealed by . . . the Nazi regime."[157] Justice Felix Frankfurter was a close friend of former Secretary of State Dean Acheson, whose comments formed a significant part of the government's brief. In addition, Frankfurter was particularly concerned with discrimination in Washington, D.C. According to Philip Elman, the principal author of the Justice Department's brief and a former clerk of the Justice, Frankfurter saw the District of Columbia as "the showcase of the nation, so called. It was the city where foreign ambassadors saw America and American democracy in action. If we had a blot on our conscience because we were not living up to our professions of equality, the place to begin to clean house was the District of Columbia."[158] As attorney general, Justice Tom Clark had told of his humiliation when the NAACP petitioned the United Nations and had cited foreign policy concerns in *amicus* briefs asking the Court to strike down racially discriminatory measures. Justice William O. Douglas's travels throughout the world had made him sensitive to how racial discrimination tarnished America's image abroad. In his 1951 book *Strange Lands and Friendly People,* describing his travels in India, Douglas wrote that "the attitude of the United States toward its colored minorities is a powerful factor in our relations with India."[159] In the opinion itself, the nation's Cold War need for civic loyalty and military strength surfaced when Chief Justice Warren stressed that education was "the very foundation of good citizenship" and essential for "service in the armed forces."[160]

The foreign policy significance of *Brown* was soon trumpeted by others. Less than an hour after the opinion was handed down, the Voice of America was broadcasting the news around the world in thirty-four languages.[161] After the decision was announced in the Senate, Herbert Lehman of New York rose and declared, "This is news which all freemen throughout the world must hail with joy. It is a victory which will have profound repercussions throughout Asia, among other places, in my judgment."[162] Later, Congressman Adam Clayton Powell called it the "shining hour of democracy" and the "greatest defeat that communism has received."[163] In a press release, the Republican National Committee claimed that the decision "falls appropriately within the Eisenhower Administration's many-frontal attack on global Communism. Human equality at home is a weapon of freedom. . . . It helps guarantee the Free World's cause."[164]

Newspapers and magazines also featured prominently the international implications of the decision:

> *Time:* In many countries, where U.S. prestige and leadership have been damaged by the fact of U.S. segregation, [the *Brown* decision] will come as a timely reassertion of the basic American principle that "all men are created equal."[165]
>
> *Newsweek:* [O]ver the years, segregation has become a symbol of inequality, not only to Negroes in the United States but to colored

peoples elsewhere in the world. It has also been a weapon of world Communism. Now that symbol lies shattered.[166]

Washington Post: [The decision] will help to refurbish American prestige in a world which looks to this land for moral inspiration.[167]

Hartford Courant: And if [the Court's decision] presents incalculable difficulties within our borders, let us not forget that it may have an even deeper and more encouraging impact outside our borders.[168]

Minneapolis Tribune: [T]he words of Chief Justice Warren will echo far beyond our borders and may greatly influence our relations with dark-skinned peoples the world over.[169]

San Francisco Chronicle: Great as the impact of the anti-segregation ruling will be upon the states of the South . . . still greater, we believe, will be its impact in South America, Africa, and Asia, to this country's lasting honor and benefit.[170]

New York Times: This nation is often criticized for its treatment of racial minorities, and particularly of the Negro. There have been grounds for this criticism. . . . When some hostile propagandist rises in Moscow or Peiping to accuse us of being a class society we can if we wish recite the courageous words of yesterday's opinion.[171]

St. Louis Post-Dispatch: The greater significance is the affirmation in the eyes of millions of people in India, Pakistan and Africa, in China, Japan, and Burma, in Indo-China, Thailand, and Indonesia that the pledge in the United States of the worth and dignity of the humblest individual means exactly what it says. Had this decision gone the other way the loss to the free world in its struggle against Communist encroachment would have been incalculable. Nine men in Washington have given us a victory that no number of divisions, arms and bombs could ever have won.[172]

Although most Southerners were sharply critical of the Court's ruling, some conceded foreign policy advantages. According to one Atlanta newspaper, "local leaders and educators" viewed the decision "as a giant step forward for democracy at home and abroad." A member of the city's board of education praised the decision as "an effective and resounding reply to the Communist criticism of our treatment of our minority group."[173]

Even if, as we shall see, the *Brown* ruling did not destroy Jim Crow, it represented the most important blow by the government on segregation and racial discrimination thus far. For many Americans, the decision was a welcome step signaling to the world that the United

States was finally living up to the ideals of democracy and equality it had been emphasizing since World War II. Yet, the Jim Crow institutions and attitudes that had been constructed over the past seventy-five years, which were built on American traditions going back to before the nation's founding, could not be made to vanish by some words of the Supreme Court. Ultimately, bringing America's traditional practices more closely in line with its newly dominant egalitarian rhetoric would require far more struggle and conflict. Indeed, unlike the Cold War, it remains today a war that has not ended.

EIGHT

"There Comes a Time"

The Civil Rights Revolution, 1954–1968

O
n the evening of December 5, 1955, a crowd of several thousand blacks gathered at the Holt Street Baptist Church in Montgomery, Alabama. The church was far too small to hold the overflow crowd. Others gathered on the grounds, across the street, and beyond. One couple could get no closer than within three blocks of the church.

The occasion for the gathering was the first mass meeting of the Montgomery Improvement Association (MIA). Only days before, black seamstress Rosa Parks had been arrested for failing to comply when a white bus driver ordered her to the back of the city bus. Although tensions over segregated buses had been building in Montgomery's black community for months, the arrest of Parks, a local activist and prominent member of the Montgomery chapter of the National Association for the Advancement of Colored People (NAACP), brought matters to a head. Several local women decided to protest Parks's arrest by organizing a boycott by blacks of the city's buses. Aided by the local NAACP and several black churches, they spread the word to the black community. To nearly everyone's surprise the next Monday morning, city buses, usually crowded with blacks on their way to work, were nearly empty.

Parks's arrest and the boycott had clearly touched a nerve in the black community, as evident in the meeting's massive turnout. Tensions and expectations ran high as that evening's main speaker mounted the podium. Though only twenty-six years old and newly installed at the Dexter Avenue Baptist Church, Reverend Martin King Jr. had nonetheless made a deep impression on Montgomery's black community. For this reason, he had been selected to head the MIA and to address the meeting.

"We are here," King told the crowd, "because first and foremost—

242

we are American citizens—and we are determined to apply our citizenship—to the fullness of its means." "And you know, my friends, there comes a time," he continued, "when people get tired of being trampled over by the iron feet of oppression." The crowd roared back its approval, fervently hoping that the time had indeed come. "There comes a time, my friends, when people get tired of being thrown across the abyss of humiliation, where they experience the bleakness of nagging despair. . . . We are here—we are here because we are tired now." The crowd's response was thunderous, but King continued, "And we are determined here in Montgomery—to work and fight until justice runs down like water, and righteousness like a mighty stream!"[1]

King's speech expressed and amplified the sentiments of many black Americans. Since War World II, America had spoken ever more forcefully about its commitment to equality and democracy but had done little to address the denial of these basic rights to its black citizens. Surely, thought many blacks, the time had come for them to demand that America make good this promise to all its citizens. The Montgomery bus boycott marked the first major step in the modern civil rights movement, in which blacks would become increasingly assertive in their quest for equal rights.

Over the next twelve years, this most storied of modern reform movements would achieve great things. Perhaps its most inspirational moment came in August 1963, when Dr. King again was the featured speaker to an unexpectedly large crowd of civil rights supporters. This time, he was standing before the Lincoln Memorial at the climax of the March on Washington, addressing a throng of nearly a quarter of million people, including some seventy thousand whites, as well as millions of broadcast listeners across the nation.[2] By the time King came to the microphones late on that hot and sunny afternoon, already Bob Dylan had sung in sorrow and anger of the death of civil rights activist Medgar Evers. Peter, Paul, and Mary had asked, "How many times can a man turn his head and pretend that he just doesn't see?" Walter Reuther had challenged one such man, the president of the United States, by insisting, "We cannot *defend* freedom in Berlin so long as we *deny* freedom in Birmingham!" But it had been Mahalia Jackson who brought the huge assembly to tears as, with fire and glorious passion, she made the old spiritual "I been 'buked and I been scorned" her personal cry. Then, after A. Philip Randolph had fulfilled his two-decades-old vision of a civil rights march on Washington by introducing the man who was now the nation's most famous civil rights champion, it was

Mahalia Jackson who prompted his most stirring improvisation when she urged, "Tell 'em about the dream, Martin."

Tell them he did, abandoning his text to say, "[E]ven though we face the difficulties of today and tomorrow, I still have a dream. It is a dream deeply rooted in the American Dream. . . ." His words made still-remote visions of simple justice achingly real and beautiful—visions of the sons of former slaves and former slaveowners sitting down together in the red hills of Georgia, of the State of Mississippi, "sweltering with the heat of oppression," transformed "into an oasis of freedom and justice," of an Alabama where "little black boys and black girls will be able to join hands with little white boys and white girls as sisters and brothers. I have a dream today," King told his fellow Americans, black and white, and hearts soared ecstatically with his sonorous words, for on that summer afternoon it seemed that this dream might at last be coming true

Almost five years later, in Memphis on April 3, 1968, King would speak of a better tomorrow one last time; but by then, the hopefulness found in Dr. King's speeches of 1955 and 1963 would be muted by the somber lessons of his subsequent experiences. By then, momentous civil rights bills had finally become the laws of the land. Yet, the everyday condition of most African Americans was little better. Racial violence had recently wracked the nation. A seemingly endless war in Vietnam demanded black manpower but drained resources for change. And as more radical black leaders challenged his dream, even King himself had begun to doubt whether the day would soon come when, as he said once more, "justice runs down like water, and righteousness like a mighty stream!" He still assured a black congregation in Memphis that "we as a people will get to the promised land"—but, he said, "I may not get there with you." The next night, as on another April night one hundred and three years before, and as on far too many other nights in America, before and since, a rifle fired, and a strong voice for racial progress was brutally silenced. Racist violence had once again struck down one who dared not only to dream but to lead the nation's unsteady march toward freedom and justice for all. And once again, violence bred violence. Quickly riots broke out across the nation. In Chicago, so often the scene of racial strife, twenty blocks were soon in flames, and Mayor Richard J. Daley encouraged his riot police to restore order by all necessary means, including shooting to kill.[3]

The great modern era of civil rights reforms was not over when Martin Luther King Jr. was slain on a motel balcony in Memphis; but the changing conditions that would bring it to an end within a decade had already begun to reset the national stage. International imperatives still favored reform, but the expanding Vietnam War increasingly devoured the funds and divided the political forces needed to achieve it. Antiracist protest efforts were splintering, as many embittered blacks rejected King's "American Dream" for more militant "Black Power" organizations. And white resistance to change, never absent, was gaining renewed determination. It all came when so much and yet so little had been achieved.

The emergence of Martin Luther King and the civil rights movement as powerful political forces came at a crucial time. Even though by the mid-1950s the Cold War was putting great pressure on the nation to reform its racial hierarchies, white obstructionism had kept the changes largely symbolic. And if many pointed to the Supreme Court's opinion in *Brown v. Board of Education* as proof of the nation's commitment to racial equality, the ruling, by itself, was accomplishing little. In part this was due to the Court's own unwillingness to push integration too quickly; in its 1955 implementation ruling on *Brown*, it ordered that desegregation proceed only "with all deliberate speed." Though the Court might have been stressing the word *speed*, most white Southerners focused on the word *deliberate* and engaged in a policy of "massive resistance" to the mandated integration. In Washington, all but a handful of the region's representatives and senators signed the "Southern Manifesto," which denounced the *Brown* decision for replacing "naked power for established law" and called on the white South "to resist forced integration by any lawful means."[4]

Back home, white Southerners began organizing grass-roots Citizens' Councils to resist integration. The first was organized in Sunflower County, Mississippi, home of archsegregationist Senator James Eastland. "By 1957," wrote John Egerton, "these 'country club' or 'white collar' Klans (formally known as the Citizens' Councils of America), together with the more traditional KKK units and various other extremist groups, would boast of having more than a half-million dues-paying members."[5] Through economic coercion and physical violence, these groups prevented integration in all but a few southern public schools. By 1960, six full years after *Brown*, only 0.16 percent of southern blacks attended school with whites. In the deep South, the situation was even worse; only 432 blacks (0.02 percent) in 1960–1961 went to integrated schools.[6]

President Eisenhower unintentionally assisted the cause of "massive resistance." After the Court's decision in *Brown*, he refused to speak publicly in favor of the decision, deeming it improper for the president to comment on the actions of another branch of government. Privately, he thought the decision a terrible mistake. More importantly, he also refused to say unequivocally that he would use the full power of the federal government, including federal troops, to enforce the Court's ruling. Underlying this reticence was Ike's own dislike of "forced" integration and the belief that patience and understanding, rather than compulsion by the federal government, could best persuade the white South to comply with the Court's decision in *Brown*. The white South, on the other hand, saw Eisenhower's caution as tacit approval of their policy of "massive resistance" and a sign that the president would never use federal troops to enforce integration.

In addition to the failure to desegregate its schools, an upsurge in racial violence following the *Brown* decision further showed that little in the South was changing for the better. According to political scientist James Sundquist, the four years following *Brown* saw "530 acts of racial violence, including six Negroes killed, twenty-nine persons shot, forty-four beaten, five stabbed, thirty homes bombed, eight burned, seven churches bombed, one burned, and four schools bombed, including a blast in Clinton, Tennessee, so powerful that it damaged thirty nearby homes as well."[7]

Perhaps the most outrageous act of violence was the murder of black fifteen-year-old Emmett Till in August 1955. Till, a Chicago native, had been visiting relatives in Sumner, Mississippi when he allegedly whistled at a white woman. For this offense, Till was beaten, shot, and dumped into the Tallahatchie River. Till's uncle, at great risk to his own life, identified the murderers, but an all-white jury deliberated for only sixty-seven minutes before finding them not guilty.[8] Compounding the outrage at the verdict felt by many Americans was the knowledge that the Till murder was a propaganda disaster for the nation. A survey of international press coverage by the American Jewish Committee found that the incident had "seriously damaged" America's global image. The *Christian Century* wrote that "the horror and indignation that are rolling in from what have been the friendliest foreign journals indicate that the townspeople [of Sumner] have engineered a local tragedy into an international calamity."[9] In addition, the United States Information Agency (USIA) found that following the Till murder and the barring of a black student, Autherine Lucy, from the University of Alabama, criticism of U.S. racial practices became an increasing part of Soviet propaganda broadcasts.[10]

The South's intransigence on desegregation and the post-*Brown* upsurge of racial violence symbolized by the Till case, however, finally forced Eisenhower's hand. Until now, the president had refused to put forward a civil rights bill, but by 1956 it was clear that any progress on civil rights required federal action. At a cabinet meeting in which Secretary of State John Foster Dulles spoke of how incidents of racial discrimination had harmed U.S. foreign relations, Eisenhower finally agreed to allow Attorney General Brownell to submit a civil rights bill to Congress.[11]

In Congress, the bill's supporters connected its purpose to the nation's Cold War struggle. Illinois senator Paul Douglas told his colleagues that incidents of racial discrimination "adversely affect the struggle of freedom against tyranny in the world. With the Communists reaching out to the uncommitted people of the Middle East and Africa and Southeast Asia, each housing riot in Illinois, each school riot in Kentucky, and each bombing of a pastor's home or intimidation of a would-be Negro voter in Alabama or Mississippi becomes not only an affront to human dignity here in this country, but a defeat for freedom in its tough world struggle for survival."[12] Senator Hubert Humphrey agreed, saying, "Just as Lincoln decided upon emancipation of the slaves, not only as an act of justice but also as a military necessity, so the achievement in America of racial equality is now urgently needed on both of these grounds."[13] Senator Joseph Clark of Pennsylvania declared that the denial of civil rights was "presently crippling the efforts of our government to create that atmosphere of mutual respect and confidence throughout the free world on which our national security and our defense against international communism both depend." Senator Jacob Javits of New York announced that the "international stake in civil rights is perhaps the most important consideration of all" regarding civil rights. "I saw this very clearly," he claimed, "in Pakistan, India, south and southeast Asia where I traveled." Javits added:

> The great contest between freedom and communism is over the approximately 1.2 billion largely Negro and Oriental population who occupy the underdeveloped areas of the Far East, the Middle East, and Africa. One of the greatest arguments used by the Communist conspirators against our leadership of the free world with these peoples has been that if they follow the cause of freedom, they too will be subjected to segregation which it is charged that we tolerate within certain areas of the United States; federal civil rights legislation is the best answer. The people are,

therefore, watching with the most pronounced concern our present international struggle on civil rights.[14]

Congress watered down the administration's bill and the former
Dixiecrat presidential candidate, now South Carolina senator Strom
Thurmond, filibustered for a record twenty-four hours, but the legislation finally passed in August 1957. The bill created a permanent
Civil Rights Commission, upgraded the Justice Department's Civil
Rights Section to a division headed by an assistant attorney general,
and established greater power for the Justice Department to protect
voting rights. Although relatively weak, the Civil Rights Act of 1957
still stands as an important achievement. For the first time since
Reconstruction, Congress had passed legislation to help protect the
civil rights of black Americans.

Yet the response to this relatively weak civil rights measure revealed just how deeply notions of racial hierarchy influenced the
personal and political identities of many whites. In his survey of
letters to Congress on the 1957 bill, historian David Alan Horowitz
found, "Feelings of helplessness concerning increased government
jurisdiction over personal life often seemed to be tied to fears that
human distinctions would be erased through miscegenation and the
emergence of one race. To some civil rights critics, racial differences
as well as ethnic and national differences were necessary to preserve
the distinctive features of human personality and culture. . . . Oblit-
eration of racial distinctions seemed to convey a vision of mass deper-
sonalization to those Americans frightened by the civil rights revolution." One correspondent from Indiana wrote, "I am perfectly willing
to sit in any part of the car assigned to me, but I do not want to
sit by just anybody." He then questioned the meaning of freedom
in a country that sought "to put everybody in the same mold, forcing the mixture of the races." A Texas man complained that the bill
would deprive whites of freedom of association and that it "means
to make one of more than one. . . . It means to mix-up and blend
into one thing two or more separate things to a degree and to and an
extent that the component parts are no longer distinguishable. . . ."[15]

As President Eisenhower signed the 1957 Civil Rights Act on September 9, events in Little Rock, Arkansas confirmed the depth of
white racial resentment suggested in these letters. When school authorities began the court-ordered desegregation of Little Rock's Central High School, Governor Orval Faubus called out the state's National Guard to block the action. Reluctant to confront him
publicly, Eisenhower tried at first to negotiate with Faubus. The gov-

ernor agreed to remove the Arkansas Guard and allow the black students to enter the school, but he then stood by as a white mob attacked blacks and white journalists. The escalating violence finally forced the black children to leave the school.

The incident compelled a reluctant Eisenhower to act. Not only had a state governor defied the orders of the federal courts, but the pictures of the incident flashed around the world powerfully contradicted America's self-proclaimed commitment to justice and equality. Historian Mary Dudziak has shown that foreign coverage of Little Rock was widespread and highly critical.[16] A Singapore newspaper contained a typical response: "What shocks the public conscience is that this rotten states of affairs is permitted in a country which, according to Eisenhower, 'has the responsibility of the free world's leadership laid upon it by destiny.' What manner of men inhabit that country?"[17]

Commentary such as this caused Secretary of State Dulles to tell Attorney General Brownell during the crisis that "this situation was ruining our foreign policy," and that its impact "in Asia and Africa will be worse for us than Hungary was for the Russians."[18] The president was well aware of these global considerations. After Faubus used the National Guard to block integration, one report to Eisenhower claimed, "Soviet media single out the Little Rock situation for special attention and take pains to point out that armed national guardsmen are not there to protect Negro children from the fanatics of the Ku Klux Klan, but to prevent them from entering school." In addition it quoted Radio Moscow as saying that U.S. ambassador to the United Nations, Henry Cabot Lodge, "tells lies stuffed with slander and makes a great deal of fuss trying to prevent the Hungarian people from living in peace and quiet, but the cries of hundreds of Negro children, ill-treated by the whites, rises from the Southern states and drown out his voice."[19] Later, in his memoirs, Eisenhower wrote, "Overseas, the mouthpieces of Soviet propaganda in Russia and Europe were blaring that 'anti-Negro violence' in Little Rock was being committed with the clear connivance of the United States government. . . ." If the crisis had continued, it would have continued "to feed the mill of Soviet propagandists who by word and picture were telling the world of the 'racial terror' in the United States."[20]

Faced with domestic discord, a constitutional crisis, and an international embarrassment, on September 24 President Eisenhower finally called in federal troops to restore order around Central High and enforce the desegregation order. Cutting short a vacation, Eisenhower flew back to Washington to speak to the nation on the crisis.

As he prepared his speech, Secretary Dulles called to suggest that the president "put in a few more sentences . . . emphasizing the harm done abroad."[21]

That evening, as the first truckloads of soldiers from the 101st Airborne Division pulled up in front of Central High, the president told the nation:

> In the South, as elsewhere, citizens are keenly aware of the tremendous disservice that has been done to the people of Arkansas in the eyes of the nation, and that has been done to the nation in the eyes of the world.
>
> At a time when we face grave situations abroad because of the hatred that Communism bears toward a system of government based on human rights, it would be difficult to exaggerate the harm that is being done to the prestige and influence, and indeed to the safety, of our nation and the world.
>
> Our enemies are gloating over this incident and using it everywhere to misrepresent our whole nation. We are portrayed as a violator of those standards of conduct which the peoples of the world united to proclaim in the Charter of the United Nations. . . .
>
> If resistance to the Federal Court orders ceases at once, the further presence of Federal troops will be unnecessary and the City of Little Rock will return to its normal habits of peace and order and a blot upon the fair name and high honor of our nation in the world will be removed.[22]

After the speech, wrote historian Robert Burk, "the Eisenhower administration immediately took steps to insure maximum international propaganda benefit from the action. . . . President Eisenhower's television address . . . was translated into forty-three languages, and the Voice of America broadcast details of the troop intervention."[23]

Press reactions to the Little Rock crisis also stressed its foreign policy implications. The *New York Times* declared, "Red Press Gloats Over Little Rock."[24] *Newsweek* called the incident "a propaganda windfall of truly major proportions for the Communists" and carried reproductions of various foreign headlines reporting the crisis and their English translations. It also wrote that "Moscow's *Pravda,* noting that Secretary of State John Foster Dulles has said U.S. foreign policy was based on moral and religious principles, commented acidly: 'The reports and pictures from Little Rock show graphically that Dulles's precious morals are in fact bespattered with innocent blood.' "[25] According to *Time,* "In Little Rock . . . the racist crowds hounded those who opposed them as pro-Communist. But it was, in fact, Orval Faubus and his followers who gave aid and comfort to Communism. . . . In Budapest, Hungary's ruthless Premier Janos Kadar fairly kicked his heels in joy. Cried he: 'Those who tolerate that a people should be persecuted because of the color of their skin have no right to preach human liberty and human rights.' In the United Nations, after a dark-skinned Ceylonese delegate denounced Soviet intervention in Hungary, Bulgaria's Peter Voutov retorted: 'Something worse could happen to you in Little Rock.' "[26] Later, the magazine editorialized that "Little Rock was a name known wherever men could read newspapers and listen to radios, a symbol to be distorted in Moscow, misinterpreted in New Delhi, painfully explained in London."[27]

In the month following Little Rock, the United States Information Agency polled people around the world regarding the Little Rock incident and American race relations in general (see table 7). The results showed that these claims of international impact were not imaginary. The report concluded that the "losses" to U.S. prestige resulting from Little Rock were "of such a magnitude as to outweigh the effects of any recent factors which have contributed to increases in U.S. standing."[28] President Eisenhower requested that United Nations ambassador Lodge come up with suggestions on how to counter the damage.[29]

The federal government was not the only institution that was made aware of how incidents like Little Rock were hurting its efforts abroad. Southern Baptist missionaries in nonwhite nations also made sure to inform their brethren at home of the problems they faced. Shortly after the Little Rock crisis, the Louisiana Southern Baptist Convention was rocked when two retired African missionaries introduced a resolution calling for "law and order" and thus implicitly condemning Governor Faubus. In Little Rock, a prominent Baptist minister was overwhelmed with critical letters from missionaries around the world.[30]

Concerns over America's image abroad pushed President Eisenhower to ask for additional civil rights legislation in 1959. In his State of the Union Address that year, the president declared, "If we hope to strengthen freedom in the world we must be ever mindful of how our own conduct reacts elsewhere. No nation has ever been so floodlighted in world opinion as the United States is today. Every thing we do is carefully scrutinized by other peoples throughout the world. . . . In other areas of human rights—freedom from discrimination in voting, in public education, in access to jobs, and in other

Table 7. USIA Survey of Foreign Opinion Regarding U.S. Race Relations, 1957

All things considered, do you think that current developments with regard to Negro-white relations in the U.S. tend more to raise or more to lower American standing in the world?	Affects, Harms, Lowers	Does Not	No Opinion
Brussels	71	14	15
London	65	11	24
Paris	61	4	35
Amsterdam	55	22	23
Frankfurt	37	10	55

Do you think the majority of the American people approve or disapprove of Negroes and whites attending the same schools?	Most Americans Favor Equality	Most Americans Oppose Equality	Don't Know	Net Approval
London	28	50	22	−22
Paris	19	43	38	−24
Frankfurt	17	27	56	−10
Brussels	44	35	21	9
Amsterdam	50	25	25	25
Oslo	50	35	15	15
Stockholm	37	43	20	−6
Copenhagen	46	36	18	10
Helsinki	44	41	15	3
Athens	39	29	32	10
New Delhi	14	33	53	−19
Tokyo	21	46	33	−25
Mexico City	26	55	19	−29

Do you have a very good opinion, good, fair, bad, or very bad opinion of the treatment of Negroes in the United States?	Very Good, Good	Fair	Bad, Very Bad	No Opinion	Net Approval
Brussels	12	13	67	8	−55
Copenhagen	5	11	82	2	−77
Helsinki	2	26	63	9	−61
Paris	2	12	74	12	−72
Frankfurt	39	23	17	21	22
London	13	20	59	8	−46
Athens	21	23	33	23	−12
New Delhi	3	7	41	49	−38
Italy	12	18	34	36	−22
Tokyo	6	16	53	25	−47
Mexico City	9	16	61	14	−52
Amsterdam	4	15	79	5	−74
Oslo	5	11	79	5	−74
Stockholm	1	7	87	5	−86

Source: Hazel Erskine, "The Polls: World Opinion of U.S. Racial Problems," *Public Opinion Quarterly* 32 (1968): 299–312.

respects—the world is likewise watching our conduct. The image of America abroad is not improved when school children . . . are deprived of their opportunity for an education. . . . By moving steadily toward the goal of greater freedom under law, for our own people, we shall be better prepared to work for the cause of freedom under law throughout the world."[31] The president's proposal eventually became the Civil Rights Act of 1960.

The bill still fell far short of a strong signal that the executive branch really meant to enforce racial reform; and even after Little Rock, the white South had gone too far down the road of massive resistance to now retreat voluntarily. As perhaps the most widely respected president of this century, Eisenhower's use of the bully pulpit could have greatly aided the cause of racial equality. In particular, his standing as a military leader would have allowed him to make a compelling case for the foreign policy necessities of civil rights. Sadly, Eisenhower did not. As a soldier and as president, Eisenhower served his country as well as any other American in the twentieth century, but in the area of civil rights he proved sorely lacking.

Black Americans were not, however, waiting on Ike. The success of the Montgomery bus boycott and the government's thus far tepid support for civil rights indicated to many that direct action was the best strategy for achieving real change. As Eisenhower prepared to leave office in 1960, a wave of sit-ins at department store lunch counters demonstrated this growing activism.

The strategies and tactics of this movement were greatly influenced by the nation's Cold War context. King and other civil rights leaders knew that foreign policy concerns provided blacks with great leverage in securing their rights. According to King, civil rights was an "issue which may well determine the destiny of our nation it its ideological struggle with communism."[32]

Drawing on several examples, from Gandhi's resistance to British colonial rule in India to domestic examples of black militancy and protest during the 1930s and 1940s, black protesters underlined to the nation and the world the contradiction between America's claims of democracy and freedom and the reality of its treatment of black Americans. When racist whites lashed out at black demonstrators, King wrote, they "were caught—as a fugitive from a penitentiary is often caught—in gigantic circling spotlights . . . a luminous glare revealing the naked truth to the whole world."[33]

Civil rights advocates also drew inspiration from the decolonization and liberation struggles in Africa and Asia. Throughout the 1950s, Britain, France, and other European nations gave up or were

forced to give up their colonial holdings in Africa and Asia. Consequently, the number of independent nonwhite nations increased significantly. In 1960 alone, sixteen African nations became independent. These changes inspired black Americans to see their struggles
as part of a global movement. In 1955, in the early months of the
Montgomery bus boycott, Martin Luther King wrote that he saw
that struggle as "a part of [an] overall movement in the world in
which oppressed people are revolting against . . . imperialism and
colonialism."[34] After attending independence ceremonies in Ghana
in 1957, King told an audience of black Americans, "Ghana tells us
that the forces of the universe are on the side of justice. . . . An old
order of colonialism, of segregation, of discrimination is passing away
now, and a new order of justice and freedom and goodwill is being
born."[35] The end of colonialism not only inspired blacks but it empowered them as well, as the changing global environment provided
a powerful tool for pressuring the government to meet their demands. While in Ghana, Martin Luther King told Vice President
Nixon, "Mr. Vice President, I'm very glad to meet you here, but I
want you come to visit us down in Alabama where we are seeking
the same kind of freedom Ghana is celebrating."[36]

The student activists who started the sit-ins made many similar
claims. In "An Appeal for Human Rights," the leaders of the Atlanta
sit-ins declared, "America is fast losing the respect of other nations
by the poor example which she sets in the area of race relations."[37]
These and other activists soon joined together to form the Student
Nonviolent Coordinating Committee (SNCC). That summer, SNCC
prepared a statement to present to the Democratic National Convention. SNCC's representative, Marion Barry, told the Democrats' Platform Committee, "America cannot fail in its responsibility to the
free world. We must be strong. Civil defense and economic power
alone will not assure the continuation of democracy. This democracy itself demands the great intangible strength of a people able to
unite in a common endeavor because they are granted a common
dignity. This challenge cannot be met unless and until all Americans,
Negro and white, enjoy the full promise of our democratic heritage—first class citizenship."[38]

Statements such this were echoed by both parties' presidential
candidates in 1960. Republican Richard Nixon and Democrat John
F. Kennedy each spoke out in favor of civil rights as a Cold War
imperative. Only weeks before their first debate, Soviet Premier Ni-
kita Khrushchev had scored propaganda points during his visit to
the United Nations by calling for the organization to move its head-

quarters from the United States. Although the United States "calls itself a free democratic country," Khrushchev cited instances "of the representatives of young African and Asian states being subjected to racial discrimination in the United States and, moreover, to attacks by gangsters." He added that "if it should be considered expedient to house the United Nations Headquarters in the Soviet Union we guarantee . . . complete freedom and security for the representatives of all states irrespective of their political or religious convictions, and of the color of their skin . . . ."[39]

Consequently, Nixon argued in the debates that in "the world-wide struggle in which we are engaged, racial and religious prejudice is a gun we point at ourselves."[40] This gun had two barrels. The first was the propaganda windfall that racial discrimination gave to the Soviets. During the second presidential debate, Nixon argued for civil rights "particularly because when we have Khrushchev in this country—a man who has enslaved millions, a man who has slaughtered thousands—we cannot continue to have a situation where he can point the finger at the United States of America and say that we are denying rights to our citizens."[41] The second barrel was the fact that racial discrimination prevented the full and efficient use of all of the nation's resources, including that of black Americans, necessary for winning the Cold War. Nixon claimed, "We also have to see that all of the people of the United States—the tremendous talents that our people have—are used adequately. That's why in this whole area of civil rights, the equality of opportunity for employment and education is not just for the benefit of the minority groups, it's for the benefit of the nation so we can get the scientists and the engineers and all the rest that we need." Only by doing so, Nixon claimed, could the United States "stay ahead of the Soviet Union and win the battle for freedom and peace."[42]

John F. Kennedy's view of civil rights was almost identical to that of Nixon. Also in their second debate, Kennedy said, "We are in a very difficult time. We need all the talent we can get. We sit on a conspicuous stage. We are a goldfish bowl before the world. We have to practice what we preach. We set a very high standard for ourselves. The Communists do not. . . . We preach in the Declaration of Independence and in the Constitution, in the statement of our greatest leaders, we preach very high standards; and if we're not going to be charged before the world with hypocrisy we have to meet those standards."[43]

Kennedy's and Nixon's rhetoric reflected a growing belief that the Cold War had taken a new and potentially dangerous turn. Decolonization of Africa and Asia created many newly independent states, the allegiance of which could prove crucial to the Cold War balance of power. "The great battle for the defense and expansion of freedom today," Kennedy told the nation, "is the whole southern half of the globe . . . the lands of the rising people."[44] And in this great battle, racial discrimination at home became even more of a Cold War liability.

Aided by the perception that he would more vigorously meet the nation's Cold War challenges, Kennedy narrowly won the 1960 election. Once in office, it quickly became clear that Kennedy's first commitment was to winning the Cold War and civil rights was seen almost solely from that perspective. In his first State of the Union message, President Kennedy's only reference to civil rights came when he said that racial discrimination "disturbs the national conscience, and subjects us to the charge of world opinion that our democracy is not equal to the high promise of our heritage."[45] In the first important statement on civil rights by an administration official, Attorney General Robert Kennedy, the president's brother, told an audience at the University of Georgia that Americans could no longer "be apathetic about their belief and respect for the law and about the necessity of placing our own house in order. As we turn to meet our enemy, to look him full in the face, we cannot afford feet of clay or an arm of glass." Kennedy added that in the "worldwide struggle, the graduation at this University of Charleyne Hunter and Hamilton Holmes [the first blacks to enroll at Georgia] will without question aid and assist the fight against communist political infiltration and guerrilla warfare." On the other hand, Kennedy warned, "We, the American people, must avoid another Little Rock or another New Orleans [where violence had recently accompanied school desegregation in that city]. We cannot afford them. . . . Such incidents hurt our country in the eyes of the world. We just can't afford another Little Rock or another New Orleans."[46]

In keeping with this focus on how the world perceived the United States, rather than on what was intrinsically the right thing to do, the Kennedy administration seemed more concerned about the symbolism of civil rights than the substance. President Kennedy failed to bar discrimination in federal housing programs with "the stroke of a presidential pen" as he had promised during the campaign, or even to ask Congress for civil rights legislation. But in February 1961, he did establish the Special Protocol Service in the State Department to deal with discrimination against diplomatic representatives from various nonwhite nations. The idea for the Protocol Service had first originated during the 1960 campaign with foreign policy advisor Chester Bowles, who told Kennedy that the "incidents involving African and other diplomats in which they have been refused service in public places are not only morally wrong but have most unfortunate repercussions abroad."[47] As ambassador to India, Bowles had seen firsthand the damage to U.S. interests caused by Jim Crow. In 1954, he wrote, "Our world responsibilities and the requirements of our national security no longer permit us the luxury of temporizing and evasion on civil rights here in America." He then explained "the painful sensitivity of all Asian peoples on this subject, and the fantastic success which Communist propaganda has had in creating anti-American feeling through the distorted pictures of our racial conflicts. . . . Despite the emphasis I have given this point, I am not yet sure that I have succeeded in making it as important as it really is in the Asian mind. Of one thing I am certain. I have not exaggerated. It is impossible to exaggerate."[48]

Under the direction of Pedro Sanjuan, the Protocol Service sought to use the influence of the State Department to convince state and local governments and private businesses that racial discrimination harmed America's foreign policy. Of particular concern to Sanjuan were the Jim Crow establishments along Maryland's Route 40, a major highway to and from Washington, D.C. In the fall of 1961, Malik Sow, the newly arrived Ambassador for Chad, was denied service at a restaurant along the highway on his way to present his credentials to President Kennedy. Later, the waitress who refused to serve him claimed, "He looked like just an ordinary run of the mill nigger to me. I couldn't tell he was an ambassador."[49] Outraged, Sow returned home, telling his government that someone more "tolerant" was required for the job.[50]

The incident was widely publicized; *Life* magazine carried it as its "Story of the Week" for December 12. Pressure from the Congress of Racial Equality (CORE) Freedom Marchers and the State Department convinced thirty-five of the seventy-five restaurants along Route 40 to serve any customers regardless of color. In addition, Sanjuan helped convince Maryland to pass a law guaranteeing equal access in public accommodations, telling the state legislature, "The issue before the world today is whether democracy works better than tyranny or tyranny better than democracy. Your aid and support in passing the Public Accommodations Bill will eliminate a source of embarrassment that greatly damages our relations with not only the neutral nations of the world, but many nations which are stoutly with us in the fight for freedom. . . . The Department of State comes to you now with a . . . request: Give us the weapons to conduct this war of human dignity. The fight for decency against Communism is everyone's war in America."[51] (Sanjuan, however, took his task much more seriously than did the president. According to Harris Wofford, Kennedy's assistant on civil rights, the president rather obtusely asked Sanjuan, "Can't you tell these African ambassadors not to drive on Route 40? It's a hell of a road—I used to drive it years ago, but why would anyone want to drive it today when you can fly? Tell these ambassadors I wouldn't think of driving from New York to Washington. Tell them to fly!")[52]

Vice President Lyndon Johnson also worked to prevent similar diplomatic embarrassments. In 1961 after the Hilton Hotel in Dallas, Texas refused to provide a room for Ghana's ambassador to the United States, Johnson told a hotel official, "[T]hese people have 20 odd votes in the United Nations. . . . It is going to be explosive internationally. We are outnumbered 17 to 1, black to white in this world." Johnson's persuasion worked and the hotel finally agreed to provide a room for the ambassador.[53]

Kennedy also recognized the symbolic importance of having more blacks in the State Department. During the 1960 campaign, Kennedy, who had chaired a Senate subcommittee on Africa, asked, "How many members of the Foreign Service are of African descent?" He then responded, "There are over 6,000 people in the whole Foreign Service—23 out of 6,000. That is not very many, when Africa will poll one-fourth of all the votes in the General Assembly by 1962."[54] Once in office, the Kennedy administration set out to add more blacks to the State Department and appoint them to more high profile foreign policy positions. One of these was Carl Rowan, journalist and State Department official who became the first black ambassador to a European nation when he was appointed Ambassador to Finland.

Events, however, were such that President Kennedy could not focus his civil rights efforts solely on token diplomatic appointments or preventing discrimination against African diplomats along Maryland's Route 40. Just like the president, black Americans were well aware of the changes in the world and civil rights activists increasingly used a strategy of direct confrontation with Jim Crow and white racists. The resulting violence shocked America and the world. In addition, the disorder raised serious questions about America's social stability at a time when it was required to "pay any price, bear any burden" in the global struggle against Communism.

The first incident came in the spring of 1961 as black and white Freedom Riders crossed the South in buses to integrate interstate transportation facilities. In Alabama, the Freedom Riders were attacked by mobs of angry whites as local police looked on. For the Kennedy administration, the Freedom Rides could not have come at a worse time. Tensions in Berlin were heating up and the president was preparing to travel to Vienna for his first summit meeting with Soviet leader Khrushchev. At one point during the crisis, Attorney General Robert Kennedy appealed for calm, saying, "I think we should all keep in mind that the President is about to embark on a mission of great importance. Whatever we do in the United States at this time which brings or causes discredit on our country can be harmful to his mission."[55] Newscaster David Brinkley condemned the rides in an on the air editorial, claiming that they were "humiliating the United States around the world."[56] The Freedom Riders were unimpressed. When a reporter asked Reverend Ralph Abernathy, "President Kennedy is about to meet with Premier Khrushchev. Aren't you afraid of embarrassing him with these demonstrations?" Abernathy replied, "Man, we've been embarrassed all of our lives."[57]

President Kennedy finally ordered federal marshals to protect the riders from violence, though not from arrest. In addition, the administration pressured the Interstate Commerce Commission to issue new rules forbidding segregation in interstate transportation facilities. Backing up this request was a letter from Secretary of State Dean Rusk (a native Georgian) claiming, "Failures and shortcomings in conduct at home do indeed create embarrassment and difficulty in foreign relations." According to Rusk, discrimination in interstate transportation created problems for nonwhite diplomats in the United States, but more importantly, "this sort of incident gives the picture of a United States where racial discrimination is accepted practice, where equal respect for the dignity of human beings is not accorded."[58]

James Farmer of CORE, one of the organizers of the Freedom Rides, hoped that they would set off "an international crisis" that would shame America in the eyes of the world.[59] He succeeded. In a survey of foreign press reactions, the USIA described the incident as "highly detrimental" to "America's image abroad." The report added that the foreign press "generally agreed that the incident had dealt a severe blow to U.S. prestige which might adversely effect its position of leadership in the free world as well as weaken the overall effectiveness of the Western alliance."[60]

The Kennedy administration sought to avoid anymore damaging incidents of racial violence like the Freedom Rides, but events were beyond their control. In September 1962, James Meredith became the first black to enroll in the University of Mississippi. In a televised address, the president asked for peace so that the nation could focus on the more important task at hand—winning the Cold War. "Let us preserve both the law and the peace and then healing those wounds that are within we can turn to the greater crises that are without and stand united as one people in our pledge to man's freedom."[61] Despite Kennedy's appeal, white mobs at Ole Miss began attacking federal marshals and Mississippi National Guardsmen assigned to protect Meredith. In response, President Kennedy sent in federal troops to restore order, just as President Eisenhower had done in Little Rock. (This was not the only parallel between the two events. Among those urging resistance to the federal government at Ole Miss was former General Edwin Walker, who had commanded the 101st Airborne at Central High. Although his conduct in Little Rock was exemplary, Walker was later forced to resign from the army for his open advocacy of the John Birch Society and other ultraright-wing causes. The following year, Walker's political views made him the target of an unsuccessful assassination attempt by Lee Harvey Oswald.)

Kennedy, like Eisenhower at Little Rock, was loath to use troops to enforce the law, but he knew he could not back down. As Howard P. Jones, the U.S. ambassador to Indonesia told Robert Kennedy, "This was a battle that had to be won. What might have been a severe set back-back to our prestige in Asia and Africa was turned into a gain."[62] Although Jones was right that a potential foreign policy disaster had been averted, the crisis at Ole Miss was hardly a gain for the U.S. abroad. A USIA survey of foreign opinion on the crisis pointed out that the president's dispatch of federal troops "evoked almost unanimous approval in free world media comment," but that "the vivid portrayal in news reports and wire photos of the more sensational aspects of the incident—such as the rioting and bloodshed—may well have left a more lasting impression of the less palatable aspects of the racial situation in the U.S."[63]

In the aftermath of the Freedom Rides and the confrontation at Ole Miss, the idea of civil rights as a Cold War imperative seemed to be embraced more firmly by a wider range of America's opinion leaders. Historian Eric Goldman wrote in the *New York Times Magazine* that the "Freedom Riders ride against segregation, and after years of cold war only the most ignorant man does not know that the existence of segregation in the United States is a tremendous liability to all Americans in the East-West struggle."[64] In 1962, author Louis Lomax wrote, "The American race problem is no longer a private matter among the citizens of this country. If one doubts this let him sit in the gallery of the United Nations during a heated exchange between this country and Russia. Always . . . the Russians are able to wash our face with the race question while the Afro-Asians suppress sardonic smiles. . . . We get our faces washed by the race issue because the implementation of segregation transgresses everything we say we stand for; thus our enemies beat our brains out by simply measuring us by our standards, not theirs!"[65]

Such comments were also evident outside of intellectual circles. Ralph M. Besse, president of the Cleveland Electric Illuminating Company, told the members of the Cleveland Rotary Club that they stood on the "battle lines" of racial discrimination. "From Cleveland's Hough to New York's Harlem, from London to Johannesburg to Bombay to Singapore the line runs, and on opposing sides Communism and the western world face each other in struggle for men's allegiance. You and I are in this struggle, whether we choose to be or not. And our personal job is simple. We must win it, not halfway around the world, but here in our own small sector of Cleveland." He added, "Today, America needs to use every available resource it has in its tremendous struggle against worldwide communism. Yet we're neglecting the Negro. We're failing to qualify one-tenth of our total population to join fully in this competitive effort, even to support himself."[66]

Perhaps the greatest significance of James Meredith's enrollment at the University of Mississippi was domestic rather than global. Although there had long been widespread white opposition to black equality in all sections of the country, over the thirty years prior to 1962 it was rarely expressed at the national level since both parties gave at least rhetorical support to the cause of racial equality. In the aftermath of the Ole Miss crisis, this began to change. White southern opinion turned sharply against the Kennedy administration and the Democratic Party, giving a great boost to Republican efforts to build their party in the South and to the realignment of the parties along racial lines.

Republican efforts to cultivate the South began in the mid-1950s when the Republican National Committee (RNC) started "Operation Dixie." Originally intended to build a moderate Republican Party in the region, this effort collapsed when President Eisenhower intervened with federal troops in Little Rock. But after the 1960 election, Republican conservatives complained that Richard Nixon had moderated his message too much in a futile effort to woo blacks and liberals, thereby missing an opportunity to build a new conservative majority by combining the traditionally Republican Midwest with the white South. To achieve this "union of corn belt and corn pone," the RNC reinvigorated Operation Dixie.

The party also began taking an increasingly conservative line on civil rights issues. Arizona senator Barry Goldwater spelled out this strategy in 1961 at a meeting of southern Republican state party chairmen. "We're not going to get the Negro vote as a bloc in 1964 and 1968," declared Goldwater, "so we ought to go hunting where the ducks are." To attract these ducks, the Republican Party relied on a distinctly segregationist call. In the 1962, the Republican candidate for the U.S. Senate in South Carolina was William Workman, author of *The Case for the South,* a prosegregation tract. In Alabama, the Republican U.S. Senate candidate, James Martin, called for "a return to the Spirit of '61—1861, when our fathers formed a new nation . . . . God willing, we will not again be forced to take up rifle and bayonet to preserve these principles. . . . Make no mistake, my friends, this will be a fight. The bugle call is loud and clear! The South has risen!" A Martin advertisement promised "vigorous action . . . to forestall collusion between the government and the NAACP to integrate schools, unions, and neighborhoods."

These efforts paid dividends for the Republican Party in the 1962 elections, held only weeks after the confrontation at Ole Miss. In an otherwise disappointing year, the Republicans managed to pick up four House seats in the South, while losing two in the North. Additionally, in South Carolina, William Workman managed to gain 43 percent of the vote against incumbent Democrat Olin Johnston. In Alabama, James D. Martin came within seven thousand votes of unseating incumbent Democratic senator Lister Hill, winning thirty of the state's sixty-seven counties. In North Carolina and Georgia, Republicans elected their first state senators since the end of Reconstruction. North Carolina Republicans also managed to defeat the incumbent Democratic speaker of the state House of Representatives. Overall, the Republicans increased their congressional vote in the South by 244 percent over 1958, as opposed to 41 percent for the Democrats.

Following the election, the RNC decided to expand Operation Dixie and the party of Lincoln became even more accommodating to racial conservatives. Journalist Robert Novak observed the following at a conference of state party chairmen in Denver in June 1963:

> Item: During one closed-door session of Republican state chairmen at the Denver Hilton Hotel, two Southern state chairmen

carried on a boisterous conversation about "niggers" and "nigger-lovers" while Negro waiters were serving lunch. "The amazing part of it was," an Eastern state chairman recalled later, "that nobody criticized them for doing it and only a few of us were uncomfortable."

Item: Some of the biggest headlines produced by the Denver meeting came from a press conference held by Wirt Yerger, the fire-eating young segregationist who was Mississippi's Republican state chairman and head of the Republican Party's Association of Southern State Chairmen. Yerger blandly accused Kennedy of fomenting that spring's racial violence in the South in order to win the election.

Item: The "omnibus resolution" adopted by the National Committee as a matter of routine came close to implicit support for Yerger's outrageous claim. The resolution's only provision dealing with civil rights condemned the Kennedy Administration for "its failure to deal effectively with the problems of civil rights and to foster an atmosphere of understanding and good will in which racial conflict can be resolved." Though the nation then was embroiled in the worst racial crisis since the Civil War, the Republican National Committee officially had no word of support—not even a lukewarm word of support—for the Negro movement. . . .

All of this pointed to an unmistakable conclusion: A good many, perhaps a majority of the party's leaders, envisioned substantial political gold to be mined in the racial crisis by becoming in fact, though not in name, the White Man's Party. "Remember," one astute party worker said quietly over the breakfast table at Denver one morning, "this isn't South Africa. The white man outnumbers the Negro 9 to 1 in this country."[67]

The significance of Operation Dixie should not be underestimated. Rather than being the unwitting beneficiaries of a white backlash against the "excesses" of the civil rights movement in the late 1960s, the Republican Party sought actively to foment and capitalize on white resistance even before that movement's main triumphs. Often the "voice of the people," as political scientist V. O. Key Jr. has reminded us, "is but an echo" of what political leaders espouse.[68] Through Operation Dixie, the Republican Party began giving a new national voice to racial conservatives. The echoes reverberate in American politics to this day.

The political realignment of the South and the Republican Party was, however, still in the future. Indeed, in early 1963 liberal Republicans in Congress were among those urging the enactment of strong civil rights legislation. In response, President Kennedy decided to introduce his own civil rights bill in February. Once again, Kennedy stressed to Cold War America the pragmatic reasons for doing so. "Race discrimination hampers our economic growth by preventing maximum development and utilization of our manpower. It hampers our world leadership by contradicting at home the message that we preach abroad. It mars the atmosphere of a united and classless society in which this Nation rose to greatness. It increases the cost of public welfare, crime, delinquency and disorder." But for the first time, the president stressed the morality of civil rights, saying of racial discrimination, "Above all, it is wrong. Therefore, let it be clear, in our own hearts and minds, that it is not merely because of the Cold War, and not merely because of the economic waste of discrimination, that we are committed to achieving true equality of opportunity. The basic reason is because it is right."[69]

This shift in emphasis was momentous; but there is little reason to think that it would have come without Cold War pressures. For over twenty years, America had been engaged in serious and far-reaching struggles with regimes that rejected many basic notions of human rights and liberties. The fight first against fascism and then against Communism compelled an ideological awakening among many Americans, as they sought to set themselves apart from their enemies by reinvigorating their commitment to liberal principles of equality and freedom. But despite his strong rhetoric, President Kennedy proposed only a rather mild voting rights measure that made no mention of desegregation.[70] The bill was even weaker than the one first proposed by President Eisenhower in 1956. Furthermore, the administration waited another month before submitting the actual legislation to Congress.

Such temporizing, however, would soon prove seriously deficient in the face of events. In April and May 1963, civil rights forces led by Martin Luther King decided to assault Jim Crow's most formidable stronghold—Birmingham, Alabama. For over twenty-five years, Public Safety Commissioner Eugene "Bull" Connor had rigidly enforced the city's segregation laws. King knew that if confronted with demonstrations and civil disobedience, Connor would not back down, setting the stage for a violent confrontation before the nation and the world. King's prediction proved correct. Connor used mass arrests, billyclubs, dogs, and firehoses against the demonstrators, many of whom were school children. Perhaps even more shocking was the bombing of black churches, homes, and establishments by white extremists.

Since then, the popular perception has grown that the scenes of violence in Birmingham so shocked the moral ideals of white Americans that they were finally convinced of the justice of and need for civil rights. "A newspaper or television picture of a snarling police dog set upon a human being is recorded in the permanent photo-electric file of every human brain," wrote journalist Eric Sevareid.[71] Although this perception has some truth to it, reality is more complicated and less sanguine. Not all or even most whites sympathized with the blacks in Birmingham. That July, 54 percent of whites thought that the Kennedy administration was "pushing racial integration too fast."[72] In December 1963, 59 percent of northern whites and 78 percent of southern whites expressed disapproval "of actions Negroes have taken to obtain civil rights."[73]

But if moral concerns over Birmingham seemed lacking, many had powerful pragmatic concerns about what the State Department described as "a veritable barrage of broadcasting to foreign audiences" on the humiliating crisis. The Soviet Union broadcast 1,420 stories, roughly a quarter of its programming, on the Birmingham crisis.[74] *Pravda*'s headline blared, "SIX-YEAR-OLDS AMONG THE ARRESTED—Monstrous Crimes of Racists in U.S.A."[75] In Africa, coverage of Birmingham was very heavy. One Ghanaian newspaper editorialized, "We are told that President Kennedy's New Frontier aims at preserving peace and democracy. But recent race incidents in the U.S. demonstrate beyond doubt that America herself is far from free and what she calls democracy is a limited liability democracy which only white men enjoy."[76] The *New York Times* reported that China used the incident to launch a propaganda campaign in the Third World against the United States, declaring that the Birmingham crisis "once again brings to light before the eyes of the world how Negroes in the United States are deprived of their rights and how ruthlessly they are repressed."[77] Another report from Beijing claimed, "It is significant that the Kennedy Administration shows up for what it is on this domestic issue of racism, just when it is going all out to force its way into Africa under the hollow slogans of 'democracy and freedom.'"[78] "Cumulatively," the USIA reported, "there is no doubt that pictures of police brutality, particularly the use of police dogs, has militated strongly against the U.S. image."[79] So great was the perceived damage to America's global image that President Kennedy directed all U.S. ambassadors to work to counteract the "extremely negative reactions" of foreigners to the Birmingham crisis.[80]

From Birmingham, Martin Luther King also saw the impact of global concerns, telling his followers, "The United States is concerned about its image. When things started happening down here, Mr. Kennedy got disturbed. For Mr. Kennedy . . . is battling for the minds and hearts of men in Asia and Africa—some one billion men in the neutralist sector of the world—and they aren't gonna respect the United States of America if she deprives men and women of the basic rights of life because of the color of their skin. Mr. Kennedy *knows* that."[81]

The media gave great play to these foreign policy problems. C. L. Sulzberger wrote in the *New York Times,* "The racial issue in the United States casts an inevitable shadow over our foreign policy by making it unquestionably more difficult to spread concepts of freedom and democracy among newly independent lands in Africa and Asia. This problem is increasingly understood by thoughtful Americans. They recognize the embarrassment caused as we seek to develop such overseas friendships when excruciating incidents accompany the long-delayed implementation of equal rights in the U.S.A."[82] *U.S. News and World Report* ran an article entitled, "Has Race Trouble Tarnished U.S. Image Abroad?" that cited "a strong reaction against the revelations of racial discrimination in the U.S. The Communist press exploits this by suggesting that a country unable to cope with its own internal problems is not ready to lead Western civilization."[83]

To reinforce the point, foreign policy officials in the Kennedy administration launched a public relations blitz to convince Americans that racial discrimination and violence were damaging U.S. foreign policy. United Nations ambassador Adlai Stevenson claimed, "Our ramparts are not just in Laos or in Vietnam or along the European defense line. They are right here, right here in every community in America where there are instances of racial prejudice."[84] A week later he told graduates of Syracuse University, "A democracy qualified by color will win no hearts in Africa and Asia."[85] McGeorge Bundy, the president's national security advisor, made similar remarks to a commencement audience at Brandeis University.[86] Secretary of State Dean Rusk in a news conference complained that racial discrimination forced the United States to run "with one of our legs in a cast" in the international race against Communism.[87]

Rusk's warning were not mere rhetoric, lent in aid to the administration's domestic policy agenda, but of no great concern to its day to day conduct of foreign policy. On the contrary, the State Department took the Birmingham crisis very seriously. Indeed, according to Taylor Branch, on June 19, Secretary Rusk cabled all U.S. embassies and consulates around the globe, instructing them to "defend the United States against the global convulsion of bad publicity about race relations."[88]

Although the most indelible images came from Birmingham, racial discord was not limited to that city. In fact, Birmingham set off the first of what were to be several summers of racial strife. According to journalist Theodore White:

> The massive Birmingham protest had triggered demonstrations all across the nation . . . all through the May and June of 1963, Negroes took to the streets. The National Guard patrolled Cambridge, Maryland; in Jacksonville, Florida, the police cleared demonstrations with tear gas; in Memphis, Tennessee, the city fathers closed the municipal pool. And everywhere from Baton Rouge, Louisiana to Charlottesville Virginia, students manned the lunch-counter front.
>
> The turbulence spread north: in Sacramento, Negroes sat-in at the State Capitol; in Detroit they invaded City Hall and demanded the city fire its chief of police and subject him to criminal trial; in New York, Negro activists dumped garbage on City Hall Plaza; in Philadelphia they clashed with police at a construction site; in Chicago, at a cemetery that refused to bury Negroes. In the ten weeks following the Birmingham uprising, the Department of Justice counted 758 demonstrations across the nation; during the course of the summer, there were 13,786 arrests of demonstrators in seventy-five cities of the eleven Southern states alone.[89]

Obviously these demonstrations and protests did great symbolic damage to America abroad, but even more importantly, like the race riots of 1943, they threatened social peace at home at a time when the nation faced grave foreign political and military threats. So great and widespread was the disorder ("more than 100,000 people took part in demonstrations over the next seven months," according to one historian) that for the first time since the Great Depression, Americans began to question the nation's fundamental stability.[90] The United States seemed to be increasingly polarized and torn apart. On the one side stood civil rights protesters. On the other were segregationist die-hards like "Bull Connor" and Alabama governor George Wallace, who that June stood in a doorway at the University of Alabama in an effort to stop its integration.

Perhaps most worrisome to white Americans was the realization that blacks were becoming increasingly impatient with the status quo and coming ever closer to the violent "fire next time" described by writer James Baldwin. In Birmingham, only the strenuous efforts of Martin Luther King and other civil rights leaders prevented blacks from striking back violently at their white tormentors. Even so, during the crisis in Birmingham black youths unconnected to King threw rocks and bottles at police and rioted at night.

Whites also feared that voices of black extremism, black Muslims in particular, were growing louder and more influential. C. L. Sulzberger wrote of the Muslims and warned of the "violence expressed or threatened by extreme activists in dissatisfied minority groups."[91] *Time* quoted Malcolm X, "The lesson of Birmingham is that Negroes have lost their fear of the white man's reprisals and will react with violence, if provoked. This could happen anywhere in the country today,"[92] For Attorney General Robert Kennedy, the very real possibility of black violence was brought home to him by Louis Martin, a black White House staffer. Martin told Kennedy that if a white man attempted to discriminate against his daughter, "I'm going to shoot him," adding, "If I, an old man, who wouldn't shoot anyone, feel that way, what about the kids?"[93] *Time* illustrated these fears with a drawing of a phalanx of angry blacks marching toward the reader. The caption read, "JUNE 1963—The moment seems to be now."[94]

For President Kennedy, the moment was now. On June 11 he addressed the nation, calling for tough and comprehensive civil rights legislation. His speech sounded several themes: the moral righteousness of civil rights, its foreign policy imperative, and the need to prevent social disorder. Kennedy told Americans, "We are confronted primarily with a moral issue. It is as old as the scriptures and is as clear as the American Constitution." He again rang the Cold War tocsin. "Today we are committed to a worldwide struggle to promote and protect the rights of all who wish to be free. And when Americans are sent to Viet-Nam or West Berlin, we do not ask for whites only." He also compared those fighting racial discrimination to those fighting the Cold War. "Like our soldiers and sailors in all parts of the world they are meeting freedom's challenge on the firing line, and I salute them for their honor and courage."

The president also placed new emphasis on the need for civil rights legislation to head off the growing threat of social chaos and violence. He spoke of "a rising tide of discontent that threatens the public safety," and he warned, "The fires of frustration and discord are burning in every city, North and South, where legal remedies are not at hand. Redress is sought in the streets, in demonstrations, parades, and protests which create tensions and threaten violence and threaten lives." "Unless Congress acts," he continued, blacks' "only remedy is in the street." Finally, he stressed, "We cannot say to 10 percent of the population . . . that the only way that they are going to get their rights is to go into the streets and demonstrate."[95]

A week later, the president reiterated these concerns in the message sent to Congress with his civil rights proposal. In it, Kennedy pointed out, "No one has been barred on account of his race from fighting or dying for America—there are no 'white' or 'colored' signs on the foxholes or graveyards of battle." He also claimed that the "fires of frustration and discord" he had warned of in his earlier speech "burned hotter than ever. . . . Rancor, violence, disunity and national shame can only hamper our national standing and security."[96]

The same mix of moral and pragmatic concerns appeared in the coalition behind the civil rights bill. As it worked its way through Congress, the bill gained widespread support from the nation's religious leaders. So great and influential was this support that Senator Richard Russell, leader of the bill's opponents, complained of "the philosophy of coercion by the men of the cloth." According to him, "We have seen cardinals, bishops, elders, stated clerks, common preachers, priests and rabbis come to Washington to press for passage of the bill. They have sought to make its passage a great moral issue. . . . They have encouraged and prompted thousands of good citizens to sign petitions supporting the bill. . . ."[97]

Foreign policy concerns remained, however, highly visible in the arguments for the new legislation. In July, Attorney General Robert Kennedy asked the Senate Commerce Committee, "How can we say to a Negro in Jackson: 'When war comes you will be an American citizen, but in the meantime you're a citizen of Mississippi and we can't help you.'?"[98] Secretary of State Rusk told the same committee that "in waging this world struggle we are seriously handicapped by racial or religious discrimination in the United States. Our failure to live up to the pledges of our Declaration of Independence and our Constitution embarrasses our friends and heartens our enemies. . . . The Communists clearly regard racial discrimination in the United States as one of their most valuable assets." If Congress did not enact the civil rights bill, "hostile propaganda might be expected to hurt us more than it has hurt us until now."[99] Although Senator Strom Thurmond claimed that Rusk was giving "tacit support to, and approval" to Communists, the rest of the committee showered praise, calling his testimony "inspiring" and "eloquent." Committee chairman John Pastore of Rhode Island told Rusk that his colleagues "feel that you have been one of the most effective witnesses that has ever appeared before this Commerce Committee." The hearing room then "broke into applause."[100]

The White House also used foreign policy arguments to mobilize the business community to support civil rights legislation. One aide told President Kennedy that when lobbying with businessmen, "it may be well to mention the foreign implications inasmuch as almost all of these companies have international activities."[101] In a meeting with corporate leaders of the Business Council, the president told them, "Clear evidence exists that the problem is being exploited abroad and has serious implications in our international relations."[102]

The military also weighed in on the importance of civil rights to its Cold War mission. In June 1963, the President's Committee on Equal Opportunity in the Armed Forces reported that discrimination near military bases was such a problem that "accomplishment of the military mission of a base confronted with such conditions is measurably impaired. There was general agreement among base commanders that the morale of both white and Negro troops suffers in the presence of such indignities and inequities. A practical pro-gram for dealing with off-base discrimination against Negro military personnel and their dependents is urgently required. . . ."[103]

Cold War concerns were not limited to the nation's governmental and business elites. Ordinary Americans were also attuned to the nation's global vulnerability on civil rights. As one self-described "thirty-four year old white homemaker" from Dearborn, Michigan wrote to President Kennedy in June 1963, "The United States stands up to this world and says, "Hey World, look at me!! You should fashion your government after mine! We're a free people and our constitution is for the people, of the people, and by the people. And the world looks down on us and says, 'Yes, this is true if your skin happens to be white.'" According to political scientist Taeku Lee, this letter was not atypical. In a survey of letters to the president on civil rights in this period, he found that nearly a third of the northern white correspondents made reference to the issue's global implications.[104]

The growing fears of social unrest also played a large role in drum-ming up support for the civil rights bill. At the same meeting with business leaders in which the president stressed the foreign policy aspects of civil rights, Robert Kennedy told them that segregation kept "the pot boiling" and "had become critical and must be dealt with directly if the situation is to be kept within bounds."[105] The proposed legislation "was the minimum that would be required to overcome the obstacles to getting people off the streets and the situation under control." The president reinforced this point, saying that "unless the emotion that is now behind the demonstrations is relieved fairly soon any real long-range solution is going to be increasingly difficult and less satisfactory."[106]

Always adept at recognizing when whites' fears made them vulnerable to organized pressure by blacks, A. Philip Randolph called again for the march on Washington that he had first proposed in 1941. In conjunction with Martin Luther King, other black civil rights leaders, and white liberals, Randolph began planning for the March on Washington for Jobs and Freedom, scheduled for August 1963. Concerned that a mass demonstration by blacks might lead to violence and undercut support for civil rights in Congress, the Kennedy administration sought to persuade King and Randolph to call off the march. Randolph (who probably challenged more presidents face to face than any other American in history) remained steadfast, recognizing that civil rights would come because of and not despite fears of social disruption. "These fires of discontent and unrest and aggressive action in the streets, highways and byways must be kept burning. . . . Congress will not act on any meaningful civil rights legislation unless it is made to act by pressure."[107]

Although it avoided violence or disorder, and its most lasting impression was the uplifting moral vision offered by Martin Luther King's "I Have a Dream" speech, the March on Washington nonetheless played on white fears. It received widespread coverage by the foreign press, and even if the absence of violence prevented what would have been an unmitigated disaster, the U.S. government could hardly have been pleased as the world witnessed thousands of American citizens marching on the capital of the Free World demanding their most basic human rights.[108] Additionally, a gathering of so many thousands of blacks triggered white paranoia. As Taylor Branch wrote, many whites feared that "marauding Negroes might sack the capital like Moors or Visigoths reincarnate."[109] The event failed to fulfill such fevered expectations, but white Americans must have been chilled at the prospect that unless something was done for civil rights, a future march might not be as peaceful.

Nor were blacks reluctant to play on these fears to press their cause. As Martin Luther King told the marchers, "Those who hope that the Negro needed to blow off steam and will now be content will have a rude awakening if the nation returns to business as usual."[110] The following month, after a bomb exploded in a black church in Birmingham, killing four girls attending Sunday school classes, King warned, "Unless some immediate steps are taken by the

U.S. Government to restore a sense of confidence in the protection of life, limb and property, my pleas [for nonviolence] will fall on deaf ears and we shall see in Birmingham and Alabama the worst racial holocaust the nation has ever seen."[111]

Though unrelated to black protests, the assassination of President Kennedy in November 1963 also contributed to the passage of civil rights legislation. His death shocked the nation, further reinforcing the growing sense of disorder that began with Birmingham. Along with Kennedy died the belief that America was basically a stable and orderly nation. Americans now had to come to grips with the presence of hatred and violence, and their tragic results. During Kennedy's funeral, Chief Justice Earl Warren declared, "What moved some misguided wretch to do this horrible deed may never be known to us, but we do know that such acts are commonly stimulated by forces of hatred and malevolence, such as are today eating their way into the bloodstream of American life. What a price we pay for such fanaticism!"[112]

In this climate, civil rights thus became one means by which Americans sought to keep together a society that seemed to be coming apart. President Lyndon Johnson and Whitney Young of the National Urban League discussed this idea only two days after the assassination:

> *Young:* Let me make a quick suggestion. I think you've just got to . . . point out that . . . with the death of President Kennedy . . . that hate anywhere that goes unchecked doesn't stop just for the week. And the [church bombing] at Birmingham—the people feel that they can react with violence when they dissent. So this thing is now bigger.
>
> *LBJ:* [Agrees.] I dictated a whole page on hate—hate internationally—hate domestically—and just say that this hate that produces inequality, this hate that produces poverty, that's why we've got to have a tax bill—the hate that produces injustice—that's why we've got to have a civil rights bill. It's a cancer that just eats out our national existence.[113]

In his first speech to the nation after becoming president, Johnson emphasized this very idea. After damning the assassination as "the foulest deed of our time," he proclaimed, "Let us continue." In particular, Johnson stated that "no memorial oration or eulogy could more eloquently honor President Kennedy's memory than the earliest possible passage of the civil rights bill for which he fought so long. . . . There could be no greater source of strength to this Nation both at home and abroad." At the end of the speech, Johnson reiterated the point. "The time has come for Americans of all races and creeds and political beliefs to understand and to respect one another. So let us put an end to the teaching and the preaching of hate and evil and violence. Let us turn away from the fanatics of the far left and the far right, from the apostles of bitterness and bigotry, from those defiant of law, and those who pour venom into our Nation's bloodstream."[114]

Not only did Johnson continue Kennedy's efforts in civil rights, but he did so with all of his overwhelming energy and political skill. The new president also continued to cite the necessities of foreign policy and domestic order as reasons for the passage of legislation. On several occasions, Johnson stated, "I can't think of any single thing we can do to strengthen American foreign policies than to pass the [civil rights bill]."[115] The president also claimed that civil rights legislation was necessary to "take these problems out of the streets and the back alleys and bring them to the courts, to let them be judiciously determined and handled." "If Congress does not act on that legislation," he warned, "we will have some very dark days in this country."[116]

Beyond these themes, Johnson also argued that blacks had earned the right to full citizenship by helping to fight America's enemies. "Today Americans of all races stand side by side in Berlin and in Vietnam," said Johnson in his first State of the Union message. "They died side by side in Korea. Surely they can work and eat and travel side by side in their own country."[117] Elsewhere, he commented, "Oh, they will let [a black] march side by side in the Marine Corps, they will let him fly in the copilot's seat in the bomber, they will let him stand at the missile launching pad and endure and indulge all the dangers of hell and war; but when he comes back home, some of them are second-class citizens."[118]

Congressional proponents of civil rights advanced the same themes. Hubert Humphrey, the leader of the civil rights forces in the Senate, told his colleagues that with outrages such as Birmingham, "I wonder that our nation can dare to claim any moral leadership in the world. Who are we to criticize excesses in the Congo, to point the finger at brutality in South Vietnam? . . . What kind of spectacle do we make in this world where we have prided ourselves on being the good society, where we have been demanding reforms from other governments—when duly constituted authority in parts of this nation not only tolerates but also incites brutality, violence, and sadism? . . . We should never again attempt to lecture any other nation until we have cleansed this blot of racial injustice from our shield."[119] To the NAACP, Humphrey claimed that the nation was "confronted with powerful adversaries in every corner of the world. . . . And what we need therefore, is the full participation, the full citizenship participation of every American regardless of race, color or creed." Moreover, the Cold War was not just a battle of manpower and resources, it was also, according to him, "a conflict of ideals" and that "the real strength of the America is its ideals. I believe that the message . . . of the American tradition of equality of opportunity and of human freedom is our most powerful force in the struggle which is being waged in the world today."[120]

These arguments were not limited to liberal Democrats like Humphrey. Republican Fred Schwengel of Iowa told the House during the debate over the civil rights bill that "not since the Civil War has the domestic tranquility of this Nation been threatened to such a massive extent as it is today. . . . Fellow members, by passing this legislation we will be lessening the possibility of violence. We will open the doors of orderly change where our citizens . . . can seek relief in the courts of this land rather than in a picket line, a sit-in, or other kinds of hazardous demonstrations." Schwengel added, "In providing for our defense today we need more than H-bombs, carriers, missiles, planes, or guns. . . . Certainly we can fight Communism in no better way than to show the world that America practices what it preaches, that the United States means what it says about the importance of democracy."[121] Republican Senator Jacob Javits of New York remarked that unless Congress passed a civil rights bill the "alternative is now so clearly disorder and possibly serious violence, not only in the South, but in other places where these racial tensions exist."[122] Senate Republican Minority Leader Everett Dirksen of Illinois pointed out that "Two and three-quarter million young Negroes served in World Wars I, II, and Korea. Some won the Congressional Medal of Honor and the Distinguished Service Cross."[123]

This confluence of forces, both global and domestic, pushed Congress to first toughen the bill originally proposed by President Kennedy and then to enact it. The bill first passed the House in February 1964 and then, after months of debate and filibusters, the Senate in June. Signed into law by President Johnson in July, the 1964 Civil Rights Act was the most far-reaching measure of its kind ever enacted. Abolishing segregation and discrimination in public accommodations and employment, the act also bars federal funds from going to racial discriminatory institutions and provides the federal government with means to enforce these and existing civil rights guarantees.

Yet despite the triumph of the Civil Rights Act, many whites, especially in the South, remained ambivalent or opposed to the idea of black equality. Only days before President Johnson signed the Act, three Mississippi civil rights workers were reported missing. Three months later, the murdered bodies of James Chaney, Andrew Goodman, and Michael Schwerner were found buried beneath an earthen dam near Philadelphia, Mississippi.

Although less violently, many northern whites also registered their disapproval of efforts to dismantle the nation's racial hierarchy. In 1963, one poll found 64 percent of whites believed that blacks were moving "too fast" in their quest for equality. In contrast 17 percent thought they moving "about right" and only 6 percent thought they were moving too slow.[124] In 1964, only 30 percent of white Americans thought blacks should have more influence in government.[125]

White unease with the course and pace of the civil rights movement was most evident in the support given to Alabama governor George Wallace in several northern Democratic presidential primaries in the spring of 1964. Wallace entered Wisconsin's April primary and waged a vigorous campaign that stressed how "an all-powerful central bureaucracy" in Washington was seeking the "destruction of property rights," a thinly veiled appeal to white fears of integrated neighborhoods. Such attacks resonated among many working class whites, including one Milwaukee supporter of Wallace who declared, "They beat up old ladies 83-years-old, rape our womenfolk. They mug people. They won't work. They are on relief. How long can we tolerate this? Did I go to Guadalcanal and come back to something like this?" To nearly everyone's surprise (including his own) Wallace took 34 percent of the vote against Governor John Reynolds, who stood in for Lyndon Johnson on the ticket. A month later in Indiana, Wallace took 30 percent of the vote against another Johnson stand-in. Two weeks later, on May 19, Wallace nearly won the Maryland primary against Johnson surrogate, Senator Daniel Brewster, losing only by the margin of 53 to 45 percent. Wallace won a majority of the white vote, and only a high black turnout and creative vote-counting in Baltimore's machine wards prevented him from winning outright. Even though he failed to win any primaries, Wallace nonetheless showed that significant numbers of northern, blue-collar Democrats were increasingly critical of their party's stand on civil rights. As one Wallace voter from Gary, Indiana remarked,

"We've got Negroes in my union and they're O.K., but eighty-five percent of the Negroes in this town are too pushy." [126]

Despite the support given to Wallace in the primaries, Lyndon Johnson won that fall in a landslide over Republican Barry Goldwater, one of the few nonsouthern senators to vote against the Civil Rights Act. The election, however, turned less on civil rights than on foreign policy and the perception that Goldwater would be trigger-happy with nuclear weapons. Although he often forcefully criticized the Civil Rights Act in his speeches, to Goldwater's credit, he refused to tap as deeply into racial resentments as Wallace had done. At his initiative, Goldwater met privately with President Johnson during the summer and agreed not to make racial appeals. Late in the campaign, when aides showed him *Choice*, a campaign film that used footage of black rioting to condemn the administration, Goldwater declared it racist, vetoed its use, and ordered all copies placed under lock and key. By not resorting to such issues, wrote campaign chronicler Theodore White, "Goldwater yielded certainly the strongest emotional appeal his campaign might have aroused." Later candidates would prove less principled in their campaign tactics. [127]

Nonetheless, there were signs in the election of the growing white resistance to racial equality. Most importantly, the South swung heavily to the Republicans. Goldwater's opposition to the Civil Rights Act won him five Deep South states: South Carolina, Georgia, Alabama, Mississippi, and Louisiana. Excluding Johnson's home state of Texas, Goldwater won a majority of the southern white vote, the first Republican ever to do so. [128] There were also signs that northern white voters were less than enthusiastic about civil rights. In California, where Johnson won 59 percent of the vote, voters rejected by an even larger margin a fair housing law passed by the state legislature. [129]

White resistance was not yet strong enough to forestall further civil rights advances, however. In January 1965, Martin Luther King began a series of demonstrations in Selma, Alabama to protest black disenfranchisement. After he and other protesters were thrown in jail for his activities, King wrote a letter that supporters placed as an ad in the *New York Times*. In it, King stressed how such injustices diminished America in the eyes of the world:

Dear Friends,

When the King of Norway participated in awarding the Nobel Prize to me he surely did not think that in less than sixty days I would be in jail. He, and almost all world opinion will be shocked because they are little aware of the unfinished business in the South.

By jailing hundreds of Negroes, the city of Selma, Alabama has revealed the persisting ugliness of segregation to the nation and the world. . . .

This is the USA in 1965. We are in jail simply because we cannot tolerate these conditions for ourselves or our nation. . . .[130]

Whatever embarrassment the nation suffered from King's arrest, far worse was to come. In March, demonstrators in Selma were beaten by sheriff's deputies and state troopers using clubs, bullwhips, and rubber hoses wrapped in barbed wire.[131] Once again, the nation and the world were shocked by the scenes of violence. ABC interrupted its showing of *Judgment at Nuremberg* to broadcast its report on Selma.[132] Civil rights leader John Lewis, who had been among those beaten, declared, "I don't see how President Johnson can send troops to Vietnam . . . and can't send troops to Selma, Alabama."[133]

In response, President Johnson issued a moving plea for legislation to protect the voting rights of black Americans. To his great credit, his speech especially stressed the nation's tradition of equality and justice and the benefits to all of overcoming the bigotry that had so deeply divided Americans for so long. But by the same token, Johnson also emphasized the importance of voting rights legislation for restoring social order, though not at any price. "In Selma as elsewhere we seek and pray for peace. We seek order. We seek unity. But we will not accept the peace of stifled rights, or the order imposed by fear, or the unity that stifles protest. For peace cannot be purchased at the cost of liberty."[134]

And voting rights, Johnson claimed in the message that accompanied his legislative request, were also crucial to American foreign policy. "In the world, America stands for—and works for—the right of all men to govern themselves through free, uninhibited elections. An ink bottle broken against an American Embassy, a fire set in an American library, an insult committed against the American flag, anywhere in the world, does far less injury to our country and our cause than the discriminatory denial of any American citizen at home to vote on the basis of race and color."[135] Beyond its very real moral motives, then, Johnson's initiative also displayed the continuing impact of concerns for America's international prestige and domestic tranquility.

With all these imperatives pressing in one direction, Congress overcame another southern filibuster and that summer passed the

Voting Rights Act of 1965. For the first time ever, all black Americans were able to exercise the suffrage freely. This measure, along with the Civil Rights Act of 1964, stand as impressive achievements, extending political and civil rights to black Americans and eradicating the legal basis for much of the racial hierarchy that had characterized American life for nearly one hundred years. Still, it is questionable whether these laws would have come without the rationale expressed in Secretary of State Rusk's comment to a television audience. He said, "[T]here is nothing that Congress has done in the past 4 years with respect to foreign policy that has been as important as what the Congress has done with civil rights and the voting rights bill. . . ."[136]

Rusk's assessment seems well advised. According to a USIA survey of foreign press commentary on the passage of the Civil Rights Act, the general theme was that the legislation had "vindicated the U.S. democratic system" and "created a new picture of the U.S. which has none of the old black spots or smears." Typical of the commentary quoted in the report is that from a Liberian newspaper: "only as of last Friday can the world say that the US is truly a great nation."[137] A USIA survey of foreign public opinion conducted in mid-1965 showed that though the "general opinion of the treatment of Negroes in the U.S. is predominantly unfavorable, usually by sweeping margins," these same respondents were much more positive in their assessment of the U.S. government's efforts to achieve civil rights and they also believed that white Americans' attitudes toward blacks was improving, largely as a result of the Civil and Voting Rights Acts.[138]

There remained, moreover, much to be done. As historic as these acts were, those dedicated to civil rights knew that inequality resulted not only from discriminatory laws but also from the systematic denial of economic opportunity to black Americans. Although not limited exclusively or even largely to blacks, President Johnson conceived of his Great Society as a civil rights measure. He told Congress that "most of the program I am recommending is a civil rights program." Equality, Johnson added, "takes much more than just legal right. It requires a trained mind and a healthy body. It requires a decent home, and the chance to find a job, and the opportunity to escape from the clutches of poverty."[139]

As with other civil rights measures, the social welfare provisions of the Great Society were not solely the result of moral concerns. Once again, fear of disorder prompted additional efforts by the government to pacify angry blacks. The passage of the Civil and Voting Rights Acts undoubtedly prevented even greater violence and bloodshed, but black anger was too great to be contained. While the economic status of blacks had improved since World War II, largely through migration to higher paying jobs in the North, increased numbers of working women, and the expansion of the welfare state, many blacks still remained stuck at the bottom of the economic ladder, locked in ghettoes, and harassed by white police.[140] In fact, by some key indicators, blacks had actually lost ground. For example, in 1950, blacks suffered from an infant mortality rate 66 percent higher than whites. By 1964, the gap had increased to 90 percent.[141] In northern cities like Detroit, the percent of black children attending predominantly black schools rose between 1961 and 1966.[142]

In 1964 and 1965, these conditions sparked major riots in several northern cities, including Harlem and the Watts section of Los Angeles. Confronted with widespread urban violence, government policymakers could not rely on the usual methods of violent repression to ensure order among unruly blacks. In the Cold War environment of the 1960s, which now included a "hot" war in Vietnam, global concerns effectively nullified a resort to such practices (though the government had few qualms about covertly using J. Edgar Hoover's FBI to undertake a wide range of surveillance and subversion activities against civil rights groups). After one riot, the USIA told President Johnson that Radio Moscow "highlighted news reports on the riots and has editorialized extensively on the economic weaknesses and the class distinction which have resulted in a breakdown of law and order." After the Watts riots, President Johnson warned that the "world is always witness to whatever we do. . . ." When America's claims of black progress are contrasted with images of riots, "the result is baffling to all the world."[143] *Newsweek* told its readers, "*Pravda* gleefully splashed a cartoon showing an LBJ-like 'Mr. Dollar' sending troops to two fronts: Vietnam—and Los Angeles."[144]

According to sociologist John Skrentny, "Stopping the riots was thus essential, but the logic of crisis management required that techniques must be quiet or congruent with the new moral boundaries of human rights." Skrentny then cited President Johnson, who wrote in his memoirs, "I knew what I had to do, but I could not erase from my mind the awful prospect of American soldiers possibly having to shoot American citizens. The thought of blood being spilled in the streets of Detroit was like a nightmare. I could imagine the inflammatory photographs appearing within hours on television and on the front pages of newspapers around the world." As a result, policymakers instead sought to prevent disorder through expanded

social welfare services and programs designed to ensure greater economic opportunities for black Americans.[145]

Fear of riots in the nation's capital also led President Johnson to
push for home rule in majority-black Washington, D.C. Less than
two weeks after Watts, Johnson claimed that "the clock is ticking"
in the District of Columbia. "I asked myself last night, what can I
do to see that we don't have any more incidents as occurred in Los
Angeles in this country. . . . So, lets act [on home rule] before its
too late."[146] In addition, the riots led to the elimination of the last
bastion of Jim Crow in the military—the National Guard. As the
Guard was increasingly used for riot control duty, the lack of black
faces in their ranks was a problem of both practical and symbolic
importance, leading the military to finally implement plans to increase black enrollment in these units.[147]

If urban riots led elites to push for greater efforts to achieve racial
equality, they only added to the anger of many ordinary whites. As
we have seen, since the end of World War II, northern whites had
tolerated civil rights for southern blacks, but when it came to integrating their own neighborhoods, they were often as reactionary as
any southern die-hard. After the Watts riots, one white resident of
the Los Angeles area wrote President Johnson that "white people . . .
are getting real tired of kinky haired, thick lipped blacks who are
giving so much trouble . . . you and the Kennedys have given them
everything they have asked for—when do you plan to stop?"[148] According to Joseph Califano, this letter was not atypical. "When Johnson had sent his fair-housing bill to Congress in 1966, it had
prompted some of the most vicious mail LBJ received on any subject
(and the only death threats I ever received as a White House assistant)."[149] The reality of northern white anger literally struck Martin
Luther King in the face in Chicago in 1966. That August, while leading a march through one of the city's white enclaves, a brick thrown
by a white counter-demonstrator grazed his head. Afterwards, King
remarked, "I've never seen anything like it. I've been in many demonstrations all across the south, but I can say that I have never
seen—even in Mississippi and Alabama—mobs as hostile and hate-
filled as I've seen in Chicago."[150]

The anti-integration sentiment of northern whites further fueled
their resistance to civil rights. By October 1966, 85 percent of whites
thought blacks were moving too fast for racial equality.[151] That summer, a Senate filibuster killed an open housing bill.[152] White resistance
manifested itself in that fall's congressional elections, contributing
to the Democrats' loss of forty-seven seats in the House, three in

the Senate, and eight governorships. The AFL-CIO found that many of their members "deserted liberal candidates for one reason only: in protest against their advocacy of civil rights."[153] One of the victims of this protest was Illinois senator Paul Douglas, an outspoken advocate of civil rights, who saw his margin plummet in those white wards of Chicago most concerned over racial integration.[154] In California, Ronald Reagan defeated liberal governor Edmund Brown, in part by denouncing open housing legislation, which he claimed, "[b]y infringement on one of our basic individual rights sets a precedent which threatens individual liberty."[155]

Despite white resistance, fears of domestic unrest remained foremost in the minds of American elites, particularly after the nation underwent another and more destructive round of riots in the summer of 1967. Racial violence struck more than a hundred cities. The worst riot was in Detroit, where forty-three people were killed and President Johnson was forced to send in federal troops to restore order. *Newsweek* declared that the riots were "a symbol of a domestic crisis grown graver than any since the Civil War."[156] *U.S. News and World Report* asked, "IS CIVIL WAR NEXT?"[157] The international implications were also clear. According to *U.S. News and World Report*, "The U.S., standing as leader of the free world, is to be profoundly affected around the globe by its epidemic of racial violence."[158]

Following the 1967 riots, President Johnson established the National Advisory Commission on Civil Disorder. In its February 1968 report, the Kerner Commission (so named for its chairman, Illinois governor Otto Kerner) stressed the importance of open housing legislation as a means to prevent more riots. Although the Kerner Commission is now usually derided as an exercise in liberal permissiveness, many Republicans also accepted such a conclusion. Everett Dirksen, whose opposition had helped to kill open housing legislation in 1966, came out in favor of the bill. According to him, the riots "put this whole thing in a different frame."[159] Comparing the United States to a sick patient, he added, "I say that because I do not want to worsen the condition of the patient, namely, the restive condition in the United States, I do not want to have the condition erupt and have a situation develop for which we do not have a cure and probably have more violence and more damage done."[160]

With Dirksen's support, the Senate passed an open housing bill in March 1968, but its prospects seemed less certain in the House. Then on April 4 came King's assassination and new eruptions of violence in black ghettoes. In all, riots broke out in 125 cities and more than seventy-five thousand National Guardsmen and federal troops were required to quell the disturbances. Thirty-nine people died, twenty thousand were arrested, and over $40 million worth of property was destroyed in the riots.[161] "Only two months after Tet," later wrote Secretary of Defense Clark Clifford, "it seemed as if we were experiencing our own national uprising."[162] The pressures were all the greater because this uprising came as the nation faced calls for even more troops in Vietnam and growing resistance to the draft undoubtedly added to concerns.

Among the cities worst hit by rioting was Washington, D.C., and for the first time, senators and congressmen could see up close the fire and smoke of black anger. It took fourteen thousand federal troops to restore order in the District. Some congressmen were so worried that they wanted President Johnson to declare martial law and complained to him that the marines stationed around the Capitol were not issued ammunition. (Despite the crisis, Johnson managed to keep his sense of humor. When told of a rumor that black militant Stokely Carmichael was organizing blacks to march on Georgetown, home of Washington's elite, Johnson responded, "Goddamn! I've waited thirty-five years for this day!")[163]

Once again, the riots put America on display to the world. As one British journalist wrote, "Television satellites flashed pictures around the world, providing instant testimony to black America's despair. In Moscow, London, and Rome people sat in the comfort of their own living rooms and watched burnings in Baltimore, killing in Chicago, and total anarchy on the streets of Washington, D.C., the capital of the United States. The riots were on a scale unprecedented except for a country on the verge of revolution."[164] Stunned by the rioting and fearful of a long, hot summer ahead, the House within a week passed the open housing bill. President Johnson signed it into law the following day.[165]

Also helping the passage of open housing was the recognition of the sacrifices of black soldiers in the Vietnam War.[166] In 1965, presidential advisor Daniel Patrick Moynihan wrote, "History may record that the single most important psychological event in race relations in the nineteen sixties was the appearance of Negro fighting men on the TV screens of the nation."[167] Though Moynihan overstated the case, civil rights advocates consistently pointed to black military service in Vietnam as a justification for their cause. This was particularly true of open housing legislation, the struggle for which coincided with the war's escalation. In each of his three special messages to Congress asking for such legislation, President Johnson pointed to the debt owed by the country to its black soldiers. In 1966, he told Congress, "Negro Americans comprise 22% of enlisted men in our Army combat units in Viet Nam—and 22% of those who have lost their lives in the battle there. We fall victim to profound hypocrisy when we say that they cannot buy or rent dwellings among citizens they fight to save."[168] The following year, he returned to the point, saying, "The bullets of our enemies do not discriminate between Negro Marines and white Marines. They kill and maim whomever they strike. . . . The bullets at the battlefront do not discriminate—but the landlords at home do. The pack of the Negro soldier is as heavy as the white soldier's—but the burden his family at home bears is far heavier. In war, the Negro American has given the nation his best—but this nation has not given him equal justice. It is time that the Negro be given equal justice. In America, the rights of citizenship are conferred by birth—not by death in battle."[169] Finally, in January 1968, the president declared, "Housing discrimination means the Negro veteran of Vietnam cannot live in an apartment which advertises vacancies."[170]

Shortly after the president spoke these words, the Viet Cong and the North Vietnamese launched the Tet Offensive, and America's involvement in Vietnam escalated to its bloodiest height. Over five hundred thousand soldiers were in Vietnam, with the Joint Chiefs of Staff requesting another two hundred thousand. And, as historian Ronald H. Spector wrote, during these months "the overall rate of men killed in Vietnam would reach an all time high and would exceed the rate of the Korean War and the Mediterranean and Pacific theaters during World War II."[171] Furthermore, black soldiers were bearing a large share of this burden (disproportionately large, many blacks argued).

These factors were clearly important in Senator Dirksen's shift in his vote on open housing. In February, as the Tet Offensive raged, he stated, "There are young men of all colors and creeds and origins who are this night fighting 12,000 miles or more away from home. They will be back. They will return. . . . They will want to be integrated into the economic and social life of our country. Unless there is fair housing . . . I do not know what the measure of their unappreciation would be for the ingratitude of their fellow citizens, after they were willing to lay their lives on the altar and in so many instances left arms and legs 12,000 miles behind."[172] After the Senate passed the open housing bill in early 1968, President Johnson pressed the same point on the House, saying, "I am shocked to even think that the boys I put on the plane at the 82d Airborne—most of whom are Negro boys going back to Vietnam the second time to protect that flag and preserve our freedom—that they can't live near the base where they have to train in this country; they must drive 15, 20, or 30 miles sometimes to get to their homes."[173] Arguments such as these helped, along with fears of more riots, to pass the open housing bill.

Indeed, the war in Vietnam also led to one of the most unlikely votes for open housing—Congressman George Bush of Texas. In 1964, when Bush ran as the Republican candidate for the U.S. Senate in Texas, he denounced the Civil Rights Act, arguing that it "trampled upon the Constitution." "The new civil rights act was passed to protect 14 percent of the people," candidate Bush told a white audience. "I'm also worried about the other 86 percent."[174] He damned the UAW's Walter Reuther because he "even donated fifty dollars to the militant Dr. Martin Luther King Jr."[175] Bush also opposed repealing the state's poll tax since without it, the "liberal bloc vote" (a.k.a. blacks and Hispanics) would "swamp" the polls.[176]

Although he failed in that race, Bush won election to the House in 1966. He knew that his overwhelmingly white and conservative Houston constituents bitterly opposed open housing, and he so voted in his first year in office. Shortly thereafter, Bush toured Vietnam and saw the many black soldiers fighting for their country. As the next vote on open housing approached, according to journalist Richard Ben Cramer, "[w]hat stuck in [Bush's] mind was Vietnam, his trip, those soldiers—black soldiers—in the jungle, in the uniform of their country . . . how could he let them come back to a nation where they couldn't live where they chose? He could not."[177] By switching his vote, Bush was the only southern Republican to vote for the bill and only one of three Texas House members to do so. "I could not have it on my conscience," Bush told the local press, "that I had voted for legislation that would have prevented a Negro serviceman, who has the funds, and who upon returning from Vietnam where he had been fighting for the ideals of this country, would know that he could not buy or rent a decent home."[178]

Bush's vote stunned and angered his white constituents. "I voted for the bill," he wrote to a friend, "and the roof is falling in—boy does the hatred surface. I have had more mail on this subject than on Vietnam and taxes and sex all put together." Some of the letters contained death threats.[179] Bush experienced this anger directly at a hostile town meeting in his district. "I had you in my house and here you would destroy everything you stood for," charged one of his former supporters.[180] Boos and catcalls came from the crowd as Bush was introduced. He later wrote, "I reminded them that even as we met, black Americans were fighting in Vietnam to protect our freedom and way of life. How did they feel about a black American veteran of Vietnam returning home, only to be denied the freedom that we, as white Americans enjoyed? . . . a man should not have a door slammed in his face because he is a Negro or speaks with a Latin American accent." When Bush finished, the crowd's anger had dissolved and it rose to give him a standing ovation. "More than twenty years later," he recalled, "I can truthfully say that nothing I've experienced in public life, before or since, has measured up to the feeling I had when I went home that night."[181]

Concern for the welfare of returning black soldiers was not, however, always so selfless. As the war dragged on, many Americans increasingly worried that black veterans, embittered over the lack of jobs and equal rights in their communities, would add a new and more threatening element to the growing problem of racial violence. In 1965, Malcolm X warned, "If it is right for America to draft us, and teach us how to be violent in defense of her, then it is right for you and me to do whatever is necessary to defend our own people right here in this country."[182] Such comments might have been expected from a radical like Malcolm X, but two years later, Whitney Young of the Urban League, one of the most moderate of national civil rights leaders, wrote ominously that black soldiers were "grimly determined—by whatever method necessary—to live in an America where his rights are fully guaranteed. In his war experience he has acquired new confidence and new skills, among them the skills of guerrilla warfare, of killing, of subversion, and the gamut of tricks of military combat." He added that "if they return to find the conditions they left unchanged, these Negro veterans might become an interested audience for the preachers of violence—and capable of being organized into a major national threat." According to Young, "they will be disillusioned and hostile—and full of fresh memories of an environment where life was cheap and where the order of the day was kill or be killed. It would then be realistic to expect that such experts of mines and booby traps and all other forms of destruction to find good reason why they should use these skills and risk their lives against the enemy of personal injustice as they did against the enemy of Communist aggression."[183] Later, Young warned that unless something changed, blacks soldiers returned from Vietnam "could make [black militant] Rap Brown look like Little Lord Fauntleroy."[184]

Although Young might have been overstating his case, black soldiers in Vietnam were disturbed by the nation's racial conflicts.

Hardly a militant then or now, Colin Powell nevertheless wrote in his memoirs, "For me and my fellow black officers at Leavenworth, Dr. King's death was an abrupt reminder that . . . racism still bedeviled America. Each of us had experienced enough racial indignities to understand the riots unleashed in black ghettoes in the wake of the King assassination. We understood the bitterness of black GIs who, if they were lucky enough to get home from Vietnam in one piece, still faced poor job prospects and fresh indignities."[185]

Concerns about black veterans ran so strong that in early 1968, an article in the *New York Times Magazine* claimed, "To the jittery Defense Department official, the returning black G.I. is both a challenge and a threat. He is a potential, and potentially lethal, opponent who has to be neutralized by getting him off the ghetto streets, or he may be an ally, newly recruited into an urban police department to help with this summer's outbreaks." To "neutralize" this threat, the Defense Department established Project Transition to provide job training to soon to be discharged vets. "Priorities for participation in the program go to minority group G.I.'s who have not learned a useful skill while in the service. Counselors who supervise the program aim to reach black G.I.'s headed back to explosive urban ghettoes and train them for jobs which will take them out of those ghettoes. As part of the program, urban police departments have also been encouraged to recruit and train black servicemen on military bases."[186]

To be sure, the Vietnam conflict did not provide positive reinforcement for domestic efforts to achieve racial equality in all respects. It was, after all, a war against an Asian enemy, even if it was fought in the name of Asian allies. Unsurprisingly, just as World War II inflamed anti-Japanese racism, many Americans became accustomed during the Vietnam years to disparaging Vietnamese "gooks" as racial and cultural inferiors. Furthermore, Vietnam was a costly war, a tremendous sinkhole of resources that might otherwise have helped Johnson's War on Poverty achieve greater success. Instead, it brought his administration into disrepute, leading him to withdraw from his campaign for reelection in 1968. His vice president and successor as the Democratic presidential nominee, Hubert Humphrey, then narrowly went down to defeat in November 1968 to a Republican who was far less concerned about the morality of civil rights, Richard Nixon.

Still, at that point great things had been achieved. The passage of open housing legislation in 1968 marked the culmination of twenty-five years of efforts to dismantle the racial hierarchy that had dominated American life since the end of Reconstruction after the Civil War. This modern Reconstruction guaranteed black Americans the right to vote, abolished state-sponsored segregation, and barred the most overt forms of private discrimination. Although blacks remained disadvantaged in important ways, the most important legal barriers confronting them had been removed. Furthermore, the government had put in place a variety of social welfare programs that sought to lessen the additional burdens of economic inequality. In no other time had America come closer to realizing the best of its ideological tradition, the belief that in regard to basic rights, "all men are created equal."

In many ways, this advance toward racial equality stands as the most important and proudest achievement of twentieth-century America. Yet, we must acknowledge honestly that most white Americans supported these changes only with great reluctance and under great pressures. For nearly thirty years, from World War II through the Cold Wars of the 1950s and 1960s, America faced unique and profound ideological and military threats first from racist fascism and then Communism. Not only did this require near total mobilization of available resources, the necessity of winning the hearts and minds of peoples around the world repeatedly forced the nation to address the damage inflicted by decades of discrimination on the hearts and minds of its own citizens. Even so, progress remained halting, with symbolic victories far more easily achieved than real substantive transformations. The nation's leaders all knew that, within the hearts of many white Americans, these changes felt profoundly disturbing and were met with great resistance. Sadly, as the imperatives of the Cold War lessened and ultimately disappeared, so would America's march toward racial equality.

NINE

"Benign Neglect"?

Post—Civil Rights America, 1968—1998

O n April 29, 1992, an all-white jury in Simi Valley, California (home of the Ronald Reagan Presidential Library) acquitted four Los Angeles police officers accused of battering black motorist Rodney King, despite the fact that the incident had been caught on all-too-vivid videotape. Within hours of the verdict, Los Angeles was in flames. The fires were so intense and widespread that an orbiting satellite observed them as "an exceptionally large thermal anomaly."[1] By the time the riot had ended, fifty-two people had died, more than twenty-three hundred were injured, and over $1 billion in property was destroyed.[2] The Los Angeles riot was the first major incident of urban unrest since 1968 and the most deadly since the New York City Draft Riots of 1863.

As with the riots of the 1960s, the 1992 Los Angeles riot embarrassed the United States before the world. According to historian Mary Dudziak, foreign coverage of the riots was both heavy and extremely critical of the United States. The *Washington Post* reported that "the riots dominated the headlines and news broadcasts in Western Europe, where the United States was portrayed as a hapless, intolerant, violent, gun-ridden nation at war with itself—and one that might be better off preaching less about the virtues of American society to other countries."[3] But unlike the 1960s, these criticisms did not seem to matter much. Almost as soon as the riot's flames died out, so too did much of the nation's concern. Given the international and domestic publicity during an election year, at least one of the three major presidential candidates might have been expected to trumpet some sort of program aimed at preventing further such uprisings. Yet none did so. Stunningly, by the time the presidential race was in full swing that fall, the L.A. riot was so little discussed that it was almost as if that vast conflagration had never occurred.

What had changed between the 1960s and 1992 to permit this indifference both to racial violence and the world's reaction to it? The past patterns of American history lead us to assign greatest weight to two factors. One is the waning of the Cold War. As the United States withdrew from Vietnam in the early 1970s and made overtures to both China and Soviet Union, the international imperatives to combat Communist charges of racial injustice that had motivated much of the nation's advance toward equal rights since the 1940s began to lessen. Although rhetorical assaults on the "evil empire" then rose again in President Reagan's first term, in the 1980s real threats from competition with the Soviets objectively declined further as the U.S.S.R. suffered through the limp final years of the "era of stagnation" under Brezhnev. Then the Cold War finally ended definitively in the early 1990s with the collapse of Communism throughout eastern Europe and the dissolution of the Soviet Union. Although there were inevitable fluctuations, the long-term pattern of these years was one of decreasing Cold War pressures to continue, much less extend, racial reforms.

The second dynamic at work in this period is that many Americans, especially but not only native-born white Americans, became increasingly uncomfortable with the transformations in American demography, institutions, and civic life wrought by the reform measures of the 1960s, just as they had done after previous reform periods. In the wake of the modern changes, native whites remained the majority and power center in America, but they were a dwindling majority that rightly felt themselves to be a less legally privileged and socially esteemed community than they had always been in the past. Unsurprisingly, many proved increasingly receptive to arguments from politicians and intellectuals suggesting covertly or overtly that whites' anxieties and resentments about these changes were more than justified.

This second dynamic was reinforced by a lesser but still significant third development. Racial progress has never come in the United States without urgent pressures from domestic reform movements, usually led by African Americans. As the high hopes of the civil rights movements were not quickly realized in the late 1960s, as instead white opposition visibly began to intensify, African Americans differed on how to respond. Leaders began exhibiting more internal disunity, with many attracted to economically or nationalistically radical movements like the Black Panthers or the Black Muslims. In the late 1960s, inner city blacks also vented anger in urban riots. In the 1970s, the riots ceased, the Panthers were decimated, and the

Nation of Islam also underwent internal difficulties, but more moderate African American organizations did not succeed in mobilizing mass support. And in the latter part of the 1980s, the separatist Nation of Islam under the direction of Louis Farrakhan gained increasing prominence.

The negative impact of these developments on reform efforts should not be overstated. As we have noted, in many ways the riots kept the fires of change burning under governmental policymakers. Thereafter, disagreements among black leaders did not prevent them from continuing to advance powerful arguments for continuing egalitarian transformations. In the 1980s, especially, Jesse Jackson played a highly visible role in presidential politics that kept issues of racial equality alive in the minds of many blacks and whites, even if he failed to achieve much in the way of concrete policy concessions. Still, on balance, the voices of black leaders calling for racially egalitarian change became somewhat more diffuse in these years than they had been at the height of the civil rights movement.

Although neither political party could ignore how domestic opposition to racial changes was gaining greater relative clout while international pressures for racial reform were fading, the Republicans were obviously better positioned to exploit these developments. This was especially true at the level of national offices, since it was the national government that had been the chief instrument of racial transformation, as it had been in previous reform eras. Once again it was the lightning rod for critical reactions; and the national government instituting these troubling changes had been overwhelmingly led by Democrats.

Beginning in the mid-1970s, many Democratic leaders tried to appear less threatening to white Americans by distancing themselves from a vigorous promotion of civil rights. But compared to Republican candidates, they could not so easily repudiate the policies their party had sponsored in the 1960s, with which many Democratic voters still identified. Hence apart from the extremely close 1976 election when Gerald Ford could not survive the overwhelming burden of having pardoned Richard Nixon's criminal conduct, Democrats lost every presidential election from 1968 to 1988 and also saw their hold on Congress weaken.

That record makes it not so astonishing after all that when a weak economy and an uncharismatic incumbent provided Democrats with an unexpected opportunity to win back the White House in 1992, their candidate chose to ignore the racial issues raised by the L.A. riots. Instead, Bill Clinton sought to show that he was a "New

Democrat" who would stand against "radical" black demands and the costly, inefficient, intrusive "big government" they tried to enlist on their behalf. In the short run, Clinton's successful course represented the logical way to ride the political tides of these years, for despite some occasional countersurges, they were clearly moving out and away from the barely touched beaches of racial equality. Whether this more conservative course was truly necessary, and whether it would serve the national interest in racial progress in the long run, remain perhaps the central questions of American politics today.

The story of just how and why the nation's commitments to further racial reforms ebbed from the late 1960s through the 1990s is pivotal for considering those questions. The high water mark of the civil rights movement of the 1960s was probably the passage of the Open Housing Act of 1968. Even though they would not exclusively determine the nation's course throughout the following years, from that point on the currents of white racial conservatism began their long resurgence. Following that spring's riots, 58 percent of whites agreed with Chicago Mayor Richard Daley's order that police should shoot looters on sight.[4] Ironically, that number matched almost exactly the 57 percent of the vote given to the two racially conservative candidates in that November's presidential election, George Wallace and Richard Nixon.

In 1968, Wallace ran in the general election as the candidate of the American Independent Party. As in 1964, Wallace avoided outright racist references, but by now he hardly needed to do so. As historian Lewis Gould pointed out, when Wallace declared that "it was never intended for the Federal Government to run the policies of local schools," Wallace's "cheering audiences knew he was talking about desegregation and civil rights."[5] Indeed, such stands had grown more popular since 1964. In September, polls had Wallace carrying 21 percent of the vote.[6] One secret poll by the AFL-CIO found that a third of its members planned to vote for Wallace.[7] Wallace's support tapered off as Election Day approached and it became clear he was unlikely to win. But even so, the Alabaman still managed to carry 13.5 percent of the vote, the best showing for a third-party candidate in over forty years.

Although he did so less obviously than Wallace, Republican Richard Nixon also played to white fears. This course was clearly opportunistic, since in his 1960 campaign Nixon had taken a relatively liberal stand on civil rights, justifying them as a Cold War necessity.

But Nixon had lost that election; and in 1968 his usual campaign calls for America to be tougher on Communism were somewhat muted by his concern not to appear to be promising to escalate the unpopular Vietnam War. Hence his Cold War racial "liberalism" succumbed to his desire to capitalize on the growing white resistance to racial equality. Not only did he endorse "freedom of choice" plans for southern school districts (a transparent dodge that allowed whites to keep their children in segregated schools), Nixon also repeatedly emphasized the decline of "law and order" in a clear effort to appeal to white fears of black riots and traditional white stereotypes of black criminality. That, he felt, was the winning message. After viewing one of his campaign spots on "law and order," Nixon told his staff, that "hits it right on the nose. It's all about law and order and the damn Negro–Puerto Rican groups out there."[8]

Nixon's choice of Maryland governor Spiro Agnew as his running mate was also designed to appeal to white racial concerns. Although elected as a moderate, Agnew had come to national attention that spring when he publicly denounced local black leaders for encouraging the riots that followed the King assassination. Agnew also spoke in favor of shooting looters and complained that "the misguided compassion of public opinion" had led to urban disorder.[9]

On Election Day in November, the new direction of the country was clear. The split in the conservative vote between Wallace and Nixon made the race a close one, but Nixon still managed to beat Democrat Hubert Humphrey, whose commitment to racial liberalism was not shared by the majority of white Americans. Humphrey suffered, too, from the unpopularity of the Vietnam War. Yet few voters could be confident that a Nixon or Wallace administration would really deal with that ill-fated conflict any more successfully than Humphrey was likely to do. Their contrasts on racial issues were far more clear.

But even though winning the support of white racial conservatives was crucial to his victory, once in office Nixon was not yet free to swing too sharply away from racially egalitarian policies. Two factors restrained him. The imperatives of the Cold War still remained quite powerful, and they were strongly reinforced by the desires of national policymakers to prevent domestic disorders for both foreign and domestic reasons.

In regard to foreign policy, the Vietnam War, after all, still raged, with much of the world critical of U.S. policy and both China and Russia looming large as North Vietnamese allies. Some scholars of race and ethnicity have noted that from the early 1960s through the

1970s, the war provided fertile soil for the derogation of southeast Asians as "gooks" who were treacherous enemies and unreliable allies.[10] Yet it also continued to impel the U.S. government to try to hold the allegiance of other nations of color abroad and of African Americans at home. United States officials did threaten to imprison the charismatic heavyweight champion Muhammad Ali when he refused military service, championed the Nation of Islam, and spoke out against U.S. policies to admiring African and Islamic countries. Such repression was, however, clearly controversial and costly. To many national leaders it still seemed far better to try to limit the black alienation for which Ali spoke.[11]

For in regard to domestic politics, no one could then know that the peak of the urban riots had passed in the spring of 1968. Instead, international and domestic pressures worked together to highlight the great need to mollify the African Americans, who were fighting for the United States abroad but rioting and protesting against it at home, with significant white liberal support. In the fall of 1969, the Nixon administration was deeply worried that student protests against the Vietnam War and ghetto riots would seriously challenge the government.[12] Nixon, Richard Harris wrote, thus confronted a dilemma: "How could the winner keep the pledges he had made to those who had elected him, and thereby maintain his power base, and at the same time do what was necessary to preserve the Union?"[13]

According to Nixon advisor John Ehrlichman, the president answered this dilemma with a "zig-zag." He alternated between racially conservative policies that would appeal to his more right-wing white supporters and measures that would maintain the nation's standing abroad and keep the peace at home by sustaining some visible national support for civil rights.[14] To satisfy conservative whites, the Nixon administration tried to slow down school desegregation in the South. It stepped up the already brutal tactics of J. Edgar Hoover's FBI toward black radicals and even more moderate civil rights leaders. It sought the appointment of more conservative Supreme Court justices. And finally, it attacked various Great Society social welfare programs. The latter were of no use to blacks anyway, Nixon reportedly told Ehrlichman, "because blacks were genetically inferior to whites."[15]

Amid the international struggles and domestic upheavals of the late 1960s, that view was, however, still far too politically damaging to be expressed openly. Instead, Nixon continued the post-1942 practice of American national elites by insisting that the United States was genuinely committed to racial equality. He also presided over two substantial pieces of civil rights legislation: the Voting Rights Act of 1970 and the Equal Employment Opportunity Enforcement Act of 1972.[16] In addition, the Nixon administration initiated affirmative action as government policy. In 1969, the administration set up the "Philadelphia Plan," which mandated that contractors on federal construction projects employ a minimum percentage of minorities. If the contractors failed to do so, they had to show a "good faith effort" to meet these standards. Those that did not could have their contracts revoked. The Nixon administration also established "set-asides" for minority businesses in federal contracts and created the Office of Minority Business Enterprise to aid them in seeking government grants and contracts.

As sociologist John Skrentny pointed out, it is one of the ironies of affirmative action that this policy was first implemented by a relatively conservative Republican administration.[17] Yet for the Nixon administration, the Philadelphia Plan had several clear political advantages. One was that it would drive a wedge between the civil rights community, which stood to benefit from affirmative action, and organized labor, particularly the construction trades, which would be forced to make room for minority workers. The Philadelphia Plan also increased the numbers of skilled workers, an important Cold War priority, and it was an effective means of providing jobs to minorities. Thus it could reduce the possibility of further riots. Labor Secretary George Shultz, a leading sponsor of the Philadelphia Plan, had earlier warned of the "explosive" problem of black unemployment and the need for "special measures" to rectify the situation. Congressional supporters of the program voiced similar concerns. Senator John Pastore of Rhode Island told his colleagues, "What we are confronted with is the fact that this Nation suffers with a difficult situation, a very distressing one, which erupted in Philadelphia not too long ago. Because the administration has the responsibility of doing something about it before it erupts all over the country, it initiated a plan it thought would solve the problem for the time being." Efforts to kill the Philadelphia Plan, Pastore added, "are disrupting that program, which I think is essential for the stabilization of the situation, which has become a quite irritable one and serious one in the Nation."[18]

Despite these initiatives, the advances of the early Nixon administration were but the last gasps of the civil rights era. Even one of the president's more liberal advisors, Daniel Patrick Moynihan, suggested that "the time may have come when the issue of race could benefit from a period of 'benign neglect.'"[19] By 1972, it had become clear that such neglect, benign or otherwise, was an increasingly safe policy. The ghettoes were once again quiet. Rifts between moderate civil rights leaders and more radical "Black Power" advocates, which had been growing since the mid-1960s, continued, but the more militant black organizations like the Black Panthers had largely succumbed to massive government suppression and their own violent internal conflicts. Although demands by organized groups to live up to the government's racially egalitarian rhetoric had by no means disappeared, they did not appear nearly as potent as they had a few years earlier.[20]

Even more importantly for an old anti-Communist like Nixon, the Cold War pressures that had proven crucial to previous advances toward racial equality were also beginning to recede. In the spring of 1972, most of the U.S. ground forces had left Vietnam. Détente was in full swing as President Nixon made his historic visits to Beijing and Moscow, and the United States and the Soviet Union had reached an agreement to limit strategic weapons. While it was a welcome relaxation in international tensions, détente nonetheless lessened the pressure for the United States to make continued racial progress on the domestic front, where white resistance to that progress was not abating. In fact, the federal courts' use of busing as a means to remedy segregation in public schools, made explicit by the Supreme Court's 1971 decision in *Swann v. Charlotte-Mecklenburg,* exacerbated the growing disenchantment with civil rights. According to Thomas and Mary Edsall, "No other issue brought home so vividly to whites the image of the federal government as intruder and oppressor."[21] With opposition to mandated integration and the new affirmative action measures in the forefront, many whites began to oppose a whole range of government social programs, and the taxes used to pay for them, as unfair, unproductive special aids to minorities.

As the 1972 election approached, the nation was sharply polarized. On the one side was mounting white conservatism. On the other were those on the left who had been mobilized by the civil rights and antiwar movements. These groups had been empowered by the recent reforms of the Democratic Party's nominating process, and they managed to select George McGovern as the Democratic nominee, perhaps the party's most liberal presidential candidate ever.[22]

These two polarities proved, however, highly unequal in their capacities to command votes. Although the Democratic Party's structure had moved to the left, much of the electorate continued to move to the right, making that fall's election a debacle for the

Democrats. This pattern was visible even in the early Democratic primaries. Just after he was seriously wounded in an unsuccessful assassination attempt, George Wallace had received more votes than any other candidate in the Democratic primaries. His 3.3 million votes far outpaced Hubert Humphrey's 2.5 million votes and George McGovern's 2.1 million. Many of Wallace's votes came in the North. He won primaries in Michigan and Maryland, and came in a close second in Wisconsin, Indiana, and Pennsylvania. Though it is unlikely that an uninjured Wallace would have actually captured the Democratic nomination, his electoral appeal dramatized how opposition to efforts to advance racial equality had growing national support.[23]

Richard Nixon therefore also began increasing his appeals to conservative white voters. In March, the president called for Congress to enact legislation banning busing, which he described in terms befitting the slave trade. Busing, he claimed, was "a symbol of helplessness, frustration and outrage—of a wrenching of children away from their families, and from the schools their families may have moved to be near, and sending them arbitrarily to others far distant."[24] Ironically, the ever-opportunistic Nixon also saw the political advantage in attacking the affirmative action policies that his administration had been instrumental in enacting. "When young people apply for jobs," Nixon argued, "and find the door closed because they don't fit into some numerical quota, despite their ability, and they object, I do not think it is right to condemn those young people as insensitive or even racist."[25] The unhappiness of young whites was indeed understandable; but like all too many American politicians before and since, Nixon took the politically easy road in response to that unhappiness. He chose to reinforce it, to inflame resentments, rather than to explain how his own administration's policies could benefit all in the long run and to seek to expand opportunities for all Americans.

Nixon's pandering to white racial conservatism allowed him to inherit the Wallace vote and added to his landslide over George McGovern. Not only did Nixon win 61 percent of the vote, he swept the South (the first Republican ever to do so) and carried large numbers of northern blue-collar voters. Their disdain for the dovish McGovern, but also their antagonism toward measures aimed at promoting racial equality, led many white workers to abandon the party of FDR for the first but not the last time.

The Watergate scandal ultimately forced Richard Nixon from office, but the racial resentments that he had tapped successfully in

1972 remained. Popular anger over busing heightened after court-ordered desegregation spread more extensively to the North. As always, many northern whites who had tolerated federal actions against southern racial hierarchies felt outrage when their own systems of segregation were challenged. They responded with violent protests and demonstrations in several northern cities, especially Boston.[26] As the uproar grew, the Supreme Court, with four Nixon appointees serving by the end of 1973, also began to back away from its commitment to integrated public schools. In the 1974 case of *Milliken v. Bradley,* the Supreme Court struck down a lower court plan to bus students between Detroit and its suburban neighbors.[27] Although the Court would continue to support vigorous desegregation remedies within individual school districts for years to come, the decision ensured that these efforts could be constitutionally circumvented by white flight from integrated schools. To be sure, many whites undoubtedly moved to the suburbs for other reasons. Yet it is an inescapable fact that they were moving to areas and schools that were and would remain overwhelmingly white. It is also undeniable that many felt more comfortable that way.

Watergate propelled Democrat Jimmy Carter into the White House in 1976 without sparking any renewed zeal for civil rights either in the electorate or in the new administration. To the contrary: as a southern white man, Carter was well equipped to reassure those who worried about the Democrats going "too far" on race. He was certainly not an advocate of racial retreat. He had been a racially liberal governor, at least by Georgia standards, and he had the endorsement of numerous civil rights leaders. Nonetheless, Carter was careful not to antagonize racially conservative whites. During the Democratic primaries, he spoke sympathetically about those who sought to maintain the "ethnic purity" of their neighborhoods against "alien groups" and "black intrusion."[28] And whether intentionally or not, Carter's anti-Washington rhetoric tapped into many of the same strains of white resentment first voiced by George Wallace. Hubert Humphrey contended in a thinly veiled criticism of Carter that "[c]andidates who make attacks on Washington are making an attack on government programs, on the poor, on blacks, on minorities, on the cities. It's a disguised new form of racism, a disguised new form of conservatism."[29] Humphrey's polemical remark was undoubtedly overstated, for then as throughout U.S. history many Americans had deep reservations about a large central government entirely apart from issues of race. Yet his claim contained an undeniable element of truth: in the mid-1970s, opposition to "Washington programs" generally inevitably threatened measures that were visibly assisting many African Americans during difficult economic times for the nation. And if many opposed big government on principle, it seems undeniable that for many others, this threat to national initiatives benefiting blacks was not irrelevant. White racial resentments had come to influence a wide range of views on government, politics, and policy.

Jimmy Carter echoed the growing white unhappiness with strong reform measures even in the Democratic Party. Although he did appoint a record numbers of blacks and other minorities to his administration and to the federal bench, the president did not push an aggressive civil rights agenda. Joseph Califano, his secretary of health, education, and welfare, found it "remarkable that a Democratic President could go through almost all of his term without delivering a fervent, ringing, major public address on civil rights. . . . It was more extraordinary that this could happen with a President who placed such emphasis on human rights abroad. . . . Carter dealt with civil rights issues when he had to, but he did not reach out with the kind of public energy and passion I thought was needed, after the setbacks of the Nixon years, to lead the nation or to break new ground."[30]

Califano perhaps failed to consider the domestic implications of the ways the global situation had changed since the Johnson years. The increasingly stultified and widely scorned Brezhnev regime in the Soviet Union had become unable to exert much credible international moral pressure. Hence a U.S. president could now emphasize human rights abroad without promoting similar substantial reforms at home.[31]

Still, the Cold War was not yet over, and the old concerns for images of progress were not wholly absent. International considerations did influence Carter's decision to appoint the first black to a high-profile foreign policy position. In 1977, he made Andrew Young, a former associate of Martin Luther King and an Atlanta congressman, the U.S. ambassador to the United Nations. According to Carter, Young's appointment left "no doubt within the developing world that ours was an honest and sincere voice."[32] While it was better than nothing, appointments like Young's were largely symbolic and a relatively noncontroversial way to reward what had now become traditional Democratic constituencies.

National leaders during the Carter years shied away, however, from more meaningful and inevitably more controversial measures. Further evidence of the declining support for racial equality came in 1978 when the Supreme Court handed down its decision in *Regents of the University of California v. Bakke.*[33] Since its inception during the Nixon administration, spurred in part by executive branch officials held over from the Great Society years and in part by civil rights groups, affirmative action had grown in scope and controversy. For many, these programs represented reverse invidious discrimination and allowed less competent minorities to secure jobs and education at the expense of whites. For others, they represented necessary means to address the inherited disadvantages and the ongoing discrimination blacks demonstrably experienced in their efforts to obtain decent jobs, housing, mortgages, and major consumer goods. Predictably perhaps, the Supreme Court arrived at a middle ground, but one that would prove increasingly shaky.

The case at hand involved Allan Bakke, an applicant to the medical school at the University of California at Davis. Of the hundred slots for incoming students, the university reserved sixteen for minority students. As a result, Bakke was denied admission despite having higher grades and test scores than some of the minority students admitted to the school. Bakke sued, claiming that he had suffered from reverse discrimination. The case did not, however, challenge the five slots that had been set aside for relatives of faculty, state politicians, and important business people and contributors. They were not forms of privilege that stirred such deep passions in the American electorate.[34]

Initially, the Carter administration, concerned over public backlash against affirmative action, planned to file an *amicus* brief that argued against the policy's constitutionality. Black and white liberals within the administration complained bitterly. The turning point came at a cabinet meeting in which Andrew Young linked the administration's efforts to pressure the whites-only government of Rhodesia to allow black majority rule to the need for a strong position in favor of affirmative action.[35] Soon thereafter, the administration changed its brief to adopt that stance.

The case deeply divided the Court as well as the Carter administration. The justices declared that hard and fast racial quotas in college admissions were unconstitutional, but that schools could use race as one factor among many to achieve the constitutionally permissible goal of a diverse student body. Although the decision thus sustained certain forms of affirmative action, it fueled the growing furor over whether any such measures were right or useful.

Carter ended up hoisted on this rather tentatively grasped petard. Neither the economy nor American foreign policy generally fared well by many measures during Carter's presidency, and the wide-spread perception of him as sympathetic to blacks and civil rights, even if he did little for them, only further contributed to his defeat by Ronald Reagan in 1980. Ever since he was first elected governor of California in 1966, Reagan had skillfully appealed to white racial resentments in covert ways. The same was true in his 1980 presidential campaign. It kicked off in Philadelphia, Mississippi, where Reagan announced, "I believe in states' rights."[36] It was here in the summer of 1964 that local whites had murdered three civil rights workers, Goodman, Chaney, and Schwerner—just the type of act of local oppression that the slogan "states' rights" had long been used to shelter. Yet, few white Americans were put off by Reagan's ugly symbolism. In fact, when President Carter condemned Reagan's remarks, the national press took him to task for being mean-spirited.[37]

Reagan also appealed to white anger at black welfare recipients by recounting vivid fables of "strapping young bucks" and Cadillac-driving "welfare queens" who abused the welfare system. Reagan professed to be opposed to virtually all "big government" aid programs. But since most Americans supported measures that assisted the white middle class, such as Social Security and Medicare, Reagan's focus on those programs most identified in white minds with blacks—welfare and food stamps—helped to make his antigovernment conservatism more saleable to the electorate.[38]

Finally, Reagan proved adept at inverting the rhetoric of racial liberalism to support his conservative ends. The 1980 Republican platform declared, "The truths we hold and the values we share affirm that no individual should be victimized by unfair discrimination because of race, sex, advanced age, physical handicap, difference of national origin or religion, or economic circumstance." On the other hand, it added that "equal opportunity should not be jeopardized by bureaucratic regulations and decisions which rely on quotas, ratios and numerical requirements to exclude some individuals in favor of others, thereby rendering such regulations and decisions inherently discriminatory."[39] The chief examples of invidious discrimination the platform provided, then, were not white racism and racial segregation. They were policies and programs that had been established to integrate society and lessen the impact of ongoing discrimination. Furthermore, despite the fact that they remained better off as a group on every conceivable economic, educational, and social measure, whites were now portrayed as the chief victims of discrimination. "If you happen to belong to an ethnic group not recognized by the federal government as entitled to special treatment, you are the victim of reverse discrimination," declared Reagan.[40]

As president, Reagan escalated the anti-Soviet rhetoric in American foreign policy and further increased the defense buildup of the late Carter administration. This racheting up of the Cold War was, however, not nearly enough to replicate the forces that had contributed to the civil rights advances of the 1960s. Reagan's rhetoric notwithstanding, the Cold War had clearly abated from its high of the early 1960s. Even with the Reagan administration's buildup, defense spending as a percent of the gross domestic product (GDP) remained significantly below the levels of the 1960s (see table 8).

Absent the strong counterpull of a genuinely competitive Cold War, the Reagan administration was safely able to scale back enforcement of civil rights. During the first two years of the administration, the budgets of the Equal Employment Opportunity Commission (EEOC) and the Office of Federal Contract Compliance Programs (OFFCP) were cut 10 and 24 percent, respectively, while their staffs were reduced by 12 and 34 percent. As a consequence, as the Edsalls pointed out, "Back-pay awards won through actions of the OFFCP . . . fell from $9.3 million paid to 4,336 recipients in 1980, to $3.6 million paid to 1,758 recipients in 1983."[41]

Reagan also appointed staunch conservatives to lead the federal government's civil rights bureaucracy. Among these was William Bradford Reynolds, who Reagan chose to head the Justice Department's Civil Rights Division and who promised to fight "the battle

Table 8. Defense Spending as a Percentage of Gross Domestic Product, 1960–1989

Year	%	Year	%	Year	%
1960	9.5	1970	8.3	1980	5.1
1961	9.6	1971	7.5	1981	5.3
1962	9.4	1972	6.9	1982	5.9
1963	9.1	1973	6.0	1983	6.3
1964	8.8	1974	5.7	1984	6.2
1965	7.5	1975	5.7	1985	6.4
1966	7.9	1976	5.3	1986	6.5
1967	9.0	1977	5.1	1987	6.3
1968	9.7	1978	4.8	1988	6.0
1969	8.9	1979	4.8	1989	5.9
Average	8.9		6.0		6.0

Source: Harold W. Stanley and Richard G. Niemi, *Vital Statistics on American Politics*, 4th ed. (Washington, D.C.: Congressional Quarterly Press, 1994), pp. 361–2.

of racial quotas, minority set-asides, and forced busing." He also challenged "the efficacy, wisdom, and indeed, in some cases, the legality,
of various sputtering and often ineffective remedial programs . . .
which the civil rights 'establishment' has advocated."[42] In a manner
reminiscent of past retreats from reform, the main thrust of federal remedial efforts on civil rights was now to war against the existing remedial efforts.

The president similarly sought to appoint racial conservatives to
the federal bench, particularly the Supreme Court. In 1986, Reagan
elevated Justice William Rehnquist to replace retiring Chief Justice
Warren Burger. Rehnquist had taken an extremely conservative line
on civil rights issues during his previous fifteen years on the Court.
And as a clerk to Justice Robert Jackson in the early 1950s, he had
written a memo arguing against declaring school segregation unconstitutional in *Brown v. Board of Education,* though he later claimed that
the memo did not represent his own views.[43] Furthermore, during his
confirmation hearings, he had to overcome well-documented stories
that as a young attorney in Phoenix, he had attacked a local civil rights
ordinance and had harassed black and Hispanic voters while working
as a Republican poll-watcher.[44] The following year, Reagan nominated
Robert Bork for associate justice. Bork had a long record of opposition
to civil rights. Most famously, in 1963, he wrote in the *New Republic* that
the proposed 1964 Civil Rights Act's ban on discrimination in public
accommodations entailed "a principle of unsurpassed ugliness" since
it limited the freedom of business owners to chose their clientele. Bork
later claimed a change of heart on this issue, but even during his confirmation hearings he spoke out in opposition to a Supreme Court
decision that struck down poll taxes in state elections.[45]

As the Bork nomination indicates, the Reagan administration did
not succeed in all of its efforts to undermine civil rights. During the
Reagan years, the Democrats retained their hold on the House and
managed in 1986 to regain the control of the Senate that they had
lost in 1980. This success in congressional elections was aided by in-
cumbency advantages in the House, by the Democrats' weakened
but continued ability to construct a biracial coalition within and
across districts, and by the manner in which many Democrats visibly
shifted in Reagan's direction on policy, though not partisanship.[46]
Senate Democrats were able to defeat Bork's nomination, largely
because his views on privacy and abortion were unpalatable to the
majority of Americans, but also because his civil rights views were
an anathema to an important part of their shaken but not yet overwhelmed coalition. Although they might distance themselves from

genuinely strong civil rights initiatives, few congressional Democrats were yet willing to repudiate openly the basic consensus in support of civil rights forged in the 1960s. In 1988, when Reagan became the first president to veto a significant civil rights bill since Andrew Johnson's attacks on Reconstruction, Congress managed to muster the two-thirds vote necessary to override the president.

Even on affirmative action, the Reagan administration was stymied in its efforts to limit the program. Early in his second term, Reagan's advisors seriously considered having him sign an executive order doing away with the program, but the perceived political costs were too high. "The internal argument was," stated William Bradford Reynolds, " 'We're expending a lot of political capital on this issue. It's getting in the way of other things that are more important. The less problems for Reagan the better. Let's don't carry this further now. We can always revisit it later.' "[47] Even though ordinary white Americans could be stirred up to oppose such programs, many white elites still supported affirmative action as a necessary crisis management tool originally forged in the Cold War era. In addition, many Democrats still thought affirmative action was useful for their constituencies, and even many Republicans found themselves pressured to support affirmative action measures benefiting women. Still, concerns about domestic disorder were probably most decisive. According to Nicholas Lemann, most members of the white elite justified affirmative action because it allowed the nation to "take some of the edge off what has been the most explosive issue in our history, the one that set off our bloodiest war and our worst civil disturbances. We create an integrated authority system. We give blacks a stake. It promotes the peace."[48]

But while liberals in support of civil rights might have been winning some of the battles, conservative Republicans, led by the charming Great Communictor, were increasingly setting the national agenda and winning the war to shape public opinion in different directions. Reagan's efforts to split the parties along racialized lines largely succeeded. Racial animosities were crucial to the making of the "Reagan Democrats"—traditional Democrats who abandoned the party to vote for Reagan in 1980 and 1984. Evidence of this appeared in a famous survey conducted after the 1984 election in Macomb County, Michigan, a largely white, blue-collar area of suburban Detroit. The county had voted heavily for John F. Kennedy in 1960 and gave a majority of its votes to Hubert Humphrey in 1968. During the 1970s, the county drifted toward the Republicans and in 1984 Reagan carried the county by a margin of two to one.[49]

To understand these shifts, in 1985 pollster Stanley Greenberg conducted a focus group with several white Macomb County Democrats who had voted for Reagan. Greenberg read them a statement from Robert Kennedy stressing the responsibility that the nation owed to blacks because of the legacy of slavery and discrimination. The response was as follows:

> "That's bullshit," shouted one participant.
> "No wonder they killed him," said another.
> "I'm fed up with it," chimed in a third.[50]

Statements like these led Greenberg to conclude that whites in Macomb County had come to view both the Democratic Party and the federal government as tools of black interests:

> These white Democratic defectors express a profound distaste for blacks, a sentiment that pervades almost everything they think about government and politics . . . Blacks constitute the explanation for their [white defectors'] vulnerability and for almost everything that has gone wrong in their lives; not being black is what constitutes middle class; not living with blacks is what makes a neighborhood a decent place to live . . . virtually all progressive symbols and themes have been redefined in racial and pejorative terms. . . . The special status of blacks is perceived by almost all of these individuals as a serious obstacle to their personal advancement. Indeed, discrimination against whites has become a well-assimilated and ready explanation for their status, vulnerability, and failures.[51]

Greenberg's report added that white voters "reject absolutely any notion that blacks suffer special circumstances that would require special treatment by employers or government. There is no historical memory of racism and no tolerance for present efforts to offset it. There is no sense of personal or collective responsibility that would support government anti-discrimination and civil rights policies."[52] Like many other policy analysts, moreover, Greenberg appeared to feel it was hopeless to combat these circumstances. Rather than calling on Democrats to argue for the national need for continued racial reforms more clearly and forcefully, political advisors increasingly recommended, implicitly or explicitly, that Democrats move away from what they perceived as the political albatross of championing racial equality. While it may have been sound political advice in the short-run, it is hard to see how this tactic helped the country heal its racial problems. And it may ultimately have harmed the Democrats electorally by further legitimizing attacks on one of their most important constituencies.

Reagan's successor, George Bush, capitalized on this racial divide in his own bid for the presidency in 1988. Running for reelection to the House in 1968, Bush had presented voters with the image of black Vietnam veterans, returning from serving their country, only to find continued discrimination at home. Twenty years later, in a move that both reflected and exacerbated the nation's retreat from racial equality, Bush embraced the image of "Willie" Horton in his 1988 presidential campaign (Horton's real name was William, but Bush's campaign used "Willie" to better convey his race to the public). The "Willie" Horton imagery served several purposes for the Republicans—it not only conjured up white fears of black crime, but also reinforced the perception of many white voters that the Democrats were overly tolerant of social deviants (read, blacks). The effort succeeded. In late October 1988, ninety-three voters in focus groups were asked about Horton. All but five of those surveyed mentioned his race and one-third mentioned it twice. All but twelve people in the groups described the women Horton raped as white.[53] Another survey of voters found that "helping blacks" was the issue that they most identified with Democratic candidate Michael Dukakis.[54] With voters so attuned to racial appeals, and with "Willie" Horton as a leading campaign issue, Bush closed what had briefly been a sizable gap and defeated Dukakis that November.

As president, the otherwise mild-mannered Bush continued to play the racial card when necessary. In 1989, the Supreme Court in a series of cases made it more difficult for plaintiffs to sue for racial and sexual discrimination under the 1964 Civil Rights Act. When Congress attempted to overturn the decision with additional legislation the next year, President Bush labeled it a "quota bill" and vetoed it in October 1990. To drive home the point, when he announced his decision to veto the bill, Bush used the word *quota* seven times in five paragraphs.[55]

The 1990 congressional elections revealed just how powerful the "quota" issue was for conservatives. That year in North Carolina, incumbent Republican Jesse Helms was running behind his black challenger, Harvey Gantt. Helms fought back by playing the race card. He ran an advertisement that showed a pair of white hands crumpling a letter as the voice-over said, "You needed that job and you were the best qualified, but they had to give it to a minority because of a racial quota."[56] Bush rejected a compromise version of the civil rights bill in 1991, once again calling it a quota bill even though this new version had a provision that expressly rejected the use of quotas.

At one time, the service of black soldiers had had a powerful influence on Bush's civil rights views. Although black soldiers served bravely during the Gulf War—and for the first time under a black chairman of the Joint Chiefs of Staff, General Colin Powell—the war was won quickly and easily, requiring none of the great sacrifices that had previously been so instrumental in advancing black equality. The Bush administration tried to cast the war as a conflict between democracy and dictatorship, fought to restore freedom to Kuwait, but this rhetoric was nullified by the undemocratic nature of the Kuwaiti regime and the refusal of the allied forces to topple Saddam Hussein from power. Finally, underlying much public sentiment in the United States during the war was an ugly streak of anti-Arab and anti-Muslim prejudice.

On the home front, Bush was not shy about using racial symbolism for political purposes in Supreme Court nominations. In 1991 when he nominated federal judge Clarence Thomas to fill the position vacated by Thurgood Marshall, Bush declared that Thomas was the "most qualified person for the job." What the president should have said was that Thomas was the most qualified black conservative who would lend legitimacy to GOP efforts to shift the Supreme Court even further to the right.

Yet ironically, the Thomas nomination helped to force the Bush administration to back off its opposition to the civil rights bill. Allegations by Anita Hill that Thomas had sexually harassed her rocked the nation; and although the nomination managed to squeak through the Senate, the Bush administration faced the possibility of a backlash against it among women. To continue to oppose civil rights legislation that would help victims of sex discrimination now seemed to carry great political risks.[57]

In addition to worries about the women's vote, the Bush administration also had to confront the specter of David Duke. For nearly two decades, Duke, a former Nazi and Klansman, had labored fruitlessly at the margins of politics. By the late 1980s, however, Duke saw a newly accommodating home for himself in the party that made "Willie" Horton a household name. Though Duke was forced to shed his brown shirts and white robes to run as a Republican, he did not shed any views. In 1989, he was elected as a Republican to the Louisiana state legislature running on standard GOP promises to oppose racial quotas, stop welfare handouts, and to get tough on crime. In 1990, he gained 59 percent of the white vote and nearly managed to defeat incumbent U.S. senator Bennett Johnston. In 1991, Duke made it into the gubernatorial runoff election and though he lost the race, he still managed to carry 55 percent of the white vote.[58] Fearing a growing gender gap and the Republican party's identification with David Duke, Bush dropped his opposition and signed the Civil Rights Restoration Act of 1991 only two weeks after the Louisiana election. Again, the Republicans judged that the nation had not moved so far to the right on race as to make people like Duke palatable; but again, their leadership was visibly moving in that direction nonetheless.

For those who insist that southern whites have undergone a fundamental change in their racial views since the 1960s, it should give pause that Duke received roughly the same share of the vote that a white supremacist candidate would probably have received thirty years earlier in Louisiana. Therefore, the most demonstrably significant change in southern politics since the 1960s is not in the attitudes of white Southerners, but the introduction of black suffrage. Nor should one dismiss the Duke phenomenon as another example of Louisiana's ongoing political carnival. Louisiana was never a typical Deep South state; historically, it possessed a more tolerant attitude (at least in New Orleans) toward black voting and a strong tradition of economic populism that tended to reduce the saliency of racial politics for a Deep South state.[59] Huey Long may have been a demagogue, but if so it was on issues of class, not race. More recently, political scientists Susan Howell and Sylvia Warren found that the racial attitudes of New Orleans area whites did not differ significantly from those in other areas of the country.[60] Finally, one should note that in 1991, 55 percent of white Louisianans voted for a (barely) ex-Klansman and former Nazi, but in 1995, only 16 percent could manage to vote for a black candidate, former congressman Cleo Fields.[61]

In any case, the image of David Duke was soon erased by those of the Los Angeles riots, offering the Republicans an even more powerful tool to excite white racial fears than "Willie" Horton. Although President Bush initially expressed his dismay at the Rodney King verdict, he quickly reverted to form, blaming the riots on "the brutality of [the] mob, pure and simple." Bush's press secretary Marlin Fitzwater added that the riots were "the result of the Great Society programs of the 1960s and 1970s."[62] Bush's ability to use the riots and the race issue more generally in that year's presidential election were, however, stymied by the character of his opponent, Democrat Bill Clinton.

Throughout his career, Clinton has often spoken movingly on matters of racial equality, especially before black audiences. But his record shows that Clinton has always been, above all else, a shrewd and pragmatic politician, well aware of the political power of white conservatism and more than willing to accommodate these sentiments to advance his own ambitions. Consequently, despite his oft-stated goal of fostering racial healing, Bill Clinton embodies the Democratic Party's retreat from liberalism, racial and otherwise, over the last two decades.

As governor of Arkansas in through most of the 1980s, Clinton followed a careful strategy of moderation designed to avoid antagonizing the state's conservative whites and powerful business interests. His success here allowed him to move into the national political arena through the Democratic Leadership Council (DLC). The council first began in the aftermath of Walter Mondale's loss in 1984. Several Democratic elected officials sought to create a conservative Democratic organization that would not only inoculate them from accusations that they were too liberal for their constituents but would also serve as a vehicle to shift the party rightward. Although the DLC criticized traditional liberal Democrats on a range of issues, the topic of race was never far below the surface of its discussions. Few were as open as former LBJ aide Harry McPherson, who declared after Mondale's loss, "Blacks own the Democratic Party. . . . White Protestant male Democrats are an endangered species." Still, many of those associated with the DLC believed that the Democratic Party had become beholden to various "special interests," usually perceived as blacks and other minorities, women, and gays and lesbians. These were precisely the terms the Reagan Republicans used to attack the Democratic Party.[63]

During Clinton's tenure as DLC chair from 1990 to 1991, the organization took a page from George Bush and David Duke's play book and approved a platform plank opposing racial "quotas." Clinton claimed disingenuously that the statement was a "reaffirmation of civil rights and affirmative action." To those who saw the statement as an effort to roll back the Democrats' commitment to racial equality, he offered the wan promise that as the DLC grew larger, their voices would ultimately be heard.[64]

Running for president in 1992, Clinton made similar efforts to distance himself from the Democrats' liberal tradition, racial and otherwise. Presenting himself as a "New Democrat," Clinton emphasized the need for greater "personal responsibility" in return for government assistance. In particular, he promised to "end welfare as we know it." To those on welfare who "refuse" to work, Clinton warned, "We will do with you. We will not do for you." There were indeed strong reasons to believe that the existing welfare system was flawed. The Clinton campaign, however, did little to combat the misperception that its problems were chiefly those of irresponsible minority recipients, nor did it provide many suggestions as to how the country would "do with" those who would lose public aid.[65]

Yet Clinton's policy appeals to conservative whites did not speak as loudly as the symbolism of his actions. In January 1992, in the crucial days before the New Hampshire primary and in the midst of his first national sex scandal, the Gennifer Flowers affair, Clinton left the campaign trail to return to Arkansas. He wished to be there for the execution of Rickey Ray Rector, a brain-damaged black man. The execution did not require Clinton's presence, but his trip sent an unmistakable message that a President Clinton would have no sympathy for black criminals—even if, like Rector, they had the mental capacity of a child. (When asked if he wanted to finish his dessert at his last meal, Rector said he would save it for later.)[66]

Perhaps the defining moment of Clinton's campaign, however, was his public feud with Jesse Jackson over the remarks of rap singer and activist Sister Souljah. In June 1992, Clinton used his address before Jackson's Rainbow Coalition to criticize the group for earlier giving a forum to Sister Souljah, who in a newspaper interview after the Los Angeles riots had purportedly stated her belief that the violence was "wise" and that it was justified for blacks to kill whites.

Despite the claims of his campaign, Clinton's criticism was not a spontaneous comment triggered by his conscience and revulsion at racial violence. Instead, it was part of a planned and deliberate strategy to reassure white voters of Clinton's toughness by attacking black extremism and alienating Jesse Jackson. Several points reinforce this assessment. First, Sister Souljah's claim that her effort to convey the views of black gang members was misquoted (which was met with great skepticism by the media) seems at least plausible, as the following transcript of the relevant part of her interview indicates:

Q: But even the people themselves who were perpetrating the violence, did they think it was wise? Was that wise reasoned action? *Sister Souljah:* Yeah, it was wise. I mean, if black people kill black people every day, why not have a week and kill white people? You understand what I'm saying? In other words, white people, this government and that mayor were well aware of the fact that black people were dying every day in Los Angeles under gang violence.

So if you're a gang member and you would normally be killing somebody, why not kill a white person? Do you think that somebody thinks that white people are better, or above and beyond dying, when they would kill their own kind?[67] (Emphasis added.)

Here Sister Souljah appears to be putting herself in the mind of a gang member. She seems to contend not that killing whites is wise but only that, for those blacks who wrongly engage in killing, it makes at least as much sense for them to kill whites as blacks. Still, the opportunity in Sister Souljah's words appears to have been too good for the Clinton campaign to pass up through a charitable (or even accurate) reading.

Second, many of Clinton's advisors had been encouraging him to confront Jackson publicly in order to reassure white voters of his toughness with Democratic Party "special interests." According to Bob Woodward, after the speech, "Clinton told [campaign advisors Paul] Begala and [George] Stephanopoulos tersely, 'Well, you got your story.' " Third, Clinton aides made sure to tip off several reporters that Clinton would use the occasion to distance himself from Jackson. Finally, Clinton originally intended to give a similar speech immediately after the Los Angeles riots, but decided to wait for a more appropriate occasion.[68]

The response to his criticism of Sister Souljah and, implicitly, Jesse Jackson was all that Clinton could have hoped. Republican polls indicated that 68 percent of the electorate were aware of the incident—twice the number who were aware of Clinton's economic plan. Moreover, whites approved of Clinton's statement by a margin of three to one, while blacks disapproved by the same margin.[69] As one blue-collar white explained, "The day he told off that fucking Jackson is the day he got my vote."[70]

Although less dramatically than during the Sister Souljah incident, Bill Clinton spent the rest of the campaign reassuring conservative whites. His campaign manifesto, *Putting People First,* scarcely mentioned the word *race* other than to oppose "racial quotas." As Andrew Hacker noted, it devoted "more space to biases based on physical disabilities and sexual preference" than to racial discrimination.[71] This strategy of exploiting or obscuring issues of racial equality appears to have had the desired effect. The Bush campaign was unable to use racial issues against Clinton in same way that they had used "Willie" Horton against Dukakis in 1988. And even though Clinton's weak position on civil rights caused black turnout to drop, increased white support for the Democratic ticket more than offset black abstentions. Still, Clinton's increased competitiveness among whites seems to have resulted from Ross Perot's draining off white support from George Bush, rather than from a surge in support for the Democrats. In 1988, Michael Dukakis received 40 percent of the white vote. Four years later, Bill Clinton managed only 39 percent.[72] Overall, Clinton's 43 percent of the popular vote was three percentage points less than Dukakis's 46 percent.

In the end, the best one can say of Clinton's gamble of offsetting lower black turnout with increased support among whites was that it worked only in the context of a three-way race. In light of American history, the notion that Democratic prospects were better if they were not identified as the party of aid to blacks was an understandable if none too admirable idea. But in fact the 1992 campaign indicated that braver strategies might have succeeded with the right candidate. Clinton did not try to be that candidate.

Clinton's strategic use of race has continued throughout his administration. After his election, he expressed a desire for a cabinet that "looks like America," but the key was "looks." Clinton's actual choices were a careful blend of women, minorities, and white men, few of whom (especially those in important cabinet positions) had the inclination or political stature to call for a strong agenda in support of racial equality. Moreover, he has quickly backed away from nominees such as Lani Guinier, Clinton's first choice for the Justice Department's Civil Rights Division, who have drawn fire from conservatives for their strong advocacy of racial justice.

Clinton never seemed to miss an opportunity to preach to black audiences about the need for more "personal responsibility" in the black community. Although he had claimed that deemphasizing racial equality was necessary for the Democrats to revive their political fortunes and achieve more liberal economic policies, Clinton was unable or unwilling to hold up the latter parts of the bargain. Not only did his health care plan fail in 1994, but in 1994 the Republicans managed to gain control of Congress for the first time since 1952. Though the result of many factors, the Republicans success in 1994 was aided by the alienation of the Democrats' base among the poor and minorities. Between 1990 and 1994, voter turnout among those making $50,000 a year or more rose from 59.2 percent to 60.1 percent, but turnout among those making under $5,000 fell from 32.2 percent to 19.9 percent, and from 30.9 percent to 23.3 percent for those making between $5,000 and $10,000. In addition, while white turnout rose slightly, from 46.7 percent in 1990 to 46.9 percent in 1994, black turnout fell from 39.2 percent to 37 percent and Hispanic turnout fell from 23.1 percent to 19.1 percent.[73]

The guiding force behind the Republican victory in 1994 was Congressman Newt Gingrich of Georgia. Although a transplant to the region, he quickly proved adept at southern-style race baiting. In his first successful race for Congress, Gingrich distributed flyers showing his opponent, Virginia Shepard, with black state senator Julian Bond. "If you like welfare cheaters, you'll love Virginia Shepard," read the flyers.[74] Gingrich's attempts to oust the Democrats from Congress also played to the nation's racial divide. As much as any recent American politician, Gingrich was keenly aware of the symbolic power of words and phrases in shaping the public debate.[75] As journalist Peter Applebome noted, "[I]t's not too hard to figure out just which teenagers [Gingrich] was talking about in his famous comment, 'It's impossible to maintain civilization with twelve-year-olds having babies, fifteen-year-olds killing each other, seventeen-year-olds dying of AIDS, and eighteen-year-olds getting diplomas they can't even read.' It wasn't the kids in white suburbs, even if the ills he cited were not limited to black inner cities."[76]

Despite the hype and spectacle generated by the media, the ensuing battles between Clinton and Republicans in the 104th Congress indicated how far to the right the political spectrum had shifted. When Clinton and the Republican leadership in Congress agreed to settle their differences on the budget in early 1996, they did so largely on the backs of the poor, minorities, and immigrants. A report by the Center on Budget and Policy Priorities found that programs for the poor made up only 23 percent of the nondefense budget, but that they accounted for over 50 percent of the reductions enacted during the 104th Congress (1995–1996).[77] In particular, the passage of welfare reform in 1996 showed the political fragility of programs perceived to disproportionately benefit racial minorities. Even though it was largely the creation of a Republican Congress, Bill Clinton nonetheless rightly claims much of the responsibility for this legislation, making his efforts to distance himself from some of its features debatable. In 1992 it was Clinton who famously set the agenda by declaring that he would "end welfare as we know it." As a Democrat attacking welfare, he succeeded chiefly in shifting the welfare policy debate further to the right. Not surprisingly, Republicans quickly responded by coming up with their own even more Dickensian welfare overhaul plans. As the 1996 election loomed, Clinton was forced to sign a bill that he acknowledged was excessively punitive, lest he be seen as too liberal on the issue.[78]

In addition to the dismantling of the welfare state, recent attacks on affirmative action also suggest a growing willingness to move away from racial equality in the post–Cold War environment. Through the 1990s, the Supreme Court became increasingly hostile to all uses of racial classifications, including efforts to assist African Americans, particularly in the 1995 case of *Adarand v. Pena*. Although the Court stopped short of striking down all affirmative action, the decision made it clear that in the future, such efforts even by the federal government would have enormous difficulty passing constitutional muster.[79]

Lower federal courts got the message and quickly began striking down state-level affirmative action programs as well. The most notable such decision was *Hopwood v. Texas* in 1996. In it, the Fifth Circuit Court of Appeals voided the affirmative action admissions program of the University of Texas Law School, holding that the school's aim of creating a diverse student body was insufficiently compelling to withstand strict scrutiny. The court also overlooked the fact that Hopwood's race was hardly the only factor in her failure to gain admission. Over a hundred whites with scores lower than hers were admitted. The Supreme Court declined to review the decision, an action that technically represented neither endorsement nor condemnation of the Fifth Circuit's stance.[80]

Supporters of affirmative action, however, had little reason to hope that the rising tide of *Hopwood*-style rulings would soon be stemmed, as opponents of affirmative action began mobilizing. In Congress, Republicans have introduced legislation to abolish various affirmative action programs. In early 1998, the House considered an amendment to forbid the use of affirmative action in college admissions. Even though the amendment failed, it did so only by the relatively narrow margin of 244 to 177. Moreover, the vote split along clear party lines, with Republicans voting for the measure 166 to 55 and Democrats voting against it 193 to 5.[81]

Opponents of affirmative action in the West were more successful with the California Civil Rights Initiative (CCRI) and the State of Washington's similar affirmative action initiative. Both banned their state from using race or gender in any of its decisions regarding employment, contracts, or admission to state universities. As Reagan had done, these initiatives used the language of the 1960s civil rights movement to oppose some of the most notable policy initiatives that era had produced. Drawing strong support from whites, the CCRI passed in 1996 despite overwhelming opposition from California blacks and substantial opposition from Latinos and Asians.[82] Subsequently, a coalition of minorities and liberal whites defeated an anti–affirmative action measure in Houston in 1997, but a court then ruled that the measure had been misleadingly worded. And in November 1998, 58 percent of the voters in Washington state voted for that state's version of the CCRI. The results of these measures for college admissions are both clear and worrisome. At UCLA and Berkeley, the two most prestigious campuses in the University of California system, the number of blacks and Latinos admitted has declined significantly, paralleling the pattern visible at the University of Texas in the wake of the *Hopwood* decision.[83]

In face of such reactions against affirmative action, Clinton launched a policy of "mend it don't end it." Although he upheld the basic goals of affirmative action, Clinton agreed there were serious problems with some existing policies and vowed to eliminate any program that "creates a quota, creates preferences for unqualified individuals, creates reverse discrimination or continues even after its equal opportunity purposes have been achieved."[84] Since rightly or wrongly critics were making those charges against virtually every form of affirmative action, it was not clear what forms the president actually supported. During one of the 1996 presidential debates Clinton proudly asserted, "I've done more to eliminate programs—affirmative action programs—I didn't think were fair. And to tighten others up than my predecessors have since affirmative action's been around." He also referred positively only to affirmative action efforts to aid women without explicitly mentioning racial minorities.[85] In addition, despite the fact that he was running well ahead of Republican Bob Dole in California, Clinton refused to take a strong stand against the CCRI. He criticized it sharply only after the election.

Perhaps because he was freed from reelection worries, President Clinton sought to pay closer attention to issues of racial equality, announcing in June 1997 his Presidential Initiative on Race. Once again, foreign policy issues played a leading role in the president's thinking. According to journalist Roger Simon:

He [Clinton] invited [his staff] to ask him the real importance of racial healing in America, and when they did, he said simply: "Foreign policy." Then he just watched the baffled expressions play across their faces as he leaned forward and explained: Empowering American minorities would ensure that America would continue to be the leading economic power in the world. American blacks who were in business in America could relate better to the African blacks wanting to do business with America. Asian Americans empowered in this country could be more competitive and do better deals with Asians in Asian countries. "That is the value of a diverse workforce," Clinton said, "making sure enterprises are globally connected. It is not just 'let's all live together in harmony.' It's about enhancing our economic power in the twenty-first century."

The press will think it is about race, Clinton told his people, but it is about foreign policy and economic policy and America's leadership role in the world.[86]

Though in many ways laudable, President Clinton's race initiative has proven less than adequate. When the presidential commission designated to lead the initiative submitted its report in September 1998, it was conspicuously lacking in substantive policy proposals. Moreover, this seems to have been the intention of the Clinton White House. "There is timidity on this question," commented Thomas Kean, a member of the panel and the former Republican governor of New Jersey. "Race is very divisive. As the year wore on, people became—not the board, but people in the Administration—became concerned. We were encouraged not to be bold. My recommendations were much bolder than anything contained in this report."[87]

At best, the initiative offered an ineffective but benign way for Clinton to play the role of "therapist in chief." Rather than attempting the more controversial and expensive effort of putting forth substantive policies to deal with the continuing impact of racial exclusion and discrimination, the initiative allowed Clinton a low-cost way to create the impression of concern and action. Yet the costs may not be so low. At worst, the president's race initiative offers a distraction from the fact that he, the Democratic party, and the nation in general have sounded an end to the modern era of civil rights reform. In his speeches on the subject, President Clinton has repeatedly stressed that the answer to the nation's racial problems requires not positive governmental action but a change in the hearts and habits of individual Americans. "We have torn down the barriers in our laws," proclaims Clinton. "Now we must break down the barriers in our lives, our minds and our hearts."[88]

These words have an eerily familiar ring. In the late nineteenth and early twentieth century, Republican Presidents, then the liberal party on race, maintained a rhetorical sympathy for equal rights but disparaged any effort by the government to achieve it, the same position as more "progressive" late-nineteenth-century Democrats. As the limited scope of his race initiative has become clear, Clinton has expressed admiration for these very leaders. He has suggested that Rutherford B. Hayes and Grover Cleveland were progressive reformers who are today underappreciated; they were, he believes, combating bigotry and economic injustices as much as was possible in their circumstances.[89] That outlook may help convince Clinton that the little he has done is all that now can be done to pursue racial progress. Yet it also suggests that, although Bill Clinton may indeed have helped the nation to build a bridge, as far as race relations are concerned it is as yet unclear whether it is a bridge to the future or to the past.

Shall We Overcome?

Few would deny that America's unsteady march toward racial equality remains remote from that grand destination. As the United States enters the twenty-first century, it may well be asked what lies ahead for American race relations. Are we stepping into that more equal, united, and harmonious America that President Clinton has repeatedly invoked, or is our bridge emptying into something akin to the troubled racial waters of the late nineteenth century? These questions are all the more urgent because the three factors that have thus far always been present when the United States has made strides toward greater racial justice—the three factors that persisted through the long stretch of the twentieth century to produce the triumphs of the modern civil rights movement—have now receded. Although African Americans continue to serve disproportionately in the nation's military, the armed forces are now voluntary and reduced in numbers. The large-scale mobilization of blacks for economic and defense purposes that prevailed through the Cold War and Vietnam years is now past. Correspondingly, the United States does not have a clearly defined enemy against which it feels compelled to stress its comparatively democratic and inclusive traditions, even if it still does so in regard to some lesser rivals like Saddam Hussein. There is also no large-scale civil rights movement pressuring the nation to live up to its more egalitarian ideals. Indeed, the largest mobilization of African Americans in the 1990s came in the Million Man March organized by the separatist Nation of Islam leader Louis Farrakhan.

Yet if the conditions always associated in the past with advancing the cause of racial equality have declined, it is also true that many things today are far different than ever before in our history. The United States is now the world's only superpower, and so it constantly plays a leadership role among many African and Asian nations still attentive to U.S. racial practices. Economic globalization also has created important incentives for the U.S. governmental and business leaders to be sensitive to the interests and attitudes of non-whites around the world. And as we have noted throughout, although progress toward racial equality has been neither constant nor irreversible in the United States, it has in certain vital regards been cumulative. Slavery, Jim Crow, and explicitly race-based immigration restrictions are gone, the latter ended by the longest period favorable to racial progress that the nation has ever experienced.

The victories of the modern civil rights movement have, moreover, transformed America in ways that may represent the irrevocable turning of a corner on race. Most major institutions of American society, from military headquarters to legislative and judicial chambers to city halls to university classrooms to professional offices to corporate boardrooms, are more racially integrated than they have ever been. With those achievements the black middle class and, indeed, the black upper class have become far larger and more prosperous than in any previous era. Michael Jordan and Oprah Winfrey are not only American icons but also hugely wealthy. And the civil rights movement's success in ending the National Origins Quota system in 1965 has meant that the United States has become more racially diverse than ever before, with fast-growing Latino and Asian populations transforming America's traditional white–black/European American–African American racial and ethnic composition. Beyond these demographic changes, opinion polls suggest that whites have by and large abandoned their old beliefs in the legitimacy of racial hierarchies. Instead, the egalitarian ideals of the civil rights movement are celebrated in American discourse, institutions, and practices to a far greater degree than those of Reconstruction ever were. Martin Luther King's birthday is a national holiday and political leaders across the spectrum invoke his example in ways that were never true of Thaddeus Stevens or Frederick Douglass.

Has the United States, then, reached a point where Americans can expect continuing declines in racial animosities and achievement of more equal opportunities for all, even in the absence of the factors that seem heretofore to have been necessary for real change to occur? Many opinion leaders and scholars argue that it has. We are not so sanguine. We do know, however, that such a stage would be truly unprecedented in U.S. history; and since history ordinarily displays continuities as well as changes, it seems prudent to be alert to the possibility that the transformation of America in regard to race has been much less than total. Perhaps some of the inegalitarian, racially divisive dynamics visible in our past are also visible in our present and future. If that is the case to any substantial degree, our history suggests that combating those dynamics should be given a very high priority in American politics.

In this conclusion we will argue that there are, in fact, abundant similarities between American political debates and developments in the late twentieth century and those of the late nineteenth century, the period when the United States stifled the advances made in the previous major era of racial egalitarian reforms, Reconstruction. Those similarities ought to restrain optimism that further racial progress will henceforth come automatically or easily. To be sure, the United States is not headed back to formal Jim Crow laws, much less slavery. But it is not so unlikely that Americans of different races, and especially blacks and whites, will live in different regions, attend different schools, concentrate in different occupations, and be governed by policies that reinforce these patterns, especially when they serve the interests and values of affluent whites and their closest allies. If so, the result is likely to be that extensive de facto segregation will be accompanied by severe inequalities in economic, educational, and political statuses and chronically fractious, sometimes explosive, racial and ethnic relations. It is not unlikely that this result will occur, we think, because despite real progress that is more or less where we are now. Moreover, many politically potent current policy positions seem likely to move us further in these directions.

Before we turn to the disturbing similarities between present policy debates and those that laid Reconstruction to rest, however, let us acknowledge the substantial case for greater optimism. Many scholars note the tremendous progress that African Americans have made in virtually every sphere of life in the last half century. Since the end of World War II, blacks have shown important improvements in income, occupations, and education. Black poverty has declined and median black income has moved closer to that of whites. Furthermore, the civil rights laws of the 1960s have provided blacks with unprecedented levels of political and legal powers and opportunities. Consequently, the once-thin ranks of black officeholders and black professionals have expanded considerably. Reflecting and reinforcing these changes are dramatic shifts in racial attitudes as reported in public opinion surveys. Over the last fifty years, overt expressions of white racial hostility have gone from being the norm to the great exception. Some scholars contend further that we have little reason to doubt those trends will continue, even if government efforts targeted at aiding blacks cease, or perhaps especially if they do.[1]

We do not dispute most of these claims. Blacks have indeed made great strides in recent decades, and these successes give us hope for further improvements in the future. We do not agree, however, that such advances will come automatically. Instead, we believe that should government measures to promote racial equality cease, there are good reasons to expect America's unsteady march toward that goal once again to stall and in certain respects to go backward.

Take, for instance, black economic progress. Although blacks did achieve economic advances from 1940 to 1960, they were aided by factors that had largely faded by the early 1970s. On the eve of World War II, 87 percent of black families lived in poverty. Then the war opened up jobs for blacks as servicemen and in the defense industries, and the defense-driven boom of the Cold War years continued to play a crucial role in black economic improvements up to 1960. Furthermore, World War II also induced the Second Great Migration, with blacks moving from brutally ill-paid rural farming occupations to industrial jobs of all types in northern cities. That shift alone accounted for most of the aggregate improvement in black economic conditions from 1940 to 1960. Even though, in total, black male incomes were only a bit over 40 percent of whites in 1940, the gap was much less in the North. Indeed, black family income in the North was 75 percent that of whites (versus only 49 percent in the South). Neither southern blacks nor northern blacks closed their respective gaps much between 1940 and 1960. Some 3 million southern blacks simply moved into the better, but not greatly improving, relative position of northern blacks. Thereafter, the southern economy began to resemble the northern industrialized economy, with the number of blacks in near-subsistence agricultural jobs diminishing to the vanishing point. Thus in 1995, when black men had annual incomes 67 percent that of whites and black women even higher percentages (though black families still had only 10 percent the material assets of white ones), blacks throughout the land might be said to have achieved the relative economic position of northern blacks in the early 1950s. That change, moreover, was chiefly due to the "northernizing" of the black population and the southern economy.[2]

Those facts represent economic progress, to be sure, but of a very limited sort. It also was dependent on factors that did not endure. There were virtually no black farm workers left to move from southern farms to better-paid northern industrial jobs.[3] And unlike the postwar boom, economic growth since 1980 largely benefited those already better off, not the less skilled, heightening a trend that began under the Republican presidents of the early 1970s. The ending of the postwar boom and favorable geographical and occupational shifts meant that black economic progress by some important measures stalled or reversed after 1970, especially during the 1980s. In 1983, the median white family had eleven times the wealth of the median nonwhite family. As Reagan era tax and spending policies took effect, this ratio increased to twenty by 1989. Overall earnings for blacks also fell relative to whites after the early 1970s. By 1996, the median incomes of black and Hispanic families relative to whites would be lower than it had been in 1972. These declines were not due to the much-decried changes in the structure of black families, often traced to War on Poverty aid policies. Whatever the sources of those changes, and we would stress limited economic and social circumstances rather than programs like Aid to Families With Dependent Children (AFDC), altered family structures account for only a portion of the economic gap between blacks and whites.[4]

The reality is that governmental aid programs, governmental antidiscrimination efforts, subsequent affirmative action initiatives, and public sector employment generally have been crucial to modern black economic progress. Their contributions have been vital especially since the end of the postwar boom and the Second Great Migration, and vital especially for the growth of the black middle class. That growth is really the "principal success story for African Americans in the past twenty-five years," because conditions for the poorest African Americans actually declined in many regards from 1975 to 1995. But the black middle class grew: in 1950, 5 pecent of employed blacks were managers or professionals, while by 1990 it was 20 percent.[5] This increased access of blacks to middle-class positions cannot be explained simply in terms of heightened black representation in largely blue-collar industrial jobs after migration to the North and the increased industrialization of the South. According to Stephan and Abigail Thernstrom, from 1940 to 1970 the largest gains in black participation in middle-class occupations came "in the less selective, less well paid, and largely female-dominated professions—school teaching, social work, and nursing." These positions were "all in the public or the quasi-public, nonprofit sector of the economy," where discriminatory practices were curbed earlier, often by state and local civil rights laws. Then, abetted by the Great Society initiatives of the 1960s, black "overrepresentation" in public sector jobs increased from 11 percent in 1960 to 36 percent in 1970, 44 percent in 1982, and 60 percent by 1994. The much more sizable growth of the black middle class since 1960 has thus been predominantly a public sector achievement.

Similarly, governmental efforts were crucial to increasing black representation in higher-paid private sector professions, since most of the increase here came only after the advent of affirmative action. In the thirty years from 1940 to 1970, black physicians increased from 4,160 only to 6,044, while in the twenty years from 1970 to 1990, 14,830 more blacks became physicians. Black lawyers increased only from 1,000 to 3,703 between 1940 to 1970, but then almost 24,000 more qualified from 1970 to 1990. Consequently, even critics of the affirmative action like the Thernstroms must acknowledge that such policies "did accelerate" the "overall rate of black progress" in these areas.[6] No one disputes, moreover, that the greatly increased presence of blacks in elective offices since the mid-1960s is traceable to the "extraordinarily effective" Voting Rights Act of 1965 and its subsequent amendments.[7]

In sum, in the last half century black entry into less selective professions has come largely via public or quasi-public sector employment, while substantial black entry into more selective ones has come only in the era of affirmative action and the Voting Rights Act. Hence it seems reasonable to judge that the growth of the black middle class has been aided significantly by federal programs, especially antidiscrimination measures and the increased federal spending on education and social programs that formed central parts of the War on Poverty of the 1960s. It has also been assisted substantially by affirmative action measures since 1970. Together, these governmental efforts have contributed substantially to all the major advances for blacks—political, educational, and economic—that have occurred in the last three decades. Indeed, it is hard to see how any progress might otherwise have continued, and in some respects even accelerated, in these years, given that the Second Great Migration and the postwar boom had already ceased. That is why it is hard to accept the argument that the opposition to national antipoverty and civil rights measures that began to emerge from 1968 on simply represented a rejection of measures that were failing to help.

Thus we think there is cause for concern when the public programs of employment, economic assistance, and affirmative action that have been largely responsible for maintaining black economic well-being in some regards since 1970 are being eliminated, while the force of the Voting Rights Act is in some respects being blunted. And since, when one moves beyond public and private workplaces,

Americans remain sharply divided by race in their schools, in their neighborhoods, and in their social lives, we are all the more dubious that racial divisions have been so thoroughly overcome that racial progress can continue to come without government actions. In 1992, for example, over a third of American black students still attended schools with more than 90 percent minority students; almost half of white students attended schools that were at least 90 percent white, a figure that rose to more than two-thirds in the Northeast and Midwest. Entering the 1990s, 44 percent of urban blacks lived in block groups that were at least 90 percent black, and the nation's urban "segregation index" still had the severely high score of 74, three-quarters of the way to complete residential segregation by race. And though social interaction among the races has increased to some degree, in 1993 almost 90 percent of American blacks still married blacks. In many respects, America remains a highly separate and unequal society.[8]

That reality leads us to the factor that many present as the most important change in recent decades and the most hopeful prospect for the future: white attitudes toward blacks. Today, public opinion has evolved to the point where the percentage of whites willing to endorse blatantly racist statements has become quite small. Blacks and whites are often also willing to express extensive support for racially egalitarian principles. Hence leading scholars like the political scientist Paul Sniderman and the Thernstroms believe that a consensual basis exists in public opinion for constructive policies on race, so long as controversial measures like affirmative action are avoided.[9]

The public opinion literature has, however, thus far not addressed one crucial question. What factors have brought about these changes? Even the most prominent recent studies are astonishingly silent on this point.[10] Yet until we know why changes have occurred, we cannot be sure that they are likely to endure. Public opinion scholars are also sharply divided on a further vital issue. How meaningful are these changes? Do they represent real agreements among white and blacks about what is to be done to address racial inequalities, or do they represent only similar willingness to espouse rather abstract ideals?

In regard to the first issue, we would stress a crucial finding of modern public opinion research: mass opinions are heavily shaped by the way issues are framed in elite discourse. Our evidence shows that with the coming of the war against Nazism, American national elites—including elected officials, judges and military officers, religious leaders, editorial writers, and educators—all began repudiating racist doctrines more emphatically, unequivocally, and unanimously than ever before.[11] Only the more extreme southern white leaders continued to use the old racist rhetoric. Moderate Southerners switched more exclusively to language of state's rights, limited government, and property rights to protect white interests—for example, by the mid-1960s, even George Wallace had dropped overt racism from his political rhetoric—and liberals actually supported reform. The elite discourse of antiracist egalitarianism then became more and more prevalent throughout the Cold War period, the years when public opinion moved steadily toward such egalitarianism, at least when people were asked directly about views easily recognizable as features of traditional racism. This change in elite discourse corresponded with a similar shift in mass opinion among whites. It thus seems reasonable to conclude that elite framing of race issues played an important role in producing the shifts in mass opinion the surveys indicate. Those shifts then made further elite reforms politically feasible.[12]

But if white Americans, as we have argued throughout, have had powerful reasons ever since slavery to defend the various racially unequal political, economic, educational, and social arrangements they inhabit, then these shifts in public opinion may be significantly limited. We might expect that popular willingness to espouse the *principles* of racial equality that elites have sponsored since 1940 may not be matched by willingness to embrace *policies* that might actually transform those arrangements in major ways. Instead, efforts to achieve such transformations are likely to be criticized on many grounds and accompanied by feelings of resentment. That is clearly what has occurred after every previous period of racial reform. And numerous studies of public opinion data provide substantial reasons to believe these reactions remain powerful in modern politics.[13]

Public opinion analysts like Michael Dawson, Donald Kinder, and Lynn Sanders have documented that though blacks and whites may largely profess agreement on racially egalitarian principles, there is in fact a huge gap between American blacks and whites on what those principles imply for policy.[14] The great majority of blacks support governmental efforts, including race-targeted measures, to reduce racial inequalities and would like to see them expanded. Most whites disagree. In all probability, the differences do not simply reflect varying judgments about whether particular sorts of policies have failed or not. As we have pointed out, "white backlash" has been a persistently recurring feature of the American political landscape. White public opinion has rarely shown strong support for any reform designed to promote racial equality until after its enactment, and on many issues support has remained weak even then.[15]

Those facts may go far toward explaining another racial gap, one that political scientist Jennifer Hochschild has explored in depth: blacks display "overwhelming pessimism" about present and future racial progress in America compared to whites. Although presumably better informed, middle-class blacks seem even more pessimistic than poorer ones.[16] It may well be that they are made so by their perceptions of how whites endorse egalitarian principles while steadfastly resisting the measures most blacks see as necessary to realize those principles in the United States today. This black pessimism, and black support for a strong governmental role in promoting black progress, may be misguided, as some suggest. Perhaps most whites really do know better than most blacks what measures are likely to help blacks today. The opposition of whites to the policy remedies favored by most blacks may understandably make African Americans cynical, but it does not *prove* that whites are significantly opposed to egalitarian racial change, much less that whites are hard-core racists. On this point, analysts like Sniderman and the Thernstroms are logically correct.

There are, however, several reasons to believe that white attitudes that are harmful toward blacks, even if not expressed in the explicit language of traditional racism, remain a serious problem and could become yet more so. For these reasons we are less sanguine that the judgments on racial policies of most whites, who are after all still the American group best off under the status quo, are more reliable than the less hopeful views of educated blacks.

Let us note first the mildest form of white attitudes that hurt blacks: support for policies that harm blacks largely due to white indifference or ignorance about the differing circumstances and interests of blacks, and hence about the highly unequal impact of those policies. For example, as blacks have migrated to the cities and as school integration has been sought, whites have moved to suburbs where few blacks live. Advances in transportation and communication, access to more and better jobs in the suburbs, lower costs for housing and consumer items outside of cities, and generally lower taxes in suburbs have all contributed to this shift. But it is important to stress that governmental policies facilitated all these developments by subsidizing the building of highways to the suburbs more than mass transit systems, by providing tax incentives for companies to relocate, and by permitting zoning laws that made it difficult for poorer blacks to purchase or rent housing in the suburbs. Whether or not most policymakers meant for these measures to aggravate the problems of urban blacks, such measures nonetheless did so. Whatever concern the predominantly white officials and voters of this era had for black interests was not sufficient to prevent those effects.[17]

Second, ongoing white hostility toward blacks is also supported by an extensive body of experimental evidence showing actual racial discrimination in housing sales, rentals, bank loans, auto sales, hiring, and other economic arenas. Such discrimination appears to contribute significantly to the creation of poverty-dominated black urban neighborhoods, and for every ethnic group, life in such neighborhoods has historically been associated with the patterns of out-of-wedlock births and high crime that cause so much concern today. Other ethnic groups, however, appear to have faced far fewer discriminatory obstacles in escaping such conditions than blacks still do. Scholars quarrel, however, over whether these studies are fully credible, and some contend they do not show high enough levels of discrimination to cause great concern. But as the renowned economist Thomas Schelling showed years ago, even relatively small levels of persistent economic discrimination can have large consequences. And though all empirical studies can be criticized, it is striking that the critics consistently have to quarrel with the methods of this research, because studies showing antiblack racial discrimination to be empirically absent are so rare.[18]

Finally, there is a substantial debate among public opinion scholars about how far white professions of commitment to principles of racial equality are in practice outweighed by ongoing white resentment toward blacks and white fear of policies that would significantly alter existing inequalities. Donald Kinder and Lynn Sanders have argued that the best predictor of white attitudes on racial policies is how whites score on what they term "racial resentment" questions. These are questions such as whether blacks on welfare "could get along if they tried" and whether if "blacks would only try harder they could be just as well off as whites." On these topics significant white majorities (just under 60 percent) said "yes" in 1986, thus indicating their belief that blacks' problems primarily reflected blacks' choices. Kinder and Sanders contend that white answers on these and other "racial resentment" questions are remarkably coherent and that they correlate strongly not only with conservative positions on race-related public policies but also with acceptance of traditional antiblack stereotypes, such as the claims that blacks are lazy, unintelligent, and prone to violence. These beliefs seem chiefly to reflect negative white views of blacks rather than white acceptance of principles of individualism, meritocracy, or opposition to reliance on government. Some analysts reject these findings because they believe that such expressions of white racial "resentment" fundamentally express acceptance of certain policy principles, not hostility toward blacks. Such criticisms, however, fail to address the claims of Kinder and Sanders, Martin Gilens, and others that high scores on "resentment" questions seem to be strongly connected to high acceptance of traditional but false antiblack stereotypes.[19]

Our analysis makes it seem likely that scholars like Kinder and Sanders and Gilens are correct. History suggests that many whites, all too understandably, are made uncomfortable if not resentful by policies threatening significant transformations in long-standing American racial hierarchies, even if those hierarchies are now de facto. Such discomfort with changes in arrangements that are familiar, valued, and advantageous is, after all, only human. And though elites under appropriate political pressures may have successfully discouraged expressions of explicit racism over the last half century, that fact does not mean that such racial discomfort has gone away.[20] If these feelings are even moderately prevalent, moreover, policy advocates who find nonracist ways of arguing for measures that will preserve the status quo are likely to find an enthusiastic hearing in many quarters. As the forces prompting racially egalitarian reforms ease, even explicitly racist arguments may be better received once again. As we have shown, that is what happened after the First Emancipation and after Reconstruction. And if we compare current policy discourses with those of the late nineteenth and early twentieth centuries, we think it is evident that once again we are indeed hearing familiar nonracist arguments against government actions to aid blacks and renewed explicit racist attacks on such policies as well.

Even so, we must stress that most if not all of the themes we will examine represent positions that people can and do find reasonable without any reference to their consequences for racial equality. But note: that reasonableness would probably be true of any discourse that was particularly effective in justifying the preservation or further entrenchment of old systems of inequality, or the creation of new, modified forms, without appearing to do so. Whites should acknowledge to themselves, moreover, that they may well be emotionally more comfortable with policies that preserve the racial status quo, even if that consequence forms no part of their conscious reflections. Hence we should be made suspicious by any similarities or parallels we find now to a time when, demonstrably, old systems of racial hierarchy were being systematically refurbished. Although the number could reasonably be expanded or contracted in various ways, we identify here, in no particular order, eleven significant similarities in the policy and political debates of the late nineteenth century and the current era. That seems to us too many to dismiss lightly.

1. The Resurgence of Arguments for State and Local Governance Instead of National Governance

We have seen that the 1860s and the 1960s were both times of great expansion in the powers, size, and range of purposes of the U.S. government. During the Civil War and Reconstruction, the federal government undertook for the first time promoting racial legal equality and punishing racial discrimination and violence. It also sought to enfranchise African Americans, to make land and financial capital available to poorer Americans, white and black, on easy terms; to assist public education for all; and even to promote immigration and naturalization on a more racially inclusionary basis. Similarly, in the 1960s, with the 1964 Civil Rights Act, the 1965 Voting Rights Act, the Elementary and Secondary Education Act, and the various elements of the "War on Poverty," it did all those things again, on an even larger scale. Hence both eras saw dramatic shifts in power to the national level, shifts that could be objected to even by those who did not oppose the egalitarian purposes to which such power was being put—along with, of course, those who did oppose those purposes.[21]

Each era then gave way to periods when political leaders and the courts condemned such expansive national governance as inefficient and dangerous. Calls to recognize the democratic advantages of local government and for the sanctity of state's rights gained renewed currency, and many federal programs were limited or terminated.

During and after Reconstruction, white Southerners consistently recited the mantra of "states' rights" to oppose federal efforts to protect black rights. Joining them were the "Liberal Republicans" who decried the "collectivism" and the "centralization of power and governmental control" Reconstruction had involved, because such centralization treated constitutional limits "with ill-disguised contempt."[22] Throughout this period, the Supreme Court also struck down various federal Reconstruction statutes under the guise of supporting "states' rights."[23]

Today, similar views prevail. "States' rights" has reentered the lexicon of mainstream politics, and both liberals and conservatives advocate the "devolution" of federal power. Among the most vocal is Bill Clinton, the leader of the modern reform party. First as governor and then as president, Clinton has repeatedly endorsed claims that "centralized bureaucracies are no longer the best or most effective way to deliver services," that "the age of big government is over" and that we need a "new government" that is "smaller" and "does more with less."[24] In fact, in 1996, Bill Clinton and a majority of congressional Democrats joined with the Republicans to end the federal government's sixty-year commitment to AFDC and transfer it to the states.[25] Not only is this the most significant devolution of federal power in memory, but it also ended one of the few national programs that had disproportionately aided racial and ethnic minorities.

Furthermore, the contemporary Supreme Court shows signs of undermining the expansive definition of federal commerce power that has prevailed since the New Deal and under which Congress passed the civil rights laws of the 1960s. In 1995, Chief Justice Rehnquist argued in *United States v. Lopez,* for example, that if the Court read federal power as expansively as the executive branch urged, "it is difficult to perceive any limitation on federal power, even in areas such as criminal law enforcement or education where States historically have been sovereign." Justice Anthony Kennedy did insist that the decisions upholding the 1964 Civil Rights Act were "not called into question" by this ruling. But Justice Clarence Thomas, who wished the Court to go further, would only say that his preferred approach did "not necessarily require a wholesale abandonment" of such modern precedents.[26]

2. Increased Prominence of Calls for Governmental Actions to Be "Color-Blind"

Such calls have resulted in the diminution of public measures consciously designed to assist racial minorities. Again the nineteenth-century Supreme Court provided a classic statement of this position: Justice Joseph Bradley's insistence in the 1883 *Civil Rights Cases* that although African Americans had perhaps merited some assistance right after the end of slavery, "there must be some stage in the progress of his elevation when he takes the rank of mere citizen, and ceases to be the special favorite of the laws." Men like Charles Francis Adams Jr. also echoed that theme, contending that the "Afro-American" must accept "the common lot of mankind. He must not ask to be held up, or protected from outside." Theodore Roosevelt concurred, contending that the problem of fully securing black rights to "equality of treatment before the law" chiefly required local assistance aimed at teaching the black man "to perform the duties" that would lead to success.[27]

Today, such calls are ubiquitous. A Supreme Court previously more receptive to affirmative action measures now says the Constitution demands "consistency of treatment regardless of the race of the burdened or benefited group." Justice Thomas has added that laws that "distribute benefits on the basis of race in order to foster some current notion of equality" are morally equivalent to "laws designed to subjugate a race." Policy analysts designating themselves liberal often agree. Former White House advisor and *American Prospect* editor Paul Starr, for example, has called for "race-neutral policies" on the ground, among others, that "[a]ffirmative action policies have helped to perpetuate racism." Similarly, the Democratic Leadership Council has repeatedly called for ending "quotas" and goals of "equal outcomes." Black Republicans like University of California trustee Ward Connerly are leading campaigns throughout the country to repeal affirmative action by direct popular vote, championing "fairness" over what they regard as unjust racial "preferences." It surely is possible that calls in the late nineteenth century to end special aid to blacks were premature, whereas the current ones are appropriate; and yet there can be no denying that their content is remarkably similar.[28]

Supporters of color-blind and race neutral policies point out that such efforts are consistent with the egalitarian demands of the civil rights movement, as represented by the Civil Rights Act of 1964. They fail, however, to acknowledge that some of the most racial discriminatory legislation meets their test of evenhandedness and racial neutrality. Poll taxes and literacy tests made no distinction according to race. Nonetheless, the clear purpose and result of such laws was to subjugate blacks to white rule. Furthermore, all efforts in American history to advance black equality, from state abolition laws, to the Civil War amendments to the Constitution, to the Civil and Voting Rights Acts of the 1960s, can be said to violate some abstract notion of race neutrality. They all afford blacks a degree of specific legal protection. We will see that contemporary conservatives are increasingly making just that claim.

3. Resurgence of Laissez-Faire Ideologies

This third parallel is linked to both the antinational government and "color blind" themes. Such ideologies contend that private market forces will provide for more progress than will public programs. The late nineteenth century Gilded Age was notoriously the era of Social Darwinism, intellectually led by men like William Graham Sumner, Yale's first professor of sociology and political science. Sumner contended that modern sciences of economics and evolution demonstrated that humanity's "combined assault on Nature" would flourish best if those individuals and "races" who failed to care for themselves were left to "the process of decline and dissolution," instead of receiving governmental protection or assistance. That basic outlook was endorsed by conservative black leaders like Booker T. Washington. His famous advice to his fellow blacks to "cast down your bucket where you are" agreed that success could and should come only through "severe and constant struggle" in the marketplace, not through public programs. Soon, the Supreme Court began writing such views into constitutional law, launching the famed *Lochner* era of opposition to economic regulation and redistribution.[29]

In the wake of the Reagan years, the similar resurgence of promarket ideologies among political leaders, policymakers, and academics will require no elaborate documentation here. It may suffice to note that black conservatives like Thomas Sowell defend the claim that "market pressures are effective against discrimination" while government policies are not by endorsing Social Darwinian scholars like law professor Richard Epstein. Epstein urges repeal of most economic regulatory legislation, including major portions of the 1964 Civil Rights Act. He not only contends that governmental "protection against poverty increases the likelihood of its occurrence" but also grounds these claims in sociobiological evolutionary theories much like those Sumner invoked. Dinesh D'Souza takes these arguments a step further, calling for the repeal of Civil Rights Act's ban on private discrimination even though extensive racial discrimination could then prevail. He contends that it is after all "universal," "defensible and in some cases even admirable" to prefer "members of one's own group over strangers." Although at this writing support for the 1964 act nonetheless remains strong, in the wake of Epstein's urgings the Supreme Court has indeed heightened scrutiny of all government regulations in the name of protecting property rights against takings without just compensation.

Leading Democrats have shifted in the same market-oriented direction. In 1991, candidate Bill Clinton urged that government be
"reinvented" along the lines of "our greatest corporations," that government "monopoly decisions" be replaced by "more choice," and
that we recognize that "work is the best social program this country
has ever devised." Accordingly, as president he supported the end
of AFDC and called on the private sector to solve unemployment
problems.[30] Few can doubt that private markets must generate most
economic opportunities in America. Yet these shifts in the direction
of pure laissez-faire undeniably threaten the antidiscrimination regulations and public employment and assistance programs that appear
to have been vital to modern black economic progress, along with
the economic hopes of many poor whites.

4. The Resurgence of "Scientific" Racism

Because people can and doubtless do oppose big government, affirmative action, government aid programs, and even federal antidiscrimination laws without harboring racism, the parallels so far may
still seem undisturbing. Such is not the case with the resurgence of
theories of nearly unalterable racial differences and inequalities,
traced both to cultural and biological factors. The evolutionary theories of the late nineteenth century generally held that humanity had
been socially and biologically formed into different races with sharply
different capacities that could be altered, if at all, only over great
stretches of time. For example, the anthropologist Daniel G. Brinton
argued in his 1895 presidential address to the American Association
for the Advancement of Science that the "black, the brown, and
red races" had a "peculiar mental temperament which has become
hereditary." It denied them "enlightenment" and left them "recreant
to the codes of civilization, and therefore technically criminal." And
he urged legislators to begin taking as their guides the "lines which
the new science dictates" instead of "older philosophies" of the
"rights of man" favored by "social reformers." Jim Crow laws were
thus, in his view, clearly advisable. Senator Henry Cabot Lodge argued similarly in urging immigration restrictions that year. He contended that each race was defined "above all" by an "unconscious
inheritance" of "moral characteristics" resulting from its distinctive
history, upon which "argument has no effect." There was no alternative but to fence out any "lower race" that sought to come
to America. Religious leaders swelled the chorus: the Rev. Josiah
Strong contended that the "mighty Anglo-Saxon race" had to pre-

vail in "the final competition of the races" he saw pending within the United States and in the world. And as we have seen, many more such quotes could be added from both Presidents Theodore Roosevelt and Woodrow Wilson as well as a host of academic luminaries.[31]

Such views are not nearly so omnipresent in the United States today, but it cannot be denied that since the end of the Cold War they have increasingly been expressed and deemed respectable. Some modern accounts stress cultural differences in contrast to biological characteristics, whereas nineteenth-century writers tended to link the two closely; but cultural differences and inequalities often appear as ineradicable now as then and are understood to have similar content. One important area where this pattern appears is in discussions of the so-called underclass or ghetto ethno-underclass. Lawrence Fuchs has argued that social analysts "commonly" use these terms to describe "a cluster of behaviors" that seem "almost foreign" to better-off Americans. These behaviors included male unemployment and low labor force participation, drug abuse and criminality, welfare dependency, high dropout rates, low birth-weight babies, high rates of teen-age motherhood, single parenting, and female-headed households, as well as "distrust of mainstream institutions," including police, government officials, and employers.[32]

These are, of course, the "behaviors" that analysts across the political spectrum stress in explaining black poverty today. Many of these analysts, moreover, dramatize the intractability of these traits in members of the "underclass" in ways that are disturbingly reminiscent of nineteenth-century arguments. In 1992, for example, the Bush administration's top mental health official, Dr. Frederick K. Goodwin, discussed recent research on aggression in primates and stated that "there are some interesting evolutionary implications." Monkeys who were "hyperaggressive" and killed each other, he said, were "also hypersexual." In the struggle for survival, they offset their mutual destruction by more frequent copulation and reproduction. Dr. Goodwin went on to wonder "if some of the loss of social structure in this society, and particularly within the high impact inner-city areas, has removed some of the civilizing evolutionary things that we have built up and that maybe it is not just the careless use of words when people call certain areas of certain cities jungles, that we may have gone back to what might be more natural, without all of the social controls that we have imposed upon ourselves as a civilization over thousands of years in our evolution."[33]

Similarly, in a July 13, 1994 hearing on President Clinton's welfare bill, New York senator Daniel Patrick Moynihan said in regard to inner city conditions, "I mean . . . if you were a biologist, you could find yourself talking about speciation here." Senator Jay Rockefeller of West Virginia replied, "[W]hen you were talking about a matter of potentially speciation, the creation of a new American person, so to speak, I think you're right about that." Both Dr. Goodwin and Senator Moynihan both later apologized because, they said, their comments seem to have offended or hurt some people, but neither actually retracted the arguments. For Moynihan, it was apparently not a new one. A couple of weeks before that hearing, nationally syndicated columnist and dean of the Washington press corps David Broder had approvingly quoted Moynihan's analysis of "speciation," which Broder defined as "the impending creation of a different kind of human, one raised outside a father-mother setting." All these far-from-extreme analysts clearly agreed that this different kind of human being might be described, in Daniel Brinton's words, as "recreant to the codes of civilization."[34] In 1997, Bill Clinton also edged close to these views. Appearing with Senator Moynihan, Clinton defended welfare reform by declaring that "when you consider the fact that the welfare population . . . is different that it used to be, and that there are some people who are on it perpetually, I think it is a good thing, not a bad thing, that we did that."[35] As commentator Adolph Reed points out, "In other words, welfare recipients aren't like you and me. They're defective—otherwise they'd have no trouble joining the middle class."[36]

The notion that humanity is profoundly divided by cultural traits that verge on biological ones, at least in regard to their intractability and their consequences, has also gained heightened currency outside the "underclass" debate. Dinesh D'Souza has argued more broadly that "America is developing something resembling a racial hierarchy—Asians and whites at the top, Hispanics in the middle, African-Americans at the bottom." But the reason, he contends, is not racism. It is rather distinct and enduring cultural endowments that render African Americans "not competitive with other groups in our society." And not just in our society, some say. In 1993 policy analyst Joel Kotkin published *Tribes: How Race, Religion, and Identity Determine Success in the New Global Economy,* arguing that though no culture or race was intrinsically superior to others, certain "global tribes" had traits that made their future success far more likely. "Tribes" of African descent were not among the favored ones. (Kotkin then was hired by the Progressive Policy Institute, the research wing of the Democratic Leadership Council).[37]

Political scientist Samuel P. Huntington subsequently published a more noted book, *The Clash of Civilizations and the Remaking of World Order*, advancing a similar thesis. Although it is far less simplistic and more balanced, his argument is especially interesting because it reflects an international climate in which ethnic, nationalist, and even racial claims to self-governance have renewed potency and legitimacy. That international setting, as opposed to the Cold War world, may be one that provides more room for American elites to argue that domestic policies should acknowledge "fundamental" ethnic and racial differences in ways that may support inegalitarian policies.[38]

That possibility is made all the greater by the fact that such arguments are already in view. In 1995, a well-placed journalist, Peter Brimelow, penned a book-length call for immigration restriction arguing that "certain ethnic cultures are more crime prone than others," specifying blacks. Education, he said, doesn't seem to help. He therefore viewed any policies leading to "an ethnic and racial transformation in America" that will end the "racial hegemony of white Americans" as highly risky. When it appeared in paperback, *Alien Nation* proudly quoted praise from a remarkable number of leading academics and policy advocates, including sociologist Nathan Glazer and former senator Eugene McCarthy.[39]

Brimelow was, however, careful neither to endorse nor reject the exhaustively discussed views of Richard Herrnstein and Charles Murray in *The Bell Curve*: that blacks are on average intellectually inferior to whites for partly genetic reasons. They used such alleged facts to argue not only against affirmative action but, again, the 1964 Civil Rights Act's antidiscrimination provisions. And explicitly biological racialism has recently been elaborated at length by scholars whom Herrnstein and Murray rely on and defend, such as social psychologist J. Philippe Rushton. In a 1995 work that self-consciously builds on late-nineteenth-century studies of race, *Race, Evolution, and Behavior*, Rushton alleges that there are two basic evolutionary strategies: have few children and nurture them to high achievement; or behave promiscuously, have many neglected children, and count on sheer numbers to ensure survival of your kind, like Dr. Goodwin's hyperaggressive, hypersexual monkeys. Rushton insists that blacks embody the latter strategy for evolutionary survival. As a result, blacks have smaller brains and less intelligence but larger genitalia and greater criminality and sexual activity than whites, just as Thomas Jefferson suggested long ago. (Herrnstein and Murray go out of their way to defend Rushton, arguing in an appendix that Rushton is not a "crackpot or a bigot," his work, according to them, "is plainly science.")[40]

Works like *The Bell Curve* and Rushton's writings are, of course, widely criticized; but their viewpoints are part of a much wider current discourse than was true a couple of decades ago.[41] Since its publication, *The Bell Curve* has sold over three hundred thousand copies. The book was reviewed respectfully in many newspapers and magazines, including the *National Review* and the *New York Times Book Review*. In the latter, the *Review*'s science reporter Malcolm Browne claimed that *The Bell Curve* made a "strong case that America's population is becoming dangerously polarized between a smart, rich, educated elite and a population of unintelligent, poor and uneducated people." Such a possibility, Browne concluded, gave society the "right— perhaps even the duty—to strengthen our species' cognitive defenses against an increasingly dangerous global environment."[42] *Newsweek* told its readers that the book's research was "overwhelmingly mainstream" and that genetics accounted for up to 70 percent of the black-white IQ difference.[43] The *National Review* recently published a lengthy and flattering interview with Murray as its featured article.[44]

While it is still widely criticized, association with the explicit racism of the type found in *The Bell Curve* no longer seems to carry the consequences that it once did. In 1998 news reports linked Republican representative Bob Bar of Georgia and Republican senate majority leader Trent Lott of Mississippi to the Council of Conservative Citizens (CCC), an avowedly racist organization descended from the white citizens' councils that fought to preserve Jim Crow in the 1950s and 1960s. In an interview, current Council CEO Gordon Lee Baum contended that *The Bell Curve* was "about right" on race. Another Council spokesman, Jared Taylor, has argued that "[i]t is certainly true that in some important traits—intelligence, law-abidingness, sexual restraint, academic performance, resistance to disease— whites can be considered 'superior' to blacks."[45]

Lott's connection with the CCC was particularly close. A column written by him ran in the CCC's newsletter alongside others that made such declarations as "No one can deny the importance of the question of miscegenation or race-mixing. Its very essence involves the preservation of the white race as well as the Negro race. It is a matter of racial survival. Compared with future interest we have at stake in this issue, all other matters fade into significance." In 1992 Lott told a meeting of the CCC, "The people in this room stand for the right principles and the right philosophy." It was also widely reported in Mississippi that the majority leader was a member of the organization. Only after the story broke in the national media did Lott deny any association with the CCC. It seems hardly thinkable that as recently as twenty years ago a national politician could have survived being associated with a group like the CCC. Yet, today Lott has received surprisingly little condemnation from his colleagues or the media and his position as majority leader seems no less secure than before the story broke.[46]

5. Arguments about the "Criminality" of Racial and Ethnic Minorities

Claims that many blacks and Latinos are by culture or biology prone to lawlessness obviously reinforce contentions that heightened governmental and community efforts to curb the "criminality" of racial and ethnic minorities are far more vital to progress than ending racial discrimination. In 1905, Theodore Roosevelt was explicit on this point. "Laziness and shiftlessness," he wrote, "and above all, vice and criminality of every kind, are evils more potent for harm to the black race than all acts of oppression of white men put together. The colored man who fails to condemn crime in another colored man . . . is the worst enemy of his own people, as well as an enemy to all the people." Roosevelt called for "relentless and unceasing warfare against lawbreaking black men."[47]

Many contemporary policy analysts clearly agree. The oft-cited facts that the United States now incarcerates a larger percentage of its population than any other nation, and that black men are so disproportionately imprisoned that between one-fourth and one-third of all young black men are in some way under the control of the criminal justice system, demonstrate that they are far from alone. Many criminologists have insisted that we must go even further, that combating racial discrimination is far less important to improving conditions in urban black America than raising incarceration rates higher yet and building more prisons as well as, perhaps, orphanages.[48] Others, especially in the wake of the O.J. Simpson trial, have also suggested that blacks generally are willing to tolerate criminality among fellow blacks, perhaps making blacks less qualified to serve on juries.[49]

Again, perhaps this is correct. Black criminality may be the real heart of America's race problem today, and blacks have to solve it themselves. Still, when the same prescription is given repeatedly and has in the past only made the disease worse, the possibility that it is a diagnosis more pleasing to the physician than helpful to the patient cannot be dismissed. Even noted conservative and Nobel laureate in economics Milton Friedman makes the same argument. According to him, the nation's drug laws have a "racist" effect by disproportionately imprisoning blacks.[50]

6. Calls for Immigration Restriction

As in the late nineteenth century, so in the late twentieth do we hear much discussion on the economic consequences of immigration, with new immigrants viewed as too poor, uneducated, and unhealthy to be safely absorbed by the United States. These are legitimate worries, whatever the solutions. But in each period, concerns focused on the racial and ethnic character of the "new immigration" also surfaced. It is true that such arguments were far more prominent one hundred years ago than they are currently. Yet late-nineteenth-century advocates of race-based immigration restrictions did not fully prevail until well into the next century, with the 1924 National Origins Quota Act; and again, the visibility of such views is similarly on the rise today.[51]

It is thus striking that the 1924 act was immediately preceded by a book that claimed to provide definitive scientific evidence for the racial theories of the turn-of-the-century era like those of Henry Cabot Lodge and his fellow Yankee patrician, Madison Grant. Princeton psychologist Carl Campbell Brigham's 1923 *Study of American Intelligence* concluded by saying, "According to all evidence available . . . American intelligence is declining, and will proceed with an accelerating rate as the racial admixture becomes more and more extensive. The decline of American intelligence will be more rapid than the decline of the intelligence of European national groups, owing to the presence here of the negro. These are the plain, if somewhat ugly, facts that our study shows. . . . The steps that should be taken to preserve or increase our present intellectual capacity must of course be dictated by science and not by political expediency. Immigration should not only be restrictive but highly selective."[52]

Compare those words not only with the passages about preserving white "racial hegemony" from Peter Brimelow cited above, but also with admonitions from *The Bell Curve*. Near the end of their review of studies of American intelligence, Herrnstein and Murray conclude that the "evidence that must also be acknowledged is that Latino and black immigrants are, at least in the short run, putting some downward pressure on the distribution of intelligence." As a result, they advise, America should "shift the flow of immigrants . . . toward those admitted under competency rules" because "present policy" cannot continue "without danger."[53] No one has sounded those dangers more clamorously than Republican presidential candidate and national media commentator Pat Buchanan, who once remarked, "I think God made all people good, but if we had to take a million immigrants in, say Zulus, next year, or Englishmen, and put them in Virginia, what group would be easier to assimilate and cause less problems?" On another occasion he asked, "Does this First World nation wish to become a Third World country? Because that is our destiny if we do not build a sea wall against the waves of immigration rolling over our shores."[54] In these comments the racial policy implications are perhaps not drawn quite so harshly, and again, many advocates of immigration restriction would not endorse these arguments; but once more it is hard not to see similarities between past and present.

7. Declining Support for and Reduced Federal Efforts at Effective Civil Rights Enforcement

We have already noted that in the late nineteenth century Congress ended most of the Reconstruction programs aimed at securing greater racial equality, while the Supreme Court read the postwar amendments and civil rights statutes increasingly narrowly. From the second Grant administration on, moreover, even presidents of the party of Lincoln generally did not push for vigorous enforcement of those statutes and amendments. Grant complained in 1875 that the "whole public are tired out" from the recurring need to use federal force against white supremacists, so that they were "ready now to condemn any interference on the part of the Government" with racist practices. Eventually the federal government instead became actively supportive of state and local efforts to construct a Jim Crow system disfranchising and segregating black Americans in every state in which they formed a large percentage of the population. African American efforts to obtain meaningful enforcement even of measures that remained on the books were generally futile.[55]

A host of funding and staffing decisions by Congress and the president and judicial rulings in areas such as standing, removal or appeal of cases from state to federal courts, standards of evidence in discrimination and desegregation cases, affirmative action, and other race-related matters have meant that federal attempts to combat racial injustice have also diminished from the end of the Carter years to the present. This decline has occurred despite studies showing continued high levels of discrimination in job, housing, and auto markets, and despite the fact that residential and school segregation remain in most regions extremely high and in some areas are on the increase. Even so, as the Equal Employment Opportunity Commission (EEOC) has suffered funding and staff reductions, it has increasingly been unable to launch antidiscrimination class action suits, even when it has been willing. The number of employment-related class action cases pursued by the commission has fallen from 1,174 in 1976 to a mere 68 in 1996. And though the 1991 Civil Rights Act did make employee discrimination cases easier to win, the reality remains that such litigation is "one of the single most unsuccessful classes of litigation for plaintiffs," according to law professor Theodore Eisenberg.[56] In April 1998, the Clinton administration did call for increased funding for civil rights enforcement. Congress, however, appropriated only a portion of that proposed increase. And although they represent a step in the right direction, these funding increases fail to make up for years of neglect. Even with the new resources, the EEOC estimates that it will only be able to reduce its backlog of cases from 64,000 to 24,000 by the year 2000.[57]

Furthermore, since 1993, appointments to the nation's top civil rights post—Assistant Attorney General for Civil Rights—have been mired in controversy, forcing the position to remain unfilled for long periods of time. President Clinton's most recent choice for the post, Bill Lann Lee, was refused a Senate hearing merely because of his stated support for affirmative action. The president then used his power of recess appointments to name Lee acting assistant attorney general, but this move drew a sharply critical response from Senate Republicans. Whether they thereby blundered by alienating Asian American voters, as White House political advisors hoped, or whether the GOP's stronger stand against affirmative action would prove more politically potent remains at this writing to be seen.

Meanwhile, the Supreme Court has not only set the hurdles that must be met to justify affirmative action at unprecedented high levels, even for congressionally authorized affirmative action. It has also ruled that the burden of proof is now on those claiming existing school segregation is due to past de jure segregation, rather on those claiming that it is not. Finally, the Court has indicated that it will not uphold even largely noncoercive judicial efforts to promote interdistrict desegregation in most instances. Yet as we have noted, influential conservative policy analysts are pushing to go even further, urging repeal of all or parts of the 1964 Civil Rights Act, the cornerstone of the "Second Reconstruction." Even if they do not ultimately succeed, such calls appear to be setting the tone of current policy debates far more than any advocacy of stronger civil rights enforcement. Moderate policy analysts such as former White House deputy domestic policy director William Galston have endorsed the view that the "rights revolution" of the 1960s sparked changes that have "exacted a fearful toll," so that traditionalist calls "for a public change of course are not on their face implausible."[58] That very plausibility is, however, what makes it vital to attend closely to the racial consequences of enforcement cutbacks.

8. Disempowerment of Black Voting

Recent years have seen the abandonment of electoral arrangements that have visibly empowered blacks. Although this parallel is, fortunately, not as strong as some of the others, we often fail to recall sufficiently that black disfranchisement came long after the demise of most Reconstruction programs. Because of its strong support among blacks, the Republican Party of the late nineteenth century had strong electoral incentives to continue to fight for black voting rights even after it had given up support for black interests in virtually all other regards. After a last-gasp Republican effort in 1890 to pass a national elections bill not only failed but helped return Grover Cleveland to the presidency, the GOP finally did surrender entirely on preserving black votes. Only then did disfranchising tactics proliferate. They were, moreover, indirect; literacy tests, Constitution tests, elaborate registration requirements, white primaries, and the infamous "grandfather clauses" all allowed whites to limit the political power of blacks severely without openly denying blacks the vote on racial grounds.[59]

To the pain of its critics, the Voting Rights Act of 1965 has in contrast not only remained one of the most successful of the 1960s reform laws but has also been significantly strengthened. Most important were the 1982 amendments that overturned contrary Supreme Court rulings and permitted litigation to focus on the racial consequences, rather than the intent, of electoral changes. That philosophy prompted the conscious creation of majority-minority districts after the 1990 census in areas where it appeared black voters had rarely had meaningful opportunities to elect candidates of their choice. The result was the most racially integrated Congress in U.S. history. But since then the Supreme Court, departing from a long line of precedents deferring to legislative districting even when done for openly partisan purposes, has firmly rejected the constitutionality of such districts in several major decisions. As things stand now, politicians can gerrymander for virtually every purpose under the sun except to strengthen the collective power of black voters. It is true that the black congressmembers elected in those districts have thus far been reelected, like most incumbents. Yet it cannot be denied that in states like North Carolina, Texas, and Georgia, new majority-minority districts were instrumental in initially electing minority candidates strongly favored by black and Latino voters.[60]

It is, moreover, striking that majority-minority districts have been singled out for rejection by a Supreme Court that generally refuses to intervene in other types of voting disputes. Those blacks not disfranchised by criminal convictions (by one recent estimate, 13 percent of black males are so disfranchised and in some states as many as one-third) are, nonetheless, by and large still able to vote. Many contend their electoral influence will be greater, not less, with the end of such deliberately crafted majority-minority districts.[61] But if it is so, it will be because, as Abigail Thernstrom has argued, those blacks will be better represented by (probably) white representatives in districts in which they are a significant minority than they would be by a representative of any race elected from a district in which they were predominant. The efficacy and desirability of majority-minority districts remains a genuinely difficult question on which unquestionably genuine champions of civil rights disagree. Still, the notion that we should prefer electoral arrangements in which whites are usually elected to represent blacks, and in which blacks do not have the power to elect candidates that they may as a community prefer, is, to say the least, not well supported by U.S. history.[62]

9. Abandonment of Efforts to Achieve High Quality, Integrated Public Education

This parallel is particularly poignant, given the role *Brown v. Board of Education* has come to play as the symbolic initiator of the modern civil rights era's victories. One of the most dramatic features of the First Reconstruction was the spread of schools in the South, both public and private, eagerly sought by an African American population starved for access to education. Many of those schools were integrated; indeed, even the University of South Carolina admitted both blacks and whites in the late 1860s. But by the early 1870s, the waning of federal support for Reconstruction initiatives meant that not only did most public schools remain or become segregated, some southern states began abandoning public schools altogether, with the result that in Louisiana white illiteracy as well as black actually increased during the 1880s.[63]

Today it is little secret that not only has the Supreme Court backed off rigorous enforcement of school desegregation, as noted above. Very few white or black leaders choose to champion the cause of school integration very vigorously. Even the National Association for the Advancement of Colored People (NAACP) has recently debated vigorously whether it will continue to uphold the cause of racially mixed schools or accept the wisdom of striving for "separate but equal" institutions. The most discussed school reforms, such as voucher systems or "school choice" and reliance on private educational firms, are not aimed at providing integrated education for all and are more likely to carry de facto segregation even further. A recent Harvard study by Gary Orfield and others confirms that, abetted by the altered judicial rulings, school segregation has risen more rapidly during the last five years than at any time since *Brown v. Board of Education* was decided. There is even growing support for de jure segregation in the form of calls by blacks as well as whites for separate schools to meet the "special needs" of young black males. It is unsurprising, then, that in 1996 *Time* magazine proclaimed the "end of integration," holding that a "four-decade effort is being abandoned." Although that eulogy may be premature, it does appear that there is not a great deal more enthusiasm for efforts to promote integrated schools now than there was at the end of the First Reconstruction.[64]

10. Rise of Doctrines of Black Nationalism and Separatism among African Americans

We have observed that the late nineteenth century was the heyday of Booker T. Washington, who publicly acquiesced in segregated schools and black disfranchisement when the Jim Crow system was being built. Blacks and whites could, he repeatedly assured all, be "separate as the fingers" in all their social and civil institutions while still working together harmoniously on matters of common interest. Marcus Garvey then was inspired by Washington's example to come to the United States and build the largest mass organization of African Americans in history, the Universal Negro Improvement Association. It, of course, explicitly rejected integrationist goals and sought to build up separate black economic, educational, and political institutions out of the bitter belief that racial harmony was a pipe dream, a belief most African Americans found all too plausible in post–World War I era.[65]

Today, in the wake of the Million Man March, one of the most visible African American leader in the nation is Louis Farrakhan, head of the separatist Nation of Islam, an organization with roots in the Garvey movement. Farrakhan, to be sure, has recently articulated a view not unlike that W. E. B. Du Bois at certain times: eventually racial separatism will be overcome within a united humanity. For the foreseeable future, however, he insists that African Americans must be united with each other without any divisive "outsider" participating in their self-direction. The Nation of Islam accordingly supports separate black institutions in every sphere, much as the Garveyites did. The fact that many black Americans now seem to be drawn once again to a movement that regards integration as a damaging and quixotic goal, along with the black pessimism that Jennifer Hochschild discusses, suggest strongly that the politics of the day display the loss of hopes for a truly unified and egalitarian America that characterized the late nineteenth century.[66]

11. Abandonment of Racial Equality by the Party of Reform

In both the late nineteenth and the late twentieth centuries, the political party that had led the reforms of the preceding era—the Republicans in the 1860s, the Democrats in the 1960s—did not explicitly abandon their professed commitment to their basic reform goals. They did, however, move to only passive support for those racially egalitarian goals, launching no further major initiatives to achieve them. Even after the infamous postelection bargaining with the South that allowed Rutherford B. Hayes to become president in 1877, he still went on to veto eight bills designed to weaken protection of blacks. His successors, James A. Garfield and Chester A. Arthur, each worked to enforce the Fifteenth Amendment guaranteeing black voting rights in certain strategic contexts, if rarely with any great vigor. It was not true even in a general political climate of retreat from Reconstruction that the Republicans did nothing to carry on its central cause.[67]

Similarly, the modern Democrats can certainly claim to have resisted the most extreme efforts to undo the changes of the modern civil rights era. President Clinton has often spoken of his commitment to racial unity and healing, and he has sought to make a major initiative on race a central theme of his second term. Overall, however, it must be said that the Democratic record on civil rights in the 1980s and 1990s has been characterized more by fairly passive resistance to conservative efforts than by any strong positive program. When the Clinton administration has found itself linked with persons identified with strong civil rights activism, such as Lani Guinier, it has quickly severed those links. Its "mend it, don't end it" approach to affirmative action has not amounted to serious resistance to judicial and legislative efforts to do only the latter. Other examples could be adduced. Whether the president's initiative on race will alter this pattern of resemblance to late-nineteenth-century Republicans on race remains at this writing to be seen, but thus far we have seen little to suggest that it will.

Recognizing these similarities is, to be sure, only the beginning of an adequate analysis of our current circumstances. The many differences between the circumstances at the start of the twentieth century and its end must equally be taken into account. We agree that a number of important conditions may well make continuing racial progress today easier to achieve than ever in our past. The most promising feature of the current context, in our view, include first, America's continuing role as a world leader with the attendant necessity to appear fair in the eyes of nations of all racial and ethnic backgrounds. Even if racial and ethnic forms of nationalism continue to gain greater power and recognitition in international politics, this leadership role will maintain pressures for the United States to treat all of its citizens justly. Second, the increasing interdependence of the U.S. economy on the economies of such nations and our reliance on favorable international trade agreements to promote economic growth also mean that American policymakers will be reluctant to take actions that might alienate our commercial and treaty partners. Third, as long as economic arrangements permit the nation to achieve substantial overall economic growth, the disadvantaged are likely to gain some share of that enhanced prosperity, however unequal; and motives to scapegoat racial minorities will also be lessened. Finally, African Americans and other racial and ethnic minorities still have far more political and economic power relative to whites than they have ever had in our nation's past. And despite the growing popularity of certain forms of separatism, they can be expected to use that power to combat any explicit efforts to restore white supremacy. In light of these changes, it need not take a war to make progress continue. Americans *have* made strides toward greater racial equality of which they can be proud and on which they can build in the present and future.

Progress is, however, likely to take far more than the "benign neglect" of the past three decades. Against those who would say the differences are so great as to make any comparisons with the past irrelevant and misleading, we do insist that, given the weakening of the factors that prompted modern progress, the sobering patterns of reaction against the First Reconstruction cannot safely be ignored today. There is little reason to think that the fundamental political dynamics at work then have no counterparts in our own time. Who could seriously deny, after all, that many white Americans have found the changes wrought by the civil rights revolution of the 1960s deeply discomforting? Who could dispute that, as Galston suggests, many now display longings for the material advantages, the ways of life, the senses of social meaning that whites enjoyed in the years before major changes were made and threatened by strong antidiscrimination laws, extensive black voting, attempts at school integration, affirmative action measures, and the whole array of modern civil rights initiatives? It is probably true that the dynamics of political reaction cannot go nearly so far today as they did in the late 1890s. But given the remarkable success of that earlier period of reaction in prolonging severe racial inequalities in the United States, the parallels need not go very far to be matters of serious concern for those committed instead to overcoming our nation's racial past. And the greater racial and ethnic diversity today may only compound the opportunities for intergroup conflicts, such as clashes between native blacks, Carribean immigrants, Latinos, and Asians, often with whites siding with newcomers to some degree in ways that maintain black subordination. Immigrants to the United States have long encountered an established racial template—whites at the top, blacks at the bottom—and from the Irish to the Italians to the Chinese to Mexicans, most have felt pressure to win acceptance by (and as) whites through distancing themselves from American blacks.[68]

What, then, should we do about race in America today? Stephan and Abigail Thernstrom have suggested we respond to our current conditions by adopting "a simple rule of thumb": "that which brings the races together is good; that which divides us is bad." We share the objective of greater unity, but not at the cost of injustice and inequality. From the earliest days of our nation, black progress has brought division and white resentments. In fact, if the Thernstroms' rule had prevailed throughout American history, it would have most likely prevented nearly every advance in black rights, from the abolition of slavery to the ending of Jim Crow. We see little reason for thinking that future black progress would be any less divisive.

Hence we think it prudent that policymakers and analysts today adopt a different guideline. We should recognize that our current conditions have been shaped by a long history of political efforts to craft hierarchical racial orders and that impulses to do so again are part of our current situation. We should therefore ask ourselves how all proposed and current policies are likely to affect our inherited racial inequalities. If we accept that racial conflicts have been "America's constant curse," as President Clinton has argued, it is irresponsible and dangerous to fail to do so.[69]

To be sure, we would not require all governmental agencies to compile formal "Racial Impact Statements" prior to promulgating regulations. We are not enthusiasts for bureaucracy or red tape any more than most Americans. But we do think policymakers and analysts should mentally post on the walls facing their desks the question, "If we go down this road, will we perpetuate or even intensify the racial inequalities government has done so much to create in this country, or will we lessen them?"

We believe that once this question is placed front and center, the case for a large number of promising reform policies becomes more clear. Having discussed so many intractable problems in this book, let us now suggest some measures that might revive the nation's flagging march toward racial justice.

1. Increased Enforcement of Civil Rights Laws

Although nearly everyone gives lip service to the idea that the government should do what it can to prosecute cases of actual discrimination, the lack of adequate funding and staff for the government's various civil rights enforcement agencies impedes this goal. We strongly support the Clinton administration's recent call for an increase in the funding for such programs. We also believe that affirmative action programs in education and employment should be continued, at least until empirical studies show antiblack discrimination has ceased and median wealth for blacks has reached 50 percent of whites.

In addition to stepped up enforcement of existing laws, we also propose the criminalization of civil rights violations. Making cases of proven discrimination a criminal offense would send a strong signal that such crimes do harm to our society as well as to their individual victims. In fact, this was the thrust of much proposed civil rights legislation until the late 1950s. Additionally, the prospect of jail terms as well as stiff fines would likely give pause to those who engage in discrimination. Finally, by making these crimes a criminal offense, the burden of proof would be on the state rather than on the individuals who have suffered from discrimination.

2. A Significant National Commitment to Reducing Economic Inequality

In addition to the continuing impact of racism and discrimination, many of America's racial minorities are also burdened by economic inequality. Ameliorating this inequality is a necessary precondition for providing all Americans with meaningful opportunity. Furthermore, reducing economic inequality will also help to lower the economic insecurity that has often played a part in working-class whites' resistance to racial equality. To achieve this, we propose the following:

Increased funding for housing and public education, directed particularly at the inner cities.

Overhauling the nation's welfare system to create a strong and universal safety net—in effect, a system of Social Security for all families with children under the age of eighteen. This would reduce poverty and provide greatly needed support to poor and working families, and its universal nature would help to remove much of the racialized stigma currently attached to welfare programs.

Index the minimum wage to increase with rising living costs.

Creation of a large-scale federal jobs programs similar to the New Deal's Works Progress Administration.

National health insurance that guarantees coverage for all citizens.

Publicly financed access to college education and/or job training for all Americans.

3. Reform of the Nation's Criminal Justice System

As we have mentioned, the nation's criminal justice system disproportionately burdens blacks and other nonwhites. Moreover, measures ostensibly aimed at curbing crime and violence have gone hand in hand with efforts to limit black equality throughout American history. To remedy this, we propose the following:

A shift in law enforcement away from incarceration (especially
for small-scale drug crimes) and toward rehabilitation.

An end to the death penalty, now hopelessly entangled with
race in America.

Restoration of suffrage to those who have completed their sentences or parole.

Ending peremptory challenges to jurors since they limit the
likelihood of racially mixed juries.

4. A Return to the Draft and Introduction of Universal National Service

As we have shown, military service has served as a powerful force
for advancing the rights of African Americans. Reinstituting the draft
on an egalitarian basis and establishing some form of civilian national
service could bring together persons from different racial and ethnic
backgrounds and help to overcome the still all-too-prevalent segregation of American life.

These proposals will strike many if not most as utopian. They are
offered more to suggest what an activist agenda committed to eradicating racial inequalities might look like, not because we expect
strong political support for such an agenda any time soon. Policy
questions are undeniably complex and some of these proposals may
not prove to be the right ones. But it is important, we are convinced,
to chart such alternative roads; we are confident that the United
States will not progress if policymakers assume that deeply entrenched racial inequalities will disappear on their own or that they
will be undone by more "conversations" or a bit of policy tinkering.
Whatever their precise forms may take, the measures needed to up-
root the centuries-long legacy of racial hierarchies will be expensive,
controversial, and divisive.

What Americans most need today is the courage to accept that
reality, the spirit to take hard but necessary steps, and faith that doing so will eventually result in better lives for us all. We acknowledge
that it is hard to see where those qualities of mind and heart will come
from; our whole analysis suggests that we are living in a time when
disillusionment and demoralization about efforts to seek racial justice
arise far more naturally than do optimism and commitment.

In part, a renewed spirit of reform can arise today from sober
assessments of America's international political and economic inter-

ests as well as the nation's concerns to achieve greater domestic tranquility. It is simply true that the United States would fare better at home and abroad if it could at last heal the deeply cut wounds of racial inequality. Yet such stark realities have never been enough by themselves to persuade white Americans to accept substantial reforms. Although the material benefits of racial progress are overwhelmingly real, they still seem more remote to most Americans than the short-term costs of sweeping change.

Yet there are within America's complex political and moral traditions examples from which inspiration for progress can justly be drawn. We believe that in reflecting on their racial challenges, Americans should pay heed to what is perhaps the greatest speech ever delivered by a democratic statesman, Abraham Lincoln's Second Inaugural in 1865. Everyone in the audience for that speech was surely exhausted by the unimaginable sacrifices of a long, horribly bloody war in which more Americans died than in any other war before or since. Every listener must have longed desperately to be told that peace was at hand, that the time for massive shared efforts was at last past. Yet like an Old Testament prophet, Lincoln delivered a sterner message. He said:

> Fondly do we hope, fervently do we pray, that this mighty scourge of war may speedily pass away. Yet, if God wills that it continue until all the wealth piled by the bondsman's two hundred and fifty years of unrequited toil shall be sunk, and until every drop of blood drawn with the lash shall be paid by another drawn with the sword, as was said three thousand years ago, so still it must be said, "The judgments of the Lord are true and righteous altogether."

This is a truly awe-inspiring demand. The suggestion that it might be just for Americans to sacrifice wealth and blood comparable to the wages of slavery, no matter how long it takes, is indeed frightening. It is all the more so when we realize that the impoverishment and violence bred by slavery have never been truly overcome, and that we are only a little over halfway through the 250 years Lincoln said it took to create those bitter conditions.

Daunting though Lincoln's message genuinely is, we believe that our whole history supports the sobering conclusion that, indeed, the road to racial harmony and justice in America remains long and steep. Powerful public commitments of the nation's will and resources, comparable to those required to win a massive war, are necessary if we are to move forward appreciably rather than fall back. Yet we also believe that these very facts about our national past and present can be a source of the conviction and devotion that are necessary if further progress is to come. There is, after all, something profoundly inspiring about being able genuinely to believe that we are a people dedicated to carrying forward our national story toward the full realization of our noblest ideals, however difficult that task may be. Such a belief enables us to see ourselves not simply as a collection of loosely allied but largely self-absorbed individuals and smaller communities, and not simply as yet another homeland born of blood and conquest and cruelty. We can see ourselves as a people who embrace a noble, indeed inspirational, historic mission, to work together to overcome past evils and achieve genuinely better lives for all of us, as persons, as families, as communities, and as builders of an ever more perfect union.

But again, Lincoln's concluding words in 1865 put it best: "With malice toward none, with charity for all, with firmness in the right as God gives us to see the right, let us strive on to finish the work we are in, to bind up the nation's wounds . . . to do all which may achieve and cherish a just and lasting peace among ourselves and with all nations."

Notes

INTRODUCTION

1. *Public Papers of the Presidents of the United States: Lyndon B. Johnson, 1965* (Washington, D.C.: Government Printing Office, 1966), pp. 281–7.

2. Dan T. Carter, *The Politics of Rage: George Wallace, the Origins of the New Conservatism, and the Transformation of American Politics* (Baton Rouge: Louisiana State University Press, 1995), p. 11.

3. See, e.g., Jennifer L. Hochschild, *Facing Up to the American Dream: Race, Class, and the Soul of the Nation* (Princeton: Princeton University Press, 1995).

4. In 1906, German historian Otto Hintze wrote, "A phenomenon repeatedly encountered in history is that fulfillment of public obligations leads in the long run to acquisition of public rights." "Military Organization and the Organization of the State," in *The Historical Essays of Otto Hintze*, ed. Felix Gilbert (New York: Oxford University Press, 1975), p. 211. Also see Peter Gourevitch, "The Second Image Reversed: The International Sources of Domestic Politics," *International Organization* 32 (autumn 1978): 881–912; Gabriel A. Almond, "The International-National Connection," *British Journal of Political Science* 19 (April 1989): 237–59.

5. Mary Frances Berry, *Military Necessity and Civil Rights Policy: Black Citizenship and the Constitution, 1861–1868* (Port Washington, N.Y.: Kennikat Press, 1977); Benjamin Quarles, *The Negro in the American Revolution* (Chapel Hill: University of North Carolina Press, 1961); Benjamin Quarles, *The Negro in the Civil War* (New York: Da Capo Press, 1953, 1989).

6. Derrick Bell, "Brown v. Board of Education and the Interest-Convergence Dilemma," *Harvard Law Review* 93 (1980): 518–29; Mary Louise Dudziak, "Cold War Civil Rights: The Relationship between Civil Rights and Foreign Affairs in the Truman Administration" (Ph.D. diss., Yale University, 1992); Mary Louise Dudziak, *Cold War Civil Rights: Equality as Cold War Policy, 1946–1968* (Princeton: Princeton University Press, forthcoming); John David Skrentny, "The Effect of the Cold War on African-American Civil Rights: America and the World Audience, 1945–1968," *Theory and Society* 27 (1998): 237–50; John David Skrentny, *The Ironies of Affirmative Action: Politics, Culture, and Justice in America* (Chicago: University of Chicago Press, 1996).

7. John Higham, "America's Three Reconstructions, *New York Review of Books*, 6 November 1997, pp. 52–6.

8. Philip Gleason, "American Identity and Americanization," in *Concepts of Ethnicity*, ed. William Petersen, Michael Novak, and Philip Gleason (Cambridge: Harvard University Press, 1982, 1980), pp. 62–3.

9. See generally Rogers M. Smith, *Civic Ideals: Conflicting Visions of Citizenship in U.S. History* (New Haven: Yale University Press, 1997).

10. W. E. B. Du Bois, *Black Reconstruction in America: 1860–1880* (New York: Atheneum, 1992, 1935), p. 700.

11. See generally Smith, *Civic Ideals.*

12. We are indebted here to Paul Frymer, *Uneasy Alliances: Race and Party Competition in America* (Princeton: Princeton University Press, 1998). Also see Philip A. Klinkner, *The Losing Parties: Out-Party National Committees, 1956–1993* (New Haven: Yale University Press, 1994).

CHAPTER ONE

1. Gary B. Nash, *Red, White and Black: The Peoples of Early America* (Englewood Cliffs, N.J.: Prentice-Hall, 1974), pp. 127–34; Edmund S. Morgan, *American Slavery—American Freedom: The Ordeal of Colonial Virginia* (New York: W. W. Norton, 1975), pp. 250–70, 328, 344–5; Ronald Takaki, *A Different Mirror: A History of Multicultural America* (Boston: Little, Brown, 1993), pp. 61–8.

2. John Hope Franklin and Alfred A. Moss Jr., *From Slavery to Freedom: A History of African Americans,* 7th ed. (New York: McGraw-Hill, 1994), p. 56; Stephen B. Weeks, "The History of Negro Suffrage in the South," *Political Science Quarterly* 9 (December 1894): 671–3; Lerone Bennett Jr., *The Shaping of Black America: The Struggles and Triumphs of African Americans, 1619 to the 1990s* (New York: Penguin Books, 1993), p. 10.

3. Bennett, *The Shaping of Black America,* pp. 64–5; Peter Kolchin, *American Slavery, 1619–1877* (New York: Hill & Wang, 1993), pp. 10–18; Donald L. Robinson, *Slavery in the Structure of American Politics, 1765–1820* (New York: Harcourt Brace Jovanovich, 1971), p. 19.

4. Robinson, *Slavery in the Structure of American Politics,* pp. 21–2; Franklin and Moss, *From Slavery to Freedom,* pp. 56–67; Kolchin, *American Slavery,* pp. 16 and 57–9; Arthur Zilversmit, *The First Emancipation: The Abolition of Slavery in the North* (Chicago: University of Chicago Press, 1967), pp. 12–24; Philip S. Foner, *From Africa to the Emergence of the Cotton Kingdom,* vol. 1 of *History of Black Americans* (Westport, Conn.: Greenwood Press, 1975), pp. 220–3.

5. Winthrop D. Jordan, *White Over Black: American Attitudes Toward the Negro, 1550–1812* (Chapel Hill: University of North Carolina Press, 1968), pp. 122–8; Weeks, "The History of Negro Suffrage in the South"; W. E. B. Du Bois, *Black Reconstruction in America* (New York: Atheneum, 1992, 1935), p. 6.

6. Kolchin, *American Slavery,* p. 240.

7. William W. Freehling, "The Founding Fathers and Slavery," *American Historical Review* 77 (1972): 86.

8. Foner, *History of Black Americans,* vol. 1, p. 280; Kolchin, *American Slavery,* pp. 63–4; Larry E. Tise, *Proslavery: A History of the Defense of Slavery in America, 1701–1840* (Athens: University of Georgia Press, 1987), pp. 14–5.

9. Robinson, *Slavery in the Structure of American Politics,* p. 72.

10. Kolchin, *American Slavery,* p. 63.

11. Rogers M. Smith, *Civic Ideals: Conflicting Visions of Citizenship in U.S. History* (New Haven: Yale University Press, 1997), pp. 38, 75–6.

12. Leslie H. Fishel Jr. and Benjamin Quarles, *The Black Americans: A Documentary History* (New York: William Morrow, 1970), p. 44.

13. Lerone Bennett Jr., *Before the Mayflower: A History of Black America,* 6th ed. (New York: Penguin Books, 1988), p. 61.

14. Benjamin Quarles, *The Negro in the American Revolution* (Chapel Hill: University of

North Carolina Press, 1961), pp. 5–6. Several others in the crowd were wounded, one of whom died a few days later.

15. Franklin and Moss, *From Slavery to Freedom*, p. 70.

16. Robinson, *Slavery in the Structure of American Politics*, pp. 74–5.

17. Foner, *History of Black Americans*, vol. 1, p. 303.

18. Merton L. Dillon, *Slavery Attacked: Southern Slaves and Their Allies, 1619–1865* (Baton Rouge: Louisiana State University Press, 1990), pp. 28–9.

19. Sidney Kaplan and Emma Nogrady Kaplan, *The Black Presence in the Era of the American Revolution*, rev. ed. (Amherst: University of Massachusetts Press, 1989), p. 11.

20. Foner, *History of Black Americans*, vol. 1, p. 299.

21. Quarles, *The Negro in the American Revolution*, pp. 38–41; and Zilversmit, *The First Emancipation*, pp. 103–8. The Rhode Island assembly, however, soon watered down the act under pressure from influential Newport slave traders.

22. Robinson, *Slavery in the Structure of American Politics*, pp. 79–80.

23. Gary B. Nash, *Race and Revolution* (Madison, Wis.: Madison House, 1990), pp. 7–20.

24. Herbert Aptheker, ed., *A Documentary History of the Negro People in the United States: From Colonial Times through the Civil War*, vol. 1 (New York: Citadel Press, 1951, 1967), p. 10.

25. Robinson, *Slavery in the Structure of American Politics*, pp. 299–300.

26. Franklin and Moss, *From Slavery to Freedom*, p. 71.

27. Smith, *Civic Ideals*, p. 76.

28. Quarles, *The Negro in the American Revolution*, p. 19.

29. Kaplan and Kaplan, *The Black Presence in the Era of the American Revolution*, pp. 24–6, 75–6; Gordon S. Wood, *The Radicalism of the American Revolution* (New York: Knopf, 1992), pp. 176–8.

30. Pete Maslowski, "National Policy Toward the Use of Black Troops in the Revolution," *South Carolina Historical Magazine* 73 (1972): 2–3.

31. Foner, *History of Black Americans*, vol. 1, p. 316.

32. Maslowski, pp. 5–6.

33. Foner, *History of Black Americans*, vol. 1, pp. 324–5; Quarles, *The Negro in the American Revolution*, pp. 52–3.

34. Foner, *History of Black Americans*, vol. 1, pp. 325–9.

35. Franklin and Moss, *From Slavery to Freedom*, p. 76.

36. Quarles, *The Negro in the American Revolution*, pp. 56–67; Foner, *History of Black Americans*, vol. 1, pp. 328–35.

37. Allan Kulikoff, "Uprooted Peoples: Black Migrants in the Age of the American Revolution, 1790–1820," in *Slavery and Freedom in the Age of the American Revolution*, ed. Ira Berlin and Ronald Hoffman (Charlottesville: University Press of Virginia, 1983), pp. 144–5. Sylvia R. Frey's, *Water From a Rock: Black Resistance in a Revolutionary Age* (Princeton: Princeton University Press, 1991), pp. 174–5, suggests that the number may be much higher.

38. Quarles, *The Negro in the American Revolution*, p. 172.

39. Kolchin, *American Slavery*, p. 73; Franklin and Moss, *From Slavery to Freedom*, p. 75.

40. Dillon, *Slavery Attacked*, pp. 36–7. Percentage calculated from U.S. Department of Commerce, Bureau of the Census, *Historical Statistics of the United States: Colonial Times to 1957* (Washington, D.C.: Government Printing Office, 1960), p. 756.

41. Zilversmit, *The First Emancipation*, pp. 112–24; Foner, *History of Black Americans*, vol. 1, pp. 347–53, 359–63.

42. Zilversmit, *The First Emancipation*, pp. 180–2, 192–3.

43. Emil Olbrich, *The Development of Sentiment on Negro Suffrage to 1860* (Madison: University of Wisconsin, 1912), pp. 22–3; Henry W. Farnam, *Chapters in the History of Social Legislation in the United States to 1860* (Washington, D.C.: Carnegie Institution, 1938), p. 470; John Codman Hurd, *The Laws of Freedom and Bondage in the United States*, vol. 2 (New York: Negro University Press, 1862, 1968), p. 57; Foner, *History of Black Americans*, vol. 1, p. 355; Charles H. Wesley, "Negro Suffrage In the Period of Constitution-Making," *Journal of Negro History* 32 (April 1947): 161–2.

44. Ira Berlin, *Slaves Without Masters: The Free Negro in the Antebellum South* (New York: Pantheon Books, 1974), pp. 46–7.

45. Quarles, *The Negro in the American Revolution*, p. 183.

46. Eli Ginzberg and Alfred S. Eichner, *Troublesome Presence: Democracy and Black Americans* (New Brunswick, N.J.: Transaction Publishers, 1964, 1993), pp. 45–6; Quarles, *The Negro in the American Revolution*, p. 187; and Kolchin, *American Slavery*, pp. 77–8. Washington's nephew and estate executor Bushrod Washington, a justice of the U.S. Supreme Court and first president of the American Colonization Society, failed to comply with his uncle's manumission order. Instead he eventually split up the slave families through sales. Elder Witt, *Congressional Quarterly's Guide to the U.S. Supreme Court*, 2d ed. (Washington, D.C.: Congressional Quarterly Press, 1990), pp. 809.

47. Nash, *Race and Revolution*, pp. 14–5; Berlin, *Slaves Without Masters*, p. 25.

48. Berlin, *Slaves Without Masters*, p. 29; Nash, *Race and Revolution*, pp. 18–9.

49. Foner, *History of Black Americans*, vol. 1, p. 508; Weeks, "The History of Negro Suffrage in the South," pp. 674–5, 677–8; Hurd, *The Laws of Freedom and Bondage in the United States*, pp. 15, 19, 74, 76, 82, 88, 90; Farnam, *Chapters in the History of Social Legislation*, pp. 363, 379, 392, 420. Georgia also formally provided the franchise on an equal basis, but there is no evidence that any free blacks voted. See Hurd, p. 101, and Weeks, p. 674.

50. Donald G. Nieman, *Promises to Keep: African-Americans and the Constitutional Order, 1776 to the Present* (New York: Oxford University Press, 1991), p. 13; Paul Finkelman, "Slavery and the Northwest Ordinance: A Study in Ambiguity," *Journal of the Early Republic* 6 (winter 1986): 346.

51. Thomas Jefferson, *Notes on the State of Virginia*, ed. W. Peden (Chapel Hill: University of North Carolina Press, 1955), pp. 87, 136–43, 155, 163.

52. Ginzberg and Eichner, *Troublesome Presence*, p. 56; Franklin and Moss, *From Slavery to Freedom*, pp. 81–3; Paul Finkelman, "Slavery and the Constitutional Convention: Making a Covenant With Death," in *Beyond Confederation: Origins of the Constitution and American National Identity*, ed. Richard Beeman, Stephen Botein, and Edward C. Carter II (Chapel Hill: University of North Carolina Press, 1987), p. 225. Calvin Jillson, in *Constitution Making: Conflict and Consensus in the Federal Convention of 1787* (New York: Agathon Press, 1988), pp. 140–50, also provides an excellent discussion of the politics of compromise over slavery.

53. Finkelman, "Slavery and the Constitutional Convention," p. 197.

54. Ibid., pp. 202–5, 212–3.

55. Ibid., pp. 210–1.

56. Ibid., pp. 214–20; Nieman, *Promises to Keep*, pp. 11–2; James Madison, *Notes of Debates in the Federal Convention of 1787* (New York: Norton & Co., 1966), p. 548.

57. Finkelman, "Slavery and the Constitutional Convention," p. 224.

58. *Annals of Cong.*, 1st Cong., 2d sess., 1223–33, 1239–47, 1501–26 (Gales & Seaton, 1834); Ginzberg and Eichman, *Troublesome Presence*, pp. 66–9; Foner, *History of Black Americans*, vol. 1, 408–12.

59. Foner, *History of Black Americans*, vol. 1, p. 451.

60. Winthrop D. Jordan, *The White Man's Burden: Historical Origins of Racism in the United States* (New York: Oxford University Press, 1974), p. 153.

61. Foner, *History of Black Americans*, vol. 1, p. 472.

62. Jordan, *The White Man's Burden*, p. 153.

63. Dillon, *Slavery Attacked*, p. 108.

64. I. A. Newby, *The South: A History* (New York: Holt, Rinehart, and Winston, 1978), p. 78.

65. Farnam, *Chapters in the History of Social Legislation*, pp. 198–200; Philip S. Foner, *From the Emergence of the Cotton Kingdom to the Eve of the Compromise of 1850*, vol. 2 of *History of Black Americans* (Westport, Conn.: Greenwood Press, 1983), pp. 105–11.

66. Franklin and Moss, *From Slavery to Freedom*, p. 124.

67. Ibid., pp. 124–6; Kolchin, *American Slavery*, pp. 127–32; and Foner, *History of Black Americans*, vol. 2, pp. 154–5.

68. Foner, *History of Black Americans*, vol. 1, p. 509.

69. Ibid., pp. 509–12; Berlin, *Slaves Without Masters*, pp. 79–107.

70. Berlin, *Slaves Without Masters*, pp. 91–2; Jordan, *The White Man's Burden*, pp. 156, 211–2; Farnam, *Chapters in the History of Social Legislation*, pp. 200–1.

71. Foner, *History of Black Americans*, vol. 1, pp. 459–61, 463–4, 472.

72. Dillon, *Slavery Attacked*, p. 54.

73. Leon F. Litwack, *North of Slavery: The Negro in the Free States, 1790–1860* (Chicago: University of Chicago Press, 1961), p. 31.

74. Foner, *History of American Blacks*, vol. 1, p. 472.

75. Litwack, *North of Slavery*, p. 31; Nieman, *Promises to Keep*, p. 17; Paul Finkelman, "The Kidnapping of John Davis and the Adoption of the Fugitive Slave Law of 1793," *Journal of Southern History* 56 (August 1990): 397–422.

76. Olbrich, *The Development of Sentiment on Negro Suffrage*, pp. 29–30; Marion Thompson Wright, "Negro Suffrage in New Jersey, 1776–1875," *Journal of Negro History* 33 (April 1948): 168–224; Henry W. Farnam, *Chapters in the History of Social Legislation*, pp. 220–1, 418, 449–50, 465; James Truslow Adams, "Disenfranchisement of Negroes in New England," *American Historical Review* 30 (April 1925): 543–7.

77. Olbrich, *The Development of Sentiment on Negro Suffrage*, pp. 26–7.

78. Franklin and Moss, *From Slavery to Freedom*, pp. 89, 91–2.

79. Foner, *History of Black Americans*, vol. 1, pp. 472–3.

80. The instructions went on to say the United States "are not prepared to sacrifice" to slave trade suppression "any of their rights as an independent nation; nor will the object in view justify the exposure of their own people to injurious and vexatious interruptions in the prosecution of their lawful pursuits." Donald Fehrenbacher, *The Dred Scott Case: Its Significance in American Law and Politics* (New York: Oxford University Press, 1978), pp. 4, 21.

81. Franklin and Moss, *From Slavery to Freedom*, p. 109.

82. Samuel Eliot Morison, Henry Steele Commager, and William E. Leuchtenburg, *The Growth of the American Republic*, vol. 1, 7th ed. (New York: Oxford University Press, 1980), 365.

83. Ibid., p. 362.

84. Franklin and Moss, *From Slavery to Freedom*, p. 108.

85. War of 1812 casualty figures from Morison, Commager, and Leuchtenburg, *The Growth of the American Republic*, p. 385. Revolutionary War figures from Allan R. Millett

and Peter Maslowski, *For the Common Defense: A Military History of the United States of America* (New York: Free Press, 1984), p. 79.

86. Lorman Ratner, *Powder Keg: Northern Opposition to the Anti-Slavery Movement, 1831–1840* (New York: Basic Books, 1968), p. 18.

87. George M. Fredrickson, *The Black Image in the White Mind: The Debate on Afro-American Character and Destiny, 1817–1914* (New York: Harper and Row, 1971), pp. 1–21.

88. Ibid., pp. 72–73; William Stanton, *The Leopard's Spots: Scientific Attitudes Toward Race in America, 1815–59* (Chicago: University of Chicago Press, 1960), pp. 19–23.

89. Foner, *History of Black Americans*, vol. 2, p. 370.

90. Fredrickson, *The Black Image in the White Mind*, pp. 78–9.

91. Josiah C. Nott and George R. Gliddon, eds., *Types of Mankind, or Ethnological Researches*, 7th ed. (Philadelphia: Lippincott, Grambo, 1855), pp. 67, 71, 77. Nott was also a close ally of the nation's leading proslavery politician, John C. Calhoun.

92. Reginald Horsman, *Race and Manifest Destiny: The Origins of American Racial Anglo-Saxonism* (Cambridge: Harvard University Press, 1981), pp. 16–38.

93. Ibid., pp. 60–1, 87.

94. Ratner, *Powder Keg*, pp. 22–3; Foner, *History of Black Americans*, vol. 2, pp. 199–200.

95. Philip F. Detweiler, "Congressional Debate on Slavery and the Declaration of Independence, 1819–1821," *American Historical Review* 63 (April 1958): 604.

96. Ibid., p. 606.

97. Foner, *History of Black Americans*, vol. 2, p. 355.

98. Dillon, *Slavery Attacked*, p. 124.

99. *Annals of Congress*, 16th Cong., 2d sess. (1820–1821), at pp. 555, 557, 615–22.

100. Olbrich, *The Development of Sentiment on Negro Suffrage*, pp. 28–9.

101. Glover Moore, *The Missouri Controversy, 1819–1821* (University of Kentucky Press, 1953; Gloucester, Mass.: Peter Smith, 1967), pp. 143–4.

102. Tise, *Proslavery*, p. 57.

103. William Yates, *Rights of Colored Men to Suffrage, Citizenship and Trial by Jury* (Philadelphia: Merrihew & Gunn, 1838), pp. 3–4.

104. Olbrich, *The Development of Sentiment on Negro Suffrage*, p. 32.

105. Yates, *Rights of Colored Men to Suffrage, Citizenship and Trial by Jury*, pp. 3–4.

106. Dixon Ryan Fox, "The Negro Vote in Old New York," *Political Science Quarterly* 32 (June 1917): 252–75; Phyllis F. Field, *The Politics of Race in New York: The Struggle for Black Suffrage in the Civil War Era* (Ithaca, N.Y.: Cornell University Press, 1982), p. 37.

107. Berlin, *Slaves Without Masters*, p. 91; Olbrich, *The Development of Sentiment on Negro Suffrage*, pp. 39–50; Wright, "Negro Suffrage in New Jersey," pp. 168–224; Farnam, *Chapters in the History of Social Legislation*, pp. 220–1, 418, 449–50, 465; Adams, "Disenfranchisement of Negroes in New England," pp. 543–7.

108. Olbrich, *The Development of Sentiment on Negro Suffrage*, p. 46.

109. Ibid., p. 48.

110. Litwack, *North of Slavery*, p. 85.

111. Olbrich, *The Development of Sentiment on Negro Suffrage*, p. 59.

112. Ibid., p. 55.

113. The corporation did so in 1829. Foner, *History of Black Americans*, vol. 1, p. 511; Constance McLaughlin Green, *The Secret City: A History of Race Relations in the Nation's Capital* (Princeton: Princeton University Press, 1967), p. 32.

114. Litwack, *North of Slavery*, pp. 114–5, 132–5.

115. Foner, *History of Black Americans,* vol. 2, pp. 197–9.

116. Ibid., pp. 200–2.

117. V. Jacque Voegeli, *Free But Not Equal: The Midwest and the Negro During the Civil War* (Chicago: University of Chicago Press, 1967), p. 1.

118. Eugene H. Berwanger, *The Frontier against Slavery: Western Anti-Negro Prejudice and the Slavery Extension Controversy* (Urbana: University of Illinois Press, 1967), pp. 21–2.

119. Ibid., pp. 23, 31–3.

120. Ibid., p. 34.

121. Ibid., p. 36.

122. Robert R. Dykstra, *Bright Radical Star: Black Freedom and White Supremacy on the Hawkeye Frontier* (Cambridge: Harvard University Press, 1993), p. 111.

123. Ibid., pp. 111–3.

124. Berwanger, *The Frontier against Slavery,* pp. 42, 45, 49, 140. In California, both the house of the state legislature passed exclusion laws, but in different forms. Berwanger, p. 76.

125. Ratner, *Powder Keg,* p. 52.

126. Ibid., p. 4.

127. Leonard P. Curry, *The Free Black in Urban America, 1800–1850: The Shadow of the Dream* (Chicago: University of Chicago Press, 1981), p. 98.

128. Leonard Richards, *"Gentlemen of Property and Standing": Anti-Abolition Mobs in Jacksonian America* (New York: Oxford University Press, 1970), p. 14.

129. Mario M. Cuomo and Harold Holzer, eds., *Lincoln on Democracy* (New York: A Cornelia and Michael Bessie Book, 1990), p. 19.

130. Charles M. Wiltse, *The New Nation: 1800–1845* (New York: Hill & Wang, 1961), pp. 166–7.

131. Horsman, *Race and Manifest Destiny,* p. 209.

132. Ibid., p. 210.

133. John H. Van Evrie, *Negroes and Negro 'Slavery;' the First, an Inferior Race—the Latter, Its Normal Condition* (Baltimore: John D. Toy, Printer, 1853). p. 18; *Congressional Globe,* 28th Cong, 1st sess. (May 20, 1844), p. 551; 2d sess. (January 14, 1845), p. 97; Takaki, *A Different Mirror,* pp. 173–6.

134. Edmund Wilson, *Patriotic Gore: Studies in the Literature of the American Civil War* (New York: Oxford University Press, 1962), pp. 133–4; Daniel Walker Howe, *The Political Culture of the American Whigs* (Chicago: University of Chicago Press, 1979), p. 273.

135. Berwanger, *The Frontier against Slavery,* pp. 125–6.

136. Ibid., p. 93.

137. Ibid., pp. 131–5.

138. Cuomo and Holzer, eds., *Lincoln on Democracy,* p. 129.

139. Foner, *History of Black Americans,* vol. 2, p. 10.

140. James M. McPherson, *Battle Cry of Freedom: The Civil War Era* (New York: Oxford University Press, 1988), p. 80.

141. Ibid., p. 81.

142. Foner, *History of Black Americans,* vol. 2, p. 17.

143. Nieman, *Promises to Keep,* p. 46.

144. Lee Epstein and Thomas G. Walker, *Constitutional Law for a Changing America: Institutional Powers and Constraints,* 2d ed. (Washington, D.C.: Congressional Quarterly Press, 1995), p. 291.

145. Nieman, *Promises to Keep,* pp. 44–9.

146. Berwanger, *The Frontier against Slavery* (Urbana: University of Illinois Press, 1967), pp. 33–4.

147. Nieman, *Promises to Keep*, pp. 40–1.

148. Abraham Lincoln, *Complete Works*, vol. 1, ed. John G. Nicolay and John Hay (New York: The Century Co., 1920), pp. 230–1.

CHAPTER TWO

1. Cartoon entered by Currier and Ives at the Clerk's Office in the District Court for the Southern District of New York, 1860; supplied to the authors by the American Antiquarian Society.

2. *The Constitution of the United States: Analysis and Interpretation* (Washington, D.C.: Government Printing Office, 1987), p. 52. Although named for Corwin, the amendment was first proposed by William Seward. R. Alton Lee, however, asserts that the idea for the amendment originated with Abraham Lincoln. See R. Alton Lee, "The Corwin Amendment in the Secession Crisis," *Ohio Historical Quarterly* 70 (January 1961): 9–18.

3. Lee, "The Corwin Amendment in the Secession Crisis," p. 23.

4. Ibid., p. 9.

5. Edward McPherson, *The Political History of the United States of America During the Great Rebellion* (Washington, D.C.: Philip & Solomons, 1865), pp. 58–64, 108.

6. Lee, "The Corwin Amendment in the Secession Crisis," p. 5.

7. James M. McPherson, *Battle Cry of Freedom: The Civil War Era* (New York: Oxford University Press, 1988), p. 224; James D. Bilotta, *Race and the Rise of the Republican Party, 1848–1865* (New York: Peter Lang, 1992), pp. 411–15.

8. McPherson, *Battle Cry of Freedom*, p. 227.

9. Benjamin Quarles, *Lincoln and the Negro* (New York: Da Capo Press, 1962, 1991), p. 64.

10. James M. McPherson, *The Struggle for Equality: Abolitionists and the Negro in the Civil War and Reconstruction* (Princeton: Princeton University Press, 1964), pp. 40–5. Quote at p. 41.

11. Illinois's approval, however, was given by a state convention, not by the state legislature, as directed by Congress when it passed the amendment. Lee, "The Corwin Amendment in the Secession Crisis," p. 25.

12. J. G. Randall and Richard N. Current, *Lincoln the President: Last Full Measure*, vol. 4 (New York: Dodd, Mead, 1955), p. 307.

13. Ibid., p. 308.

14. McPherson, *Battle Cry of Freedom*, p. 838.

15. Ibid., p. 839.

16. W. E. B. Du Bois, *Black Reconstruction in America, 1860–1880* (New York: Atheneum, 1935, 1992), pp. 207–8.

17. McPherson, *Battle Cry of Freedom*, pp. 839–40.

18. Quarles, *Lincoln and the Negro*, pp. 223–4.

19. Randall and Current, *Lincoln the President*, p. 316.

20. McPherson, *The Struggle for Equality*, p. 56.

21. Du Bois, *Black Reconstruction*, p. 56.

22. Ibid., p. 62.

23. Benjamin Quarles, *The Negro in the Civil War* (New York: Da Capo Press, 1953, 1989), p. 60; Quarles, *Lincoln and the Negro*, p. 69.

24. Ira Berlin et al., eds., *Free At Last: A Documentary History of Slavery, Freedom, and the Civil War* (New York: New Press, 1992), p. 9.

25. McPherson, *Battle Cry of Freedom*, p. 354.

26. McPherson, *The Struggle for Equality*, p. 71.

27. McPherson, *Battle Cry of Freedom*, p. 354.

28. William S. McFeely, *Frederick Douglass* (New York: Touchstone, 1991), p. 212.

29. Quarles, *The Negro in the Civil War*, pp. 94–5.

30. Ibid., p. 79.

31. Ibid., pp. 71–4, 91–3. White acclaim for Smalls, however, only went so far. Although elected as delegates from South Carolina, Smalls and three other blacks were refused seats at the 1864 Republican National Convention. Smalls later was later elected to Congress from South Carolina during Reconstruction. Du Bois, *Black Reconstruction*, p. 230.

32. John Hope Franklin and Alfred A. Moss Jr., *From Slavery to Freedom: A History of African Americans*, 7th ed. (New York: McGraw-Hill, 1994), pp. 199–200.

33. McPherson, *Battle Cry of Freedom*, p. 357.

34. Brooks D. Simpson, " 'The Doom of Slavery': Ulysses S. Grant, War Aims, and Emancipation, 1861–1863," *Civil War History* 36 (winter 1990): 41.

35. Dudley Taylor Cornish, *The Sable Arm: Negro Troops in the Union Army, 1861–1865* (New York: W. W. Norton, 1966), pp. 17–8.

36. Quarles, *The Negro in the Civil War*, p. xiv.

37. Howard C. Westwood, "Lincoln's Position on Black Enlistments," *Lincoln Herald* 86 (spring 1984): 101.

38. Cornish, *The Sable Arm*, pp. 18–9.

39. McPherson, *Battle Cry of Freedom*, pp. 357–8.

40. Ibid., p. 358.

41. Ibid., pp. 494–7.

42. Quarles, *The Negro in the Civil War*, pp. 108–12; Cornish, *The Sable Arm*, pp. 29–53.

43. Du Bois, *Black Reconstruction in America*, p. 88.

44. Ibid., p. 82.

45. McPherson, *Battle Cry of Freedom*, p. 500.

46. David Herbert Donald, *Lincoln* (New York: Simon & Schuster, 1995), p. 365.

47. Ibid., p. 364.

48. McPherson, *Battle Cry of Freedom*, p. 504.

49. Franklin and Moss, *From Slavery to Freedom*, p. 43.

50. McPherson, *Battle Cry of Freedom*, pp. 491–93.

51. Du Bois, *Black Reconstruction in America*, p. 82.

52. Ira Berlin, Joseph P. Reidy, and Leslie S. Rowland, *Freedom: A Documentary History of Emancipation, 1861–1867: Series II: The Black Military Experience* (Cambridge: Cambridge University Press, 1982), p. 84.

53. Quarles, *Lincoln and the Negro*, p. 154.

54. Berlin et al., eds., *Free At Last*, pp. 67–8.

55. Philip Shaw Paludan, *The Presidency of Abraham Lincoln* (Lawrence: University Press of Kansas, 1994), p. 222.

56. Cornish, *The Sable Arm*, pp. 229–30.

57. McPherson, *Battle Cry of Freedom*, p. 500.

58. Mary Frances Berry, *Military Necessity and Civil Rights Policy: Black Citizenship and the Constitution, 1861–1868* (Port Washington, N.Y.: Kennikat Press, 1977), pp. 42–3.

59. Ibid., pp. 42–3.

60. Quarles, *Lincoln and the Negro*, p. 154; Paludan, *The Presidency of Abraham Lincoln*, p. 146.

61. Leon F. Litwack, *Been in the Storm So Long: The Aftermath of Slavery* (New York: Vintage Books, 1979), p. 66.

62. Cornish, *The Sable Arm*, p. 73.

63. Quarles, *The Negro in the Civil War*, p. 114.

64. Ibid., p. 116.

65. Ibid., pp. 116–7.

66. Ibid., p. 118.

67. McPherson, *Battle Cry of Freedom*, p. 560.

68. Bruce Tap, "Race, Rhetoric, and Emancipation: The Election of 1862 in Illinois," *Civil War History* 39 (spring 1993): 110.

69. McPherson, *Battle Cry of Freedom*, pp. 561–2; Franklin and Moss, *From Slavery to Freedom*, p. 86.

70. Westwood, "Lincoln's Position on Black Enlistments," pp. 105–6.

71. Quarles, *Lincoln and the Negro*, pp. 154–5.

72. Franklin, *From Slavery to Freedom*, pp. 95–7.

73. Ibid., pp. 128–35.

74. Ira Berlin et al., *Freedom: A Documentary History of Emancipation, 1861–1867: Series I, Volume I: The Destruction of Slavery* (Cambridge: Cambridge University Press, 1985), p. 38; Cornish, *The Sable Arm*, p. 111.

75. Joseph T. Glatthaar, *Forged in Battle: The Civil War Alliance of Black Soldiers and White Officers* (New York: Free Press, 1990), p. 61.

76. Litwack, *Been in the Storm So Long*, p. 71.

77. Glatthaar, *Forged in Battle*, p. 40.

78. Ibid., p. 41.

79. Cornish, *The Sable Arm*, pp. 142–3.

80. Ibid., 156.

81. Joseph T. Glatthaar, "Black Glory: The African-American Role in Union Victory," in *Why the Confederacy Lost*, ed. Gabor S. Boritt (New York: Oxford, 1992), p. 156.

82. Quarles, *The Negro in the Civil War*, p. 184.

83. Glatthaar, "Black Glory," p. 152.

84. James M. McPherson, *The Negro's Civil War: How American Blacks Felt and Acted During the War for the Union* (New York: Ballantine Books, 1965, 1991), p. 202.

85. Glatthaar, *Forged in Battle*, pp. 115–9.

86. Ibid., p. 174.

87. Ibid., pp. 227–8.

88. Ibid., p. 249.

89. McPherson, *The Struggle for Equality*, p. 221.

90. Donald, *Lincoln*, p. 459.

91. Ibid., p. 466. Also see Garry Wills, *Lincoln at Gettysburg: The Words That Remade America* (New York: Simon & Schuster, 1992).

92. McPherson, *The Struggle for Equality*, p. 232.

93. Brooks D. Simpson, "Quandaries of Command: Ulyssess S. Grant and Black Soldiers," in *Union and Emancipation: Essays on Politics and Race in the Civil War Era*, ed. David W. Blight and Brooks D. Simpson (Kent, Ohio: Kent State University Press, 1997), p. 125.

94. McPherson, *Battle Cry of Freedom*, p. 702.

95. Robert R. Dykstra, *Bright Radical Star: Black Freedom and White Supremacy on the Hawkeye Frontier* (Cambridge: Harvard University Press, 1993), p. 219.

96. James M. McPherson, *What They Fought For, 1861-1865* (New York: Anchor Books, 1994), pp. 62-4.

97. John H. Van Evrie, "Free Negroism; Or, Results of Emancipation in the North, and the West India Islands, With Statistics of the Decay of Commerce, Idleness of the Negro, His Return to Savageism, and the Effect of Emancipation Upon the Farming, Mechanical and Laboring Classes," 1862, 1866, in John David Smith, *Anti-Abolition Tracts and Anti-Black Stereotypes: General Statements of "The Negro Problem,"* pt. 1 (New York: Garland, 1993), pp. 38-9.

98. McPherson, *Battle Cry of Freedom*, p. 609.

99. Ibid.

100. Cornish, *The Sable Arm*, p. i.

101. McPherson, *Battle Cry of Freedom*, p. 610.

102. Ibid., pp. 769-72.

103. Forrest G. Wood, *Black Scare: The Racist Response to Emancipation and Reconstruction* (Berkeley: University of California Press, 1968), pp. 53-5.

104. Quarles, *The Negro in the Civil War*, p. 256.

105. McPherson, *Battle Cry of Freedom*, p. 769.

106. Paludan, *The Presidency of Abraham Lincoln*, p. 284.

107. Phillip Shaw Paludan, *"A People's Contest:" The Union and Civil War, 1861-1865* (New York: Harper & Row, 1988, pp. 311-2.

108. Berlin et al., eds., *Free At Last*, p. 5.

109. Robert F. Durden, *The Gray and the Black: The Confederate Debate on Emancipation* (Baton Rouge: Louisiana State University Press, 1972), pp. 101-6.

110. Thomas M. Preisser, "The Virginia Decision to Use Negro Soldiers in the Civil War, 1864-1865," *Virginia Magazine of History and Biography* 82 (winter 1975): 99.

111. Durden, *The Gray and the Black*, p. 208.

112. Ibid., pp. 222-3.

113. Ervin L. Jordan Jr., *Black Confederates and Afro-Yankees in Civil War Virginia* (Charlottesville: University Press of Virginia, 1995), p. 242.

114. Ibid., p. 246; Quarles, *The Negro in the Civil War*, p. 280.

115. Cornish, *The Sable Arm*, p. 282.

116. Glatthaar, *Forged in Battle*, p. 10. Another twenty-nine thousand blacks served in the Union navy, constituting approximately one-fourth of that branch's total strength. McPherson, *The Negro's Civil War*, p. 160.

117. Glatthaar, "Black Glory," p. 137.

118. Ibid., p. 158.

119. Du Bois, *Black Reconstruction in America*, p. 91.

120. McPherson, *The Struggle for Equality*, p. 92.

CHAPTER THREE

1. Cited in Thomas K. McCraw, *Prophets of Regulation: Charles Francis Adams, Louis D. Brandeis, James M. Landis, Alfred E. Kahn* (Cambridge: Harvard University Press, 1984), p. 4. See also Charles Francis Adams, " 'The Solid South' and the Afro-American Race Problem," speech at the Academy of Music, Richmond, Va., Oct. 24, 1908 (Boston), p. 18; James M. McPherson, *Battle Cry of Freedom: The Civil War Era* (New York: Oxford University Press, 1988), pp. 846-7.

2. Adams, " 'The Solid South,' " pp. 15, 18-9; McCraw, *Prophets of Regulation*, pp. 1, 4.

3. Adams, " 'The Solid South,' " pp. 15-7, 19-20.

4. Ibid., pp. 16–7; Adams cited in Edward Chase Kirkland, *Charles Francis Adams, Jr., 1835–1915: The Patrician at Bay* (Cambridge: Harvard University Press, 1965), p. 29.

5. Dudley Taylor Cornish, *The Sable Arm: Negro Troops in the Union Army, 1861–1865* (New York: Norton, 1966), p. 287. In his evaluation of Adams's later comments, Cornish states, "Adams seems not to have considered that he was assuming the extraordinary in expecting his troopers to be transformed from prisoner of war guards to well-behaved cavalry on their *first* road march. March discipline . . . requires time and patience; Adams seems to have had neither. To complicate matters the more, he was worn out physically and at the point of collapse, in no mood for nonsense. His last weeks with his regiment were his worst, and his judgment of Negro troops was permanently warped by that unhappy time" (p. 315).

6. Adams, " 'The Solid South,' " pp. 16–8; Kirkland, *Charles Francis Adams, Jr.*, p. 140; Charles Francis Adams, *An Autobiography, With a Memorial Address delivered November, 17, 1915 by Henry Cabot Lodge* (New York: Houghton Mifflin, 1916), pp. xxxi, xxxiv, 177, 179.

7. Adams, " 'The Solid South,' " pp. 7, 12; McCraw, *Prophets of Regulation*, pp. 2, 4–7, 52–6.

8. This account draws on Rogers M. Smith, *Civic Ideals: Conflicting Visions of Citizenship in U.S. History* (New Haven: Yale University Press, 1997), pp. 289–327.

9. McPherson, *Battle Cry of Freedom*, pp. 698–713, 843–4, 851–2; Eric Foner, *Reconstruction: America's Unfinished Revolution, 1863–1877* (New York: Harper & Row, 1988), pp. 35–7, 61–2, 73–5.

10. W. E. B. Du Bois, *Black Reconstruction in America, 1860–1880* (New York: Atheneum, 1935, 1992), p. 201.

11. Foner, *Reconstruction*, p. 180.

12. Ibid., p. 247.

13. Du Bois, *Black Reconstruction in America*, p. 178.

14. George Sinkler, *The Racial Attitudes of American Presidents: From Abraham Lincoln to Theodore Roosevelt* (New York: Doubleday, 1971), p. 100.

15. Claude F. Oubre, *Forty Acres and a Mule: The Freedman's Bureau and Black Land Ownership* (Baton Rouge: Louisiana State University Press, 1978), pp. 12, 53–4, 57, 84–90, 95, 100, 104–7, 110–6, 129–38, 141–4, 189; Donald G. Nieman, *To Set the Law in Motion: The Freedman's Bureau and the Legal Rights of Blacks, 1865–1868* (Millwood, N.Y.: KTO Press, 1979), pp. x, xiv–xvii, 24–5, 45–9, 72–98, 111–5; Harold M. Hyman and William M. Wiecek, *Equal Justice Under Law: Constitutional Development, 1835–1875* (New York: Harper & Row, 1982), pp. 303, 314–6, 319–21, 394–8, 416–9; Foner, *Reconstruction*, pp. 68–71, 87, 158–62, 199–210, 215–6, 246–7, 404, 568; Michael L. Lanza, *Agrarianism and Reconstruction Politics: The Southern Homestead Act* (Baton Rouge : Louisiana State University, 1990), pp. 14–5, 22, 29, 53, 63, 66, 74, 80–5, 97, 113; Du Bois, *Black Reconstruction in America*, pp. 221–4, 252, 254.

16. David M. Oshinsky, *Worse Than Slavery: Parchman Farm and the Ordeal of Jim Crow Justice* (New York: Free Press, 1996), pp. 21–2.

17. Du Bois, *Black Reconstruction in America*, pp. 193, 195.

18. William Gillette, *The Right to Vote: Politics and the Passage of the Fifteenth Amendment* (Baltimore: Johns Hopkins Press, 1965), pp. 28–31; Michael Les Benedict, *A Compromise of Principle; Congressional Republicans and Reconstruction, 1863–1869* (New York: Norton, 1974), pp. 210–43, 252–6; Hyman and Wiecek, *Equal Justice Under Law*, pp. 441–5, 453–5; Foner, *Reconstruction*, pp. 272–9.

19. Data compiled from *Congressional Quarterly's Guide to U.S. Elections*, pp. 771, 774.

20. Michael Les Benedict, "The Rout of Radicalism: Republicans and the Elections of 1867," *Civil War History* 18 (winter 1972): 343.

21. John Hope Franklin, "Election of 1868," in *History of American Presidential Elections, 1789–1968*, vol. 2, ed. Arthur M. Schlesinger Jr. and Fred L. Israel (New York: Chelsea House Publishers, 1971), p. 1267–8.

22. William Gillette, *Retreat From Reconstruction, 1869–1879* (Baton Rouge: Louisiana State University Press, 1979), pp. 18–9.

23. Ibid., p. 22.

24. Act of May 31, 1870, 41st Cong., 2d sess., Ch. 114, 140–6; Act of April 20, 1871, 42d Cong., 1st sess., Ch. 22, 13–5; Eleanor Flexner, *Century of Struggle: The Woman's Rights Movement in the United States*, rev. ed. (Cambridge: Harvard University Press, 1975), pp. 145–58; Hyman and Wiecek, *Equal Justice Under Law*, pp. 467, 470–2, 489–92, 507; Foner, *Reconstruction*, pp. 454–9, 528–9, 555–6.

25. Gillette, *Retreat from Reconstruction*, pp. 31, 35, 42.

26. Ibid., pp. 48–9.

27. In 1868 national Republicans still supported Chinese immigration in the Burlingame Treaty, and they included in the 1870 civil rights laws a ban on anti-immigrant state taxes. That same year, however, the California Republican Party declared itself "inflexibly" opposed to Chinese immigration. Nevada senator William Stewart, who had earlier denounced "wicked" local laws imposing "injustice" on the Chinese, similarly abruptly switched sides. When Charles Sumner proposed extending naturalization to Chinese resident aliens as well as Africans, Stewart claimed this change would make citizens of "pagans" who were not of "our own race." An outraged Sumner then stalked to the well of the Senate, dramatically opened the chamber's Bible, and read the story of Peter renouncing Christ. In like manner, he thundered, on this day "thrice has a Senator on this floor denied the great principles of the Declaration of Independence." *Congressional Globe*, 4 July 1869, rep. 4 July 1870, p. 5150; 4 July 1870, pp. 1549–55, 1571; Ronald Takaki, *A Different Mirror: A History of Multicultural America* (Boston: Little, Brown, 1993), p. 208; Daniel J. Tichenor, "The Liberal and Illiberal Traditions in America: The Case of Immigration Policymaking" (paper presented at the annual meeting of the American Political Science Association, Chicago, August 31, 1995), pp. 3–6.

28. Charles Darwin, *The Origin of the Species and The Descent of Man* (New York: Modern Library, 1936), pp. 530–31, 539, 541, 543, 552 n. 57, 556; Herbert Spencer, *The Study of Sociology* (New York: Appleton, 1874), p. 338; I. A. Newby, *Jim Crow's Defense: Anti-Negro Thought in America, 1900–1930* (Baton Rouge: Louisiana State University Press, 1965), pp. 12–3; Anders Stephanson, *Manifest Destiny: American Expansionism and the Empire of Right* (New York: Hill & Wang, 1995), pp. 81, 84.

29. Foner, *Reconstruction*, pp. 488–511.

30. *Blyew et al. v. United States*, 80 U.S. 581, 591–4, 598–601 (1873).

31. *Slaughter-House Cases*, 16 Wall. 36, 83 U.S. 394 (1873); Robert J. Kaczorowski, *The Politics of Judicial Interpretation: The Federal Courts, Department of Justice and Civil Rights, 1866–1876* (Dobbs Ferry, N.Y.: Oceana Publications, 1985), pp. 158–66, 174–5.

32. *Slaughter-House Cases*, 16 Wall. at 403–5, 408–10, 415; Foner, *Reconstruction*, p. 530; William M. Wiecek, *Liberty Under Law: The Supreme Court in American Life* (Baltimore: Johns Hopkins University Press, 1988), pp. 114–6; Howard Gillman, *The Constitution Besieged: The Rise and Demise of Lochner Era Police Powers Jurisprudence* (Durham: Duke University Press, 1993), pp. 64–7.

33. On Miller's likely awareness of the ruling's ill consequences for blacks, see Rich-

ard L. Aynes, "Constricting the Law of Freedom: Justice Miller, the Fourteenth Amendment, and the *Slaughter-House Cases*," *Chicago-Kent Law Review* 70 (1994): 627–88. See also Kaczorowski, *The Politics of Judicial Interpretation*, pp. 143–66.

34. Gillette, *Retreat from Reconstruction*, p. 218.

35. Ibid., p. 256.

36. Ibid., p. 258.

37. Ibid., p. 217.

38. Ibid., p. 226.

39. Foner, *Reconstruction*, pp. 504–5, 532–4, 553–6; Michael W. McConnell, "Originalism and the Desegregation Decisions," *Virginia Law Review* 81 (1995): 987–90, 1049–86.

40. Gillette, *Retreat from Reconstruction*, p. 271.

41. Ibid., pp. 287–8.

42. Stuart Creighton Miller, *The Unwelcome Immigrant: The American Image of the Chinese, 1785–1882* (Berkeley: University of California Press, 1969), pp. 153–4, 159, 162, 173–77, 193–7; Foner, *Reconstruction*, pp. 553–6; Takaki, *A Different Mirror*, pp. 148–9, 209–13.

43. Gillette, *Retreat from Reconstruction*, p. 154.

44. Foner, *Reconstruction*, p. 559.

45. Gillette, *Retreat from Reconstruction*, pp. 159.

46. Foner, *Reconstruction*, p. 560.

47. *United States v. Cruikshank*, 92 U.S. 542, 551–9 (1876); Kaczorowski, *The Politics of Judicial Interpretation*, pp. 214–6.

48. *United States v. Reese*, 92 U.S. 214, 218–21 (1876); Hyman and Wiecek, *Equal Justice Under Law*, pp. 488–92; Kaczorowski, *The Politics of Judicial Interpretation*, pp. 199–204, 213–8, 226–7.

49. Richard Hofstadter and Beatrice K. Hofstadter, eds., *Great Issues in American History: From Reconstruction to the Present Day, 1864–1981* (New York: Vintage Books, 1982), pp. 44–6.

50. Gillette, *Retreat from Reconstruction*, p. 304.

51. Foner, *Reconstruction*, pp. 567–83; Du Bois, *Black Reconstruction in America*, pp. 691–3.

52. Foner, *Reconstruction*, p. 583.

53. Gillette, *Retreat from Reconstruction*, p. 348.

54. *Civil Rights Cases*, 190 U.S. 3, 13, 18–25 (1883).

55. Stephen J. Whitfield, *A Death in the Delta: The Story of Emmett Till* (New York: Free Press, 1988), p. 101.

56. Oshinsky, *Worse Than Slavery*, pp. 40–1.

57. Adolph Reed Jr., "Socializing Neo-Slavery," *Nation*, 6 May 1996.

58. Foner, *Reconstruction*, chap. 8.

59. *Ex parte Yarbrough*, 110 U.S. 651 (1884); Rayford W. Logan, *The Betrayal of the Negro; From Rutherford B. Hayes to Woodrow Wilson* (New York: Collier Books, 1965), pp. 43–5; Richard M. Valelly, "National Parties and Racial Disfranchisement," in *Classifying by Race*, ed. Paul E. Peterson (Princeton: Princeton University Press, 1995), pp. 197–9.

60. Vincent P. De Santis, "The Republican Party and the Southern Negro, 1877–1897," *Journal of Negro History* 45 (April 1960): 71–87.

61. *Congressional Record*, 51st Cong., 1st sess., p. 6543.

62. H. Wayne Morgan, *From Hayes to McKinley: National Party Politics, 1877–1896* (Syracuse: Syracuse University Press), p. 339.

63. Stanley P. Hirshson, *Farewell to the Bloody Shirt: Northern Republicans and the Southern Negro, 1877–1893* (Bloomington: Indiana University Press, 1966), p. 216.

64. Ibid., p. 222.

65. Ibid., p. 205.

66. R. Hal Williams, *Years of Decision: American Politics in the 1890s* (New York: John Wiley & Sons, 1978), p. 29.

67. Logan, *The Betrayal of the Negro*, pp. 65–89, 180–92; Newby, *Jim Crow's Defense,* pp. 14–5; C. Vann Woodward, *The Strange Career of Jim Crow,* 2d ed. (New York: Oxford University Press, 1966), pp. 90–2; J. Morgan Kousser, *The Shaping of Southern Politics: Suffrage Restriction and the Establishment of the One-Party South, 1880–1910* (New Haven: Yale University Press, 1974), pp. 27–9, 49, 241, 262.

68. John Hope Franklin and Alfred A. Moss Jr., *From Slavery to Freedom: A History of African Americans,* 7th ed. (New York: McGraw-Hill, 1994), p. 261.

69. Morgan, *From Hayes to McKinley,* p. 339.

70. *Congressional Record,* 47th Cong., 1st sess., pp. 1482–5, 1515–6, 1521–2, 1589, 2211; see also pp. 1581, 1636–7, 1645, 2126, 2207, 3267; Flexner, *Century of Struggle,* p. 177; Morton Keller, *Affairs of State: Public Life in Late Nineteenth Century America* (Cambridge: Harvard University Press, Belknap Press, 1977), pp. 133, 135, 267, 563; Tichenor, "The Liberal and Illiberal Traditions in America," p. 7.

71. Josiah Strong, *Our Country: Its Possible Future and Its Present Crisis* (New York: Baker & Taylor for the American Home Missionary Society, 1885), pp. 4–5, 14–5, 36, 43–5, 51–4, 61–2, 159–61, 165, 168, 179, 172–80, 218–9.

72. Thomas F. Gossett, *Race: The History of an Idea in America* (Dallas: Southern Methodist University Press, 1975), pp. 84–122; Newby, *Jim Crow's Defense,* pp. 52–4; John S. Haller, *Outcasts from Evolution: Scientific Attitudes of Racial Inferiority, 1859–1900* (Urbana: University of Illinois Press, 1971), pp. 121, 133; Stuart Anderson, *Race and Rapprochement: Anglo-Saxonism and Anglo-American Relations, 1895–1904* (Rutherford, N.J.: Fairleigh Dickinson University Press, 1981), pp. 42, 73–5.

73. *Congressional Record,* 54th Cong., 1st sess., pp. 2817–20; Newby, *Jim Crow's Defense,* p. 11; John Higham, *Strangers in the Land: Patterns of American Nativism 1860–1925* (New York: Atheneum Press, 1896), pp. 95–6, 101, 142, 149; Thomas G. Dyer, *Theodore Roosevelt and the Idea of Race* (Baton Rouge: Louisiana State University Press, 1980), p. 11.

74. Louis R. Harlan, *Booker T. Washington: The Making of a Black Leader, 1856–1901* (New York: Oxford University Press, 1972), pp. 60–1, 74, 204–22.

75. Ibid., pp. 218–9.

76. Louis R. Harlan, *Booker T. Washington: The Wizard of Tuskegee, 1901–1915* (New York: Oxford University Press, 1983), pp. vii–x, 32–3.

77. *Plessy v. Ferguson,* 163 U.S. 537, 550 (1896); Charles A. Lofgren, *The Plessy Case: a Legal-Historical Interpretation* (New York: Oxford University Press, 1987), pp. 110–1, 174–5.

78. Anderson, *Race and Rapprochement,* pp. 19–23; Nell Irvin Painter, *Standing at Armageddon: The United States 1877–1919* (New York: W. W. Norton & Co., 1987); Anders Stephanson, *Manifest Destiny: American Expansionism and the Empire of Right* (New York: Hill & Wang, 1995), pp. 67, 72, 77.

79. Harlan, *Booker T. Washington: The Making of a Black Leader,* pp. 236–37.

80. *Congressional Record,* 56th Cong., 1st sess., 1990, p. 711.

81. Stanley Karnow, *In Our Image: America's Empire in the Philippines* (New York: Random House, 1989), pp. 11, 109, 137, 164; A. Lawrence Lowell, "The Colonial Expansion of the United States," *Atlantic Monthly* 83 (1899): 146–50; A. Lawrence Lowell, "The Status of Our New Possessions—A Third View," *Harvard Law Review* 13 (1899): 156, 171, 176. See also Jose Cabranes, *Citizenship and the American Empire* (New Haven: Yale University Press,

1979), pp. 21, 80–101; Juan R. Torruella, *The Supreme Court and Puerto Rico: The Doctrine of Separate and Unequal* (Rio Piedras: University of Puerto Rico Press, 1988), pp. 30, 85–100; *The Insular Cases*, 182 U.S. 1 (1901); *Hawaii v. Mankichi*, 190 U.S. 197 (1903); *Balzac v. Porto Rico*, 258 U.S. 298, 308–11 (1922).

82. James M. McPherson, *The Abolitionist Legacy: From Reconstruction to the NAACP* (Princeton: Princeton University Press, 1975), p. 305.

83. Newby, *Jim Crow's Defense*, p. 69; Harlan, *Booker T. Washington: The Making of a Black Leader*, pp. 58, 244–51; Harlan, *Booker T. Washington: The Wizard of Tuskegee*, pp. 36, 50–3, 84–106, 360–78; Walter L. Williams, "United States Indian Policy and the Debate over Philippine Annexation: Implications for the Origins of American Imperialism," *Journal of American History* 66 (1980): 810, 816–7, 823–4, 829; Glenn A. May, *Social Engineering in the Philippines: The Aims, Execution, and Impact of American Colonial Policy, 1900–1913* (Westport, Conn.: Greenwood Press, 1980), pp. 9–10, 14, 89–93, 111–25; Francis Paul Prucha, *The Great Father: The United States Government and the American Indians* (Lincoln: University of Nebraska Press, 1984), pp. 763–70; Frederick E. Hoxie, *A Final Promise: The Campaign to Assimilate the Indians, 1880–1920* (Lincoln: University of Nebraska Press, 1984), pp. 96–107, 122–3, 198–210; Karnow, *In Our Image*, pp. 173–4, 242–56; and Raymond A. Cook, *Thomas Dixon* (New York: Twayne Publishers, 1974), p. 75.

84. *Giles v. Harris*, 189 U.S. 475 (1903); *Giles v. Teasley*, 193 U.S. 146 (1904); Kousser, *The Shaping of Southern Politics*, pp. 49, 241, 260–2; Benno C. Schmidt Jr., "Principle and Prejudice: The Supreme Court and Race in the Progressive Era. Part 3: Black Disfranchisement from the KKK to the Grandfather Clause," *Columbia Law Review* 82 (1982): 846–7; Harlan, *Booker T. Washingtion: The Wizard of Tuskegee*, pp. 245–7.

85. Logan, *The Betrayal of the Negro*, pp. 100–1.

86. Theodore Roosevelt, "The Negro Problem," (address to the Lincoln dinner of the Republican Club of the city of New York, February 13, 1905), in *The Works of Theodore Roosevelt*, memorial ed., vol. 43 (New York: Charles Scribner's Sons, 1925), pp. 460–75; Harlan, *Booker T. Washington: The Making of a Black Leader*, 311–23; Harlan, *Booker T. Washington: The Wizard of Tuskegee*, pp. 7, 309–10, 319–20; Dyer, *Theodore Roosevelt and the Idea of Race*, pp. 102–9; Desmond King, *Separate and Unequal: Black Americans and the US Federal Government* (Oxford: Clarendon Press, 1995), pp. 6–7.

CHAPTER FOUR

1. James L. Crouthamel, "The Springfield Race Riot of 1908," *Journal of Negro History* 47 (1962): 164–81.

2. John Hope Franklin and Alfred A. Moss Jr., *From Slavery to Freedom: A History of Negro Americans*, 7th ed. (New York: McGraw-Hill, 1994), pp. 316–7; Mary Ellison, *The Black Experience: American Blacks since 1965* (New York: Harper & Row, 1974), pp. 71–3.

3. Robert C. Bannister Jr., *Ray Stannard Baker: The Mind and Thought of a Progressive* (New Haven: Yale University Press, 1966), p. ix; Dewey W. Grantham, introduction to *Following the Colour Line*, by Ray Stannard Baker (New York: Harper & Row, 1908, 1964), p. vii.

4. Baker, *Following the Colour Line*, pp. 240, 302–5.

5. Eli Ginzburg and Alfred S. Eichner, *Troublesome Presence: Democracy and Black Americans* (New Brunswick, N.J.: Transaction Publishers, 1964, 1993), p. 273.

6. Leon F. Litwack, *Trouble In Mind: Black Southerners in the Age of Jim Crow* (New York: Knopf, 1998), p. 372.

7. Woodrow Wilson, *The State: Elements of Historical and Practical Politics*, rev. ed. (Boston:

D. C. Heath, 1918), pp. 1–2 (Wilson's editor in 1918, Edward Elliott, explicitly contended that the sections from which these quotes derive, though "written thirty years ago . . . represent substantially President Wilson's views to-day" [p. iii]); Louis R. Harlan, *Booker T. Washington: The Wizard of Tuskegee, 1901–1915* (New York: Oxford University Press, 1983), pp. 338–43; Ido Oren, "The Subjectivity of the 'Democratic' Peace: Changing U.S. Perceptions of Imperial Germany," *International Security* 20 (1995): 169–71.

8. Woodrow Wilson, *Reunion and Nationalization*, vol. 5 of *A History of the American People* (New York: Harper & Brothers, 1902), pp. 50, 58–62, 136.

9. Kenneth O'Reilly, *Nixon's Piano: Presidents and Racial Politics from Washington to Clinton* (New York: Free Press, 1995), p. 83.

10. Michael Paul Rogin, " 'The Sword Became a Flashing Vision': D.W. Griffith's *The Birth of a Nation*," in *Ronald Reagan, the Movie and Other Episodes in Political Demonology* (Berkeley: University of California Press, 1987), p. 192; Thomas R. Cripps, "The Reaction of the Negro to the Motion Picture Birth of a Nation," in *The Making of Black America: Essays in Negro Life and History*, ed. August Meier and Elliot Rudwick (New York: Atheneum, 1969), p. 152. Dixon claimed that his purpose with the film was "to revolutionize Northern sentiments by a presentation of history that would transform every man in the audience into a good Democrat!" He later told Wilson once the film was seen "there will never be an issue on your segregation policy" (Cripps, pp. 152–3). Even as late as the mid-1970s, the film was still being shown—absent any commentary or explanation—on television.

11. Ray Stannard Baker, *Woodrow Wilson: Life and Letters, President, 1913–1914*, vol. 4 (Garden City, N.Y.: Doubleday, Doran, 1931), p. 222.

12. David W. Blight, "Quarrel Forgotten or a Revolution Remembered? Reunion and Race in the Memory of the Civil War, 1875–1913," in David W. Blight and Brooks D. Simpson, *Union and Emancipation: Essays on Politics and Race in the Civil War Era* (Kent, Ohio: Kent State University Press, 1997), pp. 175–6.

13. I. A. Newby, *Jim Crow's Defense: Anti-Negro Thought in America, 1900–1930* (Baton Rouge: Louisiana State University Press, 1965), p. 167; Harlan, *Booker T. Washington*, pp. 406–11; Nell Irvin Painter, *Standing at Armageddon: The United States 1877–1919* (New York: W. W. Norton & Co., 1987), pp. 278–9; Desmond King, *Separate and Unequal: Black Americans and the US Federal Government* (Oxford: Clarendon Press, 1995), pp. 9–17.

14. E. David Cronon, *Black Moses: The Story of Marcus Garvey and the Universal Negro Improvement Association* (Madison: University of Wisconsin Press, 1955, 1969), pp. 27–8.

15. Meirion Harries and Susie Harries, *The Last Days of Innocence: America at War, 1917–1918* (New York: Random House, 1997), p. 106.

16. Leonard P. Ayres, *The War with Germany: A Statistical Summary* (Washington, D.C.: Government Printing Office, 1919), pp. 13, 90–1. In contrast, Great Britain withstood over four years of bloody fighting and far more extensive mobilization than did the United States during World War I. Consequently, the sacrifices of the working class and women played a crucial role in the expansion of the suffrage to these groups after the war. In fact, between 1910 and 1918, the British electorate grew from 8 to 21 million. Furthermore, these sacrifices also led to a more progressive tax system and an expansion of welfare state benefits. See Trevor Wilson, *The Myriad Faces of War: Britain and the Great War, 1914–1918* (Cambridge, U.K.: Polity Press, 1986), pp. 663–76 and 799–803.

17. David W. Southern, *The Malignant Heritage: Yankee Progressives and the Negro Question, 1901–1914* (Chicago: Loyola University Press, 1968), pp. 32–54.

18. Theodore Kornweibel Jr., "Apathy and Dissent: Black America's Negative Responses to World War I," *South Atlantic Quarterly* 80 (summer 1981): 325.

19. David M. Kennedy, *Over Here: The First World War and American Society* (New York: Oxford University Press, 1980), pp. 279–80; Ronald Schaffer, *America in the Great War: The Rise of the War Welfare State* (New York: Oxford University Press, 1991), pp. 78–9, 81.

20. David Levering Lewis, *W. E. B. Du Bois: Biography of a Race, 1868–1919* (New York: Henry Holt, 1993), pp. 528–31, 556. Lewis pointed out that Du Bois's burst of enthusiasm for the war was prompted in part by the promise, never fulfilled, of an officer's commission in the military intelligence section dealing with "Negro subversion." Lewis, pp. 552–60.

21. Harries and Harries, *The Last Days of Innocence*, p. 168.

22. Schaffer, *America in the Great War*, p. 80.

23. Ibid., pp. 84–9; Cronon, *Black Moses*, p. 29; Sean Dennis Cashman, *African Americans and the Quest for Civil Rights, 1900–1990* (New York: New York University Press, 1991), p. 27.

24. Carl Campbell Brigham, *A Study of American Intelligence* (Princeton: Princeton University Press, 1923), pp. 182, 190, 192, 197, 208–10; Stephen Jay Gould, *The Mismeasure of Man* (New York: W. W. Norton, 1981), pp. 192–233.

25. Franklin and Moss, *From Slavery to Freedom*, p. 347.

26. Ibid., pp. 347–8; Cashman, *African Americans and the Quest for Civil Rights*, p. 31.

27. James R. Grossman, "Blowing the Trumpet: The *Chicago Defender* and Black Migration during World War I," in *The Great Migration and After, 1917–1930*, ed. Kenneth L. Kustner (New York: Garland Publishing, 1991), p. 2; Cronon, *Black Moses*, pp. 22–25; Cashman, *African Americans and the Quest for Civil Rights*, p. 26, has somewhat lower estimates of the population shifts than older sources.

28. Franklin and Moss, *From Slavery to Freedom*, p. 353.

29. Ibid., pp. 350–1; Cronon, *Black Moses*, pp. 31–3; Theodore G. Vincent, *Black Power and the Garvey Movement* (New York: Ramparts Press, 1971), pp. 34–5; Douglas S. Massey and Nancy A. Denton, *American Apartheid: Segregation and the Making of the Underclass* (Cambridge: Harvard University Press, 1993), p. 35.

30. Massey and Denton, *American Apartheid*, pp. 20–30.

31. Vincent, *Black Power and the Garvey Movement*, pp. 114–5.

32. Ibid., pp. 33, 43, 45, 60, 151; Cronon, *Black Moses*, pp. 36–45.

33. Richard B. Sherman, *The Republican Party and Black America: From McKinley to Hoover, 1896–1933* (Charlottesville: University Press of Virginia, 1973), pp. 137, 139.

34. Francis Russell, *The Shadow of Blooming Grove: Warren G. Harding in His Times* (New York: McGraw-Hill, 1968), pp. 26, 39–40, 403–5; Geoffrey C. Ward, *A First-Class Temperament: The Emergence of Franklin Roosevelt* (New York: Harper & Row, 1989), pp. 547–8, 557–8.

35. Sherman, *The Republican Party and Black America*, pp. 149, 196; Cronon, *Black Moses*, pp. 194–5.

36. Cronon, *Black Moses*, pp. 189–91; Vincent, *Black Power and the Garvey Movement*, pp. 190–1, 209–11.

37. Horace M. Kallen, *Culture and Democracy in the United States* (New York: Boni and Liveright, 1924), p. 43; John Higham, *Send These to Me: Jews and Other Immigrants in Urban America* (New York: Atheneum, 1975), pp. 203–8, 212–3; Werner Sollors, "A Critique of Pure Pluralism," in *Reconstructing American Literary History*, ed. Sacvan Bercovitch (Cambridge: Harvard University Press, 1986), pp. 258–73.

38. Kallen, *Culture and Democracy in the United States*, p. 226; Higham, *Send These to Me*,

p. 208; Sollors, "A Critique of Pure Pluralism," pp. 260—1, 270—3; J. Christopher Eisele, "John Dewey and the Immigrants," *History of Education Quarterly* 15 (1975): 71—2.

39. Cashman, *African Americans and the Quest for Civil Rights*, pp. 22—3; *Buchanan v. Warley*, 245 U.S. 60 (1917) (banning laws imposing residential segregation); *Guinn v. United States*, 238 U.S. 347 (1915) (banning grandfather clauses).

40. See, e.g., *Corrigan v. Buckley*, 271 U.S. 323 (1926) (sustaining private racial discrimination in housing); *Grovey v. Townsend*, 295 U.S. 45 (1935) (sustaining a Democratic Party, rather than state-run, white primary).

41. Cashman, *African Americans and the Quest for Civil Rights*, pp. 22, 33; Mark V. Tushnet, *The NAACP's Legal Strategy against Segregated Education, 1925—1950* (Chapel Hill: University of North Carolina Press, 1987), pp. 1—10.

42. Dewey cited and discussed in Rogers M. Smith, *Civic Ideals: Conflicting Visions of Citizenship in U.S. History* (New Haven: Yale University Press, 1997), pp. 420—1.

43. Smith, *Civic Ideals*, pp. 420—1.

44. Sherman, *The Republican Party and Black America*, pp. 206—8; David M. Chalmers, *Hooded Americanism: The First Century of the Ku Klux Klan, 1865—1965* (Garden City, N.Y.: Doubleday, 1965), pp. 286—8; and John M. Barry, *Rising Tide: The Great Mississippi Flood of 1927 and How It Changed America* (New York: Simon & Schuster, 1997), p. 154.

45. Harvard Sitkoff, *The Depression Decade*, vol. 1 of *A New Deal for Blacks: The Emergence of Civil Rights as a National Issue* (New York: Oxford University Press, 1978), p. 28.

46. Donald J. Lisio, *Hoover, Blacks, and Lily-Whites* (Chapel Hill: University of North Carolina Press, 1985), pp. 3—20; Barry, *Rising Tide*, pp. 303—35, 365—95, 412—5.

47. Nancy J. Weiss, *Farewell to the Party of Lincoln: Black Politics in the Age of FDR* (Princeton: Princeton University Press, 1983), p. 8.

48. Sherman, *The Republican Party and Black America*, pp. 233—9.

49. Ibid., p. 247; Sitkoff, *The Depression Decade*, p. 33.

50. Sitkoff, *The Depression Decade*, pp. 34—9.

51. Weiss, *Farewell to the Party of Lincoln*, pp. 25—6.

52. Ibid., pp. 19—20; Richard B. Sherman, "The Harding Administration and the Negro: An Opportunity Lost," *Journal of Negro History* 44 (July 1964): 153; Dewey W. Grantham, *The South in Modern America: A Region at Odds* (New York: HarperPerennial, 1994), p. 118.

53. Franklin and Moss, *From Slavery to Freedom*, p. 398; Weiss, *Farewell to the Party of Lincoln*, pp. 205—8, 212; Sitkoff, *The Depression Decade*, p. 95.

54. Roger Biles, *A New Deal for the American People* (DeKalb: Northern Illinois University Press, 1991), p. 179.

55. Ibid., p. 176; Sitkoff, *The Depression Decade*, pp. 52—5. The NRA also had novelist Thomas Dixon tour the country to expound on its achievements. Raymond A. Cook, *Thomas Dixon* (New York: Twayne Publishers, 1974), p. 127.

56. Biles, *A New Deal for the American People*, p. 179; Massey and Denton, *American Apartheid*, pp. 51—5. For a brilliant analysis of the impact on housing segregation on the development of current racial politics, see Thomas Sugrue, *The Origins of the Urban Crisis: Race and Inequality in Postwar Detroit* (Princeton: Princeton University Press, 1996).

57. Robert C. Lieberman, "Race and the Organization of Welfare Policy," in *Classifying by Race*, ed. Paul E. Peterson (Princeton: Princeton University Press, 1995), p. 173; Weiss, *Farewell to the Party of Lincoln*, p. 166; Theda Skocpol, "African Americans in U.S. Social Policy," in *Classifying by Race*, ed. Peterson, pp. 142—3; Dona Cooper Hamilton and Charles V. Hamilton, "The Dual Agenda of African American Organizations since the New Deal: Social Welfare Policies and Civil Rights," *Political Science Quarterly* 107 (fall 1992): 440.

58. Lieberman, "Race and the Organization of Welfare Policy," pp. 182–3; Skocpol, "African Americans in U.S. Social Policy," pp. 143–4; and Jill Quadagno, "From Old-Age Assistance to Supplemental Security Income: The Political Economy of Relief in the South, 1935–1972," in *The Politics of Social Policy in the United States,* ed. Margaret Weir, Ann Shola Orloff, and Theda Skocpol (Princeton: Princeton University Press, 1988), pp. 239–47.

59. Robert C. Weaver, *Negro Labor: A National Problem* (New York: Harcourt, Brace, 1946), p. 15; and Weiss, *Farewell to the Party of Lincoln,* p. 269.

60. Gary Gerstle, "The Protean Character of American Liberalism," *American Historical Review* 99 (October 1994): 1058–9.

61. Peter J. Kellogg, "Northern Liberals and Black America: A History of White Attitudes, 1936–1952" (Ph.D. diss., Northwestern University, 1971), p. 3. Also see Gerstle, "The Protean Character of American Liberalism," pp. 1068–9; John B. Kirby, "The Roosevelt Administration and Blacks: An Ambivalent Legacy," in *Twentieth-Century America: Recent Interpretations,* ed. Barton J. Bernstein and Allen J. Matusow, 2d ed. (New York: Harcourt Brace Jovanovich, 1969, 1972), pp. 270–2; Alan Brinkley, *The End of Reform: New Deal Liberalism in Recession and War* (New York: Knopf, 1995), pp. 165–6.

62. Weiss, *Farewell to the Party of Lincoln,* pp. 56, 106.

63. Kellogg, "Northern Liberals and Black America," pp. 1–123; and Weiss, *Farewell to the Party of Lincoln,* p. 250.

64. Weiss, *Farewell to the Party of Lincoln,* pp. 257–65.

65. Ibid., p. 266.

66. Harold L. Ickes, *The Inside Struggle, 1936–1939,* vol. 2 of *The Secret Diary of Harold L. Ickes* (New York: Simon & Schuster, 1954), p. 115.

67. John Egerton, *Speak Now against the Day: The Generation before the Civil Rights Movement in the South* (New York: Knopf, 1994), pp. 193–4.

68. C. Vann Woodward, *The Strange Career of Jim Crow,* 2d rev. ed. (New York: Oxford University Press, 1955, 1966), pp. 117–8.

69. Sitkoff's *The Depression Decade* provides the fullest statement of this view, but also see Patricia Sullivan, *Days of Hope: Race and Democracy in the New Deal Era* (Chapel Hill: University of North Carolina Press, 1996).

70. Egerton, *Speak Now against the Day,* p. 110.

71. Cook, *Thomas Dixon,* pp. 88–90; Sitkoff, *The Depression Decade,* p. 106; Weiss, *Farewell to the Party of Lincoln,* p. 161; William Anderson, *The Wild Man from Sugar Creek: The Political Career of Eugene Talmadge* (Baton Rouge: Louisiana State University Press, 1975), pp. 136–40.

72. Sitkoff, *The Depression Decade,* p. 114; George B. Tindall, *The Emergence of the New South, 1913–1945* (Baton Rouge: Louisiana State University Press, 1967), pp. 620–1; John R. Moore, "Senator Josiah Bailey and the 'Conservative Manifesto' of 1937," *Journal of Southern History* 31 (February 1965): 21–39.

73. Robert L. Zangrando, *The NAACP Crusade against Lynching, 1909–1950* (Philadelphia: Temple University Press, 1980), p. 150; George C. Rable, "The South and the Politics of Anti-Lynching Legislation, 1920–1940," *Journal of Southern History* 51 (May 1985): 217.

74. Zangrando, *The NAACP Crusade against Lynching,* pp. 151–3; Tindall, *The Emergence of the New South,* pp. 553–4; *Congressional Record,* 75th Cong., 3d sess. (February 16, 1938), p. 2007.

75. Martin Dies, *The Trojan Horse in America* (New York: Dodd, Mead, 1940), pp. 119–20.

76. Sitkoff, *The Depression Decade*, p. 115–6; Alan Brinkley, "The New Deal and Southern Politics," in *The New Deal and the South*, ed. James C. Cobb and Michael V. Namorato (Jackson: University Press of Mississippi, 1984), p. 109.

77. Gunnar Myrdal, *An American Dilemma*, vol. 2 (New York: McGraw-Hill, 1944, 1964), p. 755.

CHAPTER FIVE

1. Jeffrey T. Sammons, "Boxing as a Reflection of Society: The Southern Reaction to Joe Louis," *Journal of Popular Culture* 16 (spring 1983): 27.

2. John Higham, *Send These to Me: Jews and Other Immigrants in Urban America* (New York: Atheneum, 1975), p. 58.

3. Carl N. Degler, *In Search of Human Nature: The Decline and Revival of Darwinism in American Social Thought* (New York: Oxford University Press, 1991), pp. 176–211; quotations from 203.

4. Gary Gerstle, "The Protean Character of American Liberalism," *American Historical Review* 99 (October 1994): 1070; Harvard Sitkoff, *The Depression Decade*, vol. 1 of *A New Deal for Blacks: The Emergence of Civil Rights as a National Issue* (New York: Oxford University Press, 1978), pp. 122, 162–3.

5. Sitkoff, *The Depression Decade*, pp. 117, 122–3, 172–3, 287.

6. Arthur R. Ashe Jr., *A Hard Road to Glory: A History of the African-American Athlete, 1919–1945*, vol. 2 (New York: Amistad Press, 1988, 1993), pp. 3, 107.

7. David Wallechinsky, *The Complete Book of the Olympics* (New York: Penguin Books, 1984), pp. 6–7, 13, 63, 84; and Sammons, "Boxing as a Reflection of Society," p. 28. After the Olympics, however, Owens, having served his purpose, was promptly ignored by white sports fans. For a time he was reduced to racing horses in degrading exhibitions to make a living.

8. Chris Mead, *Champion: Joe Louis, Black Hero in White America* (New York: Charles Scribner's Sons, 1985), pp. 23, 30; Roi Ottley, *"New World A-Coming": Inside Black America* (Boston: Houghton Mifflin, 1943), p. 193; Rayford W. Logan, *The Betrayal of the Negro: From Rutherford B. Hayes to Woodrow Wilson* (London: Collier-Macmillan, 1965), p. 364.

9. Al-Tony Gilmore, "The Myth, Legend, and Folklore of Joe Louis: The Impression of Sport on Society," *South Atlantic Quarterly* 82 (summer 1983): 258.

10. Mark D. Coburn, "America's Great Black Hope," *American Heritage*, October–November 1978, p. 85; Mead, *Champion*, pp. 67, 87.

11. James A. Cox, "The Day Joe Louis Fired the Shots Heard 'Round the World," *Smithsonian*, November 1988, p. 172; Mead, *Champion*, pp. 99–100; Brenda Gayle Plummer, *Rising Wind: Black Americans and U.S. Foreign Affairs, 1935–1960* (Chapel Hill: University of North Carolina Press, 1996), p. 42; and Coburn, "America's Great Black Hope," p. 87.

12. Mead, *Champion*, pp. 132, 141.

13. Coburn, "America's Great Black Hope," p. 88; Mead, *Champion*, pp. 132–45; and Cox, "The Day Joe Louis Fired the Shots Heard 'Round the World," pp. 172, 188–9.

14. Dominic J. Capeci Jr. and Martha Wilkerson, "Multifarious Hero: Joe Louis, American Society and Race Relations during World Crisis, 1935–1945," *Journal of Sport History* 10 (winter 1983): 11; Anthony O. Edmunds, "The Second Louis-Schmeling Fight—Sport, Symbol, and Culture," *Journal of Popular Culture* 7 (summer 1973): 45.

15. Coburn, "America's Great Black Hope," p. 90.

16. Mead, *Champion*, p. 158; Edmunds, "The Second Louis-Schmeling Fight—Sport, Symbol, and Culture," pp. 47–8.

17. Mead, *Champion*, p. 154; Cox, "The Day Joe Louis Fired the Shots Heard 'Round the World," p. 192.

18. Mead, *Champion*, p. 158.

19. These figures offer only a conservative estimate of readership, since many of these papers were saved and passed from one person to another. Lee Finkle, *Forum for Protest: The Black Press in World War II* (Rutherford, N.J.: Associated University Presses, 1975), pp. 51–4.

20. Sitkoff, *The Depression Decade*, p. 262.

21. Ibid.

22. Francis L. Broderick and August Meier, eds., *Negro Protest Thought in the Twentieth Century* (Indianapolis: Bobbs-Merrill Company, 1965), p. 183.

23. August Meier and Elliot Rudwick, "The Origins of Nonviolent Direct Action in Afro-American Protest: A Note on Historical Discontinuities," in *Along the Color Line: Explorations in the Black Experience*, ed. August Meier and Elliot Rudwick (Urbana: University of Illinois Press, 1976), pp. 314–32; Lawrence S. Wittner, "The National Negro Conference: A Reassessment," *American Quarterly* 22 (winter 1970): 883–901; and Sitkoff, *The Depression Decade*, pp. 257–63.

24. Meier and Rudwick, "The Origins of Nonviolent Direct Action in Afro-American Protest," p. 314; Lerone Bennett Jr., *Confrontation: Black and White* (Baltimore, Md.: Penguin Books, 1965), p. 142.

25. Cheryl Greenberg, "The Politics of Disorder: Reexamining Harlem's Riots of 1935 and 1943," *Journal of Urban History* 18 (August 1992): 407–8; John Hope Franklin and Alfred A. Moss Jr., *From Slavery to Freedom: A History of Negro Americans*, 7th ed. (New York: McGraw-Hill, 1994), p. 400.

26. Franklin and Moss, *From Slavery to Freedom*, p. 400; Greenberg, "The Politics of Disorder," pp. 418–9; and Cheryl Greenberg, *"Or Does It Explode?" Black Harlem in the Great Depression* (New York: Oxford University Press, 1991), p. 5.

27. Sitkoff, *The Depression Decade*, p. 210; August Meier and Elliot M. Rudwick, *From Plantation to Ghetto: An Interpretative History of American Negroes* (New York: Hill and Wang, 1966), p. 210.

28. *The Collected Poems of Langston Hughes*, ed. Arnold Rampersad and David Roessel (New York: Knopf, 1994), p. 135.

29. Barbara Dianne Savage, "Broadcasting Freedom: Radio, War, and the Roots of Civil Rights Liberalism, 1938–1948" (Ph.D. diss., Yale University, 1995), pp. 127–8.

30. James MacGregor Burns, *Roosevelt: The Lion and the Fox* (New York: Harcourt Brace Jovanovich, 1956), p. 395.

31. Only 2 percent wanted the Axis to win and 14 percent had no opinion. William E. Leuchtenberg, *Franklin Roosevelt and the New Deal, 1932–1940* (New York: Harper & Row, 1963), p. 293.

32. Robert A. Divine, *The Reluctant Belligerent: American Entry into World War II*, 2d ed. (New York: John Wiley and Sons, 1965, 1979), p. 103; U.S. Bureau of the Census, *Historical Statistics of the United States: Colonial Times to 1970*, Part 2 (Washington, D.C.: Government Printing Office, 1975), pp. 1115–6.

33. Doris Kearns Goodwin, *No Ordinary Time: Franklin and Eleanor Roosevelt: The Home Front in World War II* (New York: Simon & Schuster, 1994), p. 60.

34. Ronald Takaki, *A Different Mirror: A History of Multicultural America* (Boston: Little, Brown, 1993), p. 374.

35. Philip Gleason, "Americans All: World War II and the Shaping of American Identity," *Review of Politics* 43 (1981): 502. For an interesting examination of the role that such

moral arguments played in the success of the Allies in World War II, see Richard Overy, *Why the Allies Won* (New York: W. W. Norton, 1995), pp. 282–313.

36. Selden Menefee, *Assignment: U.S.A.* (New York: Reynal and Hitchcock, 1943), p. 168.

37. Morris J. MacGregor Jr., *Integration of the Armed Forces, 1940–1965* (Washington, D.C.: Center of Military History, 1981), p. 9.

38. Sitkoff, *The Depression Decade*, p. 301.

39. Goodwin, *No Ordinary Time*, pp. 169–70. Also see Ulysses Lee, *The United States Army in World War II, Special Studies: The Employment of Negro Troops* (Washington, D.C.: Government Printing Office, 1966), p. 44.

40. Quaker Oats Company, "Dick Tracy's Secret Detective Methods and Magic Tricks" (Chicago, 1939).

41. Neil A. Wynn, "The Impact of the Second World War on the American Negro," *Journal of Contemporary History* 6 (November 1971): 44; Goodwin, *No Ordinary Time*, p. 165.

42. Morris J. MacGregor and Bernard C. Nalty, *Black Soldiers in World War II*, vol. 5 of *Blacks in the United States Armed Forces: Basic Documents* (Wilmington, Del.: Scholarly Resources, 1977), p. 48. Ironically, the process of plasma transfusions was first pioneered by a black man, Dr. Charles R. Drew.

43. Ottley, *"New World A-Coming,"* p. 290.

44. Neil A. Wynn, *The Afro-American and the Second World War*, rev. ed. (New York: Holmes and Meier, 1975, 1993), pp. 40–41; Robert C. Weaver, *Negro Labor: A National Problem* (New York: Harcourt, Brace, 1946), pp. 15, 109.

45. Weaver, *Negro Labor*, pp. 18–9.

46. Louis Coleridge Kesselman, *The Social Politics of the FEPC: A Study in Reform Pressure Movements* (Chapel Hill: University of North Carolina Press, 1948), pp. 9–10.

47. Weaver, *Negro Labor*, p. 131.

48. Ibid.

49. Wynn, *The Afro-American and the Second World War*, pp. 40–1.

50. Sitkoff, *The Depression Decade*, p. 301.

51. Richard M. Dalfiume, *Desegregation of the U.S. Armed Forces: Fighting on Two Fronts, 1939–1953* (Columbia: University of Missouri Press, 1969), p. 27.

52. Bernard C. Nalty, *Strength for the Fight: A History of Black Americans in the Military* (New York: Free Press, 1986), p. 134.

53. Kenneth Robert Janken, *Rayford W. Logan and the Dilemma of the African-American Intellectual* (Amherst: University of Massachusetts Press, 1993), pp. 116–9; Nalty, *Strength for the Fight*, p. 132; Sitkoff, *The Depression Decade*, p. 302.

54. Wynn, *The Afro-American and the Second World War*, pp. 22–3.

55. Goodwin, *No Ordinary Time*, p. 168.

56. R. J. C. Butow, "The FDR Tapes: Secret Recordings Made in the Oval Office of the President in the Autumn of 1940," *American Heritage* 33 (February/March 1982): 23–4.

57. Ibid.

58. "Report of the Conference at the White House, 27 September 1940," in Bernard C. Nalty and Morris J. MacGregor, *Blacks in the Military: Essential Documents* (Wilmington, Del.: Scholarly Resources, 1981), pp. 104–5; Butow, "The FDR Tapes," p. 24.

59. Butow, "The FDR Tapes," p. 24.

60. Goodwin, *No Ordinary Time*, p. 169.

61. Dalfiume, *Desegregation of the U.S. Armed Forces*, p. 39.

62. Walter White, *A Man Called White* (New York: Viking Press, 1948), p. 187. The "stab in the back" comment was taken from Roosevelt's denunciation of Italy's attack on France earlier in the year.

63. Goodwin, *No Ordinary Time*, p. 171.

64. Jack D. Foner, *Blacks and the Military in American History: A New Perspective* (New York: Praeger Publishers, 1974), p. 139.

65. Nancy J. Weiss, *Farewell to the Party of Lincoln: Black Politics in the Age of FDR* (Princeton: Princeton University Press, 1983), pp. 271–82; Donald Bruce Johnson, comp., *National Party Platforms: Volume 1, 1840–1956*, rev. ed. (Urbana: University of Illinois Press, 1956, 1978), p. 393. The Democratic platform also included a section on blacks, stating, in part, "We shall continue to strive for complete legislative safeguards against discrimination in government service and benefits, and in the national defense forces." Although less forceful than the Republicans, this statement represents the Democrats' first ever positive utterance regarding civil rights. Johnson, p. 387.

66. Dalfiume, *Desegregation of the U.S. Armed Forces*, p. 40.

67. Goodwin, *No Ordinary Time*, p. 171.

68. White, *A Man Called White*, p. 188.

69. Goodwin, *No Ordinary Time*, p. 171.

70. Ibid., p. 172.

71. Weiss, *Farewell to the Party of Lincoln*, pp. 286–9.

72. Herbert Garfinkel, *When Negroes March: The March on Washington Movement in the Organizational Politics for FEPC* (Glencoe, Ill.: Free Press, 1959), p. 38.

73. Janken, *Rayford W. Logan and the Dilemma of the African-American Intellectual*, p. 121.

74. Dalfiume, *Desegregation of the U.S. Armed Forces*, pp. 115–6.

75. Goodwin, *No Ordinary Time*, p. 247.

76. Jervis Anderson, *A. Philip Randolph: A Biographical Portrait* (New York: Harcourt Brace Jovanovich, 1972, 1973), pp. 247–8.

77. Ibid., pp. 248–9.

78. Goodwin, *No Ordinary Time*, p. 248.

79. Anderson, *A. Philip Randolph*, p. 249.

80. Ibid., p. 249.

81. Paula F. Pfeffer, *A. Philip Randolph, Pioneer of the Civil Rights Movement* (Baton Rouge: Louisiana State University Press, 1990), p. 47.

82. Ibid., p. 57.

83. Ibid., pp. 57–8.

84. Ibid.

85. Gibert Osofsky, *The Burden of Race: A Documentary History of Negro-White Relations in America* (New York: Harper & Row, 1967), pp. 398–9.

86. Goodwin, *No Ordinary Time*, p. 250.

87. Kenneth O'Reilly, *Nixon's Piano: President and Racial Politics from Washington to Clinton* (New York: Free Press, 1995), p. 132.

88. Anderson, *A. Philip Randolph*, p. 255.

89. The exchange between Randolph and Roosevelt comes from Anderson, *A. Philip Randolph*, pp. 256–8. Slightly different versions of this conversation are found in Goodwin, *No Ordinary Time*, pp. 251–2; Lerone Bennett Jr., *Confrontation: Black and White* (Baltimore, Md.: Penguin Books, 1965), pp. 150–1.

90. Anderson, *A. Philip Randolph*, p. 259.

91. Goodwin, *No Ordinary Time*, p. 253.

92. Ibid., p. 255; Janken, *Rayford W. Logan and the Dilemma of the African-American Intellectual*, pp. 129–30.

93. Osofsky, *The Burden of Race*, pp. 398–9.

CHAPTER SIX

1. Gordon W. Prange, *December 7, 1941: The Day the Japanese Attacked Pearl Harbor* (New York: McGraw-Hill, 1988), pp. 149, 153; Gordon W. Prange, *At Dawn We Slept: The Untold Story of Pearl Harbor* (New York: McGraw-Hill, 1981), pp. 514–5; Bernard C. Nalty, *Strength for the Fight: A History of Black Americans in the Military* (New York: Free Press, 1986), p. 186; Dennis D. Nelson, *The Integration of the Negro into the U.S. Navy* (New York: Octagon Books, 1982, 1951), p. 25.

2. The navy also defended its policy since "the white man refuses to admit the negro to intimate family relationships leading to marriage," though it did not state how common such relationships were among its men. Richard M. Dalfiume, *Desegregation of the U.S. Armed Forces: Fighting on Two Fronts, 1939–1953* (Columbia: University of Missouri Press, 1969), p. 55.

3. Doris Kearns Goodwin, *No Ordinary Time: Franklin and Eleanor Roosevelt: The Home Front in World War II* (New York: Simon & Schuster, 1994), p. 329.

4. Patrick S. Washburn, *A Question of Sedition: The Federal Government's Investigation of the Black Press during World War II* (New York: Oxford University Press, 1986), p. 53.

5. Ibid., p. 54.

6. Brenda Gayle Plummer, *Rising Wind: Black Americans and U.S. Foreign Affairs, 1935–1960* (Chapel Hill: University of North Carolina Press, 1996), p. 85.

7. Thomas Cripps, *Making Movies Black: The Hollywood Message Movies from World War II to the Civil Rights Era* (New York: Oxford University Press, 1993), pp. 58, 76.

8. Lou Cannon, *Reagan* (New York: G. P. Putnam's Sons, 1982), p. 20.

9. Dalfiume, *Desegregation of the U.S. Armed Forces*, p. 55; Frederick S. Harrod, "Integration of the Navy," *Proceedings* 105 (October 1979): 41–2.

10. Jack D. Foner, *Blacks and the Military in American History: A New Perspective* (New York: Praeger Publishers, 1974), p. 173, Prange, *December 7, 1941*, p. 148; and Nalty, *Strength for the Fight*, p. 186. In 1973, the navy honored Miller by naming a destroyer escort (DE 1091) for him. Morris J. MacGregor Jr., *Integration of the Armed Forces, 1940–1965* (Washington, D.C.: Center of Military History, 1981), p. 58.

11. In 1943, Congress repealed the Chinese Exclusion Acts, made persons of Chinese descent eligible for naturalization, and allowed China an annual immigration quota of 105 persons—an essentially symbolic acceptance of Chinese immigration, but significant nonetheless. David M. Reimers, *Still the Golden Door: The Third World Comes to America* (New York: Columbia University Press, 1985), pp. 14–5.

12. Neil A. Wynn, *The Afro-American and the Second World War*, rev. ed. (New York: Holmes and Meier, 1975, 1993), pp. 103–5.

13. Clayton R. Koppes and Gregory D. Black, "Blacks, Loyalty, and Motion-Picture Propaganda in World War II," *Journal of American History* 73 (September 1986): 386.

14. St. Clair Drake and Horace R. Cayton, *Black Metropolis: A Study of Negro Life in a Northern City* (Chicago: University of Chicago Press, 1945, 1993), p. 745.

15. Phillip McGuire, *Taps for a Jim Crow Army: Letters from Black Soldiers in World War II* (Santa Barbara, Calif.: ABC-Clio, 1983), pp. xlii–xliii.

16. Roi Ottley, *"New World A-Coming": Inside Black America* (Boston: Houghton Mifflin, 1943), p. 314.

17. Washburn, *A Question of Sedition*, pp. 54–6. Similarly, during the Civil War, Frederick Douglass had stressed blacks' need to fight a "double battle," the first a military one against the rebels and the second a social and political one against racism and discrimination. David W. Blight, *Frederick Douglass' Civil War: Keeping Faith in Jubilee* (Baton Rouge: Louisiana State University Press, 1989), p. 167.

18. Kenneth Robert Janken, *Rayford W. Logan and the Dilemma of the African-American Intellectual* (Amherst: University of Massachusetts Press, 1993), p. 131.

19. Richard M. Dalfiume, "The 'Forgotten Years' of the Negro Revolution," *Journal of American History* 55 (June 1968): 96–7.

20. Harvard Sitkoff, *The Depression Decade*, vol. 1 of *A New Deal for Blacks: The Emergence of Civil Rights as a National Issue* (New York: Oxford University Press, 1978), p. 325.

21. Paula F. Pfeffer, *A. Philip Randolph, Pioneer of the Civil Rights Movement* (Baton Rouge: Louisiana State University Press, 1990), pp. 51–2.

22. Jervis Anderson, *A. Philip Randolph: A Biographical Portrait* (New York: Harcourt Brace Jovanovich, 1972, 1973), pp. 264–5.

23. August Meier and Elliot Rudwick, *CORE: A Study in the Civil Rights Movement, 1942(1968* (New York: Oxford University Press, 1973), p. 4.

24. Harvard Sitkoff, "American Blacks in World War II: Rethinking the Militancy-Watershed Hypothesis," in *The Home Front and War in the Twentieth Century: The American Experience in Comparative Perspective* (proceedings of the Tenth Military History Symposium, October 20–22, 1982, United States Air Force Academy), ed. James Titus (Washington, D.C.: Government Printing Office, 1984), pp. 147–55.

25. Dalfiume, "The 'Forgotten Years' of the Negro Revolution," p. 102.

26. Sitkoff, *The Depression Decade*, p. 324.

27. Wynn, *The Afro-American and the Second World War*, p. 131.

28. Drake and Cayton, *Black Metropolis*, p. 754.

29. Harvard Sitkoff, "Racial Militancy and Interracial Violence in the Second World War," *Journal of American History* 58 (December 1971): 667.

30. Approximately 75 percent of military training facilities for blacks were found in the South. Daniel Kryder, "F.D.R.'s Department of War and Black Americans" (paper presented at the annual meeting of the American Political Science Association, Chicago, August 31–September 3, 1995), p. 8.

31. Drake and Cayton, *Black Metropolis*, p. 754.

32. Kryder, "F.D.R.'s Department of War and Black Americans," pp. 21–2.

33. McGuire, *Taps for a Jim Crow Army*, p. 11.

34. Mary Penick Motley, ed., *The Invisible Soldier: The Experience of the Black Soldier, World War II* (Detroit: Wayne State University Press, 1987), p. 39.

35. Kryder, "F.D.R.'s Department of War and Black Americans," p. 18.

36. Ibid., p. 4.

37. Dalfiume, *Desegregation of the U.S. Armed Forces*, pp. 73–4.

38. Kryder, "F.D.R.'s Department of War and Black Americans," p. 26.

39. Sitkoff, "Racial Militancy and Interracial Violence in the Second World War," pp. 668–9.

40. James Albert Burran III, "Racial Violence in the South during World War II" (Ph.D. diss., University of Tennessee, 1977), p. 64.

41. Peter J. Kellogg, "Civil Rights Consciousness in the 1940s," *Historian* 42 (November 1979): 31.

42. Ibid., p. 32.

43. Ibid.

44. Ibid., p. 34.

45. Dalfiume, "The 'Forgotten Years' of the Negro Revolution," p. 103.

46. John Egerton, *Speak Now against the Day: The Generation before the Civil Rights Movement in the South* (New York: Knopf, 1994), p. 325.

47. Numan V. Bartley, *The New South, 1945–1980* (Baton Rouge: Louisiana State University Press, 1995), p. 12.

48. Charles S. Johnson, *To Stem This Tide: A Survey of Racial Tension Areas in the United States* (Boston: Pilgrim Press, 1943), p. 71.

49. Howard W. Odum, *Race and Rumors of Race: Challenge to American Crisis* (Chapel Hill: University of North Carolina Press, 1943), pp. 57, 73, 97.

50. Lerone Bennett Jr., *Confrontation: Black and White* (Baltimore, Md.: Penguin Books, 1965), p. 156.

51. Patricia Sullivan, *Days of Hope: Race and Democracy in the New Deal Era* (Chapel Hill: University of North Carolina Press, 1996), p. 158.

52. George B. Tindall, *The Emergence of the New South, 1913–1945* (Baton Rouge: Louisiana State University Press, 1967), p. 717.

53. Nat Brandt, *Harlem at War: The Black Experience in WWII* (Syracuse: Syracuse University Press, 1996), p. 95

54. Louis Ruchames, *Race, Jobs, and Politics: The Story of the FEPC* (New York: Columbia University Press, 1953), p. 29.

55. Ibid., p. 43.

56. Sullivan, *Days of Hope*, p. 158.

57. Johnson, *To Stem This Tide*, p. 66.

58. John Morton Blum, *V Was for Victory: Politics and American Culture during World War II* (New York: Harcourt Brace Jovanovich, 1976), pp. 193–4.

59. Egerton, *Speak Now against the Day*, p. 255; Dalfiume, "The 'Forgotten Years' of the Negro Revolution," p. 101; Lee Finkle, *Forum for Protest: The Black Press in World War II* (Rutherford, N.J.: Associated University Presses, 1975), p. 71.

60. Sullivan, *Days of Hope*, p. 156; Johnson, *To Stem This Tide*, p. 65.

61. Sullivan, *Days of Hope*, pp. 156–7.

62. Johnson, *To Stem This Tide*, p. 64.

63. Robert L. Zangrando, *The NAACP Crusade against Lynching, 1909–1950* (Philadelphia: Temple University Press, 1980), p. 7. Reported lynchings of blacks rose to four in 1940 and 1941, and six in 1942. The number of actual lynchings was probably higher, since growing public outrage at the practice made it "less a spectator event and more a covert act undertaken by small mobs in quick and quiet fashion." Burran, "Racial Violence in the South during World War II," p. 32.

64. Burran, "Racial Violence in the South during World War II," pp. 87–90.

65. Sullivan, *Days of Hope*, pp. 136–7.

66. Dalfiume, "The 'Forgotten Years' of the Negro Revolution," p. 103.

67. Pfeffer, *A. Philip Randolph*, pp. 46–7.

68. Alan Clive, *State of War: Michigan in World War II* (Ann Arbor: University of Michigan Press, 1979), p. 141; Robert C. Weaver, *Negro Labor: A National Problem* (New York: Harcourt Brace, 1946), pp. 222–3.

69. Dominic J. Capeci Jr., *Race Relations in Wartime Detroit: The Sojourner Truth Housing Controversy of 1942* (Philadelphia: Temple University Press, 1984), p. 70.

70. Drake and Cayton, *Black Metropolis*, pp. 90–1.

71. Thomas J. Sugrue, *The Origins of the Urban Crisis: Race and Inequality in Postwar Detroit* (Princeton: Princeton University Press, 1996), pp. 28–9.

72. Clive, *State of War*, pp. 148–9; Capeci, *Race Relations in Wartime Detroit*, pp. 96–8, 135–6; Sugrue, *The Origins of the Urban Crisis*, pp. 73–4.

73. Clive, *State of War*, p. 139; Capeci, *Race Relations in Wartime Detroit*, pp. 70–4.

74. Clive, *State of War*, p. 140.

75. Brandt, *Harlem at War*, pp. 93–4; Wynn, *The Afro-American and the Second World War*, p. 100; Koppes and Black, "Blacks, Loyalty, and Motion-Picture Propaganda in World War II," pp. 385–6.

76. Dominic J. Capeci Jr., "The Lynching of Cleo Wright: Federal Protection of Constitutional Rights during World War II," *Journal of American History* 72 (March 1986): 861–3.

77. Ibid., p. 861; Robert E. Cushman, "Our Civil Rights Become a World Issue," *New York Times Magazine*, 11 January 1948, p. 12.

78. Capeci, "The Lynching of Cleo Wright," pp. 859–69.

79. Washburn, *A Question of Sedition*, p. 99.

80. Capeci, "The Lynching of Cleo Wright," pp. 859–69.

81. Ibid., pp. 874–86.

82. Johnson, *To Stem This Tide*, p. 68.

83. *Congressional Record*, 77th Cong., 2d sess. (July 23, 1942), p. 6556.

84. *Congressional Record*, 77th Cong., 2d sess. (August 25, 1942), p. 6970.

85. Steven F. Lawson, *Black Ballots: Voting Rights in the South, 1944–1969* (New York: Columbia University Press, 1976), p. 66.

86. *Congressional Record*, 77th Cong., 2d sess. (October 13, 1942), pp. 8131–4.

87. Sullivan, *Days of Hope*, p. 119.

88. Ibid., pp. 117–9; Lawson, *Black Ballots*, pp. 61–71.

89. Dalfiume, *Desegregation of the U.S. Armed Forces*, p. 130.

90. Merl E. Reed, *Seedtime for the Modern Civil Rights Movement: The President's Committee on Fair Employment Practice, 1941–1946* (Baton Rouge: Louisiana State University Press, 1991), p. 95.

91. Koppes and Black, "Blacks, Loyalty, and Motion-Picture Propaganda in World War II," pp. 388–9.

92. Blum, *V Was for Victory*, pp. 188–9.

93. Michael S. Sherry, *In the Shadow of War: The United States since the 1930s* (New Haven: Yale University Press, 1995), p. 101

94. Koppes and Black, "Blacks, Loyalty, and Motion-Picture Propaganda in World War II," p. 390; Wynn, *The Afro-American and the Second World War*, p. 112.

95. Koppes and Black, "Blacks, Loyalty, and Motion-Picture Propaganda in World War II," pp. 391–406; Thomas Cripps, "Movies, Race, and World War II: *Tennessee Johnson* as an Anticipation of the Strategies of the Civil Rights Movement," *Prologue* 14 (spring 1982): 54–5.

96. Publicly, Louis said nothing critical of the Army's treatment of blacks, but privately he refused to accept discriminatory treatment and used his special status to secure assistance for other blacks in uniform, including Jackie Robinson. Chris Mead, *Champion: Joe Louis, Black Hero in White America* (New York: Charles Scribner's Sons, 1985), pp. 60–1, 207–36.

97. Kenneth O'Reilly, *Nixon's Piano: Presidents and Racial Politics from Washington to Clinton* (New York: Free Press, 1995), pp. 132–5.

98. Washburn, *A Question of Sedition*, p. 107.

99. Ibid., pp. 90–1.

100. Ulysses Lee, *The United States Army in World War II, Special Studies: The Employment of Negro Troops* (Washington, D.C.: Government Printing Office, 1966), p. 384; McGuire, *Taps for a Jim Crow Army*, p. 27.

101. Robert A. Garson, *The Democratic Party and the Politics of Sectionalism, 1941–1948* (Baton Rouge: Louisiana State University Press, 1974), p. 27.

102. Ibid., p. 28.

103. Ibid., pp. 94–6.

104. O'Reilly, *Nixon's Piano*, p. 137.

105. Reed, *Seedtime for the Modern Civil Rights Movement*, pp. 99–101.

106. Ruchames, *Race, Jobs, and Politics*, p. 50.

107. Morris J. MacGregor and Bernard C. Nalty, *Black Soldiers in World War II*, vol. 5 of *Blacks in the United States Armed Forces: Basic Documents* (Wilmington, Del.: Scholarly Resources, 1977), p. 48.

108. Peter Irons, *Justice at War* (New York: Oxford University Press, 1983), pp. 6–7, 38, 41, 58–59.

109. MacGregor and Nalty, *Black Soldiers in World War II*, pp. 187–243.

110. Garson, *The Democratic Party and the Politics of Sectionalism*, pp. 86–7; Goodwin, *No Ordinary Time*, p. 444.

111. Mary Frances Berry, *Black Resistance/White Law: A History of Constitutional Racism in America* (New York: Penguin Books, 1994), p. 128.

112. Ibid., p. 128; Garson, *The Democratic Party and the Politics of Sectionalism*, p. 87.

113. Robert Shogan and Tom Craig, *The Detroit Race Riot: A Study in Violence* (Philadelphia: Chilton Books, 1964), p. 9.

114. Ibid., p. 32; Selden C. Menefee, *Assignment U.S.A.* (New York: Reynal & Hitchcock, 1943), p. 150.

115. Shogan and Craig, *The Detroit Race Riot*, p. 32.

116. Capeci, *Race Relations in Wartime Detroit*, p. 168.

117. Shogan and Craig, *The Detroit Race Riot*, pp. 34–89; Alfred McClung Lee and Norman D. Humphrey, *Race Riot* (New York: Dryden Press, 1943), pp. 20–48; Sitkoff, "Racial Militancy and Interracial Violence in the Second World War," pp. 674–5.

118. Foner, *Blacks and the Military in American History*, p. 153.

119. Burran, "Racial Violence in the South during World War II," p. 131; and Kryder, "F.D.R.'s Department of War and Black Americans," pp. 31–2.

120. Nalty, *Strength for the Fight*, p. 165. After further disturbances and protests by local whites, the unit was transferred to the Aleutian Islands, where it spent the remainder of the war. Burran, "Racial Violence in the South during World War II," pp. 135–40.

121. Ibid., pp. 148–51.

122. Ibid., p. 152.

123. Kryder, "F.D.R.'s Department of War and Black Americans," p. 38.

124. Harvard Sitkoff, "The Detroit Race Riot of 1943," *Michigan History* 53 (fall 1969): 188.

125. Shogan and Craig, *The Detroit Race Riot*, p. 89.

126. Ibid., p. 90.

127. Sitkoff, "Racial Militancy and Interracial Violence in the Second World War," pp. 678–9; Wynn, *The Afro-American and the Second World War*, pp. 40–108.

128. Alfred McClung Lee, *Race Riots Aren't Necessary* (New York: Public Affairs Committee, July 1945), p. 24.

129. Menefee, *Assignment U.S.A.*, pp. 147–8.

130. Carey McWilliams, *Brothers under the Skin* (Boston: Little, Brown, 1943), p. 298.

131. Wendell L. Willkie, *One World* (New York: Simon & Schuster, 1943), p. 79; Goodwin, *No Ordinary Time*, p. 470.

. 132. Walter A. Jackson, *Gunnar Myrdal and America's Conscience: Social Engineering and Racial Liberalism, 1938–1987* (Chapel Hill: University of North Carolina Press, 1990), pp. 148–58, 162–3, 177–81. In fact, the idea for the project originated with Carnegie trustee Newton Baker, whose experiences as secretary of war during World War I made him sensitive to the problem that racial friction posed to wartime unity and mobilization. Ibid., 16–22.

133. Ibid., p. 262.

134. Gunnar Myrdal, *The Negro in a White Nation*, vol. 1 of *An American Dilemma* (New York: McGraw-Hill, 1944, 1964), pp. lxxii–lxxvi.

135. Ibid.; Stephan and Abigail Thernstorm, *America in Black and White: One Nation, Indivisible* (New York: Simon & Schuster, 1997), p. 91.

136. Gunnar Myrdal, *The Negro Social Structure*, vol. 2 of *An American Dilemma* (New York: McGraw-Hill, 1944, 1964), p. 1022.

137. David W. Southern, *Gunnar Myrdal and Black-White Relations: The Use and Abuse of an American Dilemma, 1944–1969* (Baton Rouge: Louisiana State University Press, 1987), pp. 71–99; Jackson, *Gunnar Myrdal and America's Conscience*, pp. 240–61.

138. Morton Sosna, *In Search of the Silent South: Southern Liberals and the Race Issue* (New York: Columbia University Press, 1977), p. 186.

139. Dewey W. Grantham, *The South in Modern America: A Region at Odds* (New York: HarperPerennial, 1994), p. 192.

140. Clayton R. Koppes and Gregory D. Black, *Hollywood Goes to War: How Politics, Profits, and Propaganda Shaped World War II Movies* (New York: Free Press, 1987), p. 179.

141. Thomas Cripps, *Slow Fade to Black: The Negro in American Film, 1900–1942* (New York: Oxford University Press, 1977), p. 373.

142. Koppes and Black, *Hollywood Goes to War*, pp. 180, 303.

143. Cripps, *Making Movies Black*, p. 77.

144. Ibid., p. 67.

145. Neil A. Wynn, "The Impact of the Second World War on the American Negro," *Journal of Contemporary History* 8 (1971): 50.

146. Alan Brinkley, *The End of Reform: New Deal Liberalism in Recession and War* (New York: Knopf, 1995), p. 170; Kellogg, "Civil Rights Consciousness in the 1940s," pp. 33–6.

147. Richard Polenberg, *One Nation Divisible: Class, Race, and Ethnicity in the United States Since 1938* (New York: Viking Press, 1980), p. 77.

148. MacGregor and Nalty, *Black Soldiers in World War II*, p. 270.

149. Dalfiume, *Desegregation of the U.S. Armed Forces*, p. 88.

150. MacGregor and Nalty, *Black Soldiers in World War II*, p. 315.

151. Cripps, *Making Movies Black*, p. 77.

152. Dalfiume, *Desegregation of the U.S. Armed Forces*, p. 90.

153. Wynn, *The Afro-American and the Second World War*, p. 35; Dalfiume, *Desegregation of the U.S. Armed Forces*, p. 91.

154. Nalty, *Strength for the Fight*, p. 149.

155. Ibid., p. 153; Motley, ed., *The Invisible Soldier*, pp. 195–6.

156. Dalfiume, *Desegregation of the U.S. Armed Forces*, p. 93.

157. MacGregor and Nalty, *Black Soldiers in World War II*, p. 333.

158. Nalty, *Strength for the Fight*, pp. 172–6; Hondon B. Hargrove, *Buffalo Soldiers in Italy: Black Americans in World War II* (Jefferson, N.C.: McFarland, 1985).

159. William L. O'Neill, *A Democracy at War: America's Fight at Home and Abroad in World War II* (New York: Free Press, 1993), pp. 366–74.

160. MacGregor and Nalty, *Black Soldiers in World War II*, pp. 505–6.

161. Lee, *The United States Army in World War II, Special Studies*, p. 691.

162. Goodwin, *No Ordinary Time*, p. 566.

163. Nalty, *Strength for the Fight*, pp. 176–8; O'Neill, *Nixon's Piano*, pp. 380–381; Dalfiume, *Desegregation of the U.S. Armed Forces*, p. 99.

164. Jessie Parkhurst Guzman, ed., *Negro Year Book: A Review of Events Affecting Negro Life, 1941–1946* (Tuskegee, Ala.: Tuskegee Institute, 1947), p. 361.

165. Jean Byers, "A Study of the Negro in Military Services," Department of Defense Monograph, June 1947, pp. 172–3.

166. MacGregor and Nalty, *Black Soldiers in World War II*, p. 509.

167. Nalty, *Strength for the Fight*, p. 193.

168. Ibid., pp. 193–5.

169. Wynn, *The Afro-American and the Second World War*, p. 55.

170. Weaver, *Negro Labor*, pp. 79–80.

171. Goodwin, *No Ordinary Time*, p. 540.

172. Richard Polenberg, *War and Society: The United States, 1941–1945* (Westport, Conn.: Greenwood Press, 1972), pp. 116–7.

173. Goodwin, *No Ordinary Time*, p. 538.

174. Ruchames, *Race, Jobs, and Politics*, p. 112.

175. Polenberg, *War and Society*, p. 122.

176. Allan M. Winkler, "The Philadelphia Transit Strike of 1944," *Journal of American History* 69 (1972): 86–7.

177. Ibid., p. 84.

178. Ruchames, *Race, Jobs, and Politics*, p. 118.

179. Reed, *Seedtime for the Modern Civil Rights Movement*, p. 347.

180. Guzman, ed., *Negro Year Book*, p. 141.

181. *Smith v. Allwright*, 321 U.S. 649 (1944).

182. Guzman, ed., *Negro Year Book*, p. 268.

183. 295 U.S. 45 (1935).

184. Lawson, *Black Ballots*, pp. 34–47.

185. 304 U.S. 144 (1938).

186. Alpheus T. Mason, *Harlan Fiske Stone: Pillar of the Law* (New York: Viking, 1956), p. 515.

187. 313 U.S. 299 (1941); Robert M. Cover, "The Origins of Judicial Activism in the Protection of Minorities," *Yale Law Journal* 91 (June 1982): 1292–4, 1306–7.

188. Ward E. Y. Elliott, *The Rise of Guardian Democracy: The Supreme Court's Role in Voting Rights Disputes, 1845–1969* (Cambridge: Harvard University Press, 1974), p. 80.

189. Darlene Clark Hine, in *Black Victory: The Rise and Fall of the White Primary in Texas* (Millwood, N.Y.: KTO Press, 1979), pp. 236–7.

190. Roger Daniels, *Coming to American: A History of Immigration and Ethnicity in American Life* (New York: HarperCollins, 1990), pp. 319–46; *Korematsu v. United States*, 323 U.S. 214 (1944).

191. Elliott, *The Rise of Guardian Democracy,* p. 85.

192. Polenberg, *War and Society,* pp. 111–2.

193. Garson, *The Democratic Party and the Politics of Sectionalism,* pp. 91–2.

194. David W. Southern, "Beyond Jim Crow Liberalism: Judge Waring's Fight against Segregation in South Carolina, 1942–52," *Journal of Negro History* 66 (fall 1981): 214.

195. Ibid., pp. 209–16; Lawson, *Black Ballots,* p. 51.

196. Lawson, *Black Ballots,* p. 51.

197. Donald R. Matthews and James W. Prothro, *Negroes and the New Southern Politics* (New York: Harcourt, Brace, and World, 1966), p. 17.

198. Richard Kluger, *Simple Justice: The History of Brown v. Board of Education and Black America's Struggle for Equality* (New York: Vintage Books, 1975), p. 237.

199. Lawson, *Black Ballots,* pp. 72–3; Frederic D. Ogden, *The Poll Tax in the South* (Birmingham: University of Alabama Press, 1958), p. 267.

200. Ogden, *The Poll Tax in the South,* p. 256.

201. Lawson, *Black Ballots,* p. 74; Garson, *The Democratic Party and the Politics of Sectionalism,* pp. 44–7.

202. Dominic J. Capeci Jr., *The Harlem Riot of 1943* (Philadelphia: Temple University Press, 1977), pp. 149–55.

203. O'Reilly, *Nixon's Piano,* pp. 140–2.

204. Garson, *The Democratic Party and the Politics of Sectionalism,* p. 100.

205. Ibid., pp. 106–13.

206. Sullivan, *Days of Hope,* pp. 170–1; Egerton, *Speak Now against the Day,* pp. 227–8.

207. Garson, *The Democratic Party and the Politics of Sectionalism,* pp. 113–25.

208. Lawson, *Black Ballots,* p. 47.

209. Samuel I. Rosenman, *The Public Papers and Addresses of Franklin D. Roosevelt: 1944–45 Volume, Victory and the Threshold of Peace* (New York: Harper and Brothers, 1950), p. 316.

210. Percentages computed from *Guide to U.S. Elections,* 2d ed. (Washington, D.C.: Congressional Quarterly, 1985), pp. 355–6.

211. Patricia L. Adams, "Fighting For Democracy in St. Louis: Civil Rights during World War II," *Missouri Historical Review* 80 (1985): 69.

212. Terrence M. Cole, "Jim Crow in Alaska: The Passage of the Alaska Equal Rights Act of 1945," *Western Historical Quarterly* 23 (November 1992): 429–49.

213. Dominic J. Capeci Jr., "Wartime Fair Employment Practice Committees: The Governor's Committee and the First FEPC in New York City, 1941–1943," *Afro-Americans in New York Life and History* 9 (1985): 45–63.

214. Richard Norton Smith, *Thomas E. Dewey and His Times* (New York: Simon & Schuster, 1982), pp. 445–6.

215. Ruchames, *Race, Jobs, and Politics,* pp. 164–5.

216. *Congressional Record,* 79th Cong., 1st sess. (July 23, 1945), pp. 6994–5.

217. Egerton, *Speak Now against the Day,* pp. 326–7.

218. Joe McCarthy, "GI Vision of a Better America," *New York Times,* 5 August 1945, sec. 6, p. 10.

219. Richard Morin, "Unconventional Wisdom," *Washington Post,* 6 April 1997, p. C5; Howard Schuman, Charlotte Steeh, and Lawrence Bobo, *Racial Attitudes in America: Trends and Interpretations* (Cambridge: Harvard University Press, 1985), p. 118.

220. James T. Patterson, *Grand Expectations: The United States, 1945–1974* (New York: Oxford University Press, 1996), p. 23.

221. "Jim Crow's Last Stand" (1943), in Langston Hughes, *The Collected Poems of Langston Hughes*, ed. Arnold Rampersad and David Roessel (New York: Knopf, 1994), p. 299.

CHAPTER SEVEN

1. Accounts of the Woodard beating vary. See James Albert Burran III, "Racial Violence in the South during World War II"(Ph.D. diss., University of Tennessee, 1977), pp. 226–7; Robert J. Donovan, *Conflict and Crisis: The Presidency of Harry S Truman, 1945–1948* (New York: W. W. Norton, 1977), p. 244; John Gunther, *Inside USA* (New York: Harper and Brothers, 1947), p. 686; John Egerton, *Speak Now against the Day: The Generation before the Civil Rights Movement in the South* (New York: Knopf, 1994), pp. 362–3; Bernard C. Nalty, *Strength for the Fight: A History of Black Americans in the Military* (New York: Free Press, 1986), pp. 204–5; Richard Kluger, *Simple Justice: The History of Brown v. Board of Education and Black America's Struggle for Equality* (New York: Vintage Books, 1975), pp. 298–9.

2. Burran, "Racial Violence in the South during World War II," p. 225.

3. Jessie Parkhurst Guzman, ed., *Negro Year Book: A Review of Events Affecting Negro Life, 1941–1946* (Tuskegee, Ala.: Tuskegee Institute, 1947), pp. 305–7.

4. Burran, "Racial Violence in the South during World War II," pp. 229–40.

5. Ibid., pp. 277–83.

6. Robert A. Garson, *The Democratic Party and the Politics of Sectionalism, 1941–1948* (Baton Rouge: Louisiana State University Press, 1974), pp. 180–1.

7. Ibid., p. 182.

8. Harry S. Ashmore, *Civil Rights and Wrongs: A Memoir of Race and Politics, 1944–1994* (New York: Pantheon, 1994), p. 58.

9. Steven F. Lawson, *Black Ballots: Voting Rights in the South, 1944–1969* (New York: Columbia University Press, 1976), p. 100.

10. David McCullough, *Truman* (New York: Touchstone, 1992), p. 589.

11. Jules Tygiel, *Baseball's Great Experiment: Jackie Robinson and His Legacy* (New York, Vintage Books, 1983), p. 3.

12. The topic of the Cold War's impact on civil rights has been the focus of much recent scholarly attention that has informed this and the following chapter. We are particularly indebted to the pathbreaking work of Mary Dudziak. Her forthcoming book *Cold War Civil Rights: Equality as Cold War Policy, 1946–1968* (Princeton: Princeton University Press), promises to offer the definitive treatment of this topic.

13. Walter White, *A Man Called White* (New York: Viking Press, 1948), p. 329; Mary Louise Dudziak, "Cold War Civil Rights: The Relationship between Civil Rights and Foreign Affairs in the Truman Adminstration" (Ph.D. diss., Yale University, 1992), p. 47.

14. Kenneth O'Reilly, *Nixon's Piano: Presidents and Racial Politics from Washington to Clinton* (New York: Free Press, 1995), p. 352.

15. William C. Berman, *The Politics of Civil Rights in the Truman Administration* (Columbus: Ohio State University Press, 1970), pp. 11–2; McCullough, *Truman*, p. 247.

16. William E. Leuchtenberg, "The Conversion of Harry Truman," *American Heritage*, November 1991, pp. 55–60; O'Reilly, *Nixon's Piano*, p. 146.

17. Berman, *The Politics of Civil Rights in the Truman Administration*, p. 10.

18. Leuchtenberg, "The Conversion of Harry Truman," p. 58.

19. Berman, *The Politics of Civil Rights in the Truman Administration*, pp. 25–32.

20. Ibid., pp. 33–4.

21. White, *A Man Called White*, pp. 330–1.

22. McCullough, *Truman*, p. 588.

23. *Public Papers of the Presidents of the United States: Harry S. Truman, 1946* (Washington, D.C.: Government Printing Office, 1962), p. 423.

24. John David Skrentny, *The Ironies of Affirmative Action: Politics, Culture, and Justice in America* (Chicago: University of Chicago Press, 1996), p. 157.

25. Paul Gordon Lauren, *Power and Prejudice: The Politics and Diplomacy of Racial Discrimination* (Boulder: Westview Press, 1988), p. 188.

26. Les K. Adler and Thomas G. Paterson, "Red Fascism: The Merger of Nazi Germany and Soviet Russia in the American Image of Totalitarianism, 1930's–1950's," *American Historical Review* 75 (April 1970): 1046–64.

27. Lauren, *Power and Prejudice*, pp. 188–9.

28. Whitman Bassow, "*Izvestia* Looks Inside U.S.A.," *Public Opinion Quarterly* 12 (fall 1948): 430–9. Soviet commentary on U.S. racial practices was so pervasive that it served as the subject of at least one joke among Soviet citizens. One day, the story goes, Radio Moscow decided to hold a call-in show to allow ordinary Moscovites to ask questions.

> *Caller #1:* Why don't we have a decent place to live?
> *Answer:* In America, they lynch negroes.
> *Caller #2:* Why don't we have enough food?
> *Answer:* In America, they lynch negroes.
> *Caller #3:* Why don't we have democracy?
> *Answer:* In America, they lynch negroes.

29. Dudziak, "Cold War Civil Rights," pp. 70–1.

30. *To Secure These Rights: The Report of the President's Committee on Civil Rights* (Washington, D.C.: Government Printing Office, 1947), pp. 146–7.

31. Lauren, *Power and Prejudice*, p. 173

32. Ibid., p. 191; Dudziak, "Cold War Civil Rights," p. 86. Also see Carol Anderson, "From Hope to Disillusion: African Americans, the United Nations, and the Struggle for Human Rights, 1944–1947," *Diplomatic History* 20 (1996): 531–63.

33. Gerald Horne, *Black and Red: W. E. B. Du Bois and the Afro-American Response to the Cold War, 1944–1963* (Albany: State University of New York Press, 1986), pp. 79–80.

34. Donald R. McCoy and Richard T. Ruetten, *Quest and Response: Minority Rights and the Truman Administration* (Lawrence: University Press of Kansas, 1973), p. 66.

35. Berman, *The Politics of Civil Rights in the Truman Administration*, p. 66.

36. Brenda Gayle Plummer, *Rising Wind: Black Americans and U.S. Foreign Affairs, 1935–1960* (Chapel Hill: University of North Carolina Press, 1996), p. 168.

37. Berman, *The Politics of Civil Rights in the Truman Administration*, p. 46.

38. *To Secure These Rights*, p. viii.

39. William E. Juhnke, "President Truman's Committee on Civil Rights: The Interaction of Politics, Protest, and Presidential Advisory Commission," *Presidential Studies Quarterly* 19 (1989): 594–8.

40. Ibid., 601–2.

41. Azza Salama Layton, "The International Context of the U.S. Civil Rights Movement: The Dynamics between Racial Policies and International Politics, 1941–1960" (Ph.D. diss., University of Texas, 1995), p. 106.

42. McCoy and Ruetten, *Quest and Response*, pp. 69–70; Berman, *The Politics of Civil Rights in the Truman Administration*, p. 58.

43. *The Public Papers of the Presidents of the United States: Harry S. Truman, 1947* (Washington,

D.C.: Government Printing Office, 1963), pp. 161–2 (hereafter referred to as *Truman Papers, 1947*).

44. White, *A Man Called White*, p. 348.

45. *Truman Papers, 1947*, pp. 311–3.

46. Ibid., p. 312.

47. Ibid.

48. White, *A Man Called White*, p. 348.

49. *To Secure These Rights*, pp. 79–82.

50. Ibid., pp. 82–7.

51. Ibid., pp. 151–73.

52. Ibid., pp. 100–1.

53. Ibid., pp. 147–8.

54. Ibid., p. 148.

55. Ibid., pp. 30–2.

56. Juhnke, "President Truman's Committee on Civil Rights," p. 607.

57. "You're Another," *Newsweek*, 8 March 1948, p. 52.

58. "A New Charter of Freedom," *Senior Scholastic*, 17 November 1947, pp. 10–2.

59. Robert E. Cushman, "Our Civil Rights Become a World Issue," *New York Times Magazine*, 11 January 1948, pp. 12, 22, 24.

60. McCoy and Ruetten, *Quest and Response*, pp. 92–3; *Public Papers of the Presidents of the United States: Harry S. Truman, 1948* (Washington, D.C.: Government Printing Office, 1964), p. 924 (hereafter referred to as *Truman Papers, 1948*).

61. Harry S. Truman, "Civil Rights Message," in *Freedom and Equality: Addresses by Harry S. Truman*, ed. David Horton (Columbia: University of Missouri Press, 1960), pp. 9–17.

62. *Truman Papers, 1948*, p. 126; John David Skrentny, "The Effect of the Cold War on African-American Civil Rights: America and the World Audience, 1945–1968," *Theory and Society* 27 (1998): 16.

63. Kluger, *Simple Justice*, p. 252.

64. Ibid., p. 251.

65. Tom C. Clark and Philip B. Perlman, *Prejudice and Property: An Historic Brief against Racial Covenants* (Washington, D.C.: Public Affairs Press, 1948), p. 34; Skrentny, "The Effect of the Cold War on African-American Civil Rights," p. 14.

66. Berman, *The Politics of Civil Rights in the Truman Administration*, p. 75.

67. Kluger, *Simple Justice*, pp. 246–55.

68. Ibid., p. 255.

69. McCoy and Ruetten, *Quest and Response*, p. 100.

70. Telephone interview with Grant Reynolds, December 12, 1997.

71. Stephen E. Ambrose, *Rise To Globalism: American Foreign Policy Since 1938*, 4th. rev. ed. (New York: Penguin Books, 1985), pp. 95–6; McCullough, *Truman*, pp. 603, 607.

72. Jervis Anderson, *A. Philip Randolph: A Biographical Portrait* (New York: Harcourt Brace Jovanovich, 1973), p. 276.

73. Ibid., p. 277.

74. Grant Reynolds, "A Triumph for Civil Disobedience," *Nation*, 28 August 1948, pp. 228–9.

75. Anderson, *A. Philip Randolph*, pp. 278–9; Paula F. Pfeffer, *A. Philip Randolph, Pioneer of the Civil Rights Movement* (Baton Rouge: Louisiana State University Press, 1990), p. 139.

76. "Crisis in the Making: U.S. Negroes Tussle with Issue of Resisting a Draft Law Because of Racial Segregation," *Newsweek*, 7 June 1948, pp. 28–9.

77. Telephone interview with Grant Reynolds, December 12, 1997.

78. Max Lerner, *Actions and Passions: Notes on the Multiple Revolution of Our Time* (New York: Simon & Schuster, 1949), pp. 99–102.

79. "Face the Music," *Time*, 12 April 1948, p. 21.

80. "Segregation Thorn," *Newsweek*, 12 April 1948, p. 26.

81. Berman, *The Politics of Civil Rights in the Truman Administration*, p. 117.

82. Donovan, *Conflict and Crisis*, p. 391.

83. McCoy and Ruetten, *Quest and Response*, pp. 129–31.

84. Berman, *The Politics of Civil Rights in the Truman Administration*, pp. 104–5; Donald Bruce Johnson, comp., *National Party Platforms: Volume 1, 1840–1956*, rev. ed. (Urbana: University of Illinois Press, 1956, 1978), p. 404.

85. Harvard Sitkoff, "Harry Truman and the Election of 1948: The Coming of Age of Civil Rights in American Politics," *Journal of Southern History* 37 (November 1971): 606; Peter J. Kellogg, "The Americans for Democratic Action and Civil Rights in 1948: Conscience in Politics or Politics in Conscience?" *Midwest Quarterly* 20 (1978): 49–63.

86. Paula Wilson, *The Civil Rights Rhetoric of Hubert H. Humphrey, 1948–1964* (Lanham, Md.: University Press of America, 1996), pp. 4–5; Skrentny, *The Ironies of Affirmative Action*, p. 157.

87. McCullough, *Truman*, pp. 638–40.

88. Leuchtenberg, "The Conversion of Harry Truman," p. 64.

89. Numan V. Bartley, *The New South, 1945–1980* (Baton Rouge: Louisiana State University Press, 1995), p. 87.

90. Interview with Strom Thurmond, Washington, D.C., March 1, 1991; Clark Clifford, *Counsel to the President: A Memoir* (New York: Random House, 1991), p. 207.

91. *Truman Papers, 1948*, p. 924.

92. McCullough, *Truman*, p. 590.

93. Skrentny, "The Effect of the Cold War on African-American Civil Rights," p. 25.

94. Dudziak, "Cold War Civil Rights," p. 153.

95. Era Bell Thompson, "How the Race Problem Embarrasses American," *Negro Digest*, November 1950, pp. 52–4.

96. Charles S. Johnson, "American Policies: Race and Foreign," *Negro Digest*, August 1950, pp. 82–3.

97. Berman, *The Politics of Civil Rights in the Truman Administration*, p. 191.

98. See ibid., pp. 137–91.

99. On the failure of Truman's domestic agenda, see David R. Mayhew, *Divided We Govern: Party Control, Lawmaking, and Investigations, 1946–1990* (New Haven: Yale University Press, 1991), pp. 91–2.

100. Dudziak, "Cold War Civil Rights," pp. 164–7.

101. Duane Lockard, *Toward Equal Opportunity: A Study of State and Local Antidiscrimination Laws* (New York: Macmillan, 1968), p. 24.

102. John W. Roberts, "Cold War Observer: Governor Adlai Stevenson on American Foreign Relations," *Journal of the Illinois State Historical Society* 76 (1983): 49–60.

103. Tygiel, *Baseball's Great Experiment*, p. 54.

104. Ibid., p. 34.

105. Ibid., pp. 42–3.

106. Ibid., p. 38.

107. Ronald A. Smith, "The Paul Robeson–Jackie Robinson Saga and a Political Collision," *Journal of Sport History* 6 (summer 1979): 13.

108. Tygiel, *Baseball's Great Experiment*, p. 41.

109. Ibid., p. 37.

110. Ibid., p. 69.

111. David Falkner, *Great Time Coming: The Life of Jackie Robinson, from Baseball to Birmingham* (New York: Simon & Schuster, 1995), p. 113; Tygiel, *Baseball's Great Experiment*, p. 69.

112. Tygiel, *Baseball's Great Experiment*, pp. 61–3; Falkner, *Great Time Coming* , pp. 78–86.

113. *New York Times*, 20 November 1945, p. 20.

114. Tygiel, *Baseball's Great Experiment*, pp. 72–3.

115. Robinson went hitless, but reached base on an error in his fourth at bat. Falkner, *Great Time Coming*, p. 163.

116. Ibid., p. 195.

117. Tygiel, *Baseball's Great Experiment*, p. 334; Jackie Robinson, *I Never Had It Made* (Hopewell, N.J.: Ecco Press, 1972, 1995), p. 86.

118. Hank Aaron with Lonnie Wheeler, *I Had a Hammer: The Hank Aaron Story* (New York: HarperCollins, 1991), pp. 7, 71.

119. Arnold R. Hirsch, *Making the Second Ghetto: Race and Housing in Chicago, 1940–1960* (Cambridge: Cambridge University Press, 1983), pp. 53–7.

120. Arnold R. Hirsch, "Chicago: The Cook County Democratic Organization and the Dilemma of Race, 1931–1987," in *Snowbelt Cities: Metropolitan Politics in the Northeast and Midwest Since World War II*, ed. Richard M. Bernard (Bloomington: Indiana University Press, 1990), pp. 70–1.

121. Thomas J. Sugrue, "Crabgrass-Roots Politics: Race, Rights, and the Reaction against Liberalism in the Urban North, 1940–1964," *Journal of American History* 82 (September 1995): 569–71.

122. The list of works advancing this argument is long and growing. The fullest statement is found in Thomas Byrne Edsall and Mary D. Edsall, *Chain Reaction: The Impact of Race, Rights, and Taxes on American Politics* (New York: Norton, 1991, 1992). One of the more recent versions is in Ronald Radosh, *Divided They Fell: The Demise of the Democratic Party, 1964–1996* (New York: Free Press, 1996).

123. Robert Korstad and Nelson Lichtenstein, "Opportunities Found and Lost: Labor, Radicals, and the Early Civil Rights Movement," *Journal of American History* 75 (December 1988): 786–811.

124. Thomas J. Sugrue, *The Origins of the Urban Crisis: Race and Inequality in Postwar Detroit* (Princeton: Princeton University Press, 1996), p.170.

125. Korstad and Lichtenstein, "Opportunities Found and Lost: Labor, Radicals, and the Early Civil Rights Movement," p. 809.

126. Ibid., p. 811.

127. Michael S. Sherry, *In the Shadow of War: The United States since the 1930s* (New Haven: Yale University Press, 1995), p. 148.

128. Korstad and Lichtenstein, "Opportunities Found and Lost: Labor, Radicals, and the Early Civil Rights Movement," p. 811. On the role of white elite support for the civil rights movement, see David Alan Horowitz's insightful article, "White Southerners' Alienation and Civil Rights: The Response to Corporate Liberalism, 1956–1965," *Journal of Southern History* 54 (May 1988): 173–200.

129. W. E. B. Du Bois, *The Autobiography of W. E. B. DuBois: A Soliloquy on Viewing My Life from the Last Decade of Its First Century* (New York: International Publishers, 1968), p. 333.

130. Lee Nichols, *Breakthrough on the Color Front* (New York: Random House, 1954), p. 112.

131. Richard M. Dalfiume, *Desegregation of the U.S. Armed Forces: Fighting on Two Fronts, 1939–1953* (Columbia: University of Missouri Press, 1969), p. 218.

132. Jack D. Foner, *Blacks and the Military in American History: A New Perspective* (New York: Praeger Publishers, 1974), p. 189.

133. Harry S. Truman, "Fair Deal for the Negro," in *Freedom and Equality*, ed. Horton, pp. 19–26.

134. Ernest Leiser, "For Negroes, It's a New Army Now," *Saturday Evening Post*, 13 December 1952, p. 27.

135. Ibid., p. 26.

136. Dudziak, "Cold War Civil Rights," p. 170.

137. Kluger, *Simple Justice*, p. 617.

138. Ibid., pp. 645–6.

139. Dudziak, "Cold War Civil Rights," p. 177.

140. Kluger, *Simple Justice*, p. 558.

141. Philip B. Kurland and Gerhard Casper, eds., *Brown v. Board of Education, 1954 & 1955*, vol. 49 of *Landmark Briefs and Arguments of the Supreme Court of the United States: Constitutional Law* (Arlington, Va.: University Publications of America, 1975), p. 121.

142. Ibid., pp. 121–3.

143. Ibid., pp. 146–7.

144. O'Reilly, *Nixon's Piano*, pp. 165–6; Stephen E. Ambrose, *Eisenhower: The President* (New York: Simon & Schuster, 1984), pp. 125–7, 142–3, 308–9, 336–8, 387.

145. Ambrose, *Eisenhower*, p. 190.

146. Robert Fredrick Burk, *The Eisenhower Administration and Black Civil Rights* (Knoxville: University of Tennessee Press, 1984), p. 28.

147. Sherry, *In the Shadow of War*, p. 147.

148. Burk, *The Eisenhower Administration and Black Civil Rights*, p. 24.

149. Ibid., pp. 45–6.

150. Dudziak, "Cold War Civil Rights," pp. 27–8.

151. Skrentny, "The Effect of the Cold War on African-American Civil Rights," p. 18.

152. Burk, *The Eisenhower Administration and Black Civil Rights*, pp. 49–50.

153. Skrentny, *The Ironies of Affirmative Action*, pp. 157–8.

154. Kluger, *Simple Justice*, pp. 613–6, 657–67, 678–99.

155. 347 U.S. 483 (1954).

156. Dudziak, "Cold War Civil Rights," p. 182.

157. Kluger, *Simple Justice*, p. 690.

158. Philip Elman, "The Solicitor General's Office, Justice Frankfurter, and Civil Rights Litigation, 1946–1960," *Harvard Law Review* 100 (1987): 823.

159. Dudziak, "Cold War Civil Rights," pp. 179–80.

160. 347 U.S. 483 (1954).

161. " 'Voice' Speaks in 34 Languages to Flash Court Ruling to the World," *New York Times*, 18 May 1954, p. 1.

162. *Congressional Record*, 83d Cong., 2d sess. (May 17, 1954), p. 6647.

163. Ibid., 6859.

164. Dudziak, "Cold War Civil Rights," pp. 188–9.

165. "The Nation: 'To All on Equal Terms,' " *Time*, 24 May 1954, pp. 21–2.

166. "Supreme Court: Historic Decision," *Newsweek*, 24 May 1954, pp. 25–6.

167. "Editorial Excerpts from the Nation's Press on Segregation Ruling," *New York Times*, 18 May 1954, p. 19.

168. Ibid.

169. Ibid.

170. Ibid.

171. "All God's Chillun," *New York Times*, 18 May 1954, p. 28.

172. "Editorial Excerpts on School Bias Ruling," *New York Times*, 19 May 1954, p. 20.

173. Dudziak, "Cold War Civil Rights," pp. 191–2.

CHAPTER EIGHT

1. Taylor Branch, *Parting the Waters: America in the King Years, 1954–1963* (New York: Simon & Schuster, 1988), pp. 138–41.

2. Ibid., pp. 881–3; Harvard Sitkoff, *The Struggle for Black Equality, 1954–1980* (Toronto: Collins Publishers, 1981), pp. 161–4.

3. Sitkoff, *The Struggle for Black Equality*, pp. 220–1.

4. In the House, 101 of the South's 128 representatives signed the document and of the twenty-two southern senators, only Lyndon Johnson of Texas, and Albert Gore Sr. and Estes Kefauver of Tennessee refused to join in. Numan V. Bartley, *The Rise of Massive Resistance: Race and Politics in the South during the 1950s* (Baton Rouge: Louisiana State University Press, 1969), p. 116.

5. John Egerton, *Speak Now against the Day: The Generation before the Civil Rights Movement in the South* (New York: Knopf, 1994), p. 617; Bartley, *The Rise of Massive Resistance*, p. 85.

6. Gerald N. Rosenberg, *The Hollow Hope: Can Courts Bring About Social Change?* (Chicago: University of Chicago Press, 1991), p. 50.

7. James L. Sundquist, *Politics and Policy: The Eisenhower, Kennedy, and Johnson Years* (Washington, D.C.: Brookings Institution, 1968), pp. 238–9.

8. David Halberstam, *The Fifties* (New York: Villard Books, 1993), pp. 431–41.

9. Stephen J. Whitfield, *A Death in the Delta: The Story of Emmett Till* (New York: Free Press, 1988), p. 46.

10. United States Information Agency, Office of Research and Analysis, "Communist Exploitation of American Racial Incidents: Moscow Lets U.S. News Items and Pix Tell Its Story Abroad," 3 December 1962. National Archives (NWDT2-306-RREPS-1962R(174)).

11. Herbert Brownell, *Advising Ike: The Memoirs of Attorney General Herbert Brownell* (Lawrence: University of Kansas Press, 1993), p. 219.

12. *Congressional Digest*, April 1957, pp. 116–8.

13. Paula Wilson, *The Civil Rights Rhetoric of Hubert H. Humphrey, 1948–1964* (Lanham, Md.: University Press of America, 1996), p. 36.

14. Azza Salama Layton, "The International Context of the U.S. Civil Rights Movement: The Dynamics between Racial Policies and International Politics, 1941–1960" (Ph.D. diss., University of Texas, 1995), pp. 119–20.

15. David Alan Horowitz, "White Southerners' Alienation and Civil Rights: The Response to Corporate Liberalism, 1956–1965," *Journal of Southern History* 54 (May 1988): 173–200.

16. Mary L. Dudziak, "The Little Rock Crisis and Foreign Affairs: Race, Resistance and the Image of American Democracy," *Southern California Law Review* 70 (1997).

17. "Singapore Paper Taunts U.S.," *New York Times*, 27 September 1957, p. 12.

18. Kenneth O'Reilly, *Nixon's Piano: President and Racial Politics from Washington to Clinton* (New York: Free Press, 1995), p. 181. Less than a year earlier, Soviet troops had brutally suppressed a revolt against Hungary's Communist regime.

19. Steven R. Goldzwig and George Dionisopoulos, "Crisis at Little Rock: Eisenhower,

History, and Mediated Political Realities," in *Eisenhower's War of Words: Rhetoric and Leadership,* ed. Martin J. Medhurst (East Lansing: Michigan State University Press, 1994), p. 220.

20. Dwight D. Eisenhower, *The White House Years: Waging the Peace, 1956–1961* (Garden City, N.Y.: Doubleday, 1965), pp. 168, 171.

21. Dudziak, "The Little Rock Crisis and Foreign Affairs," p. 67.

22. *Public Papers of the Presidents of the United States: Dwight D. Eisenhower, 1957* (Washington, D.C.: Government Printing Office, 1958), pp. 693–4.

23. Robert Fredrick Burk, *The Eisenhower Administration and Black Civil Rights* (Knoxville: University of Tennessee Press, 1984), p. 186.

24. "Red Press Gloats Over Little Rock," *New York Times,* 26 September 1957, p. 14. Also see "Vatican Decries Racial Bias in U.S.," *New York Times,* 7 September 1957, p. 9.

25. "As Others See Us: U.S. and Little Rock," *Newsweek,* 7 October 1957, p. 34.

26. "What Orval Hath Wrought," *Time,* 23 September 1957, p. 13.

27. "The Meaning of Little Rock," *Time,* 7 October 1957, p. 15.

28. Azza Salama Layton, "International Pressure and the U.S. Government's Response to Little Rock," *Arkansas Historical Quarterly* 56 (autumn 1997): 263.

29. Goldzwig and Dionisopoulos, "Crisis at Little Rock," p. 221.

30. Harold R. Isaacs, "World Affairs and U.S. Race Relations: A Note on Little Rock," *Public Opinion Quarterly* 22 (fall 1958): 369.

31. *Public Papers of the Presidents of the United States: Dwight D. Eisenhower, 1959* (Washington, D.C.: Government Printing Office, 1960), pp. 16–8.

32. Martin Luther King, "A Realistic Look at the Question of Progress in the Area of Race Relations," address at Freedom Rally, St. Louis, Missouri, April 10, 1957.

33. Michael S. Sherry, *In the Shadow of War: The United States since the 1930s* (New Haven: Yale University Press, 1995), p. 209.

34. James H. Cone, "Martin Luther King, Jr., and the Third World," in *We Shall Overcome: Martin Luther King, Jr., and the Black Freedom Struggle,* ed. Peter J. Albert and Ronald Hoffman (New York: Pantheon and United States Capitol Historical Society, 1990), p. 199.

35. Martin Luther King, "The Birth of a New Nation," sermon given at Dexter Avenue Baptist Church, Montgomery, Alabama, April 7, 1957.

36. John David Skrentny, "The Effect of the Cold War on African-American Civil Rights: America and the World Audience, 1945–1968," *Theory and Society* 27 (1998).

37. "An Appeal for Human Rights," in *Atlanta Georgia, 1960–1961: Sit-Ins and Student Activism,* ed. David J. Garrow (Brooklyn, N.Y.: Carlson Publishing, 1989), p. 186.

38. "Democratic Convention Statement, July 1960," in Julian Bond and Andrew Lewis, *Gonna Sit at the Welcome Table,* 2d ed. (New York: American Heritage, 1995), p. 429.

39. "Russian Premier, in 2-Hour Address, Outlines Proposals for Reorganizing United Nations," *New York Times,* 24 September 1960, p. 9.

40. Burk, *The Eisenhower Administration and Black Civil Rights,* p. 257.

41. "The Second Kennedy-Nixon Debate: October 13, 1963," online document available at <http://www.netcapitol.com/Debates/60-2nd.htm>.

42. "The Third Kennedy-Nixon Debate: October 7, 1963," online document available at <http://www.netcapitol.com/Debates/60-3rd.htm>.

43. "The Second Kennedy-Nixon Debate: October 13, 1963," online document available at <http://www.netcapitol.com/Debates/60-2nd.htm>.

44. Stephen E. Ambrose, *Rise to Globalism: American Foreign Policy since 1938,* 4th rev. ed. (New York: Penguin Books, 1985), p. 182.

45. Carl M. Brauer, *John F. Kennedy and the Second Reconstruction* (New York: Columbia University Press, 1977), pp. 75–6.

46. Robert F. Kennedy, "Civil Rights: Conflict of Law and Local Customs," *Vital Speeches of the Day*, 1 June 1961, pp. 483–4.

47. Timothy P. Maga, "Battling the 'Ugly American' at Home: The Special Protocol Service and the New Frontier, 1961–63," *Diplomacy and Statecraft* 3 (1993): 127–8.

48. Chester Bowles, *Ambassador's Report* (New York: Harper & Brothers, 1954), pp. 395–6.

49. "Big Step Ahead on a High Road," *Life*, 8 December 1961, p. 32.

50. Maga, "Battling the 'Ugly American' at Home," p. 130.

51. "Department Urges Maryland to Pass Public Accommodations Bill," *Department of State Bulletin*, 2 October 1961, p. 552.

52. Harris Wofford, *Of Kennedys and Kings: Making Sense of the Sixties* (New York: Farrar, Straus, and Giroux, 1980), p. 127.

53. Layton, "The International Context of the U.S. Civil Rights Movement," p. 137.

54. Brauer, *John F. Kennedy and the Second Reconstruction*, pp. 43–4, 77.

55. Branch, *Parting the Waters*, pp. 434, 472–3; Brauer, *John F. Kennedy and the Second Reconstruction*, pp. 106–7.

56. Paul Jones, "Brinkley Takes Stand against 'Freedom Rides,' " *Atlanta Constitution*, 26 May 1961, p. 30, reprinted in Bond and Lewis, *Gonna Sit at the Welcome Table*, p. 503.

57. Wofford, *Of Kennedys and Kings*, p. 156.

58. "Department Supports Desegregation in Interstate Bus Facilities," *Department of State Bulletin*, 19 June 1961, pp. 975–6.

59. O'Reilly, *Nixon's Piano*, p. 211.

60. United States Information Agency, Office of Research and Analysis, "Worldwide Reactions to Racial Incidents in Alabama," 29 May 1961. National Archives (NWDT2-306-SREPS-1961S(17)).

61. *Public Papers of the Presidents of the United States: John F. Kennedy, 1962* (Washington, D.C.: Government Printing Office, 1963), pp. 726–8.

62. Brauer, *John F. Kennedy and the Second Reconstruction*, p. 203.

63. United States Information Agency, Research and Reference Service, "Media Comment on the Mississippi Crisis," 5 October 1962. National Archives (NWDT2-306-RREPS-1962R(109)).

64. Eric F. Goldman, "Progress—By Moderation *and* Agitation," *New York Times Magazine*, 18 June 1961, p. 12.

65. Louis E. Lomax, *The Negro Revolt* (New York: Harper & Brothers, 1962), p. 242.

66. Ralph M. Besse, "The Line Around the World: The Negro Situation Today," *Vital Speeches of the Day*, 1 April 1962, pp. 377, 379.

67. This and other references to Operation Dixie are found in Philip A. Klinkner, *The Losing Parties: Out-Party National Committees, 1956–1993* (New Haven: Yale University Press, 1994), pp. 41–70.

68. V. O. Key Jr., *The Responsible Electorate: Rationality in Presidential Voting, 1936–1960* (Cambridge: Harvard University Press, 1966), p. 2.

69. Brauer, *John F. Kennedy and the Second Reconstruction*, pp. 221–2.

70. Steven F. Lawson, *Black Ballots: Voting Rights in the South, 1944–1969* (New York: Columbia University Press, 1976), pp. 294–5; Brauer, *John F. Kennedy and the Second Reconstruction*, p. 222.

71. Sundquist, *Politics and Policy*, p. 260.

72. Hazel Erskine, "The Polls: The Speed of Racial Integration," *Public Opinion Quarterly* 32 (fall 1968): 514.

73. Paul B. Sheatsley, "White Attitudes toward the Negro," *Daedalus* 95 (winter 1996): 231.

74. Branch, *Parting the Waters*, p. 807; Brauer, *John F. Kennedy and the Second Reconstruction*, p. 240.

75. "Six-Year-Olds among the Arrested," *Current Digest of the Soviet Press* 15 (June 5, 1963): 20.

76. United States Information Agency, Research and Reference Service, "Reaction to Racial Tension in Birmingham, Alabama," 13 May 1963. National Archives (NWDT2-306-RREPS-1963R(85)).

77. "China Press Taunts U.S. on Civil Rights," *New York Times*, 1 June 1963, p. 8; Robert Trumbull, "Peking Exploits U.S. Racial Strife," *New York Times*, 3 June 1963, p. 5.

78. Jacques Nevard, "Red China Calls Kennedy Racist; Steps Up Attacks on Negro Issue," *New York Times*, 6 June 1963, p. 20.

79. United States Information Agency, Research and Reference Service, "Reaction to Racial Tension in Birmingham, Alabama," 13 May 1963. National Archives (NWDT2-306-RREPS-1963R(85)). Most USIA reports on world opinion of U.S. race relations were classified, but a copy of this document was obviously leaked to the *New York Times*. See "Foreign Reaction to Race Rift Mild," *New York Times*, 29 May 1963, p. 16. The article's headline belied its content.

80. Branch, *Parting the Waters*, p. 835.

81. Ibid., p. 791.

82. C. L. Sulzberger, "Racism in the Communist Orbit," *New York Times*, 5 June 1963, p. 40.

83. "Has Race Trouble Tarnished U.S. Image Abroad?" *U.S. News and World Report*, 19 August 1963, p. 66.

84. "Stevenson Faces U.S. Racial Plight," *New York Times*, 27 May 1963, p. 20.

85. "Stevenson Calls Bigotry Harmful to U.S. Abroad," *New York Times*, 3 June 1963, p. 59.

86. "Racial Bias Called Test for Republic," *New York Times*, 10 June 1963, p. 44.

87. "Problems of Discrimination and U.S. Foreign Policy," *Department of State Bulletin*, 17 June 1963, p. 935.

88. Taylor Branch, *Pillar of Fire: America in the King Years, 1963–1965* (New York: Simon & Schuster, 1998), p. 114.

89. Theodore H. White, *The Making of the President: 1964* (New York: Atheneum Publishers, 1965), p. 179.

90. James T. Patterson, *Grand Expectations: The United States, 1945–1974* (New York: Oxford University Press, 1996), p. 480.

91. C. L. Sulzberger, "American Extremist Shadows," *New York Times*, 29 May 1963, p. 32.

92. "Freedom Now," *Time*, 17 May 1963, pp. 23–5.

93. Wofford, *Of Kennedys and Kings*, p. 174.

94. *Time*, 21 June 1963, p. 13.

95. *Public Papers of the Presidents of the United States: John F. Kennedy, 1963* (Washington, D.C.: Government Printing Office, 1964), pp. 468–71 (hereafter referred to as *Kennedy Papers, 1963*).

96. *Kennedy Papers, 1963*, pp. 483–94.

97. Sundquist, *Politics and Policy,* p. 268.

98. Brauer, *John F. Kennedy and the Second Reconstruction,* p. 279.

99. Dean Rusk, "Fulfilling Our Basic Commitments as a Nation," *Department of State Bulletin,* 29 July 1963, pp. 154–9.

100. E. W. Kenworthy, "Rusk and Thurmond Clash Coldly over Civil Rights," *New York Times,* 11 July 1963, p. 1; Dean Rusk, *As I Saw It* (New York: W. W. Norton, 1990), pp. 579–89.

101. Brauer, *John F. Kennedy and the Second Reconstruction,* p. 276.

102. Skrentny, "The Effect of the Cold War on African-American Civil Rights."

103. Bernard C. Nalty and Morris J. MacGregor, eds., *Blacks in the Military: Essential Documents* (Wilmington, Del.: Scholarly Resources, 1981), p. 330.

104. Taeku Lee, "Collective Agency and Frame Contestation: Black Insurgency and the Dynamics of Racial Attitudes during the Civil Rights Era, 1948–1965" (paper presented at the annual meeting of the Midwest Political Science Association, Chicago, April 1997), pp. 19–21, 33.

105. Brauer, *John F. Kennedy and the Second Reconstruction,* pp. 276–7; Horowitz, "White Southerners' Alienation and Civil Rights," p. 193.

106. Brauer, *John F. Kennedy and the Second Reconstruction,* pp. 276–7.

107. Paula F. Pfeffer, *A. Philip Randolph, Pioneer of the Civil Rights Movement* (Baton Rouge: Louisiana State University Press, 1990), pp. 244–5.

108. United States Information Agency, Research and Reference Service, "Worldwide Comment on the Washington Civil Rights March," 6 September 1963. National Archives (NWDT2-306-RREPS-1963S(172)).

109. Branch, *Parting the Waters,* p. 872.

110. Ibid., p. 875.

111. Robert D. Loevy, *To End All Segregation: The Politics of the Passage of the Civil Rights Act of 1964* (Lanham, Md.: University Press of America, 1990), pp. 63–4.

112. Michael R. Beschloss, ed., *Taking Charge: The Johnson White House Tapes, 1963–1964* (New York: Simon & Schuster, 1997), p. 64.

113. Ibid., pp. 29–30. Also see Robert Dallek, *Flawed Giant: Lyndon Johnson and His Times, 1961–1973* (New York: Oxford University Press, 1998), p. 112.

114. *Public Papers of the Presidents of the United States: Lyndon B. Johnson, 1963–1964* (Washington, D.C.: Government Printing Office, 1965), pp. 8–10 (hereafter referred to as *Johnson Papers, 1963–1964*).

115. Ibid., p. 374.

116. Ibid., p. 684.

117. Ibid., p. 116.

118. Ibid., pp. 142–3.

119. "Sen. Humphrey on the 'Raw and Ugly Shame' of American Society," *Congressional Quarterly Weekly Report,* 20 September 1963, pp. 1635–6.

120. Paula Wilson, *The Civil Rights Rhetoric of Hubert H. Humphrey, 1948–1964* (Lanham, Md.: University Press of America, 1996), pp. 86, 90.

121. *Congressional Record,* House of Representatives, 88th Cong., 2d sess. (February 10, 1964), p. 2763.

122. "Washington Reacts as Rights Crisis Grows," *Congressional Quarterly,* 31 May 1963, p. 837.

123. *Congressional Record,* Senate, 88th Cong., 2d sess. (June 9, 1964), p. 13119.

124. William Brink and Louis Harris, *Black and White: A Study of U.S. Racial Attitudes*

Today (New York: Simon & Schuster, 1967), pp. 220–1. This attitude was remarkably uniform across the country. Those whites selecting "too fast" ranged from a high of 81 percent in the South to a low of 64 percent in the East.

125. Lloyd A. Free and Hadley Cantril, *The Political Beliefs of Americans: A Study of Public Opinion* (New Brunswick, N.J.: Rutgers University Press, 1967), p. 124.

126. Dan T. Carter, *The Politics of Rage: George Wallace, the Origins of the New Conservatism, and the Transformation of American Politics* (New York: Simon & Schuster, 1995), pp. 205–15.

127. White, *The Making of the President*, pp. 247–8 and 348–50.

128. Michael Barone, *Our Country: The Shaping of America from Roosevelt to Reagan* (New York: Free Press, 1990), p. 380.

129. Lou Cannon, *Reagan* (New York: G. P. Putnam's Sons, 1982), p. 111.

130. Skrentny, "The Effect of the Cold War on African-American Civil Rights."

131. Patterson, *Grand Expectations*, p. 581.

132. Robert Weisbrot, *Freedom Bound: A History of America's Civil Rights Movement* (New York: W. W. Norton, 1990), p. 138.

133. Patterson, *Grand Expectations*, p. 581.

134. *Public Papers of the Presidents of the United States: Lyndon B. Johnson, 1965* (Washington, D.C.: Government Printing Office, 1966), pp. 281(7 (hereafter referred to as *Johnson Papers, 1965*).

135. Ibid., p. 289.

136. "Secretary Rusk Appears on NBC's 'American White Paper,' " *Department of State Bulletin*, 27 September 1965, p. 510.

137. United States Information Agency, Research and Reference Service, "Foreign Reaction to Senate Passage of the Civil Rights Bill," 25 June 1964. National Archives (NWDT2-306-RREPS-1964R(89)).

138. United States Information Agency, Research and Reference Service, "A Note on Worldwide Opinion about U.S. Race Relations," World Survey III Series, December 1965. National Archives (NWDT2-306-RREPS-1965R(204)).

139. *Johnson Papers, 1965*, p. 286.

140. Mark J. Stern, "Poverty and Family Composition since 1940," in *The "Underclass" Debate: Views from History*, ed. Michael B. Katz (Princeton: Princeton University Press, 1993), pp. 220–53; Douglas S. Massey and Nancy A. Denton, *American Apartheid: Segregation and the Making of the Underclass* (Cambridge: Harvard University Press, 1993), pp. 42–57; Thomas J. Sugrue, *The Origins of the Urban Crisis: Race and Inequality in Postwar Detroit* (Princeton: Princeton University Press, 1996), pp. 259–71; Norval D. Glenn, "Some Changes in the Relative Status of American Nonwhites, 1940 to 1960," *Phylon* 24 (summer 1963): 109–22.

141. Weisbrot, *Freedom Bound*, p. 158.

142. David English, *Divided They Stand* (Englewood Cliffs, N.J.: Prentice-Hall, 1969), p. 141.

143. *Johnson Papers, 1965*, p. 899.

144. "After the Blood Bath," *Newsweek*, 30 August 1965, p. 14.

145. John David Skrentny, *The Ironies of Affirmative Action: Politics, Culture, and Justice in America* (Chicago: University of Chicago Press, 1996), p. 108; Joseph A. Califano Jr., *The Triumph and Tragedy of Lyndon Johnson* (New York: Simon & Schuster, 1991), pp. 207–26.

146. Califano, *The Triumph and Tragedy of Lyndon Johnson*, pp. 228–9.

147. Nalty and MacGregor, eds., *Blacks in the Military*, pp. 342–3.

148. Gerald Horne, *Fire This Time: The Watts Uprising and the 1960s* (Charlottesville: University Press of Virginia, 1995), p. 280.

149. Califano, *The Triumph and Tragedy of Lyndon Johnson*, p. 276.

150. Weisbrot, *Freedom Bound*, p. 183.

151. Erskine, "The Polls: The Speed of Racial Integration," p. 522.

152. Hugh Davis Graham, *The Civil Rights Era: Origins and Development of National Policy, 1960–1972* (New York: Oxford University Press, 1990), pp. 258–62.

153. Lewis L. Gould, *1968: The Election That Changed America* (Chicago: Ivan R. Dee, 1993), p. 13.

154. Thomas Byrne Edsall and Mary D. Edsall, *Chain Reaction: The Impact of Race, Rights, and Taxes on American Politics* (New York: Norton, 1991, 1992), pp. 59–61.

155. Cannon, *Reagan*, p. 111.

156. "An American Tragedy, 1967—Detroit," *Newsweek*, 7 August 1967, p. 18.

157. "Is Civil War Next?" *U.S. News and World Report*, 7 August 1967, p. 30.

158. "As Outside World Sees Riots in America," *U.S. News and World Report*, 7 August 1967, p. 12.

159. Graham, *The Civil Rights Era*, p. 272 n. 3.

160. *Congressional Record*, 90th Cong., 2d sess. (February 28, 1968), p. 4574.

161. English, *Divided They Stand*, p. 130.

162. Clark Clifford, *Counsel to the President: A Memoir* (New York: Random House, 1991), p. 530.

163. Califano, *The Triumph and the Tragedy of Lyndon Johnson*, pp. 278–80.

164. English, *Divided They Stand*, pp. 130–1.

165. Irving Bernstein, *Guns or Butter: The Presidency of Lyndon Johnson* (New York: Oxford University Press, 1996), pp. 497–9; Graham, *The Civil Rights Era*, pp. 270–3.

166. Steven R. Goldzwig, "Rhetorical History and Democratic Ideals in Conflict: LBJ, the Assassination of Martin Luther King, Jr., and the Civil Rights Act of 1968" (paper presented at the annual meeting of the American Political Science Association, San Francisco, August 29–September 1, 1996), p. 11.

167. Peter B. Levy, "Blacks and the Vietnam War," in *The Legacy: The Vietnam War and the American Imagination*, ed. D. Michael Shafer (Boston: Beacon Press, 1990), p. 209.

168. Public Papers of the Presidents of the United States: Lyndon B. Johnson, 1966 (Washington, D.C.: Government Printing Office, 1967), pp. 468–9.

169. *Public Papers of the Presidents of the United States: Lyndon B. Johnson, 1967* (Washington, D.C.: Government Printing Office, 1968), p. 194.

170. *Public Papers of the Presidents of the United States: Lyndon B. Johnson, 1968–1969, Volume 1* (Washington, D.C.: Government Printing Office, 1970), p. 62 (hereafter referred to as *Johnson Papers, 1968–1969, Volume 1*).

171. Ronald H. Spector, *After Tet: The Bloodiest Year in Vietnam* (New York: Free Press, 1993), p. xvi.

172. *Congressional Record*, 90th Cong., 2d sess. (February 28, 1968), p. 4574.

173. *Johnson Papers, 1968–1969, Volume 1*, p. 446.

174. Jefferson Morley, "Bush and the Blacks: An Unknown Story," *New York Review of Books*, 16 January 1992, p. 21.

175. Herbert S. Parment, *George Bush: The Life of a Lone Star Yankee* (New York: Scribner, 1997), p. 109.

176. Andrew Delbanco, "Self-Remade Man," *New York Times Book Review*, 14 December 1997, p. 9.

177. Richard Ben Cramer, *What It Takes: The Way to the White House* (New York: Random House, 1992), pp. 593–4.

178. Parmet, *George Bush*, p. 132.

179. Ibid., pp. 132–3.

180. Morley, "Bush and the Blacks," p. 24.

181. George Bush, *Looking Forward* (New York: Doubleday, 1987), pp. 92–3.

182. Levy, "Blacks and the Vietnam War," p. 217.

183. Whitney M. Young Jr., "When the Negroes in Vietnam Come Home," *Harper's,* June 1967, p. 65.

184. Sol Stern, "When the Black G.I. Comes Back from Vietnam," *New York Times Magazine,* 24 March 1968, p. 40.

185. Colin L. Powell, *My American Journey* (New York: Random House, 1995), p. 124.

186. Stern, "When the Black G.I. Comes Back from Vietnam," pp. 37, 40.

CHAPTER NINE

1. Mike Davis, *Ecology of Fear: Los Angeles and the Imagination of Disaster* (New York: Metropolitan Books, 1998), p. 421.

2. Gerald Horne, *Fire This Time: The Watts Uprising and the 1960s* (Charlottesville: University Press of Virginia, 1995), p. 355.

3. Mary Louise Dudziak, "Cold War Civil Rights: The Relationship between Civil Rights and Foreign Affairs in the Truman Adminstration" (Ph.D. diss., Yale University, 1992), pp. 201–9.

4. Hazel Erskine, "The Polls: Recent Opinion on Racial Problems," *Public Opinion Quarterly* 32 (winter 1968–1969): 696.

5. Lewis L. Gould, *1968: The Election That Changed America* (Chicago: Ivan R. Dee, 1993), pp. 65–6.

6. Ibid., p. 137.

7. Dan T. Carter, *The Politics of Rage: George Wallace, the Origins of the New Conservatism, and the Transformation of American Politics* (New York: Simon & Schuster, 1995), p. 352.

8. Ibid., p. 348.

9. Lewis Chester, Godfrey Hodgson, and Bruce Page, *An American Melodrama: The Presidential Campaign of 1968* (New York: Viking Press, 1969), pp. 491–2.

10. Moon H. Jo and Daniel D. Mast, "Changing Images of Asian Americans," *International Journal of Politics, Culture and Society* 6 (1993): 417–41; Peter Kivisto, *Americans All: Race and Ethnic Relations in Historical, Structural, and Comparative Perspectives* (Belmont, Calif.: Wadsworth Publishing Company, 1995), p. 428; David M. Reimers, *Still the Golden Door: The Third World Comes to America* (New York: Columbia University Press, 1985), pp. 175–6.

11. John Hope Franklin and Alfred A. Moss Jr., *From Slavery to Freedom: A History of Negro Americans,* 6th ed. (New York: Knopf, 1988), pp. 433, 435.

12. Kenneth O'Reilly, *Nixon's Piano: Presidents and Racial Politics from Washington to Clinton* (New York: Free Press, 1995), p. 291.

13. Richard Harris, *Justice: The Crisis of Law, Order, and Freedom in America* (New York: Dutton, 1970), pp. 144–5.

14. O'Reilly, *Nixon's Piano,* p. 318.

15. Ibid., p. 327.

16. Hugh Davis Graham, "Richard Nixon and Civil Rights: Explaining an Enigma," *Presidential Studies Quarterly* 26 (winter 1996): 97.

17. John David Skrentny, *The Ironies of Affirmative Action: Politics, Culture, and Justice in America* (Chicago: University of Chicago Press, 1996), pp. 177–221.

18. Ibid., p. 102.

19. Alonzo L. Hamby, *Liberalism and Its Challengers: From F.D.R. to Bush*, 2d ed. (New York: Oxford University Press, 1992), p. 320.

20. Franklin and Moss, *From Slavery to Freedom*, pp. 459–66.

21. *Swann v. Charlotte-Mecklenburg Board of Education*, 402 U.S. 1 (1971); Thomas Byrne Edsall and Mary D. Edsall, *Chain Reaction: The Impact of Race, Rights, and Taxes on American Politics* (New York: W. W. Norton, 1991, 1992), p. 87.

22. Theodore H. White, *America in Search of Itself: The Making of the President, 1956–1980* (New York: Warner Books, 1982), pp. 118, 255, 286, 378, 431.

23. Dan T. Carter, *From George Wallace to Newt Gingrich: Race in the Conservative Counterrevolution, 1963–1994* (Baton Rouge: Louisiana State University Press, 1996), p. 52.

24. Edsall and Edsall, *Chain Reaction*, p. 89.

25. Ibid., p. 97.

26. J. Anthony Lukas, *Common Ground: A Turbulent Decade in the Lives of Three American Families* (New York: Knopf, 1985) offers a thorough and powerful treatment of the Boston school desegregation crisis.

27. 418 U.S. 717 (1974).

28. Jules Witcover, *Marathon: The Pursuit of the Presidency, 1972–1976* (New York: Viking Press, 1977), pp. 302–9.

29. Ibid., pp. 293–4.

30. O'Reilly, *Nixon's Piano*, p. 353.

31. In his memoirs, Carter's only mention of domestic civil rights was two sentences in a chapter focused on his foreign policy emphasis on human rights. Jimmy Carter, *Keeping Faith: Memoirs of a President* (Norwalk, Conn.: Easton Press, 1982), p. 151.

32. Ibid., p. 150.

33. 438 U.S. 265 (1978).

34. Godfrey Hodgson, *The World Turned Right Side Up: A History of the Conservative Ascendancy in America* (Boston: Houghton Mifflin, 1996), p. 154.

35. Joseph A. Califano Jr., *Governing America: An Insider's Report from the White House and the Cabinet* (New York: Simon & Schuster, 1981), p. 241.

36. Lou Cannon, *Reagan* (New York: G. P. Putnam's Sons, 1982), pp. 269–70.

37. Ibid., pp. 280–281.

38. Edsall and Edsall, *Chain Reaction*, p. 152.

39. Ibid., p. 144.

40. O'Reilly, *Nixon's Piano*, p. 361.

41. Edsall and Edsall, *Chain Reaction*, pp. 187–8.

42. O'Reilly, *Nixon's Piano*, p. 363.

43. Richard Kluger, *Simple Justice: The History of Brown v. Board of Education and Black America's Struggle for Equality* (New York: Vintage Books, 1975), pp. 605–9.

44. O'Reilly, *Nixon's Piano*, p. 368.

45. Ethan Bronner, *Battle for Justice: How the Bork Nomination Shook America* (New York: Anchor Books, 1989), pp. 67–8, 224–5.

46. Wayne King and Warren Weaver Jr., "Washington Talk: Briefing; The Black Factor," *New York Times*, 5 January 1987, p. A14; Mark J. Penn and Douglas E. Schoen, "Reagan's Revolution Ended?" *New York Times Magazine*, 9 November 1986, pp. 4–23.

47. Nicholas Lemann, "Taking Affirmative Action Apart," *New York Times Magazine*, 2 July 1995, p. 54.

48. Ibid.

49. Edsall and Edsall, *Chain Reaction*, p. 181.

50. Peter Brown, *Minority Party: Why Democrats Face Defeat in 1992 and Beyond* (Washington, D.C.: Regnery Gateway, 1991), p. 25.

51. Edsall and Edsall, *Chain Reaction*, pp. 181–2.

52. Brown, *Minority Party*, p. 28.

53. Kathleen Hall Jamieson, *Dirty Politics: Deception, Distraction, and Democracy* (New York: Oxford University Press, 1992), pp. 34–5.

54. Jeremy D. Mayer and Molly W. Sonner, "Did Lee Atwater and Willie Horton Matter? Racial Environment, National Partisan Elites, and the Presidential Elections of 1988 and 1992" (paper presented at the annual meeting of the American Political Science Association Meeting, San Francisco, August 29–September 1, 1996), p. 7.

55. *Public Papers of the Presidents of the United States: George Bush, 1990, Volume II* (Washington, D.C.: Government Printing Office, 1991), pp. 1435–6.

56. O'Reilly, *Nixon's Piano*, pp. 392–3.

57. Steven Shull, *A Kinder, Gentler Racism? The Reagan-Bush Civil Rights Legacy* (Armonk, N.Y.: M. E. Sharp, 1993), p. 90.

58. Tyler Bridges, *The Rise of David Duke* (Jackson: University Press of Mississippi, 1994), pp. 193, 236–7.

59. V. O. Key Jr., *Southern Politics in State and Nation* (Knoxville: University of Tennessee Press, 1949, 1977), pp. 156–82, 519.

60. Susan E. Howell and Sylvia Warren, "Public Opinion and David Duke," in *The Emergence of David Duke and the Politics of Race*, ed. Douglas D. Rose (Chapel Hill: University of North Carolina Press, 1992), pp. 80–93.

61. Stephanie Grace, "Voting Split along Race Line," *New Orleans Times-Picayune*, 19 November 1995, p. A1.

62. Carter, *From George Wallace to Newt Gingrich*, p. 98.

63. James R. Dickenson, "Democrats Seek Identity after Loss," *Washington Post*, 17 December 1984, p. A6. For more on the creation of the DLC, see Philip A. Klinkner, *The Losing Parties: Out-Party National Committees, 1956–1993* (New Haven: Yale University Press, 1994), pp. 179–88; John F. Hale, "A Different Kind of Democrat: Bill Clinton, The DLC and the Construction of a New Party Identity" (paper presented at the annual meeting of the American Political Science Association, Washington, D.C., September 2–5, 1993).

64. Gwen Ifill, "Democratic Group Argues Over Goals," *New York Times*, 7 May 1991, p. A21; Dan Balz and David S. Broder, "Democrats Argue Over Quota Clause," *Washington Post*, 7 May 1991, p. A8.

65. Michael Kramer, "The Brains behind Clinton," *Time*, 4 May 1992, p. 45.

66. Marshall Frady, "Death in Arkansas," *New Yorker*, 22 February 1993, p. 132; Christopher Hitchens, "Minority Report," *Nation*, 2 March 1992, p. 258.

67. *Washington Post*, 16 June 1993, p. A7; Sheila Rule, "Rapper Chided by Clinton, Calls Him a Hypocrite," *New York Times*, 17 June 1992, p. A22; Chuck Philips, " 'I Do Not Advocate . . . Murdering,' " *Los Angeles Times*, 17 June 1992, p. F1.

68. Jack W. Germond and Jules Witcover, *Mad as Hell: Revolt at the Ballot Box, 1992* (New York: Warner Books, 1993), p. 303; David S. Broder and Thomas B. Edsall, "Clinton Finds Biracial Support for Criticism of Rap Singer," *Washington Post*, 16 June 1993, p. A7; David S. Broder, "Clinton's Gamble with Jesse Jackson," *Washington Post*, 17 June 1993, p. A25.

69. Thomas B. Edsall, "Black Leaders View Clinton Strategy with Mix of Pragmatism, Optimism," *Washington Post*, 28 October 1992, p. A16.

70. Germond and Witcover, *Mad as Hell*, p. 304.

71. Andrew Hacker, "The Blacks and Clinton," *New York Review of Books*, 28 August

1993, p. 14; Bill Clinton and Al Gore, *Putting People First: How We Can All Change America* (New York: Times Books, 1992), p. 64.

72. Paul J. Quirk and Jon K. Dalager, "The Election: A 'New Democrat' and a New Kind of Presidential Campaign," in *The Elections of 1992,* ed. Michael Nelson (Washington, D.C.: Congressional Quarterly Press, 1993), p. 78; Stanley and Niemi, *Vital Statistics on American Politics,* p. 100.

73. Philip A. Klinkner, "Court and Country in American Politics: The Democratic Party in 1994," in *Midterm: The Elections of 1994,* ed. Philip A. Klinkner (Boulder: Westview Press, 1996).

74. Peter Applebome, *Dixie Rising: How the South Is Shaping American Values, Politics, and Culture* (New York: Times Books, 1996), pp. 108–9.

75. David Maraniss and Michael Weisskopf, *"Tell Newt to Shut Up!" Prizewinning Washington Post Journalists Reveal How Reality Gagged the Gingrich Revolution* (New York: Touchstone, 1996), pp. 128–45.

76. Applebome, *Dixie Rising,* p. 109.

77. Press release from the Center on Budget and Policy Priorities, December 4, 1996.

78. Since its passage, supporters of the legislation have pointed to a sharp drop in welfare case loads. Such declines have indeed been impressive in some areas, but the number of people on welfare had been declining even before the passage of the law. Additionally, this drop in welfare cases comes during what is perhaps the best job market in over twenty years. The true test of a safety net comes when people are falling. Therefore the verdict remains out on the new legislation until the next economic downturn. Even with a booming economy, recent reports by several private charities noted a sharp upturn in those seeking assistance from food kitchens and homeless shelters. Furthermore, the new law's two-year time limit for assistance has yet to expire, leaving open the question of what will happen to those who are unable to find work once their support is cut off. Noah Isackson, "Demand Grows for Basic Needs," *Chicago Tribune,* 11 December 1997, p. 7; Dennis O'Brien, "City's 30 Shelters Filled to Capacity," *Baltimore Sun,* 5 December 1997, p. 1B; Laura Griffin, "News Charities Puts Focus on Emergency Aid Agencies," *Dallas Morning News,* 27 November 1997, p. 1.

79. *Fullilove v. Klutznick,* 448 U.S. 448 (1980); *Metro Broadcasting, Inc. v. FCC,* 497 U.S. 547 (1990); *Adarand Constructors, Inc. v. Pena,* 115 S. Ct. 2097 (1995).

80. *Hopwood v. Texas,* 78 F.3d 932, *cert. denied,* 116 S. Ct. 2581 (1996); A. Leon Higginbotham Jr., "Breaking Thurgood Marshall's Promise," *New York Times Magazine,* 18 January 1998, p. 28.

81. *Congressional Quarterly Weekly Report,* May 9, 1998, p. 1246.

82. "State Propositions: A Snapshot of Voters," *Los Angeles Times,* 7 November 1996, p. 29.

83. Karla Haworth, "Minority Admissions Fall on 3 U. of California Campuses," *Chronicle of Higher Education,* 27 March 1998, p. A41; "No Black Students Say They Will Enter Texas Law School's Class," *Chronicle of Higher Education,* 30 May 1997, p. A36. Some preferences, however, have avoided controversy. For example, according to the *Chronicle of Higher Education,* in 1994, Texas A&M University "reversed admissions denials for 17 applicants at the request of regents, 7 for legislators and other state officials, 4 for former students, and 10 for campus administrators. Sixty-seven other students were admitted, with no reversals of denials, in part because of sponsorship from one of those four groups. Of the 67, Dr. Bowen [President of Texas A&M] said, 'I assume they might not have gotten in' without the request of the groups. Of the total of 105, six did not even

meet minimum entrance criteria." Patrick Healy, "Texas Universities Open Doors for Well-Connected Applicants," *Chronicle of Higher Education,* 13 June 1997, p. A29.

84. Holly Idelson, "Clinton Comes to Defense of Affirmative Action," *Congressional Quarterly Weekly Report,* 22 July 1995, p. 2194.

85. "Transcript of Second Presidential Debate," *New York Times,* 17 October 1996, p. B11.

86. Roger Simon, *Show Time: The American Political Circus and the Race for the White House* (New York: Times Books, 1998), pp. 315–6.

87. Steven A. Holmes, "Clinton Panel on Race Urges Variety of Modest Measures," *New York Times,* 18 September 1998, p. A1.

88. "Remarks by the President at University of California at San Diego Commencement," White House Press Release, June 12, 1997.

89. Kenneth T. Walsh, "Learning from Big Jumbo: Why Clinton Scrutinizes Presidents Obscure and Legendary," *U.S. News & World Report,* 26 January 1998, p. 33.

CONCLUSION

1. Here, we rely primarily on the arguments offered in Stephan Thernstrom and Abigail Thernstrom, *America in Black and White: One Nation, Indivisible* (New York: Simon & Schuster, 1997), esp. pp. 18–9, 140, 157, 184–7, 190–2, 234, 289, 499, 526.

2. Ibid., pp. 18, 34, 68, 79–81, 178, 195, 197, 233–235, 550 n. 34, 560 n. 61. On black–white wealth disparities, see Melvin L. Oliver and Thomas M. Shapiro, *Black Wealth, White Wealth: A New Perspective on Racial Inequality* (New York: Routledge, 1995).

3. Thernstrom and Thernstrom, *America in Black and White,* pp. 35, 116–7.

4. *Economic Report of the President, 1998,* pp. 124–5, 131–3, 144–5; Edward N. Wolff, *Top Heavy: The Increasing Inequality of Wealth in America and What Can Be Done about It* (New York: New Press, 1995), p. 2.

5. William G. Bowen and Derek Bok, *The Shape of the River: Long-Term Consequences of Considering Race in College and University Admissions* (Princeton: Princeton University Press, 1998), pp. 10–11.

6. Thernstrom and Thernstrom, *American in Black and White,* pp. 186–8, 538, 581 n. 7.

7. Ibid., pp. 156–8, 301, 462.

8. Ibid., pp. 215–6, 341, 526.

9. Ibid., pp. 68, 104, 141, 521, 524; Paul M. Sniderman and Thomas Piazza, *The Scar of Race* (Cambridge: Harvard University Press, Belknap Press, 1993); Paul M. Sniderman and Edward G. Carmines, *Reaching beyond Race* (Cambridge: Harvard University Press, 1997).

10. Sniderman and Piazza are faulted for this shortcoming in Donald R. Kinder, Adam Berinsky, and Nicholas Winter, "Racism's End? Stability and Change in White Americans' Opinions on Matters of Race" (paper prepared for the annual meeting of the American Political Science Association, Boston, Mass., August 1998), p. 6. Kinder and his colleagues suggest, as we do here, that "moral instruction" by opinion leaders, including "editorial writers" and "presidents," along with "education" may account for the decline of overtly prejudicial survey responses (p. 24 n. 9).

11. The Thernstroms might well agree. They note that "World War II was an ideological struggle" in which U.S. leaders contrasted American principles of "freedom and democracy" to "Nazi racism," but faced the difficulty that "common beliefs about the eternal superiority of the white race and the inferiority of the Negro race bore more than a passing resemblance to the doctrines preached by Hitler" (*America in Black and*

White, p. 70). They do not, however, discuss the relationship of elite opinion to mass opinion.

12. Donald R. Kinder and Lynn M. Sanders argue in *Divided by Color: Racial Politics and Democratic Ideals* (Chicago: University of Chicago Press, 1996), for example, that "[m]embers of Congress, presidents, corporate public affairs officers, activists, policy analysts, reporters and editors," and other opinion leaders can powerfully affect "the underpinnings of opinion" and "the very meaning of opinion" by "inducing citizens to think about issues in particular ways." They believe that modern American elites frame racial issues in ways that do reinforce espousal of racial equality "*in principle*" but also legitimate opposition to any major changes in racial statuses (pp. 192, 270).

13. Personally, we remain skeptical of how sincerely many whites have accepted recent changes in the racial status quo. We each grew up in rather typical Midwestern towns, places probably worse than some but better than others when it came to white racial attitudes. Growing up in the 1960s, 1970s, and 1980s, racist language and stereotypes remained pervasive among our extended families, friends, and acquaintances. Yet we have no doubt that if asked in opinion surveys, they would have expressed nominally liberal views on race. Today, travels outside of the halls of academia (and sometimes within) reinforce this impression. We find that many ordinary whites, of all education and income levels, are often quite open in expressing their racial prejudices to other whites in informal settings.

14. Thernstrom and Thernstrom, *America in Black and White*, p. 304; Kinder and Sanders, *Divided by Color*, pp. 17–9, 27–31, 92, 135, 145; Sam Howe Verhovek, "In Poll, Americans Reject Means but Not Ends of Racial Diversity," *New York Times*, 14 December 1997, pp. 1, 32.

15. Thernstrom and Thernstrom, *America in Black and White*, pp. 142, 151, 177, 179, 506–7, 574 n. 18.

16. Jennifer L. Hochschild, *Facing Up to the American Dream: Race, Class, and the Soul of the Nation* (Princeton: Princeton University Press, 1995), pp. 4–5.

17. Thernstrom and Thernstrom, *America in Black and White*, pp. 248–9.

18. Douglas S. Massey and Nancy A. Denton, *American Apartheid: Segregation and the Making of the Underclass* (Cambridge: Harvard University Press, 1993), pp. 32–3, 96–109, 179–80; Ian Ayres, "Fair Driving: Gender and Race Discrimination in Retail Car Negotiations," *Harvard Law Review* 104 (1991): 817; Richard A. Epstein, *Forbidden Grounds: The Case against Employment Discrimination Laws* (Cambridge: Harvard University Press, 1992), pp. 47–58; Thernstrom and Thernstrom, *America in Black and White*, pp. 224–5.

19. Kinder and Sanders, *Divided by Color*, pp. 92–127; Thernstrom and Thernstrom, *America in Black and White*, pp. 614–5 n. 153; Martin Gilens, " 'Race Coding' and White Opposition to Welfare," *American Political Science Review* 90 (September 1996): 593–604. Kinder, Berinsky, and Winter, "Racism's End," add that the average survey "thermometer scores" of white feelings toward blacks did not grow significantly warmer from 1964 to 1996. They remained only mildly favorable throughout that time (pp. 8–10).

20. One recent poll suggests large and growing support for the concept of "separate but equal" among those between the ages of 15 to 24, exactly the age cohort that has had the least exposure to the antiracist discourse of the Cold War. According to this poll, in 1991, 41 percent of those aged 15 to 24 agreed that it was "OK if the races are basically separate from one another as long as everyone has equal opportunities," while 57 percent disagreed. In 1997, those numbers had reversed themselves, with 68 percent expressing support for "separate but equal" and only 31 percent disagreeing. Although

merely suggestive, these results are disturbing nonetheless. "Racial Separation Is OK, Say 68 Percent in MTV Poll," *Atlanta Constitution*, 5 December 1997, p. 7G.

21. Rogers M. Smith, *Civic Ideals: Conflicting Visions of Citizenship in U.S. History* (New Haven: Yale University Press, 1997), pp. 277–83, 296–324.

22. Charles Francis Adams, " 'The Solid South' and the Afro-American Race Problem" (speech to the Academy of Music, Richmond, Va., October 24, 1908), pp. 4, 7, 12, 16–9.

23. Smith, *Civic Ideals*, pp. 330–7, 375–6; *Slaughter-House Cases*, 83 U.S. 394 (1873); *Civil Rights Cases*, 109 U.S. 3 (1883).

24. Alice M. Rivlin, *Reviving the American Dream: The Economy, the States and the Federal Government* (Washington, D.C.: Brookings Institution, 1992), pp. 9, 118, 126; Thomas Sowell, "The Right to Be Wrong," *Forbes*, 17 June 1996, p. 50; Democratic Leadership Council (Gov. Bill Clinton, Chairman), *The New American Choice*, Washington, D.C., 1991, p. 8; William J. Clinton, Second Inaugural Address, Washington, D.C., January 20, 1997.

25. In the final House vote on welfare reform, Democrats divided evenly, 98 to 98. In the Senate, 25 Democrats voted in favor with only 21 opposed to the bill. Only one Senate Democrat running for reelection that year, Paul Wellstone of Minnesota, voted against the bill. He was reelected.

26. *United States v. Lopez*, 115 S. Ct. 1624 (1995); *Printz v. United States*, 117 S. Ct. 2365 (1997) (striking down certain provisions of the Brady Handgun Violence Prevention Act requiring state enforcement officials to participate in administering a federal regulatory measure).

27. *Civil Rights Cases*, 109 U.S. 3, 18–25 (1883); Adams, " 'The Solid South,' " p. 18; Theodore Roosevelt, "The Negro Problem," address to the Republican Club of the city of New York, February 13, 1905, in *The Works of Theodore Roosevelt: Memorial Edition*, vol. 18 (New York: Charles Scribner's Sons, 1925), pp. 462–3.

28. *Adarand Constructors. Inc. v. Pena*, 115 S. Ct. 2097 (1995); Democratic Leadership Council, *American Choice*, p. 8; Paul Starr, "Civil Reconstruction: What to Do Without Affirmative Action," *The American Prospect*, winter 1992, pp. 9–10; Eric Pooley, "Fairness or Folly? Ward Connerly Brings His Campaign against Affirmative Action to a Wider Stage Just as Clinton Rolls Out a New Set of Race Initiatives," *Time*, 23 June 1997, p. 32.

29. Smith, *Civic Ideals*, pp. 351–2, 412, 417–8, 424–6.

30. Sowell, "Right to Be Wrong," p. 50; Richard A. Epstein, *Takings: Private Property and the Power of Eminent Domain* (Cambridge: Harvard University Press, 1985), pp. 320, 341; Richard A. Epstein, "A Taste for Privacy? Evolution and the Emergence of a Naturalistic Ethic," *Journal of Legal Studies* 9 (1980): 665–78; Thernstrom and Thernstrom, *America in Black and White*, pp. 562 n. 101, 649 n. 129; Dinesh D'Souza, *The End of Racism: Principles for a Multiracial Society* (New York: Free Press, 1995), pp. 544–5; *Dolan v. City of Tigard*, 114 S. Ct. 2309 (1994); Democratic Leadership Conference, *American Choice*, p. 5; Clinton, Second Inaugural.

31. Smith, *Civic Ideals*, pp. 355–6, 364–5, 410–9.

32. Lawrence H. Fuchs, *The American Kaleidoscope: Race, Ethnicity, and the Civic Culture* (Hanover: University Press of New England, 1990), pp. 485–9.

33. Philip J. Hilts, "Federal Official Apologizes for Remarks on Inner Cities," *New York Times*, 22 February 1992, sec. 1, p. 6.

34. Moynihan quoted in *Newsday*, 14 July 1994, p. AO4, with his apology in a letter to the *Buffalo News*, 2 August 1994, p. 2; David S. Broder, syndicated column, *Denver Post*, 26 June 1994, p. D-01.

35. "Remarks by the President in Roundtable Discussion on Welfare Reform," White House Press Release, February 18, 1997.

36. Adolph Reed Jr., "A New Minimum: $10 an Hour," *Progressive,* April 1997, p. 16.

37. Dinesh D'Souza, "Improving Culture to End Racism," *Harvard Journal of Law and Public Policy* 19S (1996): 788–9; Joel Kotkin, *Tribes: How Race, Religion and Identity Determine Success in the New Global Economy* (New York: Random House, 1993), pp. 1–10.

38. Samuel P. Huntington, *The Clash of Civilization and the Remaking of World Order* (New York: Simon & Schuster, 1996).

39. Peter Brimelow, *Alien Nation: Common Sense about America's Immigration Disaster* (New York: HarperPerennials, 1996), pp. 9–10, 55–6, 122, 184.

40. Richard J. Herrnstein and Charles Murray, *The Bell Curve: Intelligence and Class Structure in American Life* (New York: Free Press, 1994), pp. 642–3.

41. Brimelow, *Alien Nation,* pp. 9–10, 55–6, 122, 184; Herrnstein and Murray, *The Bell Curve,* pp. 1–16, 269–315, 642–3; J. Philippe Rushton, *Race, Evolution and Behavior: A Life History Perspective* (New Brunswick, N.J.: Transaction Publishers, 1995), pp. 1–16.

42. Malcolm Browne, "What Is Intelligence and Who Has It?" *New York Times Book Review,* 16 October 1994, pp. 3, 41, 45.

43. Geoffrey Cowley, "Testing the Science of Intelligence," *Newsweek,* 24 October 1994, pp. 55–60.

44. Dan Seligman and Charles Murray, "As the Bell Curves," *National Review,* 8 December 1997.

45. Thomas B. Edsall, "Lott Renounces White 'Racialist' Group He Praised in 1992," *Washington Post,* 16 December 1998, p. 82; Bob Herbert, "Mr. Lott's 'Big Mistake,' " *New York Times,* 7 January 1999, p. A31.

46. John Kifner, "Lott, and Shadow of a Pro-White Group," *New York Times,* 14 January 1999, p. A1.

47. Roosevelt, "The Negro Problem," p. 445.

48. Michael Tonry, *Malign Neglect—Race, Crime, and Punishment in America* (New York: Oxford University Press, 1995), p. 3; John J. DiIulio Jr., "The Question of Black Crime," *Public Interest* 117 (1994): 3–32; Glenn C. Loury, *One by One from the Inside Out: Essays and Reviews on Race and Responsibility in America* (New York: Free Press, 1995), pp. 45, 72. Cf. Glenn C. Loury, "The Conservative Line on Race," *Atlantic Monthly,* November 1997, pp. 148, 153; Glenn C. Loury, "An American Tragedy: the Legacy of Slavery Lingers in Our Cities' Ghettos," *Brookings Review,* spring 1998, pp. 41–42.

49. Michael Weiss and Karl Zinsmeister, "When Race Trumps in Court," *American Enterprise,* January/February 1996, pp. 54–57.

50. Milton Friedman, "There's No Justice in the War on Drugs," *New York Times,* 11 January 1998, sec. 4, p. 19.

51. Smith, *Civic Ideals,* pp. 357–69, 441–3.

52. Carl Campbell Brigham, *A Study of American Intelligence* (Princeton: Princeton University Press, 1923), p. 210.

53. Herrnstein and Murray, *The Bell Curve,* pp. 360–1, 549.

54. Tyler Bridges, *The Rise of David Duke* (Jackson: University Press of Mississippi, 1994), pp. 193, 244–5.

55. Smith, *Civic Ideals,* pp. 371–85, 448–53; Eric Foner, *Reconstruction: America's Unfinished Revolution, 1863–1877* (New York: Harper & Row, 1988), p. 560.

56. Douglas S. Massey and Nancy A. Denton, *American Apartheid: Segregation and the Making of the Underclass* (Cambridge: Harvard University Press, 1993), pp. 4–16, 60–82, 96–

109, 207–212; Ian Ayres, "Fair Driving: Gender and Race Discrimination in Retail Car Negotiations," *Harvard Law Review* 104 (1991): 817; Amy Saltzman, "Suppose They Sue? Why Companies Shouldn't Fret So Much about Bias Cases," *U.S. News & World Report,* 22 September 1997, p. 69.

57. Terry M. Neal, "Gore Makes Civil Rights Pledge," *Washington Post,* 20 January 1998, p. A1; Leadership Conference on Civil Rights, Press Release, October 22, 1998, Washington D.C.

58. *Freeman v. Pitts,* 503 U.S. 467 (1992); *Missouri v. Jenkins,* 115 S. Ct. 2038 (1995); Richard A. Epstein, *Forbidden Grounds;* Sowell, "The Right to Be Wrong," p. 50; Herrnstein and Murray, *The Bell Curve,* pp. 447–508; William A. Galston, *Liberal Purposes: Goods, Virtues and Diversity in the Liberal State* (Cambridge: Cambridge University Press, 1991), pp. 268–73, 287.

59. Smith, *Civic Ideals,* pp. 383–5, 451–3.

60. *Shaw v. Reno; Miller v. Johnson,* 115 S. Ct. 2475 (1995); *Shaw v. Hunt; Bush v. Vera,* 116 S. Ct. 1941 (1996); Thernstrom and Thernstrom, *America in Black and White,* pp. 288–9, 299–309, 484–6.

61. Marc Mauer, "Intended and Unintended Consequences: State Racial Disparities in Inprisonment," The Sentencing Project, 1997; Tamar Lewin, "Crime Costs Many Black Men the Vote, Study Says," *New York Times,* 23 October 1998, p. A14.

62. Abigail Thernstrom, *Whose Votes Count? Affirmative Action and Minority Voting Rights* (Cambridge: Harvard University Press, 1987), pp. 1–10, 208–15, 220–31.

63. Smith, *Civic Ideals,* pp. 320–4, 396–400, 464–8.

64. James S. Kunen, "The End of Integration: A Four-Decade Effort Is Being Abandoned, as Exhausted Courts and Frustrated Blacks Dust Off the Concept of 'Separate but Equal,' " *Time,* 29 April 1996, p. 38; Gary Orfield et al., "Deepening Segregation in American Public Schools," Harvard Project on School Desegregation, April 5, 1997, p. 11; Peter Applebome, "Schools Experience Reemergence of 'Separate but Equal,' " *New York Times,* 8 April 1997, p. A10; Steven A. Holmes, "At N.A.A.C.P., Talk of Shift on Integration," *New York Times,* 23 June 1997, p. A1.

65. Smith, *Civic Ideals,* pp. 417–8; Theodore G. Vincent, *Black Power and the Garvey Movement* (Berkeley: Ramparts Press, 1971).

66. For Farrakhan's views, see, e.g., "Giving New Meaning to Race," accessible from *The Final Call Online,* vol. 12, no. 24, 1996.

67. Rayford W. Logan, *The Betrayal of the Negro: From Rutherford B. Hayes to Woodrow Wilson* (New York: Collier Books, 1965), pp. 43–5.

68. See, e.g., David R. Roediger, *The Wages of Whiteness: Race and the Making of the American Working Class* (New York: Verso, 1991); Jeannie Sclafani Rhee, "In Black and White: Chinese in the Mississippi Delta," *Journal of Supreme Court History* (1994): 117–32.

69. Clinton, Second Inaugural; Thernstrom and Thernstrom, *America in Black and White,* p. 539.

Index